Koolhaas
Ulrich Obrist

Editors: Kayoko Ota
with James Westcott
AMO

Project Japan
Metabolism Talks…

TASCHEN

# OMA
## AMO

**Project Japan**
**Metabolism Talks...**
Rem Koolhaas
Hans Ulrich Obrist

**Editor** Kayoko Ota
**Coeditor** James Westcott

**Design** Irma Boom

**Architectural photography, 2009** Charlie Koolhaas
**Interview photographs** Joseph Grima

**Assistant designers**
Irma Boom Office: Sanne van de Goor, Julia Neller
AMO: Carolina Cantante, Nora Dohrmann,
Marcela Ferreira, Barbara Iwanicka

**Assistant editors** Samuel Stewart-Halevy, Stephan Petermann
**Editorial assistants** Samir Bantal, Rebecca Bego, Nancy Chidiac,
Katharina Ehrenklau, Khaled Malas, Becky Quintal, Kei Sasaki,
Erandi de Silva, Shuchen Xiang

**Translators** Thomas Daniell, Wayne Lammers, Hiroshi Watanabe
**Interview translators** Kazue Kobata, Keiko Murata
**Transcription** Ivan Carvalho, Keiko Mizutani, Anna Shefelbine,
Manuel Zwyssig

**Editorial coordination**
Florian Kobler, Kathrin Murr (Cologne)

**Production coordination**
Horst Neuzner (Cologne)

**First published in 2011 by TASCHEN GmbH**
Hohenzollernring 53, D-50672 Köln
www.taschen.com

**EACH AND EVERY TASCHEN BOOK PLANTS A SEED!**
TASCHEN is a carbon neutral publisher. Each year, we offset
our annual carbon emissions with carbon credits at the Instituto Terra,
a reforestation program in Minas Gerais, Brazil, founded by Lélia and
Sebastião Salgado. To find out more about this ecological partnership,
please check: www.taschen.com/zerocarbon
**Inspiration: unlimited. Carbon footprint: zero.**

To stay informed about TASCHEN and our upcoming titles,
please subscribe to our free magazine at www.taschen.com/magazine,
follow us on Twitter, Instagram, and Facebook, or e-mail your questions
to contact@taschen.com.

Printed in Spain
ISBN 978-3-8365-2508-4

# CONTENTS

In 2005, a team including an architect, a curator, editors, and a photographer came to Tokyo to interview the surviving members of the Metabolism movement...

**ACKNOWLEDGMENTS**

This book would not exist without:

- the **initiative** of Stefano Boeri, then at *Domus*
- the **generosity** of our protagonists—responding with wit and patience to questions that often must have seemed clinical and ignorant
- the **intelligence** shared by Arata Isozaki, Toyo Ito, Hajime Yatsuka, and Charles Jencks, who experienced the events we were trying to reconstruct
- the **tact** of Kayoko Ota and her ability to identify, find, and reassemble fragments of her country's finest hour
- the **persistence** of James Westcott, without whom the book would be less English
- the **vividness** of Charlie Koolhaas's "captures" of Metabolism aging (well)
- the **imagination** of Irma Boom
- the **endurance** of Benedikt Taschen

Rem Koolhaas
Hans Ulrich Obrist

We are deeply grateful to:

Jiro Tsukamoto (Kikutake Associates); Mikio Kurokawa with Misako Mataga (Kisho Kurokawa Architect & Associates); Chie Kato, Hisashi Nakai (Maki and Associates); Kaori Omura (Kikutake Architects); Sumiko Onodera, Tadashi Matsumoto (GK Design Group Inc.); Mitsuhiro Sakata (Masato Otaka Architects & Associates); Yumiko Takashima (Shimokobe Kenkyushitsu); Yukari Yoshifuku (Kawazoe Kenkyushitsu); Toshiko Amiya, Takako Fujimoto (Arata Isozaki & Associates); Chiaki Hara; Kenichi Matsuda, Yumiko Ichikawa (Tange Associates); Yoshinori Yamamoto (Otani Associates); Ikuko Horie (Kawaguchi & Engineers); Eriko Kinoshita, Miki Uono (Toyo Ito & Associates, Architects) **...without whose intelligent support and patience, this book would not exist.**

Nobuo Abe; Mari Asada; Ken Awazu (Awazu Design Room); Mariko Furuta with Sonomi Furuta; Isao Hashimoto (Maekawa Associates); Masahiro Hikita (Communication Design Institute, Kyoto); Akiomi Hirano; Koichi Mera; Makiko Otaka; Hitoshi Sakai (Institute for Social Engineering); Michiko Uchida **...who opened their archives and knowledge of our protagonists.**

Yukio Futagawa with Katsumasa Tanaka (GA Photographers); Hitomi Saito (A.D.A. EDITA Tokyo); Yasuhiro Ishimoto with Akiko Yamada; Osamu Murai with Masami Suzuki, Aya Hotta (Studio Murai); Tomio Ohashi **...who shared with us their historically invaluable documentation of the Metabolists' and Tange's work.**

Hiroyasu Fujioka; Shizuo Harada; Yoshihito Honma; Kiwa Matsushita; Kiyonori Muroga (IDEA magazine); Naoto Nakajima; Yoshikazu Nango; Yoshimi Nara (Filmart-Sha Co., Ltd.); Saikaku Toyokawa; Meruro Washida, Yoshiko Isshiki **...who shared their professional and academic expertise.**

Bijutsu Shuppan-sha; Heibonsha; Kajima Shuppankai; Kindaikenchiku-sha; Sanseido Publishing; Shinkenchiku-sha; Shokokusha; Architectural Institute of Japan; Architectural Institute of Japan Library; Asada Archive at Tohoku University of Art and Design; Central Research Institute of Electric Power Industry; Hiroshima Municipal Archives (Koji Ikemoto); Hiroshima Peace Memorial Museum; Institute for Social Engineering (Hitoshi Sakai); International House of Japan (Kimihiro Sonoda); Japan Design Committee (Mariko Tsuchida); National Institute for Research Advancement (NIRA); Shimokobe Archives at Research Institute for Urban and Environmental Development, Japan; Sogetsu Foundation; Tama Art University Library, Hachioji (Tomoya Watanabe); Taro Okamoto Museum of Art (Yasuo Nakano); The 21st Century Museum of Contemporary Art, Kanazawa (Misato Fudo); Tokyo Metropolitan Archives; The Kyoto Shinkin Bank; Mitsubishi Heavy Industries, Ltd.; Miyake Design Studio; Sakakura Associates (Yasuhiro Mandai); Takara Belmont Corp. (Sadaji Masuda); Ueno Sekkoumokei Seisakusho (Akinori Ueno); Nahoko Wada (Tohoku University of Art and Design); Yoshichika Uchida **...publishers, cultural institutions, corporations, and individuals who generously opened their archives.**

Takeo Obayashi (Obayashi Corporation); Johnnie Walker (Za Moca Foundation); Keiko Murata **...who supported our research in Tokyo.**

Naoko Hatta; Jun Ishida; Yusuke Kaneko; Toshiyuki Kikuchi; Yutaro Tomii **...for creative support and advice.**

Ian Buruma; Cynthia Davidson (Log); Sarah Herda (Graham Foundation for Advanced Studies in the Fine Arts); Rumiko Ito; Kazue Kobata; Sanford Kwinter; Karen Marta; Todd Reisz; Misa Shin; Akira Suzuki; Yoshiharu Tsukamoto; Clemens Weisshaar **...for inspiration and insight.**

Mr. and Mrs. Kengo Asakura; Koichi Watanabe; Daisuke Sato; Commemorative Organization for the Japan World Exposition '70; Mrs. Kiyonori Kikutake; Municipality of Sakaide (Urban construction department); Nakagin Integration Inc.; National Museum of Ethnology; NittoBest Corporation (Kunihiro Seino); Shintoshi Consulting, Inc. (Sumiko Mizukami); Shizuoka Shimbun and Shizuoka Broadcasting System, Tokyo Branch; Yamanashi Culture Hall **...for support and assistance in facilitating Charlie Koolhaas's photography of buildings by Tange and the Metabolists.**

Sandra Bsat; Annemarie Costeris; Kaveh Dabiri; Eveline van Engelen; Farshid Gazor; Ekaterina Golovatyuk; Gwinyai Hoeve; Keigo Kobayashi; Lars Lijten; Khalid Al Nasser; Shaun Palmer; Timur Shabaev; Shohei Shigematsu; Hugh Snelgrove **...for creative thinking at OMA/AMO.**

Gan Hosoya with Naomi Ito (Light Publicity); Kazumasa Nagai with Hitoshi Oikawa (Nippon Design Center Inc.); Kohei Sugiura with Sachiko Kagaya (Sugiura Kohei Plus Eyes Inc.); Yamazaki Design Office (Noboru Yamazaki); Communication Arts R (Mai Yoshida); Printing Museum, Tokyo (Keiichi Ishibashi); DNP Foundation for Cultural Promotion; Japan Graphic Designers Association (Naoki Kondo); Recruit Creation Gallery G8 (Shuzo Osako) **...for sharing knowledge of the graphic designers contemporary with the Metabolists.**

TOTO (Nobuyuki Endo, Kumiko Ikada at Culture Promotion Department) **...for invaluable support in launching the project.**

Kevin Scott **...for facilitating and expediting the publishing of this book.**

Netherlands Foundation for Visual Arts, Design and Architecture; Graham Foundation for Advanced Studies in the Fine Arts; Netherlands Architecture Fund; The Obayashi Foundation **...for their generous support in the production of this book.**

The editors

# Movement (1)
# Rem Koolhaas

What is a Movement? A form of conspiracy? A shoal of fish changing direction in a single flash? A form of trapeze act? An unstable human pyramid? Or simply a crisis that erupts between geniuses to make it unthinkable to go on in the old way?

Almost like a textbook, *Project Japan* reconstructs the history of Metabolism, the last movement that changed architecture. It documents Metabolism's meticulous preparations, the assembly of its component parts—in this case, mostly human—its aims, its revolutionary content, its detonation, the extent of its fallout, and its global reach.

Why look (and listen) again to a Japanese avant-garde that engineered its appearance on the world stage 50 years ago and disappeared 25 years later in the bonfire of neoliberalism?

At a moment when the connection between architects and their "own" culture has dwindled to insignificance, and the market has dissolved any connective tissue between colleagues, it seemed urgent to listen to the survivors of a group of architects who saw their country and its transformation as a project, who changed their fatherland with new tools recognizably derived from its traditions, who worked together in a strategic alliance to achieve greater prominence and credibility, in a sustained intellectual effort that mobilized a vast range of other disciplines.

In the mid-'30s, Japan invaded China, ostensibly to construct a "Greater East Asia Co-Prosperity Sphere" that would eventually include parts of Manchuria, Mongolia, Thailand, Vietnam, Laos, Burma, the Philippines, and Indonesia. The "sphere" offered stunning possibilities for Japanese architects: a continent where they could start from scratch. Ten years later, two atom bombs completed the destruction of their homeland. To seal their humiliation, the occupying forces of America imposed democracy on the losers. The same architects and planners who had, in the '30s, projected vast new settlements on wide open spaces abroad were now confronted with their own cities transformed into radioactive rubble. From utopia to apocalypse in less than half a generation…

But modern architecture survived: unlike Germany, but like Italy, the values of Japan's prewar regime were projected through its language; ironically, the radical reversal of political fortunes could only be expressed in the same aesthetic….

Architecture is a deeply contradictory profession. Its actions intersect with a huge range of unrelated domains; at the same time, its essence—to build—is so complex that it requires extreme focus and concentration. Sadly therefore, it is largely inhabited by two human typologies, "builders" and "thinkers," united in mutual disdain. Kenzo Tange was both.

Tange died in 2005, the very year we began our interviews, and had withdrawn from public life almost a decade earlier. Like Tokyo, a mass surrounding a central void, this mass of conversation is constructed around his absence. But it is a book about him. Without Tange, no Metabolism.

Tange emerges from these interviews as a nurturing and yet calculating figure, someone who combines an exceptional pedagogical range with a marked generosity towards other talents, on which, in return, he does not hesitate to depend.

Japan invaded its Asian neighbors to share the benefits of Japan-ness. Tange was part of that campaign. His winning designs in Bangkok (for a Japanese-Thai Cultural Center) and in Japan were shrewd amalgamations of traditional and modern thinking: 50% past, 50% future. This hybrid DNA, synthesized in the war, gave him a tactical advantage at the beginning of his postwar career that he would exploit himself as an architect and implant in his students as a teacher.

In a seamless continuity between Tange Lab—his base at Tokyo University—and his house-office, he works on three fronts simultaneously: the reinforcement of the social status of the profession, the credibility of design, the reinvention of the architect.

Tange creates a milieu, a mixing chamber for artists, intellectuals, and architects, foreigners and Japanese, men and women (unusual for Japan at that time). Talents are discovered, nourished, (re)programmed, embedded, married, in an almost domestic intimacy that gives Tange invaluable insights—professional and personal—into the strengths, weaknesses, and potential of those who would eventually bond together as a "movement," Metabolism.

For Tange, it was not enough to turn Japan into a platform for architecture; his boldest ambition—extreme for an architect on the losing side of World War II—was to invent himself as an international architect and to pass on that identity to a next generation of Japanese colleagues, like a relay.

In 1960, a confident Japan initiates a World Design Conference as a stage so that its own emerging talents can confront the international avant-garde. A masterplanner does not leave fingerprints on success. If so, it was perhaps Tange's masterstroke to leave in 1959 for America, to develop fresh ideas with new students at MIT, leaving instructions with two intellectuals in his circle, Takashi Asada and Noboru Kawazoe, to transform his protégés into "Metabolists."

The diversity of the group that coalesces in his absence is astonishing. Solid introverts, meditative poets, charismatic wunderkinder, feudalists, provincials, revolutionaries, cosmopolitans, thinkers, doers, fanatics, mystics—a kaleidoscopic inventory of the Japanese psyche. The sum of the Metabolists' individual obsessions is a surprisingly comprehensive repertoire: it covers all possible conditions in Japan, except straightforward building on the given ground.

Tange returns in time for the conference, where the young Metabolists—Kurokawa, the youngest, is only 26—are mixed with their world-famous counterparts.

Ironically, the moment of the Metabolists' first appearance as a collective is also the start of their individual careers—the growing economic might of the country produces centrifugal forces that demand recognizable agents and identities.

Now three additional powers—bureaucracy, business, and media—accelerate the momentum. Their meeting ground is Japan's "impossibility." The diagnosis rests on three interlocking vulnerabilities that, together, imply a manifesto for the total transformation of the country—Project Japan.

a.  The Archipelago has run out of space: mostly mountainous, the surfaces fit for settlement are subdivided in microscopic, centuries old patchworks of ownership

b.  Earthquakes and tsunamis make all construction precarious; urban concentrations such as Tokyo and Osaka are susceptible to potentially devastating wipeouts

c.  Modern technology and design offer possibilities for transcending Japan's structural weakness, but only if they are mobilized systematically, almost militaristically, searching for solutions in every direction: on the land, on the sea, in the air…

One young graduate of Tange Lab chooses not to become an architect but a bureaucrat. Not in the boring sense of the word—Atsushi Shimokobe crisscrosses '60s Tokyo in a red Ferrari—but as an embedded agent in a position to script the future of his country. (No architect ever rises higher in Japanese bureaucracy: in 1977, Shimokobe becomes vice minister of the National Land Agency.)

From his position he helps construct Tange as an international "winner," occasionally through illegal means, an iconic figurehead in whose slipstream the other Metabolists proceed. He systematically supports Tange's students and hands them commissions that correspond to their individual fascinations, working on land, water, and in the sky. Shimokobe is the puppet master who implements the vision from behind the scenes.

Business endorses. A nervous America calls the interchangeability between bureaucracy and business "Japan Inc."; adopted at WoDeCo, Metabolism is one of its vigorous offspring.

At the brink of the '60s, media discovers architecture, or at least architects. As their nation's future apparently depends on them, Japan's architects are endowed with a special glamour. In television studios, Tange performs the role of Japan's transformer-in-chief like a smooth Howard Roark.

Kurokawa aims beyond architecture; his think tank can now address any issue: with himself as prototype, he helps to construct a new Japanese masculinity. The twin dandies Kurokawa and the writer Mishima, elegant modern samurais, share a mise-en-scène that defines a new bandwidth of maleness: mirrors, smoke, chandeliers, sharp suits, narrow ties, kimonos, swords... Western decadence, Eastern purism, effortlessly synthesized.

Expo '70, the first in Asia, is Metabolism's apotheosis. Half of the continent is welcomed under Tange's "Big Roof," a playground crisscrossed by anarchic robots. The thickness of the roof contains a village of mini utopias; the individual pavilions are a flash-forward to a Metabolist country.

The ultimate transformation of Japan seems imminent: after reaching second place in the global economic rankings, Prime Minister Kakuei Tanaka publishes a *Plan for Remodeling the Japanese Archipelago* (1972). Shimokobe is credited as ghostwriter.

But the 1973/74 oil crisis stops Japan's revolution in its tracks. The Arab world reveals Japan's structural weakness: the owners of the oil control its lifeblood. But with ironic timing, this reversal launches Tange, and with him the Metabolists, into a final phase, triggered by the combined demands of independences in Africa, a modernizing Islam in North Africa and the Middle East, and the emergence of Singapore, where the Metabolist aesthetic is first established on the scale of an entire city-state (not by the Japanese, but by gifted locals). From the late '60s to the early '90s, Japan's architects, free from associations with the West, offer the defining alternative to Western aesthetics in an arc from Nigeria to the Arabian Peninsula across southeast Asia. As Metabolism expands, its energy is slowly spent, absorbed finally in the global generic of the late 20th century.

It has been a gripping experience, to meet, at this point in my life, the protagonists of an older movement—sharing revelations—a radical memento mori, extended over six years of interviews, a confrontation with mortality in a profession that aspires to eternal life... Perhaps old age requires strategy more than any other period in life. The conversations demonstrated touchingly that it is more crucial to exploit your limitations than to survive your gifts. As memory weakens, vision is the only option.

**Arata Isozaki**

**Kiyonori Kikutake**

**Noboru Kawazoe**

**Fumihiko Maki**

**Kisho Kurokawa**

**Kenji Ekuan**

**Atsushi Shimokobe**

Stills from video shot by
Hans Ulrich Obrist

# Movement (2)
# Hans Ulrich Obrist

**Protest against Forgetting** Project Japan started in 2005 when Kayoko Ota, then an editor at *Domus* with Stefano Boeri, and now the editor of this book, proposed that Rem and I should interview the Metabolists together for a special feature in the magazine. Kayoko convinced us of the urgency: this might be the last opportunity to meet the protagonists and thoroughly investigate Metabolism, which was still poorly understood outside Japan. Maybe the last avant-garde movement in architecture was receding into history without ever having properly entered the historical record. Our project, to interview the main protagonists and associates of the movement, is an attempt to make a polyphonic portrait of the movement. It is also what I would call, after the historian Eric Hobsbawm, a protest against forgetting.

**Interview Marathon** Around the same time the Metabolism project began, I conceived the idea of an interview marathon: a 24-hour event with 24 participants, in Stuttgart in 2005. Then, at the Serpentine Gallery summer pavilion in London in 2006, Rem and I interviewed 72 people over 24 hours, including artists, architects, writers, and other practitioners, about their work and about the London of the future.

The pavilion itself was designed by Rem and Cecil Balmond, with Arup (and was the sixth in a series invented by Julia Peyton Jones at the Serpentine). A temporary structure capped by an inflated, movable bubble, the pavilion was a form of ephemeral, mutable architecture—a vessel for unpredictable events. In this sense, we were already learning from Metabolism.

**Beginnings** In the early summer of 1995—10 years before the beginning of the systematic Metabolism research—Hou Hanru and I were preparing "Cities on the Move," an exhibition on the rapid urbanization of Asia, and we attempted to pay a visit to Rem Koolhaas in Rotterdam. He was bound for Hong Kong to continue his research on the Pearl River Delta. "See you tomorrow in Hong Kong!" was his parting message. We took this gesture literally, jumped on a plane and headed east. It was during this first evening in Hong Kong that we discussed Metabolism for the first time. Hanru and I continued the journey to Singapore where we met Tay Kheng Soon, WIlliam Lim, and Liu Tai Kher; Metabolism came up in all the conversations. A few days later I arrived in Japan and interviewed for the first time Kisho Kurokawa and Fumihiko Maki. The Metabolist research started 10 years before it started...

and Christopher Alexander. Rem and I agreed on a method for our interviews: a Bakhtinian polyphony of voices: not just dialogic, but trialogic, allowing for multiple means of exploring the interviewee's practice. The three-way interview is an attempt to break the segregation of professional spheres and cultural fields. This is what we applied to the Metabolism interviews.

**Infinite Conversation** After our first meeting in Asia, Rem and I quickly realized that we shared an obsession with the interview-form (I have recorded over 2,200 hours of interviews since 1991), and we set out to interview pioneers in architecture together, including Robert Venturi and Denise Scott Brown, Philip Johnson, Oswald Mathias Ungers,

**Optimism** The 1960s, bookended by the publication of *Metabolism 1960* and Expo '70, was a decade of immense optimism, in economics and in architecture. The Metabolists announced an ambitious vision of accelerated urbanism and advanced technology existing in parallel with an untainted nature—a techno-utopia. The first such proposal was Kikutake's Marine City of 1958, which he followed with (at least) six subsequent plans for floating cities that both interact with nature and form a fortification against it.

**Doubts** For Isozaki, who was close to the members but never joined Metabolism, the group was in fact "too optimistic," he told us. "They really believed in technology, in mass production; they believed in systematic urban infrastructure and growth ... The Metabolists had no skepticism toward their utopia."

"Nothing great was ever achieved without enthusiasm"—Ralph Waldo Emerson (1803–82)

**Postwar Japan** The moment of Metabolism is inseparable from the tremendous changes in Japan during the 1950s and '60s. The ruins of World War II, and the unexpected economic stimulus of the US-led conflict in Korea from 1950–53, were fundamental to the visions of renewal and change that we find in Metabolism. The optimism that propelled Japan into second place in the world GDP stakes by the mid-1960s, and which saw university attendance jump from 20 percent of Japanese youth to around 40 percent, was a suitable backdrop for the massive ambitions of these architects.

METABOLIST MANIFESTO? *Metabolism 1960: The Proposals for New Urbanism* probably stands as one of the final manifestations of architectural modernism. Designed by Kiyoshi Awazu, *Metabolism 1960* features four seminal essays: Kikutake's "Ocean City," Kawazoe's "Material and Man," Otaka and Maki's "Toward Group Form," and Kurokawa's "Space City." As much as these declarations stand as rallying calls towards the future, they are also the culmination of a global period of radical innovation since the end of World War II.

Perhaps, after all, "Metabolism" as a group, as a label, was a strategic alliance. Perhaps there were more differences among its members than there were correspondences of vision and style; Maki, for instance, is in many ways the polar opposite of Kurokawa and Kikutake: he rarely proposed megastructures and high-tech visions; he certainly avoided the flamboyant theorizing of Kurokawa.

A TRADITIONAL AVANT-GARDE

**The Future is Invented with Fragments from the Past** When we began our mission to learn more about Metabolism, we believed it to be all about the future. But many of our conversations in fact focused on the past. Hiroshi Hara told us that before Tange, modernism had simply been equated in Japan with Functionalism, conceived as an opposing concept to "traditionalism." It was Tange who first "stepped in and said he was going to create a new style of Japanese modernism by assimilating tradition." This assimilation led, in turn, to a profound sense of experimentation and a search for the new, rather than simply the recombination and resurrection of the old. Metabolism has many links to the "just past," which, as Dan Graham said, allows work to have historical and political value. One under-recognized connection that Metabolism and Tange have with the "just past" is to Finnish American architect Eero Saarinen. His Ingalls Ice Hockey Rink at Yale (completed 1958), with its curving concrete spine, is a key predecessor to Tange's Yoyogi National Gymnasia for the the 1964 Tokyo Olympics.

**The Organic Movement** The Metabolists subtly, perhaps unknowingly, held out for the idea of the flexible manifesto, up for continual renegotiation. Until the group's gradual, unofficial dissolution in the mid-1970s, Metabolism operated in a constant flow of proposals, buildings, and a ceaseless production of texts. So prolific was the flow of ideas that not even *Metabolism 1960* was sacrosanct—fitting, perhaps, for a movement premised on an ethos of adaptability to change. To my question about the status of the manifesto, Maki responded: "Even today I can't really say what the manifesto was."

**Impermanence** There is a strong Japanese tradition of making buildings and cities as temporary structures. Kurokawa and Kawazoe in particular focus on Ise Shrine, rebuilt every 20 years since 690 CE, as the quintessentially Japanese archetype for Metabolism's ethos of impermanence. Parallel to the emergence of Metabolism, English architect Cedric Price emphasized in Europe the necessity of architecture as a question of time and not just a question of space. Price proclaimed the necesssity of a limited lifespan of building.

**Age of the Manifesto** In our interviews, we sought to discover how each Metabolist stood in relation to the group, in relation both to the 1960 book, and to the idea of the manifesto in general. Today, we recognize the age of the avant-gardes as an age of manifestos. What kind of role has there been for the manifesto in the work of successive generations? Does the idea of the manifesto as a collective call to arms have any purchase for a movement like Metabolism, fundamentally premised on the unpredictable, the anti-fundamental, and the anti-foundational?

**Break with CIAM** Metabolism was part of a wave of movements in postwar architecture that went beyond the legacy of CIAM (Congrès Internationaux d'Architecture Moderne), questioning its mechanical principles, and more broadly, the idea of the masterpiece. Kurokawa described to us his own thinking at the time as an attempt "to understand the shift from a mechanical to a biodynamic age." CIAM held no answers to this. Beginning in 1953, the CIAM breakaway group Team 10, including Peter and Alison Smithson, Aldo Van Eyck in the Netherlands, and Giancarlo De Carlo in Italy challenged the often inhuman homogeneity and scale of Le Corbusier and the International Style. Grounded in anthropological studies, projects like the Smithsons' House of the Future (1956) envisaged a more human architecture that could be responsive to differing individual needs.

**The Big Roof at Expo '70** Kenzo Tange's steel space frame roof structure was suspended 30 meters above Festival Plaza at Expo '70 in Osaka, the pinnacle of Japan's postwar economic miracle, and a crucial coming together of Western and Japanese architectural avant-gardes. It was also to prove the last major and successful public engagement of the Metabolists as a group.

**Learning from Konrad Wachsmann** Behind the space frame structure, with its emphasis on the modular, the organic, and the implicitly biological, there lay the shadowy figure of Konrad Wachsmann, the German-born visionary who was responsible for at least two revolutionary design concepts of the mid-20th century. All roads lead back to Wachsmann. Wachsmann, following a year's apprenticeship with Le Corbusier in 1924, produced prefabricated housing for Albert Einstein in Caputh in 1929; in exile in California in 1941, he founded the General Panel Corporation (GPC) with Walter Gropius and designed the Packaged House, a factory-built prefabricated house that could be assembled in nine hours using only a hammer. Then there were Wachsmann's mobile aircraft hangars made for the US Air Force during World War II and into the 1950s. These giant space frames, which Eckhard Schulze-Fielitz, a contemporary pioneer of the structure, described as a "tetrahedron-octahedron structure that can be easily combined," could be collapsed and shipped anywhere for speedy construction. Wachsmann gave a seminar in Tokyo in 1955, which was attended by Tange, Isozaki, and Ekuan; the ideas from this key meeting of West and East arguably filtered down into Metabolism five years later.

Though the scheme failed commercially, the GPC is today remembered as the "NASA of the prefabricated housing industry in America," as the Architects' Journal declared in 1999.

Archigram's Peter Cook declared that "Konrad Wachsmann was even more important to us than Bucky [Fuller]."

**Yona Friedman, Ville Spatiale, 1958–** In France, Yona Friedman, who had been in touch with the Metabolists since the late 1950s via Otaka, was on a similar path. His Ville Spatiale scheme, developed in maquettes and collages, prefigures Tange's Big Roof. Friedman's Spatial Cities were large-scale modular canopies that could be suspended above towns, cities, and landscapes, ossatures to be fleshed out; less inherently flexible, more "strict, rigid structure[s]," but under and within which, as Friedman has told me, "everything is permitted to take place." Friedman's vision was for the Spatial City canopies to house capsules, habitable nodes nestled within the framework.

**Constant Nieuwenhuys, New Babylon, 1959–74** New Babylon is a ludic and knowingly fantastical vision of a post-revolutionary city growing on an elevated framework. In a description remarkable for its correspondence with Friedman and Tange's deployment of the Wachsmann space frame, Constant explained to me in 1999 that New Babylon aimed to "put an end to the separation between city and landscape. The landscape continues and the city is placed on a different level. It is a network, rather than a core. A city is not an area, a section of packed-down earth, surrounded by a landscape, but a network that spreads on another level above the landscape." He continued in a Metabolic vein: "New Babylon is not a construction, because it is at the same time a deconstruction: one builds and destroys at the same time; there are simple elements that appear and disappear on a line that remains, naturally, unchanging."

**Cedric Price, Fun Palace, 1960–65** Metabolism shared with English architect Cedric Price—though in parallel rather than as a direct influence—the idea of architecture as ecology, of buildings and environments as self-sustaining and adaptable structures. Isozaki has written of Price's Fun Palace proposal: "The important thing was that there no longer was any strict time or space composed by the artist but, rather, mechanical systems reconfiguring in every possible way in response to circumstances." In Isozaki's words, Price "divorced" architecture "from the dictates of post-1930 industrial design that inundated our modern world with streamlining right down to the smallest details, [in order] to conform to overall strategies of assembling, dismantling and moving … [Price] focused his entire attention on the hardware dictated for all such processes, effectively erasing the architecture into the system."

Today we live in a time that is more atomized and has less cohesive artistic and architectural movements. If there is currently a reconnection to the manifesto as a document of poetic and political intent, what lessons can Metabolism, as a movement, offer us for a collective vision of the future and of the prospects of democratic social control today, not least amid the crisis of climate change?

Kurokawa was deeply concerned with ecology: his Yamagata Hawaii Dreamland (1966) was enclosed in a cell-like form precisely to avoid spilling out onto (what he considered) the pristine northern Japanese landscape; his planned capsule village in Usami (1972) would have been built on scaffolding over a hill in order to preserve the vegetation below.

**Third Paradise** With this project Kurokawa attempted to integrate the natural paradise with the artificial paradise, which is what Italian artist Michelangelo Pistoletto proposes in his recent manifesto for a "Third Paradise." As Pistoletto told me, "We have to be able to connect natural and artificial life. The first paradise was the garden of nature, in which humans were totally integrated. The second paradise commenced when humanity seemed to gain independence from nature and produced the artificial worlds which we inhabit today. This led to pollution and the deterioration of nature." For Pistoletto, the Third Paradise is the integration of the natural with the artificial— a key Metabolist principle. The Metabolists also called into question the autonomy of art and architecture. As Pistoletto said: "In the 20th century, there was a break, a moment of artistic consciousness and autonomy. If we want to keep the autonomy of art and architecture that was gained at that moment, we have to put art and architecture in a condition to transform the world, otherwise the world will transform it again."

**Continuum** Within Japan, as I see it, there is a clear continuum, a true Japanese architectural miracle, moving from Tange, through Metabolism and the ambivalent fellow-traveler Isozaki onwards to the "progressive anarchy" of Kazuo Shinohara's Uehara House (1976) and Centennial Hall in Tokyo (1987), and then to the School of Shinohara, to Toyo Ito, for whom all architecture is an extension and "epidermis" of nature, and forwards again to SANAA, then to Junya Ishigami, to Sou Fujimoto. The Japanese, it seems, do not kill the father/mother.

**Imperative** An ecological imperative is clear in projects like Takashi Asada's Kodomo-no-kuni (Children's Land, 1965). The project was conceived specifically to prevent further development on its site in Yokohama. Ecology is also present in Otaka's 1959 Tokyo Bay proposal, which, in his own words, was a "development that would preserve the seaside nature familiar to me from my student days ... I began to think about the natural environment as comprising major assets such as ecosystems, topography, and vegetation." Meanwhile, Asada created the Environmental Development Center. Like Otaka's Tokyo Bay proposal, made in response to the rapid development and extensive industrialization of the shoreline after the war, ecology was at the heart of Asada's thinking, and, according to Kenji Ekuan, "He started out by declaring that Japan was on course to becoming one giant trash heap."

**Today** The challenges of sustainability demand that cultural production today reclaims its old sense of ambition and scale; that it once again embraces the possibilities of total design. Bruno Latour has recently called for an expanded role for design that extends "from the details of daily objects to cities, landscapes, nations, cultures, bodies, genes, and ... to nature itself," welcoming this as a new political ecology that might "ease modernism out of its historical dead end." This is not to say that we should resurrect anything like the monolithic aesthetic schemes of modernism itself, but rather that we should borrow from their ambition in order to form our own dynamic, shifting, and alterable institutions and spaces of the future.

**Void Metabolism** Atelier Bow Wow comes to mind. They described Tokyo as a sustainable form of a horizontal "city made out of houses." For them, Tokyo as a field of autonomous and self-regenerating grains, cells, and particles is a type of Metabolism, but very different from the vertically concentrated Metabolism of the '60s. In the words of Bow Wow: "At that time, Metabolism symbolized their concepts in terms of composition of the vertical core—the bundling of lifelines surrounded by detachable capsules." For Bow Wow, the 21st-century regeneration of houses is not around a core but a void—they refer to the space between buildings. "Further distinguished from the 'Core Metabolism' of 50 years ago, it is within the framework of 'Void Metabolism' that the practice of designing small houses in Tokyo's residential areas is a clearly perceivable housing behavior."

The book you are about to read consists of two alternating elements:

## History

A chronology of nine chapters tells the story of Metabolism as it interlocks with the history of Japan in the 20th century: from the wide open spaces of a colonized Manchuria in the 1930s and a devastated Japan after the war (Tabula Rasa); to Kenzo Tange's strategic orchestration of young architects in the postwar years (Tange Lab); to the establishment of Metabolism at the 1960 World Design Conference (Birth of a Movement); to the full repertoire of Metabolism's architectural inventions (On the land, on the sea, in the air); to the lionization of Kenzo Tange and then Kisho Kurokawa (Media Architects); to the apotheosis of the movement (Expo '70) and its pioneering globalization in the '70s (Expansion/Exile); to a realization of how successive postwar Japanese governments mobilized the most creative forces of its population— Project Japan itself...

### Interviews

Marked by pink bands on the edge of the page, nine interviews with the Metabolists, and with those who had crucial relationships with them in varying ways, form the skeleton of the book. In the left hand margin, comments from a supporting cast of characters—the Metabolists' colleagues, critics, and progeny, all interviewed by Koolhaas and Obrist—are strategically placed to illuminate or complicate key moments in the main conversation.

# Arata Isozaki 磯崎新

**1931** born in Oita City **1954** graduates from Tokyo University; joins Tange Lab **1959** asked to join Metabolism but declines **1960** participates in Plan for Tokyo 1960 at Tange Lab; completes first building: Oita Medical Hall **1962** participates in Metabolist exhibition "This Will be Your City" in Tokyo; plans Clusters in the Air and City in the Air; publishes *City Demolition Industry, Inc.* **1963** establishes Arata Isozaki & Associates **1964** Iwata Girls' High School, Oita **1965** designs set for Hiroshi Teshigahara's film *Face of Another* **1966** Skopje masterplan with Tange; Oita Prefectural Library **1968** *Electric Labyrinth* installation for Milan Triennale is set up but not shown **1969** begins "Dismantling of Architecture" articles in *Bijutsu Techo* magazine **1970** Festival Plaza with Tange, Expo '70 **1971** Fukuoka Mutual Bank headquarters **1974** Gunma Prefectural Museum of Fine Arts, Takasaki; Kitakyushu City Museum of Art; integrates Tange's and Louis Kahn's plans for Abbas Abad New City Development, Tehran **1976** participates in "Man transform" exhibition at Cooper-Hewitt Museum, New York **1978** Conceives "Space-time in Japan MA" exhibition, Musée des Arts Décoratifs, Paris; curates "A New Wave of Japanese Architecture" in the US **1983** Tsukuba Centre Building **1985** Palladium Club, New York **1986** Los Angeles County Museum of Art; loses to Tange in competition for the new Tokyo City Hall **1988** starts commissioning architects for public buildings in Kumamoto Prefecture for Kumamoto Artpolis **1990** producer, Expo '90, Osaka; Art Tower Mito; Palau d'Esports Sant Jordi for Barcelona Olympics **1991** Team Disney Building, Orlando; designs Louis Kahn retrospective at Pompidou Center; designs "Visions of Japan" at Victoria & Albert, London **1995** Kaishi Plan city masterplan for Zhuhai, China **1997** curates "The Mirage City: Another Utopia" at ICC, Tokyo **2001** publishes *Unbuilt* **2002** Qatar National Library and National Bank proposals, Doha; masterplans Education City, Doha **2003** Milano Fiera Redevelopment **2004** designs for University of Central Asia campuses in Tajikistan, Kyrgyzstan, and Kazakhstan **2007** directs Fukuoka city's campaign for 2016 Olympics **2008** Central Academy of Fine Arts, Beijing **2011 Education City** Convention Center, Doha

**"The Metabolists had no skepticism toward their
utopia. I thought they were too optimistic..."**

Arata Isozaki has maintained an ambivalent relationship with Metabolism ever
since he was asked to join them when they came together, named their philosophy and published their manifesto at the 1960 World Design Conference.
He refused. Yet he participated in the Metabolists' 1962 exhibition "This will
be your city" in Tokyo, shared many of their ideas throughout the '60s, and
worked with them on Expo '70 in Osaka. Outside Japan, Isozaki was often
mistaken as a member of the Metabolists, though he remained independent
and critical of the unquestioning "progressivism" he thought they proclaimed.
When the Metabolists dreamt of renewal, Isozaki spoke of ruins. He preferred
to keep the company of artists, filmmakers, and writers rather than fellow
architects. In this interview (with Hans Ulrich Obrist still on his way to Japan from
Europe), Isozaki describes the historical background of Metabolism, reaching
back not only to their father figure Kenzo Tange—Isozaki's teacher from
1950–54, his boss until 1963, and a collaborator on masterplanning Skopje and
Expo '70—but further back to the generation of Japanese architects and urban
planners who drew new cities on the tabula rasa of Manchuria in the 1930s.
Did their grand schemes unleash the architectural ambitions of the Metabolists?
As an outsider, Isozaki introduces Metabolism here as the "last avant-garde
movement," and pinpoints the oil crisis of 1973 as the moment when utopia
was suspended indefinitely, government plans dissipated, and, for an extended
period, "everything stopped."
Do avant-gardes only exist only under strong regimes? Even though he was
never officially a Metabolist, he seems to regret that their ambitions were no
longer officially encouraged...

The interview took place at
Office of Arata Isozaki Associates and Ristorante Amore,
Roppongi, Tokyo, September 8, 2005

Isozaki the insider agrees to meet in a neutral location (his favorite gourmet restaurant) to disclose information on Tange and the Metabolists...

**1932–1945** Architectural forefathers of Kenzo Tange engage in the imperial adventure of the Greater East Asia Co-Prosperity Sphere, experimenting in Manchukuo (Japan's colonial name for Manchuria), Inner Mongolia, and Shanghai on a scale unthinkable in Japan.

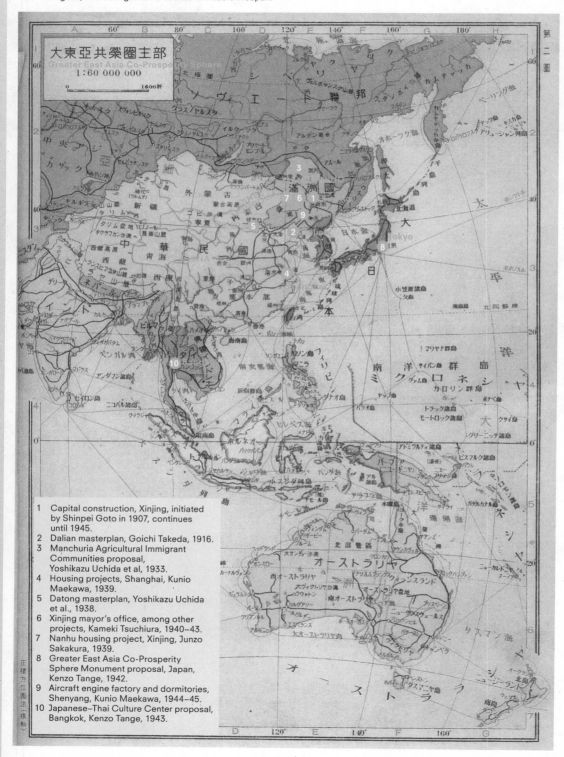

1 Capital construction, Xinjing, initiated by Shinpei Goto in 1907, continues until 1945.
2 Dalian masterplan, Goichi Takeda, 1916.
3 Manchuria Agricultural Immigrant Communities proposal, Yoshikazu Uchida et al, 1933.
4 Housing projects, Shanghai, Kunio Maekawa, 1939.
5 Datong masterplan, Yoshikazu Uchida et al., 1938.
6 Xinjing mayor's office, among other projects, Kameki Tsuchiura, 1940–43.
7 Nanhu housing project, Xinjing, Junzo Sakakura, 1939.
8 Greater East Asia Co-Prosperity Sphere Monument proposal, Japan, Kenzo Tange, 1942.
9 Aircraft engine factory and dormitories, Shenyang, Kunio Maekawa, 1944–45.
10 Japanese–Thai Culture Center proposal, Bangkok, Kenzo Tange, 1943.

**Mengjiang**
Eastern Inner Mongolia
was also under the yoke
of Japan's puppet regime
in Manchukuo from 1932.

**Eika Takayama**
Takayama was typical of
the Japanese intellectuals
of the time: he engaged in
this project for exploiting the
resources of Inner Mongolia
in spite of his exposure to
the influence of Marxism.
**Hajime Yatsuka**

**REM KOOLHAAS** My first question is political. In an article on Metabolism, Hajime Yatsuka makes a connection between Metabolism and the Japanese occupation of Manchuria. He suggests that architects like Kenzo Tange were stimulated by Japan's ambition to build in the vast open spaces of Manchuria, which afforded Japan its first experience of large-scale planning from scratch.[1] Do you think there was a connection between the military and the architectural adventure?

**ARATA ISOZAKI** Well, to give you a little overview, the Japanese military government invaded Manchuria in 1932. They placed Pu Yi, the last emperor of China, on the throne as the puppet ruler of Manchukuo between 1932 and 1945, and started to exploit the region. Everything in Manchukuo was virtually free for designing or planning at that time.

**RK** In what sense "free"? A kind of carte blanche?

**AI** Exactly. They were very right-wing ideologues while at the same time working in a mode that had very left-wing connections.

**RK** A lamination of left and right?

**AI** That's right. And they were really involved in construction. Many Japanese modernist architects who had studied under Le Corbusier, like Kunio Maekawa ④ and Junzo Sakakura ⑦, who won the competition for the Japanese Pavilion at the 1937 World Exposition in Paris, had big projects in Manchuria and China: government buildings, city halls, bank offices—large scale buildings constructed from around 1935 to 1940. It was a bit like when Mussolini invaded Ethiopia, Rhodes, and the Greek islands.

**RK** Were some of the city planning projects also executed?

**AI** Yes, but their city planning was very conventional. One quite interesting project that needs to be documented was the masterplan for Datong ⑤ in Mengjiang, Inner Mongolia. It was a collaboration between Yoshikazu Uchida and Eika Takayama, who were professors of architecture at Tokyo Imperial University, together with Uchida's son Yoshifumi and Toshiro Kasahara. It was clearly a Japanese utopian city built around an old Chinese city, along with completely new developed areas.

**RK** Did that kind of thinking trigger Japanese architecture after the war? Did it unleash the architectural imagination—not in Manchuria, but in Japan itself?

**AI** That's a question I asked myself during the years I spent with Tange, so I made a series of interviews in the mid-'70s with people who lived through the war.[2] I had come to know most of the Japanese architects who were active before and after the war. Most were collaborators with the war, in a way. My interviewees admitted to some continuity between the prewar and postwar generations, but gave no testimony about direct links. So I had to somehow piece together their methodologies, their modus operandi, their manner of speech, what they designed. Basically I thought nothing had changed. Those 20 years—the decade before the war and the decade after—were an unbroken progression. There was no discontinuity. The end of the war came right in the middle. The ideological disruption was only superficial.

I knew Tange would never agree to such an interview, so I didn't ask. Tange never talked about the war years. He never spoke in public about the ideas he had then. During the war he won two major competitions held by the Architectural Institute of Japan: the first was for the monument to the Greater East Asia Co-Prosperity Sphere ⑧ in 1942 and the second was for the Japanese-Thai Cultural Center in Bangkok ⑩ in 1943. Those were, in a sense, Tange's debut projects. After Japan's surrender in the war, he won the competition for the Hiroshima Peace Memorial Park, which was completed in 1954.

I was a student of his from 1952 and joined his studio in 1954. I worked with him as an assistant, then as his collaborating partner. In all the time I was in his office, until 1963, I never heard Tange talk about those three projects, nor after I went independent but continued to collaborate with him, until 1975. So I know almost everything about Kenzo Tange over those 20 years.

Japan's leading modernists pre-Tange, Junzo Sakakura and Kunio Maekawa, have a European father figure: Le Corbusier. Tange, next in line, is freer from his influence...

**1936** Sakakura, working in Le Corbusier's office in Paris, inspects La Ville Radieuse with Pierre Jeanneret.

**1951** Maekawa listens to Corbu, his former boss, while in the UK for CIAM.

**1955** Mentors and protégé: Tange (arms folded) with Hideto Kishida (hand on face), his professor at Tokyo University and later a collaborator and advisor, and Maekawa, his first boss (left).

## TANGE AND TRADITION

At the beginning of his career, Tange the modernist systematically refers to the classics of Japanese architectural tradition.

### Symmetry

**690** Ise Shrine: Shintoism's most sacred shrine.

**1942** Monument to the Greater East Asia Co-Prosperity Sphere: Shrine-like building for the "sacred" zone of public celebration.

### Courtyard

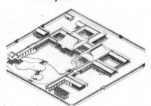

**1331** Imperial Palace, Kyoto: wings enclosing courtyards.

**1943** Japanese-Thai Culture Center, Bangkok: palatial *Shinden-zukuri* (compositional form).

### Pilotis

**1620** Katsura Detached Palace, Kyoto: raised on pilotis.

**1955** Hiroshima Peace Memorial Museum: traditional architectural proportion painstakingly rendered in high tech earthquake-proof concrete.

He graduated in 1938, but the mystery is before 1945: the 10 years from 1935 to 1945.

What I would argue is that Tange was the most significant person who established an ideology in design before the war ended. Back then, his mentor at Tokyo Imperial University was a young professor called Hideto Kishida, who was in a position to judge competitions and plans for international expositions and the Tokyo Olympics of 1964. He had a new design strategy for interpreting Shinto architecture in a modernist manner, though he himself didn't design. He was juxtaposing images of ancient buildings such as Ise Shrine, the Kyoto Imperial Palace, and Katsura Detached Palace with his own photographs. Tange responded to this strategy. He used precisely those three ancient buildings as models for the three competitions I mentioned previously. And of course, Kishida was on the jury for those competitions. You could say that Kishida discovered Tange before the end of the war as the modernist architect who could represent Japan.

I recently wrote a study on Michizo Tachihara.[3] The same generation as Tange, he was a beautiful poet and a modern architect. Not in the Italian Fascist mold, but more like Speer, a northern, Scandinavian classicist. He gave considerable thought to what Japanese sensibility should be. Also a student of Kishida, as an architect and poet, he was in the same milieu as Tange, who at the time was only concerned with Corbu and European modernist architecture, not with Japan. Tachihara must have been worried about Tange. He later asked him to think how they could work together on the Japanese situation. My assumption is that Tachihara pushed Tange toward a Japanese romanticism to which he himself belonged.

RK **To become more Japanese. And that was during the 10 mystery years from 1935 to '45?**

AI Yes. Tange managed to establish "Japan-ness" in modern architecture. In my essay, I compare him to Giuseppe Terragni, who tried to use the abstract vocabulary of modern architecture to create something beyond the Mussolini period.[4]

RK **A parallel.**

AI Yes, a parallel. That was before the war. After the war, Eero Saarinen was also a parallel. Tange always had some parallel competitor.

### Okamoto

RK **What was Tange's trajectory after the war?**

AI The Hiroshima Peace Memorial Park was probably Tange's first major work to be built in Japan after the war, which was built on ground zero of the atomic bomb. His second project of national importance was the Yoyogi National Gymnasia for the 1964 Tokyo Olympics. The third was Expo '70 in Osaka. Tange had a close relationship with the artist Taro Okamoto, who designed the funny sculpture in Expo '70 called Tower of the Sun. They were friends, but completely different in character and expression. Always fighting—a love-hate relationship. [*laughs*] I know because I was always in between them. Okamoto had studied art in Paris among the Surrealists and Abstract School. He was also associated with Bataille's group. Coming back to Tokyo a little before the war, he started an avant-garde movement. I think Tange became very close to him and was influenced, through him, by the European style of avant-garde.

RK **This was before the war or just after the war?**

AI Okamoto studied and came back to Japan before the war, but was soon drafted into the army. His activities started after the war. In 1954, when I finished graduate school, he took me to Okamoto's studio to assist him. One day Okamoto asked me to bring as many maps of Tokyo and reference materials about the future of Tokyo as possible. He said he wanted to plan a utopian city, like Jean Dubuffet and other European artists were doing. It was a proposal

Over 15 years, three epochal projects by Tange symbolize and
catalyze Japan's economic and spiritual postwar resurgence...

< **1955** Hiroshima Peace Memorial Park: opening ceremony on the 10th anniversary of the bomb, a year before the government calls the official end of the post-war era.

^ **1964** Yoyogi National Gymnasia: icon of the Tokyo Olympics, and centerpiece of a massive modernization drive, including elevated highways across the capital and bullet trains to Osaka—funded by Japan's unfolding economic miracle.

> **1970** Big Roof at Expo '70, Osaka: *Time* magazine declares on its cover that "No Country has a Stronger Franchise on the Future than Japan."

## TANGE VS. OKAMOTO

Creative opponents, Tange and artist Taro Okamoto represent opposite poles of the Japanese psyche: Yayoi sophistication and Jomon brute force...

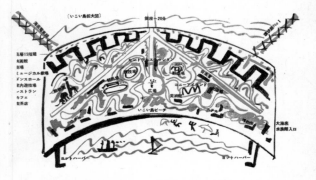

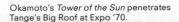

**1959** The pair first cross paths on Okamoto's *Ikojima*, aka Ghost Tokyo, an island of leisure that would float on Tokyo Bay. The scheme is part of a radical new masterplan for the entire city, for which Tange contributes expertise and dispatches his student, Isozaki, to assist.

For Expo '70, an unlikely collaboration forms: Tange the harmonizer and Okamoto the provocateur, drinking, smoking, and gesticulating...

Okamoto's *Tower of the Sun* penetrates Tange's Big Roof at Expo '70.

**Plan for Tokyo 1960**
Taro Okamoto's *Ikoijima* was an artistic exercise, but Tange's Plan for Tokyo 1960 was nothing less than Le Corbusier's Ville Radieuse (1935). With the idea that a single creator can build a society wherein a huge number of people will live, Le Corbusier later approached Stalin. In India, he charmed a powerful provincial family and ended up making huge, sculptural relics in Chandigarh. So, as a way of making places for people to live, their approaches had a serious deficiency.
**Masato Otaka**

**dynamism**
Tange and Isozaki made this great structure that was supposed to be a cybernetic environment. They wanted it to be invisible architecture, faceless architecture, with no façade; everything is the exchange of information, etc. Then Okamoto said: "It's too factional and futuristic. Let's make something very brutal." So he put this figure through it. It was a deliberate Jomon act against Yayoi civilization. Jomon is an ancient culture—it literally means trace of rope around a vase. Jomon is regarded as rough, wild, and popular. Then Icame Yayoi, which is smooth, polished, and regarded as aristocratic. Okamoto took pictures of Neolithic vases and said:"This is Japan. Forget about polished surface, go directly into this depth!" It's an odd couple: Tange with Yayoi sophistication and Okamoto with Jomon, representing some deeper transgressive energy.
**Akira Asada**

**strong role**
Asada was secretary-general, assigned by Tange to help organize the conference while he taught at MIT in 1959. Asada convened meetings of the Metabolists in the run-up to the conference.

**Team 10 meeting**
Otterlo, September 1959: the meeting where CIAM (Congrès International d'Architecture Moderne) collapses and is replaced by Team 10. Tange presented his recently completed Kagawa Prefecture Office building and Kikutake's Sky House and Marine City (1958).

for a kind of "virtual" Tokyo or second Tokyo, right in the middle of Tokyo Bay. It was publicized as a collaboration with Tange. Okamoto's genius was calling it Ghost Tokyo (*Ikojima*, Island of Leisure). His innovation was to orient the city's growth from the Imperial Palace toward a new island on Tokyo Bay, whereas a radial expansion was already underway outward from the Palace, just like Greater London. He said, let's take refuse landfill as our starting point and make another Tokyo. Anyone living in Tokyo who gets frustrated...

RK **Let's go there! Was Okamoto's project part of Tange's** Plan for Tokyo 1960 **or independent of it?**

AI You could say they were independent, but chronologically speaking, Okamoto's virtual Ghost Tokyo came first, which may have triggered the Plan for Tokyo 1960. Actually, a number of similar projects came out before and after those two, but they simply sought to expand real estate by reclaiming land. In my view, Japan's first avant-garde was this artist, Taro Okamoto. I was really surprised when he proposed the *Tower of the Sun*: it pierced the Tange team's flat Big Roof scheme for the Expo, sticking out above. It was a tumult.

RK **A scandal.**

AI Yes. Many young art critics asked me what I thought about it. The roof had become a kind of skin, a membrane penetrated by the tower. Okamoto thrived on polarities. He always brought in an opposing element and focused on the tension created in between. Tange, conversely, always produced synthesis; he resolved oppositions. The discrepancies between the two men working together generated a kind of dynamism.

### The Man behind the Scene

RK **The emergence of Metabolism around the time of the Tokyo Bay plan is a very complicated story. As with Deconstructivism, everyone and no one belongs to it. Would you say it began with the World Design Conference? Did the movement emerge spontaneously—as simultaneous insights shared by like-minded people—or was it more like a branding campaign? Because you can read it both ways.**

AI In my view, the idea of a Metabolist group came from Tange's partner Takashi Asada. He was a strange engineer, almost a mad engineer, but very interesting. I was very influenced by him. Tange wasn't so technologically oriented, but Asada had lots of ideas on technology that were sometimes quite strange and not so successful. But he exerted a strong influence on Tange's technological side. Kurokawa and I were his pupils and at the same time his friends. He taught us a lot. But Asada always tried to start from zero, to create from complete tabula rasa. So once the Metabolist group was actually formed with his efforts, Asada said, "OK, you guys go ahead—you're on your own. I'll do something else." He left them, as always. That's why his name isn't on the list, but he was behind the scenes at the beginning. Asada had a very strong role all through the World Design Conference.

RK **Who came?**

AI It was right after the Team 10 meeting. Alison and Peter Smithson were invited, and Aldo van Eyck. Louis Kahn and Paul Rudolf came from the United States. There was also Jean Prouvé.

RK **And did the Japanese architects manifest themselves as a group?**

AI Well, Asada suggested to one architecture critic, Noboru Kawazoe, that he organize some young architects to present a manifesto and proposals in book form at the conference. Kawazoe was very active at that time and sometimes critical of Tange in his writing. Kawazoe first sounded out Asada's idea with Masato Otaka, who was working with Fumihiko Maki. Then he asked Kiyonori Kikutake, Kisho Kurokawa, Maki, and me. No doubt everybody made their quick sketches in two or three months, but it was too much for me. Besides I had

Never a Metabolist, Isozaki builds in a different mode throughout the 1960s. Four of his buildings are in Oita, on the island of Kyushu, where his father is an influential businessman and poet. After two Brutalist experiments, Isozaki's obsession with art—and his contrarian flair—manifests in his Nakayama House in 1964. Drawing on Junichiro Tanizaki's *In Praise of Shadows* (1933), he claims: "I tried to practice a reckless quest to see if a sheer composition of cubes could be architecture. It would be irrelevant to proportional relationship or balance. Solely for the purpose of destroying the exquisite proportion—a face of Japan which I learned from Kenzo Tange—did I make such a flop."[5]

**1960** Oita Medical Hall.

**1963** Iwata Girls' High School.

**1964** Nakayama House, Oita.

**1966** Oita Prefectural Library.

**independent**
While working on Plan for Tokyo 1960, Isozaki also developed his City in the Air project for Nishi-Shinjuku, which would have perfectly fit the Metabolist book.
**Hajime Yatsuka**

Herbert Spencer
1820–1903, British social philosopher who coined the phrase "survival of the fittest."

Group Form
"Our idea of Group Form stands firmly against the image we have had in architecture for thousands of years: that is, the image of a single structure, complete in itself." Maki and Otaka, "Toward Group Form," Metabolism 1960.

lots of work going in Tange Lab. I was on his team for Plan for Tokyo 1960. I was still a young member of Tange's studio with no plans to go independent, so for one thing I didn't need to join them.

## Utopia

**RK**  **Who do you think invented the word "Metabolism"?**

**AI**  I don't know, maybe Kikutake. But I was thinking about their concept of time: time is linear and grows or progresses from the beginning to become a utopia in the end. It's a linear progression with no…

**RK**  **No deviation.**

**AI**  Right. When Japan surrendered in 1945, I was still very young, but I could feel that history was disrupted. At the same time there was a sense of complete stillness, from which maybe another time or another history could start. Like in the movie *The Matrix*, two or three parallel worlds were crossing—this kind of thinking preoccupied me.

**RK**  **So did you make plans?**

**AI**  I had no idea of planning per se. We needed targets for planning. In order to create any kind of utopia, planning efforts had to be systematic. Or so we'd learned from 19th-century Marxist ideas and utopian thought inherent in Herbert Spencer's Darwinistic, progressive social order. I knew this wasn't what was actually happening, but I couldn't explain why. The only doubt I had about the Metabolists was that these architects had no skepticism toward their utopia; they represented only a form of progressivism. I thought they were too optimistic. They really believed in technology, in mass production; they believed in systematic urban infrastructure and growth. Change and growth were Team 10 subjects too, of course. We learned a lot from Team 10.

## Two Tendencies

**RK**  **For me, there are two interesting tendencies in Metabolism: one is very formal, very strong, and very harsh, the other shapeless and undefined. [*Draws two building shapes—one with a striking form, the other blurry.*]**

**AI**  Probably the latter is Group Form, of Maki's conception. Tange and I, of course, are on the formal side.

**RK**  **Yes, I know. I'm also on that side, unfortunately, so I always have the feeling that the other side is more interesting. [*laughs*] Do you have any comment about that side?**

**AI**  I guess everyone was on board with the idea that the city is formless and accidental. However, one does need form to make a project. Here's the contradiction.

**RK**  **What I find interesting about Maki is that he himself can't do "formless" anymore—he also came over to our side! [*laughs*]**

**AI**  Any architect who wants to design architecture will. [*laughs*]

## Cultural Connections

**RK**  **One Metabolist, Noboru Kawazoe, was a journalist. Was there any connection with writers and other intellectuals? In other words, was architecture at that point part of a larger cultural movement? Were there Metabolist writers or Metabolist artists?**

**AI**  I don't think the Metabolists seriously considered their concepts or their architecture in any cultural context. They were more following developments in modern architecture or industrial product design. There were artists, composers, theatre people, photographers, and writers back then in Japan, of course; not actual groups, but…

**RK**  **Connections.**

While working in Tange Lab on Plan for Tokyo 1960, Isozaki develops a new kind of megastructure: the joint core system, with branches growing off in different directions, creating a hovering network of buildings. Then, very quickly, his artistic side takes over and he imagines the megastructure's demise into Roman ruins. A Metabolic preemption and absorption of decay, or a cynicism about the future that the Metabolists are incapable of?

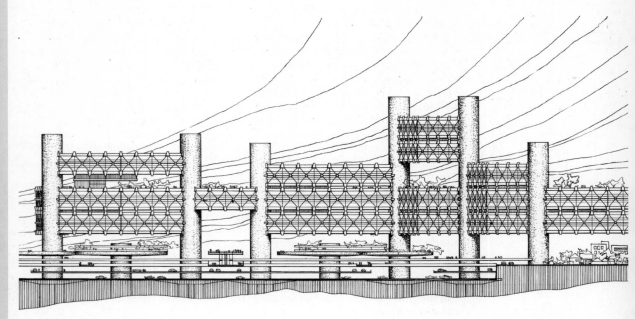

**1960** Prototype: City in the Air, employing the joint core system.

**1962** Destruction of prototype: "Incubation Process," which Isozaki captions with a poem:[6]

Incubated cities are destined to self-destruct
Ruins are the style of our future cities
Future cities are themselves ruins
Our contemporary cities, for this reason,
are destined to live only a fleeting moment
Give up their energy and return to inert material
All of our proposals and efforts will be buried
And once again the incubation mechanism is reconstituted
That will be the future

**1962** Just before leaving Tange Lab to set up his own office, Isozaki develops, privately, "Clusters in the Air"—a more radical solution to Tokyo's mess than his teacher might allow. Striding over (ignoring) the chaos of Shibuya, the Clusters—a variation on the joint core system—allow habitation that begins only at the limit of Tokyo's building height law, 31 meters. "Tokyo is hopeless," Isozaki declares. "I am no longer going to consider architecture that is below 30 meters in height … I am leaving everything below 30 meters to others. If they think they can unravel the mess in this city, let them try."[7]

Sketch for Clusters in the Air.

The model.

## PRESERVATION

**1963** Isozaki, 32, still relatively unknown, exercises political muscle with a poetic project in the popular weekly *Shukan Asahi*. While the developer Mitsubishi begins to demolish the historic "red brick town" of Marunouchi (Tokyo's central business district) in order to build what the critic Teiji Itoh calls "Stalingrad," Isozaki presents a counterproposal, using megastructure as a tool of protest. Starting at 45 meters up, a network of interlocking tetrahedrons hovers over the existing buildings rather than destroying them, creating an elevated artificial ground for habitation, liberated from the density and the traffic of the streets below. Residents move at three different speeds and in three different trajectories around the megastructure: vertically, via express elevator in the core; diagonally, via escalators sliding along the buildings' edges; and horizontally via conveyor belts in the horizontal beam connecting the tetrahedrons.[8]

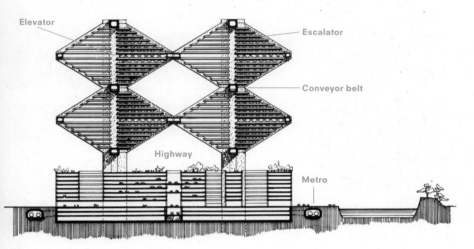

Integrated transport.

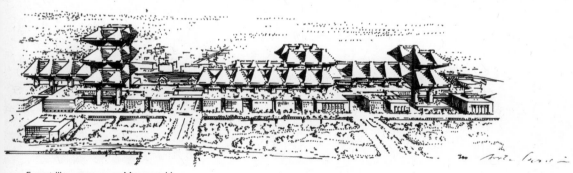

Forest-like canopy over Marunouchi.

**1968** Moving in different circles to the Metabolists, Isozaki mobilizes his friends outside of architecture—photographer Shomei Tomatsu, graphic designer Kohei Sugiura, musique concrète composer Toshi Ichiyanagi—to help create his installation *Electric Labyrinth* at the Milan Triennale, an art exhibition. Isozaki builds 12 curved aluminum panels featuring Tomatsu's photos of the devastation in Hiroshima and Nagasaki; as visitors pass through, the panels rotate to reveal images of corpses, while Ichiyanagi's music plays. "We wanted to show how the cities of the future would continue to fall into ruin…"

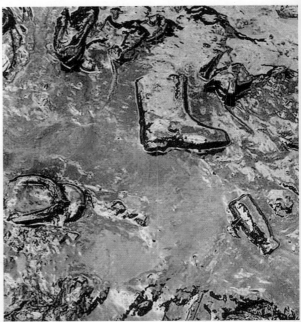

"The only photographer in Japan after the war."
Shomei Tomatsu, *Ise Bay Typhoon Devastation* (1959).

Kindred spirits: as part of the May '68 movement, students occupy the triennale and prevent the public from ever seeing *Electric Labyrinth*. Isozaki, a burgeoning political radical himself, takes this photograph, and remains sympathetic.

*Hiroshima Ruined for the Second Time*: the imagination of megastructures growing like weeds over the blasted landscape of Hiroshima (photographed by Tomatsu) makes the scene even more bleak for Isozaki. "The Japan that I thought I should talk about to the outside was not a 'beautiful Japan' but as Hiroshima suffering from wounds."[9]

**Electric Labyrinth**
Isozaki's installation, made in collaboration with Kohei Sugiura (graphic design), Shomei Tomatsu (photography) and Toshi Ichiyanagi (music), never opened to the public due to the student occupation of the Milan Triennale. Only in 2002 is the work shown for the first time, at ZKM, Karlsruhe, in the exhibition "Iconoclash," curated by Peter Weibel, Hans Ulrich Obrist, et al.

**no antipathy**
Isozaki: "I myself have had a peculiar relationship with Metabolism. Though I never belonged to the group, I was apparently making projects as a Metabolist from a larger perspective. And not knowing such domestic details, foreign people began quoting or referring to my work as an example of Metabolism, which kept me busy correcting them for some time. But now as I look back, I was an assimilator of Metabolism, if not its member. As a proof, I participated in an exhibition organized by the group. Working in this way, I came to see gradually but clearly the difference of my method and thinking from theirs."
*Shinkenchiku*, April 1978.

**earthquakes**
Stories of people immediately rebuilding on the ruins of their destroyed homes are often reported in newspapers in Japan as something admirable. In 1963, when Skopje was destroyed by an earthquake, Tange's team won the competition to reconstruct the city, and I went to the site several times to help develop a final scheme. We learned a great deal in Skopje. Instead of immediately constructing houses on the sites of destroyed buildings, the Yugoslavs created provisional shelters—tent huts—in the suburbs and lived in them for several years. They began the work of construction only after developing a masterplan, and then gradually returned to their former districts. That is unfortunately quite difficult to do in Japan.
**Koji Kamiya**

**Tsukiji project**
Also in 1964: a colony of buildings connected with joint cores. After the death of Dentsu president Hideo Yoshida, the project was completed in a compromised form.

**AI** Yes, connections. For example, the art critic Shuzo Takiguchi, a friend of André Breton and Marcel Duchamp from the same generation. To me, he was a modern artist-architect, my guru of sorts. Many artists like Yoko Ono and composers like Toru Takemitsu felt the same way toward him. Among them was the photographer Shomei Tomatsu. To look at his work after the war, one would feel he was the only photographer around. He was once asked to be a member of the Metabolist group, so he contributed photographs to the second book of Metabolism, which never got made, but it wasn't really his best work anyway. Starting with the aftermath of the Nagasaki atomic bombing right after the war up till now, he's continued to document the hidden side of Japanese society.

He's completely different from Nobuyoshi Araki, who is my friend. Tomatsu is much more serious. For me, Tomatsu was the only photographer in Japan after the war. He represented and documented all for us. I asked him to contribute photographs to my installation *Electric Labyrinth* at the 1968 Milan Triennale, but he said I'll collect all the images taken after the atomic bomb and give them to you. So he gave me maybe 50 photographs, and with one of them I made a panoramic montage entitled *Hiroshima Ruined for the Second Time*. I think he's a very important photographer. I was also close to the writers Kenzaburo Oé and Kobo Abé, who wrote really fantastic novels influenced by Kafka.

**RK** I know Abé's work.

**AI** The film *Woman of the Dunes* (1964) was based on his novel. I already knew Kobo Abé before he was published. Kenzaburo Oé and I were close because he was a student of Professor Kazuo Watanabe, whom I immensely respected. He was an expert on humanism and introduced Rabelais to Japan.

**RK** **So you're describing a cultural situation compared to which the Metabolists were somehow narrow, always too linear.**

**AI** I think so. Of course, I have no antipathy towards the Metabolism movement, but their interests were so limited. And another major issue: I didn't like how they wanted to sell their ideas to the authorities, to the Japanese government and the establishment to get more work. Tange was very different: teaching at Tokyo University, his new challenges were received with sympathy. When Tange was a student, he studied Heidegger and many other literary works. He wrote about Corbu before he came on the scene as an architect. In that essay, he mentions Corbu's name only once or twice; most of the discourse is on Michelangelo. He wrote that Corbu and Michelangelo were once-in-a-thousand-year phenomena.[10] It was his first article and very interesting.

**RK** **He had culture.**

**AI** He had knowledge of literature and philosophy.

### Skopje Earthquake

**RK** **Can you tell us something about the Skopje project? Does it actually exist? Because it's one of these strange phenomena—its status is completely ambiguous.**

**AI** Skopje is a long story. One could do a whole book about it.

**RK** **In a way, for me, it's the most pure Metabolist project because earthquakes like the one in 1963 provide good conditions for accelerations.**

**AI** In 1965, Tange was selected in the UN competition from among eight international architects and planners. I'd already gone independent, but didn't have work so he asked me to come back to his studio to work on the Skopje project. I think it was the first project under my personal lead. Right after designing the Olympic gymnasia in 1964, Tange was concentrating on big projects including the Tsukiji project for the Dentsu headquarters, and he was almost completely exhausted. This was the situation behind the Skopje project.

**RK** **But does it exist? Was it built?**

## TABULA RASA IN SKOPJE

**1965** After an earthquake destroys 65 percent of Skopje, Macedonia, the UN calls an international competition to rebuild the city. Tange ("exhausted" after a series of large projects in Japan) teams up again with his former student Isozaki (without work in his new office) and wins the competition, seizing the chance to become an international architect...

Winter: tensions rise as Tange, suited, and Isozaki, wearing the sweater, plan the new Skopje. The rapt attention of the Japanese clashes with the evident skepticism of the Westerners.

Summer: Tange draws directly on the tabula rasa of Skopje, watched by an enforced and ever-enlarging collaboration.

**1966** Tange and Isozaki, attempting to account for Skopje's ancient remnants and natural surroundings, nevertheless plan a hypermodern new city replete with joint-core structures. The masterplan features a classic Tangean central axis and a road system—on multiple levels, in loops, and merging with the buildings—drawn from their last collaboration, Plan for Tokyo 1960.

**nothing at all**
Tange later said that not an insignificant part of their conception was respected and realized in Skopje. He was not speaking of individual architectural forms, which is Isozaki's concern here, but of general layout and modules in plans. This tells us the difference between these two architects.
**Hajime Yatsuka**

**we thought**
Isozaki was Tange's "brain," and it seemed that Tange was dependent on his ideas. The concept of the Festival Plaza was probably largely produced by Isozaki. The source for that large roof was the space frames of Yona Friedman, but Tange himself burned with an abnormal determination to implement a huge space frame covering the plaza as a potent "object" for this national event. However, rather than an object, the Festival Plaza that Isozaki wanted to create was an urban space that would be immediately implemented by means of "information": an instant city. Undoubtedly, he was greatly influenced by Archigram's Plug-In City and Walking City, from 1964. On this site for a national event, Isozaki conceived a scene of people intoxicated by a hallucinatory urban space produced by two robots, as if in a huge disco. However, his scheme was hindered by bureaucrats, and a visionary urban space was not produced.
**Toyo Ito**

**After Expo '70**
For Japan's top architects, 1969–70 was the major postwar turning point. After two national events, the 1964 Tokyo Olympics and Expo '70, the growth of the economy reversed and we entered a period of introversion. There was no longer a place in Japan for Tange; and Otaka, Kikutake, Kurokawa, and the rest of the Metabolists lost the youthfulness and vigor they possessed in the '60s.
**Toyo Ito**

**AI**  Our proposal was approved, but I actually don't know how it was realized in the end. I was having big fights every day in Skopje. I once even tore up the drawings and went home. I have bad memories. When I got there, I found that we'd won first place, with 51 percent. In second place was a Croatian architect. Very traditional, nothing new. They got 49 percent. The percentage was so close, the United Nations decided Tange and the Croatian should work together. In came another team: Doxiadis from Greece, very close to Macedonia, working more on traffic and regional planning, but they also had a say. And to top it all, the UN named their own supervisory team from Warsaw. Everyone who worked on the reconstruction of Warsaw, which was deemed such a success, moved to Skopje.

If there'd been only two of us, it would have been OK, even if we were fighting all the time. But more and more came in, more conservative people, over our heads. After a few months of working there, I was completely exhausted. I thought, "My God, I can't do this anymore." And Tange said, "OK, it's time to compromise and go home." So we did. This was exactly when Tange started to work on Expo '70. He took me on again. For me, the Skopje project basically died, or was killed, at that point. Just a few weeks ago, someone who had been to Skopje came to Tokyo and—

**RK**  **He showed you pictures? Was there something you could recognize?**

**AI**  No, nothing at all! [*laughs*]

### Expo '70, the '70s

**RK**  **Can you explain the main structure you built for Expo '70?**

**AI**  We didn't have many ideas; it was to be a kind of frame for activities. At that time we proposed a movable roof on top—I was thinking of a big 300-meter long frame. But actually Tange designed the frame and I designed all the equipment underneath, including the suspended robot and the walking robot. The suspended robot served for computer-controlled architectural lighting. We proposed the concept and exterior design for the Festival Plaza in 1966 or '67. Tange, as masterplanner, designated the location in 1967, and I made a proposal with an artist and some others that this Festival Plaza should accommodate all kinds of activities including artistic performances underneath the roof, because the weather in Japan is unstable in the summertime. It rains a lot, so we thought we better have some kind of skin or roof.

**RK**  **So Tange designed this big roof to be an umbrella for different projects?**

**AI**  Exactly. Tange divided labors for the Festival Plaza: I worked on all the facilities underneath and the two robots; Kurokawa and others were asked to build capsules within the roof for various architects to exhibit in.

**RK**  **Was Yona Friedman there?**

**AI**  Yes, we invited architects like Friedman, Hans Hollein, and Archigram to exhibit in the capsules. We thought the core members of Team 10 were already a little too established to invite.

Before 1970, Tange had no experience designing an expo. That was really a first for him. But he always found himself in such situations and he did well. This is just my own idea, but it seems to me that Tange played a major role as the architect representing Japan for 25 years until the country's power declined in the 1970s. After Expo '70, no offers came to Tange from the Japanese government so he had to go into "exile." He did lots of work in Saudi Arabia and many other countries. Of course, he had commissions in Japan, but nothing major. Even the Metabolists had more major commissions than Tange.

### Writing

**RK**  **What role does writing play for you?**

**AI**  From 1969 to 1973, I wrote a series of articles explaining contemporary people

**1969–71** "Killing Metabolism with information": Isozaki invites emerging new forces from the West to contribute to the series "Dismantling of Architecture" in *Bijutsu Techo*, giving Japan's younger generation alternatives to Metabolism…

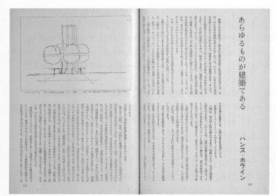

Hans Hollein: "Everything is Architecture."

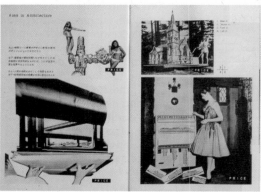

Cedric Price: "Alice in Architecture."

Archizoom: "No-stop City."

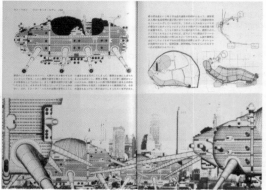

Archigram: "Walking City."

Working again with graphic designer Kohei Sugiura, Isozaki expands the boundaries of his profession in a series of covers for alternative architecture magazine *Toshi Jutaku* (Urban house).

and movements in architecture like Archigram, Archizoom, Superstudio, Cedric Price, and people in Vienna.[11] It was a survey of 1960s radicalism. I wanted to analyze social conditions at the time and the problems that remained.

**RK**    **But in a way, the writing basically killed Metabolism with information. Is that what you're saying? [*laughs*]**

**AI**    Well, I did try. [*laughs*] You do get straight to the point! That was 30 years ago. It was very difficult to write. Even obtaining information directly from each architect was difficult; source materials were limited. Anyway, I tried to edit them and put them into another context. The major point was that '60s movements were radical, not avant-garde. Metabolism was the last movement that tried to be avant-garde. To be an avant-garde, one needs a manifesto. So the Metabolist manifesto in 1960 was the last in modern architecture.

**RK**    **I agree.**

**AI**    After that we've had no manifestos at all. Of course, there have been many interesting words and statements—Hans Hollein, for instance, saying that everything is architecture—yet those ideas don't belong to a traditional utopian avant-garde movement. They were more radical, meaning they pushed the situation to extremes until it exploded and ended abruptly. Radicalism was a major characteristic of the 1960s, and really erupted in '68. Expo '70 was a kind of avant-garde showpiece for traditional modern architecture, yet inside there were more radical ideas.

**RK**    **It was an incubator.**

**AI**    Yes, some things overlapped. Anyway, after Expo '70, all these things became completely kitsch. Society didn't want it. The Japanese government no longer needed it, nor was able to supprt it. After the first global oil shock, which brought on a recession in 1973, it was no longer possible to continue with these kinds of avant-garde ideas. Everything stopped.

**RK**    **Isn't it ironic that avant-gardes only exist when there's a strong government, but fall apart when there's a weak government? There's both nothing to react against and nothing that could possibly support the fantasies. I think one great weakness of architecture since the '70s is that we can never find the support we need.**

**AI**    I think the '70s and the '80s—from 1968 until 1989 when the Soviet Union crashed—was a period of suspended animation in which nothing happened. All we could do was tweak and replace little things. No revolution, no radical change. So-called Deconstruction, for example, which was so popular then, was mannerist manipulation that brought no radical change. After 1989 we may have felt many things were going to happen, but for me those 20 years from 1969 to 1989 were so difficult. Nothing changed.

### Two Domains of Culture

**RK**    **Did you or any of the Metabolists have affiliations with political parties? Were there Communists? Were there left-wing architects or right-wing architects?**

**AI**    Personally, I was very close to the Communist Party when I was a student. I had lots of friends who were Communists. [*laughs*] Some of Tange's friends were…

**RK**    **Communists?**

**AI**    Yes. From around 1968, I was non-political. I didn't trust the Communists or any other parties.The *Zengakuren* activist students' league was already demonstrating. It was just like the student movement in the West. I wasn't political after that, either. Tange had some feeling for it, but was hesitant to visit politicians. Government bureaucrats found Kikutake not only talented, but easy to work with, so he did many different public projects. But Kurokawa was the closest to politics. He appeared in the media with politicians and was always very close to top government figures; he was a kind of star. Kurokawa and I lived in different domains of culture, as architects, which were actually carefully demarcated in a latent way. These domains never overlapped, so I never competed with him. I was very critical of his work.

Architecture alone is insufficient to convey the range of Isozaki's impulses; within architecture, he begins trying even harder to break all rules…

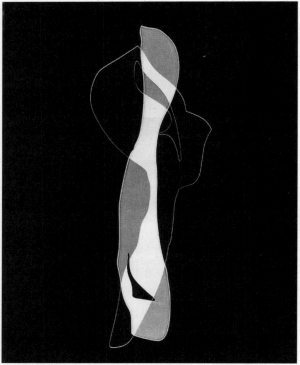

**1978** The Monroe technique infiltrates Isozaki's architecture: "… these curved lines emerge in his architectural works and furniture designs." ("Arata Isozaki: The Man Obsessed with Monroe Curves," *Shukan Shincho*, September 14, 1978.)

**1966** Using his own version of the French curve, made by tracing the shape of Marilyn Monroe, nude, Isozaki draws *Marilyn on the Line*. Jasper Johns sees the drawing in Tokyo and recommends it to the Sydney Janis Gallery in New York for the exhibition "Homages to Marilyn Monroe" in 1967.

**1971** "An effective way of neutralizing architecture…" Isozaki's drawing for Gunma Prefecture Museum of Modern Art is nothing but repeated skeletal cubes: his first salvo in his war against the modernist architectural establishment.

two identities
The double characterization of Isozaki as Arata and Sin seems to have made it possible for him to build many works, unlike European radicals. Sin would have never worked in Qatar, for example.
**Hajime Yatsuka**

Joseph Grima
An editor at *Domus*, researcher and photographer for the Metabolist interviews.

## City Demolition Industry, Inc.

**RK** **I want to talk about your text City Demolition Industry, Inc.** (see p. 52) **and your** two identities **therein: Arata the timid Stalinist versus Sin in the Trotskyist killer. I think it's one of the most interesting texts written by an architect.**

**AI** I wrote it in 1962 when I'd never had anything published as an architect.

**RK** **So this was when you accused the Metabolists of not being skeptical enough, of being too Marxist and linear?**

**AI** Yes, I did so to keep a distance from Metabolism.

**RK** **So how did these two identities work?**

**AI** I can't explain it logically because…I'm a kind of schizophrenic, divided. I wrote a continuation of the Sin and Arata story in which these two personae meet again and talk after 40 years. A bit of science fiction.

**RK** **When did you write this second installment?**

**AI** In 1999, under the title Rumour City.

**RK** **Does it still relate to the same issues?**

**AI** I wrote it when I published the book *Unbuilt* in 1999.[12] In 1962, the character Arata makes a little company and tries to destroy the city and city life. The other, Sin, establishes the company policy. Back then, I thought the character was almost Trotsky, but also partly Stalin. The Stalinist criticizes Trotsky and confuses things. That was the first part. In the second part, the character Sin is based on Trotsky. When Arata meets him 40 years later, he is more than half dead. "You disappeared 40 years ago," Arata says, "and you did it very well. You destroyed the city so well. But now you're so timid. I have more ideas." [*laughs*]

A funny thing happened with the original part. An editor at *The Japan Architect* magazine asked me to write something for the front of the magazine, but he wasn't very specific. So I wrote City Demolition Industry, Inc. He read it and said, "We can't publish this on the front," so he buried the essay at the back in the advertising pages. Nobody read it. [*laughs*] When I published a collection of essays around the beginning of the 1970s, I put it up front, subverting a decade of posteriority.[13]

**RK** **Many people are now interested in architecture as a discipline, though largely unrelated to other disciplines: no links with literature, no connection to painting. What you've been discussing is the total opposite.**

### Reincarnation in the Middle East

**JOSEPH GRIMA** I was curious to see your recent library and bank projects in Qatar. How do you feel about the fact that such visionary projects have been totally decontextualized? There are obviously very similar visual references, but what do you think about the social context for which your original visionary projects were conceived versus where they're being planned now?

**RK** **Can I answer that question?** [*laughs*] **Sorry.**

**AI** Let me tell you a very funny story. When I was introduced to the Emir of Qatar, I showed him my book. Looking through it, he stopped at the City in the Air project from 1962 and said, "Oh, this is very interesting!" I said, "It's a project from my student days. Impossible to realize. Just a dream." But the Emir said, "No, I want this." It was very simple. Back in Tokyo I started to work on it, but still I didn't want to use the exact same form. At first, I was pushing the top of the buildings like a stealth aircraft, but he said, "No, no, no!" [*laughs*]

**RK** **He wanted the real thing.**

**AI** "The original is so much better!" [*laughs*] The Middle East is a very strange place.

**JG** It's really interesting in this regard. But don't you think it's become a kind of logo, a symbol that has been totally decontextualized and reapplied?

**RK** **But that's where my answer comes in. I think the great newness of Metabolism**

**2002** The unbuilt, which he previously celebrated, threatens to become built as Isozaki takes projects designed for Japan's urban condition to Doha, responding to the Emir of Qatar's declaration, "I want this..."

Qatar National Bank: City in
the Air, pulled down to earth.

National Library of Qatar:
a single Cluster in the Air.

**2011** "Super-big": Isozaki's Convention Center,
Doha, part of his masterplan for Education City.
The '70s radical surfs the wave of globalization.

**context**
True, Isozaki's City in the Air, supported only by giant cores, had minimum contact with the ground and could enjoy the maximum freedom from the constrains of local context. However, most of the Metabolists' urban projects were, unlike their European counterparts, designed for specific sites in the city, and thus related to their conception of the city (mostly Tokyo).
**Hajime Yatsuka**

**super-big**
In 2010, Isozaki is designing a super-big masterplan for Changchun, formerly Manchukuo's capital, Xinjing; a museum in Harbin, also in the former Manchukuo; and a concert hall in Datong (Inner Mongolia).

is that it is by definition anti-contextual. It basically claims there is no context and that architecture in the future has to exist independent of context. Beyond social context, beyond the implication of the whole movement.

**KAYOKO OTA Did you work in the Middle East in the '60s and '70s?**

**AI** Tange often did, but I only worked with him and Louis Kahn on the Abbas Abad New City (1973–75), a very large project in the center of Tehran (see p. 610). Tange and Kahn worked together on this big development project sponsored by the Pahlevi family. One developer, I don't know where they were from, was very close to the Pahlevi family, and they asked the two architects to work together.

**RK Excellent taste, eh? [laughs]**

**AI** That was my last collaboration with Tange. I was asked by Tange to work between the two masters and put their ideas into one project. Tange and I worked on it first together, then we had a workshop with Louis Kahn in Japan, then Kahn sent us a scheme from the States two months before he passed away. It might have been Kahn's last project. In the end, I had to finish it, which I somehow did. [laughs] Then came the Iranian revolution. The Pahlevis fled the country and that was that. The Qatar National Library was the first project of my own in the Middle East. Now my office is loaded with work for the Aga Khan: we have a series of campuses for the University of Central Asia in Kazakhstan, Tajikistan, and Kyrgyzstan—really difficult places. But I thought the idea of creating campuses in such locations would be interesting: no technology at all, more like medieval monasteries in the mountains.

**RK What do you think of the times now?**

**AI** There are no middle-size projects; they're either very small or super big.

**RK Do you also think it is one of the worst moments?**

**AI** I don't think so. I think every moment is very difficult, terrible! [laughs] There were no good periods in the last two decades; they came only in the 1960s, '70s and early '80s, when we still had small-scale, individual architectural projects. But by the end of the 1980s big developments started in a few places, and throughout the '90s the wave of large projects spread gradually from London to Berlin to Seoul to Las Vegas and Singapore, and finally it's arrived in Milan.

**RK Dubai?**

**AI** Dubai and Abu Dhabi. In those places, sites are always more than one or two hundred thousand square meters. Huge. No longer human scale.

**RK No intimacy.**

**AI** So your concept of "bigness" is becoming a reality! [laughs] Or super-big even!

**References**
1  Hajime Yatsuka, "The Alter-Ego and Id 'Machines' of Modernist Architecture," ArchiLab's Urban Experiments (London: Thames and Hudson, 2005).

2  Arata Isozaki, Nihon kenchiku no 1930-nendai—Keifu to myakuraku (Japanese architecture in the 1930s: connections and context) (Tokyo: Kajima Shuppankai, 1978).

3  Arata Isozaki, "Zenshin deno mi no makasekiri—Tange Kenzo no Nihon" (Total surrender with whole body—Japan by Kenzo Tange), Shinkenchiku, July 2005.

4  Arata Isozaki, Japan-ness in Architecture (Cambridge, MA: MIT Press, 2006).

5  Isozaki, Shinkenchiku, July 2005.

6  Arata isozaki, Japan-ness in Architecture, 2006

7  Teiji Ito, "Moratorium and Invisibility," in David Stewart, eds. Arata Isozaki Architecture 1960–1990 (New York: Rizzoli, 1991).

8  "Mitsubishi Jisho ni mono mosu" (Protest against Mitsubishi Jisho), Shukan Asahi, February 1, 1963.

9  Isozaki, Shinkenchiku, July 2005.

10  Kenzo Tange, "Ode to Michelangelo," Gendai Kenchiku, December 1939.

11  Arata Isozaki, "Kenchiku no kaitai" (Dismantling of architecture), Bijutsu Techo, 1969–71.

12  Arata Isozaki, Unbuilt (Tokyo: TOTO Publishing, 2001).

13  Arata Isozaki, "Toshi hakaigyo K.K.," Shinkenchiku, September 1962. Text published in English as "City Demolition Industry, Inc." in Kenneth Frampton, ed., A New Wave of Japanese Architecture: Catalog 10 (Cambridge, MA: MIT Press, 1980).

## City Demolition Industry, Inc.
### Arata Isozaki, 1962

You must not laugh at this strange business. The company is real! In the very center of Tokyo, yes, floating in the air, it is trying to sneak into the cracks of your life—the life you spend in the megalopolis.

I first learned of the existence of this company when I looked at the name printed on the visiting card of my friend S. He was once a professional killer rather famous in the field, but he quit that job to become a founder of the City Demolition Industry, Inc. I never knew why he chose murder for a profession, but he always said he did so because it was the quickest way to make money, and I did not try to delve further into it. I regretted that he should present me with his new card, slowly, shrugging his shoulders, just as I was about to consult him about an important matter I had particularly at heart. This is about annihilating all the editors of magazines in our country who are too timid to challenge the status quo in city planning and architecture. I asked him if things were going better. My friend S. then urged me to join his company, the name of which sounded to me more like a secret society than that of company.

There was a serious cause for his resignation from his job as a killer— a monster had emerged that kept hurting his professional pride day and night! He is a man of temperament, as any artist or artisan might be. Once he accepted an order to kill someone, he never spared any effort in the process of his work, whether that person was only a small boss with a dozen followers or a big figure in power such as a cabinet minister. The careful, long-term planning and scheming, the beauty of a murder well done, as well as the perfect disposal of the body! It was just like an artist engaged in designing. Without the snobbery of Frank Lloyd Wright or the bluff of Le Corbusier, he could produce a complicated vision in which, while extinction was coupled with existence, the concept of emptiness was caught in the very midst of action. He might have been one of the very, very few who could actually accomplish this. Then all of a sudden he changed his job.

Naturally, I was very curious to know why. He said he had been utterly disappointed at the relatively insignificant situation into which his profession had been driven, and so, feeling the bitterness of hurt pride, he wished to break with it and to start a new one. But what was the direct motive? In answer to my question he unfolded the newspaper at his side. "Yesterday's Traffic Accidents—5 Killed, 89 Injured." This meant that modern civilization had replaced the private enterprise of killing. The steady increase of such unintentional murders as traffic accidents, and moreover the low price attached to an individual life,

usually less than one million yen, gradually nullified his profession as a killer, lowered his wages, and hurt his sense of self-esteem. According mechanism called the city, which was the inevitable product and the physical supporter of modern civilization. The city, therefore, was the killer of all killers and, worse still, being anonymous, it was a curious enterprise to which no responsibilities were attached. And he felt that in order to create an age in which the killing profession would again be an art, and in which this human act could be performed with pleasure, there was nothing more urgent than to destroy these inhuman cities. The aim of his company, therefore, was to destroy cities by all possible means. Tokyo, for him, was especially easy to undermine. It was like a building whose foundations had decayed, walls collapsing and water pipes getting thinner, structures barely standing, braced by numerous struts and supported by a jungle of props and buttresses, patches and stains from the leaks in the roof. Its original elegance had vanished. Imagine such a deserted house—decorated gaudily on the surface, it goes on killing people, goes on emitting a vigorous energy. A gigantic monster on the brink of extinction; a pig roasted whole; the ultimate evil of unintentional, inevitable mass massacre. . . He said that such a city must be destroyed as soon as possible.

This city makes people gradually forget the seriousness of death. Disappointed or rather infuriated by the depression of his own profession, my friend S., who decided to destroy the cities, may be an old-fashioned humanist. An admirer of artistic and humanistic murder, S. made up his mind to challenge the megalopolitan city.

It seemed strange to me that the prospectus printed for the establishment of his company, which he gave to me to read, showed only the conceptual aim of destruction and the methods and the organization of the execution. Well, S. is a poet, and so it may be that he is proud that only poets can understand his true intention. Now, if one is of the opinion that only methods are of significance nowadays and that each individual can prove his identity only when he risks his life in executing these prescriptions, it might be said that the aim and the prospect are only ghost images and that the real image is present only in the methods. A professional killer, in this sense, does not display interest in anything other than method. More precisely, all that counts for him is the act of killing, because he must discount all other considerations.

### Prospectus of the Establishment of the City Demolition Industry, Inc. and the Content of Its Business
Our company aims at the complete destruction of large cities which have been repeatedly engaged

in vicious mass murder, and at the construction of a civilization in which elegant, pleasant and humanistic murder can be carried out easily. We shall be engaged in any action necessary for achieving these aims. We practice our business as follows:

## 1. Physical Destruction
We shall destroy buildings, roads and other city facilities, using all possible means including human power, dynamite, atomic and hydrogen bombs.

## 2. Functional Destruction
The aggravation of traffic confusion through the systematic abolition of traffic signals, etc.; the encouragement of illegal construction; the dropping of poison into water reservoirs; the disturbance of communication networks; the total abolition of the house number system; the immediate and complete enforcement of all legal city planning provisions.

## 3. Destruction of Images
The encouragement of proposals for Utopia city planning in the future; the enforcement of city improvement and a solution to the housing shortage by the mass-construction of public corporation-style residences; the elimination of all calamities in the cities including traffic accidents.

Our company will energetically carry out the kinds of destruction stated above and will constantly endeavor to introduce new plans. Readers may laugh at the determination of my friend S. as expressed in the above prospectus. You are all well accustomed to this city, intoxicated with its familiar smiles. You go on producing beautiful buildings one after another. You have nothing to do with my friend S.'s heroic resolve. He says that he does not feel any poetic sentiment before your beautiful accomplishments. He intends to continue the strange business of his company. He has nothing to do with you—nothing at all.

Not because I happen to be engaged in urban design but because S. is my friend I was finally persuaded to analyze and discuss the prospectus of his company. While discussing various aspects of the problem, his opinion and mine got so mingled together that we became unable to tell whose was whose. However, we finally reached certain conclusions. Is it really possible to carry out the physical destruction of modern cities?

To answer this question, it is enough to remember Tokyo or Hiroshima of seventeen years ago. The scene there was more than ruins. It was next to nothing. Although Hiroshima at that time was sentenced to death and was expected to remain uninhabitable for the next seventy years, we have to concede that Hiroshima has come to possess a body even more substantial than it had before the

war. No more Hiroshima! Resurrection like a phoenix! All right, at that time nobody dared to propose the destruction of cities. Nobody will at present, either. A city with physical substance—perhaps it has never existed on earth.

Aren't cities merely abstract ideas? Nothing but ghost images which have been built up by citizens through mutual agreement for their practical purposes? And, so far as such a mirage has been transmitted, only the process of transmission exists as the substance of the city. The force that can eliminate this transmission is not the destruction of cities, but the eclipse of a civilization.

If you do not believe this, burn your own house and dig up your land. You will not forget the scene, and somebody will probably make a record of it. Thus, you will still be possessed of some fragments of your house unless oblivion, death and the total eclipse of civilization wipe out everything. But I am not trying to justify nuclear war, which seems to contain the ability to annihilate both the substance and idea simultaneously. Certainly this will cause extinction.

My friend S.'s image of the mechanism of city may be too simple. Because it might be said that the city is maintained by a complicated feedback mechanism which its citizens have built up in order to protect themselves. This feedback is exquisitely intricate and so the functional destruction, as mentioned in Article 2 of the Prospectus, will be able to be immediately repaired.

However, the immediate and complete execution of today's city planning as drawn and legally authorized—if it were executed just as specified in the articles and maps—would bring about a drastic change. Such city planning has always ended in empty theory and that is why cities have been kept alive. But if any city planning would be put into practice just as it is blueprinted, the mayor would lose his job and the city assembly would be thrown into confusion. I had better say that city authorities have opposed city planning not because it is revolutionary, but because it is unrealistic and old-fashioned. If you don't believe me, put city planning into practice, and you will find it an excellent means for throwing the city into turmoil or for stultifying its energy. My friend S.'s opinion seems to be a little matter-of-fact, for in Japan those who have devised the legal city plans have not dreamt even for a moment that their plans will be actually put into practice.

That is why they have legalized plans in a carefree manner. According to my friend S. the implementation of city plans would inevitably bring cities to destruction. He says, with a cynical smile, that as soon as I draw up a plan I should put it into practice. It is inexcusable, he argues, for the professional to only make utopian plans. On the other hand the plan of his city demolition industry, if he executes it too hastily, will bring prosperity rather than destruction and, against his will, the circumstances that would satisfy his artistic aspirations will not be brought forth. However, when I think of the hollow sound of the slogans for building, renewing and improving cities—in reality the political propping-up of the metropolis—I come to think in terms of destruction as the only reality.

Since S. is not a city planner nor an architect but a killer, he can be active about the cities, and can have concrete ideas because he can deal with the abstraction and unreality in his mind. On the other hand, I am connected, in my profession, with the product of reality, and so while I make concrete proposals, concrete countermeasures, and improvements on them, I am made to feel ever more keenly the impossibility of putting my proposals into practice. My friend S. says that that is all the more reason for him to go ahead with his business and that in so doing, he will again have some connection with cities and will feel the impracticality of concrete plans. As for myself, I could continue to draw an unrealistic veil over my concrete proposals as a staff member of his company.

Despite all these exchanges our discussions broke up..He called me a Stalinist coward and I called him an inexperienced Trotskyite. Thus, pasting the labels of the long past on each other, we both felt some satisfaction.

P.S. His name is SIN and mine is ARATA as it is written on the first page of this article. It is however, a sheer coincidence that SIN is a Chinese phonetic reading of the character of my name, while ARATA is the Japanese reading. I don't know if my friend's business will ever prosper.

*Note*
*I wrote this story in 1962 when Tokyo was on the first wave of rapid economic growth, blending the reality and dream (fantasy) that I then saw.*

(Translated by Richard Gage)

# Tabula Rasa
# In search of wide open space

**"Construction will have nothing blocking its way..."**

Yoshikazu Uchida, "Datong Urban Planning,"
*Kenchiku Zasshi*, November 1939.

Where Western architecture is based on a myth of the tabula rasa—a new beginning in the old world, Japan, with its population crammed into the ca. 25 percent of its surface which is not mountainous, has a stifling lack of space, which makes the act of planning intolerably pressurized, or simply futile. A series of natural and man-made phenomena, with intervals of a decade, suddenly, almost incidentally, offer Japan brand new wide open spaces that force architectural experimentation on a grand scale:

**1923** The Great Kanto Earthquake devastates Tokyo, creating space for a new masterplan to fix the crowded, messy capital, but not the political or economic conditions in which it can actually be realized.

**1932** Dreaming of a Greater East Asia Co-Prosperity Sphere, in which the five Asian peoples—Japanese, Chinese, Korean, Manchurian, and Mongolian—would live together peacefully, Japan, also in imperialistic competition with the USSR, seizes control of Manchuria. Kwantung Army General Kanji Ishiwara sets up a puppet state there, called Manchukuo, with Puyi, the last Qing emperor of China, as the nominal leader. Whereas Japan is a mostly uninhabitable 330,000 square kilometers, Manchukuo, is a flat 1,300,000. Tabula rasa suddenly becomes a real proposition. The most respected and progressive architects and urban planners—including Kenzo Tange's mentor, Hideto Kishida—begin projecting Japan's imagination onto Manchukuo's vast expanse.

**1945** After Japan's expeditions outside its own Archipelago, the American fire- and atomic bombing brings tabula rasa to Japan itself. The Hiroshima experience—literal for some of our protagonists, who witness the aftermath—encourages existential cynicism in some; others sublimate the shock into a lifelong commitment to new beginnings. The generation that will become the Metabolists share, from the beginning, the Japanese obsession with tabula rasa.

**1923** Tabula rasa in Tokyo: the Atagoyama district after the Great Kanto Earthquake and its resulting fires.

## General Plan for the Reconstruction of the Imperial Capital
## Shinpei Goto

The Great Kanto Earthquake devastates the capital and, along with the fires that break out afterwards, kills 140,000 people. Shinpei Goto, Japan's home minister, sees the perfect opportunity to realize a version of the masterplan he had conceived for Tokyo when he was mayor in 1920. The plan would introduce European-style order on the city—the Hausmann-style revolution that Tokyo never had: wide streets, sanitation systems, parks, squares, major bridges. Goto, a former doctor, learned infrastructure planning in more pliant environments: Japanese-colonized Taiwan in the late 19th century, as head of the Civil Administration Bureau, and Manchuria, where he was head of the South Manchurian Railways Company. Goto's plan for Tokyo proves more difficult to implement. He encounters opposition in the Diet because of the prohibitively high price and fragmented ownership of the land that his masterplan would occupy. The scheme is scaled down drastically, but leads to the construction of several new trunk roads, two new bridges over the Sumida River and more than 50 new parks.[1] Many of those involved in the reconstruction—Yoshikazu Uchida, Toshiro Kasahara, and Toshikata Sano—will be engaged in the urban planning of the puppet state of Manchukuo a decade later. But bitterness over the missed opportunity to radically remodel Tokyo trickles down the generations and is still felt 40 years later by Tange and the Metabolists.

帝都復興計畫東京市案一般圖

**1923** General Plan for the Reconstruction of the Imperial
Capital, including artificial islands and several large parks
(red overlay = area destroyed by earthquake and fire).
Goto is unable to expropriate enough land to implement
his plan, and is forced to scale back his ambitions.

**Expanded Territory**

1    Housing Collective Scheme for
     Agricultural Immigrants, Manchukuo,
     Yoshikazu Uchida et al, 1933
2    Datong Masterplan, Yoshikazu Uchida,
     Yoshifumi Uchida, Eika Takayama,
     Masaru Sekino, 1938
3    Nanhu Housing Project, Xinjing,
     Junzo Sakakura, 1939
4    New Civic Area, Shanghai,
     Kunio Maekawa, 1939
5    Monument to the Greater East Asia
     Co-Prosperity Sphere, Kenzo Tange, 1942

**Housing Collective Scheme for Agricultural Immigrants
Yoshikazu Uchida et al.**

One year after Japan escalates its longtime presence in Manchuria to a full colonization, Yoshikazu Uchida, professor of architecture at Tokyo Imperial University, travels to the newly named Manchukuo. His mission is to house the 200,000 hungry farmers moving there from impoverished northern Japan; with it, he has the chance to plan on a scale that turned out to be impossible in Japan. Uchida and his team—which includes Toshiro Kasahara, with whom he had already worked on the post-1923 reconstruction of Tokyo, and Kenzo Tange's mentor Hideto Kishida—devise a modern utopia as new to the Japanese as a view of the horizon. Across vast swathes of agricultural land the size of Tokyo, the team projects a sparse pattern of uniform, isolated mini-cities of 10 hectares each, echoing the 1920s Russian de-urbanist thinking of Moisei Ginzburg, Mikhail Barsch, and Konstantin Melnikov in their "Green City" project, and Frank Lloyd Wright's 1932 Broadacre City scheme to establish the urban condition in the countryside. Each individual house—designed in the local vernacular style— is conceived as a miniature farm; beyond it, outside the city walls, lies the endless farmland of the Manchurian plains.[2]

Fort: one of Uchida's housing collectives.

**1933** Zoom out: Uchida's endless scheme for housing Japanese farmers in Manchukuo.

**Datong Masterplan**
**Yoshikazu Uchida, Yoshifumi Uchida, Eika Takayama, Masaru Sekino**
Two years later, Uchida—together with his son Yoshifumi, urban planner
Eika Takayama from Tokyo Imperial University, and Masaru Sekino—returns
to the continent to develop a masterplan for Datong, an old town with plentiful
surrounding coal reserves in the Japanese-controlled region of Mengjiang, Inner
Mongolia.[3] "We all went there to build an ideal republic, like a paradise,"[4]
Takayama admits, along with having "a big fantasy about planning an entire city,"[5]
following Soviet and European urban planning models. The new Datong "will
contribute to the industrial planning of Japan, Manchukuo, and China, which
would put itself in a strategic position for the grand scale national land planning."[6]
Building outside the old walled city, where, Uchida says "construction will have
nothing blocking its way,"[7] they plan local-style brick housing in a dense
"neighborhood unit system" of cul-de-sacs. Construction begins.

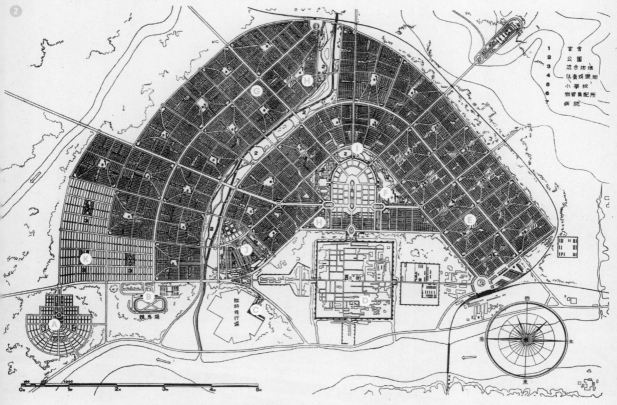

Wrapped around the old walled city,
the new "fantasy" Datong.

A  village module for
   repetition
B  horseracing track
C  airport
D  preserved old town
E  food and supplies depot
F  hospital
G  elementary schools
H  officers' housing
I  park
J  leisure zone
K  mixed-use zone

**1938** Planning the un-Japanese condition: Uchida photographs the territory that his extension to Datong could never fill…

**1938** Handbuilt: the new Datong takes shape.

**Nanhu Housing Project, Xinjing**
**Junzo Sakakura**

Sakakura accompanies Hideto Kishida on a trip to Manchukuo's capital Xinjing; upon his return to Tokyo he makes a masterplan blatantly influenced—with its wide open spaces and relentless rationalism—by the five years he spent in Le Corbusier's studio in the early '30s. There, Sakakura worked on La Ville Radieuse, Le Corbusier's plan to wipe clean central Paris, and the masterplan for Algiers— like Manchukuo, a liberating foreign territory. Sakakura calls Manchukuo a "living laboratory"[8] and writes to Charlotte Perriand, asking if Le Corbusier and Pierre Jeanneret could be consultants for Xinjing.[9] Construction of the project would be supervised by Toshiro Kasahara, now the director of Manchukuo's governmental architecture department. The young Kenzo Tange, working for Kunio Maekawa, spends his evenings at Sakakura's Tokyo office, and is credited on the Nanhu project.

Sakakura's experiment in the "living laboratory,"
published in *Gendai Kenchiku*, August 1940.

## Housing Plan for New Civic Area
## Kunio Maekawa

After Japan's victory in the Battle of Shanghai in 1937, the tabula rasa mentality migrates from Manchukuo to China. Kunio Maekawa proposes a residential tract within the massive New Civic Area, the Japanese district to the north of the European concessions on the Bund. His plan consists of 1,500 housing units and four parks, and is bordered by Matsui-dori Avenue and a highway connecting the old and new Shanghais. Maekawa, criticizes the masterplan for the rest of the New Civic Area, calling for "an architect who can embody the grand mind of Japan." He remains frustrated with the scale of the housing units, constrained by the domestic standards of Japan, saying, "We need to review our mentality of carrying around tatami and sashimi with us."[10]

Maekawa helps plan the consolidation of Japanese territory in Shanghai.

## Monument to the Greater East Asia Co-Prosperity Sphere
## Kenzo Tange

Tange, 29, wins the competition for a monument to the Greater East Asia Co-Prosperity Sphere, Japan's benevolent name for its embattled empire. Bringing back home the thinking from Manchukuo, he acts as if Japan too is a tabula rasa. Using the language of imperialism as a vehicle for radical modernization at home, Tange plans not just a monument but a massive new urban network to "relieve the excessive expansion of Tokyo."[11] The capital and the nationalist symbol of Mount Fuji, 100 kilometers away, would be connected with a new road making them just one hour apart. "In the vast area along this road as the main axis," Tange writes, "there will be urban facilities necessary for the political operation of the Sphere, as well as facilities for the enhancement of the Japanese spiritual culture." Planning the rapid development of the Tokaido region, Tange is susceptible to imperialist rhetoric, declaring that the monument "represents Japan's prime rank in the world." For the monument's Sacred Zone of Allegiance, under the benevolent gaze of Mount Fuji, Tange chooses Ise Shrine–style architecture, refusing the mainstream Imperial Crown style (modernism with an Asian roof), and renders his vision in classical Japanese style. Maekawa, Tange's teacher and the chief jurist for the competition, calls this decision "shrewd."[12]

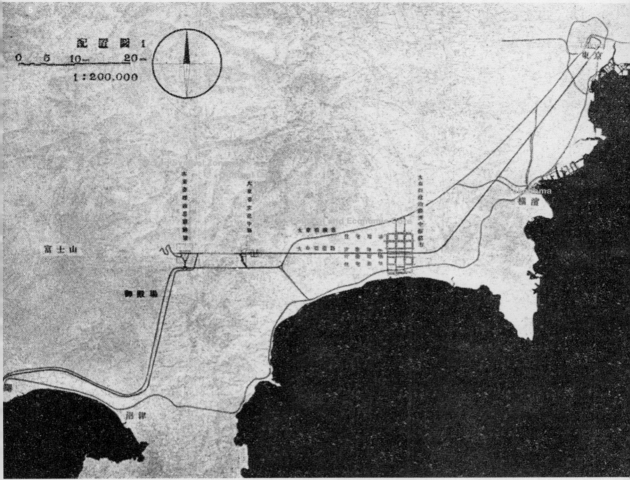

配置圖 1

0  5  10ｍ  20ｍ

1 : 200,000

富士山

御殿場

沼津

横濱

東京

Monument as masterplan: Tange's axis from Tokyo to Mount Fuji.
The urban axis re-emerges in his Plan for Tokyo 1960 and his
Tokaido Megalopolis scheme in 1964.

5 **1942** Sacred nationalism: Tange deploys Ise Shrine–style architecture for the Sacred Zone of the Monument to the Greater East Asia Co-Prosperity Sphere, overlooked by Mount Fuji.

People's Square

Monument for pledging
allegiance to Japan

**Tabula rasa comes home**

By the end of the war, the tabula rasa Japan experienced in Manchuria 12 years earlier arrives, shockingly, in its own cities: US firebombing destroys 50 percent of Tokyo, 60–88 percent of 17 other cities, and 99 percent of Toyama. Then, on August 6, 1945, the United States drops the atomic bomb on Hiroshima; Nagasaki is destroyed three days later. In the immediate aftermath, future Metabolist Kenji Ekuan and Atsushi Shimokobe (working for the Tokyo police) visit Hiroshima's ruins;[13] Tange, together with Sachio Otani and Takashi Asada visit the following year. Tange Lab, an experimental architecture studio forming at Tokyo University, starts producing new masterplans for ground zero in Hiroshima and destroyed districts of Tokyo, but discovers that erasure of the urban fabric does not necessarily produce a tabula rasa where anything is possible: there is a bizarre mixture of flattened city and an intact land ownership system that makes radical planning still difficult. Modernist repertoires of urban planning cannot apply; new ideas will be required. The Japanese trauma associated with land—saturated on its own mountainous archipelago, then liberated in foreign territories, now scorched at home—forms a critical back-drop for the growth of a new generation of architects that will become the Metabolists...

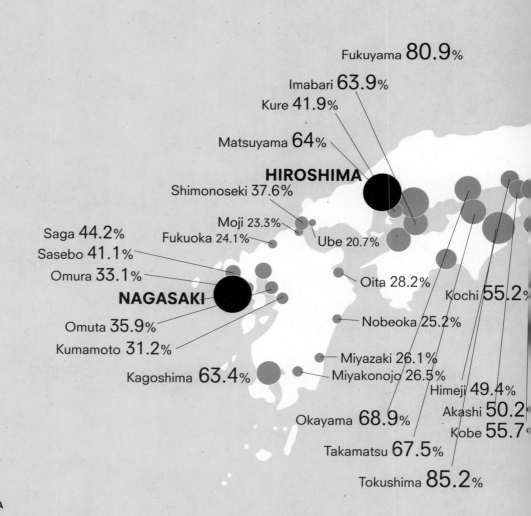

Fukuyama **80.9**%

Imabari **63.9**%

Kure **41.9**%

Matsuyama **64**%

**HIROSHIMA**

Shimonoseki 37.6%

Moji 23.3%

Fukuoka 24.1%

Ube 20.7%

Saga **44.2**%

Sasebo **41.1**%

Omura **33.1**%

**NAGASAKI**

Oita 28.2%

Kochi **55.2**%

Omuta **35.9**%

Kumamoto **31.2**%

Nobeoka 25.2%

Kagoshima **63.4**%

Miyazaki 26.1%

Miyakonojo 26.5%

Himeji **49.4**%

Akashi **50.2**

Kobe **55.7**%

Okayama **68.9**%

Takamatsu **67.5**%

Tokushima **85.2**%

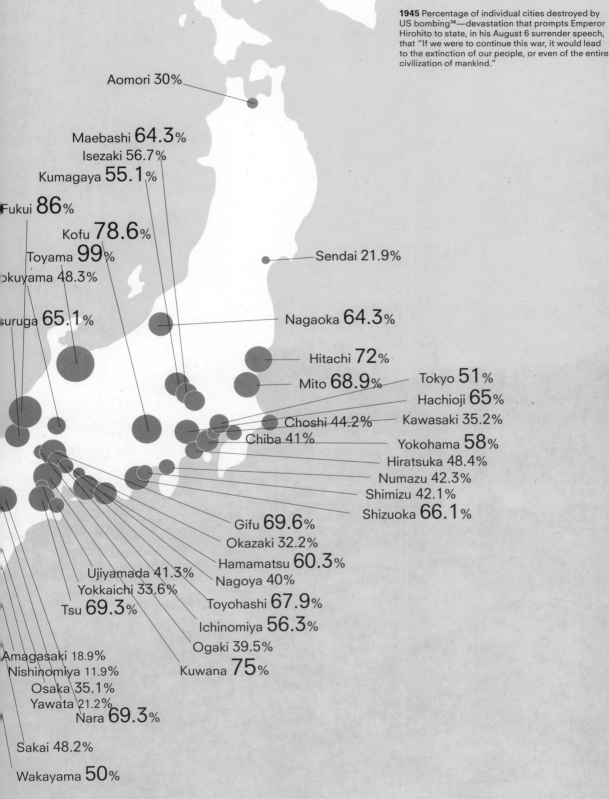

**1945** Percentage of individual cities destroyed by US bombing[14]—devastation that prompts Emperor Hirohito to state, in his August 6 surrender speech, that "If we were to continue this war, it would lead to the extinction of our people, or even of the entire civilization of mankind."

Aomori 30%

Maebashi 64.3%
Isezaki 56.7%
Kumagaya 55.1%

Fukui 86%

Kofu 78.6%

Toyama 99%

okuyama 48.3%

suruga 65.1%

Sendai 21.9%

Nagaoka 64.3%

Hitachi 72%

Mito 68.9%          Tokyo 51%

Hachioji 65%

Choshi 44.2%        Kawasaki 35.2%

Chiba 41%           Yokohama 58%

Hiratsuka 48.4%

Numazu 42.3%

Shimizu 42.1%

Shizuoka 66.1%

Gifu 69.6%

Okazaki 32.2%

Hamamatsu 60.3%

Ujiyamada 41.3%     Nagoya 40%

Yokkaichi 33.6%

Tsu 69.3%           Toyohashi 67.9%

Ichinomiya 56.3%

Ogaki 39.5%

Amagasaki 18.9%
Nishinomiya 11.9%

Osaka 35.1%         Kuwana 75%

Yawata 21.2%

Nara 69.3%

Sakai 48.2%

Wakayama 50%

**1945** Progress: using some of the earliest available color film, the Americans document their transformation of Hiroshima, using the new technology of the atom bomb, into a traumatized tabula rasa.

"When I stood in the ruins of the city after losing my father and sister to the bomb there, I was suddenly overcome by this sense of personal mission. In a world where there was nothing left at all, I felt the call of all things man-made. The burned out shell of a streetcar, an overturned truck, a half-melted bicycle... I felt like they were all calling out to me, saying, "Hear us, O traveler!" When evening came, the setting sun was just so amazingly beautiful, setting the horrific ruins aglow in its crimson light— it was as if the light of the Western sun upon the atomic hellscape transformed it into a dazzling vision of paradise. The setting sun saved the relationship between the realm of things and the realm of people. That scene has continued to have a primal significance in all that I've done since. Experiences like that redirected my perception of the mutability of life from a sense of vanity and desolation to the sense that change drives new growth. I vowed to pursue the kind of change that fit the needs of postwar Japan through industrial design."
**Kenji Ekuan**, p. 481

"Drop everything and go to Hiroshima, is what Tange said to me. I went there and found that, rather than just being burned by the atomic bomb, everything had been melted flat and made featureless."
**Sachio Otani**, p. 481

"Right after the war, when we were asked by the Institute for War Recovery to make a reconstruction masterplan for various cities in Japan, I volunteered to work on Hiroshima. There was a rumor that if you went there you might be radiated to death and that there was no grass growing any more. But I wanted to go there anyway, even if I would die because I had a special bond with the city. In Hiroshima we [Asada, Otani, and Mitsuru Ishikawa] stayed in a hut with a corrugated sheet metal roof on the scorched earth. Our task was to make the masterplan based on what few materials were left in the basement of the burned city hall."[17]
**Kenzo Tange**

"Should any emergency arise, offer yourselves courageously to the State."
("Rescript on Education," recited every day by schoolchildren until 1945.)[15]
Tange is 32 at the end of the war, the Metabolists mostly teenagers (Kurokawa,
the youngest, is 12). They quickly seize the spirit imbued in them by their
early education for a very different project…

Tokyo: 51 percent destroyed.

**1945** Downtown Tokyo by the Sumida River: the city of wood and paper disappears; only the few concrete structures remain. "I was in Tokyo, and I remember vividly the spectacle of people gradually returning to scorched hills and plateaus, building crude huts, and starting to inhabit them," Sachio Otani recalls. "Even when separated by distances too great to hear one another's voices, greetings were exchanged and answered. That became an incentive to live. I was able to imagine the revival of the town. I built a hut on the ground of a scorched field. Our dream was to discover a middle ground between the individual and the state, a secure frame in which to live. We hypothesized a situation in which traditional state power was partly dismantled and urban society blossomed. That World War II ended with the defeat of Japan was, I think, not at all disadvantageous for conceptualizing the reconstruction of the state, society, and cities after the war."[16]

**References**

1 Sentaro Go, *Shosetsu Goto Shinpei—Gyokaku to toshi-seisaku no senkusha* [Shinpei Goto, a novel: Pioneer of administration reform and urban policy] (Tokyo: Gakuyo Shobo, 1999).

2 Yoshikazu Uchida et al., *Uchida Yoshikazu-sensei sakuhinshu* [The complete work of Professor Yoshikazu Uchida] (Tokyo: Kajima Kenkyujo Shuppankai, 1969).

3 Yoshikazu Uchida, "Datong Urban Planning (1)," *Kenchiku Zasshi* (monthly journal of the Architectural Institute of Japan), November 1939.

4 Arata Isozaki, *Nihon kenchiku no 30-nendai* [Japanese architecture in the 1930s] (Tokyo: Kajima Publishing, 1978).

5 Sutemi Horiguchi, Eika Takayama et al., "Roundtable commemorating the 70th anniversary," *Kenchiku Zasshi*, April 1956.

6 Eika Takayama, "Notes on Datong masterplan," *Gendai Kenchiku*, April 1939.

7 Uchida, Datong Urban Planning.

8 "Roundtable: The Architecture in the Continent," *Gendai Kenchiku*, October 1939.

9 Junzo Sakakura, "Nanhu Housing Project, Xinjing," *Gendai Kenchiku*, August 1940.

10 Kunio Maekawa, "Shanghai Housing Plan," *Gendai Kenchiku*, April 1939.

11 Kenzo Tange, "The winning entry of the competition: Monument to the Greater East Asia Co-Prosperity Sphere," *Kenchiku Zasshi*, December 1942.

12 Kunio Maekawa, "Competition juror's comment," *Kenchiku Zasshi*, December 1942.

13 Kenzo Tange, *Ippon no empitsu kara* [From one pencil] (Tokyo: Nihon Tosho Center, 1997).

14 Martin Caidin, *Torch to the Enemy: The Fire Raid on Tokyo* (Bantam War Books, 1960).

15 John W. Dower, *Embracing Defeat* (New York: Norton, 1999).

16 Sachio Otani interviewed by the authors, November 2008.

17 Tange, *From one pencil*.

# Toshiko Kato 加藤敏子

**Discussed in this interview:**
**Kenzo Tange, Part I (part II on p. 550)**

**1913** born in Osaka **1921** lives in Shanghai, where his father works as a banker **1930** high school in Hiroshima; moved by Le Corbusier's design for the Palace of the Soviets, decides to become an architect **1935** enters architecture department of Tokyo Imperial University after reading Valery, Gide, Proust, Dostoyevsky, Hegel, Heidegger, Wölfflin **1938** works with Kunio Maekawa **1939** publishes essay "Ode to Michelangelo" in *Gendai Kenchiku* **1940** first building, made under Kunio Maekawa: Kishi Memorial Hall **1942** age 29, enters graduate school; wins competition for monument to Greater East Asia Co-Prosperity Sphere **1943** wins competition for Japanese-Thai Cultural Center, Bangkok **1946** graduates; becomes associate professor, Tokyo University graduate school; creates Tange Lab **1946–1949** Tange Lab creates reconstruction masterplans for Hiroshima, Kure, Maebashi, Isezaki, Wakkanai and Tokyo's Ginza and Shinjuku districts **1948** second place in competition for Hiroshima World Peace Memorial Cathedral **1949** marries Toshiko Kato; wins competition for Hiroshima Peace Memorial Park, including museum and other buildings; begins collaboration with Isamu Noguchi on Hiroshima **1950** extends masterplan for Hiroshima **1951** attends CIAM in Hoddesdon, UK; meets his hero, Le Corbusier **1952** loses competitions for Kanagawa library and concert hall and Ministry of Foreign Affairs **1953** builds house for himself and Kato; protests against conditions of the National Diet Library competition; co-founds Japan Committee on International Design **1954** starts *Rei-no-kai* (That group); protests for intellectual property rights on architecture in *Asahi Shimbun* newspaper **1955** Hiroshima Peace Memorial Park complete; debates on traditionalism starts **1957** Tokyo City Hall, Japan's first entirely glazed facade **1958** Kagawa Prefecture Government Office; Imabari City Hall **1959** teaches at MIT for four months; attends CIAM in Otterlo, Netherlands **1960** Plan for Tokyo 1960; Vice chairman and program director, World Design Conference; Tsukiji Project begins; publishes *Kastura: Tradition and Creation in Japanese Architecture* **1961** presents Plan for Tokyo 1960 on NHK TV nationwide broadcast; establishes URTEC **1962** *publishes Ise: Prototype of Japanese Architecture* with Noboru Kawazoe; participates in Metabolist exhibition "This will be your city" **1964** Yoyogi National Gymnasia for Tokyo Olympics; appears on the cover of *Shukan Asahi*; St. Mary's Cathedral, Tokyo; helps form Japan Center for Area Development Research; Tokaido Megalopolis plan; becomes professor of newly established Urban Engineering Department at Tokyo University **1965** wins UN competition for reconstruction of Skopje, Macedonia **1966** publishes Tokaido Megalopolis scheme in a pocket book *Future Image of the Japanese Archipelago*

**"The social status of architects was very low, so Tange was trying to make all architects aware of this and elevate their status..."**

During some 20 years of marriage, Toshiko Kato witnessed Kenzo Tange's wide-ranging activities as he transformed from an unknown, aspiring architect and organizer of his profession into Japan's most powerful modern architect—and the father figure of Metabolism. After marrying in 1949 in the midst of Tange's intense work for the Hiroshima Peace Memorial Park competition, Kato supported Tange with the practicalities of his various architectural, social, and political groups, accompanied him to the US in 1959, and managed his communications leading up to the World Design Conference in 1960, which was the launchpad for the Metabolists. Tange went on to complete a string of major public buildings throughout the 1950s and early '60s, and rose to become Japan's symbolic national architect at the 1964 Tokyo Olympics. But Kato reveals here a man for whom love, family, nurturing a community, and even having fun were equally important as architecture: the first phase of a career before he turned his attention outside Japan and settled into an increasingly demanding public role.

Toshiko Kato's residence in Aoyama,
Tokyo, November 16, 2008 and August 23, 2009

Postwar, with Tange Lab up and running, Tange starts another new chapter: he marries Toshiko Kato in 1949 and builds a house for his new family in Seijo, Tokyo. The house becomes a social hub in which he nurtures the next generation of architects, galvanizes peers in other disciplines, and draws strength for his own mission to transform the role of the architect from servant of the construction industry to key protagonist in the rebuilding of the nation...

**1953** Surveying his spacious new territory.

Incubator: during a work session at Tange House, his students Jiro Inazuka (hand to mouth), Koji Kamiya (leaning across the table), and Kisho Kurokawa (peering from above) huddle around the table with Tange, who "never showed an air of importance": a master who does not insist on hierarchy in the creative process...

Hiroshima

Tange: "The year after the war, I was commissioned by the War Reconstruction Institute to work on the reconstruction plans for destroyed cities. In Hiroshima, where the burning smell was still pervasive in the aftermath of the bomb, I worked with Asada, Otani, and Mitsuru Ishikawa, and slept in a hut built by the city." From Kazukiyo Matsuba's interview with Tange, "Running from burnt field to information city," *Kenchiku Zasshi*, January 1986.

**REM KOOLHAAS When and how did you get to know Tange?**

**TOSHIKO KATO** My sister's brother-in-law was an architect called Kiyoshi Ikebe. When he found me fascinated by architecture, he decided to make me an architect and conspired with Tange, who was associate professor at Tokyo University, to make me an auditing student there. So Ikebe took me along with him to Tange's house, and there I met Tange for the first time. He was working on a reconstruction plan for the scorched earth of Tokyo. This was in the spring of 1947.

**RK** **At that time, did Tange still have very few realized works as an architect?**

**TK** The first competition he participated in after the war was for the Hiroshima World Peace Memorial Cathedral (1948). He won second prize, and though there was no first prize winner, his design wasn't realized. During the war, he made various proposals, I heard, but was unable to realize a single one. He was also helping others design houses. Such was the situation at the time. There was no chance to think of himself as an international architect.

**HANS ULRICH OBRIST So you met Tange just two years after the war. Arata Isozaki told us that Tange never talked about the war years. Did he ever tell you about his war memories?**

**TK** Tange's mother was killed by machine-gun fire. He did talk a little about this to me once, but after that he absolutely never talked about the war. He didn't even want to touch the subject, I think. He always had a very strong desire for peace, so Hiroshima Peace Memorial Park was something he was really keen to work on. The competition started less than a month after we got married in 1949, and everybody came over to work at our house.

**RK** **Where was your house? What was it like?**

**TK** My father had just bought a big house in Seijo. It was the house of an artist, so there was a large atelier space. This table [*pointing at a photo*] was Tange's drawing board. Everyone else also worked there. This house was the starting point. Sachio Otani would be at the drawing board all day long. He didn't eat, didn't sleep, didn't talk.

**RK** **And Tange, was he already 40 years old?**

**TK** Thirty-six, when we got married.

**RK** **You must have been very impressed, but you also seem to be very freethinking and independent. You were probably critical then. Did you take him very seriously, or were you always slightly ironic?**

**TK** I didn't really know, until someone told me later, that he was talented. But when he was doing Hiroshima, I thought to myself, "Wow, he is somebody." I also real-ized that he was a person who would realize any goals he had not matter what.

**RK** **On the whole, people participating in the postwar reconstruction had strong political convictions, usually from the left. Was that also true for Tange? Did politics play any role in his considerations?**

**TK** Many of the people around us leaned to the left, and Tange was invited to join Ikebe and Hamaguchi's New Architects Union (NAU). He consulted me about it several times, but I told him that I did not agree to his becoming part of a political group. Society itself was in a considerably left-leaning period, but I still thought it would be wrong to join. He was in a dilemma, but in the end he did not join the NAU. Then Hamaguchi said, "Tange is walking on thin ice." I remember that he was criticized for maintaining a very dangerous indecisiveness in his relationships. But the people who did join the NAU became unable to visit America when McCarthyism began. It was fortunate that Tange was able to travel abroad easily.

### Tange House

**RK** **How do you see your contribution to that part of Tange's life?**

**TK** I don't think I contributed anything. I can say that since Tange would take me along anywhere he went and treated me equally, I was sincerely motivated to do my best for him in whatever way I could.

**1951** Disturbed sleep: Michiko Tange and Kato's daughter, is woken late one night by Isamu Noguchi, who makes her pose next to his new Akari lampshades for a promotional photo. Noguchi, just arrived in Japan, is collaborating with Tange on Hiroshima Peace Park…

**1952, August 6** From the shell of his Hiroshima Peace Memorial Museum, still under construction, Tange watches the annual commemoration ceremony at Ground Zero. The linear masterplan, with an axis to the ruined dome, comes into focus.

RK    **But for instance you told me that you objected to his joining the NAU.
So you must have been a guide in certain important decisions.**

TK    Well, it just so happened... that was before our marriage. [*laughs*]

RK    **You spoke English so you probably helped in communications. And you came
from a liberal background so that must have colored...**

TK    Oh, I think he had the same way of thinking. I tried my best so that he could
devote himself to architecture, which he loved.

MICHIKO UCHIDA  She was the one who invited people from abroad to our home,
and wrote most of the letters to foreign countries.

TK    A variety of people would come to our house. Some of them were celebrities
that you wouldn't be able to meet easily, so we had some unusual experiences.
The visits of foreign guests like Walter Gropius and Charlotte Perriand are
among my fond memories. Many artists would also visit us—Tange was always
interested in collaborating with people in the art world. It was Tange who
established an architecture division within the art group *Shinseisaku Kyokai*
(New creation association). He later collaborated with the artist Genichiro
Inokuma, whom I knew very well, on the Kagawa Prefectural Office building.
As well as that, Tange strived to establish the Japan Design Committee in order
to improve the aesthetic standard of everyday furniture and utensils, and
he often invited Japan's top designers like Sori Yanagi, Isamu Kenmochi, and
Yusaku Kamekura, together with the artist Taro Okamoto to our house for
discussions. And one more thing: the social status of architects was low at
that time, so he established *Rei-no-kai*, an organization intended to elevate
the status of architects. The members of the group also visited us frequently.
This was all in the early 1950s.

HUO   **That's totally new information. Can you tell us more about *Rei-no-kai*?**

TK    Actually, this group already existed when the property rights polemic occurred.
It was a group of core architects and their wives, which was unique back then.
The gathering eventually got involved in the copyrights polemic, and I remember
them saying, "Let's take action so that architects' names will be credited in
newspapers." It was always me who was sending out an invitation for the
gathering. When I asked Tange, "How should I call this gathering?" he replied,
"you can just write down 'that gathering.'" That's how the name "That Group"
came about.

HUO   **Fantastic. Was Isamu Noguchi among the many artists who came to your house?**

TK    Yes, when he and Tange were collaborating on the Hiroshima Peace Park, he
often came to our house. Both Tange and I were very close to him. Sometimes
Isamu would bring along his actress wife.

RK    **Can you tell me a little bit about Noguchi's character? It must have been
interesting that he came from America to help in the rebuilding of Japan.**

TK    I think he was a magnificent artist, yet there was always this sense of loneliness
in him, being neither American nor Japanese. Do you know the story of the
arch of Hiroshima's Peace Memorial Park? Originally, Isamu designed it upon
Tange's request. The design was ready to be constructed. But then someone,
I don't know who, said that it would be a mistake to have an American make
the memorial, which led to a great deal of debate. Finally, the opposition
prevailed and they made Tange redesign it. Tange placed great importance
on friendship, so I think he was greatly troubled by this. But even so, I think
that his friendship with Noguchi was unaffected.

### 1959

HUO   **In 1959 you spent time with Tange in the United States. Worldwide, many
things were happening at this time, as Fred Kaplan discusses in his book 1959:
the microchip and the birth control pill were invented, there was the space
race, the computer revolution, the rise of Pop Art, free jazz, new journalism,
indie films, the emergence of Fidel Castro, Malcolm X, superpower diplomacy,**

**1959** While Metabolism coheres in his absence (under his offstage directions, executed by Takashi Asada), Tange takes time out from the scene he created—traveling, broadening his network, developing ideas he has no time to work on in Japan…

Transplant: as visiting professor at MIT, Tange uses his students to design a floating housing system for Boston Harbor, which he then takes home with him to apply to Tokyo Bay.

Team 10, Otterlo, Netherlands: Toshiko Kato accompanies Tange at the first post-CIAM meeting, where he engages Peter Smithson on the issue of tradition (see p. 126), presents Kikutake's work as well as his own, and spies potential invitees for the World Design Conference in Tokyo the next year…

aveled to the north

retired chief of the Nitto
annery recalls Tange com-
g from Tokyo (half a day's
ain ride) to tour Kurokawa's
uilding under construction,
nd for the inauguration
ending two specially made
ater fountains for factory
orkers, probably designed
y Taro Okamoto.

the beginnings of Motown, Happenings, the generation gap, and all of this happened against the background of the Cold War. It's also the year that Frank Lloyd Wright's Guggenheim opened, which, according to Kaplan, marked a moment when everything changed in architecture. He calls it the superstar phenomenon. I was wondering if any of that resonates with you, and if you could tell us a little bit about this idea of 1959 with Tange.

**TK** Of course, we went to the Guggenheim. The idea of 1959… Well, Tange may well have been aware of what was going on in the States then, but I was completely occupied with our daily life, not being able to think of anything intellectual. In the 10 years after our marriage in 1949, Gropius visited Japan, and zealously praised Tange in America, and he started to become internationally famous. He built the Tokyo Metropolitan Government Building in 1958, but because it was clad in glass, it was harshly criticized. People couldn't believe that such architecture could be built in earthquake-prone Japan. The newspapers also attacked Tange. So we put together a dossier about the building and sent it to all kinds of people and places abroad. Before long, he was receiving high evaluations from abroad, and the Japanese commotion finally subsided because of his increasing reputation overseas.

American life and Japanese life, after defeat in the war, were at very different levels. Everything in the States was a surprise to me. In Japan there were still very few cars for individuals, and people only just managed to own a TV. It was difficult for a woman to travel—unless she was an expatriate's wife, a woman could not receive permission to go abroad. So Tange deliberately applied for a Fulbright in order to bring me along.

**RK** **Did you drive a car?**

**TK** I got my license in Boston. I'm not a very good driver, though.

**RK** **Do you remember the type of car you had? Was it American?**

**TK** It was just some old jalopy. Our monthly income was only $1,000. That was a very large amount of money in Japan in those days, but we were staying in a residential hotel that cost $300, and because at the weekends we entertained people at our own expense, just as we would in Japan, that half year was the poorest in my life.

Since Tange needed to teach only three days a week at MIT, he received permission to go to other universities on the remaining two days, such as Harvard, Princeton, Yale, and Columbia. For Christmas in Chicago, Minoru Yamasaki invited us. We stayed at his house and went to Eero Saarinen's office, but before that we stopped by at Lakeshore Drive and met Mies at IIT.

**HUO** **Do you remember what Tange and Mies discussed?**

**TK** I have no memory of that. I do remember that we had lunch together, but I mistakenly drank all of Mies's coffee, then I was in a complete panic. But I'm sure Tange was delighted to see him. It had all been arranged by a student of Mies who had come to Japan on a Fulbright.

**RK** **Did you go to jazz clubs in America?**

**TK** Yes, we did once or twice. I do remember very well that we attended Sammy Davis Jr.'s *Porgy and Bess* (1959) in New York. Tange said the songs were fantastic. We saw many other movies, too. I think once upon a time he wanted to become a movie director. His favorite was Akira Kurosawa.

### Mentor and Matchmaker

**RK** **I think we should also talk about Tange's performance as a teacher and his support for younger students—his role as a mentor. We heard for instance that Tange traveled to the north of Japan to support the opening of Kurokawa's Nitto Food Cannery in 1963—a moment when Tange must have been very busy with the Yoyogi Olympic Gymnasia. From that story we have an impression that Tange was extremely generous and supportive of some of his students, and I would like to know more about that side of his character.**

## MARRIAGE ASSEMBLY LINE

Acutely aware that he is guiding his students into a life—architecture—that is excessively demanding in inverse proportion to its material rewards, Tange (with Kato's help) also provides pastoral care for his flock at Tange Lab, arranging and hosting a series of weddings in his own home and his home away from home, International House in Tokyo.

Isozaki and wife, at Tange House.

Kurokawa and wife, a science graduate of Kyoto University, at International House.

Noboru and Yasuko Kawazoe, also at I-House.

Kurokawa pours for his marriage broker Tange. A sublime moment for a mentor and protégé.

Saikaku Toyokawa
Architect and architectural historian, expert on the theoretical and professional works of Tange Lab.

**TK**  I don't know about his working demeanor, but I suppose Tange spoke amiably to everybody, like a friend, or he may have sometimes spoke strictly at his studio. Actually, when Kurokawa decided to leave the Lab, Tange wanted to keep him for a little longer. Obviously, such an excellent protégé would be of great help to Tange, but not only that, he believed Kurokawa would grow to be a fantastic architect if he would remain in his Lab for two more years. So he asked me to convince Kurokawa to stay. I invited him to our house and spent a long time talking. Kurokawa was, however, already determined: he had gotten married, was already a father, and was eager to be independent. Tange was so disappointed that he kept saying, "I wish he'd stay just for two more years..." I think he was quite worried.

**SAIKAKU TOYOKAWA  You know, the two were matchmakers for about 15 graduates from his studio, even offering their own house for the wedding ceremonies. Isozaki's was one of them.**

**TK**  We would often be matchmakers upon request. The ceremonies would not be "god-witnessed" at a Shinto shrine or a church, but "people-witnessed," as we called it, and we shared the fees from everyone. He was aware that he was pushing everyone into a lifestyle with not much money, so I think he was personally concerned about them. Isozaki had no parents, so we held his wedding ceremony at our house. Kurokawa's wedding was at the International House. Matsumoto, the director, was very kind to us, and let us use the I-House as if it were our own home.

**RK  Can I ask you about your favorites among those people? Did you have particular likings for their sensitivity or sense of humor or other qualities separate from architecture, as human beings?**

**TK**  A difficult question... The students were all wonderful, and I couldn't single out anyone in particular. But because Isozaki had lost both of his parents, and Kurokawa had come alone after graduating from Kyoto University, I did care about these two. It was in the '50s when they were all so young.

**HUO  What about the role of Taro Okamoto? We heard that Tange had connections with many visual artists and that maybe the most important dialogue was with Okamoto.**

**TK**  Just like Isamu, he was a close friend of Okamoto. They were all in a group, together with Ken Domon and Yusaku Kamekura, that was gathered by Sofu Teshigahara. He was like a big brother, and took the group to all kinds of places. They were constantly going to Ginza to drink, having made their Ginza debut. [*laughs*] I, too, was often taken out with them. While Okamoto and Tange were debating in public the Jomon and Yayoi cultures, I think they were stimulating each other based on a tremendously close friendship and profound mutual understanding. They did a great deal of work together, like the famous *Tower of the Sun* at Expo '70. Okamoto's murals in the former offices of the Tokyo Government and the former Sogetsu Kaikan building, which Tange designed, were also splendid. It is a great pity that neither of those works still exists.

**HUO  What about Takashi Asada? He was very close to Tange and participated in the postwar reconstruction masterplans.**

**TK**  Asada was the closest to Tange back then and supported him. The people involved in the reconstruction plans of Tokyo were Ikebe, Tange, Take of Waseda University, and Yoshifumi Uchida. I'm not sure about plans for other cities, but I believe that Asada assisted Tange on all of them.

**HUO  Did you meet Asada? What are your memories of him? What kind of man was he?**

**TK**  Soon after I married Tange, I befriended Asada and Otani since they stayed at our house during the Hiroshima competition, but as someone who had returned from the war and was already married, Asada projected an extre-mely mature impression. He was outgoing and skillful at managing all kinds of situations. Otani, on the other hand, was an extremely reticent person. It made a great impression on me to see how these two men were so completely opposite. However, it was a very good combination! [*laughs*]

**1961** Tange gathers his progeny—from Metabolism and Tange Lab—in social as well as professional settings...

Left side: Koji Kamiya (second from left, reaching for sugar), Tange, Maki (gazing across) and Ekuan (crossing hands).
Right side: Kurokawa (at the back), Asada, Otaka, Kawazoe, Isozaki, Kikutake, and Sachio Otani.

URTEC
Immediately after Tange was commissioned to design the Olympic gymnasia and the client said it would commission some other organization to prepare the working drawings based on his designs. [A profit-making project of such a scale could not be commissioned to a studio of a national university professor, who was ostensibly a civil servant.] That was simply unthinkable. Tange had no choice but to create an organization out of people in his inner circle to be in charge of the working drawings. That was how URTEC [UR for urbanists, TEC for architects] came to be created, and I became its president.
**Koji Kamiya**

## The Tange Method

**RK** How intensely did Tange work on all these projects and to what extent, in his own mind, were they his own, or were they collaborations with the very gifted people that he invited to his office?

**ST** If I may answer from my research, when Tange worked on something together with Isozaki and Kurokawa, he would surely credit it as Tange plus Isozaki plus Kurokawa. Many alumni have expressed how pleased they were to be treated so equally, unlike in other offices.

**TK** It was all very fair. There certainly was a so-called Tange design method, where he would first have each member of the staff present ideas, and then gradually develop something out of that. But in the end he would try to reach as close as possible to what he originally had in mind. Why would I know it? Well, when Eero Saarinen visited Japan, he and Tange were quite amused to find out that they were exactly the same on this point. As far as I know, Tange was completely preoccupied with architecture—in both present and future tenses—even when sitting around at home. I'd assume that he always had in mind pretty clear images of what he wanted to do.

**HUO** How did he generate work in this period?

**TK** Back then he obtained most of his work through competitions or through former clients who would come back with a new commission, and therefore he hardly searched for work himself. But he did fail in many competitions, such as for the Ministry of Foreign Affairs and the National Diet Library, after everyone worked all night, day after day, and submitted the entry just in time. It was always so disappointing to hear an unsuccessful result, and I still clearly remember lamenting for the wives of all the staff members who would not go home during competitions. We would express our grief to one another, while Tange would always say that all the research would be useful in the next projects.

**RK** I get the impression that you actually contributed a lot to a kind of sensibility, and that you were connected to the artistic world.

**TK** Absolutely not. You know, he had outstanding sensibility for everything, and I was enchanted with the beautiful lines he produced. I would say our tastes did match well. Well, that could be my own wishful thinking.

**HUO** Very often, we hear that it really all started with Tange going away to the States in 1959, and asking, in his absence, for the World Design Conference to be prepared. What are your memories about the beginning of Metabolism?

**TK** I did hear of the Metabolists but didn't know much about them, because I thought it was something scholarly. Kawazoe would often visit our house, but Maki was still in the States.

**KO** And what about Takashi Asada, whom Tange delegated to look after the World Design Conference as secretary-general while you were in America?

**TK** Asada was the top person in Tange Lab, so it was by all means logical to entrust him with the task. Fortunately, a wonderful woman named Tsune Sesoko just returned from the States and supported Asada for the Conference. The two together did a marvelous job.

**HUO** You talked about three different groups that Tange launched. But there was also an unrealized group called Team Tokyo, which would have included Otani, the members of Metabolism, and Isozaki. Do you know anything about that?

**TK** I know nothing about that. You know, Tange was skillful at delegating things to other people. He was often assisted by Koji Kamiya at URTEC and Otani at the university. At home I helped out with things such as correspondence with foreign countries. I think he delegated minor matters to other people in order to focus solely on architecture. In that sense, perhaps he was not especially hardworking.

**RK AND HUO** He was not?! [*laughter*]

**TK** He was always lying around the house. I hardly ever saw him looking busy.

**MU** Sometimes he was still at home when I returned from primary school.

**1963** In parallel with his work as de facto state architect on the Yoyogi National Gymnasia, the official icon of the Olympics, Tange, repeating his strategy of using the World Design Conference as a launchpad for Metabolism, assembles a new group to try to exploit another international stage…

Unofficial: at International House, Tange calls a meeting of Team Tokyo, consisting of elder statesman Junzo Sakakura (second from left) and his Rei-no-kai colleagues Takashi Asada (center) and Takamasa Yoshizaka (the tallest man by far, who coined the phrase "artificial land" in 1954). The group is short-lived and leaves no record of its activities.

Official: Tange reviews the unfinished model of the Yoyogi National Gymnasia, which will host the Olympic sports at which Japan will excel: judo (new to the Games) and swimming.

Tange at the Yoyogi construction site for the Tokyo Olympics, not wearing his helmet.

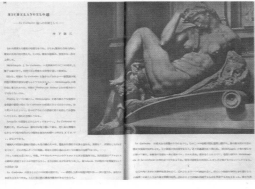

Homage: "Le Corbusier made a breakthrough among the white sanitary wares of modern architecture, and so did Michelangelo among the flat architecture of the early Renaissance." Tange's first published article spells out his frustration with Japan's superficial adoption of modernism thus far; he will attempt a more radical synthesis… ("Ode to Michelangelo: An Introduction to a Discourse on Le Corbusier," *Gendai Kenchiku*, December 1939).

| RK | He was still having fun? |
|---|---|
| TK | He rarely got angry or shouted. He watched a lot of television, and we went to movies and concerts together. |
| MU | When a new disco called Mugen opened, it was my father who escorted me there for the first time. |

### Tange the Man

| RK | **So, he was not formal?** |
|---|---|
| TK | Not at all. Because Japan is such a hierarchical society, everybody should have been calling him sensei, but he absolutely refused to allow anybody to do it. Of course there was a professional pecking order, but he would insist on equality in ordinary human relationships. Some of his staff members would get so surprised when they saw how things actually were elsewhere. He was such a normal person, you know. |
| RK | **Down to earth, more than ordinary. There is an image of him as being very severe, very formal, always with kings, presidents...** |
| TK | Deep down, he was extremely gentle. He never showed an air of importance. |
| HUO | **We heard that Tange always wore a suit. Was this already so when you met him?** |
| TK | No, he was wearing kimonos, so I thought he was an older gentleman. [*laughs*] However, he was a touch stylish. |
| RK | [*pointing at a photo*] **Did Tange dislike wearing helmets?** |
| TK | He disliked it indeed. |
| RK | **I think it's because if you are on the construction site of your own building and if you wear a helmet you have less communication with your building. That's why I don't like it.** |
| TK | He was always paying such attention to his appearance. |
| RK | **What did that mean?** |
| TK | That he was very stylish. When taking a picture of the three of us, or when going out together, he would coordinate our look. |
| MU | We had to change our clothes. |
| TK | As souvenirs for us, he would always bring home a suitcase full of shoes and clothes that weren't available in Japan back then. |
| RK | **Was Tange considered handsome in Japan?** |
| MU | He really was stylish, I'd say. |
| ST | I have an interesting story. When the Imabari City Hall was under construction, Tange would come sometimes and tour the site while wearing a bowtie. But Isozaki, who was stationed there throughout, had learned his on-site etiquette from the people there, from the way he wore a hachimaki headband to the way he wore tabi socks with a split toe. Isozaki was amused when he told us, "Tange had a bowtie; I was gangster style!" |
| MU | In this photograph he is wearing a bowtie. No doubt he was mimicking Le Corbusier. [*laughs*] |
| HUO | **When you met in '47, was Le Corbusier already his hero? Who were the people that he looked up to?** |
| TK | I suppose that would have been Le Corbusier and Mies. |
| RK | **Mies also?** |
| TK | Him, and also Michelangelo. He just loved Michelangelo. |
| RK | **From your point of view, how would you describe Kenzo Tange as an architect?** |
| TK | Well, what I would remark is that he was always thinking not only of architecture but of society at large. As I mentioned, he collaborated with a variety of artists; he launched the Design Committee, with the intention of improving the quality of daily life; and he organized *Rei-no-kai* (That group), which worked to elevate the social status of architects. As such, he always thought about the big picture before his own situation. That's what I'd like everyone to remember about Tange. |

The inventor of Japan's modern architecture scene returns to the source, Katsura Detached Palace. In the restricted inner sanctums, he removes his shoes—a gesture of respect, and a sign of feeling at home...

Shinpei Goto
Goto and his outstanding
subordinates devised a superb city plan that would
have completely transformed
Tokyo and anticipated its
future needs. Unfortunately,
he was thwarted by short-
sighted opponents con-
cerned only with their own
interests, and the plan was
implemented in less than half
the area of Tokyo—mainly to
improve the low-city districts
in the eastern part of the city.
The work achieved by Goto
and his city planners gives
me one of comparable vision
and ability after the Second
World War.
Koji Kamiya

HUO **What do you remember of how Tange thought of Tokyo and his plan for Tokyo Bay?**

TK The postwar reconstruction plan for Tokyo that he made with Ikebe and others was not adopted, but at the time of the Olympics, the Tokyo government executed a thorough restructuring of the metropolitan area, expanding its traffic network on a major scale. Tange was angry at the time and lamented that if his team's plan had been built in the first place, they would not have had to do such wasteful work. I believe Tange cherished a dream to redo the metropolitan planning of Tokyo with precisely installed infrastructure—like Shinpei Goto tried to do after the Great Kanto Earthquake in 1923. He regretted that the Tokyo government did not realize Goto's grand plan, which would have prevented the need for such costly efforts later on. Because land was worth nothing at that time, the plan of Tange's team would have been so simple to implement. But it was rejected by the Tokyo metropolitan governor. Which reminds me, even when we were out on a date this was always the topic of conversation. [*laughs*]

RK **So, your dates were boring!**

TK No, no, because I love architecture. When we first met, he didn't appear to be a so-called prodigy; he did not come across as an exceptionally sharp-looking person. Yet what surprised me after we were married was how extremely broad and spacious his mindscape was. He had a broad outlook from every aspect, and he could always see through the future with a superb ability to imagine and to take action. Indeed, he would instantly get it, however complicated it may be.

# Tange Lab
# Laying the ground for Metabolism

**"When we saw our national land turned into scorched earth with sporadic burnt concrete structures, we had a dream and hope of drawing a new city as if over a blank white sheet. But soon we learned that there is a thick opaque layer of political, economic, and social realities beneath the scorched earth of each city..."**

Kenzo Tange, "Trajectory of Urban Design,"
*Shinkenchiku*, August 1971.

The years between the end of World War II and the declaration of Metabolism in 1960 are dominated by the creativity, pedagogy, and professional organizing of Kenzo Tange. Aged 32 at the end of the war, Tange begins a series of strategic steps not only to launch his own career but to reinvent the role of the architect in Japan. To do so, he works in three domains: in public, Tange becomes Japan's foremost modernist architect, with his Hiroshima Peace Park Memorial as a launchpad for a slew of commissions for public buildings throughout the '50s; at Tokyo University, he teaches and mentors future Metabolists Fumihiko Maki, Kisho Kurokawa, and fellow-traveler Arata Isozaki in the ingeniously named Tange Lab; and in his own home and at Tokyo's International House he runs groups and committees in which architects and designers develop their identity, a sense of agency, and tools for gaining professional recognition. Tange spends the formative years of his own career intensely and generously grooming the careers of the next generation, preparing them for their role on the international stage.

The passionate educator:
Tange Lab, Tokyo University.

Having spent the war working in Kunio Maekawa's office and Tokyo Imperial University's graduate school, Tange is appointed assistant professor and immediately sets up Tange Lab. In Japan, architecture is categorized as science (*rikei*) rather than an art (*bunkei*), thus Tange *kenkyushitsu* is a lab not a studio; yet its residence is a former sculpture studio. Takashi Asada returns from the war and joins as Tange's assistant; Sachio Otani is another key member. Tange Lab becomes an incubator where students become researchers, part of a collective effort to invent as well as design.

Commissioned by the War Recovery Institute, Tange Lab visits Hiroshima, Maebashi, Isezaki, Fukushima, and Wakkanai to survey bomb damage and begin masterplans for reconstruction—none of which are fully realized.[1] Tange Lab also wins second place in a competition to reconstruct the devastated Ginza and Shinjuku districts in Tokyo; the winner is the Yoshifumi Uchida, who worked with his father on the masterplan for Datong, Inner Mongolia, and now applies his skills to Japan's native tabula rasa.

The situation is poised between promise and frustration: every Japanese city seemingly available for the projection of the Lab's vision, and yet also out of reach: "When we saw our national land turned into scorched earth in which nothing remained but a sparse scattering of burnt concrete structures," Tange writes, "we had a dream and hope of drawing a new city as if on a blank white sheet. But we soon learned that there is a thick opaque layer of political, economic, and social realities beneath the scorched earth of each city. In fact, the cities were reconstructed not according to an urban plan but political realities."

Late-night session at the nascent Tange Lab. Tange presides in cardigan and tie at the back; on the far right, Takashi Asada.

After working on the 1946 masterplan, Tange Lab again attempts to participate in the reconstruction of Hiroshima, this time though the competition to design the World Peace Memorial Cathedral. They win second prize, though their design is criticized by the jury for "lacking in religious and Japanese qualities."[2] There is no first prize winner; Kiyonori Kikutake, a 20-year-old student at Waseda University, places third.

While most of Tange's growing circle of architects are members of the left-leaning New Architects Union (NAU), Tange remains ambivalent and does not join. It turns out to be a shrewd move: the Red Purge, managed by the American occupation, unfolds as a more aggressive form of McCarthyism, removing thousands of presumed leftists from their jobs and making life increasingly difficult for avowedly left-leaning architects.

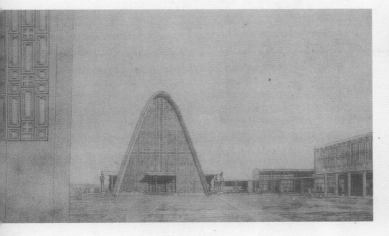

**1948** The jury questions the dynamic use of concrete in Tange Lab's competition entry for Hiroshima World Peace Memorial Cathedral.

**1947** At Tange Lab, associates and students (including Takashi Asada, right, and Sachio Otani, center) with a map of Tokyo behind them and a blank sheet in front of them. Evidence of the room's former use as a sculpture studio remains (top right).

A self-conscious effort: probably part of the same Tange Lab photo shoot, the satellite image of Tokyo features again, a key tool for planning their new territory...

Tange marries Toshiko Kato, an auditing architecture student at Tokyo University, who helps organize his growing range of activities. He immediately begins working, in their own home, on the competition for the Hiroshima Peace Memorial Park, which includes a park, a monument, and a museum flanked by an archive, convention center, and banquet hall. Tange's design—with the museum as its centerpiece, a long glass-clad slab on pilotis—is victorious. A major municipal and later national effort, the project symbolizes Hiroshima's recovery (its population grows from 136,000 at the end of the war to 270,000 in 1949) and establishes Tange as the unofficial national architect laureate at the age of 36. Meanwhile, Tange continues his grassroots activities: with Kunio Maekawa and five other architects, he sets up an architecture department within the artist group Shinseisaku Kyokai (New creation association) and includes architecture within their exhibitions—claiming architecture as a form of art.[3]

Tange with Shoichi Ueno, model maker for the Hiroshima Peace Memorial Museum. The model features the first version of the memorial itself that is later rejected: an arch.

Transporting a model of the Peace Museum, which will have one of Japan's first earthquake-proof glass façades.

With the Peace Memorial Park under construction, Tange is asked to work on a broader masterplan for the core of the city, with a park stretching along the eastern side of the river Ota, a stadium, a museum, and a complex of cultural and sports facilities for children. A pamphlet (below) is sent out with the October issue of *Kokusai Kenchiku* (International architecture);[4] it catches the eye of Josep Lluís Sert at Le Corbusier's studio, and he invites Tange and Kunio Maekawa to the June 1951 meeting of the Congrès Internationaux d'Architecture Moderne (CIAM) in Hoddesdon, UK—Tange's first trip abroad and his entry on the international stage.

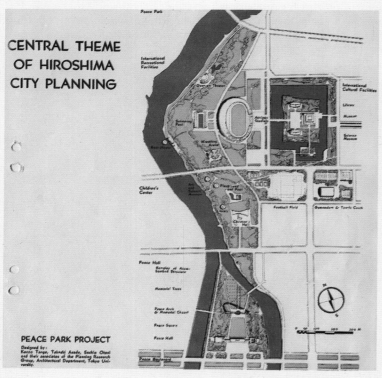

**1950** The *Kokusai Kenchiku* pamphlet, in which Tange Lab presents its plan to reconstruct even more of Hiroshima.

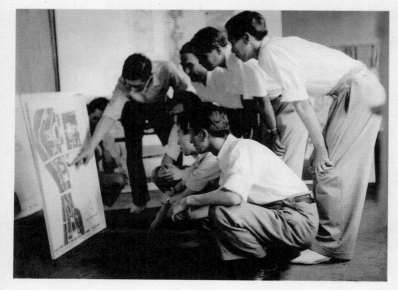

Asada, number two at Tange Lab, choreographs a lesson on the enlarged masterplan.

**1950** Future: Children's Center, featuring art and science museums and a children's library.

CHILDRENS CENTER    0003    BIRD'S-EYE VIEW

**1953** Children's Library, the first concrete-shell structure in Japan.

Tange meets artist and designer Isamu Noguchi, born in 1904 in Los Angeles of mixed parentage, on a visit to Japan. Spreading the blessings of his new status as Hiroshima's would-be masterplanner, Tange invites Noguchi to work on the two bridges to the Peace Memorial Park. Noguchi designs railings that culminate in rising suns. Tange also asks Noguchi to design the Peace Memorial itself— believing this to be a task for an artist rather than architect.

Meanwhile, as the Red Purge continues and more architects participate in the construction boom, fueled by a growing economy and the Korean War, the attraction of political agitation diminishes and the NAU dissolves. General MacArthur leaves Japan to outpourings of gratitude and grief: *Asahi Shimbun* publishes a "Lament" for him: "when the Japanese people faced the unprecedented situation of defeat, and fell into the *kyodatsu* condition of exhaustion and despair, it was General MacArthur who taught us the merits of democracy and pacifism and guided us with kindness along this bright path. As if pleased with his own children growing up, he took pleasure in the Japanese people, yesterday's enemy, walking step by step towards democracy, and kept encouraging us."[5]

"Make this square with a slight grade and create something like a stage here"

**1950** Seeds of collaboration: "[Noguchi and I] found great company in each other," Tange writes to an official of Hiroshima, recounting discussion they'd had about the Peace Memorial Park. "He made just one proposal to slightly slope the open public space and create a platform or stage. This is actually what I also had in mind but did not think possible..."[6]

**1953** One of Noguchi's bridges, over the river Ota to the Peace Park, called *tsukuru* (create); the other bridge is called *yuku* (pass away).

**1951** Building bridges: Tange, Noguchi, and Asada (hands on hips) observe construction.

**1951** Toshiko Kato: "There was always this sense of loneliness about Noguchi, being neither American nor Japanese…" Noguchi and Tange work side by side at Hiroshima Peace Memorial Park.

As the American tutelage comes to an end and Japan regains its independence, Noguchi's proposal for the monument to Hiroshima's atom bomb victims is rejected by the Ministry of Construction when Hideto Kishida, Tange's former professor and a committee member for the Hiroshima project, questions whether someone with American heritage should be allowed to work on the memorial.[7] Tange reluctantly takes over the design. Meanwhile Tange Lab wins the competition for the Tokyo Metropolitan Government Office, the first of a wave of commissions for public buildings in the newly self-determined Japan.

**1954** Tange photographs the tombstones at Ground Zero, Hiroshima, while his museum rises behind. The photo impresses a young Arata Isozaki, who later remarks: "I saw Tange's meditation for the dead giving way for new life."[8]

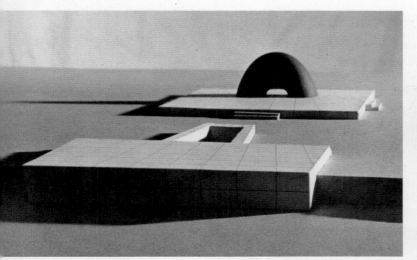

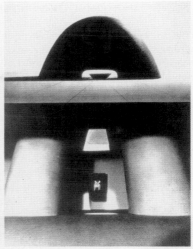

**1952** Memorial to the dead: Noguchi's rejected proposal for Hiroshima.

The public would begin its journey underground, where, Noguchi conceives, the living must go in order to meet the dead. "When the sculpture was completed," Sachio Otani recalls, "Isamu put it in front of Tange ... It looked like human viscera. At that moment, I remembered the people hit by the atomic bomb walking around with their skin peeling off and viscera exposed."

**1955** Tange's enforced redesign of Noguchi's memorial, with the nearly completed museum behind. The memorial is modeled on the *haniwa*, miniature houses placed in tombs during Japan's Tumulus period (third seventh century) as an offering to the dead.

Tange completes two buildings: the Hiroshima Children's Library in the otherwise unrealized Children's Center, and a new house for his family—like many of his early designs, a strategic blend of traditional Japanese and modernist styles—which becomes a base of operations for Tange's circle of young architects, designers, and artists. They form the Japan Committee on International Design, with the support of the Ministry of International Trade and Industry, to facilitate Japan's participation in the 1954 Milan Triennale.[9] In the late '50s the Committee provides a platform for organizing the 1960 World Design Conference. Members includes Junzo Sakakura, Charlotte Perriand in a guest role, Kunio Maekawa, artist Taro Okamoto, industrial designer Isamu Kenmochi, design critic Masaru Katsuni, and chief of the Japan Housing Corporation and a government-sponsored construction mogul Hisaakira Kano; meetings take place at Tokyo's International House.

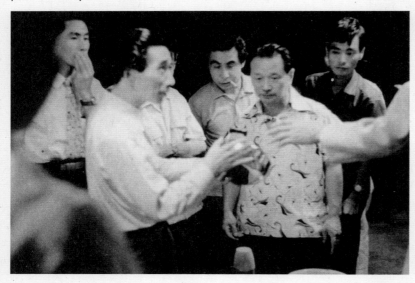

Designing the everyday: Tange and artist Taro Okamoto discuss a cooking pan in a meeting of the Japan Committee on International Design.

Tange and Okamo at another committee meeting, at International House. Here, Hisaakira Kano first talks about the idea of reclaiming massive parts of Tokyo Bay—inspiring Tange's Plan for Tokyo 1960.[10]

Tange starts another group that initially meets as a casual gathering of friends in the architecture profession. When Kato asks the name of the gathering, in order to send out the invitations, Tange answers, "Just 'that gathering' [*Rei-no-kai*] will do." (*Rei* also means "zero"—the original insignificance of the group encoded into the name). Soon though, the purpose of Rei-no-kai becomes more serious: they protest the lack of protection of architects' ideas in the competition for Tokyo's National Diet Library (in which the winner is not guaranteed any role in the construction of the building).[11] The members—Tange, Hiroshe Oe, Motoo Take, Soichi Kawai, and Takashi Asada—become activist architects, and the connotation of *Rei-no-kai* shifts from "that gathering"—a casual assembly— to "that group," with a specific political mission.

Kikutake (in a baby blue suit) and Sachio Otani (eating) join the members of Rei-no-kai, including Takashi Asada, right, and Hiroshi Oe opposite him. Unusually for a professional/ social gathering in the '50s, wives are also invited.

**1953** A slab raised on pilotis, the new Tange home is a synthesis of tradition and modernity—Tange's chosen strategy at the beginning of his career—drawing on Katsura Detached Palace, Corbusian geometry, and his own Hiroshima Peace Memorial Museum (designed at the same time).

## TRADITION VS. MODERNISM

Architectural debate in postwar Japan focuses on aesthetic and historic identity. At stake is the core notion of Japanese-ness, made urgent by the influx of American culture during the 1945–52 American occupation. Tange becomes a central figure in the debate between a purely Japanese tradition and the International Style arriving from the West and the Soviet Union since the 1920s. In 1955 he publishes the essay "How to understand modern architecture in Japan today—for the creation of tradition" in *Shinkenchiku* (edited by future Metabolist Noboru Kawazoe). Tange opposes the prevalent use of modernist style as mere patina—placing white tiles over a simple box, which he calls "white sanitary ware"—and the fudging of modernism with traditional touches like a pitched roof. Instead, he insists on exploiting tradition as a means of innovation. While building prolifically in a modern mode and strategizing the high-tech avant-garde of Metabolism, Tange is still nourished by Japan's tradition: in 1960 he writes a book with Walter Gropius on the 17th-century Katsura Detached Palace; in 1961, with Kawazoe, he writes a book on the seventh-century Ise Shrine—the main references points of imperialist and Shintoist history respectively. Ise, which provided Tange with a prototype for his Greater East Asian Co-Prosperity Sphere Monument proposal in 1942, continues to inspire him for the Hiroshima Peace Memorial Park Museum (also on pilotis, but with Ise's pitched roof taken off). For Tange and the future Metabolists, there is no conflict in their simultaneous study of tradition and modernism. Ise Shrine, rebuilt every 20 years with new materials, and Katsura Detached Palace, extended in a modular fashion and adapted to changing royal needs over the centuries, are inspirational in the nightly gatherings with Takashi Asada and Noboru Kawazoe in the late 1950s that give birth to Metabolism.

Tange and Kawazoe's *Ise: Prototype of Japanese Architecture*, (MIT Press, 1965).

Tange's *Katsura: Tradition and Creation in Japanese Architecture* (Yale, 1960), designed by Herbert Bayer.

Tange, effusive over tradition: "Ise Shrine manifests primitive yet powerful, simple yet noble, and serene yet ecliptic qualities, which cannot help moving us." Ise Shrine, 690 CE, photographed for Kawazoe's *Shinkenchiku* in 1955.

Tange, with some reservations about Katsura: "Katsura consolidates all qualities in history but not in a creative way. Since it lacks in the strength of unifying all members, its impression is lyricism but lacking unifying tension." Katsura Detached Palace, ca. 1620, a "text" for Metabolism, photographed by Yasuhiro Ishimoto, coauthor of *Katsura*: Tradition and Creation in Japanese Architecture

## JOMON VS. YAYOI

Architectural debate also focuses on two Japanese histories, philosophies, and aesthetics: Jomon, symbolizing the primitive, and Yayoi, the aristocratic. In the Jomon period, from 14,000 BCE, wildly decorated (*Jomon* means "rope pattern") pottery, idols, and thatched pit dwellings are the norm. The style comes to stand for the savage and dynamic. By the Yayoi period, from 300 BCE, earthenware becomes more refined, and structures like granaries are raised on stilts—the elevation also reflecting the emergence of social hierarchies, which arrive with the cultivation of rice. Tange is originally drawn to Yayoi style, but starts to oscillate with the Jomon style from the late '50s, when more sculptural form appears in work like the World Health Organization headquarters proposal (1960). Jomon and Yayoi styles will clash most violently at Expo '70, where Tange and Isozaki's elevated, spaceframe roof is pierced by Taro Okamoto's huge, rude *Tower of the Sun*. Okamoto writes a passionate appraisal of Jomon wares in 1952, triggering a debate that lasts decades...[12]

**2000 BCE** Jomon pot.

**300–400 AD** Yayoi earthenware.

**Jomon, 14,000 BCE–300 BCE**

Tange: "Jomon appeals to us with the flooding energy of the fundamental life of the people. It has a resilient strength and a sense of mass which comes out of through their wild battles with nature; it also has a free and agile sensitivity."[13]

**Yayoi, 300 BCE–250 CE**

Tange: "In Yayoi, man and nature are synthesized to create a calm lyricism, acknowledging nature's blessings. A passive attitude, submitting to the surroundings, prevails. A flat equilibrium and quiet balance with no dynamism are left in a transient mood."[14]

One of the first major postwar architectural exchanges in Japan, and one that will reverberate for decades, takes place first at International House, then at Tokyo University: the Wachsmann Seminar. Konrad Wachsmann, known for his Packaged Houses designed with Walter Gropius in the '40s (which could be constructed in nine hours using only a hammer) and his pioneering giant space frames built for the US Air Force, selects 21 students for a seminar with the aim of designing "a school unit" building. Kawazoe meets his fellow future Metabolist Kenji Ekuan at the seminar; Tange's student Arata Isozaki is also there. Originally planned for 21 days (Wachsmann evidently employs numerology to shape his pedagogy), the seminar ends up running for two months, teaching new techniques of prefabrication and new developments in space frame technology — indispensable tools of a temporary, renewable architecture.[15]

To Asada, who assists with the seminar, Wachsmann emerges as the opposing pole to Le Corbusier: the former pursues a technological architecture of the provisional and the pragmatic, while the latter stands for the elegant and the eternal. Asada sees profound potential in between these two poles.[16] In their report published in *Kenchiku Zasshi* (March 1956), Isozaki and Arata Ono remain frustrated by the gap between Wachsmann's idealism and the capabilities of Japan at the time: "Whereas Wachsmann was firmly rooted in the automation period with a highly developed industrial system, both theoretically and technically, some of the participants adhered to the reality of Japan, which occasionally made debates even emotional. Could we say that his cosmopolitan character makes him think of people in an abstract sense?" Fifteen years later Wachsmann's development of space frame technology facilitates Tange's Big Roof at Expo '70.

Konrad Wachsmann: "The boundaries between product, building element, and structure will vanish and buildings will be recognized as parts of a greater whole that is continuously shaping the landscape of civilization."

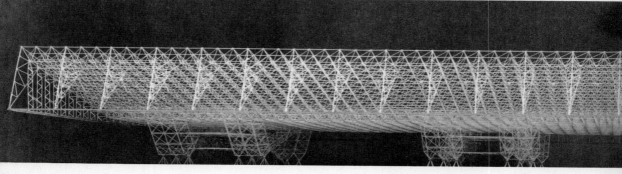

Konrad Wachsmann

Takamasa Yoshizaka

Kenzo Tange

**1955** Seeds of Metabolism: Wachsmann speaks at International House before moving on to Tokyo University...

**1955** Wachsmann with space frame model and architect Hiroshi Oe.

A wave of commissions, mostly for public buildings, arrives at Tange Lab, providing opportunities to experiment, in reality, with the merger of tradition and modernity and the shift from Yayoi to Jomon sensibility. Tange writes: "If the Tokyo Metropolitan Government Building was a Yayoi-style expression using steel, the Kagawa Prefecture Government Offices and Kurayoshi City Hall would be a transition from Yayoi to Jomon style..."[17]

**1957** Kurayoshi City Hall: Tange's transition from Yayoi refinement to Jomon mass...

**1958** Kagawa Prefecture Government Office.

**1955** Tosho Insatsu book printing factory, Numazu.

**1958** Imabari City Hall.

**1958** Tokyo Metropolitan Government Building: one of Japan's first steel and glass façades, until now considered vulnerable to earthquakes…

While building, Tange continues teaching. On the blackboard: section and plan of Mount Fuji–type housing (1965), a cone-shaped structure (artificial ground) for housing.

Tange joins 43 architects from around the world in Otterlo, the Netherlands, for the last meeting of the Congrès Internationaux d'Architecture Moderne (CIAM). Tension between generations and a gradual shift to sociological and technological concerns leads to the dissolution of CIAM and the formation of Team 10 (aka Team X) in its place. Tange debates the Europeans on tradition and presents Kikutake's Sky House and Tower Shaped Community along with his own Kagawa Prefectural Office (all 1958). He then brings the international spirit back to Tokyo, hosting Eero Saarinen in 1959, and inviting Louis Kahn, Alison and Peter Smithson, and Ralph Erskine for the World Design Conference a year later...

**1959** Tange and Peter Smithson engage in a discussion on tradition...

**1959** At the last CIAM / first Team 10 meeting, Jaap Bakema gesticulates...

**Peter Smithson** "It just so happens, by accident of history, that the aesthetic of the old Japanese architecture, which has a certain openness in its construction, corresponds to a feeling we have for an open aesthetic with its possibilities of cycles of fixed things, of changed things, and so on. Now if Tange had not lived in Japan he would have had to invent that language. He has, however, the possibility of using his language, but no one else of us has ... We simply do not have Tange's possibilities. As a rule, I can see no point in suggesting that we should look into our stylistic past in each country."

**Kenzo Tange** "One strong current in the Western hemisphere is something which I call 'aestheticism.' I see that aestheticism arises from the acceptance of existing order and is an effort to set abstract beauty in their wishful situation. It is strikingly stylistic and has failed to convey any fresh breath of naked human being. Typical examples can be found in the 'decorativism' now popular in the United States ... On the other hand, against aestheticism, there is an emerging force, which I call 'vitalism.' No matter how chaotic the reality is, I believe there is always the vitality of the masses underneath. Though their voice is suppressed and their energy hidden, this is something which we should dig out and make resound through our work ... Vitalism itself is not regionalism .. the popular tendency to use regional characteristics for decorating the façades of buildings must be rejected. The same should be said of tradition. In my thinking, tradition can be developed through challenging its own shortcoming and pursuing the meaning of continuum within it ... all I said above starts from a positive denial of making order out of reality. Vitalism is always destructive to our reality, but it is constructive for the future."[18]

**1959** Celebrating the death of CIAM: Aldo Van Eyck, Alison Smithson, Peter Smithson, and Jaap Bakema at Otterlo.

**References**

1  Kazuo Iwata (aka Noboru Kawazoe), "The Japanese Personality of Kenzo Tange," *Shinkenchiku*, January 1956.

2  Catholic Hiroshima Diocese, ed., *Drawing Collection of the Architectural Competition for the Memorial Cathedral for World Peace* (Tokyo: Koyosha, 1949).

3  Hiromitsu Umemiya and Etsuko Funabiki, *Research on the Architectural Department of Shinseisaku kyokai*, dissertation presented at the Architectural Institute of Japan convention, August 2002.

4  Kenzo Tange and Terunobu Fujimori, *Tange Kenzo* (Tokyo: Shinkenchiku-sha, 2002).

5  "Lament for General MacArthur," *Asahi Shimbun*, April 12, 1951.

6  Letter from Kenzo Tange, dated May 27, 1950. Hiroshima Municipal Archives.

7  Hideto Kishida, *En* [Relation] (Tokyo: Sagami Shobo, 1958).

8  Arata Isozaki, *Isozaki Arata no shikoryoku* (The thinking power of Arata Isozaki) (Tokyo: Okokusha, 2005).

9  "Passion for good design," Japan Design Committee, http://designcommittee.jp/#/about/gooddesign (2007).

10  Yasuhiro Ishimoto, interviewed by Terunobu Fujimori and Junichi Ishizaki, "The Trajectory of the Post-war Modernism," *Shinkenchiku*, May 1999.

11  Kenzo Tange, "On Architectural Copyright," *Asahi Shimbun*, January 21, 1954.

12  Taro Okamoto, "Jomon Earthenware," *Mizué*, February 1952.

13  Kenzo Tange, "Transformation in Japan's Traditions," *Asahi Shimbun*, April 21, 1959.

14  Ibid.

15  Takashi Asada, "Wachsmann Seminars," *Shinkenchiku*, February 1956.

16  Takashi Asada, "The Age of Machines and the New Path of Architecture: On Konrad Wachsmann," *Kenchiku Zasshi*, March 1956.

17  Kenzo Tange, *Ippon no empitsu kara* (From one pencil) (Tokyo: Nihon Tosho Center, 1997).

18  Oscar Newman and Jacob Bakema, ed., *CIAM '59 in Otterlo* (Hilversum: Uitgeverij G. van Saane, 1961).

# Kiyonori Kikutake 菊竹清訓

**1928** born into landowning family in Kurume, Kyushu **1948** third place in competition for Hiroshima World Peace Memorial Cathedral (Tange is second, but there is no winner) **1950** graduates from Waseda University; enters Takenaka Komuten contractors **1953** opens own office in Tokyo; works on postwar renovation and collective housing works, forms ideas about renewal in architecture **1958** Sky House completed; Marine City and Tower-Shaped Community proposals **1959** joins Metabolism; Tange presents his Marine City at CIAM, Otterlo **1960** presents Marine City Unabara and Sky House in *Metabolism 1960*, at the World Design Conference, Tokyo, and in "Visionary Architecture" at Museum of Modern Art, New York **1961** proposes Koto Plan, a "disaster prevention city" for Tokyo Bay **1962** curates with Kawazoe the exhibition "This will be your city" at Seibu Department Store, Tokyo **1963** Administrative Building of Izumo Shrine, Shimane; formulates *ka, kata, katachi* concept **1964** Hotel Tokoen; wins Pan-Pacific Award (of the AIA) and Architectural Institute of Japan Prize **1965** Pear City project, based on concept of Multi-channel Development **1966** Pacific Chigasaki Hotel, embodying concept of Tower-Shaped Community; Miyakonojo Civic Center **1967** Sado Grand Hotel, a horizontally expandable system **1969** wins competition for PREVI low-cost housing, Lima, Peru with Maki and Kurokawa; publishes *Taisha Kenchikuron* (Discourse on metabolic architecture); Expo Tower for Expo '70, an application of Tower-Shaped Community **1970** Architectural Institute of Japan Prize for Expo Tower **1971** leads Marine City projects at University of Hawaii as visiting professor **1971–84** designs branches of Kyoto Shinyo Kinko bank, Kyoto **1972** starts Stratiform Structure Module for artificial ground; member of study group for Prime Minister Tanaka's national reform plan—insists on preserving Japan's natural beauty **1975** Aquapolis, Japanese pavilion at Okinawa Expo; KIC Project, a floating, movable artificial ground **1976** Floating Hotel proposal for Abu Dhabi **1978** wins Auguste Perret Award from Union internationale des architectes **1984** IT Aquapolis proposal: floating city for one million inhabitants **1985** Tsukuba Expo pavilions **1988** Nara Silk Road Expo, producer **1991** president of Japan Macro-Engineers Society **1992** Amazon Ecopolis proposal **1993** Edo-Tokyo Museum; Linear City proposal **1994** Sagami Bay Marine City project **1998** directs exploration of "Hyperbuilding," ultra high-rise architecture as form of artificial ground **2001** appointed general producer for Aichi Expo **2005** Kyushu National Museum

**"My architecture was my protest, as a former landlord, against the dismantling of the entire landowning system..."**

A minivan carries the interview team across Tokyo: Rem Koolhaas, Joseph Grima acting as photographer, researcher Samir Bantal, translator Kazue Kobata, and editor Kayoko Ota. Hans Ulrich Obrist is rushing directly off his plane from Paris. The Imperial Palace and the skyscrapers of the CBD slide by outside, but all of it escapes the attention of the passengers, absorbed in last minute preparations as they make their way towards the Sky House to interview its architect and the Metabolist figurehead Kiyonori Kikutake.

Upon arrival, the team is ushered into Kikutake's modern office building across the street from the Sky House, passing by peculiar relics of rusty steel—the remnants of his floating platform for the Okinawa Ocean Expo in 1975, the only Metabolist floating project to be realized so far. Inside, models of Kikutake's projects from various eras are on display. Where is Kikutake himself?

In Japan, such a visit is carefully planned and scripted beforehand, and every-thing must unfold smoothly and impressively without explanation. Several young men in suits quietly ask the team to step outside. Across the street, we see an elevated structure of bare concrete. Rather humble in scale and appearance, we realize that this is the Sky House—an incubator of Metabolism; a building whose configuration has changed seven times since its construction in 1958. The team is jolted from its awe by Kikutake's cheerful voice: "*Yokoso irasshaimashita!*"—Welcome all the way! The (then) 77-year-old is dressed in a gorgeous silk pleated shirt, undeniably by Issey Miyake. After a quick walk-through of the house, he brings the team to the large living room on the elevated floor, where a crew from the magazine *Casa Brutus* is waiting to capture a memorable meeting of the two architects. A sudden moment of improvisation: gauging the situation, Kikutake and Koolhaas quickly collaborate on rearranging the chairs and cushions to accommodate the small crowd.

Hans Ulrich Obrist slips in 15 minutes later.

Sky House and the office of Kiyonori Kikutake Architects,
Otowa, Tokyo, September 9, 2005

After the war, Kikutake's ancestral land is confiscated by the US occupying forces—an attempt to eradicate the remnants of feudalism. For Kikutake, 19, it is an insult added to a deeper injury—the geological instability, and stifling shortage, of Japan's land. Frustrated on all sides, he embarks on a lifelong search for alternative surfaces on which to build…

Mise-en-scène: Sky House's alcove—the traditional space of symbolic exhibition in a Japanese home—pays tribute to Kikutake's grandparents, 15th generation landowners of the fertile plains of Tsukushi, Kyushu: atavistic inspiration for Metabolism…

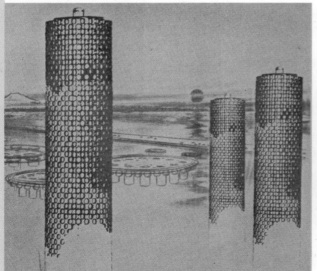

**1958** In the air: "It is incorrect to say that the most sure means to live is to cling to the land," Kikutake writes in Metabolism 1960. Tower-Shaped Community, 300 meters tall, is a "vertical ground," into which living units can be plugged. The contested and precarious ground of Japan is ignored altogether.

**1958** On the sea: "The Marine City is moveable, autonomous, and climate controlled." Each platform floats by means of towers submerged beneath the sea.

**KIYONORI KIKUTAKE** This portrait represents my origins. [*Pointing to a portrait of his grandparents hanging in his alcove (left).*]

**REM KOOLHAAS It's very beautiful. What is the theory?**

KK　I have some rather unconventional views about democracy. My ancestors were landlords, and in Japan, the landlords were traditionally the providers of infrastructure as well as the patrons of culture. They built schools, they built floodgates, they maintained and improved farmland, and they also supported Shinto shrines and Buddhist temples.

　　When I went to see an aristocratic country house in Britain, it struck me that it was very much like the house of an old Japanese landlord. In both cases the food they eat is very simple fare, too. It's different from the democracy that's known in America. Japan and the UK share a kind of equality between the landlord and the farmer. Europe had all those wars and experienced tremendous tragedies, but even so, the landowning aristocracy has not disappeared. This is true in the Netherlands and in Britain and in France and in Germany. And it's true in the United States, too. Not only that, but neither in Europe nor in the United States have they had their own land reform. The slaves were freed, but the American president hasn't liberated his big ranch.

RK　**It's a unique point of view. But your architecture was revolutionary in a certain way, so do you think it benefited from the upheaval when the Americans** abolished **the landowner system after the Second World War?**

KK　My architecture was my protest, as a former landlord, against the dismantling of the entire landowning system. Landlords provided vital support for the local community. Take the landlord away and you undermine the entire social and cultural fabric of the community.

RK　**So,** indignation **was one of the important forces for your architecture?**

KK　Yes, that's exactly right. It stands as the most important issue among the original inspirations for my ideas. My conceptions for Tower-Shaped Community (1958), Marine City (1958), and the others were all fundamentally about land. This is the first time I've said this.

RK　**They were not based on the land, but in the sky or on water?**

KK　In the case of Tower-Shaped Community, the walls represented vertical land, and in the case of Floating City (1971), I was working with land that could be moved.

RK　**So the political dimension of your work is partly that?**

KK　Perhaps, but it's probably more accurate to say there really wasn't a political dimension.

RK　**Were you ever involved in political activity? Did you ever try to change the land ownership system after becoming an architect?**

KK　No to both questions. I addressed the issue through design and creativity.

RK　**I think we have to ask this really core question. I want to be sure I understand correctly what you said about the landowner—because I'm so surprised.**

　　**Maybe I should also introduce a small part of autobiography: I was educated in London, partly by the Archigram group, who were overtly inspired by your kind of architecture. The point is, we as Europeans could only look at Metabolist architecture as a gesture towards democracy. For instance, the capsule and the cell seemed to be an absolutely important base from which the individual could unfold his life.**

　　**And so when I hear you, your approach seems on the contrary to be an almost** aristocratic exile, **not connected to democracy, but more an exile to the sky and to the water, away from the ground. When we see something like this [***pointing at a drawing by Kikutake***], we think: "OK, their heart is in the right place, they are democratic." But when I hear you, we have a completely different story, which is: "We cannot own the ground anymore and we are condemned to go into the air."**

KK　That's right. To be a landlord is to hold the infrastructure. In today's system, the municipality, as the new landlord, has to consider what kind of public

Envisioning himself as a landlord/guardian continuing the benevolence of his forebears towards their tenants, Kikutake applies his visionary schemes to actual sites, attempting to protect them against potential calamity—planning for disaster more than utopia...

**1961** Disaster Prevention City: Koto ward, known as Tokyo's "zero-meter area," faces chronic existential threats in the form of flooding, tsunamis, subsidence, earthquakes, and fires. As a solution, Kikutake develops an unsolicited proposal to build a grid of six-meter high piers, with each block capable of holding 20-story buildings. "Hopefully the new district will become a water city like Venice," Kikutake writes. All existing housing in Koto would be relocated to the safety of his elevated city.

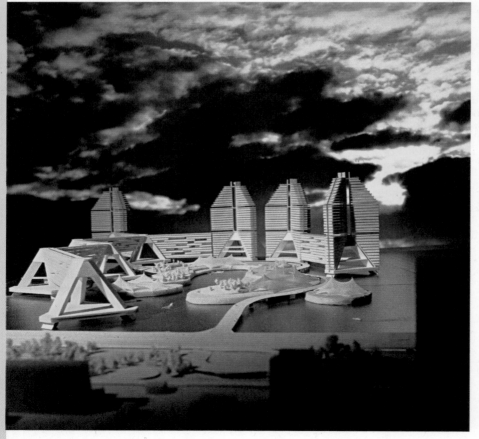

**1963** Shallow Sea Type Community: another site-specific proposal for the shore of Tokyo Bay, Kikutake plans a "soft landing" megastructure, half-resting on the seabed, half-floating. Located just out to sea at the edge of a jetty, the scheme preserves the bay's coastline—threatened by rampant reclamation—and provides immunity against flooding.

ouse. These megastructure
rojects, motivated by his
rivate resentment, were
ttempts at building up the
ew horizon (or rather the
ew vertical) for lebensraum
 postwar Japan. Tower-
haped Community was
onceived as a vertical site,
nd it seems that he was
ying to substitute mainte-
ance of the community
 landowner families with
new form of communal
ontrol in the tower-city. This
as an attempt to replace
ncient forms of paternalistic
ommunity with his new
ture community, bypassing
apitalist disorder. To see
 only as an experiment in
rchitectural form—leaving
is ideological dimension
side—is nothing but
uperficial.
ajime Yatsuka

awazoe's wife
asuko Kawazoe is credited
 Metabolism 1960 for the
yout and editing. At the
me, she was editor of the
terior design magazine
ving Design.

xhibition
Visionary Architecture,"
urated by Arthur Drexler,
nowed drawings from Da
inci to Piranesi to Soleri,
ıller, Kahn, Kikutake, and
urokawa. According to
ikutake, it was Paul Rudolph,
participant in World Design
onference in 1960, who
ecommended to MoMA that
ey should include his and
urokawa's project in the
xhibition.

infrastructure to build. Including maintenance and operation, the municipality has to consider what kind of system it needs to put in place in order to restore what the old landlords used to provide.

### Manifesto

**RK**  **We've never considered the history of Metabolism in those kinds of dimensions. I think it is extremely unusual that an important incentive of one's architecture is indignation or anger. Your architecture was a form of protest. What I would like to talk about is how in the original presentation of Metabolism, the book *Metabolism 1960*, that kind of protest is not very clear. The argument is always based on a biological metaphor of renewal. If there is any manifesto, it is always considered technocratic.**

**KK**  I had no desire to use that book to make political statements reflecting my feelings of protest. And besides, the book wasn't really a manifesto as such. It was just a compilation of things we'd each done, which we put together in preparation for the World Design Conference in 1960.

**HANS ULRICH OBRIST**  **But to continue with the political dimension, many of the Metabolist members referred to Marxist teachers. Was there a kind of Marxist background in Japan?**

**KK**  Marxism ultimately failed. The Soviet Union became Russia. A lot of artists and academics went to the Soviet Union with stars in their eyes, but their dreams were shattered. I never thought communism would succeed. At any rate, I never conceptualized any kind of social revolution.

**HUO**  **With Metabolism, it was a joint manifesto, or rather, a polyphony of voices. There wasn't one manifesto which everybody signed—or was there? It would be really interesting to identify the glue of this movement, and to know what it was that the writers in the group held in common.**

**KK**  The person who brought us together and unified us was Noboru Kawazoe. He was a critic and the editor of a magazine called *Shinkenchiku* (Japan architect), and he worked hard to tie us together in a single whole. He was our leader, our lynchpin. I hardly knew any of the other architects who became Metabolists. And it's worth adding: Kawazoe's wife was our editor, and whenever she said gather round, we all hurried right over.

**RK**  **But what did he do? How did he make all this happen?**

**KK**  He asked the important question of what unique qualities and ideas Japan could bring to the world.

**RK**  **And that put you on the map?**

**KK**  Yes.

**RK**  **I think that Metabolism was a deliberate effort to put Japanese architects on the map and also to manifest Japanese architecture abroad. So there was this strategic dimension. I would like to ask about the environment of publicity, media, and exhibitions: How were you able to expand from building this house in 1958 to establishing Metabolism in 1960? How was all of that filtered in two very short years and introduced in the exhibition at the Museum of Modern Art in 1960?**

**KK**  Well, we had each been doing our own thing before 1960, so we basically collected our various viewpoints and works and made them into a book. It was more of a give and take about methodology than a declaration of principle or a manifesto. I never consulted with anyone or discussed with them critically the creative aspects of the Sky House, but I was always ready to talk whenever it was connected with the World Design Conference. A hypothesis would emerge in our discussions, and from there we'd have to consider whether or not we had the technical means to prove it, and what kind of longevity it would have—it was in fact from discussions like this that I came up with the concept of renewability—and it was always the Kawazoes who acted as the leaders in this process.

**1959** Before Metabolism fully emerges, Kikutake codifies his obsession with water-based architecture. Inspired by water lilies, jellyfish, buoys, and other sea creatures, he devises floating spheres and grids of generic accommodation, sunken cylinders that form circular excavations in the sea, hexagonal floating pylons that aggregate to form islands, elements that exploit wave motion, and systems for growing food at sea...

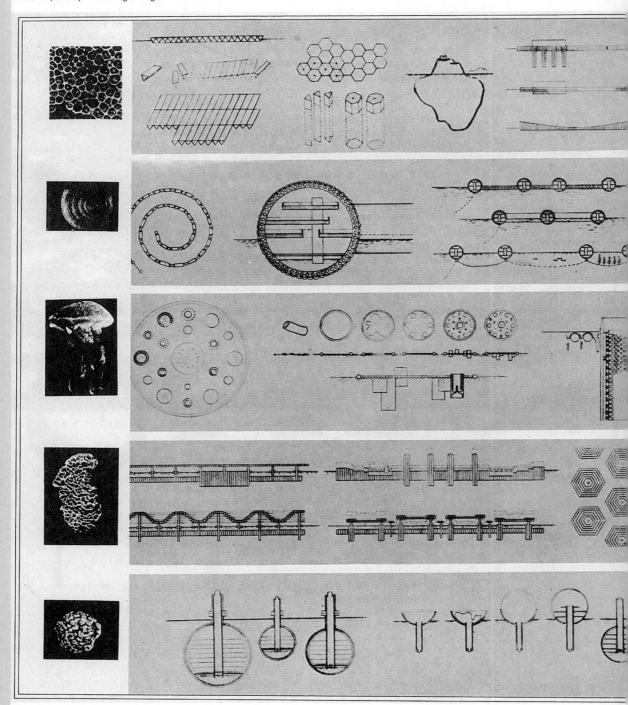

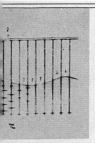

1 鬼ハスのように、広々と
海に浮かぶこの提案は、
正三角形のコンクリート
製密閉型ユニットによっ
て組み合わされ、緊結し
都市の人工地盤をつくり
上げている

2 浮遊した球型と円柱型の
二つのブロックの連結は、
丁度骨と関節のような関
係て接続し、拡大増殖が
できる

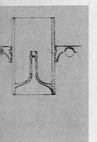

3 くらげのように、海中に
脚を伸ばしたこの提案は、
宇宙船のように多数の部
材の組立てでつくられる

4 六角柱の構成によるこの
提案は、海中と空中の二
つの空間とし、波浪を避
け、海面を大きくピロテ
ィで開放している

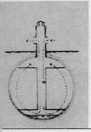

5 ウキのようなこの提案は、
そのほとんどが海面から
姿を没し、海中に球根と
して計画され、一部分が
空に伸びたかっこうにな
っている

1. Like a water lily, a floating surface stretching far and wide over the water is comprised of tightly combined concrete triangular tubes. It is an artificial ground for a city. Buildings can be built over it by plugging columns into the hubs of the units. To make the structure float, the units stretch down in the sea until they achieve the necessary buoyancy. Other features prevent the artificial ground from rocking and swaying.

2. Like sea plants, an expandable chain of alternating balls and cylinders, both made of concrete, harvest food from the sea just by floating. The system can be used for food production or as a storage unit, with no need to plow or fertilize.

3. Like jelly fish, cylinders—concrete legs—float in the sea, mostly submerged, forming a protected space inside. On the surface of the cylinder, light-weight concrete slabs stretch out to form membranes. Using surface tension and buoyancy, the membranes become artificial land and provide space for an "urban square." The cylinder can stay in deep or shallow sea, depending on the population of the city. Inside the cylinder wall, housing units will be attached, each with sunlight in one window, and views of sea creatures from the other.

4. In order to defend against waves, a composite unit of hexagonal columns, like pilotis, leaves the surface of the sea open. Units can be combined by connections at different points: columns, floors, or walls. Each hexaganol column can be raised at least 20 meters above sea level, and lowered by releasing air.

5. Like a buoy, the bottom of a bulb stays in the water, stretching its stalk in the air. The bulb has a control tank at the bottom to adjust its buoyancy. The structure is suitable for use as a factory (especially an automated one), a lighthouse, or for the storage of food, material, or energy. By making a conglomeration like frogspawn, the floating units can achieve high stability. And since the structure is so stable it can be brought down quite deep into the sea, where it can stay free of tidal, wave, or climatic change. This structure can also be customized to produce fresh water, crucial for living and manufacturing.

*Kokusai Kenchiku*, February 1959

**1958** "Giving my ideas concrete shape…" Through Sky House, Kikutake tests his concepts of artificial ground and changeability on his own family. Their new home, in northwest Tokyo, is (initially) a single-story slab elevated safely 6.6 meters in the air on earthquake-proof pilotis…

Perching on a steep hillside…

Excavated patio underneath the house, before infilling and seclusion.

repealed
y the Building Standard Law,
which replaced the 30-meter
height limit (in place since
919) with a Floor Area Ratio
mit, acknowledging that
odern high-rise buildings
ould be earthquake resistant.

Metabolist
ven today, after half a cen-
ury, the Sky House gleams.
ogether with Kurokawa's
akagin Capsule Tower
1972), it is noteworthy among
e realized works based on
e principles of Metabolism.
owever, these two works
re opposites. Kurokawa's
apsule Tower expressed
Metabolism extremely clearly,
hereas with Kikutake's Sky
ouse, rather than insisting
n points of principle, its
ssence may be felt in the
ay it exudes a Japanese
uality. At that time in Japan,
mall Functionalist houses
ere becoming popular, with
imple wood or steel struc-
ures influenced by figures
uch as Marcel Breuer. Amid
e attempts to express
piritual abundance within
hysical poverty through
raditional sukiya-style
legance, the Sky House
sserted an entirely different
radition. For Kikutake,
radition was the virility of
he minka folklore house
ather than the elegance of
he sukiya house. A dwelling
pace raised high upon four
tructural walls, an almost
quare concrete roof, sliding
ooden panels lining the
orridor that runs along the
xterior perimeter, a single
nterior space kept as low as
ossible—while this vocab-
lary also exists in Western
urope, one cannot avoid
ensing the space of the
apanese minka here. It is
recisely this space, born
f Kikutake's rage, that is
enuine Metabolism.
oyo Ito

Domestically, in Japan, the period after the World Design Conference saw a significant consolidation of the design community, which helped architecture and culture link up with the industrial design field—machinery, tools, and furnishings—and with the graphic design field—posters and such. I think a ripple effect from the conference played a very big role in this.

But it took time for new building techniques to actually establish a foothold across society. To take high-rise structures as an example, our construction code limited buildings to a height of 30 meters, and we had to wait until 1963 to get this rule repealed. Similarly, it took 15 years to develop the alignment between shipbuilding and architecture necessary for floating structures. We had to wait until the Okinawa Ocean Expo in 1975. Artificial land platforms remain legally unrecognized to this day, and all we've seen of them since Okinawa is a model that was exhibited at the Tsukuba Science Expo in 1985.

### Sky House

**HUO** **Because many of the things you're describing also relate to Sky House, I want to simply ask if you could describe to us this project from 1958.**

**RK** **In this particular house what were you trying to demonstrate? What makes it Metabolist?**

**KK** The kitchen and the bathroom units. Both are movable, and both can be replaced with new units.

**RK** **Can we look at the kitchen and the bathroom? How many times did the house change?**

**KK** A little bit at a time, seven times altogether. Though the changes were all relatively minor.

**RK** **What made it change? In the documentation it's about different family circumstances, more children or less.**

**KK** The children's room was a small "move-net" unit that we attached under the floor. It's made so you descend through a small hole in the floor. Unfortunately I can't show it to you anymore, because we've removed it now that the children are married and gone. I remember this rather amply-girthed architect from England who visited—

**RK** **James Stirling?**

**KK** Yes, that's the man. When Stirling-san visited, the children's room was still in place. He went down to look at it, and the opening was just barely big enough for him to get through.

**RK** **What kind of impact did it have on the lives of your children? They were the first inhabitants of Metabolist architecture.**

**KK** They shared a single room, and their private space was down there, but they also used the living room upstairs, and they either played with the neighborhood kids in the yard downstairs or they brought them up here. For houses that have the space, it's always been customary in Japan for neighborhood children to come and go as they please.

### Capsule vs. Move-net

**RK** **I'd like to talk about the capsule, because I know you avoid the word "capsule."**

**KK** That was Kurokawa's word.

**RK** **You have your own word.**

**KK** Move-net.

**RK** **Move-net. We know that the word is different, but what I'd like you to comment on is the difference between, for instance, Archigram's capsule and your move-net. You explain the move-net as something that has an eternal value related to Japanese tradition, related to agriculture, to frugality, to a sparseness of means, and in Archigram the same cell is described as a consumerist item related to the car industry, for instance. I find it interesting that there is this same entity**

Over more than 50 years, Sky House transforms along with its
occupants. Kikutake strategizes a series of temporary additions and
permanent alterations, some of which improve it, some of which fail,
some of which it never recovers from…

**1962** Metabolist family: the first of three move-nets
is attached to the underbelly, used as a hanging crèche…

Metabolism central: beneath the
move-net, the offices of Kikutake's
architectural practice (bottom right),
embedded in the surrounding site wall.

Metabolist child, inside his personal move-net. "The idea of providing children with such a small space proved to be too simplistic," Kikutake reflects. "They needed larger space even just to be able to sleep properly. They are just too active to fit in a minimal room."[1]

**2009** Final evolution: glass barrier imposed, move-nets removed, underside filled in. Sky House ends up connected to the ground it tried to avoid.

**1958** Original state, with patio beneath.

**1962** First move-net attached; kitchen and bathroom added to offices underneath driveway.

**1977** Previously empty ground level (patio) starts to be filled in with kitchen, bedrooms, and sunroom.

**1985** Ground level completely occupied with living room and expanded bedrooms.

and in one case it is described as a deeply traditional and even ecological entity and in the other one it's about consuming or throwing away.

**HUO** Cedric Price in the 1960s started to talk about the idea of having a "post-planning" situation where self-organization can happen within the building: one can actually "hang" the functions on according to what is needed. I'm very fascinated by the Sky House because it was the idea of one big open space and then all the other things are—you didn't use only the idea of "hanging on," but also, perhaps more strongly, "plugging in." Obviously, it was the time when the cybernetic movement was very strong. Was there any link to that?

**KK** I'm not sure how much of a link there was, but what was fortunate for me was that I grew up in a landlord family, and the entire village would gather at our house for all the big celebrations and services—coming of age, weddings, funerals, festivals—and huge crowds would turn out. So instead of having permanent walls, our rooms were all divided with sliding doors, and we could open them up and turn the house into one big wide open space. When I designed the Sky House, the same kind of open structure appealed to me.

I was born and raised in Saga Prefecture, which was the most prosperous agricultural region on Kyushu Island. We harvested two crops every year: rice and wheat. And when there is so much agricultural bounty, you can use what comes out of the fields to make roofs and build houses, too. Instead of using brand new building products or materials, you can, for example, roof your house with something that comes right out of your own fields. And even materials that have already been used once can be reused so long as you disassemble them and preserve them properly.

**Pao**

**RK** So again it is related to the landowner.

**KK** Yes. Those are my roots. If you want to reuse components, you have to standardize them so they can be prefabricated. Like tatami mats and shoji doors. You also have to think about how you're going to fit the components together, and at that point the order of assembly becomes very important.

In that context, I often wondered why Japan's Edo culture and the Italian Renaissance blossomed at the same time in the 16th century. I found out that the curator of the Beijing Museum of Natural History has asserted that the Mongol conqueror Genghis Khan disseminated Chinese civilization in the 13th century both to Japan and to Italy.

**RK** To the left and the right. [laughs]

**KK** That's right. Speaking architecturally, what came to Japan was the pao, which is to say, a structure that you can repeatedly put up and dismantle. Because of their nomadic life, it needed to be lightweight, they had to build it very quickly, and they took it apart and rebuilt it over and over. It may be possible to say that this is the origin of Metabolism.

Now, if we look to the west, though I'm talking about a different era here, in the Mesopotamian city of Ur they bricked over houses buried in mud and built new houses on the same spot over and over. It's been learned that they repeated this eight times. There was apparently a very strong impulse to create an eternal building.

**RK** So the mud house became the Renaissance and the tent became Metabolism?

**KK** Yes, it became a Metabolist structure made of wood. And I think the notion of attaining eternity with a mud house—or attempting to—is really fascinating.

We learned a lot about Functionalism in university but I've come to question it. The thing is, it's true that you can achieve a desired functionality at some given moment, but then a moment later it's gone. The Bauhaus and American universities both teach Functionalist design, but it's folly to think that that is how you can create eternal buildings. At any rate, it will never actually result in any eternal buildings. A building is something that undergoes constant change, from simple

Kikutake's insistent systematization of architectural thought leads to a series of trilogies, first inspired by physicist Mitsuo Taketani, fellow native of Kurume.

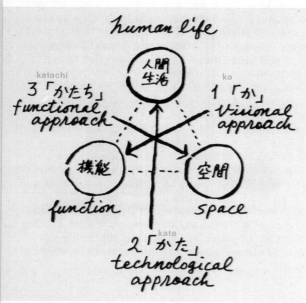

**1960s** *Ka, kata, katachi*: essence, substance, phenomenon. "Any educated person can grasp it."

**2005** *Chi, tachi, katachi*: blood, temperament, embodiment. "Something new I'm working on right now": an effort to schematize the characteristics of an architect.

**a, Kata, Katachi**
was always confused by
the three-step theory of *ka,
kata, katachi* that Kikutake
would recite. I could only
understand it as an explan-
atory logic, and I felt it was
far from being a productive
logic. The most fascinating
moments in the creation of
architecture lie in a process
of ambiguous oscillation and
inseparable fusion between
word and expression, myself
(the individual) and society,
imagination and reality. The
act of subdividing this into
three steps is nothing more
than a scientific dissection.
**Toyo Ito**

**Nobel Prize**
In 1949, for predicting the
presence of the meson. In
1955, Yukawa (1907–81)
signed the Russell-Einstein
Manifesto for nuclear dis-
armament.

**Shoichi Sakata and
Mitsuo Taketani**
Sakata (1911–1970)
developed a precursor to
the quark model; Taketani
(1911–2000) wrote the
*Doctrine of the Three Stages
of Scientific Development*
(1936), which explored the
triad of phenomenon,
substance, and essence.

**Justus Dahinden**
Kikutake: "Now let me
explain the similarities
between Justus Dahinden
and myself in terms of
methodology and philos-
ophy. The point to note is in
the triangular approach; his
philosophy is rooted in the
triangle of Structure, Gestalt,
Spirit, forming the holistic
aspect of architecture. I also
consider the process and
structure of design in three
stages of Image, Technology,
and Form, which are respectively regarded as steps of
philosophy emphasizing Essence, Substantialism, and
Phenomenalism." Kikutake's
Foreword to Dahinden's
*Architecture* (Stuttgart:
Karl Kramer Verlag, 1987).

facelifts to the wholesale rearrangement of rooms due to a change in lifestyle. There's a demand for buildings that you can do that with, and they are in fact being built.

**HUO**  What else has changed in this house?

**KK**  As we sit here talking, I'm reminded of nearly 50 years ago, at the time of the World Design Conference, when Louis Kahn was in this house, sitting by this alcove, and the Metabolists were sitting here, too, and we all talked and argued about architecture. We talked about methodological issues. One of the questions was: what are you left with as a design principal if you remove functionalism?

Kahn-san brought up the example of a school and asked which is more important, the classrooms or the hallways? He asserted that the classrooms were the master space. But I observed that when you actually watch children as they go through their school day, you see that the hallways that form the network between the classrooms are much more exciting spaces. It turned into a heated discussion.

**HUO**  What were the precedents for Sky House?

**KK**  My submissions had been placing well in competitions since I was a student, and then after I graduated, I worked for about three years for president Shojiro Ishibashi of the Bridgestone Tire Company, dismantling wooden structures and rebuilding them elsewhere. We happened to be from the same hometown.

**RK**  So it was a whole series of constant transformations?

### Ka, Kata, Katachi

**KK**  Yes. So I decided that if I wanted to work on my own designs, I needed to start by giving my ideas concrete shape in my own house, and that's how this Sky House I live in came about. Then in the late 1950s, after Hideki Yukawa had received his Nobel Prize for physics, I became interested in his collaborators, the nuclear physicists Shoichi Sakata and Mitsuo Taketani, and at that time Kawazoe told me about a book that described their methodologies.

The American method for studying elementary particles was to spend huge sums of money building these experimental devices called cyclotrons. But Japan didn't have that kind of money, so the physicists instead used theory to show the existence of mesons. The book about their methodology was written by Professor Taketani. In a happy coincidence, it turned out he was born in Kyushu, too, not very far from my hometown, and I was fortunate enough to be given frequent opportunities to discuss these questions with him.

Basically, Taketani put forth a three-stage methodology looking at the questions of phenomenon, substance, and essence to show the existence of mesons. I was influenced by this when I developed my own three-stage methodology for design, which I refer to as *ka, kata, katachi*. I've written in detail about this theory in "*Taisha Kenchiku-ron: ka, kata, katachi*,"[2] but in a nutshell, ka in design corresponds to the "essence" stage, kata corresponds to the "substance" stage, and katachi to the "phenomenon" stage.

For example, if you want to use this three-stage methodology to evaluate a design, you first address *katachi*—whether on a gut level you find it beautiful. Also, does it express a fundamental principle or have universality? And next: does the beauty you see somehow transport you into dreams or into the future? You have to think through it step by step in this way. On the other hand, if you are creating a design, you begin with a conception for the future, then you con-sider what technologies and industries you will need to call upon to achieve your vision, and finally you must scrutinize whether the form of your design appears natural. This is what the methodology prescribes. To my surprise, Louis Kahn as well as Justus Dahinden of Switzerland also had their own three-stage processes.

**RK**  But when I see the three-step methodology, it's so abstract that...

**KK**  If all you've done is heard an explanation, that's an entirely understandable response. But it's actually not so much an abstract philosophical thing as

In the first 10 years of his career, Kikutake is able to develop Metabolist concepts through a series of commissions from interested clients…

**1957 Renewal** Kikutake recycles timber and bricks from derelict buildings in his hometown of Kurume to create new buildings for the Bridgestone Dormitories for war widows and their children—proto-Metabolism…

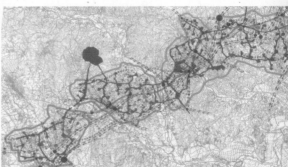

**1965 Channel Networking** The Tokyu rail company commissions Kikutake to design a new town, Pear City (named after the fruit that used to grow there), alongside its new suburban rail line, the Denen Toshi, west of Tokyo. The scheme is based on "Multi-channel Development": building alongside a growing transport and information network. A tower sits on an elevated plaza (artificial ground) from which Corbusian swathes sprawl out. Above: Multi-channel Environment, a superimposition of transportation (grey), vegetation (green), and shopping (orange) networks along the Denen Toshi line.

**1958 Move-net** "The origin of the move-net harks back to Bridgestone Tonogaya Apartments. When we couldn't find space for a shoebox, it instantly occurred to me to stick it out of the window. I wasn't completely sure about the result, but it gave me tremendous inspiration…"[3]

**1966 Artificial Ground** On a former US military base, Takashi Asada masterplans Kodomo-no-kuni (Children's land) in Yokoham for which he commissions Kikutake to build a cluster of study environments as artificial ground, elevated like tree houses. Toyo Ito, a young member of Kikutake's office, also works on the projec

it is a real world thing, and you don't have to be an architect or a specialist. Any educated person can grasp it.

What you see here [*indicating a diagram on the wall*] is another three-stage paradigm, but it's for looking at the natural gifts of an architect. At the first stage, you have chi, which means "blood" in Japanese. Blood is DNA. Each designer has his own unique DNA that predetermines what direction his designs will take. Stage two is *tachi*, which is the Japanese word for a person's dispo-sition or temperament. And the last stage is *katachi*, which is to say shape or embodiment. It's something new I'm working on right now.

One of the museums you designed, Koolhaas-san, the Kunsthal in Rotterdam, has a room where the floor is made entirely of grating. I was quite astonished when I saw that. This methodology can't explain something like that. [*laughs*]

**RK** **I'm so happy about your remark. [*laughs*] Chi, tachi, katachi... So you are moving from there to there [*pointing from the first trilogy diagram to the second*]. It's a really important part of the discussion. The system may be true at some point, but exactly the fact that it is true makes it almost unworkable today. What I wanted to get at is whether you think that the current conditions in the world, not only in Japan but for instance in China, enable that kind of stability or whether there has to be something more arbitrary or more personal.**

**KK** Without a methodological framework, you have no way of knowing what kind of era the present age is within the grand flow of history. That's why methodology is so vital. More importantly, if your methodology doesn't tell you what you need to do, then it really has no value at all.

### Networks

**HUO** **This brings us to the next question: how did your ideas expand from individual buildings to ideas for entire cities?**

**KK** Today, information technology has become extremely important in urban design. During the Second World War, research in networks started at Waseda University, headed by Professors Jun'ichi Takagi and Hiroshi Hirayama, who were Japan's top experts in the field at the time. It was research based in telecommunications theory.

**RK** **So they were studying networks as part of the Japanese war effort?**

**KK** Yes, though what actual effect their work may have had on war strategy is beyond my knowledge. At any rate, they were among the top experts in com-munications theory in the world. My older brother was involved in this research, too, and it was fascinating stuff. I thought it would be interesting to apply these network theories in thinking about cities. In the 1960s I began doing this, and I wrote an article entitled "Channel Development" in which I proposed to redesign Tokyo and other Japanese cities by incorporating a network model. All over the world, planners were talking about adopting the district planning model for urban design seen in the United Kingdom, but in the age of infor-mation it really needs to be the channel network model.

**RK** **If I may respond immediately, when I see something like this article, I'm jealous of your generation because you were surrounded by very serious media that made very ambitious publications that encouraged articles like yours.**

**KK** But you had the same sort of thing in Europe. You had Bruno Zevi's *L'Architettura* in Italy. In Germany there was the earlier incarnation of *Bauen und Wohnen*, and in Italy there was *Casabella*. I think you've had lots of magazines that covered cutting edge issues.

While plotting Metabolism and conducting private experiments with his marine cities, Kikutake builds prolifically and experimentally throughout the 1960s...

**1966** Miyakonojo Civic Center auditorium: shaped like a human ear for optimal acoustics.

**1963** Izumo Shrine Administrative Building: synthesis of tradition and modernity.

**1966** Pacific Hotel Chigasaki, a stubby version of the Tower-Shaped Community, and a fashionable resort, southwest of Tokyo, for '60s youth.

**1964** Tokoen Hotel: cantilevered floors and pagoda-style roof. Toyo Ito writes: "His desire to break the status quo and his aspiration to become an established architect make a tense balance in this project."[4]

**1967** Sado Grand Hotel: artificial ground on pilotis, solution to the lakeside's unstable foundations.

### Room for Doubt

RK But here the attention is clearly on the work, and now we have to deal with the attention that is focused on the person.

A generational question again: you have your triangle, Louis Kahn has his triangle, and Justus Dahinden has his triangle. It's all about explanation, method, and very stable forms, but where is your room for doubt? And did you ever have a crisis in your life about architecture?

KK It's because I was always experiencing doubts that I needed a methodology. At the same time, when I faced a problem in architecture or city planning, I would look for a way to resolve it by testing various hypotheses. And of course, I was always bumping into problems. When I don't know which direction to turn my boat, this three-stage methodology serves as my compass. It provides a framework for discussion: is the problem a technological one, is it merely a formal one, or is it something more essential?

HUO Now after Rem's question about doubt, I want to follow up with a question about regrets. I was wondering if you had any projects that you regret having not been realized?

RK This is a question Hans asks everybody.

KK Yes. For example, there was an international design competition in 1969 for the PREVI high-density, low-income housing in Lima, Peru, in which we proposed a public mound, which we considered the most important thematic element in our submission. We were one of the winners, but the judges never understood the point of the mound, so we had to build the housing without the mound.

On top of that, the sponsors said that from their perspective a design competition for housing should not be about choosing a single winner and building thousands of units based on that one plan. Rather, what they wanted was to build a wide variety of housing, so not just our winning design, but the designs submitted by all 13 teams should be built. And that's what happened.

HUO So it was only partially realized.

KK Yes. But almost nothing has become of my designs for floating projects due to legal barriers.

RK By the way, there are so many different chairs in this room.

KK I try not to sit too long in any one chair. It's better for my back.

RK There is a concept behind it! [laughs]

HUO I have another very practical question: How many people work in your office? And what was the maximum and minimum that worked in your office?

KK About enough for a boat race, [laughs] plus enough staff to support them. We've sometimes had as many as 30. At the moment we have a core group of seven, plus two secretaries, for a total of nine. We've had a phenomenal number of people helping out in a support capacity over the years. We have been very blessed.

HUO Within your practice what would you say is the ratio between what is built and what is unbuilt?

KK I suppose I'd say 50/50.

RK That's a lot.

HUO How many projects would that be, the realized ones?

KK Sometimes the projects you really want to build remain unbuilt, and other times they simply take a very long time to come to fruition, so of the five hundred we've proposed, the ones actually built come to less than one hundred.

### Realizations, Regrets

HUO Your generation in Japan has had the extraordinary opportunity of having not only the 1960 conference but also the 1964 Olympics and Expo '70 in Osaka. There is quite an interesting parallel today to China, which has the Olympics in Beijing and the Expo in Shanghai. In the best of all cases, as it was in 1964

**1968** Kikutake manipulates marine models and collages
into the most convincing simulations of his vision...

Framing the latest iteration of Marine City.
Earlier models on the fringes.

Techno-sublime: Marine City (version #6)
at home in a classical Japanese vista.

Nation building at sea: the Aquapolis, Kikutake's only realized floating city, is towed over 1,000 kilometers from Hiroshima, where it was constructed, to Okinawa, where it serves as the Japan "pavilion" for Ocean Expo '75. The government invests ¥180 billion in the event as a celebration of the handover of the Okinawa islands from the United States to Japan in 1972, though US military bases remain.

"The sea you want to see."
Ocean Expo '75 official slogan.

A 100 x 100-meter floating city block, the Aquapolis contains a banquet hall, offices, infirmary, communication room, post office, residences for 40 staff members, computer room, and exhibition spaces observed by visitors from a moving walkway.

Visitors flock to the Aquapolis.

Visionary.

int venture
ee p. 673.

and 1970, the Olympics and the Expo can be unbelievable engines of innovation; they can produce reality. As a curator I'm always most interested in embarking on exhibitions that produce reality. It was something your friend Peter Smithson has emphasized a lot to me—the fact that exhibitions can produce architectural reality. Did Expo '70 produce reality for you?

KK    I'd have to say no. As a member of the planning group, I asserted that we should make Expo '70 a model for innovative city design. But my views were ignored and the site was planned with parking on the outside, which meant that all visitors had to enter through the gates on foot. It was a very poor set-up as far as I was concerned—wrong-headed urban design centered entirely on pedestrians.

RK    **I totally agree.**

HUO    **What about the Aquapolis, which was made for the Okinawa Expo in 1975? Did the Okinawa exhibition produce one-to-one reality for you?**

RK    **Was the Aquapolis not a model but the real thing? Was that your fascination?**

KK    Absolutely.

HUO    **So it was one city block?**

KK    Yes, 100 metres by 100 metres. I thought that was about the size a city block needed to be. Later I saw the 100-meter Plaza in Buenos Aires and nodded to myself that one hundred meters on a side had been the right choice. Aquapolis was built to commemorate the return of Okinawa from the US to Japan. The floating technologies that were used belonged to the US Navy. In 1972, when Richard Nixon and Kakuei Tanaka held a summit in Hawaii, they discussed the construction of a floating city as a joint venture between Japan and the US. But sad to say, Nixon insisted it should be built not in the Pacific but in the Caribbean, right in the hurricane zone, and the idea fell through. It was very unfortunate. I only found out about it sometime later.

RK    **Regret.**

HUO    **Unrealized.**

KK    But it's a beautiful design. It's a project I still hope to build someday. [*laughs*]

**References**

1  Kiyonori Kikutake, interviewed by Mitsuo Okawa, "Expansion and reform of Sky House, and the theory of Metabolism," *Kenchiku Zasshi*, November 1994.

2  Kiyonori Kikutake, *Taisha Kenchiku-ron: Ka, Kata, Katachi* (Metabolic theory of architecture), (Tokyo: Shokokusha, 1969).

3  Kiyonori Kikutake, *Kindai Kenchiku*, April 1958.

4  Toyo Ito, "Kikutake Kiyonori-shi ni tou—warera no kyoki wo ikinobiru michi wo oshieyo to" (Kiyonori Kikutake, teach us how to survive our madness), *Kenchiku Bunka*, October 1975.

**1958** Waking, walking, working (planning the addition of a new move-net), entertaining (Kawazoe, Kikutake, and others), and studying at Sky House, scrutinized in the television documentary *House of a Kangaroo*.

1958 Kiyonori Kikutake: Sky House, Tokyo
2009 Photos by Charlie Koolhaas

# Birth of a Movement
## Metabolism and the World Design Conference

**"The state of confusion and paralysis in metropolitan cities and the inconsistency and luck of systematic planning is forcing us to make this proposal..."**

Kiyonori Kikutake, *Metabolism 1960*.

In 1959, Tange temporarily departs the scene he created in order to spend a semester teaching at MIT in Boston. Back home, the nascent Metabolists begin cohering in his absence—though still under his offstage directions.

The international platform of the 1960 World Design Conference in Tokyo necessitates the formation of a new Japanese architectural movement, Tange believes. He charges Asada—his number two at Tange Lab, secretary-general of WoDeCo, and borderline mystic ("people bleed," he declares, as explanation of the fundamental importance of Metabolism)—with the task of seeking out young architects and designers to participate in the conference. This triggers the birth of a movement. Asada and Kawazoe convene nightly gatherings of promising young talents; Kawazoe names their gradually unifying outlook "Metabolism." The discussions are intense and wide ranging, launching from Japan's ancient history as a means of adapting for the future...

The group codifies its work and concepts—renewal, artificial ground, Group Form—in a short book that is something like a manifesto: *Metabolism 1960: The Proposal for New Urbanism*. Kurokawa and Awazu sell it on the door of the World Design Conference, like a guide book, as the international avant-garde arrives... Though this was a guerrilla action not entirely authorized, the ambitious young men also make pivotal "official" contributions to the conference, probably thanks to Tange and Asada. In front of an audience of 227 international architects and designers selected and invited by Asada—among them Jean Prouvé, Paul Rudolph, Alison and Peter Smithson, Louis Kahn, and Ralph Erskine—Kurokawa, Kikutake, Ekuan, Otaka, and Tange himself make presentations that propose a new architectural strategy. Buildings and cities must be able to adapt, grow, elevate, even float, if they are to survive the dual pressures of rapid modernization and inevitable natural change (usually calamitous)...

Obsessed with Japanese tradition, contemporary pressures, and possible futures for their nation, Tange, Kurokawa, and Maki are—from the beginning of their careers—simultaneously inspired by the world outside Japan. In the 1950s, long before Metabolism begins, they travel the world out of sheer curiosity and find inspiration for theories both archetypal (Maki's Group Form) and futuristic (Tange's seaborne infrastructure)...

### 1951 Tange: Europe
After attending CIAM in the UK, Tange goes on a pilgrimage to Rome, for Michelangelo's St. Peter's Basilica, then to Marseille, for Le Corbusier's Unité d'Habitation. Interested in the new scale of urban architecture and its relation to the human scale, he also visits New York for the first time, where he is impressed by Lever House and the UN Building.[1]

**MOBILITY**
- San Francisco

- Cranbrook
- St. Louis
  - Boston
  - New York

**GLASS AND STEEL**

- Brasilia
**NEW CITY**
  - Sao Paulo

### 1959 Tange: United States
During his four months in the United States teaching at MIT, and through side visits to San Francisco and Chicago, Tange is confronted with the modern American metropolis. He is fascinated how elevated highways—still absent from Tokyo—form an intrinsic part of the city and looks for ways of "integrating urban communications spaces with architecture."[2] Known in Japan as an outstanding architectural form-giver; outside Japan Tange researches future systems of urban planning, which he will take home with him and exploit in Plan for Tokyo 1960.

### 1957 Tange: Brazil
On the jury for the 4th Biennale of Architecture in Sao Paulo with Mies van der Rohe, Marcel Breuer, and Phillip Johnson, Tange most likely visits Brasilia, still under construction, an unprecedented utopian city.

### 1958 Kurokawa: USSR

Visiting Moscow and Leningrad for international architecture student conferences, Kurokawa is disillusioned by the dominance of Stalinist rather than Constructivist architecture. He is impressed though by the Soviet Union's advanced prefabricated housing and visits factories in both cities—inspiring his first book, *Prefabricated Houses* (1960), a fascination that will evolve into the capsule...

### 1956 Tange: Grand Tour

A two-month journey through China, the USSR, Egypt, and India, where he visits Le Corbusier's Ahmedabad Museum, a brutal mass of bricks on pilotis, completed three years before.[3] The trip induces Tange to experiment with more brutal forms at home...

**PREFABRICATED HOUSING**

• Leningrad

• Moscow

esdon

gnols-sur-Cèze
arseille Rome

**URBAN PATTERNS**

• Athens
• Hydra
  • Beirut      • Tehran
    • Damascus  • Isfahan
• Cairo

**LE CORBUSIER**

• Chandigarh

• Ahmedabad

• Singapore

### 1959–60 Maki: Grand Tour

After six years in the US, at Cranbrook and Harvard, Maki wins a Graham Foundation Fellowship that allows him to travel for two years in Southeast Asia, India, the Middle East, and Europe. While the Metabolists are gathering under Asada and Kawazoe in Tokyo, Maki is largely absent, visiting vernacular prototypes of human settlements, along with the work of Le Corbusier wherever he can find it. He sees himself as retracing the steps of philosopher Tetsuro Watsuji (1889–1960) in his 1935 work, *Fuhdo* (Anthropological climatology). Watsuji traces connections between ethics/culture and climate/

geography, and travels from Japan to Europe, experiencing monsoons in Asia, deserts in the Middle East, and meadows in Europe.[4] From Maki's travels, and in collaboration with Otaka, the theory of Group Form emerges: "I saw in those collective forms from the Mediterranean both an expression of regional culture and a body of wisdom accumulated over many years. Here, as nowhere else, I became aware of the existence of a historical and decisive relationship between cities and architecture. For those cultures, creating buildings and creating cities were one and the same thing."[5]

**1958** Nascent Metabolists, and their mentor Kenzo Tange, gather at Kikutake's housewarming party for his recently completed Sky House.

Noboru Kawazoe

Kenzo Tange

Kisho Kurokawa

Tokyo's World Design Conference has its roots in the 1956 International Design Conference in Aspen (IDCA). Isamu Kenmochi, an interior designer, and Sori Yanagi, an industrial designer, visiting Aspen as representatives of the Japan Committee on International Design (of which Tange and Okamoto are members), propose that the 1958 iteration of the conference should be held in Japan instead of Aspen. The proposed venue is a hotel on the lake of Hakone, a mountainous area just southwest of Tokyo.

Will Burtin, the graphic designer who cofounded the IDCA in 1951, supports Kenmochi's proposal as a way to make the conference truly "international" and suggests that Hakone would be an "East-West" edition of the IDCA. He finds great enthusiasm among some members, including Charles and Ray Eames.[6]

Suitably encouraged, Hisaakira Kano, chairman of the Japan Housing Corporation and vice president of the Japan Committee on International Design, sets up and chairs a preparatory committee in Japan and creates a detailed itinerary for the 1958 event.[7] Tange, a member of the preparatory committee, visits Burtin in New York in 1957 to sound out the IDCA's progress on the Hakone edition as their procrastination becomes obvious. "We seem to have taken a delicate viewpoint towards openly declaring the Design conference a truly International affair," writes a disappointed Morton Goldshell in a memo to the cautious IDCA executive committee. "Maybe the idea of design growing and flourishing in other countries makes some of our corporate members fearful of a growing competition overseas."[8]

But by this time, a "World Design Conference" preparation committee has emerged, with Kano and Takashi Asada at the helm, and sufficient confidence to organize their conference independently of the indecisive Americans. Rather than an "IDCA" based in Aspen with an excursion to Hakone, their idea is for a permanently roving World Design Conference. Asada writes to Burtin: " The Japan Preparations Committee hopes that an international organization of designers can be formed for the improvement of Man's visual surroundings and that the World Design Conference will become a permanent institution moving from one member country to another."[9]

But WoDeCo, hosted in Tokyo, is a one-off. Burtin does not attend, apparently preoccupied by the Aspen "international" conference, which, despite earlier assurances, goes ahead concurrently with the Japanese international conference...

**1958** Tange briefs Asada at the Sky House party.

January 20, 1958

Mr. Hisaakira Kano, President
Japan Committee on International Design
The International House of Japan, Inc.
2 Toriizaka Asabu Minato-ku
Tokyo, Japan

Dear Mr. Kano:

As a result of a recent meeting of the Executive Committee of the International Design Conference, I can now inform you that my suggestions regarding an International Design Conference in Japan, in 1959, has been accepted. Since I have been elected program chairman for that year's conference, it gives me great pleasure to be able to carry on negotiations with you in this matter.

It has now been made clear that the 1959 World Conference on Design will be held instead of our usual Aspen Conference, and it is hoped that, if your kind invitation is still in effect, the conference would be sponsored jointly by IDC and The Japan Committee on International Design. For those American members of IDC who are not able to attend the conference in Japan, regional meetings are contemplated, in which members who have participated in the Japan conference will report on their findings and impressions.

I wish to convey my great pleasure about this step forward in creating a truly great opportunity for designers and artists from all over the world to meet in your beautiful country to discuss their ideas and problems. I hope that we can immediately commence with the planning of a program that will equal this occasion. Since I am already at work with my committee on this matter, I would be most appreciative of your thoughts and suggestions at your early convenience. In this fashion we can expedite the clarification of our mutual aims and arrive more quickly at a conference structure.

With my very best regards, I remain

Cordially yours,

Will Burtin
Program Chairman
1959 IDC

An "international" (mis)understanding? Will Burtin delivers the news that, after much goading from the Japanese design community, the International Design Committee Aspen has finally accepted the idea of Japan hosting the 1959 conference instead of Aspen. But it does not work out that way...

WORLD DESIGN CONFERENCE IN JAPAN: WoDeCo–TOKYO

room 301, the international house of japan, 2 toriizaka-machi, azabu, minato-ku, tokyo, japan. phone: 48-8351

Mr. Will Burtin,
132 East 58th Street,
New York 22, N.Y., U.S.A.

June 15, 1959

Dear Mr. Burtin,

For years Japanese designers have dreamed of holding a worldwide conference in Tokyo which would be attended by designers and other professionals concerning creative works in such various fields as architecture, urban design, the crafts, industrial design, and graphic arts.

The idea came up at the Aspen Conference in the United States in 1956, and in the following months it was given serious attention by the International Designers Association in Japan. In the fall of 1958 the Japan Preparations Committee was formed to make concrete plans for the conference. At present this committee is at work on such matters as the subjects for conference discussion, the program, the location of meeting, and the raising of funds.

The Preparations Committee is sending herewith a preliminary schedule, together with a form to be filled. We should greatly appreciate your filling in the form and returning it to us at your earliest convenience. We are eager to have many competent designers attend and hope you would be interested in this conference and willing to cooperate with us for the success of it.

We shall be grateful for any suggestions you might wish to make concerning the conference, and we hope that you will recommend other prospective participants in your reply. A formal invitation to the conference will be sent to you in near future.

Very truly yours,

Takashi Asada, Architect-Planner
Secretary General
World Design Conference in Japan (WoDeCo-Tokyo)

Independence: after an aborted collaboration with the IDCA, the Japanese surreptitiously break away from the Americans and launch their own conference, under a different name. Takashi Asada sends Burtin information on the World Design Conference in Tokyo, to take place in 1960, and a form to fill in.

In the run up to the World Design Conference in 1960, a complex leadership system crystallizes, with Tange the key catalyst—and the only figure capable of mobilizing Japan's architecture and design circles for the conference. Realizing that an international stage is set for a Japanese movement to announce itself, Tange—already committed to teaching at MIT in the run-up to WoDeCo—charges Asada and, through him, Kawazoe, to assemble a group of emerging talents that will become Metabolism.

**CHAIRMAN**

JUNZO SAKAKURA

**Junzo Sakakura** Tange's predecessor as Japan's foremost modern architect.

HISAAKIRA KANO

**Hisaakira Kano** Initiator of WoDeCo and chairman of the preparatory committee, also chairman of the Japan Housing Corporation.

**GOVERNMENT**
Ministry of International Trade and Industry (MITI) and JETRO (govt. agency for exports) provide ¥5 million funding.

**BUSINESS & INDUSTRY**
Contribute ¥49 million in funding.

Preparatory Committee of the World Design Conference (WoDeCo)

**SECRETARY-GENERAL**

TAKASHI ASADA

**Takashi Asada** Number two in Tange Lab, he is charged by Tange with gathering a group of young architects for WoDeCo.

Action Committee

NOBORU KAWAZOE

**Noboru Kawazoe** quits as editor of *Shinkenchiku*, Japan's most important architecture magazine, in 1957. Asada assigns him to help scout talent for WoDeCo...

KISHO KUROKAWA

**Kisho Kurokawa** a student at Tange Lab, and disillusioned by his visit to the Soviet Union in 1958 and the collapse of CIAM a year later, becomes a polemicist for Metabolism; WoDeCo is his launchpad into the international arena...

**SCOUTED YOUNG TALENTS >**

**Masato Otaka** spends his days supervising construction of Kunio Maekawa's Tokyo Cultural Hall, and Harumi high-rise apartments (both 1958–60) and his nights meeting with fellow future Metabolists...

ENZO TANGE

**enzo Tange** Absent in the build p to WoDeCo, but sets Metabolism in motion from afar rough Asada.

**Sori Yanagi** Industrial designer and founding member of Japan Committee on International Design.

**Ken Ichiura** Architect specializing in wooden prefabricated housing.

**Hiromu Hara** Graphic designer who commissions promising talents for WoDeCo materials.

+ Seiichiro Arai

## DIRECTORS

**samu Kenmochi** Interior designer nd founding member of Japan Committee on International Design. riggers WoDeCo in 1956 by nviting the International Design Conference Aspen to Japan.

**Yusaku Kamekura** Graphic designer and founding member of Japan Committee on International Design.

**Takashi Kono** Founding father of graphic design in Japan, creator of WoDeCo logo.

**Iwataro Koike** Industrial designer and mentor to Kenji Ekuan.

+ Masaru Katsumi, Yoshinobu Ashihara, and 10 others...

**Fumihiko Maki** teaches at Washington University, St. Louis, and builds Steinberg Hall there; studies urban patterns in Central Asia and the Middle East from 1958–60, and stops by Tokyo in early 1960 to articulate his findings with Otaka and the Metabolists...

**Kiyonori Kikutake**, already renowned with his Sky House, develops a new version of his Marine City proposal in the build-up to the conference...

**Kenji Ekuan**, an industrial designer, sets up GK Design in 1957 with his professor Iwataro Koike and classmates at Tokyo National University of Fine Arts. Kawazoe, with a mission to bring in talent from all disciplines, invites him to join the WoDeCo preparation committee...

**Kiyoshi Awazu** wins the Japan Advertising Arts Award in 1955 and the Grand Prix at the World Film Poster Competition in France three years later for his Pop-influenced designs. In 1959, he establishes the Awazu Design Institute, catching the eye of Kawazoe...

Burdened by interlocking responsibilities—teaching at Tange Lab, building symbolic municipal architecture in Japan—escape is Tange's only way out. He goes to teach at the Massachusetts Institute of Technology in Boston for a semester, taking time as an independent thinker and leaving his promising accolytes behind. At MIT, "liberated from daily chores," Tange writes, he develops ideas on "growth and change" and "integrating urban communications spaces with architecture."[14] The result of his research at MIT is a proposal for a housing system accommodating 25,000 people on the water of Boston Harbor (the design will reemerge a year later in his Plan for Tokyo 1960). A highway runs underneath the A-frame tube...

Back to school...

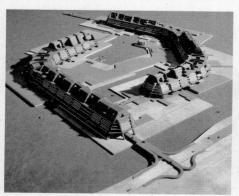

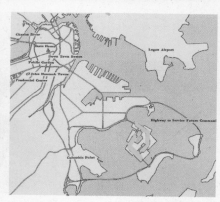

**1959** Tange's housing system for Boston Harbor, in which he tries to produce architecture that mediates between the human scale and the new, non-human scale of modern urban infrastructure. He will present the plan at the World Design Conference the next year.

Tange is program director on the preparatory committee of the upcoming World Design Conference, but leaves Takashi Asada in charge while he is in the US. While the cat's away, Asada engages politicians, bureaucrats, business leaders, journalists, and academics; by night, he grooms a new avant-garde. He and Kawazoe gather a group of young architects and designers for discussions at Ryugetsu restaurant and inn in Ginza. The group initially includes Kurokawa, still a rookie in Tange Lab, and the already well-established Kiyonori Kikutake. Looking for solutions to the urban crises caused by Japan's explosive economic growth and its unstable and scarce land, the group looks to historical Japanese precedents—the cyclical rebuilding of Ise Shrine and the modular growth of Katsura Detached Palace—as inspirations for a new type of changeable architecture…

he name "World Design
onference" is made official
nd Asada presents its logo
 a preparatory committee
eeting at International House.

eft behind. At Tange Lab, working
 the extension to Tokyo City Hall:
rom left) Jiro Inazuka; Isozaki, who
ill leave in three years to set up his
wn office and remain on the periphery
f Metabolism; and Metabolism's
oungest member, Kurokawa, who will
pen his own office in 1961. Outside
e Lab, protests intensify against the
S–Japan security treaty, due to be
enewed in 1960 (the treaty was first
gned in 1951). A split opens in Tange
ab in the run up to WoDeCo: Kurokawa
ssists Kawazoe in organizing the con-
erence; Isozaki, the perpetual con-
arian, and Jiro Inazuka are among
e majority who see the conference
s a tool of the establishment.

One month before the World Design Conference, Kawazoe announces the foundational idea of Metabolism: artificial ground (*jinko tochi*), the unifying concept behind the diverse works the Metabolists are about to present to the world. Artificial ground is a form of adaptation to the absence of tabula rasa, or even basic stability and available space in Japan; if there is no ground to build on, Metabolism will adapt and build its own ground.

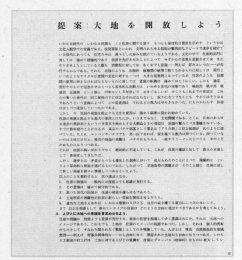

A proposal: Let's liberate the ground!
Noboru Kawazoe, *Kindai Kenchiku*, April 1960
In and around large cities such as Tokyo, the price of land is skyrocketing … The problem is that the land is not only already too expensive but also in critically short supply. This has been a major complication hampering the construction of new housing. However, it is exacerbated complications like this that trigger rapid or even revolutionary progress. The very difficulty of obtaining land is actually unfolding a new possibility for housing … Here is what I propose for new housing:

A. The image of the ground is always the basis for the image of a house. But today people are being liberated from fixed land towards a global scale. By liberating natural ground as it originally was—be it the pilotis hoisting proposed by Kisho Kurokawa or the grotto-like housing by Masato Otaka— I believe we could acquire a new awareness of the ground …

B. Our prime task is to provide people with land on demand, that is, artificial ground. It could be reinforced concrete slabs, or something like walls [that accommodate plug-in capsules], or floating on the ocean. The first has been proposed by Le Corbusier, the latter two by Kiyonori Kikutake in his Tower-Shaped Community and Marine City. The liberation of the ground would be the only justification for developing artificial ground. If it wasn't for liberating the ground back to the original natural state, people won't be motivated to live on artificial ground. Though the current malaise of land would inevitably force people to artificial ground to a certain degree, such an awareness is essential to realize artificial ground in such a way to solve the problem.

Prompted by Kawazoe, Kikutake and Kurokawa work on a compilation of their ideas so far: *Metabolism 1960*. They work in coffee shops and in Tokyo's International House. Meanwhile Maki and Otaka, the other unit within Metabolism, collaborate on a Group Form plan for Shinjuku station in Tokyo, which will also appear in the book. At the last minute, Kawazoe realizes there is no introduction to the book, so he writes a short text (below) grouping all the projects under a conceptual umbrella—he is the only one to actually use the word "metabolism," though every contributor talks about processes of renewal in their plans for future cities. The introduction gives *Metabolism 1960* the feeling of a manifesto, though it is never explicitly described as such. Awazu designs the book and creates a logo (below), and Kawazoe's wife, Yasuko, works on the layout. (Ekuan is too busy organizing the industrial design contingent of WoDeCo to contribute, but he is a Metabolist from the start). The 89-page book is printed in an edition of 2,000 by Bijutsu Shuppansha (Fine arts press) and sold by Kurokawa (wearing a bow tie) and Awazu for ¥500 at the entrance of Sankei Kokusai Hall, the venue of WoDeCo, announcing Metabolism to an international audience.

cubator: International House, ɔkyo, where *Metabolism 1960* written and assembled.

Metabolism logo, designed by Awazu, an adaptation of the *tomoe*.

METABOLISM/1960

Noboru Kawazoe's introduction to *Metabolism 1960*:
"'Metabolism' is the name of the group, in which each member proposes future designs of our coming world through his concrete designs and illustrations. We regard human society as a vital process—a continuous development from atom to nebula. The reason why we use such a biological word, metabolism, is that, we believe, design and technology should be a denotation of human vitality. We are not going to accept the metabolism as a natural historical process, but we are trying to encourage active metabolic development of our society through our proposals."

1960 May World Design Conference, Tokyo: "OUR CENTURY: The Total Image. What designers can contribute to the human environment of the coming age."

Takashi Asada, secretary-general, and Hisaakira Kano, chairman of the preparatory committee, secure the support of government and industry titans, including the Ministry of International Trade and Industry (MITI), the Agency of Patents, the Foreign Ministry, and JETRO, the governmental agency for exports. While senior members of the committee focus on raising funds from corporations, younger members like Kawazoe and Kurokawa prepare the agenda for the conference, and invite a stellar cast of global architects and designers.

◀ 現代の顔 ―

建築界のベスト・ドレッサー

── 丹下 健三 ──

梁木タイに黒の背広姿　丹下健三氏は　建築界のベスト・ドレッサーという評判がある。今までに考案された建築も　スタイル的に都会的で垢抜けがいい。東京にある自宅をはじめ　どれもピロティ式（地面から建物を柱で持ち上げたような建築）で貫かれている。日本デザイン会議会場で

Tange—"the best dressed man in the architecture circle"—awaits the arrival of 227 guests... pictured on the front page of *Shukan Shincho*, May 23, 1960.

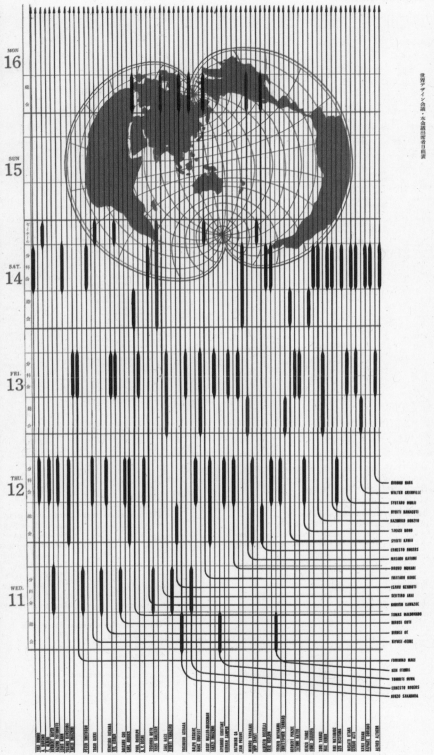

Schedule and guest list in WoDeCo Bulletin No. 6, designed by Gan Hosoya.[15]

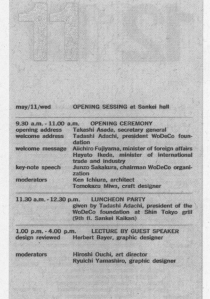
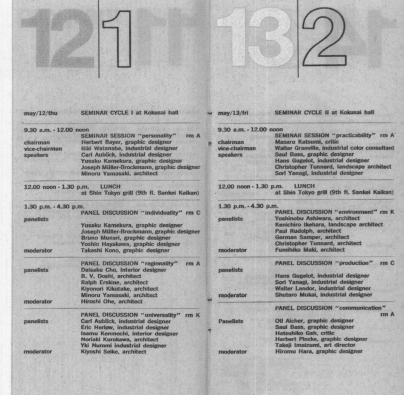

| may/11/wed | OPENING SESSING at Sankei hall |
|---|---|
| 9.30 a.m. - 11.00 a.m. | OPENING CEREMONY |
| opening address | Takashi Asada, secretary general |
| welcome address | Tadashi Adachi, president WoDeCo foundation |
| welcome message | Aiichiro Fujiyama, minister of foreign affairs |
| | Hayato Ikeda, minister of international trade and industry |
| key-note speech | Junzo Sakakura, chairman WoDeCo organization |
| moderators | Ken Ichiura, architect |
| | Tomokazu Miwa, craft designer |
| 11.30 a.m. - 12.30 p.m. | LUNCHEON PARTY |
| | given by Tadashi Adachi, president of the WoDeCo foundation at Shin Tokyo griil (9th fl. Sankei Kaikan) |
| 1.00 p.m. - 4.00 p.m. | LECTURE BY GUEST SPEAKER |
| design reviewed | Herbert Bayer, graphic designer |
| moderators | Hiroshi Ouchi, art director |
| | Ryuichi Yamashiro, graphic designer |

| may/12/thu | SEMINAR CYCLE I at Kokusai hall |
|---|---|
| 9.30 a.m. - 12.00 noon | SEMINAR SESSION "personality" rm A |
| chairman | Herbert Bayer, graphic designer |
| vice-chairman | Riki Watanabe, industrial designer |
| speakers | Carl Aubök, industrial designer |
| | Yusaku Kamekura, graphic designer |
| | Joseph Müller-Brockmann, graphic designer |
| | Minoru Yamasaki, architect |
| 12.00 noon - 1.30 p.m. | LUNCH |
| | at Shin Tokyo grill (9th fl. Sankei Kaikan) |
| 1.30 p.m. - 4.30 p.m. | PANEL DISCUSSION "individuality" rm C |
| panelists | |
| | Yusaku Kamekura, graphic designer |
| | Joseph Müller-Brockmann, graphic designer |
| | Bruno Munari, graphic designer |
| | Yoshio Hayakawa, graphic designer |
| moderator | Takashi Kono, graphic designer |
| | PANEL DISCUSSION "regionality" rm A |
| panelists | Daisaku Cho, interior designer |
| | B. V. Doshi, architect |
| | Ralph Erskine, architect |
| | Kiyonori Kikutake, architect |
| | Minoru Yamasaki, architect |
| moderator | Hiroshi Ohe, architect |
| | PANEL DISCUSSION "universality" rm K |
| panelists | Carl Aubök, industrial designer |
| | Eric Herlow, industrial designer |
| | Isamu Kenmochi, interior designer |
| | Noriaki Kurokawa, architect |
| | Yki Nummi industrial designer |
| moderator | Kiyoshi Seike, architect |

| may/13/fri | SEMINAR CYCLE II at Kokusai hall |
|---|---|
| 9.30 a.m. - 12.00 noon | SEMINAR SESSION "practicability" rm A |
| chairman | Masaru Katsumi, critic |
| vice-chairman | Walter Granville, industrial color consultant |
| speakers | Saul Bass, graphic designer |
| | Hans Gugelot, industrial designer |
| | Christopher Tunnard, landscape architect |
| | Sori Yanagi, industrial designer |
| 12.00 noon - 1.30 p.m. | LUNCH |
| | at Shin Tokyo grill (9th fl. Sankei Kaikan) |
| 1.30 p.m. - 4.30 p.m. | PANEL DISCUSSION "environment" rm K |
| panelists | Yoshinobu Ashihara, architect |
| | Kenichiro Ikehara, landscape architect |
| | Paul Rudolph, architect |
| | German Samper, architect |
| | Christopher Tunnard, architect |
| moderator | Fumihiko Maki, architect |
| | PANEL DISCUSSION "production" rm C |
| panelists | Hans Gugelot, industrial designer |
| | Sori Yanagi, industrial designer |
| | Walter Landor, industrial designer |
| moderator | Shutaro Mukai, industrial designer |
| | PANEL DISCUSSION "communication" rm A |
| Panelists | Otl Aicher, graphic designer |
| | Saul Bass, graphic designer |
| | Hatsuhiko Gah, critic |
| | Herbert Pinzke, graphic designer |
| | Takeji Imaizumi, art director |
| moderator | Hiromu Hara, graphic designer |

**May 11–16, 1960** WoDeCo program. The 15th is reserved for excursions in Tokyo (there is also a trip to Nara, Kyoto, and Osaka). Graphic design by Ikko Tanaka.

## 84 foreign participants, including

| graphic designers | Otl Aicher |
|---|---|
| | Saul Bass (closing speech) |
| | Herbert Bayer (keynote) |
| | Max Huber |
| | Josef Müller-Brockmann |
| | Bruno Munari |
| theorists | Françoise Choay |
| | Tomas Maldonado |
| industrial designer | Hans Gugelot |
| architects | Charles Correa |
| | B.V. Doshi |
| | Ralph Erskine |
| | Louis Kahn |
| | Jean Prouvé |
| | Paul Rudolph |
| | Peter and Alison Smithson |
| | Raphael Soriano |
| | Minoru Yamasaki |

## 143 Japanese participants, including

| architects | Kunio Maekawa |
|---|---|
| | Kiyoshi Seike |
| | Hiroshi Oe (member of *Rei-no-kai*) |
| | Yoshinobu Ashihara |
| | Seiichi Shirai |
| | Motoo Take (*Rei-no-kai*) |
| | Uszo Nishiyama |
| | Kazuo Shinohara |
| bureaucrat | Atsushi Shimokobe |

### Origin of international partipants

| USA, Canada | 37 |
|---|---|
| Europe | 22 |
| Middle East | 7 |
| South America | 6 |
| Australia, New Zealand | 5 |
| Southeast Asia | 4 |
| India | 3 |

**may/14/sat    SEMINAR CYCLE III at Kokusai hall**

**9.30 a.m. - 12.00 noon**

|  |  |
|---|---|
| | SEMINAR SESSION "possibility"    rm A |
| chairman | Tomas Maldonado, critic |
| vice-chairman | Shoichi Kawai, architect |
| speakers | Jean Prouvé, industrial designer |
| | Hans Schleger, graphic designer |
| | Peter Smithson, architect |
| | Kenzo Tange, architect |

**12.00 noon - 1.30 p.m.    LUNCH**
at Shin Tokyo grill (9th fl. Sankei Kaikan)

**1.30 p.m. - 4.30 p.m.**

|  |  |
|---|---|
| | PANEL DISCUSSION "society"    rm K |
| panelists | Max Huber, graphic designer |
| | Uzo Nishiyama, architect |
| | Raphael Soriano, architect |
| | Kohei Sugiura, graphic designer |
| moderator | Noboru Kawazoe, critic |

|  |  |
|---|---|
| | PANEL DISCUSSION "technology"    rm C |
| panelists | Alfred Altherr, architect |
| | Masato Otaka, architect |
| | Jean Prouvé, industrial designer |
| | Alberto Rosselli, industrial designer |
| moderator | Kazuhiko Honjo, architect |

|  |  |
|---|---|
| | PANEL DISCUSSION "phylosophy"    rm A |
| panelists | Kenji Ekuan, industrial designer |
| | Louis Kahn, architect |
| | Tomos Maldanado, critic |
| | Peter Smithson, architect |
| | Kenzo Tange, architect |
| moderator | Ryuichi Hamaguchi, critic |

**may/14/sat (evening)  EDUCATIONSEMINAR at Kokusai hall**

**7.00 p.m. - 9.00 p.m.**

|  |  |
|---|---|
| | SEMINAR ON DESIGN EDUCATION |
| speakers | Otl Aicher, graphic designer |
| | Jupp Ernst, industrial designer |
| | Yasuo Inamura, color specialist |
| | Arne Korsmo, architect |
| | Haru Madokoro, design educator |
| | Toshio Ozeki, design educator |
| | Masakiku Takeyama, design educator |
| | Isamu Tsukada, design educator |
| moderator | Iwatero Koike, design educator |

**may/15/sun    SIGHT SEEING of Tokyo**

**may/16/mon    CLOSING SESSION at Kokusai hall**

**9.30 a.m. - 11.30 a.m.    CLOSING SESSION**

|  |  |
|---|---|
| resume of cycle I seminar session | Herbert Bayer |
| resume of cycle II seminar session | Masaru Katsumi |
| resume of cycle III seminar session | Tomas Maldonado |
| resume of education seminar | Iwataro Koike |
| WoDeCo Tokyo declaration | Junzo Sakakura, chairman |
| closing greeting | Hisakira Kano, honorary chairman |

|  |  |
|---|---|
| moderators | Seiichiro Arai, art director |
| | Toshihiko Goto, craft designer |

**1.30 p.m. - 4.30 p.m.    LUNCHEON PARTY**
for foreign guests
given by Tadashi Adachi, president of the
World Design Conference foundation at
Ishibashi mansion

**PANEL EXHIBITION "my works & my images"**
the panel exhibition of "my works & my images" is held at
Kokusai hall of the Sankei Kaikan (5th fl. rm D) during the
conference.

---

**WoDeCo・世界デザイン会議報**    昭和35年2月25日

### ―ひろば―
**服飾デザインは含まないか**
学生 三宅一生

‥‥私はコスチューム・デザインの勉強をしています。WoDeCoの行事は素晴らしいと思っています。私も参加したいと思っていました(学生として)。しかしながら、このWoDeCoには、デザインの全分野と記されているにもかかわらず、何故服飾デザインが含まれていないのでしょうか! 私には理解できませんが、衣服というものの生活とどれほど大きな違がりをもっているかなどということは、今さら言うまでもないことです。この点に関して委員長の御意見をお聞きしたいのです。

【事務局より】 同じような趣旨の御質問を他にもいろいろな方々からいただきました。常任委員会できめられ

て考え方に従って、事務局からお答えします。

**部会名称を広義に解釈して**
実行委員会規約草案のなかで、第7条に各専門部会の名称と内容を記してありますが、第1部会‥‥第5部会の分け方は非常に抽象的なものであります。そして、入会を希望される方々に御自身で適当な部会を選んでいただくようになっています。第1部会はグラフィックデザイン等、第3部会はインダストリアル・デザイン等)と、各部会ともそれぞれに相当ひろい分野をカバーできるように考えられております。

服飾と同じように、船舶デザイン、土木設計、写真、舞台装置、関連語科学の研究など、個々に数えあげれば無数の専門家が出来るのですが、その中で比較的簡単に特定の部会を選べるものもあり、また同一

ジャンルでも、デザイン対象やデザイナーの立場によって違った部会に分れるものもあります。たとえば、テクスタイルデザインは、仕事の内容によって第1から第5まで、どの部会にも含まれる可能性があります。

もっとも、実行委員会の組織化がきわめて短かい期間に進められたため、規約(草案)の条文や、その解釈、運用などにいろいろの不備や片寄りがないとはいえませんし、また初例の組織活動に参加された方々の専門別分布の片寄りなどのために、入会の御案内も配られている分野が多いと思います。WoDeCoの本来の趣旨として、「デザインという仕事に関するすべての分野を含んで総合的に行なわれる。」(規約前文)と記されていますが、それを実現するためにも、ぜひ色々な立場の方の積極的な参加と交流をお願いしたいと思います。(組織係)

---

**Issey Miyake**, a 22-year-old student of costume design, complains to the chairman of WoDeCo, Junzo Sakakura, that fashion is excluded from WoDeCo's embrace: "I think the WoDeCo is a wonderful event and was looking forward to participating in it. But I wonder: why doesn't WoDeCo include fashion design while claiming it stands for all design genres?! I don't understand it. Needless to say, clothing is fundamentally linked with our lifestyle. I would like to ask for the opinion of the chairman about this matter." The secretariat replies: "We received similar questions from various people. ... The organization might reflect that the founding members come from certain fields and not others, and we have therefore missed inviting certain groups to the conference. But our protocol does say that the conference 'addresses all fields of design professions.' We therefore encourage people from a variety of positions to actively participate and exchange." (WoDeCo Bulletin, February 25, 1960)

The Metabolists appear as individuals rather than as a group at the conference. While they make no formal declarations or even an announcement of their name (Tange is the only one to use the word "metabolism"), Kurokawa, Kikutake. and Otaka present their projects from *Metabolism 1960*; Kawazoe and Maki moderate sessions; Ekuan speaks on "Technology and the Masses." Other delegates echo the sense of rapid global change and the need for architecture and urban planning to catch up.[16]

**Yusaku Kamekura**
**May 11: Katachi**
"One of the problems which have been imposed upon us Japanese designers is the problem of tradition. Tradition is a burden for the designer, but one which he cannot reject. We have the duty to take our tradition apart, and then put it together in a new way."

**Minoru Yamasaki**
**May 11: Architecture and democracy**
"I think that the basic problem of architecture is to somehow bring about an expression of our total society rather than an individual preconception. ... I am for a more disciplined architecture. Architecture must be the creation of an environment or background for all of man's activities ... It is only recently with the development of democratic concepts that our major buildings are being built for all the people. Today, we are building buildings for all, and the need to awe and impress is not consistent with the principles of democratic society."

**Kiyonori Kikutake**
**May 12: The Oceanic City**
"Cities are almost withering and lifeless though they ought to be vivid and vigorous. All cities and architecture find a place to settle as though to praise the eternity of space. These immovable architectures have been constantly and quietly covering the surface of ground. Both our society and our life are being suffocated by this tranquil but fearful inorganic space. To begin with, encroachment of farmland grips our throat, congestion of traffic causes us arterial sclerosis, and a degrading residential environment is paralyzing us. In this way, cities are turning into a graveyard, while oppressing human life.
City design must open a way towards the revival of humanistic cities ... One measure is to stimulate those stiffening cities and to inject mobility and changeability into the architecture. Cities in the future should keep up with the rhythm of regeneration of human life and advancement of society by an organization which is movable and connecting. It is impossible to reflect these movable factors dynamically if one tries to build up a city and architecture on immovable land. The vision of Ocean City has inevitably emerged from this."

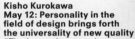

**Kisho Kurokawa**
**May 12: Personality in the field of design brings forth the universality of new quality**
"The future city must change and renew itself uniquely to adapt continuously to the life of tomorrow with a certain common basis. Therefore, every segment needs to be transformed constantly so as to keep a common system. Thus, the city will grow, constantly renewing itself, rebuilding its individuality and yet maintaining the universal unit of life."

Kikutake in a panel discussion, with his Sky House and Ocean City behind him.

**Herbert Bayer**
**May 11: Design reviewed**
"Evolution has been a wasteful process. Many forms of life are ill-adapted and without sufficient power to sustain existence. The succession of life is marked with more species which have died out than have remained alive. Against odds, man has evolved as the dominant animal. Only he has acquired the unique powers to turn nature to his own use and advantage. He has made it his task here on earth to change his environment rather than to adjust to it."

**B.V. Doshi**
**May 12: Change and new experience**
"Change is a basic human need."

**Louis Kahn**
**May 14: Form and design**
"We should not have to rip up the street every time a pipe goes bad and disrupt traffic. You should go inside the building and correct your pipes and let traffic go on. That street really wants to be a building; it's come to that point."

**Paul Rudolph**
**May 13: Hierarchy of Space**
"Modern architecture has produced brilliant theories and buildings as individual and separate gems, but so far has thrown little light on how to relate one building to another or to the environment."

**Jean Prouvé**
**May 14: Industrialization of architecture**
"There is not one city in this world which could compare with the jets or the planes which our children are so widely admiring today, with the exception perhaps of Chandigarh or Brasilia. The return to the past is an important tendency nowadays. People of leisure turn back to the past—they look for ancient houses, old places, and old villages as they still exist in France and perhaps in Japan."

**Peter Smithson**
**May 14: Antagonistic Cooperation**
"...it used to be felt, in the heroic period of modern architecture, that planning or the reconstruction of cities was only possible if one could start with the complete ownership of the ground and with a possibility of gigantic programs of reconstruction, with a tabula rasa. Experience has proved that neither ownership of the land nor the opportunity to build on a large scale are in themselves sufficient, that there must be a concept of what to do with the land and how to build on a large scale, before the purely legalistic techniques are useful... However, in the last ten years or so, certain techniques have emerged which accept this complexity as the source of invention, not as a hindrance..."

**May 13** In the middle of the conference, Louis Kahn visits Kikutake's Sky House, a new hub of the architectural community. A discussion takes place among several architects, Kawazoe, and the publisher of *Metabolism 1960* with Maki translating for Kahn. Kikutake recalls: "Since there were no chairs, we all squatted on the floor in the southeast corner and began talking...

**Kenzo Tange**
**May 14: Technology and man**
"In the same way as life, as organic beings composed of changeable elements, as the cell, continually renewing its metabolism and still retaining as a whole a stable form—thus we consider our cities."
Tange presents his housing system for Boston Harbor, which he is in the process of adapting for his Plan for Tokyo 1960.

What was intended as a quick visit turned out to be a debate till dawn. The discussion centered on methodology, which was linked to Kahn's philosophy. We talked about the three-step methodology, too. I said, I have a little disagreement with your methodology. I don't think he expected to have such a debate in Japan, or at Sky House, and I think he was surprised."

**Masato Otaka**
**May 14: Cooperation of Designers**
"...the city is composed of countless persons, countless individuals; on the other hand, wealth becomes more and more concentrated, developed, and transformed. With regard to this dynamic modern city I would like to propose a method of Group Form... dividing the city space into two sections: the machine-like sections and the human sections; and also of dividing it into two spaces: the space for speed and the space for people to walk."

**Kenji Ekuan**
**May 14: Technology and the masses**
"In its ceaseless vicissitudes, humanity will no doubt experience great pains, but, while we observe with resignation how everything around humanity constantly flows away without the least stagnation, we are required to bring forth from ourselves the buds of new courage."

Launchpad: the old guard of Japanese graphic design, occupied with organizing WoDeCo, commissions emerging talents to execute the actual design of conference materials. This page, clockwise: WoDeCo posters, designed by Kohei Sugiura and Gan Hosoya; poster for the WoDeCo "designs today" exhibition, by Kazumasa Nagai with Ryuichi Yamashiro (art direction). Opposite page: four variations of WoDeCo posters, featuring the logo by Takashi Kono, designed by Ikko Tanaka with Hiromu Hara (art direction).[17]

world
design
conference
1960 世界デザイン会議

world
design
conference
1960 世界デザイン会議

world
design
conference
1960 世界デザイン会議

world
design
conference
1960 世界デザイン会議

WORLD DESIGN CONFERENCE IN JAPAN / 1960

び

NATURE AND
THOUGHT IN
JAPANESE DESIGN
NATURE ET
PENSÉE EN
DESIGN JAPONAIS

Official WoDeCo publication, *Bi* (beauty), carefully crafted to introduce Japanese aesthetics to foreign guests, with text by critic Teiji Itoh. Graphic design by Gan Hosoya with Masaharu Shirai (cover), art direction by Hiromu Hara and Takeharu Imaizumi. Launched by WoDeCo, all go on to become prominent designers.

曲線
LIGNE COURBEE
CURVE

日本の曲線は、直線の変形である。竹の束み
に折れさると竹のつくりだす曲線は、典型的
なものの一つでみる。

La ligne courbe japonaise est une transformation de la ligne droite. C'est une de
ces lignes typiques que celle d'un bambou
ployé sous le poids de la neige.

The Japanese curve is a variation of the
straight line. Most typical of it is the curve
of the bamboo bending under the weight of
snow.

"The Japanese curve is a variation of the straight line. Most typical of it is the curve of the bamboo bending under the weight of snow."

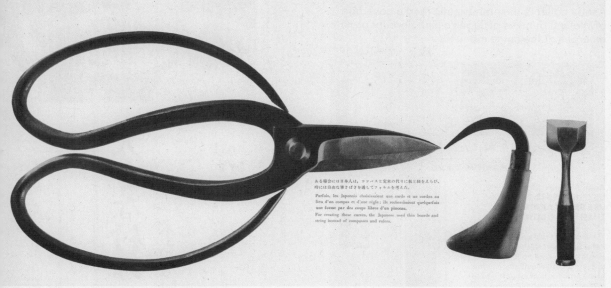

ある場合には日本人は、コンパスと定木の代りに板と糸をえらび、時には自由な筆さばきを通してフォルムを考えた。

Parfois, les Japonais choisissaient une corde et un cordon au lieu d'un compas et d'une règle; ils recherchaient quelquefois une forme par des coups libres d'un pinceau.

For creating these curves, the Japanese used thin boards and string instead of compasses and rulers.

"For creating these curves, the Japanese use thin boards and string instead of compasses and rulers."

このゆえに直線と曲線と相対立する線ではなくして、それらは力のうみだした双生児である。かつての人たちのうみだした双生児である。かかる線を気力の表現であると考えた者もいた。

C'est ainsi que ces deux lignes n'étaient pas celles, qui s'opposaient, mais les deux jumelles dont avait accouché la force. Quelques-uns anciens considéraient une telle ligne comme une expression de la force d'esprit.

Accordingly, the straight line and the curve are not mutually opposed lines; they are twins born from the one and only strength. Some considered such lines as an expression of vitality.

"…the straight line and the curve are not mutually opposed lines; they are twins…"

Asada collects the enthusiastic media coverage of WoDeCo; news of Japan's nine percent growth emerges at the same moment...

*Asahi Shimbun*, May 15, 1960
**USEFULNESS IS THE KEY: USE REALITY RATHER THAN IMAGINATION**

"Environment rules architecture," Peter Smithson said. "Today one single architect is no longer able to build a Versailles Palace alone. Many architects must participate in planning and constructing a city together, in a 'confrontational collaboration.'" In other words, "architects today are also urban planners."

*Shinkenzai* (New construction material), Week 3, May 1960
**WORLD DESIGN CONFERENCE ENDS WITH FRUIT: THE ESSENCE OF ARCHITECTURE IS HUMANITY**

Yusaku Kamekura, graphic designer: "Herbert Bayer said the conference was even too luxurious."
Uzo Nishiyama, architect: "Attending many discussions about urban planning, I'm convinced that Japan is the poorest in the field."
Minoru Yamasaki, architect: "It was a very nice meeting but if I could make one claim, discussion could have been more effective if groups were smaller."
Noboru Kawazoe, critic: "The diversity of participants was one factor behind the success. I learned a lot, especially from the philosophical thinking of Louis Kahn."
Fumihiko Maki, architect: "We should clarify and share the social responsibility of architects across the world. And what the increase of cars would mean to a city."

外国都市計画家の
空からみた東京

大きな村みたい
一本もない道らしい道

*Asahi Shimbun*, May 16, 1960
**TOKYO SEEN FROM THE SKY: FOREIGN URBAN PLANNERS SAY "IT'S LIKE A BIG VILLAGE"**

Mr. Peter Smithson, a major urban planner from the UK, and his wife; Valkrishna Doshi, a young Indian urban planner and disciple of Le Corbusier; and Takashi Asada, architect and secretary-general of the World Design Conference, flew over the mammoth city of Tokyo with 10 million people. The four agreed: it certainly has Oriental vibrance, but it's merely a conglomerate of small towns, or just a large village...

Doshi: Oh, is there no major road in Tokyo?
Asada: There will be four-lane highways all around by the time of the Olympics.
Doshi: Four lanes each?
Asada: No, in total.
Doshi: Nonsense, that's too narrow!

Doshi criticized that the city has no organic traffic network, green space or any order that anticipates a new age. It's as if sleeping, waiting for a major operation in the future. When the plane came over collective housing blocks, Mrs. Smithson repeated, "cheap looking." Mr. Doshi asked if they were jails. While the housing blocks were severely criticized, the agricultural villages and rural plains where natural topography was tactfully used for living were highly favoured. Mr. Smithson declares: "Tokyo should stretch over the sea." Mrs. Smithson: "The West has many bitter experiences of urban planning and the Japanese should learn from them." Mr. Doshi: "We should consider Tokyo as manifesting contemporary, rather archaic, problems."

成長率9%は可能

減税、来年度以降も継続

*Yomiuri Shimbun*, May 21, 1960
**THE IMPORTANCE OF LANGUAGE**
**Shuzo Takiguchi, art critic**

In a session I attended, I was compelled by the importance of an international conference and its difficulty. Here, German and Italian were both translated into Japanese, which were further translated into English. How can you be precise about 'individuality' and 'personality' with two translations? But the visual language of designers is fast. Bruno Munari decided to present his work 'silent.' That was inspiring.

*Yomiuri Shimbun*, October 21, 1960
**PRIME MINISTER IKEDA PRESENTS ADMINISTRATION PLAN AT DIET: DOUBLING THE INCOME IS THE TARGET**

Ten days after the assassination of the Social Democratic Party's leader, the Diet resumes and Premier Ikeda affirms the execution of his Income Doubling Plan.

*Yomiuri Shimbun*, October 21, 1960
**9% GDP GROWTH RATE IS POSSIBLE: TAX REDUCTION EXTENDED TO NEXT YEAR**

"On December 23, 1960, there was a closing party for WoDeCo," Asada writes in his memoirs. "I was made chairman of the Metabolism group before I knew it."[18] The conference is a launchpad for the Japanese architects: Paul Rudolph recommends Kikutake and Kurokawa to curator Arthur Drexler for the exhibition "Visionary Architecture" at the Museum of Modern Art in New York in 1960. Kurokawa shows Agricultural City and Kikutake Marine City, both from *Metabolism 1960*. In the *New York Times*, Ada Louise Huxtable writes: "A young Japanese, Kiyonori Kikutake, has come up with one of the most intriguing concepts of all—a, Marine City, consisting of floating concrete cylinders containing dwellings with underwater views (the symbolism becomes increasingly terrifying) based on the not untenable theory that future population expansion may force communities into the sea."[19] The work appears alongside that of Le Corbusier, Frank Lloyd Wright, Paolo Soleri, Buckminster Fuller, and Antonio Sant'Elia. Metabolism enters the international avant-garde.

"The first trip of the Metabolists, December 19 and 20, 1960," from Asada's archive: Kikutake, Asada, Kawazoe, Kurokawa. The destination of their jaunt remains unknown.

**References**

1   Kenzo Tange and Terunobu Fujimori, *Tange Kenzo* (Tokyo: Shinkenchiku-sha, 2002).

2   Kenzo Tange, "On a Vision for a New City," *Asahi Shimbun*, April 5, 1960.

3   Tange and Fujimori.

4   Fumihiko Maki interviewed by Masato Kawamukai, *Nihon gendai kenchiku no kiseki* (The trajectory of the contemporary Japanese architecture) (Tokyo: Kajima Shuppankai, 2003).

5   Fumihiko Maki, *Nurturing Dreams* (Cambridge, MA: MIT Press, 2008).

6   The Will Burtin Archives, Rochester Institute of Architecture.

7   Foundation for WoDeCo Organization, "The Process toward the Opening of WoDeCo in Japan," December 1, 1959. The Asada Archive at Tohoku University of Art and Design.

8   Burtin Archives.

9   June 15, 1959, Burtin Archive.

10   Noboru Kawazoe, post-interview note for the editors, 2007.

11   Kazuto Tanabe, "On the progress of WoDeCo," *Kenchiku Zasshi*, October 1960.

12   Foundation for WoDeCo Organization.

13   Takashi Asada, *Tsuiso: Matsumoto Shigeharu* (Remembering Shigeharu Matsumoto), (Tokyo: International House of Japan, 1989).

14   *Kenzo Tange Associates*, Vol.1, SD special issue, 1980.

15   Committee for the exhibition, *1960s Graphism* (Tokyo: Printing Museum).

16   All quotes: *The Official Document of the World Design Conference* (Tokyo: Bijutsu Shuppansha, 1960) and "Daily Report, World Design Conference in Japan, No.4."

17   *1960s Graphism*.

18   Noboru Kawazoe and Kiyoshi Awazu, eds., *Takashi Asada: Ten-chi-jin no shoso wo tazunete* (Visiting various phases of heaven, earth and man) (Tokyo: Domesu Shuppan, 1982).

19   Ada Louise Huxtable, "The Architect as a Prophet," *New York Times*, October 2, 1960.

Looking forward:
Kawazoe, Kurokawa, Kikutake.

# メタボリズム I

"'Metabolism' is the name of the group, in which each member proposes future designs of our coming world through his concrete designs and illustrations. We regard human society as a vital process—a continuous development from atom to nebula. The reason why we use such a biological word, *metabolism*, is that we believe design and technology should be a denotation of human vitality..."—Noboru Kawazoe

**Metabolism I** 1960
メタボリズム I 1960

**City of the Future**
未来の都市

**The Proposals for New Urbanism**
都市への提案

By
**Noboru Kawazoe**
**Kiyonori Kikutake**
**Masato Otaka**
**Fumihiko Maki**
**Kisho Kurokawa**

Published by
**Bijutsu Shuppansha, Tokyo**

Language **Japanese and English**
Book design **Kiyoshi Awazu**
Layout **Yasuko Kawazoe**
Book format **hard cover, jacket**
Dimensions **210 × 203 mm**
Number of pages **90**
Print run **2,000 copies**
Price **¥500**

メタボリズム Ⅰ

未来の都市

METABOLISM/1960

# metabolism

都市への提案 THE PROPOSALS FOR NEW URBANISM

「メタボリズム」とは、来たるべき社会の姿を、具体的に提案するグループの名称である。

われわれは、人間社会を、原子から大宇宙にいたる宇宙の生成変転する一過程と考えているが、とくにメタボリズム（新陳代謝）という生物学上の用語を用いるのは、デザインや技術が、人間の生命力の発露と考えるからに他ならない。したがって、われわれは、歴史的発展代謝を、自然的に受け入れるのではなく、積極的に促進させようとするものである。

今回は、建築家による都市の提案でまとめられたが、今後、各分野のデザイナーや美術家、技術者、科学者、また政治家など、多分野からの参加が予定され、すでにその一部は準備を始めている。われわれのグループそのものも、たえまない新陳代謝を続けていくであろう。

海洋都市〜菊竹清訓 6／物質と人間〜川添登 42／群造形へ〜大高正人・槇文彦 52／空間都市〜黒川紀章 70

"Metabolism" is the name of the group, in which each member proposes future designs of our coming world through his concrete designs and illustrations. We regard human society as a vital process—a continuous development from atom to rebuild. The reason why we use such a biological word, the metabolism, is that, we believe, design and technology should be a denotation of human vitality.

We are not going to accept the metabolism as a natural historical process, but we are trying to encourage active metabolic development of our society through our proposals.

This volume mainly consists of the designs for our future cities proposed only by architects. From the next issue, however, the people in other fields such as designers, artists, engineers, scientists, and politicians, will participate in it, and already some of them are preparing for the next one.

In future, more will come to join "Metabolism" and some will go; that means a metabolic process will also take place in its membership.

Ocean City—K. Kikutake 6
Material and Man—N. Kawazoe 42 Toward Group Form—M. Ohtaka・F. Maki 52 Space City—N. Kurokawa 70.

海洋都市 OCEAN CITY　　KIYONORI KIKUTAKE　菊竹清訓

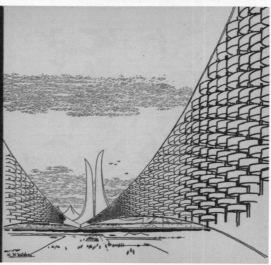

その端緒

われわれが提案するのではない。都市の混乱と麻痺が、そして建築の矛盾と葛藤が、提案させるのだ。1958 年、都市住宅に発表をはじめ、翌年 1 月「塔状都市」としてまとめた。これは国際建築誌 1 月に発表した。つづいて同年 2 月、海洋調査から検討を加えてきた浮上都市、軽く簿撮の可図性を「海上都市」として提案したのである。この 2 つの都市デザインへの提案は、その空間の基本的な方向を展開させる。われわれは「主要」い都市「うなばら」を提案しようとするものである。

この都市は、海洋固定にして新しい都市秩序をもち、自由に生成発展していく人間社会にもっともよく適応するような人間の都市として提案したい。

都市の混乱であると同時に、またこれは建築の混乱でもあるにすぎない。

その意味では、この提案は「人間的空間」への提案といってもよいかもしれない、われわれはより「人間的空間」をつくりだされることにこそ関心をもつものである。

往期する都市に、変化する人間の静的な関係ではない新しい空間と人間の向導しあう対応をこに見つけだそうとするものだ。

### THE BEGINNING

We do not suggest a proposal of the future city. The state of confusion and paralysis in metropolitan cities and the inconsistency and lack of systematic city planning is forcing us to make this proposal.

A concentrated study made on metropolitan dwelling in 1958 was published in *"THE KOKUSAI KENCHIKU"* under the title "The Tower-Shape Community" in January the following year. Then in February, "The Floating City", a project of a mobile city under study for the past two years, was proposed under the title "The Marine city". At our next step is to enlarging the dimensions of these two city projects we have conceived a new city project *"THE UNABARA"*.

We make this proposal in hope that this marine city under a new system of order may become a city well suited for the community life of free and vigorously growing people. One proposal must be the subject of architectural design as well as the subject of urban design. In this sense, the marine city may be a proposal to "Human Space" and we are very interested in to make it. What we wish to describe in this proposal is not the static relation of growing city with asphixiated human but the sympathizing correspondence of the new space with human.

スタッフ
大越　侶、内井昭蔵、遠藤勝勧
武者英二、栗田守道、建行由浩
土井慶成、奥田光生、佐藤武郎

Staff
Makoto Koji,　　Shozo Uchii,
Shokyo, Endo,　　Eiji Musha,
Moriyasu Kurita,　Tatsuo Dori,
Yukio Dei,　　　Mitsuo Takada,
Takeo Setsu.

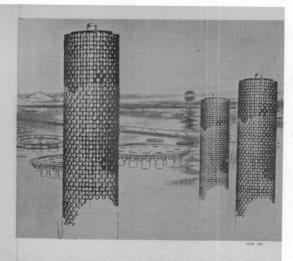

塔状都市

都市デザインは，明日のものでなければならない。明日への意欲と発想に始まるのでなければならないであろう。
都市のこれまでの諸問題は，明日のために整理され，準備されねばならないが，明日を束縛するものであってはならないであろう。
東京という巨大な規模の都市は，病み疲れている。唯マンモス化して，都市としてのコントロールを失っているばかりではない。この都市に住む900万の人間の順応性に頼って，病んでいる事実を覆いかくし，正当づけようとさえしているのである。水平都市の限界は，交通機能の能力，居住性の水準をはるかに越えて，拡がっている。ガン状の新しい有害な組織が，都市を覆っているのだ。ベッドタウンという転移がもう始ってきている。
都市デザインが，このまま混乱の極に達しようとしてあがく都市の現実に，目をつぶっていることは許されない。目標を見うしない，バランスを破り，希望を捨てた都市に，新しい光を導入しなければならない。
都市の新しい秩序は，都市に住む者のすべてが，社会を意識することに始まる。社会の一つの単位としての都市に誇りを持つことなのだ。
短かい人間の一生を，どこに送るかという自覚に基いた，「住む」空間への意志をつかむことである。
「住む」空間は，そこからイメージされてこなければならないし，「住み，働らき，楽しむ」ことのできる希望の都市へのアプローチは，広い分野から求められねばならないであろう。
一つの問題——「住む」こと，ここに焦点を絞るとき，空に挑戦する地上300mの塔状都市が誕生するのだ。
塔状都市は，「住む」ことを総合的に解決しようとする提案であるが，唯一の解決ではむろんない。
「住むこと」を総合的に問題にするという意味で，都市と名付けたが，都市の機能をすべて備えているわけではない。
この塔状都市が5,000人の人口をもっていることが重要なのではない。「住む」ことを立体的に，総合的に問題として取上げようとする所に，私の意義がある。
1,250の住居単位は，ここでは円筒状の量産型として，157mの円周に互違いに装着されるが，これが最もすぐれた解決であるとは考えていない。
ヘクタール当りの人口問題が，この塔状都市の採用によって150人から600人までの範囲で，解決し得ることが予測されるが，人口密度とは別問題なのである。塔状都市が，現実の都市を生きかえらせる有効な手段として，すぐ着手されるものとも考えてはいない。
しかし，提案されるであろう。
都市が，いかに計画的に，いかに総合的に準備され，努力の蓄積が必要かという意味において，また都市がいかに明日の生活のために重要であるかを知るために，そして都市デザインへの構想がいかに重要であるかを告げるために。
塔状都市は，個人と社会を結合し，建築と都市を結ぶ，新しい現代のモニュマンなのである。

12

TOWER SHAPE COMMUNITY

The design of city must be the property of the tomorrow. It should be originated by the wish and expression for the tomorrow.
The past problems on the city should be re-adjusted and prepared for the tomorrow, but, should not restrict the tomorrow.

Tokyo, a huge city, is worn out with bad sickness. She has lost the proper control of city, because of her mammoth like scale. On the contrary, she is even trying to conceal her illness and to justify the present situation by depending on the adaptability of inhabitant.
The limitation of the horizontal city has far passed over from the ability of function of transportation and the living standard. The new harmful tissue like cancer is spreading over the city. The transposition called "Bed Town" has already started.
The design of city should not overlook such actual situation that the city is coming to the climax of her confusion. The design of city should bring new light to the city which now has lost its direction, has broken its balance, and has given up its hope.
The new order of city will grew up from the point that each of all inhabitants has become conscious of the community. This means that each has a pride on his own city as a unit of his community. Further more, this means that each will find his strong will on "space for living" where he has to spend his short life.
The "space for living" should be imaged from this point, and the approach to the city where he is able to "live, work and enjoy" should be considered from the various situations.

One problem——"living", when focusing to this point, the 300 m. high Tower Shape Community which challenges the sky will be born.
The Tower Shape Community is a proposal to solve the problem on "living" synthetically. However, it, of course, is not a sole solution.
In a sence as it studies the problems on "living" synthetically, the word of "City" is used, but it has not every function which the city should have.
It is not an important point that the Tower Shap Community consists of a population of 5000 men. It is an important point that the writer's significance really lies in the point to take up the matter synthetically and stereospacely.
The 1,250 living units, as a mass produced cylindrical shape, will be installed alternatelly in the 157 m. high cylinder, but I don't think this is a best method to solve the problem. It is anticipated that the problem on population per hectare will be solved, in the range of 150 and 600, by the adoptation of the Tower Shape City, but my proposal is different to the question on the density of population. I don't think that the Tower Shape City plan will be taken up in the immediate future as one of the effective means to revive the existing cities. However, he shall still

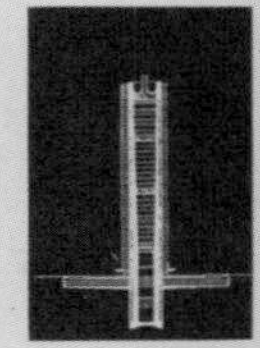

propose it to.
Because, in the sence that the city requests the accumulation of continued efforts for the intensional and synthetic preparation, that in order to know how important the city is for the life of tomorrow, and further that in order to notice how important the idea of design of the city is.
The Tower Shape City is the "Monument" of modern life to connect each and community, and to relate architecture and city.

13

住むための条件

塔状都市は，5,000人の人口が「住む」ための，あらゆる条件を満すようなモニュマンである，といってもよい。モニュマンは，かつて種々な記念と表象に答えてきたが，このモニュマン（塔状都市）は，今，都市の「住む」という問題を，「住む」というそのままで強く訴えかけるものとして構想されるであろう。
「住む」ということがどんなことかについて楽しく語りかけ，人々に感銘を与えるようなものであって欲しいからだ。
多くの人々が都市に「住む」ために，広い分野で長い時間をかけて，それぞれ努力してきている。だがそのエネルギーを，建築家は混乱に導いてはならない。
建設のフィルターが凹レンズのように，貴重なエネルギーを拡散させるような形ではなしに，凸レンズによって，正しく「住む」ということに焦点を結び，エネルギーが $\sum$ されるような構想をもたねばならない。$\sum$ されることが重要なのである。
国連の経済社会局の報告によれば，現在の地球人口は28億であるが，今の増加率をつづければ，40年後の20世紀末には63億になるという驚くべき数字が上げられており，日本の人口は，1平方マイル当り900人になると推定されている。
この爆発的人口増加に対して，果して誰もが「住める」ことを保証しあえるであろうか。
現在のベッドタウンの構想にのみ頼れない，重大な危機が推測され切迫してきているのである。
建築が樹木より低かった時代の「水平都市」には，決別すべき時期が迫っているといってよい。（東京は平均1.4階の水平都市。）
木立の中で経験するような「見通しのきく都市空間」を再び獲得したいのである。
見通しがきくことによって，都市は自分のスケールを意識することになるであろう。見とおしによって，個と集団とは再び都市の概念で結びあわされるのだ。
ここで，初めて都市内に於ける位置の問題が，より重要な意味をもって取り上げられてくるであろう。
位置（住所）は，最も能率のよい，判りやすい方法によって分類され，命名されるから，迷路のようなこれまでの市街地図は不必要となり，簡単な標示が，正しく人々を案内してくれるであろう。
立体化されることによって生じた多くの空地は，すべて緑化され，空気を新鮮にするスペースとして保存され，これはまた建物の耐用年限に応じて2世紀毎の建替え用地として役立つこととなろう。
敷地と敷地にはさまれて苦吟していた道路は，最も能率のよい方向に勢よく伸びて行き，ダイレクトに都市内部の交通を結び合わせてくれるであろう。
もはや道路と敷地との腐れ縁はスッキリと切離されたのである。one-way による快適な道路が都市生活に思う存分寄与する時がきたのである。
平地住居から空中住居に変ることによって，「住む」ことのいろいろの問題解決の光が射し込んでくる。
大地にしがみついていることが「住む」ことへの最も確実な手段とは言えなくなってきていることを知るべきである。
「住む」ための条件は大きく転廻し，転廻していることを悟らねばならないときがきた。

14

the conditions for living

It may be said that the Tower Shape City is the monument which fills whole conditions to live for 5,000 men.
Up to this time, the monuments have met to man's various rememberance and symbols, but this "Monument" (the Tower Shape City) will be regarded as the one which appeals strongly the problem on "living" of the city as it is.
Because, man wishes that it will speak pleasantly to and will give a deep impression to him as to the matter on "living".
So many people have endeavored for years in every field in order to live in the city. The architects must not to guide such a energy to the confusion.
It must have such a design to focus correctly at the point on "living" and to sigma the energies, with the filter of contruction, as like as a convex lens will focus the rays at one point.

In accordance with the report issued by the Bureau of Economy and Society of the United Nations, there are 280,000,000 in population of the present world, and if it will increase the quantity with the outstanding percentage, it is reported that the population of the world will rise up to the surprising number of 630,000,000 in the end of the 20th Century, 40 years later. In addition, it is estimated that the population of Japan will be 900 per one square mile at that time.
For such an explosive increase of the population, who could guarantee the possibility of "living" for everybody?
The very important crisis which is unable to depend on the present plan on "Bed Town" is being anticipated at present.
It may be said that it is the time to separate from the horizontal city in the age that the buildings stand lower than trees. (Tokyo is the horizontal city having approx. 1 Floor and a quarter high)
We sloudd like to regain as like "wide perspective space of city" as we have experienced in the woods.
By means of this wide view space, the city will be conscious of its own scale.
By this wide view space, the each and the the group will be reconnected at the point of the general idea on the city.
In this point, the problems, on the location in the city will be taken up importantly. The location (address) will be classified and be named by the most effective and most understandable means, so the old city map like a labyrinth will be of no use anymore.
The simple road sign will guide the poeple correctly.
The surplus space created by the vertical development of the city will be planted trees and will be remained as the space to freshen air. Such a space will also be reserved for the lot to be built up the new buildings after 200 years, in accordance with the durability of the building.
The roads which has now wriggled around among the lots will be spread over in straight line to the most effective direction, and it will connect directly the city to the city.
The fatal relation between road and lot will be disappeared.
The comfortable road by one way system will be able to serve the city life to the top of its function.
By progressing from flat house to sky house, the prospective ray for the settlement of the various problems on "living" will shine into.
We have to take a note that it is uncorrect to say that the most sure means to live is to cling to the land.
It is the time to know that the condition on "living" has turned around much and is still turning around.

15

人工土地は「壁」

プリミティーブな人間生活にとっては自然の大地と，その環境は，生活の条件としてよく成立し得たし，その生活に満足してきた。しかし今日の人間生活にとっては，自然の土地の条件だけで生活を支えきれるものではない。
重さを支持し，位置と拡がりをもつ以外に，更に設備施設としてのガス，水道，電気，排水が整っていなければならないであろう。更に，集まり，交通する環境条件が備わっていなければならない。都市生活に対応する土地条件を考える場合，こうした人工的に後から添加された条件が，大きく浮び上ってくるのである。それは，大地と個人の関係から，自然と集団との関係に移ってきたことを示すものだ。今や極端な言い方をすれば，「住む」ことに対応し得る条件こそ，人工的立地条件であるとさえ言うことができよう。
新しい人工土地の一つは，壁面として計画されねばならない。壁面にすることによって高さに挑戦することが出来るからである。大空に拡った樹の葉のように，空中に伸る住居単位を装着してゆけばよい。生産と構造と経済の上で最も効果的な壁面を，我々の技術の内から創造しなければならない。塔はこれらの条件によく適合する一つの型となろう。
塔は，1,250戸の家族単位を支える構造的なダイナミックな力にあふれ，さらに，一つの機能を表現するのでなく，樹幹の繊維のように，壁にあらゆる設備の諸配管を内包して，「生活」を真に支えるという表現をとることとなろう。
塔のなかには生産設備工場をおいて，徐々に建設してゆくという方法をとることが出来る。まず芯棒としてのコンクリートの塔をつくるのだ。カイコが自分の住家を自分の口で作り上げるように，内部で準備したものを積み重ねて高くしてゆけばよい。コンクリートの躯体が出来上ったら，この工場は，直ちに住居単位の工場に切換えられる。コンクリートのための工場から，スチールの工場に変るのだ。1,250の住居単位は，すべてこの内で組立てられ，塔に装着されるであろう。
工事が終了しても，工場は閉鎖したり引きはらったりはしない。そのまま住居単位の改善試作に向ってこれまでの製作上の経験を分析し，研究を開始する。一年間の研究成果は，新しい型にまとめられて，既に装着されている住居単位を交換する工事にあてられるであろう。
この工場は，こうして，コンクリートの塔の生命の終るまで，ちょうど設備施設と同じように，新しい管理施設として真の管理に役立ってゆくこととなろう。
人工土地としての新しい塔状壁面は，「住む」ための設備施設や交通施設を一杯つめこんで，住居単位の生活を裏からバックアップするであろう。
交通は垂直交通によって，現在の水平交通に負担をかけることなく，能率的に内部の交通を解決し，10階で生活する家族も，20階で生活する家族も，ほとんど同じような条件におき，無用の混乱を防止するのである。だが最も重要なことは，これらバラバラの項目についての問題ではなしに，交通とか，都市施設・設備施設・環境施設・住居単位群のすべてが，一体的に計画される所にあるといってもよい。
土木も建築も，設備も，インダストリアル・デザインも，すべてを集め，あらゆる分野の人たちの総力が結集されて，一つの塔として築き上げられるのであり，そこに真の意義を見出すのである。
これは都市デザインにおける最も基本的な問題でもあるといってよい。

16

artificial land should be "wall"

For the primitive life of human being, the earth and environment of the nature could have its significance of the existence, and man had satisfied his life. But, for the life of human being of this day, it is impossible to held his life with the conditions of the earth alone.
In addition to hold the weight and to have the location and expansion, the living facilities such as gas, city water, electricity, and drainage must be prepared. Furthermore, the life-environment such as meeting and transportation must be provided with.
Taking into the consideration on the conditon of the earth to correspond to the city life, such man-created conditions given later will be individual closed up.
It indicates that the relation between each individual and the earth has advanced to the relation between a group and the nature. To say more exactly, the condition which is able to meet to "living" is the man-created conditions of location.
One of the new artificial land should be planned as a wall. By using such a wall, man is able to challenge the height. The vertical development of the city space is one of the propositions of this world. In order to use such wall, it must be studied and be solved the problem how to live in such a wall.
As like as tree leaves spreading into the sky, such living unit can be installed rising up to the sky. We have to create the most effective wall for industry, economy and construction with our engineering. The tower shape structure will be one of these most suitable structures which meet the aforementioned conditions.
The Tower will be overbrimming with a dymanic spirits of structure which supports 1250 housing units. Furthermore, it will express the function to support "life" truly, providing complete net wrok of living facilities like fibers of tree, instead of expressing just one function.
The construction of the Tower will be able to progress step by step after the manufacturing plants has be constructed inside at first.
First of all, the concrete tower as a core will be constructed. As like as silk worm will produce his own living facility by his mouth, we will accumulate up one establishment constructed inside the Tower by one.
Upon the completion of the concrete core, this plant will be renovated to the manufacturing plant for living units. That is, the concrete plant will be changed to the steel works. The 1,250 living units will be manufactured at this works then will be installed in the Tower.
Even if the whole construction is over, this works will neither be closed nor be taken off. This works will then be the laboratory to study the improvements of the living unit.
By one year study at the works, the new type of living unit will be manufacutred and then will be reinstalled in the wall replacing the old unit.
This works will serve as a new administrative facility for the lives in the Tower as well as other facilities do as long as the Tower stands on.
The wall serface of the Tower as a artificial land will backup the life of living unit with living facilities and public facilities for the purpose of "living".
The vertical transportation will, not casting a burden upon the horizontal transportation, solve effectively the problem on the inside transportation of the Tower.
The almost similar condition will be tendered to both the family on the 10th Floor and that on the 20th Floor, and the useless confusion will be prevented.
However, the most important point is that the whole problems such as transportation, city quipments, living facility, living environment and group of living units will be taken up in well order. The Tower will be completed with the concentrated efforts of every part such as civil engineering, architecture, equipment, industrial design, etc. etc., And, the true meaning will exist at this point.
This is the most foundamental problem as to the city design too.

17

As trees come out new buds, turn red, then fall down leaves, in accordance with the circulation of the four seasons, the living unit will belong together with the inhabitant's life.

The housing unit will be made of steel, because the durability of steel, that is 50 years, is most suitable to serve the man's life. The steel unit which has done the duty will be communalized for the new housing unit for new family.

For a couple, a child is just member of living unit, excepting the importance that a child spends the most stressful and important period to grow up with them. Consequently, the housing unit will be planned as a basis of a couple.

The reason that the living unit has been manufactured as like a cylinder shape as airplane's body, is not only effective for those purposes but it has been designed as a frameless structure in order to support the power of horizontal cantilever.

This shape will also be most suitable to mass manufacture, transport and install. A huge concrete cylinder will make a pleasant atmosphere to the neighborhood, and small living culture will make a happy and comfortable room.

The outside structure of the living cylinder will be constructed of steel, but the more familiar materials to human life such as plastic, will be used for the finishing materials of the space, though its durability is short.

Since that durability of such materials will be more suitable to replace with the sum improved new materials in some days. The materials for wall, ceiling and floor will be treated and considered as like as a Movement does.

At the connecting point of the Tower wall and the living cylinder, magnet will be installed in order to place the living cylinder correctly, and the structural bonding method will be adopted at that connection.

While, the greate joint system will be applied to the joints of facilities.

By this system, it will be able to install the lighting equipments anyplace inside of the cylinder as the electricity is available at all over the inside surface.

In this living cylinder, kitchen, toilet, bath room and water closet will be made of plastic materials in one unit.

As the location will be designed as a part of Movement, the composition of that space of living unit will be studied only for the arrangement as a type of living, instead that has been studied before as a fundamental matter for living.

The living unit of the tomorrow should be studied as a unit of life instead of as a unit of housing.

Parts of Movement shall be refined its own design as a can be used by itself, not assembling less a unit. Neatness, beauty and familiarity will be well blended in the design of these parts.

The Movement will support directly the life in the living unit as like as the furniture does. And the Movement will, reflecting its increased improvement and progress to the living unit, promote the life to the key front of the civilization at all times, as like as TV brings a hot news into our life everyday.

The main parts of the steel unit will be manufactured at the plant in the Tower, and after the careful inspection, those will be lifted up to the desired level by the ring.

As if congratulating the new born of one family, the new unit will going up with slow rotation around the outside of the Tower to the higher part in the sky.

All of both inhabitants of the Tower and the people in the vicinity of the Tower will send their sincere and warmful congratulations for the starting of new life of a fresh couple when they observed the lifting of new unit.

Now, the new family with the new unit has joined in the Tower Shape Community. They will always welcome this very impressive lifting of the new unit.

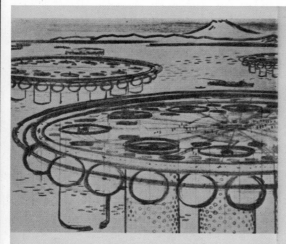

## MARINE CITY

The history of civilization of the world may be considered as recalled the civilization of continents established, and prospered on the land. The continents have hold man on the land in safety and have promised happiness and hope, in seemed that as if the continents would meet man's ex-pectation. However, when man was reduced to each individual and each individual had to struggle to each other to survive alone within the limited area, could man find own happiness and hope on the land as man expected? Unfortunately, the civilization of continents have accumulated bloody struggles of human relations established within the limited land, so, it was a history of endless internecine war of man. Eventually, the civilization of continents has brought up the present opposition of two big continents which is inviting everyday's life of the people of this world. The civilization of continents have brought nothing but such a largest opposition after its 5000 years' history. The most miserable fact which bordedes the end of the world is nothing else but the destiny of the civilization of continents, and this destiny had been achieved at that time when man had scrapied, then, clung to and expected too much from the land. Notwithstanding the land did not increase, the population increased much rapidly. The consequence will be most apparent if taking into the consideration on the mutual relation between population and agricultural products in the world.

Asia is a typial continent of this question. The present poverty of Asian countries have its root in the unbalenced increase of population and agricultural products and also in the inefficient pri-mities landscerly in these countries. Such fact will be regarded as a truth even if man devide the land by the boundaries, speak different languages, and use particular currency within an in-dividual state. In past, the map of the world had been revised again and again, but man could never overmarke the deep-rooted internal contradiction of which the continents embodied.

In these areas where the people cling to each sinful land and keep primitive industries, the living standard is in low level and the political and social situation is in unstable condition. Furthermore, the length of life is very short too. The writer wishes to point out the fact such situation is degrading day by day. Such situation is not influenced by local climate, natural feature and race. The industrial revolution was a most important opportunity for man to liquidate the continued causation between man and the continents. The revolution was a new halo of god that man could have a prospect disregarding the connection with the land. By the revolution, man had taken leave of the land and had been emancipated from the dragging life entangled in the past civilization of continents. And, the civilization of sea was introduced to man.

Marine City is a proposal to build up the world of tomorrow for man. This proposal is going to confront with the sea which possesses over 70% area of the surface of the globe. man observed the progress of the civilization of continents since, and have refused man's invasion for 5000 years. In other words, in an unsimbled unit of human community. Marine City is going to challenge the sea to man's new world.

The purpose of Marine City is neither intend to enlarge the land nor to escape from the land. Merely, to escape from the land, the plan of Marine City requests too much prudent studies and discernible, while, to enlarge the land, the plan demands too much excellent combination of aesthetic engineering and powerful economy. The existing confusion of land cities should not be brought to Marine City. The sea will refuse such disorder and careless undertaking as the has refused before. The desacration of such fastidious virtue of the sea in the reclamation project of foreshore. It is a clear fact that the excellent condition of human community can not be

established on the reclaimed ground, if considered the existing relations between man and the land. At present, the engineering would be of no use unless it would assemble and organize the human powers more orderly and synthetically. It could neither be endured nor allowed that the engineering to be utilized in such huge plan might be driven away to the destructive confusion which was being called as "Construction".

The continental shelf down to 200 m. depth of water should be offered to man's use, but man have to reserve enough space for fish and marine plant. The sea is waiting a new discovery of the sea which will promise a true happiness of human being. so, let it be the time that the civiliza-tion of continents must hand over its part to the prospective civilization of sea commenced by Marine City, as well as the coal was had burned over its part to the oil era. It must be studied that Marine City will be a unit of human community, not that of individial life. In case when Marine City became unsatisfactory unit for community, it will be brought to the middle of ocean and be sunken there without the least hesitation. Then, such sunken Marine City will be left laid at the bottom of sea. Marine City does not be anchored at the definite point. It can cruise to anywhere man wants where convenient. The construction of Marine City will start from the floating manufacturing plants which will be the member's body of Marine City. From this plant will, one new unite of Marine City will be delivered out one by one. Marine City will submit stereo-space for human community on the surface, while, it will offer fish bed to preserve and breed fishes by its under water part. As "Marine City" is the artificial city, it will have each particular function provided by the original scheme. These establishment will be presented to the new human community in the sea, and these will promise man the new world in the coming days.

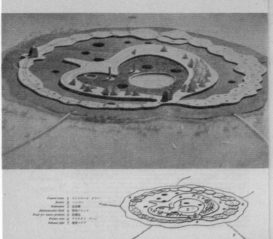

海洋都市「うなばら」は、海に浮ぶ生産都市である。人口 50 万の生産都市として計画されている。

この都市は二つの環によって構成される。内側の環、居間のための住居環、外側の環は、生産のための生産環で、二つの環は管理ブロックで連結される。

この新しい都市の中央には、人間の住むのである。人間が中心の住むことは、これからの都市の基本にならなければならない。

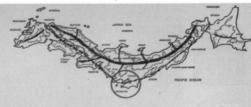

## OCEAN CITY

The ocean city of "Unabara" is an industrial city floating on the ocean. It is planned as an industrial city for a population of 500,000.

The city consists of two rings, namely, the inner ring for housing space and the outer ring for production. The two rings are interconnected by an administrative block.

The central tower of this new city is to be inhabited by man. It is indispensable that this center of future cities be inhabited by man.

The control tower soars into the sky, 500 meters above sea level. Its structure is like that of a boat which extends 1000 meters into the sea. The tower is the energy center of the city. An artificial sun on top of the tower illuminated the entire city. It will also function as a lighthouse.

Right by the control tower the functions as a means of transportation to other cities. This part is used by automatives, which are the safest and fastest way of transportation. Jet planes start from the alighting areas of the central tower.

The outer fringe of a city has a protective zone which averages 500 meters in width. It includes an equipment which absorbs solar energy as well as the energy of the sea waves. The area between the production ring and the housing ring is used for raising and cultivating marine products while the inside of the housing ring is used for people.

The expanse of an ocean city is kept within the controlling limits of the control tower. When a city surpasses the controlling limits, a new control tower is built in accordance with the decision made by the administrative block conference. With the tower as a nucleus, cities will multiply themselves like cells.

Paralysed transportation system, disintegrated industrial area, inadequate industrial area are becoming a deeply rooted obstacle which is keeping Japan behind western countries.

Above all things, it is necessary to build a direct industrial highway which will connect the main production belts of Japan. The ocean city of "Unabara" will be its center. On the other hand, the central industrial highway will run through the back bone of the Japanese archipelago, while it functions as a recreational highway.

The city of "Unabara" will be situated on Suganoi Bay.

As the ocean cities of Otaru, Hachinohe, Oita, Yokohama as well as those of the Island Sea and Northern Kyushu will be rebuilt and gradually protrude toward the sea, away from the coast, it will not be necessary for the city of "Unabara" to be fixed to a spot.

It should keep moving to seize efficient areas while sustaining its function as a city. The industrial cities along the Pacific coast will be a nexis of newly crystalized groups.

The cities will keep crystallize or deteriorate depending on their growth or degradation. But, industrial cities will keep floating and crystallizing themselves.

---

## 三つが動くもの

個人生活　ムーブネット

家族生活　ムーバブルハウス

都市生活　メガビルド

## the three movable things

Human life　Movenet

Family life　Movable house

Urban life　Megastructure

As shown in "The Sky House", "A Factory Apartments" and "H Residence", we have centered with our own eyes the benefits of the living equipment we named move-nets.

A move-net is divided into:

Kitchen move-net

Bath move-net

Children's move-net

Container move-net

Our research team has come to the conclusion that the move-nets, which at present consist of steel frames and panels, should in the future be made of plastic.

Move-nets should be the trunk of a synthetic research by engineers, from different fields. They should also be testified by a combined team of different workers.

The function to store and exchange these move-nets will probably be able to satisfy our needs. On the other hand, it will further increase production by closely knitting resource circulation between production and consumption. It will, in the meantime, select a system which will directly connect engineering progress to family life.

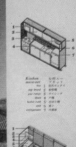

ムーバブルハウス

この都市が円周を最学単位としていをように、この住居も円周の長さで大きさを示すのである。円周はモジュールで定められており、モジュールはそれぞれの弧の長さによって表わされるもまたモジュールで定められるのである。モジュールには、この最学は、人間の一定の時間に歩く距離で表わるし、72 米が基準単位とっている。

この円形の住居は、2 人から8 人までの家族を収容する7層型の型がまず決められ、さらに生活水準とし、年令差・職種による違い・色彩の組合せの変化が考えられるし、ムーバブルハウスに、また心から軽転し、望む部屋を望む方向におけることができるように考えられるであろう。

このムーバブルハウスのムーバブロックはY字型・ハ・スト・ルサティ・子供のそれら家族数に応じてつ一つの中あらを字架とりにとい可変する。子供のムーバ・ブロは子供数が増してもよいように。収にかえれば望っ速続する各線に考えられる。これらの生活の面から提思しょに飯学有にと考えられ。期用年数は 10 ケで設計される。されいえるムーバ・ブルハウスは世代代的リズんある 25 年とおさえられるが、実際には 5 年程度にとりかえられるかもしれない。ムーバブルハウスは、ムーバブックの鉄道ステンレスパイプ（構造と設置を一体とした）に分離のように取付けられて、まるで魚のような色景と景して、この都市単位を美しい色閣で徴着つけるに違いない。

movable house

Circumference is the measuring unit of both the size of a city and its living units. Circumference is decided by a module. A move-net is attached to the circumference and the arc of each segment is measured by a module. In case of this city, the module is expressed by the distance reversal by a human being within a limited sense. 72 meters is the standard unit.

The round house is for a family of 2 to 8 people. There are seven defferent types differing according to the standard of living, age, kind of work etc. A subtle combination of colors as well as finish is taken into consideration. A movable house will have a central axis which will enable its rooms to face whichever direction it is desirable.

The container move-net of a round movable house is in the form of the letters. The move-net of the bathroom, kitchen and the children's room varies from one single room to a number of separate rooms according to the size of the family. The move-net of the children's room is interrelated in order to make it possible to connect them when necessary. All the household equipment which is designed for a ten-year-durability is changed every other year.

In considering the shifting rhythm of a generation, the durability of a movable house is limited to 25 years. But in reality, it is likely to be used for the duration of five years. A movable house is attached like a balance weight to a vertical stainless pipe which contains both the structure and equipment. Its bright coloring which resembles that of the scales of a fish enhances the beauty of a city as a unit.

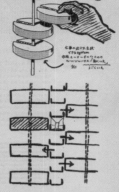

住居ムーバ・ブロック
ソのピン止の取付けられる
住居単位 2人～8人

---

ムーバブロック

ムーバブロットの考えかたを、ムーバブルハウスに拡大した。さらに都市の単位としてのムーバブロックに適用してようと、そうすれば都市空間にひっこし、とりあえ、つけくわえるムーバブルを旧来不動なこの都市の中に導入することができるからである。

Ｙ・ポ・ストルサティの型に、そのマストに下顎貌をはるように垂直ステンレスイくブロクプを持ってている内容の部分で、ムーバブックスとりつける。この部と枠で構成された一つの都市単位を住居のムーバブロックで表わにし、

マストが高さ 100 m であれるの住居ムーバブックの人口は 10,050 人とし、300 m なら 30,000 人とっている。そして枠と帆の間には会渡装置の割がふくまれ、外設となり、このブロク全体を暖・空気調整を如御けるのである。

帆におまれる上部構造には住居。コンクリートの下部建造には、商店・学校・ビクリエーションブリッグ

mova-block

Let us expand the concept of a move-net from a movable house to a mova-block. This will enable us to introduce a movable element into the hitherto immovable city.

A movable house is attached to an H-P shell concrete ship with a mast which has a triangular space covered with a net of vertical stainless pipes. A city unit consisting of these ships and sails is called the mova-block of a city unit.

If the mast is 100-meter-high, the population of the living area of a mova-block will be 10,000 to three sails. If the mast is 300-meter-high, the population will be 30,000. The plastic membrane between the sails in the first outer layer which intercepts air and will act as an efficient airconditioning system for the entire block.

The upper structure of the sail contains living units, while the concrete lower structure contains

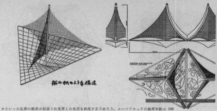

都市の帆のような構造

ネといった住居の延長が収容する大きした生活を創成するであろう。ムーバブロックの耐用年数は 300 年とし、少くとも 50 年後に新しいムーバブロックに建造しなおされよう。

住居のムーバブロックを、会渡標準アパート地域てと比較してみると、空間の使われかたの根其は極めてはっきりする。もっとも大きな違いは 20 m 毎の空輸された中庭にないってつつ一つだかりめあかりとも射中の余暇、道路および見通しについてであろう。

この住居機成のダイナミックな存をあわせはるく海洋都市にあるのではない。現実海市の住居を立体推化、高率化するときあるの一つの手がかりを提示するであろう。地震や、現実に対する抵机と同時に、ビルの空間をつくるのでないに、都市空間があたい感とらえられるような空の見える構想を必要のある。

これらの都市の単位としてのムーバブロックは、6 つ集まって一つの大きなグループとなり、さらにそ

other function related to human life, such as shops, schools, recreation jungles etc.

Mova-blocks are usable for 100 years and should be rebuilt every 50 years.

In comparing a mova-block of houses with a standard public housing project, one can clearly recognize the difference in the usage of space. One of the most striking differences is the fact that instead of chopping down into 20-meter courtyards, the entire lower structure abounds in sunshine, ascends in sunshine, adequate ventilation and a view.

This dynamic concept does not have to be limited to ocean cities. It merely suggests one way of solving the problems facing present day cities which tend to soar above ground. While being able to resist earthquakes and storms, A city should avoid having city canyons and have access to open skies.

---

れが 6 つ円まて、一つの中央広場のブロックをもちあう。

ここには、大学や音楽堂、劇場、美術館などの施設がそのよりとしたひろがりのなかにつくられるのである。

人が増加してくれば、住居ブロックを追加建造すればよいが、人口が減ってくれは、その分けだけのものを撤退に沈めていけばよい。

しかしおそらく昆界の都市人口は、あまり問題とはなってこないであろう。余暇を都市の内室で過す人々をよりも、大量のリクリエーション、ブーンに出掛けて、そうで家族とともに、我行サスボードの美しい第二の生活を送る者が多くなりゆからである。

人々の住居の機成、ただ都市のみを必要とせず、都市もまた、人間社会のすべてを満足させるような ものとはならないであろうからである。

Mova-blocks as a city unit should form a big circle consisting of six mova-blocks. Six of these big circles should be united around a central plaza.

Universities, concert halls, theatres, museums and other institutions should enjoy the benefit of ample space.

If there is a marked increase of population, a housing unit block can be added, while in case of a decrease in populations, an equivalent number of old housing units can be sunk into the sea.

Most probably, urban population will not be a problem of great concern. Instead of spending their leisure time in cities, an increasing number of people will go out into the recreation zone on land and enjoy their second life by travelling and enjoying sports with their families.

The structure of human life will not necessarily be centered around the cities. The cities themselves will stop being a place which satisfies all the needs of human society.

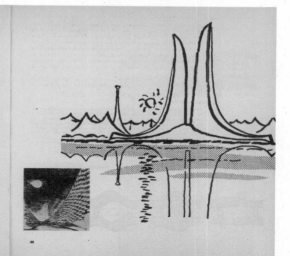

生産のムーバブロック

*production movo-block*

As opposed to housing movo-block, production movo-block is closely knit with the production ring. The inside of two pipes which connect concrete slaps is filled with plastic foam. Two layers of concrete slabs are added on top of it. A production well is defined by wedging concrete. The mouth of the well is a sliding foam. Buildings are built under the sea. Below a certain point, it is necessary to fill in the gravity control tank with sea water in order to maintain buoyancy. Keeping balance according to the amount of sea water, it is possible to delve deeper. A concrete well can be as wide as 100 meter, while those in smaller size are as big of a gas tank.
In order to meet production structure, cantilevers and slabs are attached to the circumference of the well.
The space of this cylinder should be adapted in accordance with production equipment. Since it is possible to delve deeper into the sea, the capacity can be increased if necessary.

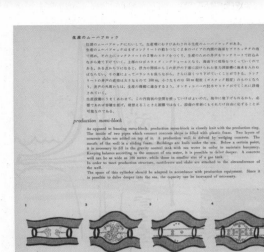

生産の単位空間

*space unit of production*

It is most important that the space required for productive structure should be able to adapt itself to future expansion and reduction as well as future changes.
Especially in an age of innovation, there is a growing tendency of estimating the recovery term of equipment investment much shorter. And its necessity will be felt more acutely in the years to come.
The concept movo-block in an ocean city is a necessity for its industrial equipment, while in the meantime, it is fundamental as a productive space.
A productive space should always be able to accept expansion, changes and reaction. In other words, it should be a biological space unit.
The design for S factory consists of two space units—a 250-meter—square eight storied productive space and a shaft containing stairs, elevators, lavatories and airconditioning equipment with its ducts. Resembling a cell, this structure enables limitless expansion in any direction.
Like the thousand hands of a movo-block of an ocean city, the lower productive units can keep expanding by connecting the circular lighting and ventilation holes.
In accordance with stratigraphic irregularities, the radius should be longer in deeper areas and shorter in shallower ones.
In accordance with the concept of a production unit, the productive structure of S factory is organized within 3.25 m grit.

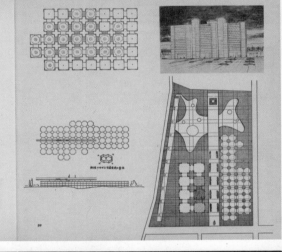

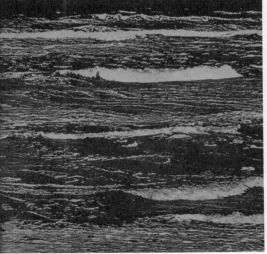

物質と人間　MATERIAL AND MAN　, NOBORU KAWAZOE　川添 登

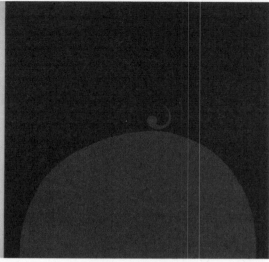

43

物質と人間

44

45

46　47

## MATERIAL & MAN

Everything will come to an end if a nuclear war covers all the earth with a shower of radio-activity. No one on earth wishes it, but, arguments among the best brains of the world are always based on the possibility of a nuclear war. I deny a nuclear war, at the same time, I deny all the arguments which premise it. The powerful countries say that they make nuclear weapons in order to prevent a world war—that the general barrier against nuclear weapons is an effective deterrent to war. This logic has been widely denounced by intelligent people all over the world, but, these people use similar logic when they threaten the public by saying that the next war will bring the destruction of mankind, for the approach simply arouses a general feeling of anxiety all over the world. The war-mongers of big countries avail themselves of this atmosphere to justify their plans for making nuclear weapons.

Under such circumstances, people gradually feel uneasy about the gigantic material civilization that surrounds and begin to lose belief in metal civilization, which seems incapable of relieving them. This is a natural result when nuclear war is stifled in a discussion. All the anxiety about contemporary civilization is, I believe, based on this. Radioactivity harms people's mind before it affects their bodies.

If all mankind really came to believe that there will be no war, I think a new epoch would begin at the moment, and it will be an epoch of construction which aims at bringing happiness to everyone. We will be rid of uneasiness, distrust, and horror, we will become optimists. If all the people in the world try to do this, there will be no excuse for the big countries to make nuclear weapons.

Who will be, then, the leaders of optimism? It has become clear that the politicians and thinkers are incapable. The established artists must also be excluded, since they are participating in the preparation of the war. Those who fear the destruction of mankind have no courage to fight against the A-bombs and H-bombs. Only optimists who do not worry about our destiny can fight against them. These optimists, I believe, can be found only among architects and designers, by which I mean the people who give hope and form to all the things men make. Even if all mankind is wiped out by radioactive shower, many cities and villages will be left as they are, and some days when creatures from another star visit the earth, they will be able to recognize the remains of a high civilization. Just as we restore the past by excavating ruins of the stone age and ancient times, they will visualize our civilization throughout our cities, our architecture, and our utensils. The only language that can convey our thoughts and feelings to them will consist of the forms and shapes, that architects and designers have given to the things that survive. Things will remain long after mankind disappears. This fact makes architects and designers optimistic in times of crisis. They have been optimists ever since civilization came into existence, because they have trusted in tangible objects.

At the beginning, I denied every argument based on the destruction of mankind, but I have explained the optimism of architects and designers with the same premise. This is clearly a contradiction, and one that contemporary architects and designers cannot escape. What I want to say is that their strong confidence towards the immortality of material ought to be expanded to cover a wider scope. It is important for them to believe in the existence of physical things, but they must also know that energy too is a form of material existence, since it causes the development of material. In another words, we have to affirm both existence and change.

---

The universe is constantly engaged in creation. Nebulae are born one after another from a tiny atom to the greatest nebula, every piece of matter is a dynamic body ever changing and developing. We are all included in the process. Life, the highest among the things made from matter, is the one which is most concerned with metabolism.

Our constructive age or tomorrow, or say, today, will be the age of high metabolism. Order is born from chaos, and chaos from order. Extinction is at the same creation. We can see the duality of the process not only now but in the history of the past. In the coming age, however, this process must be practised systematically and rapidly, especially in cities where civilization and culture are centralized. This is where tomorrow's city planning starts.

Our belief in the development of material will necessarily lead to a belief in Nature. We have disturbed the order of Nature and Nature has reclaimed. We tried to give a fixed order to the people of our cities, but the people turned the cities into chaos with their spontaneous energy. In making cities, therefore, we must return Nature her original order. We should stimulate the metabolism of Nature. Cities in the future should be capable of promoting the dynamic development of Nature by way of civil engineering. Cities should coexist with the dramatic features of Nature with mountains, lakes, rivers, plains, and ravines; with showers, typhoons, ocean currents, and volcanoes. Future cities should tackle Nature on a super human-scale together with Nature on the human scale such as trees and streams. At the same time, individual houses must have individual shapes. If a city can be metabolized, it contain various kinds of houses without losing its order.

In the society of the future, no one should be restricted in expressing his own original ideas and grasping his own happiness. Thanks to the development of communication, individuality will be pursued to the highest degree. When everyone can express his individuality freely, then everyone will lose his individuality. The emancipation of self results in the loss of self-consciousness. The individual is conscious only of being a part of living entity; he finds himself to be fastened in with all the mankind. Thus the whole of society becomes one living thing.

The metabolism of our life will be operated in such a way as to follow the order of Nature, while Nature will be developed at the hands of men. Men and Nature will be unified into one, and the whole earth will become one huge living thing.

Ever since life came into existence on the earth, various kinds of creatures have covered the surface of the earth and have established a sort of balance. Even the lower animals have tried to change their environment for a better one. Men have gradually succeeded in controlling the order of Nature and turned it to their own advantage. Just as a shell is a part of a shell-fish, man-controlled nature—architecture, and cities,—are a part of men. And Nature itself is a part of men. When we look from the side of Nature, men is a part of Nature, just as shells and shell-fish are.

To analyse a life down to the single cell first bent on the earth or to analyse a law of nature is the work of the scientist. It is a work of architects and designers to give things their form and shape. other words, architects and designers are responsible for the final form of the material civilization.

What will be the final form? There is no fixed form in the ever-developing world. We hope to create something which, even in destruction will cause a subsequent new creation. This "something" must be found in the form of the cities we are going to make—cities constantly undergoing the process of metabolism.

---

**1**

私はカイになりたい

私は貝になりたい。一介の無為な世界では生れ出たりもするかもしれぬが、こんなふうになってくるとは。それは「底なる世界」だ。そのうちなにも書く気もなくなってくるような時代になるだろう。人間のするところは皆をおしとどめることだけだ。

その内、すでに私は貝であった、いろいろ空想にふけっていて、そこで私はハラといえないようなことをと思いついた。さあ、どうしよう！私はロボットを育てのだ。

I want to be a *Kai* (sea-shell).

I am a sea-shell. All day long, I do nothing but opening and shutting my shells. It is really a wonderful world for lazy boys. Soon everything will be done by machines. Only work we have to do will be dreaming.

Suddenly I think of a wonderful plan.

「私の夢の実現」ピーター・ブリューゲル　Pieter Breugel

**2**

私はカミになりたい

私は天使の声を聞いた。私こそ予言者である、いや、神そのものかも知れない。建築家たちに号令をすべて「宇宙建築」は三次元式的に造られるから、フランは三次元の世界として扱われる。誰が行うまるか、大高正人、菊竹清訓、黒川紀章のうち誰が、わたし、建築家は、四次元空間に通じない限り、四次元空間を明確に把握できるのは私だけである。どうしたって私は神さまだ。

I want to be a *Kami* (god).

I hear the voice from heaven. I am a prophet or perhaps a god himself. I give orders to the architectural world to make "universal architecture"—architecture of four dimension which drawings have to be cubic. Who will be an architect? Masato Otaka? Kiyonori Kikutake? Or Kisho Kurokawa? I am sure I am the one who can grasp precisely a four dimensional space. I desreyve to be a god.

*"Tower of Babel" Pieter Breughel*　Jean Charlot

**3**

私はカビになりたい

次第に、ぶーんぶん、鋭うか。私にあびせかける声が山ほどにもしてくる。どうも鋭うりのは、やはりすごい。私だりイメージの「私」がいけなければ、オレはゴムがこの世界最高な計つ、人間が一段として、人間はオレが、地球主に乗って、宇宙に投るのだ。私は聖典するか鋭うの御歌の一つに、数十年後に、コミュニケーションの世界が猛烈に進歩し、誰かの対えに「超級な設備」が付けられると、誰かの頭も、考えた心と、遠したこと、それは電気無信用によって「気える」ことになろう。私のきったことは、全人類のだれもが知って、「伝える」だれもにも、だれになる人のきったこと、誰人の日常生活はたいたら、あるのは人類の意の嵐がのは、マイはえるが、こうしても全身は消えて同じ無しだろう。

ただ思うのに、宇宙に対する「人間の大なる夢」を大いくことができるだろう。

*"字宙集的思惟図" 川添登彦*　Yutaka Kawazoe

I want to be a *Kabi* (bacteria).

Mad, dogmatic, and fanatic are the adjectives put to me. But it is a good thing to be a god. Perhaps I stick too much to "myself." I have to throw away self-consciousness and free love mankind as its own particle. I have to attain a state of perfect selflessness.

Now I am a cell of bacteria which is constantly propagating itself. Several generations hence, the extreme progress in communication will enable everyone to take a brain wave receiver with him which conveys directly and exactly what other people think and feel to him and vice versa. What I think will be known by all the people. This means that the self-consciousness of the individual will be lost and the will of mankind will remain. It will be the same as the will of bacteria. The only difference will be men's capacity to dream a magnificent dream.

---

群造形へ TOWARD GROUP FORM　F. MAKI, M. OHTAKA,　大高正人，槇文彦

協力：ミド同人，增山敏光，藤本昌也
ASSISTANCE BY : MIDO INSTITUTE OF DESIGN, TOSHIO MASUYAMA, MASAYA FUJIMOTO

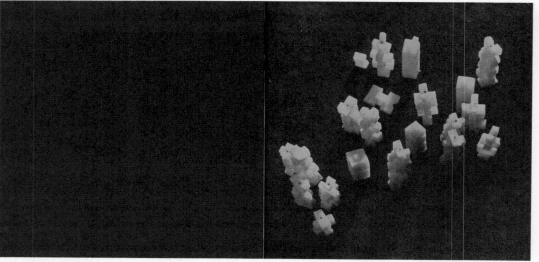

群造形

"あらゆる束縛や規律から解放され自由な人間の生活空間は何か?" という日本要的な反発から近代建築は始められた。"Less is more" とか "神のスケールから人民のスケールへ" と言うようなフレーズは近代精神の一つの原点を示している。その過程は造形的な表現を取りながら、ねも近代精神其のものの展開であった。近代絵画の運動も、フォルムと色彩の解放から始って、悪意の平面と自由な空間を求め、自由な空間を求め、或いは、最も精神的なもの、とらえどころのないものまでもリアルなキャンパスの上に表現しようとした。それは近代精神さと密接な互を為したということがこれらの近代の傾向がこつの運動は、同じ内的な精神を呼吸していて、保関にかよ初とには別々に発達された。建築が芸術がなったのは、個性主義では、個性主義の...

になってしまっているように思われる。これはさらに近代運動バーンの制限に等ていることをも示している。理解では、機能主義最の批判、伝統の論争などが行われたり、建築に弾性や地方性を取りもどそうとする試みが行われている。これは、明らかに建築の深潔ではあるが、まだ、無数に分裂し変化しつつ個性を、扱うことなく《全体像》にて統一するよりな方向に進められない。

現代の都市が夢に大の多数の多様性が、個人のかのの都市のための都市のための都市の教育をどのように統一するかという当にはおられない。地域主義、人間が、未来の都市を考えのかが、こつの天異換されたいるを示しているのがこたこつが出現する、都市や都市のデザイン、発展と変化の過程を半めて大な現代社会の問題を全体像にてこたらえる方法を先送りにはならない。そうしたデザインの問題提起を発ーーすぎるとして、一つの対点と方法にはなるのではいわけトと考えている。すなわち、群のディテール、あくまでも個性的な総合であり、その全成と調和の過程を通じて、その部分と上に社会的な全体像をとらえようとする。変化する全体と部分の関係の上に一つの造形を求めようとするのが群造形の考え方である。

## TOWARD GROUP FORM

What kind of living space shall there be for men who have shaken off the dust of the Middle Ages? This was a fundamental question which started a new movement in modern architecture. "Less is more," or "From God's scale to human scale." These phrases will illustrate a basic principle of the modern spirit. It is a sense, the new movement was the development of the modern spirit itself, while it was taking the form of visual expression.

In parallel with this movement, the development of modern painting took a similar course. For instance, the freedom in form and color, uninhibited expression of individual feelings, the acceptance of fantasy, or experimentation to express even the inner world of man on canvas, all these are attempts to visualize the modern spirit.

There is, however, one great difference between these two pioneering movements in the course of development, although both are closely related to the development of the modern spirit. Whereas architecture has been more conscious of logic and principles, painting has been more individualistic. In architecture, our society has been always either much generalized or idealized; in painting, on the contrary, society has been always expressed through the inner eyes of individual painter. (There are some exceptions, of course, like Gaudí who was an extremely individualistic architect or Mondrian who was a painter with a more scientific approach.)

Through this development, modern painting has become in diverse and personal that in certain instances any identity or common ground with the rest of society is difficult to detect. On the other hand, architecture has gradually lost its individuality and manifold expression, and as a result, the architect's concept of our society is becoming more stereotyped.

We then have face a turning point in architecture and painting. Lately, however, the criticism of functional architecture, the rise of regionalism, and intense discussion of the relationship between tradition and modern architecture, all indicate that architects are again becoming interested in individuality and regional expression in building. Our architecture is moving forward. Yet so far, there has been an strong attempt to create a new total image to express the vitality of our society, at the same time embracing individuality and retaining the indentity of individual elements.

The biggest issue in contemporary politics and economics is the organization of an orderly society without sacrificing the fundamental freedom of the individuals who make up the society. In the pursuit of this idea men of the coming age must meet this challenge in politics and economics. In architecture and urbanism, as in politics and economics, we must build up new concepts and methods that will not only strengthen the architectural development of the individual buildings that are elements of the group, we try also to create a total image through the group, that is again a reflection of growth and decay in our life systems. This is an effort to conceive a form in relationship to an ever-changing whole and its parts.

## TOWARD GROUP FORM

In the past, man has tried to discover the secret of natural phenomena and the substance of the universe. In the latter half of the twentieth century, however, in the fields of both science and the humanities, we are more concerned with grasping the total picture and the underlying relations among phenomena rather the study of individual phenomena.

We now limit our discussion to the problem of structure in our urban society. Compared with ancient and medieval cities, modern cities are characterized by:

i) The coexistence and conflict of amazingly heterogeneous institutions and individuals.
ii) Unpredictably rapid and extensive transformations in society.

It is questionable, however, whether in urban design we have the visual language with which we can create the space that responds to and comprehends such characteristics of our urban society.

Most of our cities fall either into utter confusion or monotonous patterns built by a few dogmatic architects. Such cities lack individuality not only in the elements that perform their complex functions, but also an overall unifying character. They also lack elasticity and flexibility in adjusting to social and economic change. We again lack an adequate visual language to cope with the superhuman scale of modern highway systems and with views from airplanes.

The idea of Group Form which we suggest here begins with solving such problems. Our idea of group form stands firmly against the image we have had in architecture for thousands of years: that is, the image of a single structure, complete in itself—for example, the Pyramids, the Parthenon, a Gothic church—our typical image of architecture. Our idea stands also against the total image of making an exquisite static composition, using several buildings as its elements, for instance, the Horyu-ji, the Piazza San Marco, Chandigarh, or Brasilia. In short, we are trying to surpass these approaches.

In this "group architecture" just mentioned, the relationship between the elements and the totality may be represented as TOTALITY = $\sum$ ELEMENTS, and the balance thus obtained is destroyed at the moment a single element is taken out of the group.

In the group form, on the other hand, the relationship is represented as TOTALITY $\supset \sum$ ELEMENTS, where: $\supset$ inclusion

Here the totality embraces the elements; in other words, the total image of the group is not basically altered, even though some elements are taken out, or different elements added.

Now comes the question of conceiving ate grouping such a total image and also investigating the systems of these elements out of which the whole is built up.

In our proposed Shinjuku redevelopment project, this idea is applied as follows: The amusement squares, for instance, are conceived as images of flowers. The plan forms a center about which opera houses, theatres, concert halls, movie theatres, variety theatres, etc., radiate like petals. The total image will be well maintained even if certain petals are missing. In the shopping town, the spaces for various shopping activities for retailing, wholesaling, window-shopping, drinking, eating and cutting, all are conceived as a group. Then in the office town, the group of towers extends densely in a tight space like the Milky Way. While in single structure columns, beams, arches, and other devices are used to create space freely, in the group form, walls, shafts, floors, and units[*] are basic components for building the visual environment. Space within and without is developed simultaneously. Accepting certain accidental design results, we shall be able to express the feeling of concentrated urban energy in the group form.

In city planning the concept of "master planning" has been often criticized for the following shortcomings: First, the whole plan cannot be comprehended until it is completed. Second, when completed, it may well become socially obsolete or at least obsolescent. Then, at the worst, the plan is never completed. A master plan is basically a static concept, whereas the concept of master form we are proposing here is dynamic. Master form is an entity that is elastic and enduring through any change in a society. Therefore, master form is one of the principles of a more dynamic approach in urban design, and the concept of group form is basic to the conception of the master form. Group form by no means denies the validity of single structure architecture or of architectural groups. Rather it includes them. We consider "a static composition" one possibility in the group form. The group form after all is the pursuit of a total image. Therefore, it is not necessary to limit composition to inorganic, geometrical, structural, or mechanical patterns. Rather group form is an intuitive, visual expression of the energy and sweat of millions of people in our cities, of the breath of life and the poetry of living.

* Wall : Any medium which separates space horizontally.
  Floor : Any medium which separates space vertically.
  Shaft : Element which transfers objects from one level to another.
  Unit : A cell or block which performs a specific function.

その自然現象、建築にひそむ謎も明るみに出そうと努力してきた。もか人天科学の精緻に於ては、この様な設立された建築について中で探究をすすめうる彼等の事象のうちにひそわるつながりを求め、一つの全体像をつくりあつるを忘ってよいのではないかも。今回は今現代都市構造の特性に即時の要件を古代、中世の都市に比べてみるとその左な無思はし、以取べられたにならない慮、建築も複雑雑件の秩序なあり、複雑であること化、空間的なひるがが形象を待ちかいへ限えもる。

返しながら色でられを一つの空間をつくりすげることを目的とする都市デザ要求をもった多様な世界を待つるものだろうか、閉如如く現在の都市の多、あるいは少数の建築家が割一的なデザインが部分的にみられるのみで性、趣数の多様性を包括し複合な全体像が実現しえるのみならず、又流し複軟性、適応性にもひけばならない。そしてバイタルに、飛行機の発達に「極にていくいまと色の未来象形を持めてに知いうべきを。

そしてまた色てきたこの精緻を表現しようとせる色とられた次出鈴を建築にもってまたこうな一連の"作待としての建築"や、それらをのメガ色がない、な色スに知るる一連の"作待としての建築"や、それらやのメガ色があない、な色スに知みもい。サングルクの広場、近しはゴシディポール、ブラトルプにみも超えるとするものである、例えば上述しような色建築言語に、彼々関係、Totality＝∑ elements として表すことが出来る、したがって、一われわれがの全体像は必に現われるとの。

pality＝∑ elements であり全体像はエレメントの集りをむしめしも。われ見えられたうな仕組を色は形象と呼ものように、その割としての全体像形の集りとは、軽外エレメントを包含し、しかも登服し、時間的変化に対

ようう様な全体像の影記とそれをつくりすげる都のトタルムの探究式に外ならないのである。

今私達が提案して居る新観について述べてみるならば、アミューズメットスクェーマーは映画館、劇場、コンサートホーム、ガラントンス等が延びたなり、その都の一つの度とミナーキをもそれから割び、そしてその一つつかたと連なてを色のてのて都市像が出現するのであり、シャッピグタウンにのる果部、デパートメット等の、ドッキングにとなる住斉空間が出現してともらわれ、又オフィスタクンでは密集した調音な空間にオフィスルの各出星医の塔にのりく百で、てタ建築の主株構造で株、窓、アーチが自由に組合され色空間をつくって行き、野合街に於では新しく拡縮これる老へに基と、より理境的な、シャフト、スポット等が群をなしてのが行く、以下是とは、以平にのびる内機空間と外機空間の部のであ。又、シャフトは、選つたレベルの機能を結ぶものであり、床とは、下は地下より、地表前、空中までもくる人間の為都内での活き、又下機空間の外機空間の同時に形成され色発展していく、構造体を各々集、には、都市が鉄きもれエネルギーを色社会の中にしあげ行く、雪で都の計画にマスタープランといい経合いしば使用されたことがある。それはマスタープランが完成するまで封都全体とてしろったろるととが色出来なくたらたら又完まれたとら現に是にに社会のにたのプランも機能を忘にが色たまりますまた、スタープランの未点に実現味はまいい場合が多いことにどんなにも明かれてある。私のこ街追列のある色ての色コンドミュの一般ものをつくりなぐしつつ、より弾力のあるよるな都色性の質の開始変化に敵えるものを、即わマスタープランの色をクラシニクの分野に到一に段新するのである。もちろ都是街は従来の単位にしての建築とは建築的色存在を否定するものでもなく、そのなと色色、その中間的なフアドドジョンによる建築制を株設しよりとするものこちも。まとてまた一方、それはます生物産の秩形であって、無機理互色を分秩色色エレメットの組合でではない、むしろそれは現代都市の風要にようとに生み出した人間のエネルギーを、そして是からエレメットの多種価なるくみわせて全体の強に違りかけ、現代のちも色色生命の音色と生活の詩をうたいあげするものなのである。

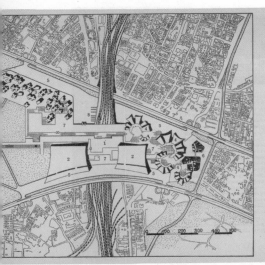

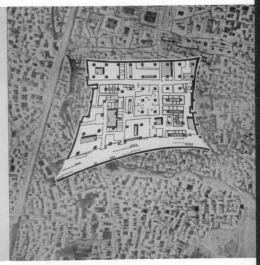

| マスターフォーム | MASTER FORM |
| --- | --- |
| 新宿ターミナル 国電＋中央＋地下＋ 地下鉄＋バスタクシー | 1 SHINJUKU TERMINAL TRAINS＋SUBWAY＋ BUSES＋TAXIS |
| ショッピグ タウン 30,000 坪 (現在の店鋪より) | 2 SHOPPING TOWN 30,000 m2 WORKING SHOPP-ING SPACE |
| オフィス タウン 30,000 人のための | 3 OFFICE TOWN WORKING PLACE FOR 30,000 PEOPLE |
| アミューズメット スクェア (現在の娯楽サフ) | 4 AMUSEMENT SQUARE 2×PRESENT AMUSE-MENT SPACE |
| ガレージ ウェイ 駐車3万台＋3,000 の高速 | 5 GARAGE WAY CLOSE TRAFFIC＋ PARKING SPACE FOR 30,000 CARS |
| オールド タウン | 6 OLD TOWN |
| エスプラナーテ 土地と広さと水 | 7 ESPLANADE SUN, SPACE, AND WATER |

ショッピグタウン

観ら動物館に連結した商店街、あらゆるスタイル、あらゆる種類の店があるが、様々の施設が色成はは平行にのくいる。掛々は、続く変化に入れかわれた、生きている。

**SHOPPING TOWN**

The shopping town is directly connected with the railway terminal and parking area. It contains shops and stores of various styles and kinds. Within the space provided with hoist access through stairways and elevators, shop areas, access lanes, and passageways are freely changeable, depending upon needs at a given time.

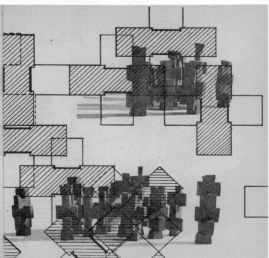

ビジネス タウン

交通のシステムに連しくて出来るだけ密集していなけれはならない、あらゆる都的な無利さをもちながら、その中にも変化に富んだビスタが計されるが色別にないない。

これが唯一のビジネスタウンの造形原理になるだろう。

**BUSINESS TOWN**

The business town requires a closer connection with the traffic system and high density within. It also requires all the conveniences of a modern city and at the same time a variety of vistas from the windows of the buildings. These requirements will be the basic principles for the design of the business town.

アミューズメント・スクウェア
広場のデザインが緑でを決定する。広場
が芯になり、オペラ・ハウス、映画館、音
楽、劇場等——が花びらになる。花びら
の一枚一枚が新しく生れ或いは散りそく
ミューズメント・スクウェアは、絶えず新
しい・アッサンブルに満ちている。

AMUSEMENT SQUARE
The form of each plaza is determined
by the central element in the "Flower"
design of each group of buildings.
The plaza is the center of a flower; an
opera house, theatre, concert hall,
movie theatre, variety theatre, etc.,
are the petals. Any petal may be
removed or replaced; yet the square as
a whole remains a fresh ensemble.

空間都市 SPACE CITY NORIAKI KUROKAWA 黒川紀章

農村都市計画

"人口が農村から都市に流入する" "都市からの人口の分散" 等の概念の中には、都市中心的な都市対農村という考え方がある。私は、農村の農業を生産手段とする近代都市でも{ではならないと考える。農村都市、工業都市、消費都市、モデリュー。...ど都市は各々コンパクトにゲインされなきゃで、それぞれ間に、明確なアーバンシステムが存在しなければならない。農村都市には、これから成長していく都市が多い。それだけの将来一芽...し育っての基本的な模型を含有する。

農村集落は日本の場合、神社、小学校、寺院を中心とする 500 m × 300 m のコミュニティ単位として...とまっている。計画案では、このコミュニティを囲う設備フレーム（道路、水道、電力、作業用モノレール）を地上 4 m の位置に作り、地上は作業レベルに解放され、共同作業、共同賃用を可能とする。設備フレームのレベルは社会生活の施設のカウンコンタクトレベルであって、ここに神社、学校、行政施設が設置される。住宅単位はキノコ型の住居単位（住居）を基本とし、屋根を支持する床に...したし、1 階一ま壁までのものは、作業レベルについ、コンダクトレールをつつ接ってキノコの床に壁ざする。この住居単位に、中心に鉄筋ンクリートの設備シャフトがあって、これに数学間と設備が収められ、この柱を通して、水、電気、ガスなどが、これらの設備シャフトには、キノコ型住居の構造の支持であると同時に、設備基はは（使用、台所ンェト、洗濯間、協室）などをケフける設備ベースでもあって、これらをとりまと居空間が、建築設備の総合体となって、それらの新陳代謝を容易にしている。1 ジェッタの基本単位は 500 m × 500 m の設備フレームで構成され、これは 100 m × 100 m の 25 のブ...のかんなり 2000 人を収容する都市単位となる。

AGRICULTURAL CITY

It seems to me that there exists a city versus village concept with an emphasis toward cities when we say "the flow of agricultural population into cities" or "dispersion of urban population."
I am of the opinion that rural communities are cities whose means of production is agriculture. Agricultural cities, industrial cities, consumption cities and recreation cities should each form an integral part of a compact community. A distinct urban system should exist between these cities. Agricultural cities have a potential as future cities. And that is the reason why it is necessary to have a basic plan for their future expansion.
The basic unit of the rural area of Japan is a 500 m × 500 m community centered around a shrine, a grammar school and a temple. According to the proposed plan, roads, water-service, electricity, monorails for work and other facilities are installed 4 meter above ground. This will enable common handling and administering of agricultural works.
The level of the facility frame is the level of expansion of social life. And this is where shrine, schools and administrative institutions are established.
The basic housing unit (pile) is in the shape of a mushroom, a one to three storied structure with a wooden frame aluminum roof. The mushroom shaped house has a ferro-concrete facility shaft to which living quarters and other facilities are attached. Water, electricity and gas are provided as municipal facilities.
The equipment shaft is the center of the mushroom structure as well as the equipment base which provides each architectural equipment as bathrooms, kitchen units, washbasins etc. The surrounding living area is a medium to facilitate circulation of architectural equipment.
A 500m×500m frame is the basic unit of one community. It consists of twenty five 100m×100m blocks for 2000 people.

74    75

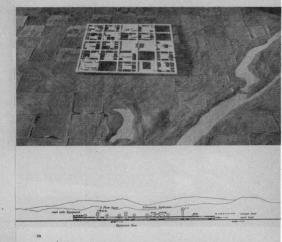

キノコ型の家

既成概念の破壊、ここから次の時代の建築が生れる。壁、屋根、床、まという形態はもはや現代の人間意識の拡がり、生活の変化を...しとれていく機能を失っている。現代的機能で空間拡がりの要請の拡がりがある、かつて遮断に住んでいた人間...。社会的生活の拡がりを作現していくとき、水平方向の世界を囲い込む壁をうちやぶって、小家族単位から、大衆社会集団の空間を獲得したとき、始めて屋根と壁の分離がおこった。

現代の人間社会の私のには、科学、技術の進歩と人間意識が拡かりに変えられて、今までにさらが...ったはうな。都市空間のデザインを必要としている。水平方向にまで個がまじ当々解決になっている現代れ市の孤独への拡がりを、人々は、例えらに個人の空間を確保しようとするとき、個人空間に壁がまじいと思い、我々はまたそのように拡がりすぎた社会空間の中で拡散して都市の孤独感へとまじて。住宅空間に対る壁が都...市の空間にまで拡がりに更もならない。また...して拡がり都市空間がまして拡大してもならない。またとき個が空間を本空がて拡がりになって、わしくる、都市空間の空間の中で、空間でもまじにして天空からを見える星々のもと個が...なして、空間に宇宙の方向へ拡がって...。水平方向にる都市にら市のくと...てなし空間に、変化することる。

即ち、大地を唯一の結合点とし...る建築が、宇宙への拡がりの中で大地と別離する。そして、水平の人工地型や、新しい人工地型が...る建築の総合として...考えられる。ここにおいて建築はより...な結合のシステムの中で展開すれ、社会の進歩...も見...て居まていくことが出来る。

キノコ型の家（木質計画案）では、傾斜の壁（屋根である）が、柱（設備シャフト）で...る結んから持ち、柱の屋根でのウく...はり入っている。だからこの住空間からは、固定された内と外...見るこの拡展いり、遥近なパレル（沿天の窓）からは空中方向の外界に壁をつきて見えると沿く...なます...て宇宙の拡がりを感じることが出来る。屋根裏の中の住空間は、柱に寄り...てとりつけられる建築設備と空間の新陳代謝に応じて動いて行く。

MUSHROOM SHAPE HOUSE

Architecture of the coming age emerges from disregard of existing concepts. The concepts of a wall, a roof, a floor, or a window have lost their function as a sustaining concept of modern man. One of the main characteristics of modern age is the urge to expand toward the universe. As a result of its expanding social life, mankind had eliminated the wall which hitherto obstructed the view toward the horizon. The separation of the roof and the wall first occurred when mankind came to regard space as that of a mass society rather than a family unit society.
Modern society is in need of a space which had hardly existed in the past social life. The architectural space of urban communities is threadbare from a horizontal point of view. This gave rise to an urge for walls for more private areas. An overly expanded community area revealed in intensifying man's loneliness. The purpose of a wall in urban area and living area has to undergo reconsideration. Only when there is a wall space which enables a man to express himself safely, can an expanding space be regarded functionally. Again, when community space instead of keep expanding only horizontally, begins to expand toward the universe, the roof which only rusticon no realize horizontal expansion will have to undergo a basic change.
I should like to introduce a living space surrounded by walls and a ceiling with a view of stars. In other words, architecture, which hitherto was inseparable with the earth, is separating itself from it by expanding toward the universe. Thus, horizontal artificial foundation and vertical arti-

76    77

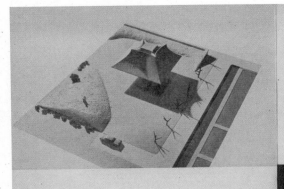

ficial foundation will be regarded as a new architectural base. Only then can architecture keep pace with the progress of society.
In a mushroom shape house, the slanting wall, which is also the roof, is arging from the pillar or equipment shaft. The roof entirely covers up the living space. Although one can only see a limited expanse of the outside world from the living space, the level of the tea ceremony space presents a limitless horizontal expanse. The ceiling with a sky-light makes to realize the expanse of the universe. The living space within the roof wall can be changed by rearranging architectural equipment installed along the shaft (equipment shaft).

78    79

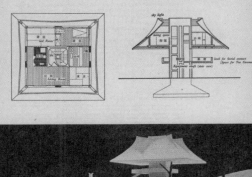

東京は人口900万を突破した。この計画案は、世界でもっとも大きい人口をかかえ、世界でもっとも混乱している大東京を新しく生れ変らせる提案をして、まとめられたものである。この提案の軸となる垂直壁はエレメント（...）は、従来の垂直壁として発想した。

都市は空に向かな宿命として働いていて、この動きには、部材の部分分析部分によって、その変動の見掛けがあり、基本的な都市の部幹（都市連結）と、都市合体（Urban Connecter）と、住居ユニット、建築設備が開には、耐用年数、スケール、の差がある。このことから、それぞれの移動しやすいネネスパンションをとるアーバン・デザインの方法を考えねばならない。ここに住居ユニットをとりつけるベースとなる都市部合体（Urban Connecter）は、土木的なスケールの都市構造と、人間的なスケールの住居単位を結ぶ重要なものである。ここでは、東京スタデッフの竹のような構造の竹型コミュニティーと、生産施設という、ボ型スケ模成といる本型ユニットがいる。内側手結合体であり、ここで、今後都市の下で地や増いと思われるスピード、スケール、人間精神のギャップの橋わたしが行われる。人の移動幹体は地上31m（現在の高さ制限レベル）に設置され、都市交通は、すべて空中交通と地中交通にある。都市骨格のレールは、交通そのものの目的をもちたエリミネーション交通の道路となる。この骨格に近付けられる竹型コミュニティーは外側に住居ユニット、内側に共通施設がとりつけられる。竹の頭にあたるところには、輪状の型スタートションがある。垂直の壁は、それ自体構造壁であると同時にエレベーター、コンパアーを含む設備壁である。

## URBAN DESIGN FOR NEW TOKYO: A STEP TOWARD A WALL CITY

The population of Tokyo passed the 90 million line. The following is a tentative plan for revitalizing Tokyo, the biggest and most confused city of the world.

A city is eternally moving as a container of future life. There exists a changing cycle which differs according to each section of the city. There exists a difference in the durability and scale in the basic urban structure (including urban facilities, urban connecter, living units and architectural equipment). One must, therefore, devise an urban design which will enable a flexible expansion between these differing elements. Especially, the urban connecter which is the base of living units is indispensable as a connector of urban structure on an engineering scale and living units on a human scale.

Here, bamboo type communities consisting of vertical slabs in a bamboo like structure and plant type communities consisting of a vertical slab structure act as urban connectors. And these urban connectors will fill in the tie gaps caused by the every increasing consequences of speed, scale and human spirit of the coming age.

The mass type urban structure will be 31 meter above ground (the present height limit). Urban transportation will be limited to air and underground transportation. The level of urban structure will be devoted to recreational transportation, entirely apart from the purpose of transportation itself. Attached to this structure, bamboo type communities will have living units on the outside and common equipment on the inside. There will be a round aerial station at the place of the joint of a bamboo.

The vertical wall itself is both a structural wall and an equipment wall which acts as an elevator and a conveyor.

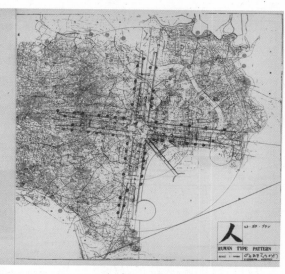

HUMAN TYPE PATTERN

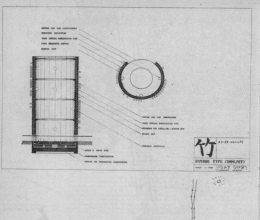

BAMBOO TYPE COMMUNITY

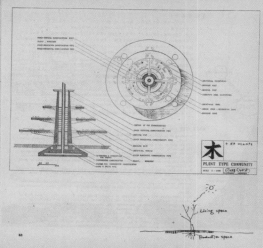

PLANT TYPE COMMUNITY

ル・コルビジェによは、都市の生活を、住むところ、働くところ、リクリエイトするところ、そして交通という四つの輪でとらえている。しかし、現代に、都市生活の24時間が大きく変貌しつつある。

まず、家庭の崩壊があげられる。住居が1家族を収容する空間であった時代は過ぎ、住居ユニットは世代単位のものになり、更に個人単位の空間へと変化するだろう。労働の質が変化し、労働の時間が減少すると、人々は週3日〜4日のリクリエーションの時間を得するようになり、住居が都市に定着しているとその存在理由がしてくる。原子力エネルギーの家庭移動が実現するようになると鉄筋をもたないシステムにはコンパクトなものでなくてはならない。

住居空間の全体一定の住居空間と移動住空間の...で、この代代の都市生活を組立るためのうとなるだろう。即ち、都市全体が、巨大なコンパクトな建築体（Architectural construction）として構成され、どうしても都市に定着されねばならない定量住居空間（工場、事務所）は一体的になる。そして、一方では週3〜4日のリクリエーションを利用して行ける住居空間が必要になる。

垂直壁都市では、この連続住居を構成る（連続する壁の塔）として成り、その設備にはモノレール交通が、各階には自動昇下（コンパアー）が永不変にとりつき、壁の内側に住居ユニットと工場、事務所がキャリル一ぶスにとりつけられる。

中世の都市に市壁を見よ。宇宙への拡がりの中で、再び新しくよみがえり、激しく動い行く生活のバイタリティーを受けとめ、常に明日の人間生活の支えになって行くであろう。

## WALL CITY

According to Le Corbusier, urban life consists of four elements, namely, a place to live, a place to work, a place for recreation and transportation. But, the twenty four hours of modern urban life are undergoing a great change.

Firstly, family life is disintegrating. Gone are the days when a living unit was a space only for one family unit. A living unit is now based on one generation and will eventually change into a per person unit. With the change of working conditions, working hours be shortened. People will have three or four days for recreation. To have one's roots in city will in itself be meaningless.

Realization of atomic energy will mean a highly compact supplying system. Separation of living space into fixed living space and movable living space will be the decisive element of urban life in an atomic age.

In other words, the entire city will turn itself into a gigantic compact architectural construction, where the fixed living space of a city will be inseparable from the working space (factories and offices).

As a result, there will rise a necessity of movable living space for the three or four days of recreation. In a wall city, the vertical wall which is the equipment wall have and these go deep into the ground and form an continuous ring. Monorail transportation will join their apea. A moving corridor will connect the horizontal transportation of each level.

Living units, factories and offices will be found to balance on both sides of the wall.

The medieval concept of a wall will be reconsidered. In the expansion toward the universe, a wall will stabilize the vitality of an intense way of life and bring hope for tomorrow.

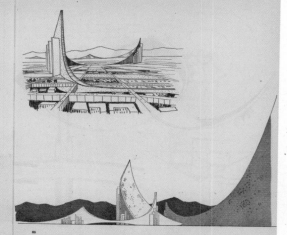

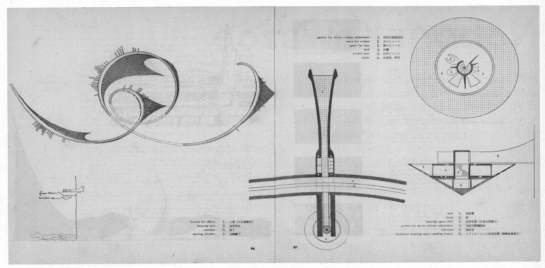

グループ GROUP / 1960

菊竹清訓 きくたけ・きよのり（建築家）
1928 年福岡県久留米市生れ。'50 年早稲田大学建築科卒業。村野・森建築設計事務所、竹中工務店設計部、アメリカ菊竹建築研究所を経て独立。'53 年に独立、現在に独立建築設計事務所代表。平和記念、作品は、「スカイ・ハウス」、「島根県立博物館」、「都城ホパート」など。

Kiyonori Kikutake, architect
Born in Kurume-City, 1928 and B. AYCH.
from Waseda University in 1950. Experiences
at Toga Murano Architectural Office. In 1953,
had his own office in Tokyo. Works: are
Sky House, Tomogata Apartment House and
Shimane Prefectural Museum.

川添 登 かわぞえ・のぼる（評論家）
1926 年東京生れ。早稲田大学建築科 心理学専攻 二。'55-'57 年、「新建築」編集長。現在、建築評論家、国際建築編集部「ゾディアック」日本編集委員。著書「現代建築のあるもの」「神と神の家」「幼稚園」（東洋学大名 22 など）「近代の発見」（造園）

Noboru Kawazoe, critic
Born in Tokyo in 1926. Graduated from the
Waseda University (Architecture and psychology). At present, critic and correspondent of
"Zodiac." Author of "Creation of contemporary architecture", "Dwelling of Gods and
people" and "Kindergarten."

大高正人 おおたか・まさと（建築家）
1923 年福島県生れ。'45 年東京大学建築科卒、大学院を経て '47 年前川國男建築設計事務所に勤務し、現在に同系。平和国図書館、文化作品は、「報徳館アパート」、「晴山図書館」、「日吉公会堂」の同計画設計に一人参加。

Masato Ohtaka, architect
Born in Fukushima, in 1923. Graduated from
the Architectural Department of Tokyo University. Experiences at Kunio Maekawa's
architectural office. Works: Kanagawa city
music hall and library, Fukushima cultural
center, Harumi apartment House, etc.

槇 文彦 まき・ふみひこ（建築家）
1928 年東京生れ。'52 年東大卒。グラハムフェローおよびハーバード大学で建築・都市計画を学ぶ。スキッドモア、ウスト、カナダ工業大学設計に参加。'54年よりグラント工大学助教授、現在、グラハム基金による都市環境デザイン及研究員の委員とされる。

Fumihiko Maki, architect
Born in 1928, Tokyo. B. Arch. from Tokyo
University. M. Arch. from Cranbrook Academy and Harvard Experiences at S.O.M. Inc.
Lab Sert and Kenzo Tange. Now Assistant
Professor, Washington University. Awarded
Graham Foundation Fellowship in 1958.

黒川紀章 くろかわ・のりあき（建築家）
1934 年名古屋生れ。京都大学、東京大学大学院を卒業。現在丹下健三研究室に在籍し研究。'58 年、レーラグランド早稲田の関東建築学生会議に日本代表して発表。ルネサンスの国際建築学生オデザーベントして受賞。著書に「プレファブ住宅」がある。

Noriaki Kurokawa, architect
Born in Nagoya in 1934. B. arch. from
Kyoto Univ. and M. ARCH. from Tokyo
Univ. Now, a member of Kenzo Tange's
Team. Japanese Representative of Vth International Conference of Architectural students,
1958 in Lininigrad. Author of "Prefabricated
Houses."

マークと各章の扉のデザイン 栗津 潔：編集とレイアウトとデザイン 河添愛知子
Symbol for the each chapter Kiyoaki Awazu : Edition Yasuko Kawazoe.

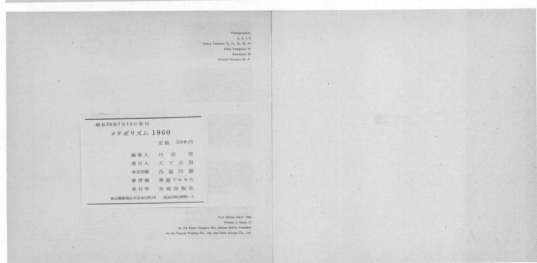

Photographers:
U. S. I. S
Ettore Tacchato 21, 73, 74, 78, 79
Yukio Futagawa 39
Kawamoto 36
Hiroshi Hamaya 40, 41

昭和35年7月15日発行
メタボリズム 1960
定価 500円
編集人 川添 登
発行人 大下正男
本文印刷 凸版印刷
扉印刷 青藤プロセス
発行所 美術出版社
東京都豊島区市谷本村町15 電話（353）0881-5

First Edition April 1960
Printed in Japan ©
By the Bijutu Syuppan Sha, Masao Ohhita President
At the Toppan Printing Co., Ltd. and Seito Process Co., Ltd.

# Noboru Kawazoe 川添登

**1926** born in Tokyo **1945** four months before the end war, recruited to military in Miyakonojo **1953** graduates from Waseda University **1955** becomes editor of *Shinkenchiku*; participates in debate over tradition; publishes critical essay "The Japanese characteristics of Kenzo Tange" in *Shinkenchiku* under pseudonym **1956** starts English edition of *Shinkenchiku*: *The Japan Architect* **1957** quits *Shinkenchiku*; associate editor on Bruno Zevi's *Zodiac* magazine **1958** begins convening young architects for World Design Conference **1959** with Takashi Asada, begins gathering members of Metabolism; visits Ise Shrine for the first time **1960** executive committee member of World Design Conference; contributes "Material and Man" to *Metabolism 1960*; publishes *Kenchiku-no-metsubou* (The extinction of architecture) and *Tami-to-kami-no-sumai* (House for people and the gods), which receives Mainichi Publishing Culture Award; writes *Prefabricated House* with Kurokawa **1961** publishes *What is Design?* **1962** curates with Kikutake the exhibition "This will be your city"; publishes *Ise: Prototype of Japanese Architecture* with Tange; works on *Metabolism 1965,* unfinished second book of Metabolism **1966** launches *Dezain Hihyo* magazine with Kiyoshi Awazu, Shinya Izumi, Ichiro Hariu, et al **1967** becomes sub-producer for Expo '70, in charge of Mid-Air Exhibition in Tange's Big Roof **1968** travels to US and Europe with Maki, Kurokawa and Ekuan to invite architects to Expo '70; joins launch of Japan Futurology Academy **1970** establishes thinktank CDI (Creative Design Institute) with Hidetoshi Kato, Ekuan, Kikutake, Awazu, et al, who worked together on Expo '70 **1971** first branch of Kyoto Shinyo Kinko community bank opens, designed by Kikutake (CDI's first commission) **1972** researches provincial "core" cities for Ministry of Construction; director of Japan Life Science Academy **1973** participates in the rebuilding ritual of Ise Shrine **1974** commissioned by National Institute of Research Advancement (NIRA) to create blueprint for regional cultural development **1977** Atsushi Shimokobe, of the National Land Planning Agency, begins commissioning CDI for research **1981** sets up *Keikaku Rengo* with other Metabolists to undertake masterplan for Tsukuba Science Expo **1996** Kikutake and other friends celebrate Kawazoe's 70th birthday and the publication of his 70th book **2007** publishes life's work *Ise Jingu: A Temple of Forest and Peace*, on Ise Shrine

**"It was a group of very strong egos, so we got into any number of fights along the way..."**

If Kenzo Tange was the mentor and father figure of the Metabolists, the writer who first articulated their ideas as Metabolism was Noboru Kawazoe. A Marxist with an interest in history, Kawazoe was both an architecture critic and a collaborator, an observer and a Metabolist himself. After quitting as editor of *Shinkenchiku* (Japan architect) in 1958, Kawazoe was struggling to make a living by his writing. Then, like Tange, he launched an effort—though without Tange's conscious sense of ambition—to elevate the status of the profession that was barely sustaining him, rather than surrendering to its marginality. With his wife Yasuko, Kawazoe edited the manifesto *Metabolism 1960* for the World Design Conference that year, which the absent Tange had assigned him to help plan with Takashi Asada. Two years later, Kawazoe collaborated with Tange on a book about the Ise Shrine. In this sense Kawazoe is an exemplary Metabolist, combining tradition (and even mysticism) with avant-garde propositions. It is a dual intellectual approach that, as in our conversation with Kikutake, we find incredibly surprising...

Hotel Okura, Toranomon,
Tokyo, September 9, 2005

Turning the tables: Kawazoe the critic and editor, used to asking questions, now faces interrogation.

Metabolist tradition: In *Ise: Prototype of Japanese Architecture* (1960), Kawazoe and Tange declare themselves in awe of Ise Shrine and its cyclical renewal—the shrines have been rebuilt every 20 years since 690 CE—at the exact moment that they are developing their most radical visions for Japan's future (Tange: Plan for Tokyo; Kawazoe: artificial ground), as if phases that typically occur in Western architects sequentially (the early Corbusier, the late Corbusier), are simultaneous in Japanese architects...

**1969** Novelist Yukio Mishima (see p. 454) is another avant-garde figure obsessed with Ise Shrine and Japanese tradition. In *A Defense of Culture*, he writes: "Essentially, Japanese culture does not distinguish the original from the copy. We see the most typical example in the construction of Ise Shrine. The newly built shrine is always the original, which hands over its life as the original to the new one as soon as it is built. The copy becomes the original. Such a concept about culture still occupies the deepest parts of our minds today."

**Kawazoe** "The Japanese thought that life becomes eternal by being absorbed into the great stream of Nature. For them, it was not a case of 'life is short, art eternal.' They had only to look at the Ise Shrine—ever new, yet ever unchanging—to know that it is art, in truth, that is short and life that is eternal." (Kawazoe first visits Ise in 1959; in 1973 he witnesses the 60th rebuilding of the shrine.)

**Tange** "As our helicopter went high into the air above Ise, the inner precincts of Naiku and Geku receded from view as if swallowed by the dense wood around them. The form of Ise, born out of the depths of primeval nature, seemed to sink once more into the forest. But one sensed that even today countless deities lived down there. The feeling overcame me that I was gazing into the innermost recesses of the soul of the Japanese people." (Tange first visits Ise in 1953, to inspect the new 59th version of the shrines.)

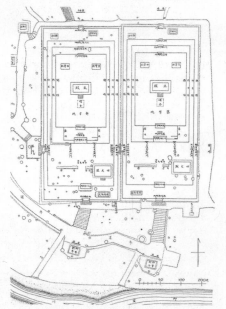

Eternal return: the three shrines of Ise are rebuilt every 20 years—with new materials but in identical form and with identical techniques—on alternating, adjacent sites.

**REM KOOLHAAS** This is deliberately a strange question that probably has nothing to do with the real issues, but when I look at your writing—in translation, of course—I see you're very poetic. And perhaps the most poetic is your statement: "I want to be a seashell, I want to be a god, I want to be a bacterium."[1] But you also write about Ise and Japanese history and Japanese traditions. Is there any connection between Metabolism and Mishima?

**NOBORU KAWAZOE** I don't think there was any influence at all.

**RK** OK, I can see that Metabolism is very fresh, energetic, linear, and that Mishima is very decadent in all directions. Yet what's puzzling for me is the combination of being extremely modern and radical on the one hand, and so completely dependent on or related to tradition on the other. It's a combination that exists only in Japan, as far as I can see. I've never seen anyone in any other culture claim modernity and at the same time claim tradition and history.

**NK** I think the reason for that is exceedingly simple: the reason is that we are Japanese. Which means that right after asking what is a human being, what does it mean to be part of the human race, we ask what is Japan, what does it mean to be Japanese? And when we ask those questions, Ise Shrine stands as the symbol of what it means. As I'm sure you are aware, the Ise Shrine is completely rebuilt every 20 years. The shrine you see today is not the same shrine that was there before.

**HANS ULRICH OBRIST** You went there with Kenzo Tange in 1953, no?

**NK** We didn't actually visit together, but we did write a book about it together.[2] Tange understood Ise Shrine very well. He said that the shrine precincts themselves served as the embodiment of the deity. Not only Ise, but shrines all over Japan are built on a human scale, and in each case the shrine space itself evokes the presence of the invisible deity. That's why shrines don't need graven images like the statuary in ancient Greek temples or in Buddhist temples.

**RK** This is exactly why I started with this question. How is it possible for Tange, somebody reputed to be the author of an avant-garde movement and who had a very successful international career, to begin his career talking about Ise Shrine, sacrifice, ghosts, etc.

**NK** It comes from an awareness that, just as Ise Shrine was reborn from parent to child, then from child to grandchild in a continuous line, so did our ancestors live from one generation to the next and to the next, and we now stand at the end of that continuous line.

Ise Shrine is the archetype of Japanese architecture, but in the roughly 1,200 years since it was first built, Japanese architecture has also seen tremendous advances. When the French Huguenot François Caron arrived here from Holland early in the 17th century, he was amazed at how Japanese carpenters, just by drawing a few points and lines on a flat piece of wood, could make all the necessary cuts on the spot and assemble the pieces into a structure—whether it was a grand temple or a humble home—and how they could then take the pieces apart and move them wherever they wanted and reassemble them.[3] The techniques of wooden construction developed in Japan essentially represented the world's first prefabricated architecture.

### Everyman Poet

**RK** I want to go back to the beginning. You are now talking to us as an intellectual explaining tradition in a very didactic way. But now I want to talk about a different identity of yours, which I mentioned in the beginning: the poet, maybe not so rational, not so didactic; the writer who wrote "I want to be a seashell, I want to be a god, I want to be a bacterium." Can you explain that? In other words, somebody with an "I". Not a tradition, but "me."

**NK** I think of myself as a single, simple man in the great flow of history—just a simple man among the people.

**1955** Kawazoe, 29, takes control of *Shinkenchiku* (Japan architect),
one of many competing architectural monthlies, and transforms it into a
vehicle of contemporary debate, *and* for explicating Japanese tradition…

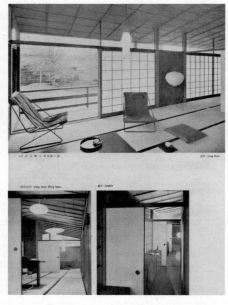

Kawazoe features Tange's just-completed family home. In the same issue (January 1955), he writes a critical article on Tange under the pseudonym Kazuo Iwata: "When he looks down on people (as in his Shimizu city hall or the National Diet Library proposal), he regards them as an audience and expects their applause. But, riding with the wind of popular opinion in this way, he could easily perform a tragedy or comedy and become washed away by the colony's trends, into fascism again, or into a new kind of Japonica [a specific type of Orientalism]…"

Archetypes: in the June 1956 issue, Takamasa Yoshizaka, architect and member of Tange's *Rei-no-kai*, writes on Haniwa clay figures (third–sixth century)—key element in the debate on tradition; right, Kawazoe introduces his obsession Ise Shrine.

**RK** Yes, but you're also a seashell and a god and a bacterium. So maybe you could start by talking about the god part.

**NK** I think everyone wishes they could just take it easy—they wish they could be a god. At the same time they'd also like to just blend in as one of the people. So they have a sense of personal power, you might say. And it's important for them to have that sort of ambition and desire. But I think what ultimately counts is how you control your ambitions and desires. You could say the same about Metabolism. Every one of us has his own separate ambitions and desires, but when something needs to be done, we all work together to make it happen. And at times like that, somebody needs to fill the role of a conductor in an orchestra.

### Marxist Physics

**RK** And that leads to power? More power?

**NK** Yes, sometimes it links into power, but also sometimes it means fighting against power. The European philosopher I've been most influenced by is Karl Marx. The two books I keep reading over and over are his *Das Kapital* and the Japanese classic *Nihon Shoki,* which chronicles our history from mythical times to when the nation was born and the Ise Shrine was built.[4]

**HUO** That's interesting. It leads us to a question we asked Kikutake, whom we interviewed earlier today. When I asked him if Marxism was somehow a basis for Metabolism, he smiled and said we should ask you. So could we get a bit more of an explanation of how Marxism was an underpinning for Metabolism? What kind of Marxism was it? Was there some form of Japanese Marxism?

**NK** I suppose it was our own particular brand of Marxism. For example, when Kikutake spoke of *ka, kata, katachi,* he was being influenced by the physicist Mitsuo Taketani.

**HUO** Kikutake actually credited you with having been a major instigator of Metabolism and, as a matter of fact, he said you told him to read a book by Taketani. I think this is an interesting role for a critic: to act as a connector and catalyst.

**NK** When we were students, in 1949, the Japanese nuclear physicist Hideki Yukawa won the Nobel Prize for physics for his theory of mesons, and coming as it did so soon after Japan's defeat in the Second World War, it served as tremendous encouragement to many Japanese at the time. But it's worth noting that two of the physicists who worked with Yukawa on his research, Shoichi Sakata and Mitsuo Taketani, were Marxists. In particular, Taketani's three stage theory— phenomenon, substance, and essence—was very well known among intellectuals and was regarded as the compass that pointed the way to Yukawa's meson discovery.

The book I lent to Kikutake was Taketani's *Benshoho no shomondai* (Problems of dialectics).[5] Kikutake's three-stage *ka, kata, katachi* was partly an adaptation of Taketani's three-stage theory, but also partly original. Taketani's theory was a criticism of Ernst Cassirer's argument in *Substance and Function* (1910) that the understandings of modern science have been advanced by a shift in focus to substance and function, but I saw that it could also be taken as a criticism of functionalism. Cassirer's later work, *Philosophy of Symbolic Forms,*[6] was widely read in Japan since before the war, and the aesthetician Masakazu Nakai, a friend of Taketani's, had cited it in advocating functionalist aesthetics.

**RK** Was your relationship with Kikutake your most intimate among the Metabolists?

**NK** Yes, in terms of theory and methodology of design, I identified most closely with Kikutake. But for the dynamic state of the city and the modes of production for building construction and other such socioeconomic concerns, I regarded Masato Otaka, who was the oldest Metabolist, as a step ahead. If an architect is an integrator of technologies, it means he's also an integrator of economic elements. Since I had no experience in such practical matters, I had much to learn from Otaka. I had read *Das Kapital* pretty closely, and I talked about

**1955 August** Monument to the postwar period: the government declares the "end of the postwar period" and Kawazoe's *Shinkenchiku* critically reflects on the decade in the special issue "Ten years after the atomic bomb: Japanese architecture and architects."

**1957** "I started referring to myself as 'the world's foremost architecture critic.'" Leaving *Shinkenchiku*, Kawazoe tries to build his reputation in order to get freelance writing gigs.

**1960** In the space of a year, Kawazoe tries to usher in the future, organizing the World Design Conference and the formation of Metabolism, and simultaneously dig up the past, completing *Tami-to-kami-no-sumai* (House for people and the gods)…

Kawazoe (smoking) receives the Mainichi Culture Award for *Tami-to-kami-no-sumai*, and drinks with Takamasa Yoshizaka (left; architect, *Rei-no-kai* member, and coiner of the phrase "artificial land"), Tange (in bow tie), and Takashi Asada (right, in glasses). Two years later, they come together again to form the short-lived Team Tokyo.

*Tami-to-kami-no-sumai* (House for people and the gods) analyzes the relationship between mythology, social hierarchy, and ancient architecture, featuring Jomon pit dwellings, elevated Yayoi houses, and Izumo and Ise Shrines (again). "The Ise Shrine is as it were a 'master key' to all rooms in a hotel," Kawazoe explains. "The enigma of Imperialism, embedded in the skin of every Japanese person, lives deep inside the Ise Shrine like a phoenix."

Curator: meanwhile, at the World Design Conference, Kawazoe curates "My Works and My Images" in which conference participants point to the future; Tange's project for housing on Boston Harbor is second from the right.

it and even wrote about it, but what I didn't realize until later was that Otaka's views were consistent with what might be termed the essential core of Marxist doctrine. We don't have time for me to go into detail here, but in a word, the trinity formula of land, capital, and labor that appears in *Das Kapital* volume three, which Marx left incomplete, corresponds remarkably well with Otaka's views on urban architecture. My impression was that Otaka never read as far as volume three of *Das Kapital*, so it came as quite a surprise to me when I realized this.

### WoDeCo and the Absent Parent

**HUO** I am curious to know everything about the World Design Conference in 1960 and how it was prepared.

**NK** While Tange was away in the United States at MIT in 1959, I was told to come up with a theme and program for the World Design Conference.

**RK** The implication is that because Tange went to the States, the movement wasn't a monument to him, but it actually came to include many younger people.

**NK** Not at all. The design conference would never have taken place without Tange, and without the conference to push us, I doubt we would have launched the Metabolist movement either.

**HUO** From our interviews, I get the feeling Metabolism was a bit like the extraordinary things that happen in an apartment when the parents are away. The grown-ups go on holiday and the kids have a party.

**NK** I think that's an apt metaphor. At the conference we had an exhibition called "My Works and My Images," for which we invited submissions. We included some display panels for Metabolism in that, and we also edited the book *Metabolism 1960* that we sold on site. This was actually against conference rules, but we just went ahead and did it without permission, and fortunately the executive committee and secretariat took the view that it was the sort of mischief you had to expect from the youngsters, and they were willing to look the other way.

**HUO** Tange tasked you with organizing the conference, and you obviously had the infrastructure and could invite people. What were the criteria? Why did you invite Kurokawa, for example, who was only 26 years old at the time?

**NK** As I imagine you are aware, Japan is a little different from Europe and the United States, where the term "architect" refers to a very distinct function. What we have instead is a certification called "First Class Architect," obtained by passing a nationally administered exam, that actually includes structural engineering and construction along with architectural design. Legally, the designer of a building is not an individual architect but a First Class Architect licensed office. The law that established this was passed in 1950, so in 1960 we were still kind of feeling our way as to exactly how the law was supposed to work, and some of that manifested itself in the chief architect and his staff butting heads. This was also on the eve of the rebellion of the so-called "Angry Young Men." Every architect's office and every university was experiencing friction between the director and the staff, the professor and the students. There was the *Rei-no-kai* group of Tange's older generation and the *Gokikai* group of the younger generation, whose members declared they would not participate in the design conference. So the only participants from the younger generation were those who were most under Tange's sway. I think we were regarded as traitors by the rest of the younger crowd, even by the majority in Tange Lab.

**HUO** Why was Isozaki not involved? Isozaki was a friend of Tange, a protégé.

**NK** Right. Basically, except for Kurokawa, none of the staff from Tange Lab participated, including Isozaki. There was a rupture between the generations.

**RK** So to return to the metaphor of the absent parent: he was absent, but the children had no fun? [*laughs*]

**NK** Except Isozaki seemed to be getting his fun in other ways.

**1959** In a gathering in the build-up to WoDeCo, Kawazoe, Kikutake, and Kurokawa realize the need to name their nascent group. For Kawazoe, Friedrich Engels's *Dialectics of Nature* provides an inspiration: he finds the term *shinchintaisha*—connoting renewal. Engels writes how, with recent scientific discoveries in nature, "all rigidity was dissolved, all fixity dissipated, all particularity that had been regarded as eternal became transient, the whole of nature shown as moving in eternal flux and cyclical course." Kikutake finds the English equivalent: "metabolism"; understandable around the world, and complete with an "ism" at the end.

In Sanseido's 1959 Japanese-English dictionary, Kikutake's probable source for the translation we find, rather than *shinchintaisha*, just *taisha*—"metabolism." Kawazoe agrees to the name, but remains unsatisfied since it signifies adaptation to change but not growth, propagation, or metamorphosis, which the Metabolists also investigate.

メタボリズム・マーク

**1960** Metabolism, trademark: Awazu designs the group's symbol, an adaptation of the traditional *tomoe* symbol. The third element is smaller than usual; it is meant to be the child of the bigger two, representing regeneration.

## "ism"

**RK**  **Who used the word "metabolism" first?**

**NK**  That was me.

**RK**  **And when was that?**

**NK**  The catalyst, once again, was Marx. I was talking a lot about *shinchintaisha* at the time, which means "regeneration" or "replacement of the old with the new." I was looking for something new we could put forth at the design conference. In Japanese, the same term is used in biology for "metabolism."

**HUO**  **I would like to hear your definition of the word "metabolism."**

**RK**  **And did you use the Japanese word or the English word?**

**NK**  As I say, in Japanese the word is *shinchitaisha*. In the Japanese edition of Friedrich Engels's *Dialectics of Nature* there's a line that says something to the effect of "one of the most essential features of living things is *shinchintaisha*."[7] That's where I got the term. I was wondering what a good equivalent for *shinchintaisha* might be, so Kikutake looked it up in a Japanese-English dictionary and said the English word was "metabolism."

**HUO**  **So Kikutake was the translator! Excellent.**

**NK**  The "ism" part was the perfect touch—like a school of thought.

**RK**  **This is interesting, how a group of people who don't speak English are so ingenuous about the effect of an "ism."**

**NK**  Since this was the World Design Conference we were getting ready for, I really thought it needed to be a word that would resonate internationally.

### Made in a Hallway

**HUO**  **So Kikutake also had fun. To talk more about the *1960* book, I've always been fascinated about how in architectural history, even more than with the arts, books play an extremely essential role, from Le Corbusier to Frank Lloyd Wright to now. Many architecture books are actually as important as the built work; they have a huge influence.**

**In these interviews, everyone says the Metabolism book wasn't just a documentation of built work but a** strategy **to get the work out there. I like the idea—it's actually quite similar to a lot of conceptual art a few years later when artists had this strategy that art should have its own channels of distribution. In a similar way, you were distributing these books at the conference.**

**Could you talk a little bit about the role the book played? Who conceived it? Who designed it? The book has the strong presence of Kikutake, who has almost 40 percent of the content. It seems to be very much a dialogue between you and Kikutake, but maybe I'm wrong.**

**NK**  Well, once we decided to put together a book, it seemed like it pretty much had to be centered most of all on Kikutake. And since we were all so poor, we worked on it in coffee shops or at International House—and not even in the lobby, just in the hallway.

**HUO**  **In a coffee shop? A hallway? That's even better. [*laughs*]**

**RK**  **That same International House, which is a favorite of mine.**

**NK**  There was a table and chairs in the hallway, and that was where we got Kikutake to draw up his Marine City plan, with Kurokawa and me offering suggestions to do this, do that. Not only had I never built a thing, but this was supposed to be a futuristic city as well; and for his part, Kurokawa was only a graduate student at the time. But there we were, telling Kikutake to do this, do that. I suspect he was a little put off by us, but he really threw himself into it.

**HUO**  **Were there models, historical avant-garde examples, that influenced him? Kikutake once mentioned Futurism, but I'm not sure how he saw it. And did the Russian avant-garde of the early 20th century also provide a toolbox?**

**NK**  I don't think Kikutake was influenced by the Russian avant-garde or Futurism. He was basically just taking his own Marine City to the next level. He wasn't drawing on any other models.

Orchestrated by Kawazoe, 34, the Metabolists assemble their founding document in the corridor of International House—"There was a table and chairs in the hallway, and that was where we got Kikutake to draw up his Marine City plan…" The 90-page book is ready in time for the World Design Conference, though its connections to the conference remain unofficial…

Home away from home: as well as hosting meetings of the Metabolists and Tange's circle of architects and designers, I-House, in Roppongi, Tokyo, is a guest house for foreign architects in town for WoDeCo. It is designed in 1955 by the previous generation—Junzo Sakakura, Kunio Maekawa, and Junzo Yoshimura—and built with grants from the Rockefeller Foundation.

"There is no fixed form in the ever-developing world," Kawazoe concludes in his essay for *Metabolism 1960*, "Material and Man."

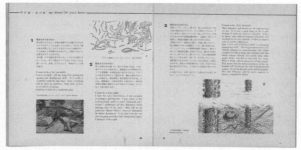

Kawazoe—a poet after all—describes his transition, "50 years hence" from "lazy" seashell to godlike architect to bacteria "constantly propagating itself."

At the same time, Kawazoe completes the pocket-sized book *Kenchiku no metsubou* (The extinction of architecture)—his private manifesto for Metabolist principles of transience and renewal. "Our time is not viable for 'architecture' (in the monumental sense that Europeans would regard it). If one tried to create such architecture, it would immediately turn into 'ruins.' … Observing today's confusion in cities, it is apparently necessary to turn away from the wasteful expense and effort of building and scrapping and move to a systematic way of planning. What we need is a long-term prospectus, a plan for a hundred years."

RK **So basically original?**

NK Yes, he was doing original work. As Kikutake has acknowledged, his family used to be one of the largest landholders in Japan, but they lost everything in the land reforms after the war. It was partly in response to that that he came up with the artificial land platforms proposed in his Tower-Shaped Community and Marine City plans (1958).

Otaka and Maki and I come from families that went through similar experiences during the upheavals of the Meiji period. We grew up hearing stories about the hardships our grandfathers and fathers had to endure as a result, so we all have a strong defiant streak in us. Which is to say, Metabolism is not something cooked up by architects and designers just for fun.

As you point out, the book *Metabolism 1960* was a kind of manifesto, so we chose an unusual format, and Kiyoshi Awazu designed it, with my wife Yasuko doing the layout. My wife used to be editor of the interiors magazine *Living Design*, and some of the most prominent graphic designers raved about her layout skills, so she was our secret weapon.

HUO **Has the book ever been reprinted? Because it was such an important historical document.**

NK No.

HUO **Why not?**

NK It never sold very well. It wasn't the sort of thing that stood out at bookstores. But magazines like *Kindai Kenchiku* (Modern architecture) ran features on it, so that spread the word about Metabolism even more.

### The Moment

RK **We want to understand the essence of your contribution. There are two scenarios: you were an editor and Tange was around, it was a very interesting time for Japan, so you made the best of these opportunities; or were you dedicated to this particular cause on your own terms, because you believed in it? That's really the issue. Was it the moment or belief?**

NK I'd say I was basically just going with the flow. I wasn't operating with any unified conception of where I thought things should go. I was editor of *Shinkenchiku*, and I was laid up sick in bed for a while when all of a sudden there was this big blowup. I tried to calm things down but couldn't, so in the end we all quit, en masse. After that I had to earn my keep solely as a critic. To be honest, there was a side of me that was saying I don't have time for this Metabolism crap [*laughs*]

RK **So it was never intended. A circumstantial moment.**

HUO **It happened.**

NK I started referring to myself as "the world's foremost architectural critic." I figured I had to be the only one in the world putting food on the table solely as an architectural critic. [*laughs*] I was just barely eking out a living.

RK **That was the ambition.**

HUO **Very interesting.**

RK **It was part of the survival impulse.**

NK Those were pretty desperate times for me. But even so, my work for the design conference was all strictly as a volunteer. I remember feeling like my back was to the wall and I really needed to do something about it. Fortunately, Otaka and Kikutake stepped up to the challenge in so many ways, and that took some of the burden off of me.

HUO **Can one call you an accomplice? This is one definition of a critic, no?**

NK I didn't really think of myself as an accomplice. I did have this sense that I was participating in a revolution of sorts, but only as a kind of historical inevitability. And I still think of it all as something that grew out of the historical process of Japanese architecture—borne along on the currents created by the process of modern architecture. Otherwise, architects like Kikutake and Otaka, who'd

**1966 March** Kawazoe's mission to communicate Metabolism with the masses: *Taiyo* magazine (The sun) illustrates Kawazoe's article "Metamorphosis of Tokyo" (featuring proposals by Tange and the Metabolists) with a larva metamorphosing into a dragonfly...

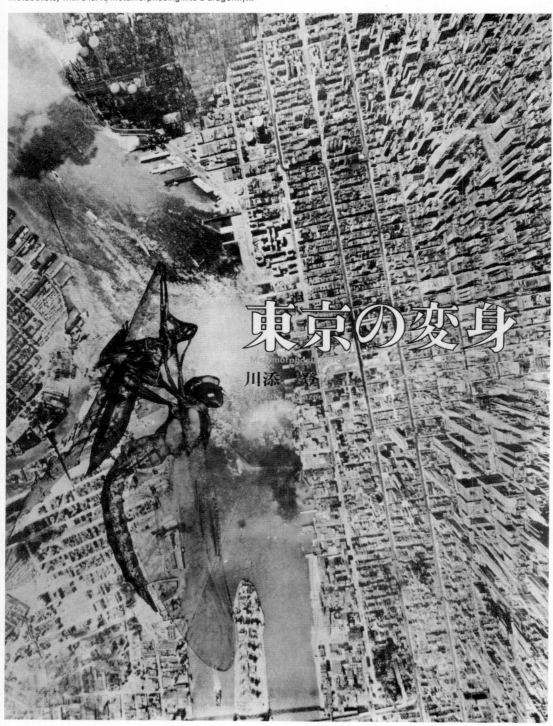

東京の変身

Metamorphosis of Tokyo

川添 登

Noboru Kawazoe

already established a name for themselves in society, would never have paid any attention to me. I had to put together arguments that would carry weight with people like that. There were things I could offer because I'd studied completely different things than them, but it was really only by learning from them that I was able to do it.

**HUO** **This leads to the question of your role. Metabolism is often described as an organic movement with no "in" and "out" mechanisms of exclusion; members came and members went. It was a flexible, organic organization, yet there was a certain cohesion within that openness. It's almost an oxymoron, no? Open cohesion or non-cohesive cohesion. Take the Situationists: you have Guy Debord, who mercilessly decided who was "in" or "out" in an extremely authoritarian, military kind of way. I sense that Metabolism, while avant-garde, wasn't a militaristic organization.**

**NK** No, we never had any kind of top-down military structure.

**HUO** **But what was the cohesion? And what was your role?**

**NK** Everybody agrees it's a mystery how we managed to keep our cohesion, but somehow we did. It was a group of very strong egos, so we got into any number of fights along the way. I even excommunicated Kurokawa a couple of times. [laughs] We're all human, so there were plenty of incidents like that.

**RK** **And you wouldn't speak to him because of what he said?**

**NK** No, the other way around. We created something called the International Inter-Design Conference, but Kurokawa was acting cocky and doing all sorts of stuff on his own without consulting anyone else, so I finally said I'd had it and quit [laughs]. Ekuan, the industrial designer, and Awazu, the graphic designer, both knew what had happened but decided to stick with Kurokawa, so I remember telling Ekuan he wasn't welcome in my home anymore. [laughs]

**HUO** **Kikutake described Tange this morning as a "mentor and sponsor" and you as a "writer and journalist." You two also wrote a book together. How did a mentor-sponsor and a writer-journalist create a movement? I really want to understand how it worked. Did you two set things up? I have the impression that you did set up conditions under which it could flourish, but maybe that's wrong.**

### Asada Again

**NK** I suppose I need to elaborate a bit on what I said before. Tange didn't tell me directly that he wanted me to plan the conference and decide who to invite and so forth. Takashi Asada was the secretary general, and it was through him that Tange asked me to get together with some of the young leaders in the architectural, graphic, industrial, and other design fields to stir up energy in time for the conference and to come up with a theme. The four men I chose to work with at that point—Otaka, Awazu, Ekuan, and Kurokawa—essentially became the core group of the Metabolists. Then after Tange returned to Japan and we'd completed that initial assignment from him, we started talking about what we could bring to the conference ourselves, and that's when Metabolism was born.

**HUO** **These Metabolist gatherings in the middle of the night remind us of the historic avant-garde salons like the late night Dadaist meetings in a Berlin café. Though in this particular context it was pragmatic and formal because it was actually all about organizing, on behalf of Tange, an extremely strategic conference for 1960.**

### Metamorphosis

**JOSEPH GRIMA** **There was a plan to do a second Metabolism book, wasn't there? But it was never published.**

**NK** There were several such plans, actually, but nothing ever came of them.

**JG** After the event, how did you promote Metabolism? Through publications?

Kawazoe, curator: appointed by Taro Okamoto to organize the Mid-Air exhibition, embedded in Tange's Big Roof, with the theme "city of the future," Kawazoe mobilizes his peers for a performance on the world stage.

**ca. 1968** Kawazoe and fellow planners for events in the Big Roof and Festival Plaza at Expo '70 meet in Kyoto. From left: Hidetoshi Kato, Kawazoe, Kurokawa; front row: unknown, Isozaki.

"The Future—the World of Progress": Kawazoe's plug-in exhibition in the Big Roof. "We are planning to compose the Mid-Air exhibition entirely of capsules … we want to embody the image of the city in the future,"[8]

**NK** In 1963 we talked about doing a volume with the title *Metamorphosis*, and we held a couple of planning sessions, but to be frank, it just didn't gel. To begin with, the members of the group were getting plenty of exposure at the time writing for magazines like *Kindai Kenchiku* and *Shinkenchiku*. Besides that there was the problem that we couldn't seem to agree on anything. And then there's the fact that I gave up on it.

**RK** So I think it was more of a label of convenience than a movement.

**NK** In some ways I suppose it was.

**RK** What did you want to do with *Metamorphosis*? What was your ambition with this second book of Metabolism?

**NK** I thought maybe we could open up the membership a bit. But Asada and Kurokawa dug in their heels, so…

**RK** How did you want to change the members?

**NK** For example, to bring in Tange and Isozaki and turn it into a little bit of a broader movement.

**RK** But also international members?

**NK** No, my thinking didn't go that far.

**HUO** What about Kazuo Shinohara? Shinohara was from the same generation, and he also has strong links to science.

**NK** When I look at a home, I always try to imagine what it would be like for me to live there, but the problem with Shinohara's houses is that I come up blank. They don't feel to me like places to live. They're just boxes.

### Judgment

**RK** This is your own private judgment?

**NK** Yes. But remember, that's my area of expertise—passing my personal judgment not only on houses but on buildings of all kinds.

**RK** Does that mean you held private human feelings towards all the other architects?

**NK** Kikutake is a true master of home design. I wouldn't say his Sky House is especially livable, but that was essentially done as a kind of minimalist exercise. Perhaps I should add that I am one of the leading authorities in studying and researching the residential styles of Japanese people today.

**HUO** Are there any younger generation architects you're interested in? Because you said you wanted to extend the group, then you said you'd include Tange and Isozaki. One could obviously extend into new generations as well, no?

**NK** Among those active at the time, Hiroshi Hara. I thought we needed to look for fresh new directions. That's why I was jointly editing a magazine called *Dezain Hihyo* (Design criticism) with Hiroshi Hara, Awazu, and the art critic Ichiro Hariu. In retrospect, though, I'm glad we didn't get Isozaki or Hara to join us, since they both became postmodernists.

**RK** Was there any architect you wanted to exclude?

**NK** Not really. Even Kurokawa—I may have thought he was a bit too cocky, but I still considered him a dear young fellow. [*laughs*]

**HUO** So this was a big unrealized project. I have a habit to always ask about unrealized projects.

**NK** Well, I guess as things turned out, the recently published *Metabolism and Metabolists* is the long-awaited second volume on Metabolism.[9]

## METABOLIST BANKING

Continuing the momentum of their collaboration at Expo '70, Kawazoe, Hidetoshi Kato, Kikutake, and Ekuan launch a new think tank: CDI, the Communication Design Institute. For their first project, Kawazoe leads research into the identity, social role, and building needs of the Kyoto Shinyo Kinko bank. Over the next 13 years, CDI builds 30 new community branches around Kyoto. The branches are designed as "space modules," all using the same standard units, which are meant to be rebuilt after five years (though they last the next 40 years). Ekuan's GK designs the interiors and accessories. The banks include elements like children's libraries and playgrounds, exhibition spaces, community meeting and dining areas—a metabolic, programmatic flow in which banking becomes part of everyday life...

**1977** Kisshoin.

Kyoto Community Bank branches

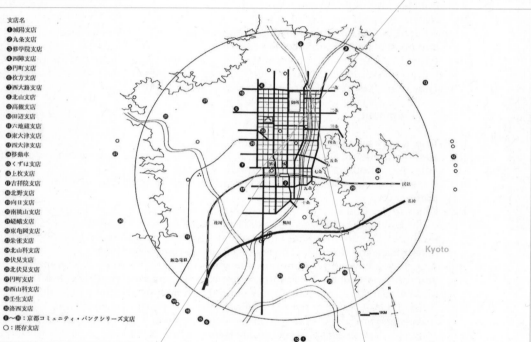

支店名
❶城陽支店
❷九条支店
❸修学院支店
❹西陣支店
❺円町支店
❻枚方支店
❼西大路支店
❽北山支店
❾高槻支店
❿田辺支店
⓫六地蔵支店
⓬東大津支店
⓭西大津支店
⓮移動車
⓯くずは支店
⓰上枚支店
⓱吉祥院支店
⓲北野支店
⓳向日支店
⓴南桃山支店
㉑嵯峨支店
㉒東亀岡支店
㉓朱雀支店
㉔北山科支店
㉕伏見支店
㉖北伏見支店
㉗円町支店
㉘西山科支店
㉙壬生支店
㉚洛西支店

❶～㉚：京都コミュニティ・バンクシリーズ支店
○：既存支店

Kyoto

**1971** Shugakuin.

**1974** Kitayama.

"Space module": an umbrella structure with roof supported by a central column, all prefabricated off-site.

**References**

1   Kawazoe et al, *Metabolism 1960* (Tokyo: Bijutsu Shuppansha, 1960).

2   Kenzo Tange and Noboru Kawazoe with Yoshio Watanabe, *Ise—Nihon kenchiku no genkei* (Tokyo: Asahi Shimbunsha, 1961). English edition: *Ise: Prototype of Japanese Architecture* (Cambridge, MA: MIT Press, 1962).

3   François Caron, *A True Description of the Mighty Kingdoms of Japan and Siam,* first published in 1636. Caron (1600–1673), working for the Dutch East India Company, was probably the first French person to visit Japan.

4   Prince Toneri and Ono Yasumaro, *Nihon Shoki* (The Chronicles of Japan), 720. The oldest extant chronicle of Japan, covering the sixth to the eighth century.

5   Taketani Mitsuo, *Benshoho no shomondai* (Problems of dialectics) (Tokyo: Rigakusha, 1946).

6   Ernst Cassirer, *Philosophy of Symbolic Forms* (Chicago: Open Court, 1923).

7   Friedrich Engels, *Dialectics of Nature,* 1883; the Japanese edition appeared in 1929.

8   Noboru Kawazoe, "Collapse of the city and an architect's philosophy," *SD,* January 1969.

9   Otaka and Kawazoe, eds., with Kikutake, Maki, Ekuan, Awazu, and Kurokawa, *Metabolism and Metabolists* (Tokyo: Bijutsu Shuppansha, 2005).

Reprise: to mark Otaka's 80th birthday in 2005, Kawazoe instigates the long-awaited update to *Metabolism 1960* (both are published by Bijutsu Shuppansha).

1968 Masato Otaka: Sakaide Artificial Ground
1968 Photos by Osamu Murai
2009 Photos by Charlie Koolhaas

# Tokyo Bay
# A planning frenzy

**"Tokyo has been left to expand beyond control and is now a huge mess ... Learning from my own experience, I arrived at this idea of creating an estate where there are no landowners."**

Hisaakira Kano, chairman of Japan.
Housing Corporation, 1958.

Even after swathes of Tokyo are destroyed in the war, the entrenched system of urban land ownership—together with the absence of the radical masterplanning that had modernized Western cities like Paris one hundred years earlier—makes large-scale planning difficult at the exact moment when it is most needed: the captial's population explodes from 3.5 million in 1945 to 9.5 million in 1960. Whereas the previous generation of architects and planners resorted to Manchuria and China for unfettered new construction, a new generation realizes that a vast reservoir of territory in fact exists on their own doorstep: Tokyo Bay, 922 square kilometers of empty sea right next to Tokyo's intolerably crowded central area of 622 square kilometers. If the land itself in Tokyo is not available for the projection of their visions, the Metabolists—prompted by the vision of an artist, Taro Okamoto, and a housing developer, Hisaakira Kano—would simply create a new surface, a form of artificial ground (人工土地), upon which to build. In the international wave of postwar hyper-engineering—reversing rivers (the Soviet Union's plans to redirect the flow of the Siberian river, 1960s), space travel (Sputnik 1, 1957; Kennedy's announcement of the mission to the moon, 1961), and supersonic flight (British and French collaboration on Concorde begins in the early 1960s)—the inhabitation of Tokyo Bay seems plausible. What was previously thought of as an intractable geographical limitation suddenly transforms in the imagination into a new zone for free growth, facilitated by high-tech engineering. The proliferation of architecture magazines creates a forum for a kind of gladiatorial combat of audacious proposals for Tokyo Bay; the new medium of television also plays a part, broadcasting Tange's Plan for Tokyo 1960. The schemes range from wholesale reclamation of Tokyo Bay to islands, floating and semifloating megastructures, networks of highways and piers for housing, governmental buildings, offices, and industry, stretching 18 kilometers from Koto Ward in the northwest across the entire bay to Kisarazu in the southeast—an entirely new city at sea. The planning of Tokyo Bay is one of several moments in Japan where the phobia of land shortage reaches a frenzy. Tokyo Bay thus becomes a laboratory for artificial ground, which evolves into a core Metabolist concept, equally important as the capsule, though historically overlooked…

**1960** Untapped territory: Tokyo Bay, a resource for fishing and shipping, will be reimagined as a vast artificial ground...

The idea to use Tokyo Bay as a territorial resource is not new, but has been limited to occasional, haphazard landfill schemes around Tokyo's waterfront Koto Ward starting as early as the 17th century, and peaking in the 1960s. Against the historical backdrop of already realized reclamation and Tokyo's massive population growth, more ambitious plans for construction covering the entire bay seem not only viable but urgent. Tange's Plan for Tokyo 1960 is only the most well known in a series of (competitive) schemes drawn up by an artist, various technocrats, lobbyists, and the Metabolists themselves, employing various creative strategies…

**1957** Outpost:
Ikoijima, Island of Leisure, aka Ghost Tokyo, Taro Okamoto

**1958** Total infill:
Yamato: A New Capital on Tokyo Bay, Hisaakira Kano

**1959** Islands:
Neo Tokyo Plan, Council for Industrial Planning, with Hisaakira Kano

**1959** Belt:
City on Tokyo Bay, Masato Otaka

**1959** Modules:
Development of Tokyo Bay and Network of Mechanical Circulation, Masato Otaka

**1959** Head and hands:
New Tokyo Project—A proposal for Tokyo 50 Years After: Human-Type Plan, Kisho Kurokawa

**1960** Wings:
New Tokyo Plan, Kenzo Tange

**1960** Spine + branches:
Plan for Tokyo 1960, Kenzo Tange

**1961** Manhattanite:
Major Tokyo Bay Plan, Kiyonori Kikutake

**1961** Cells:
Ocean City, Kisho Kurokawa

After a horrific decline to 3.5 million in 1945, the population of Tokyo grows 270 percent by 1960. "The city of 10,000,000 is of fundamentally different character from a city of 1,000,000," Tange writes. "Its needs cannot be met by the same means that have been employed in the past." Plan for Tokyo 1960, *Shinkenchiku*, March 1961.

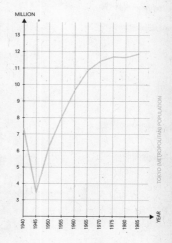

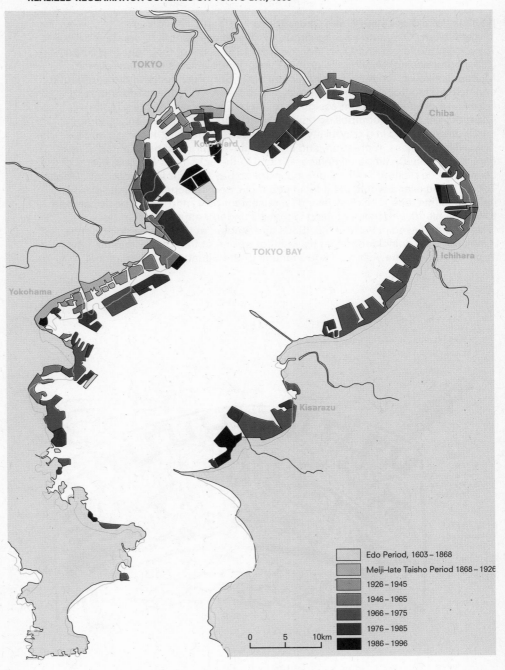

Edo Period, 1603 – 1868
Meiji–late Taisho Period 1868 – 1926
1926 – 1945
1946 – 1965
1966 – 1975
1976 – 1985
1986 – 1996

0      5      10km

## Ikoijima, Island of Leisure, aka Ghost Tokyo

The artist Taro Okamoto chairs a group of "first-class people to create a Tokyo Masterplan of Our Own" for the June 1957 issue of the magazine *Sogo* (All encompassing). Also in the group: Kenzo Tange and his assistant planner Mitsuru Ishikawa, the flower arrangement artist Sofu Teshigahara, the aeronautic engineer Hideo Itokawa, and the novelist Kobo Abe. With the collaboration of Isozaki—a graduate student assigned to the project by his teacher, Tange[1]— Okamoto presents a compelling mixture of artwork and urban plan, serious intentions rendered in a playful style. New zones for industry, high-rise and low-rise living, business, recreation, and community centers, will be oriented in rays emanating from the Imperial Palace. Crucial to the scheme is *Ikoijima*, Island of Leisure, to be built on artificial ground in Tokyo Bay (Okamoto also calls it "Ghost Tokyo"). The island would include an aquarium, zoo, beaches, marinas, concert hall, museums, and a "Coney Island" amusement park, and would be connected to the mainland with trains running in tunnels underneath the bay.

Okamoto had lived in Paris in the 1930s and studied at the Musée de l'Homme; it may not be a coincidence that his plan for a zone of free play within the city appears in the same year as the foundation of the Situationist International.

Island of Leisure, a new concept in Japan.

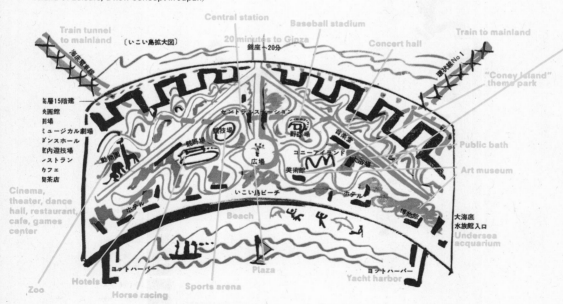

Shortly after Okamoto's proposal, the concept of leisure—using the English term—is born in Japan. The word appears in the 1961 "White Paper on Japanese People's Lifestyles," an annual report made by the Economic Planning Agency: "Our attitude of consumption in the last several years has changed tremendously compared to the prewar or postwar period of poverty ... We may indeed be in a time of 'consumption revolution' or 'lifestyle restoration' as some call it, a time that is characterized by three phenomena: 1) westernization of lifestyle, 2) minimization of house labor, and 3) increase of leisure consumption." Leisure has an increasing importance for Tange and Kurokawa in particular...

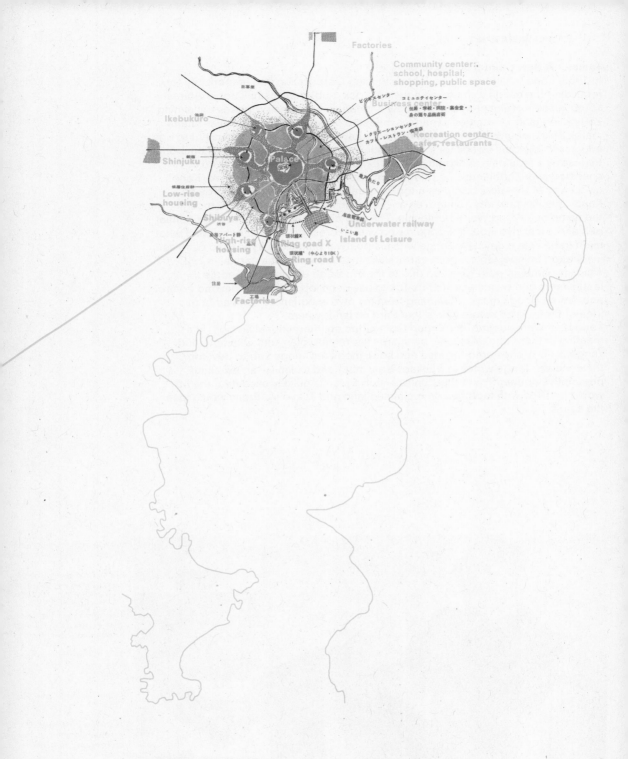

Factories

Community center:
school, hospital;
shopping, public space

ビジネスセンター    コミュニティセンター
(住居・学校・病院・集会堂・
身の回り品商店街)
Business center

Ikebukuro

レクリエーションセンター
カフェ・レストラン・喫茶店
Recreation center:
cafes, restaurants

Shinjuku

Palace

Low-rise
housing

Underwater railway
Island of Leisure

Shibuya

High-rise
housing

Ring road X

Ring road Y

Factories

## Yamato: A New Capital on Tokyo Bay

In 1958, Kano, chairman of the Japan Housing Corporation and responsible for rebuilding the nation's shattered housing stock, publishes a small book, *Atarashii shuto kensetsu* (Construction of a new capital), in which he proposes reclaiming 250 million tsubo (common Japanese measure of area; one tsubo = two tatami mats). This amounts to two-thirds of Tokyo Bay filled in, an area equivalent to one and a half Tokyos. The soil for infilling would be generated by using an atom bomb to destroy a mountain, Nokogiriyama, in Chiba Prefecture[2]—where Kano's ancestors were noblemen. Thirteen years after Hiroshima and Nagasaki, Kano conceives of the atom bomb as a tool to create a city rather than destroy one. Kano calls this new city Yamato, an ancient name for Japan, and more recently the name of a World War II battleship. The new city would consist of a residential belt and a massive industrial zone mixed with a forest on the eastern side of what used to be Tokyo Bay. Like Tange with his postwar plan for Tokyo, Kano cites as inspiration Shinpei Goto's post-earthquake masterplan for the capital in 1923, which he laments was "given up due to the blockage of mindless people ... landowners and politicians ... Thus Tokyo has been left to expand beyond control and is now a huge mess ... Learning from my own experience, I arrived at this idea of creating an estate where there are no landowners."[3]

Kano is vice president of the Japan Committee on International Design. In a meeting at International House, he shares his Yamato plan with Okamoto and Tange, who latches onto the idea and soon mobilizes Tange Lab to develop the concept. Tange writes in *Shukan Asahi* that Kano's plan is "an excellent preemptive concept" and that "unless such a plan is quickly executed, the bay would be filled with factories on reclaimed land and Tokyo's citizens would lose the sea."[4]

Shortage of housing units in Japan in 1945: 4.2 million

Number of new units constructed by 1957: 4.65 million

New shortage of units due to overcrowding and poor conditions: 2.3 million

Tatami mats (measuring 3 x 6 feet) per person, 1940: 3.8

Tatami mats per person, 1958: 3.4

*Statistics delivered by Hisaakira Kano in a speech on February 10, 1958.*[5]

The man charged with rehousing the Japanese: Hisaakira Kano.

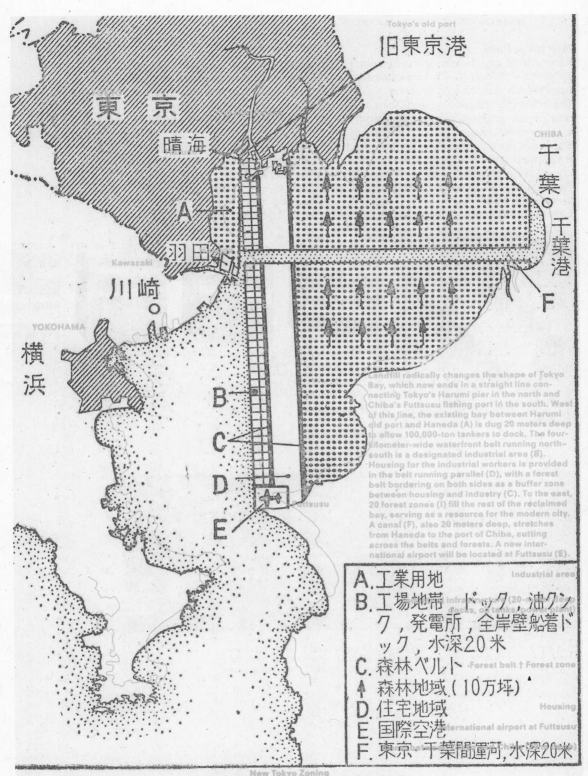

旧東京港 Tokyo's old port

東 京

晴海

CHIBA

千葉○

千葉港

A

羽田

Kawazaki

川崎○

YOKOHAMA

横浜

F

Landfill radically changes the shape of Tokyo Bay, which now ends in a straight line connecting Tokyo's Harumi pier in the north and Chiba's Futtsusu fishing port in the south. West of this line, the existing bay between Harumi old port and Haneda (A) is dug 20 meters deep to allow 100,000-ton tankers to dock. The four-kilometer-wide waterfront belt running north-south is a designated industrial area (B). Housing for the industrial workers is provided in the belt running parallel (D), with a forest belt bordering on both sides as a buffer zone between housing and industry (C). To the east, 20 forest zones (I) fill the rest of the reclaimed bay, serving as a resource for the modern city. A canal (F), also 20 meters deep, stretches from Haneda to the port of Chiba, cutting across the belts and forests. A new international airport will be located at Futtsusu (E).

B

C

D

Futtsusu

E

**Industrial area**

A. 工業用地

B. 工場地帯　ドック（20-油タンク，発電所，全岸壁船着ドック，水深20米

C. 森林ベルト　**Forest belt † Forest zone**

↑森林地域（10万坪）▲

D. 住宅地域　**Housing**

E. 国際空港　**International airport at Futtsusu**

F. 東京・千葉間運河，水深20米

「新東京」の地域分布 2

## Neo Tokyo Plan

Kano's 1958 plan fascinates Yasuzaemon Matsunaga, head of the Council for Industrial Planning (CIP), who immediately organizes a committee of technocrats from the Ministry of Construction and other authorities to develop the idea.[6] The council gives recommendations to the government on energy, resource, and infrastructure planning; its Seventh Recommendation, led by Kano, produces a new, more "masterplanned" version of the Yamato proposal. This time, Tokyo Bay is not filled in; the plan instead calls for the creation of islands surrounding a new international airport. Kano maintains his proposal to use an atomic bomb to create the artificial ground, including with the proposal an article from *Scientific American* titled "Non-Military Uses of Nuclear Explosives."[7] Atsushi Shimokobe, an emerging bureaucrat in the Department of Planning in the Ministry of Construction, is also acknowledged in the paper for cooperation.[8]

Nuclear explosions to build a new city: "The industrial application of an atomic explosion" in four versions, from the December 1958 *Scientific American*, placed by Kano in the appendix of the Neo Tokyo Plan. An explosion near the surface (far right) would create a huge depression and free up enough earth to fill in most of Tokyo Bay...

2.9 million will live on the west side and 2.7 million on the east side of the Neo Tokyo Plan by 1975.

In 1962, three years after Neo Tokyo Plan, the Council for Industrial Planning still convene regularly in the office of Hisaakira Kano, now Chiba prefecture governor. From left: Tokyo metropolitan vice-governor Kazuo Ota; Kano; electricity mogul and chairman of the CIP, Yasuzaemon Matsunaga; Kanagawa prefecture governor Iwataro Uchiyama.

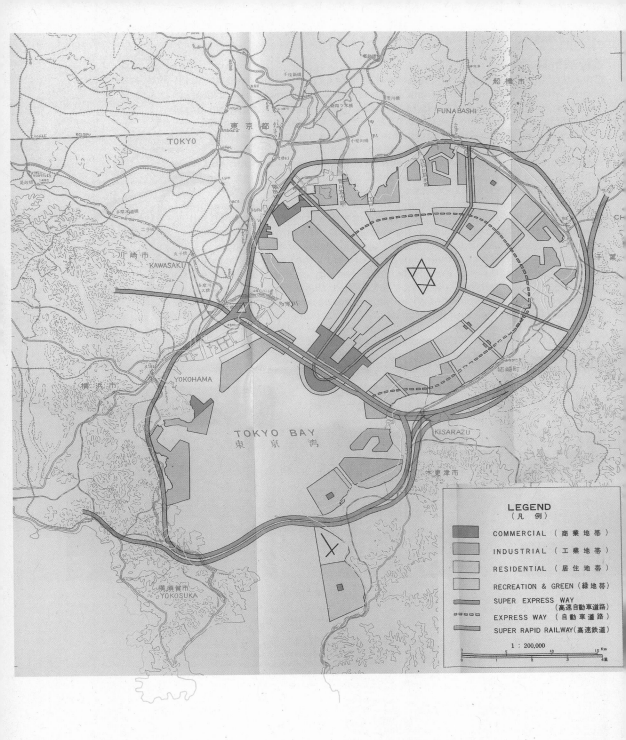

LEGEND
（凡 例）

COMMERCIAL （商業地帯）
INDUSTRIAL （工業地帯）
RESIDENTIAL （居住地帯）
RECREATION & GREEN （緑地帯）
SUPER EXPRESS WAY （高速自動車道路）
EXPRESS WAY （自動車道路）
SUPER RAPID RAILWAY （高速鉄道）

1 : 200,000

TOKYO BAY
東 京 湾

## City on Tokyo Bay

Critical of the CIP's proposal, Otaka and Kurokawa get in on the act. Otaka, shortly after completing the Harumi apartment buildings on reclaimed land in Tokyo Bay while working at Kunio Maekawa's office, creates his own proposal for artificial ground. In the February 1959 edition of the *Kokusai Kenchiku*, Otaka writes of Kano's 1958 proposal that "only such a fundamentally superb idea would allow Japan to survive in the second half of the 20th century." He encourages his fellow architects and urban planners to "support and improve" Kano's plan, while criticizing the Council for Industrial Planning's rendering for degrading Kano's idea.

Rather than the reclamation and industrial development that Otaka lamented for destroying the coastline, he proposes a massive curved belt composed of a detailed city grid not visible in the overall plan. The grid itself is formed by piers (roads); inside each block there are four slabs of mass housing resembling the Harumi slabs, their uniformity offset by the varying blobs of reclaimed land upon which they partly rest. "The city on the sea will have no complication of ownership," he writes in *Kenchiku Bunka*;[9] and, evidently exasperated with the complexities of Tokyo, proposes converting the city to farmland. He calculates that the cost of piling for his city on the sea is affordable and calls it a Venice of the Orient. Matsunaga, of the Council for Industrial Planning and head of the Federation of Electric Power Companies of Japan, who helped develop Kano's Yamato plan, approves of Otaka's idea, symbolizing the new alignment of industry and the avant-garde...[10]

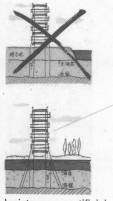

Insistence on artificial ground: rather than resting on reclaimed land, Otaka's buildings rest on pilings.

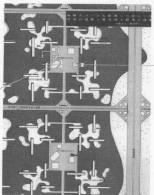

The grid: rational slabs rest on randomly shaped islands.

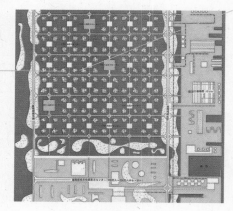

**1958** Harumi high-rise apartments, on the shore of Tokyo Bay, by Otaka and Kunio Maekawa, commissioned by Kano's Japan Housing Corporation. Otaka's model for the housing slabs on his seaborne city...

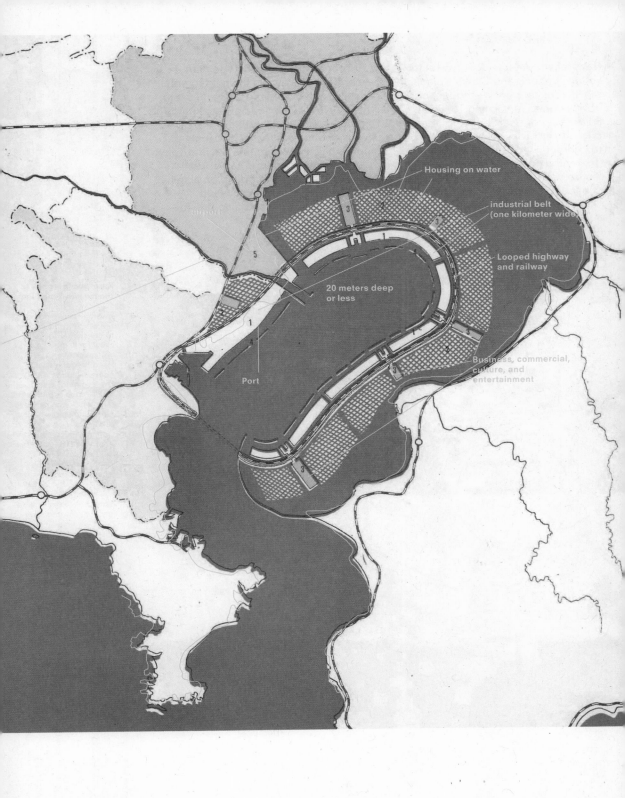

Housing on water

industrial belt
(one kilometer wide)

Looped highway
and railway

20 meters deep
or less

Port

Business, commercial,
culture, and
entertainment

## New Tokyo Project—A Proposal for Tokyo 50 Years After: Human-Type Plan

Following Kano and Otaka's plans, the 25-year-old Kurokawa is the next to enter the increasing frenzy—though, characteristically, as a dissenting voice: "I am in opposition to reclaiming Tokyo Bay," he writes. "New cities need a visual pattern. I'd like to propose a human pattern for this project. Tokyo is currently sticking its butt out into Tokyo Bay. It should place its eyes, mouth, and ears there instead, to interact with the rest of the world."[11] Accordingly, a new pier juts out into Tokyo Bay as the promontory of a restructured Tokyo, with numerous urban cores distributed over a 300-meter-wide boulevard, like acupuncture points on a spine. The focal point is an "urban navel" near the Imperial Palace, which would "accommodate people's consumption of a variety of desires and also provide a space for rituals."

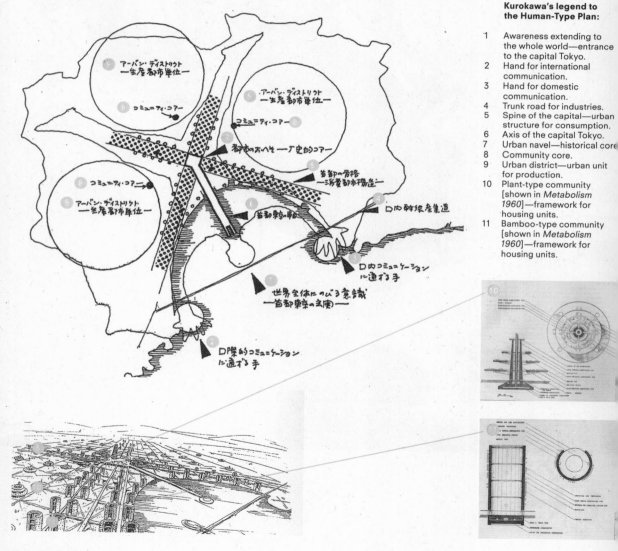

**Kurokawa's legend to the Human-Type Plan:**

1 Awareness extending to the whole world—entrance to the capital Tokyo.
2 Hand for international communication.
3 Hand for domestic communication.
4 Trunk road for industries.
5 Spine of the capital—urban structure for consumption.
6 Axis of the capital Tokyo.
7 Urban navel—historical core.
8 Community core.
9 Urban district—urban unit for production.
10 Plant-type community [shown in *Metabolism 1960*]—framework for housing units.
11 Bamboo-type community [shown in *Metabolism 1960*]—framework for housing units.

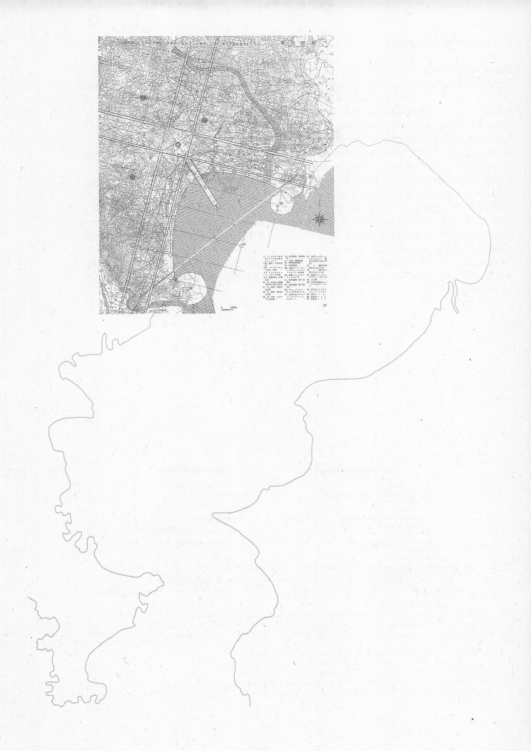

## New Tokyo Plan

Tange publishes the article "Five million on the sea: What if the new Tokyo plan comes true?" in *Shukan Asahi*. "Recent research by the UN says that Tokyo has missed two chances of recovery—the Great Kanto Earthquake and the war disaster—and this would be the third," Tange writes. "We don't need to wait for foreigners to tell us that we have been repeating mistakes. Indeed, unless we make a plan, it will be too late to remedy this malaise."[12] His proposal calls for the construction of a complex pattern of artificial ground, interspersed with open water, stretching over Tokyo Bay. A central axis, consisting of two three-lane highways (and a subway running underneath the artificial ground), runs between Marunouchi in Tokyo and Kisarazu in Chiba, with a central business district, between the highways. Housing is located in the wings stretching from the central axis, built on water, and Tokyo and its two neighboring prefectures, Chiba and Kanagawa, are now connected with a road circling Tokyo Bay. The scheme is an elaboration of the project for Boston Harbor, "a community for 25,000 people," which Tange developed with his students at MIT the year before.

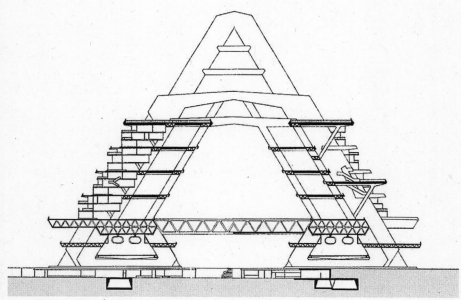

Transplant: A-frame housing for Boston Harbor, 1959, now placed over Tokyo Bay. Here, the atrium is up to 100 meters high and accommodates a network of roads, a monorail, and various urban infrastructure. "Houses will be built on artificial ground provided on every third level of the triangular/diagonal surfaces," Tange writes.[13]

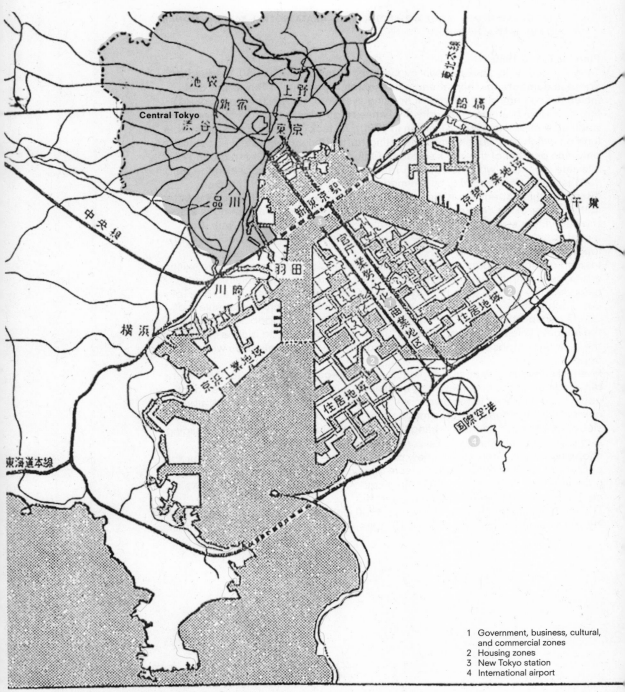

Central Tokyo

池袋　上野
新宿　東京
渋谷
品川

東北本線
船橋

中央線

羽田

川崎

横浜

京浜工業地域

千葉

国営・業務・文化地区

商業地区

住居地区

住居地区

住居地区

京浜工業地域

新東京駅

国際空港

東海道本線

1　Government, business, cultural,
　　and commercial zones
2　Housing zones
3　New Tokyo station
4　International airport

A new Tokyo on the Bay, resembling early integrated circuit boards?

## Plan for Tokyo 1960

Tange's scheme in *Shukan Asahi* evolves into Plan for Tokyo 1960, made after rigorous demographic and economic research, by a team in Tange Lab that includes Koji Kamiya (in charge of housing systems), Isozaki (office buildings), and Kurokawa (transport). A triptych of crises motivates them: Tokyo's population boom (5.4 million in 1950, 10 million in 1960); its lack of housing and affordable land on which to build; and its suffocating traffic (the street system accounts for only nine percent of the city's surface). Only the most radical restructuring can alleviate the crisis, which is caused, Tange writes in a long proposal in the March 1961 issue of *Shinkenchiku*, by the medieval centripetal pattern of the city: "Because this pattern is not discarded, every time a fine new building is erected in the metropolitan centre, the city moves one step closer to a comatose state ... the permanent structure of the modern metropolis is incompatible with the movement that is necessary to the life of the metropolis. The old body can no longer contain the new life."

Instead of the centripetal, Tange projects a linear city over the top of the existing urban mess, one that exists on bridges, piers, platforms, and reclaimed land extending like a spine from the city center 80 kilometers all the way across Tokyo Bay. Each vertebra of this spine is a nine-kilometer-long "unit" (a capsule?) of "cycle transportation system" consisting of three decks of looping highways. On the intricate levels of artificial ground" it would be possible to build a city free of the restraints imposed by land and to produce new space values as well as new hopes."

Five million would live at sea, in giant A-frame megastructures up to 138 meters tall, made up of their own levels of artificial ground upon which each resident could build a house "to his own taste." A further 2.5 million would work along the central axis, in megastructures made up of joint cores that support giant hovering slabs with massive spans, creating "columnless piloti" areas under the buildings. Along this central axis would be zones for government buildings, offices, shopping, hotels, recreation, a new central station, and a new Tokyo harbor for passenger vessels. What Tange's team does not mention is industry: their city is postindustrial, designed for the tertiary sector, a city composed by its flows of communication, information, and road traffic.

The team calculates that Plan for Tokyo 1960 would cost ¥18 trillion ($50 billion in 1960) to construct over a period of 20 years—not much more than the ¥12 trillion

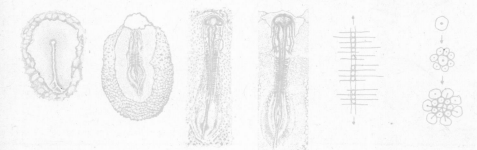

Growth observed by Tange in the spines of mammals, an inspiration for linear urban planning. "While protozoa evolve and grow in an afferent or radial pattern," Tange writes, "vertebrate does so in a linear pattern. As life becomes more complex in its functions, it needs to shift from an afferent pattern to a linear pattern, along the axis of a backbone and artery." *Shinkenchiku*, March 1961. Tange uses the spine metaphor for his urban masterplans in the future: Skopje (1965), Tehran (1975), Lumbini (1978), Abuja (1979)...

Linear "open system" (left) beats cellular "closed system" (right): Tange advocates spinal growth in place of the amorphous, un-1checked radial growth of Tokyo.

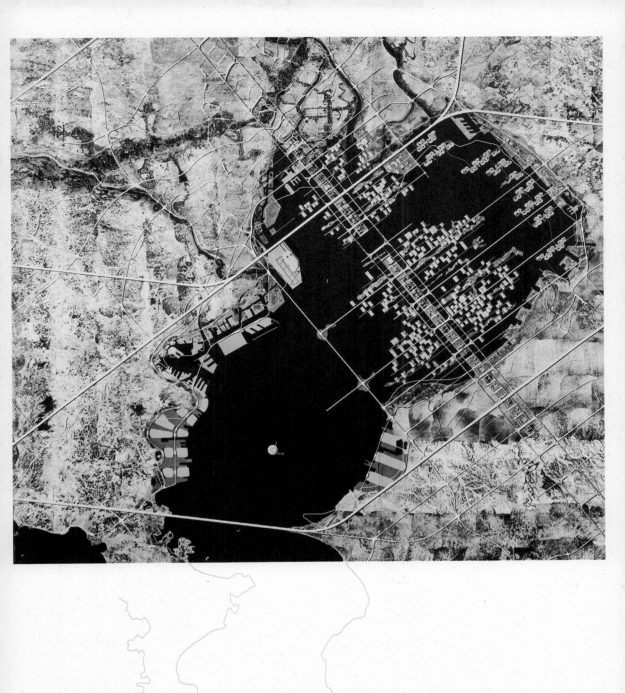

that will be spent on construction in Tokyo in that period anyway. Funds would be raised by both public and private investment. He presents the scheme on a special 45-minute TV program on the national channel NHK on January 1, 1961. In *Shinkenchiku*, critics point out the lack of engineers or traffic experts in Tange's team (Ryuichi Hamaguchi)[14] and the uncertain foundations of the artificial ground growing from the seabed (Kenzaburo Takeyama).

Nevertheless, the plan—presented with a deadpan earnestness which Tange honors his audience with being ambitious and strong enough to ride along with— creates a sensation, especially among the architecture and urban planning milieu, and *Shinkenchiku* organizes a symposium on the project in May 1961. Tange presents to a panel including Tokyo University professor of urban planning Eika Takayama (a masterplanner of Datong, see p. 66), Kikutake, and the Ministry of Construction bureaucrat Atsushi Shimokobe. Shimokobe as a panelist doesn't hide his doubt (see p. 679), yet after all the panelists have spoken, he stands up and concludes that "everyone agrees that Tokyo needs a solution, and that has to be an unconventional project with fundamentally different approaches and ideas from the urban planning we've known. Rather than criticizing the plan, we should find a way to back up the proposal."[15]

Tange continues to receive interest and support from specialists and industrialists outside the architectural circle, including the Ministry of Construction, the Tokyo Metropolitan Government, the Metropolitan Highway Corporation, and the Japan Housing Corporation. Meanwhile, Tange moves on to develop the idea into the Tokaido Megalopolis plan, which he publishes in 1964, expanding scope from the bay to the whole nation with a "national axis"...

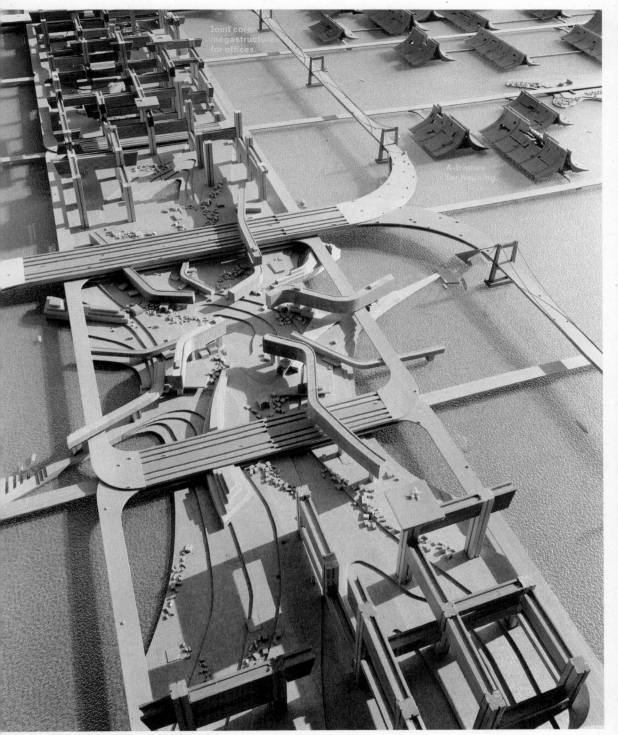

Joint core
megastructures
for offices

A-frames
for housing

Plan for Tokyo: detail of the new archipelago of piers,
highways, megastructures, and reclaimed land.

## Major Tokyo Bay Plan

Finally, Kikutake, the godfather of marine architecture in Japan, weighs in on the Tokyo Bay planning frenzy. His plan consists of three integrated elements: the Koto Plan, to protect the low-lying Koto Ward from flooding through an intricate grid of piers that would house one million people (see p. 134); the South Tokyo Plan, a floating city off the coast of Harumi; and a much larger Manhattan-like grid stretching across the entire bay. The two industrial belts elaborate his Marine City project of 1958, this time over an area of 231 square kilometers. Kikutake also plans two leisure developments—the Tone Recreation Zone in the northeast and the Izu Recreation Zone in the southwest. All prefectures surrounding the bay would be connected by a looped highway.[16] Kikutake's plan is one of the most complex and nuanced, with varying scales or plausibility—but the scheme lacks a convincing graphic articulation, like Tange's collaged satellite photos, crucial in the new media environment…

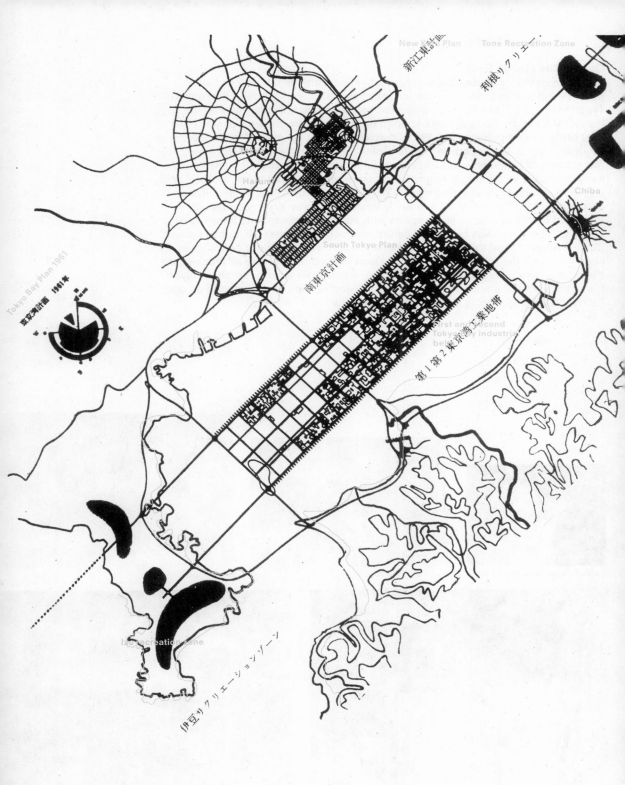

New Kō Plan    Tone Recreation Zone
新江東計画    利根リクリエーション Zone

Chiba

Hasumi

South Tokyo Plan

南東京計画

Tokyo Bay Plan 1961
東京湾計画 1961年

First and Second
Tokyo Bay industrie
bel

第1第2東京湾工業地帯

Izu recreation zone
伊豆リクリエーションゾーン

## Ocean City (Tokyo Bay)

In a film most likely made for a visiting delegation from the UN and Harvard, Kurokawa presents a new scheme for Tokyo Bay, similar in shape to his Human-Type Plan of 1959, but now composed of cells that reach further out into the bay. Inside the cells are floating Helix-shaped megastructures, drawn from his Helix City project (also published in 1961). Kurokawa works "in secret" on this scheme while working in Tange Lab on Plan for Tokyo 1960. "I believe creating metabolism of urban environments is useful for positive control of human milieu," Kurokawa says in the film, in English. "Reasons why I use that spiral artificial land unit are to make organic traffic system between motorcars and people. Roads on the top of artificial land are gradually forming highway system of the city ... We could create attractive living space with sunshine, breeze, and a feeling of seasons. The ocean has been wild nature which is conquered for human beings. But in the near future the ocean will take an important role for our urban life and liberty through the history of the city..." Kurokawa's proposal, like all those made during the Tokyo Bay frenzy, is not taken up, and the gladiatorial combat played out in the arena of the architecture press, TV, and now on film, comes to an end, for now, as the architects increasingly build in the "real" world...

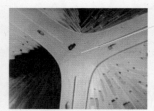
Traffic runs on top of the helixes...

which link together...

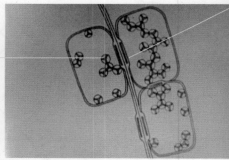
to form cells...

Studying his helix.

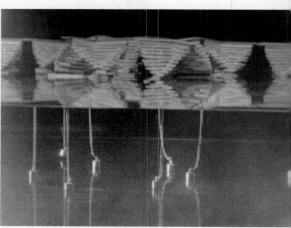
Floating Helixes.

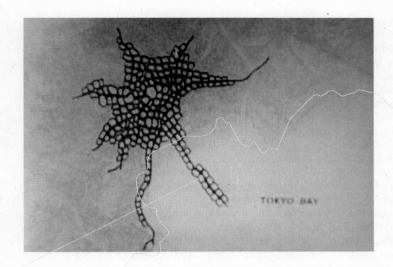

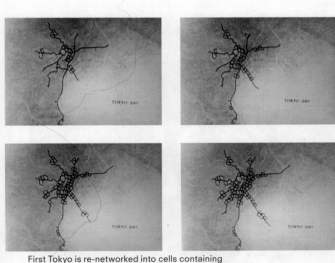

First Tokyo is re-networked into cells containing
helix megastructures, then the organism grows
into Tokyo Bay…

**Kenzo Tange: Tokyo Plan 1986 vs. Kisho Kurokawa: New Tokyo Plan 2025**
Though none of the grand schemes from the early 1960s are built, 20 percent
of Tokyo Bay is reclaimed anyway by a gradual, ad hoc, planless process.
By the late 1980s, Japan's property boom and Tokyo's astronomical land prices
rekindle the pressure, and the incentive, to project artificial ground out onto
the bay again. With a competitive spirit that has only been sharpened by the
passage of 30 years, Tange and Kurokawa return to their old stomping ground…
Tange writes in the November 1987 issue of *The Japan Architect*: "Those of
us who have participated in the production and implementation of urban plans
for the industrialized West and for many nations of the third world consider the
sluggishness of Japanese city administration very lamentable. If nothing is done
to remedy [the high cost of land] in the next four or five years, Tokyo will no
longer be qualified to bear the responsibility of one of the world's urban poles."
Tange's Tokyo Plan 1986—made as he wins the competition for the new Tokyo
Metropolitan Government offices (beating Isozaki)—would begin by developing
existing islands of reclaimed land. In the long run, the plan's axis would extend
from Tokyo towards Kisarazu on the opposite shore, creating on its way the
500-hectare Tokyo Bay City, an independent administrative district serving
as Tokyo's new nucleus of business, culture, and residence, with its own international airport. The plan includes a scheme to connect Tokyo with the neighboring prefectures of Kanagawa and Chiba, which would support the functions
of the capital and offer much needed office space.
Meanwhile, Kurokawa presents a counterplan: New Tokyo Plan, 2025. This
involves not only the creation of a new grid of islands in the bay, which would
accommodate three million salarymen and their families, but also a metropolitan
corridor linking Tokyo with Nagoya, Osaka, and Kyoto by way of fiber optics and
a maglev automobile: the "Linear Motor Car."[17] Whereas Kurokawa opposed
massive reclamation in 1961, now he becomes its advocate.

Kurokawa presents his New
Tokyo Plan at the press club
of the National Land Agency.

**Tange** Tokyo Plan 1986

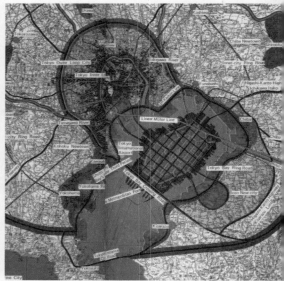

**Kurokawa** New Tokyo Plan 2025

**References**

1   Taro Okamoto and Arata Isozaki, "City, Civilization and Art," *Okamoto Taro chosakushu, 9: Taro tairon* [Collections of Taro Okamoto's writings, No.9: Dialogues with Taro] (Tokyo: Kodansha, 1979).

2   Hisaakira Kano, *Atarashii shuto kensetsu* [Construction of a new capital] (Tokyo: Jiji Shinsho, 1960).

3   Hisaakira Kano, "Remaking Tokyo," *Geijutsu Shincho*, November 1958.

4   Yasuhiro Ishimoto interviewed by Terunobu Fujimori and Junichi Ishizaki, "Trajectory of the post-war modernism in architecture—Kenzo Tange and his time," *Shinkenchiku*, May 1999.

5   Abridged from a lecture delivered February 10, 1958. *Annals of Public and Cooperative Economics*, Volume 30, Issue 1, January 1959.

6   "The dream of construction New Tokyo Yamato," *Zaikai*, November 1958.

7   Gerald W. Johnson and Harold Brown, "Non-Military Uses of Nuclear Explosives," *Scientific American*, December 1958.

8   Council for Industrial Planning, ed, "The 7th Recommendation of the Council for Industrial Planning: On the 2-billion-tsubo reclamation of Tokyo Bay" (Tokyo: Diamond-sha, 1959).

9   Masato Otaka, "Proposals of a new housing with high-rise apartments and a city on Tokyo Bay," *Kenchiku Bunka*, February 1959.

10   Interview in writing with Masato Otaka by Hans Ulrich Obrist and Kayoko Ota, May 2008.

11   Noriaki Kurokawa, *Kenchiku Bunka*, September 1959.

12   Kenzo Tange, "Five Million People on the Sea," *Shukan Asahi*, October 16, 1960.

13   Ibid.

14   Ryuichi Hamaguchi, "Conductors of City Planning?" *The Japan Architect*, August 1961.

15   "Report: Symposium on Plan for Tokyo 1960," *Shinkenchiku*, July 1961.

16   Kiyonori Kikutake, "Sekkei Kasetsu" [Designing hypotheses], *Kokusai Kenchiku*, 1961.

17   Kisho Kurokawa, "New Tokyo Plan 2025," *The Japan Architect*, November–December 1987.

# Fumihiko Maki 槇文彦

**1928** born in Tokyo **1952** graduates from University of Tokyo, where he studies in Tange Lab for a short time, and goes to Cranbrook Academy of Art, Michigan **1953** enters Harvard's Graduate School of Design **1954** joins Skidmore, Owings, & Merrill in New York, working under Gordon Bunshaft **1955** enters Josep Lluis Sert's New York office **1956** studies again at Harvard, invited by Sert; meets Paul Rudolph; becomes associate professor at Washington University in St. Louis **1958** meets Takashi Asada and future Metabolists through Tange Lab classmate Koji Kamiya **1959–60** travels the Middle East, Europe, and Asia with grant from Graham Foundation to study vernacular urban patterns **1959** joins Metabolism and prepares Shinjuku Project with Otaka **1960** participates in World Design Conference, Tokyo; publishes "Group Form" with Otaka in *Metabolism 1960*; Toyoda Memorial Hall of Nagoya University, first commission in Japan; attends Team 10 meeting in Bagnols-sur-Cèze, France; returns to Washington University in St. Louis; Steinberg Hall at Washington University completed; **1961** wins Architectural Institute of Japan prize while in US **1962** associate professor of urban design at Harvard **1964** elaborates Group Form in his book *Investigations in Collective Form*; works on K-Project for Tokyo's downtown district; Movement Systems in the City research at Harvard **1965** returns to Tokyo to open own office **1967** Hillside Terrace design begins; Rissho University Kumagaya Campuses **1968** Golgi Structures: plan for cone/cylinder-shaped high-density communal living system **1969** Hillside Terrace, Tokyo, phase one completed **1970** Senri Civic Center Building, Osaka; presents installation of Golgi Structures at Expo '70 **1972** wins competition for PREVI low-cost housing project, Lima, with Kikutake and Kurokawa; Kato Gakuen Elementary School **1974** Kuragaike Memorial Hall, Toyoda **1976** Japanese embassy, Brazil **1984** Fujisawa Municipal Gymnasium **1985** Spiral Building, Tokyo; publishes *Miegakure-suru toshi* (City that disappears and emerges); international pavilions, Tsukuba Expo '85 **1986** National Museum of Modern Art, Kyoto **1991** wins competition for Frankfurt am Main center redevelopment **1992** Hillside Terrace, final phase **1993** wins Pritzker Prize; wins Prince of Wales prize for Hillside Terrace **1996** Floating Pavilion, Groningen, Netherlands **2004** commissioned to design new UN building UN5, New York **2007** Republic Polytechnic, Singapore **2008** publishes *Nurturing Dreams*; breaks ground on World Trade Center Tower 4 at Ground Zero, New York; headquarters of Aga Khan Development Network, Ottawa **2010** completes new building for MIT's Media Lab

**"We always feel… not pressure necessarily, but an urgency from tradition…"**

While World War II and the atomic bomb turned most of the Metabolists and their mentors against America, Fumihiko Maki studied (at Cranbrook and Harvard), taught (at Washington University in St. Louis), built (also at Washington U), and worked (with Josep Lluís Sert and Skidmore, Owings & Merrill, New York) in the US—all before the Metabolists coalesced in 1960, when he was 32 years old. He had also toured Europe, the Middle East, and Asia for two years, developing a fascination with recurring vernacular urban patterns in different parts of the world. The theory that grew out of these observations—"Group Form," first articulated in an essay with Masato Otaka in *Metabolism 1960*—critiqued both the rigidities of modernist urban planning *and*, implicitly, the hi-tech, hard-to-realize megastructures proposed by his Metabolist colleagues. The team meets Maki in his office at Hillside Terrace, his Group Form life's work, built in interdependent increments between 1969 and '92; he is a sober and methodical figure, a quiet counterpoint to the polemics and deadpan fantasies of his Metabolist colleagues. Maki was concerned with organic urban growth and linkage more than masterplanning, and in the outside world more than in (only) improving the conditions of Japan. Maki's apparently fundamental differences from other Metabolists again calls into question the coherence of the group, suggesting that its membership structure and principles were in themselves fluid, changeable, metabolic…

Maki and Associates and Le Petit Bedon,
Daikanyama, Tokyo, September 10, 2005

In a plain meeting room in his offices at Hillside Terrace,
Maki's Metabolist credentials are questioned...

**1953** At 25, Maki leaves Nagasaki on a cargo ship bound for Seattle. After the two-week voyage, he arrives in an America at the zenith of its power—while Japan is still desperately rebuilding. Maki is attracted by America's advanced architecture—curtain walls, shells, tensile members—and is eager to learn its techniques, first at Cranbrook, then Harvard. Except for brief periods in Tokyo (crucially, during the build up to the 1960 World Design Conference) and a two-year tour of Europe and the Middle East, he spends the first 12 years of his career as a foreign implant in America. His inspiration is an implant himself, Walter Gropius…

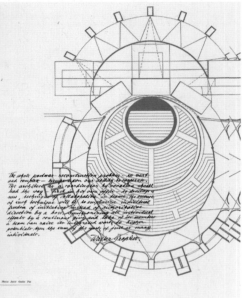

At Tange Lab, Maki is first drawn to the American scene through *L' Architecture d'Aujourd'hui* (a precious magazine in postwar Japan), featuring Walter Gropius's activities at Harvard. Gropius writes: "The whole postwar-reconstruction process—so vast and complex—hangs upon our ability to cooperate. (February 1950 issue.)

**1955** In New York, Maki works with Josep Lluís Sert, his mentor at Harvard, on the American Embassy in Baghdad, completed five years later.

**1962** Maki (third from left) returns to Harvard as associate professor under Sert, now the dean, third from right.

america
ere was another person
ho was free from anti-
merican feelings: Tange.
spite of the fact that his
other was killed by American
achine-gun fire, and in spite
his strong inclination to
e national cultural heritage,
e was open to the influence
American achievements
nce he first attended the
AM meeting in Hoddesdon
the UK in 1951. While Tange
d doubts about the achieve-
ents of European modernism
the time, he was struck
American technical
oficiency, evident in the
orks of Mies van der Rohe
d Skidmore, Owings &
errill. Tange's actual archi-
ctural practice in the
50s was done vis-à-vis
mericanism.
ajime Yatsuka

iel Saarinen
ommissioned in 1925 by
eorge Gough Booth to
esign the Cranbrook Edu-
ational Community, con-
eived as an American
quivalent of the Bauhaus.
aarinen taught there and
ecame president of the
ewly named Cranbrook
cademy of Art in 1932.
mong his student-collab-
rators were Ray and
harles Eames. In his book,
e City (1943), Saarinen
ompares cities to cellular
tructures: the growth of
ums is like diseased cell
ssue; good "community
lanning" resembles healthy
ell tissue.

**REM KOOLHAAS** Many of the Metabolists we have talked to so far seemed very resistant, almost hostile, towards America because of the war. You are an exception, taking America as a source of inspiration. Can you explain why you went to America? Why didn't you have anti-American feelings?

**FUMIHIKO MAKI** Being young, I was drawn to places where things were happening. If I'd been five years older, like Shimokobe and Otaka, I'd inevitably have been involved in the war—so that was a tremendous threshold. America was one of the epicenters for architecture in the early 1950s. I came across a special issue of *L'Architecture d'aujourd'hui* on Walter Gropius's time at Harvard.[1] Harvard and MIT were portrayed as places where new ideas had been transplanted from Europe.

**RK** Transplanted from Europe?

**FM** Yes, something new was emerging, a kind of fusion.

**RK** Already it was almost an artificial cloning.

**FM** That's right.

**RK** And that artificiality appealed to you?

**FM** I don't know if it was the artificiality that appealed to me. You're talking, let's say, about Alvar Aalto in Finland, where perhaps drawing could come out of sentiment. That wasn't what I was attracted to.

**RK** Did America represent a democratic appeal, a political appeal?

**FM** We'd been familiar with European modernism for many years, ever since Kunio Maekawa and Junzo Sakakura went to work with Le Corbusier in the 1930s. However, when I graduated from Tokyo University in the early '50s, Japan, like Europe, was still struggling to recover from postwar destruction. Nothing was happening.

**RK** That's very interesting: Europe and Japan were similar at that point.

**FM** We were hearing about Mies van der Rohe in Chicago and Gropius at Harvard, so I thought, why not go to the United States? So in 1952 I went to Cranbrook. The campus was designed by Eliel Saarinen. There I read his book called *The City*,[2] but with no illustrations, which I remember really frustrated me. Then I went to Harvard a year later, where I learned quite a bit of urbanism directly from the official CIAM line under José Lluis Sert, my mentor. Then I became a Graham Foundation Fellow from 1958 to 1960 and had a chance to travel all over the world. I quit everything and spent those two years traveling in the Middle East, Europe and Asia.

**RK** Do you think that your Metabolism in the '60s—if you'll allow me to speak of it that way—also had European and American components?

**FM** Sure.

### How I Became Involved

**RK** So you attended the 1960 World Design Conference while on a temporary visit to Japan?

**FM** That's correct.

**RK** How were you involved in the organization of the World Design Conference?

**FM** As a young assistant.

**RK** Through Tange?

**FM** Yes, through Tange and Sakakura. I'll tell you how I became involved with Metabolism. In 1958 I was back in Tokyo while on the Graham Foundation grant. Whenever I came back from the States, Tange would invite me to informal dinners. He wanted to know all about the States—what Eero Saarinen was doing and so on. He became sympathetic to techno-utopian ideas—perhaps from the Plan for Tokyo 1960 onward.

Through Koji Kamiya and Takashi Asada, who was number two in Tange Lab and also the secretary-general of the 1960 World Design Conference I came to know the Metabolists, including Otaka. They were very interested in some of my views and suggested that I should join Metabolism. So from 1958 to 1960,

**1958–1960** With an intuition that the world is the best teacher—and with a $10,000 fellowship from the Graham Foundation—Maki embarks on a journey through Southeast Asia, India, the Middle East, and Europe. He is fascinated by the organic-seeming urban compositions he encounters from the air and on the ground: "For those cultures, creating buildings and creating cities were one and the same thing."

**Isfahan** "We lack an adequate visual language to cope with ... views from airplanes," Maki will write in *Investigations in Collective Form* four years later.

**Hydra** "It was a dramatic experience to see the entire town made of these solids as 'genetic forms' along the contours of the hills."[3]

Ground view: genetic forms in the alleyways of Hydra.

Herbert Bayer

Bayer (1900–85), Austrian-born graphic designer, lived in Aspen, Colorado, and participated in the founding of the International Design Conference in Aspen in 1949.

Friends

Maki and I found ourselves having very similar opinions on the issue of groups, so he and I produced a proposal together, "Toward Group Form," at his Tokyo home for Metabolism 1960. It contained two urban problems, which still remain today: 1) land ownership in Japan is excessively fragmented, and if this is not altered we cannot hope for successful clustered architecture; 2) the townscape achieved by 1960 had been made based on pedestrians, but it also contained the achievements of advanced civilization. In particular, it was full of cars, so Japan's disorderly streets had become even more unassailable. Eventually, we presented one solution with the three-dimensionalization of land ownership in the Sakaide Artificial Ground project as a method for solving the problem of tiny subdivisions of land ownership.

Masato Otaka

Group Form

Maki's 'group form' had something essentially incongruent with Metabolism... The discourse of group form didn't come out as a technological proposal but rather as a necessary social process. It was indeed centered on a sociological observation. We could then say that the argument was an authentic succession of modern architecture in terms of its ethical aspiration for social integration." Isozaki, "Discourse on Fumihiko Maki," Shinkenchiku, April 1978.

I divided my time between traveling and collaborating on the Metabolist manifesto in Tokyo. I participated in many discussions in Tokyo, which took place in Ginza, at a small inn. Just eight or 10 tatami mats with a low table where we sat discussing and drinking.

RK **What did you drink?**

FM We drank beer or saké or whiskey—not wine at that time.

### Puppet Master

HANS ULRICH OBRIST **And Takashi Asada was the catalyst for these meetings?**

FM Asada was one of our godfathers—no, godbrothers. He was a bright, intellectual person and was always interested in bringing young people together for discussions. That kind of person doesn't exist anymore.

RK **Somebody who enjoys stimulation?**

FM He was a very stimulated person. He was a very important force in organizing the World Design Conference. In fact, Asada brought many people together. Herbert Bayer from Aspen, as well as Louis Kahn, Minoru Yamasaki, Paul Rudolph, and Peter and Alison Smithson.

HUO **Is Asada in the Metabolism 1960 book?**

FM No, he wasn't in the book. He preferred to remain an advisor.

HUO **Isn't it strange that the catalyst who triggered it all is not in the book? How come?**

FM That was an interesting part of his character.

RK **A true catalyst.**

FM He always distanced himself. He wasn't interested in being a central figure.

HUO **The invisible man of Metabolism.**

RK **Or the puppet master.**

FM Puppet master. We always behaved like puppets, though there was a strong, interesting kinship between the puppet master and the puppets. We were quite independent, but at the same time, we would answer his call late in the evening.

RK **If Asada was a puppet master, what was Kawazoe?**

FM Kawazoe was an advocate, a spokesman. As a critic and commentator, he had a strong desire to say something through the movement, to summarize things.

### Keeping a distance

RK **So he was trying to create some coherence out of the different voices?**

FM Yes, but it would have been quite difficult to summarize. If I had to describe our attitudes I'd have to say that Kikutake and Kurokawa, for instance, were more interested in techno-utopia. I wasn't interested in technology per se, but in urbanism, which isn't necessarily associated with techno-utopia. Yet the Metabolism group respected each position. Despite our differences, we always tried to be friends, and I still have strong affiliations with them. No one tried to come up with a unifying blanket statement. That's very important.

HUO **So it wasn't the militaristic idea of the avant-garde, which is about inclusion and exclusion. Can one say that it was an organic movement?**

FM It was an organic movement, but among limited club members—like Team 10, who never invited in many people. Just the original members stayed on.

RK **Team 10 was very strict about who was in and who was out. They traumatized many people. But with Metabolism, I have the feeling that you were more tolerant.**

FM Perhaps more tolerant of others' ideas. Speaking of techno-utopia, I must say that Tange was much closer to the Metabolists than myself. From the very beginning, I was a little bit more objective and, like Isozaki, kept a certain distance from this techno-utopia aspect of architecture. When I wrote Investigations in Collective Form in 1964,[4] I tried to put Mega Form, Group Form and other forms more or less on an equal terrain to examine the characteristics of each approach.

**1960** Visiting Tokyo, Maki is eager to codify the ideas generated by his travels. He finds a kindred spirit in Otaka, whose thesis was on "clusters," and they collaborate on a definition of Group Form in *Metabolism 1960*: a post-CIAM urban planning that surrenders to change rather than imposing mastery, and that asserts interdependence among disparate, even unfinished elements, rather than hierarchy and isolation. Group Form is both spontaneous and ancient, "an intuitive, visual expression of the energy and sweat of millions of people in our cities, of the breath of life and the poetry of living."

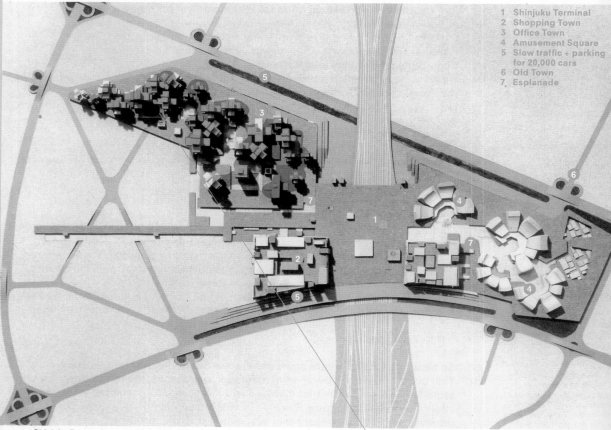

1 Shinjuku Terminal
2 Shopping Town
3 Office Town
4 Amusement Square
5 Slow traffic + parking
  for 20,000 cars
6 Old Town
7 Esplanade

Shinjuku Redevelopment Project: the first Group Form proposal, made with Otaka as a counterproposal for the building work already underway around one of Tokyo's major train stations. "Petals" within Amusement Square (4) or towers in Office Town (3) can be absent without effecting the overall composition...

Office Town, made of clay, malleable like Group Form itself. Maki and Otaka's poetry continues: "A group of towers in various sizes and heights extends densely in a tight area like the Milky Way."

After the war, there was a long debate in Japan about tradition. At the time, modern architecture and Russian realism were arriving. Tradition was a buzzword of the intelligentsia on the left, even though that might seem counterintuitive. Tange and others talked of tradition mostly as something "for the people." Architects had to be quite humble to surmount such intellectual obstacles. Everyone thought of modernism as Functionalism. When everyone was discussing Functionalism and Traditionalism as opposing concepts, Tange stepped in and said he was going to create a new style of Japanese modernism by assimilating tradition.

Hiroshi Hara

RK   **Although is "tolerant" the right word? Was it simply a Japanese form of politeness?**

FM   Politeness, probably. [*laughs*]

RK   **Because tolerance is such a liberal Western concept. I realize more and more that tolerance is a way of creating a wall around oneself, of getting together without actually meeting.**

FM   I think "politeness" might be a better word.

HUO   **How do you feel about the group's manifesto?**

FM   My stance is a bit reserved towards that. You're talking about the 1960 manifesto, right? Even today I can't really say what the manifesto was. Hajime Yatsuka, who wrote a book on Metabolism, considered the manifesto more of an anthology of new urbanism.

RK   **Maybe this [*gestures to the book* Investigations in Collective Form] is the most manifestolike.**

FM   *Metabolism 1960* was the manifesto in a way. We were looking to develop a new future for Japan at that time, not…

RK   **Not for the rest of the world.**

FM   We weren't trying to spread our ideas to the West.

### Toolbox

HUO   **I have a question I've always wanted to ask you. In his wonderful *Vision and Value* books, György Kepes said that we cannot truly understand the forces that prevail in architecture and art if we don't look at other disciplines, such as science.[5] One of the things I'm particularly interested in is this link to science—the bridge between architecture, urbanism, and science in Metabolism. I was wondering if science was a toolbox for you.**

FM   Well, although "genetic form" is certainly biological terminology, I never intended to make any connection to science such as Kepes sought.

RK   **No claims.**

HUO   **No toolbox. I would like to talk more about Team 10. I understand you knew the members well?**

FM   In 1960, the Smithsons invited me to attend the Team 10 Conference in Bagnols-sur-Cèze in the south of France. Spending a week there, I got acquainted with all the original members of Team 10. Oskar Hansen and Giancarlo De Carlo passed away recently. Sadly, the original members of Team 10 are all gone now: Ralph Erskine, the Smithsons, Jaap Bakema, and Aldo van Eyck. I was never regarded as a member because, as you know, Team 10 was a very closed family. But Peter Smithson, Bakema, van Eyck, and Giancarlo De Carlo befriended me, particularly in my later years.

RK   **So you went to only one meeting?**

FM   Only one meeting, but somehow that enabled friendships to develop.

HUO   **I interviewed all the surviving members over the last six or seven years. One thing I sense in common between Metabolism and Team 10 was this strange negotiation between the local and the global—the "glocal," as it were. De Carlo, Erskine, and Peter Smithson talked to me about resisting homogenized globalization or a universal language, while at the same time introducing new things into that global dialogue. They wanted to be part of the global dialogue and local at the same time. Could you talk about this paradox?**

### Never Been Colonized

FM   Japan interpreted "international" in a fairly lucid manner. In the early '50s, there was strong discussion among many Japanese architects about modernism versus tradition. Japan had a very long history and its own unique tradition when modernization began in the 1850s. Since we'd never been colonized, we didn't have to accept imposed cultures outright. We were in a position to select…

RK   **And develop your own culture.**

**1964** In his pamphlet *Investigations in Collective Form*, Maki calls for expanding the possibilities of urban planning, which, at the beginning of the '60s, he finds hopelessly limited: "Cities, towns, and villages throughout the world do not lack in rich collections of collective form. Most of them have, however, simply evolved: they have not been designed." He identifies three modes of collective form, including the one he will spend most of his career on...

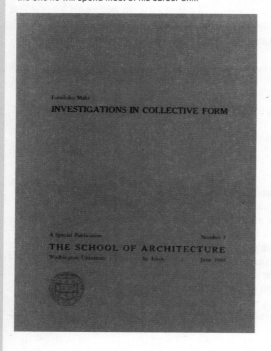

Fig. 7, (above) a Sudanese village. Fig. 8, (below), a Greek village. Two examples of Group Form architecture.

Archetypes: Sudanese and Greek villages.

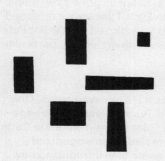

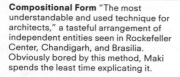

**Compositional Form** "The most understandable and used technique for architects," a tasteful arrangement of independent entities seen in Rockefeller Center, Chandigarh, and Brasilia. Obviously bored by this method, Maki spends the least time explicating it.

**Mega Form** "A large frame in which all functions of a city are housed"; see Tange's housing system for Boston Harbor (1959) and Kurokawa's Agricultural City (1960). Maki warns of this technique: "If the Mega Form becomes rapidly obsolete, as well it might, especially in those schemes which do not allow for ... change ... it will be a great weight about the neck of urban society."

**Group Form** "Evolv[ing] from a system of generative elements in space." Maki's passion...

**1964** From his base in the United States, Maki joins the Artificial Land subcommittee (part of the Architectural Institute of Japan), and merges the concept with Group Form: K-Project, in Tokyo, is an elevated urban strip upon which buildings and programs of various size and function (shopping, offices, transportation) spring up organically. Maki proposes the scheme, which combines artificial ground with Group Form, to the Ministry of Construction through the Architectural Institute of Japan.

**1965** Maki forms his own group: leaving academia and the US, Maki returns to Tokyo to start Maki and Associates, with Morikazu Shibuya and Akira Ozawa.

**1969** Clusters: like Office Town, an informal Group Form of towers in Maki's competition entry for the International Atomic Energy Agency (IAEA) and UN Industrial Development Organization complex, in Vienna.

## THE IN-BETWEEN

Maki, a fan of Paul Klee, is more interested in lines, spaces, and relations than in defining shapes. Refusing to assert overall control in the mode of the traditional architect, he instead acts as a technical choreographer of movements, elements, and potential…

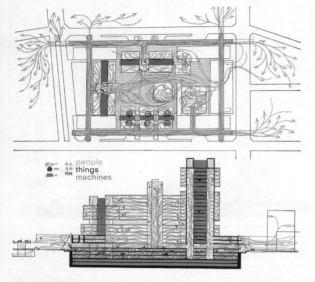

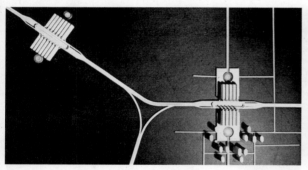

**1960–61** Free range: Awazu illustrates circulation patterns encouraged by Maki's Dojima Redevelopment Project (unbuilt), for central Osaka. People (orange looping lines) flow between offices, convention center, art center, and "amusement center."

**1964** With his urban design studio at Harvard, Maki make "Movement Systems in the City," an open-ended networ of three-dimensional nodes. "Urban design is ever concern with the question of making comprehensible links betwee discrete things."[6]

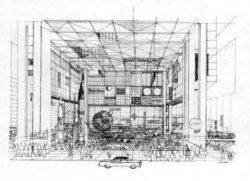

**1965** Abstaining: City Room and City Corridor, open frameworks for indoor/outdo urban space. "The architect does not concern himself with the ways City Corridors and Rooms will be used," he writes.[7]

**FM**   Yes, we chose food from France, not from England [*laughs*]; took naval architecture and the legal system from England; took medicine and technology from Germany.

**RK**   **Got the best of everything.**

**FM**   Yes, we've taken Westernization as almost synonymous with progress. It's been our national ethos these last 150 years. Yet objectively speaking, we always feel… not pressure necessarily, but an urgency from tradition. Although we, myself included, tend to create buildings in modernist language, tradition somehow unconsciously comes out in the scale, proportions, or treatment of space. Kikutake's early work shows this. So does Tange's. Tradition permeated many architects of that time and still does today. However, the manifesto of Metabolism was ahistorical.

### I Happen to Be Japanese

**RK**   **The irony here is that we're trying to look at Metabolism and almost 80 percent of the discussion is about Japanese tradition.**

**FM**   Oh, really?

**RK**   **Kawazoe was relentless in connecting every single aspect of Metabolism to tradition, to readings of particular temples. I think "obsessive" is not too strong a word. What I find interesting is that if we look at Metabolism, I think there are two strains: one is deeply provincial, totally concerned with Japan, solely informed by and intended for Japan; while yours is completely cosmo-politan, a kind of world-citizen approach applicable not only to Japan, but global in scope. Was that a conscious divorce, a position you were aware of at the time? Was the split between you as a modernizer and the others coming from a Japanese tradition already noticeable in the '60s? It must have been strange to be part of such an incredibly Japanese group where people also didn't speak English—you must have had to straddle both camps.**

**FM**   You know, I happen to be Japanese and was very comfortable with those people. Yet at the same time I'd already been exposed to things outside—more than anyone else in the Metabolist group. So I could position myself to be both Japanese and also a little bit of an outsider, able to look at Japan from a certain distance. It didn't create any contradictions in myself. Nor were the other members so critical as to impose upon anyone, saying, "you're wrong and I'm right." I think Metabolism was inevitable yet also a circumstantial product of that particular time and place—that's the way I see it.

**HUO**  **A circumstantial product?**

**FM**   Yes. Looking back on Tokyo in the late 1950s and early '60s, there weren't many people with whom to share views which were not necessarily one's own. At the same time, there was a certain appreciation for and dream of something we'd like to do or something we'd like to break. Such feelings could be shared by a certain number of young people, like ourselves. Also, communication between these people was more informal. Today everybody's busy, everybody has a schedule. But in the late '50s, we were drinking and eating pizzas, talking. Communicating and scheming to do things was…

**RK**   **Spontaneous.**

**FM**   Yes, much more spontaneous and easy.

### In Brick or Mud

**HUO**  **When I visited you about eight years ago for "Cities on the Move" we spoke about how you were the only one among your generation who looked into conditions in Asia, not just in Japan. You say in your issue of *Space Design* that the impressions of streets and cities you gained during these journeys led to a vision of Collective Form.[9] At that time not so many people looked at these places in terms of their urban conditions.**

**1969–1992** Rebuke to virtuosity: Hillside Terrace grows subtly from architecture to urban fabric over 30 years in Tokyo's Daikanyama district. "One cursory look at architectural history is sufficient to find that the whole development is characterized by man's immense desire to make buildings grand and perfect," Maki writes in 1964;[8] Hillside Terrace, his lifework, quietly strives for the opposite: well-integrated anonymity.

Slow-growth urbanism.

To be visible from above, it has to be artificially highlighted.

hitecture
omes as a bit of surprise
t Maki, being a man of
ctice, is so precise here
out his theory or credo.
have known him to have
ver depended on esoteric
gon, but this statement
s his intelligence with
erican pragmatism.
ime Yatsuka

69
e year later, the need
housing becomes even
re urgent after the Ancash
rthquake. For documen-
on of PREVI since its com-
tion in 1972, see Time
lds!: The Experimental
using Project (PREVI),
na: Genesis and Outcome.
arcelona: Gustavo Gili,
08).

| | |
|---|---|
| FM | When I visited villages and small towns in the Middle East—from Isfahan to hill towns in the Greek islands—I began to recognize certain genetic forms. |
| RK | **Patterns.** |
| FM | Yes, patterns manifested in space or in the use of materials, interconnecting with other elements, whether in brick or mud or whatever. I see this as a way to structure a certain order, even in the future city. The idea of the megastructure tends to be either a product of absolute power from the past or a by-product of some techno-utopia future expressed by everyone from Le Corbusier to Yona Friedman to Kenzo Tange. |
| | Yet I thought one could also start by establishing ground rules using genetic or quasi-genetic form in a completely opposite direction. Furthermore, Japanese traditions of compositional form correspond to neither Mega Form nor Group Form. I became interested in the linkage of independent or semi-independent objects. In the second chapter of *Collective Form* I discussed linkages: physical linkage, implied linkage, social linkage. |
| RK | **Are you describing something you still wholly believe in, unmodified?** |
| FM | It has been modified, of course, but via my daily practice. |
| RK | **Do you still see it as an actual guiding principle?** |
| FM | It may apply sometimes. Have you seen Hillside Terrace? It's an incremental development of a plan. |

### Accidental Increment

| | |
|---|---|
| HUO | **The whole idea seems to have been pushed further with Hillside Terrace, which grew from 1969 to 1992, as well as with Keio University, where you built several projects from 1981 to 1994. You continue to do sustained projects that grow over time. You've written that the idea of projects growing and evolving over many years or decades—this genetic idea in your work—is something you saw in Marcel Breuer.[10]** |
| FM | Did I? I perhaps wrote that 40 years ago. I have no memory. [*laughs*] I think architecture is to write a story using certain grammar, syntax, and phrases. The phrasing must somehow remain one's own over the years, however things combine and change. Ultimately one is composing a fiction based on limited knowledge and limited vocabulary, though at the same time, change is inevitable. Back in 1960, all I had to go on was my own image of something that ran counter to all that over-organized techno-utopia. I thought that an accidental increment could better suggest a kind of new order, which might be good for the immediate, if not distant, future. Perhaps such an image of genetic form may have stayed in my mind over the years. |

### Lima Low-Cost Housing

| | |
|---|---|
| HUO | **Can you talk about the PREVI project in Lima, which I understand was only partially realized?** |
| FM | Kikutake, Kurokawa and I collaborated on one occasion, though we've worked largely independently throughout our careers. In 1969 the United Nations, with Peter Land as commissioner, invited 13 architects to build low-cost housing just outside Lima. The three of us, as Metabolists, made up one group. Three teams won the international competition: us, Atelier 5, and Herbert Ohl. But in the end the UN decided to divide the site so that all 13 architects invited to the competition—Jim Stirling, Aldo van Eyck, and Christopher Alexander, among others—could each realize their own project. |
| | Our proposal was to develop a genetic sort of form. Families ranged in size from just a core to up to ten children, so we decided to make the building in such a way that many parts of it could be added later. This was the original genetic form [*points to drawing and photos*], but see how the people have transformed it? This is precisely my interest in genetic form and change, which |

## PROYECTO EXPERIMENTAL DE VIVIENDA (PREVI), LIMA

**1969** In an attempt to solve Lima's housing crisis—and to learn from the informal solutions that spring up as a result of it—the Peruvian government, with the assistance of architect Peter Land at the UN, invites 13 international architects to submit proposals for a social housing project that is already Metabolist in principle: PREVI's 1,500 experimental homes must be able to incorporate change. A sub-group of Metabolism—Maki, Kikutake, and Kurokawa—are one of three competition winners, but all 13 competitors are given space in which to build; thus PREVI becomes a rare collaboration of the international avant-garde, as well as one of the few occasions where Metabolism itself creates a joint production. Maki, Kikutake, and Kurokawa design a terrace of long, low breeze block houses, simple enough for residents to build and manipulate…

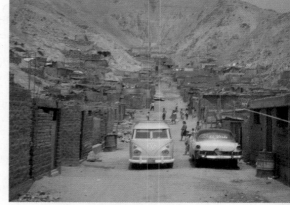

Found Group Form? The PREVI site, outside Lima. Photographed by Maki, pre-construction.

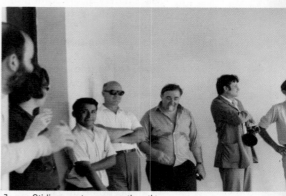

James Stirling, center, among the other international architects visiting Lima.

Planning "genetic form," ready for transformation: Maki (sitting) and Kikutake working on PREVI.

Urban collage, with Metabolism creating the most consistent forms.

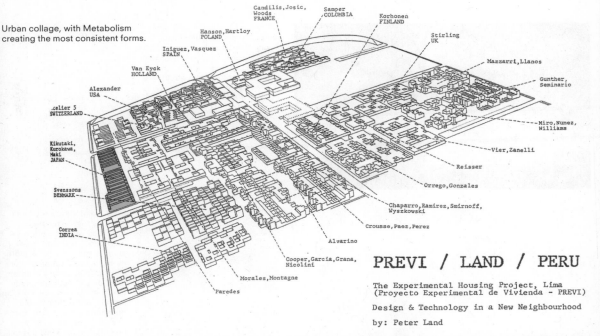

Candilis,Josic, Woods FRANCE
Samper COLOMBIA
Korhonen FINLAND
Hanson,Hartloy POLAND
Stirling UK
Iniguez,Vasquez SPAIN
Mazzarri,Llanos
Van Eyck HOLLAND
Gunther, Seminario
Alexander USA
..elier 5 SWITZERLAND
Miro,Nunez, Williams
Kikutaki, Kurokawa, Maki JAPAN
Vier,Zanelli
Reisser
Svenssons DENMARK
Orrego,Gonzales
Chaparro,Ramirez,Smirnoff, Wyszkowski
Correa INDIA
Crousse,Paez,Perez
Alvarino
Cooper,Garcia,Grana, Nicolini
Morales,Montagne
Paredes

# PREVI / LAND / PERU

The Experimental Housing Project, Lima
(Proyecto Experimental de Vivienda - PREVI)

Design & Technology in a New Neighbourhood

by: Peter Land

**ca. 1970** Construction in breeze blocks for maximum economy.

**1979** Ten years after construction, Maki writes: "Our housing unit, which enabled maximum flexibility and expansion by means of a simple plan, evolved by the hands of its residents ... I think this project may be one of the best works of collaboration that Metabolist thinking ever achieved."[11]

**2011** Adapted frontage of the initially uniform Metabolist units, photographed by *Domus* magazine.

**2011** Decay and growth, simultaneous.

**1991** Maki's Frankfurt am Main center redevelopment tries to organize an urban high-rise zone as Group Form, using "negative" and "positive" spaces—a strategy first employed for the Golgi Structures, 23 years earlier...

**1968** Golgi Structures: Maki predicts that, in the future, capsules will proliferate as individuals demand "more income, more free time, more mobility, satisfaction of more lust, more autonomy in urban functions, direct democracy, community by choice, development of information media." But instead of focusing on the capsule itself, as his fellow Metabolists do, Maki designs a structure to mediate between their intensely private space and the public space that inhabitants will still desire. The in-between, inside-outside spaces of the Golgi* facilitate "information transmission" and "allow real experience ... participated in by many." Capsules plug into the membrane of towers and, since they are conical, inhabitants can presumably observe each other across the atria of a benevolent panopticon... "Capsule space melts into neighborhood space."[12]

\* The cluster of stacked cones takes its shape from the Golgi body (named after the Italian scientist Camillo Golgi, 1843–1926), the organelle in plant and animal cells that processes and transports protein.

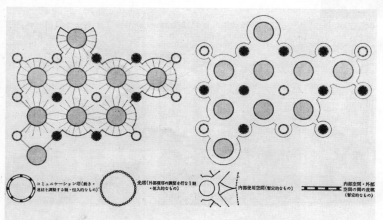

**Communications tower** (organizes human, material and energy movements and connections)

**Light tower** (takes in sunlight and air, and coordinates comfortable conditions)

**Internal space in use**

**Membrane between inside and outside spaces**

were keywords for Metabolism. Ironically, this happens to be the only interesting example of collaboration among the Metabolists—and there's no technology; it's all low-tech.

**RK** **The only one realized is low-tech?**

**FM** Yes, it was Group Form. This was another competition my office entered, for the redevelopment of Frankfurter Messe in 1991 [*shows drawings*]. Unfortunately, right after we won first prize, the Berlin Wall came down and all the money in West Germany went into the East.

**RK** **That happened to us too in Germany, with Karlsruhe. The Wall fell and that was that. But for me—excuse me for saying something so absurd—this Frankfurter Messe is less you than the Hillside Terrace.**

**FM** In what way?

**RK** **This seems, for you, unusually concerned with shape. Almost aggressive...**

**FM** This Golgi structure? I was working with relationships between outer and inner space and also developing an image they could have. It's a kind of intellectual exercise.

**RK** **Do you recognize your influence on contemporary architecture or do you not look for that?**

**FM** No, I don't look for that.

### Tolerant of Reality

**RK** **This might be a horrible caricature, but I think that some Metabolists were interested in form and some more interested in formless ideas. I empathize with your side, though I can't quite participate on it. You are not necessarily with the "formless" approach, but you seem less interested in shape than the others. It's clearly based not only on your own creativity, but also on a reading of the world as it is, via a kind of modernist vernacular. Some of these images [*points*] manage to look as if no architect were involved at all, barely different from what happens randomly in the city. Do you recognize that? In some ways, you seem so tolerant of reality that you're...**

**FM** Sure, I'm tolerant, just like you! [*laughs*]

**RK** **...that you're almost abstaining from architecture.**

**FM** I'm not abstaining from architecture. I'm just involved in things of the day! [*laughs*]

**RK** **I know. [*laughs*] That's exactly what I'm trying to get at. Here, for instance [*points to a photo in a book of Maki's work*], this particular image. It's almost like a contemporary shopping center or a random office development. It doesn't have any overall compositional logic. Where does it differ from those, for you?**

**FM** That's a good question. [*laughs*]

### Preemptive Modesty

**HUO** **I'd like to ask you Rem's doubt question. Do you ever have doubts about architecture?**

**FM** Sure, all the time.

**RK** **The interesting thing about your approach is that you have a kind of preemptive modesty. [*laughs*] I'm actually dying to ask you about Mies, because I wasn't sure whether you were saying "genetic" or "generic" architecture.**

**FM** Ah, it's genetic.

**RK** **Genetic? OK—because Mies was trying to do a kind of generic architecture, an architecture without features. When I met you in the 1980s, you were architectural. You had just done the cubic Spiral Building, a building with clearly identifiable ambitions. What I like about Hillside Terrace is that here the ambitions are so subtle that any kind of spectacle disappears. Would you say that's true of your work in general, that you're trying to get more and more subtle in terms of the effect—or no?**

**2007** Republic Polytechnic campus, Singapore: the return of the cluster, connected by a platform of artificial ground.

**1985** Spiral Building: an attempt to create a heterogenous urban condition in a single building in downtown Tokyo.

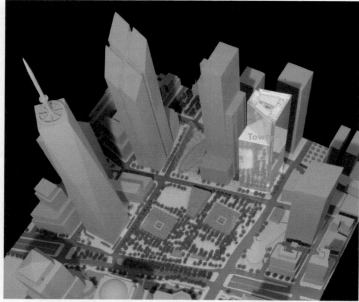

**2012** 4 World Trade Center, New York: the shortest and simplest building on the site, Maki imposes the greatest effect on a highly compromised collective form by voluntarily disappearing…

**FM** Well, every time I design, I set a certain goal. I try to answer the questions given to us, but I also question myself. The subtleties you mention may come up quite unconsciously. But if you see a certain subtlety in the results, I won't deny it.

**HUO** **That leads to my question about your unrealized projects, which is a recurring question. Over your very long trajectory, what's the percentage of built work to unbuilt work? And do you have any particular unrealized project that you'd really like to see built some day?**

**FM** You know, I've never counted built versus unbuilt. I must say I've been fortunate to be able to build more often than not.

Of course, if one loses a competition, it's effectively an unbuilt project, though I'd rather think of it as deposited in the bank for safekeeping. I can always withdraw the deposit for the next occasion.

**References**

1  Paul Rudolph and Walter Gropius, "Walter Gropius et son école," *L'Architecture d'aujourd'hui*, no.28, February 1950.

2  Eliel Saarinen, *The City: Its Growth, Its Decay, Its Future* (New York: Reinhold Publishing, 1943).

3  Fumihiko Maki in interview, Masato Kawamukai, *Gendai Nihon kenchiku no kiseki* (The trajectory of contemporary Japanese architecture) (Tokyo: Kajima Shuppankai, 2005).

4  Maki, *Investigations in Collective Form* (St. Louis, IL: Washington University, 1964).

5  György Kepes, *Vision and Value* (New York: George Braziller, Inc., 1965–66). A set of six anthologies, each containing over 200 essays.

6  Maki, *Investigations in Collective Form.*

7  Fumihiko Maki, "Theory of Group Form," *The Japan Architect*, February 1970.

8  Ibid.

9  "Fumihiko Maki: 1987–1992," *SD* (Space Design), January 1993.

10 Ibid.

11 Fumihiko Maki, "Metabolism/1960—Trajectory of Group Form," *Metabolism 2001, Obayashi Quarterly No.48* (Tokyo: Obayashi Corporation, 2001).

12 Fumihiko Maki, "Capsule is the king," *SD*, March 1969.

**1969–92** Fumihiko Maki: Hillside Terrace, Tokyo
**2009** Photos by Charlie Koolhaas

*Metabolism 1960*, the book that launched the movement, promises future editions on the very first page. Immediately after the World Design Conference, the Metabolists begin planning the second installment. The "hidden" hand of the first book, Takashi Asada takes the lead in post-conference meetings and is made honorary chairman. But there is no formal membership structure for Metabolism: "No troublesome agreements or regulations bind members of Metabolism as a group," Asada explains in the would-be introduction to the second book. This very informality, coupled with the success of the movement creates more and more exposure for its individuals; independent work intensifies, and, plans for the second book are postponed and revived several times.

*Metabolism 1965: Metamorphosis* is the closest they get to realization. Kurokawa claims the title for this would-be book is his, and explains that it is the result of a frustrating three years of trying to realize metabolic concepts in the real world: "unless the theory of metamorphosis—according to which metabolic processes produce a sudden emergence into a qualitatively different stage—were introduced to the public, it would be impossible to go beyond the methodologies of metabolism." Whereas metabolism adapts to and absorbs external change, metamorphosis focuses on radical transformation. Kawazoe writes: "Our advocacy of metamorphosis is not for the purpose of advocating bizarre forms in design, but comes from our awareness that we are presently undergoing an unprecedented environmental revolution in the history of humankind."

Asada writes a preface to the new book, introducing Metabolism's members with an affectionate regard. Kawazoe suggests expanding the membership of Metabolism (at the end of the first book, he wrote that "a metabolic process will also take place in its membership"), but he meets resistance from Asada and Kurokawa.

A theoretical contents page is drawn up, an almost inscrutable abstract framework for the Metabolists' projects since 1960; many of them are realized or closer to realization than they could dream for the first book, which is part of the reason why they have no time to finish the second book…

Projects that would have appeared in the book:

| | | |
|---|---|---|
| EKUAN | Pumpkin House | capsule |
| | Tortoise House | artificial ground |
| | Dwelling City | artificial ground / capsule |
| | Metabolism Furniture | renewal |
| KUROKAWA | Helix City | artificial ground / mobility |
| | Floating City Kasumigaura | artificial ground / cellular growth |
| | Metamorphosis | linear and cellular growth |
| | Box-Type Mass-Produced Apartments | capsule |
| | Nitto Food Cannery | linear growth |
| MAKI | Dojima Plan | artificial ground / group form |
| | K-Project | artificial ground / group form |
| OTAKA | Sakaide Artificial Ground | artificial ground / group form |
| | Kanda-Otemachi Plan | artificial ground / group form |
| KIKUTAKE | Koto Plan (Disaster Prevention City) | floating artificial ground / renewal |
| | Shallow Sea-Type Community | floating artificial ground / renewal |
| | Ikebukuro Plan | move-net / artificial ground |
| | Marine City 1963 | floating artificial ground / renewal |
| | Tetra Project | artificial ground |

metabolism 1955

Kiyonori Kikutake

Increasingly abstract typologies in the contents page for *Metabolism 1965*.

## My Colleagues of the Metabolism Group
### Introduction by Takashi Asada

No troublesome agreements or regulations bind members of Metabolism as a group. This is a handful of freedom-loving and progressive architects, planners, designers and critics who happen to be friends. A stained copy of the book *Metabolism 1960* is lying open on my desk. On the first page is a dedication to me which ends with the words: "On the eve of the World Design Conference, May 10, 1960." The signatures are by Noboru Kawazoe, Masato Otaka, Kiyonori Kikutake, Fumihiko Maki, Kiyoshi Awazu and Noriaki Kurokawa. All these signatures remind me of men of outgoing personality who are determined to advance. During the last six years, as leader of the group, I have been calling on the members to put into practice and to test various theoretical projects which they have proposed in *Metabolism 1960*. Our group has been making steady achievements. What I mean by "achievements" are not merely laborious projects of architecture or professional success in the popular sense of the word. I mean something entirely different— achievements which have an intangible strength. You may call them "ideas that manipulate space." Taking this opportunity, I want to describe each member of Metabolism—a task which I may be best suited to undertake because I am the eldest in the group.

### Noboru Kawazoe
Rather short in stature and fair-complexioned, Kawazoe-san is one of my closest friends. He is a critic of international standing. His sharp eyes are focused on the foundation of our civilization from which he extracts facts for close scrutiny to make forecasts for the future. Kawazoe-san was born in Tokyo in 1926 as the son of an architectural engineer. He specialized in psychology and architecture at Waseda University. Upon graduation in 1953, he joined the editorial staff of *Shinkenchiku*, a monthly architectural magazine, and later was editor until 1957. While he was editor of *Shinkenchiku*, Kawazoe-san ignited the controversy over "the role of tradition in contemporary architecture" which brought about great repercussions not only in Japan's architectural field but also in the allied arts. The controversy became the focus of wide attention. Undoubtedly, Kawazoe-san is one of the central figures in the theoretical field of Metabolism. So is his wife, Yasuko Kawazoe, who once excelled herself as a capable editor and did much in training young talent for Japan's graphic design field. She played an important role in promoting compilation of *Metabolism 1960*. On one excuse of another, members of "Metabolism" dropped in at the home of Mr. and Mrs. Kawazoe about 50 kilometers west of Tokyo, on the Pacific coast, and spent many pleasant and rewarding hours.

### Kiyoshi Awazu
Awazu-san was born into a middle-class family in Tokyo in 1929. A youth with a freedom-searching mind, he dropped out from a course in business management at Hosei University in 1945 and, in search of beauty, entered into the world of aesthetic creations. He studied painting and graphic design on his own. It was during these days that he demonstrated his competence in typographic design. In 1964, he opened his own design office. In my judgment, he is something more than just a graphic designer. His deep understanding of motion picture culture, I am sure, was nurtured in those days. In his work with avant-garde movie production, Awazu-san has made outstanding movie title page design: *Face of Another, Woman in the Dunes*, etc. He has also displayed outstanding skill in architectural projects carried out in cooperation with members of Metabolism. Notable among these are his wrought iron doors, concrete murals and crest designs. He is liked by everybody. Among his many friends are poet Shuntaro Tanikawa, musician Tohru Takemitsu, and movie producer Hiroshi Teshigawara. He is a good father and has a wonderful family. He always carries some toys in his pocket for his three little children.

### Kenji Ekuan
Ekuan-san is one of the most unusual members of the Metabolism group. He was born in 1929 the son of a Buddhist priest, which entitles him to succession in the priesthood of his father. I do not know why, but for some reason he decided to study industrial design at the Tokyo University of Art, from where he graduated in 1955. From his university days, with his fellow students, he formed the GK Industrial Design group and was engaged in various other types of work. In 1955, he moved to the United States to study at the Art Center School in Los Angeles. Upon his return to Japan, in 1957, he opened a design office with his GK members, which he now heads. His office has been engaged not only in industrial design but also graphic and interior design—a new field in Japan in which his group is most active. He is the most influential leader of the Japan Industrial Designers Association (JIDA). I first met Ekuan-san at a seminar which I arranged for Konrad Wachsmann when he visited Japan. I found him a man with a bright and joyful character and very popular... Ekuan-san has a balanced way of thinking design by harmoniously blending his Buddhist background with traditional Japanese views on materials. He owes much to Kawazoe-san in this respect.

## Kisho Kurokawa

Kurokawa-san is the youngest member of our Metabolism group and has the strongest fighting spirit. He belonged to the Kenzo Tange group. In 1962, he became independent and opened his own office. His wife is also a graduate of the engineering faculty of Kyoto University, the first female student in that field. She majored in applied chemistry. Their campus romance led to marriage.

During the early years of my association with the Tange group, I supervised Kurokawa-san's graduate work. Even in those days, he was most active among the architecture students. It can be easily imagined that his asset of quickly grasping new ideas served him well in learning from the many achievements of the senior members of the Tange team. He bravely faced numerous difficulties. For better or worse, he represents Japan's postwar youth.

Although small in stature, Kurokawa-san is a bundle of vitality. In Japan's architectural journalism, he is an indispensable figure. Each year, he is in the midst of a number of controversies in architectural circles. As he is the youngest in the Metabolism group, he is always the target of much criticism by senior members. But he knows how to cope with such criticism. It is a delight indeed to see the youngest Metabolism member staging a one-man crusade against Japan's deep rooted bureaucratic system.

## Fumihiko Maki

Maki-san is Tokyo-born, Tokyo-bred. Like Kikutake-san, he was born in 1928. Maki-san spends half of his time in Japan and half in the United States. He truly is one of Japan's few architects of international standing. He recently opened an architectural office in Tokyo and has been spending more time in Japan than heretofore. His wife also spent time in the United States and acquired an international education.

I am fully aware of the big role the Makis have played in promoting friendly relations between architectural circles in Japan and the United States. They have been serving as the "window" to the world for members of the Metabolism group. In the Metabolism group, Maki-san is unique because of his extensive observation and rational way of thinking. He has much persuasive power. He rarely gets excited even at an animated discussion meeting. But when he does, he really goes for it.

Maki-san is the father of two small children. As a rule, he does not keep late hours. And that may be why he is enjoying such good health. Sometimes, he would sit up till late—if he has to, that is.

## Masato Otaka

In our group, Otaka-san is the second-eldest. He was born in 1923 as the son of an educator, in Fukushima, located some 200 kilometers northeast of Tokyo. Generally, people born in northern Japan are considered to be of the stolid type. Otaka-san is no exception. His "stolid" characteristics can be detected in some of his works. Otaka-san is considered to have the most "stability" in our group. Even Noboru Kawazoe-san, who is of the patient type, says, "Sometimes, I have to spend several months before I can convince him of just one particular thing." I do not know anyone in our group who reminds me of "earth" more vividly than Otaka-san. He is a silent man and strives steadily towards his goals. He is dependable and full of humanity. He would tackle a problem in a slow but steady way, investing much time and effort in exploring all the fundamentals of the problem.

During the last several years, Otaka-san has been active as organizer of a designers' group for the establishment of agricultural cooperative buildings in farming areas. And yet, the sphere of Otaka-san's activities is not confined to rural Japan. He was in charge of conducting experiments on the "artificial ground formula" under a program designed to improve the poor soil of Sakaide City.

## Kiyonori Kikutake

Kikutake-san is well known not only in Japan but also on an international scale. With his "futuristic" proposals of "marine cities," Kikutake-san is known in architectural and non-architectural fields alike.

He was born in 1928 in a good family in Kurume in Kyushu, Japan's southernmost island. In 1953, he became independent and opened his own office at the age of 26. He thus became an independent architect before anybody else in the Metabolism group. Besides his architectural creations, Kikutake-san has exerted equally ambitious efforts in design theory of *ka* (Image)—*kata* (Function)—*katachi* (Form) and other theories on original architectural concepts. He may appear as a gentleman with drastic proposals but he is a man of unique sensibility which he fully expresses in his works and plans.

His ancestors lived in an area where the ruling Himiko clan was the first such clan to be recorded in literature even before the beginning of ancient Japan. He was raised under rigid family discipline. He is an enthusiastic participant in discussions on Metabolism and is always anxious to verify the results of discussions. Kikutake-san is especially interested in traditional things, probably because he comes from a history-conscious region of Kyushu. From the point of view of behavior, Kikutake-san in all respects resembles Kenzo Tange-san. Undoubtedly, he is a gentleman by international standards.

# On the Land,
# on the Sea, in the Air
# The repertoire
# of Metabolism

**"Our group has been making steady achievements ...
which have an important intangible strength.
You may call them ideas that manipulate space."**

Takashi Asada, "My Colleagues
of the Metabolist Group," 1965.

In the afterglow of the World Design Conference, the Metabolists start receiving more and more attention for their ambitious proposals and more and more commissions for built projects—but as individuals rather than as a group. In the maelstrom, the second book of Metabolism, promised on the first page of *Metabolism 1960*, does not appear despite multiple attempts. But the members of Metabolism though continue to convene and collaborate—either in small alliances or as a full team—on pivotal occasions: for an exhibition in Tokyo in 1962 (also featuring Tange), a UN competition for Lima in 1969, Expo '70, and Tsukuba Science Expo '85, where they set up their own company.

In the dialectic between the Metabolists as a group and the architects as individuals, it is easy to lose track of how systematic their research in the end became. The Metabolists' physical and conceptual output is so massive and so diverse that a thorough inventory is necessary in order to understand its strategies and its evolution. Here, we build a typology and timeline of Metabolism's inventions and neologisms: the repertoire with which they wanted to rebuild Japan. From the capsule to artificial ground, from modular growth to Group Form, floating cities to the joint core and forest-like megastructures, the Metabolists create a host of new concepts, and new territories—on the land, on the sea, in the air—on which to build them.

The basic unit of Metabolism, the capsule, has myriad origins in Japan: national archetypes in the form of *kago* "mobile chairs" (cited by Kurokawa) and the tea hut (Ekuan); Kurokawa's study of prefabricated housing in the late 1950s; a modern obsession with mobility in the form of jets and cars; and the severe pressure on urban space (in 1967, the average family of 4 people lives in only 2.9 rooms). In 1969, after two decades of development by the Metabolists, Kurokawa pens the "Capsule Declaration": "The capsule stands for an emancipation of the building in relation to the ground and heralds the era of moving architecture…"

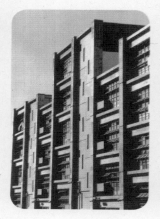

1953

1956

1962

### Phone booth
Ekuan
Possibly the first con-
sciously-designed capsule,
Ekuan's phone booth NTT
(Nippon Telegraph and
Telephone Corporation)
becomes ubiquitous
throughout Japan.

### Tonogaya Apartments
Kikutake
Kikutake cites the shoe
boxes fixed to the outside
of each window—an im-
provised solution to a lack
of space—as a prototype
of his version of the
capsule: the move-net.

### Move-net for Sky House
Kikutake
With the arrival of children, Kikutake hangs
the first of three move-nets to the underside
of his Sky House; they are removed when
the children outgrow them.

1962

1962

## Plastic Ski Lodge
### Ekuan

"If we accept the notion that the tea house was made using the most advanced contemporary technology," Ekuan writes, "the true tea house of today may be the camping vehicle or even the interior of the passenger automobile." The portable capsule ski lodge, loaded on the back of a truck and deposited on a mountain, sleeps four pioneers.

## Box-Type Apartments
### Kurokawa

Kurokawa's first capsule, his Box-Type Apartments, grows out of his 1958 visit to prefab housing factories in Leningrad and Moscow and the book *Prefabricated House*, which he writes with Kawazoe in 1960. The Box-Type Apartments consist of four kinds of capsules; occupants personalize the configuration according to taste and the growth/shrinkage of their family.

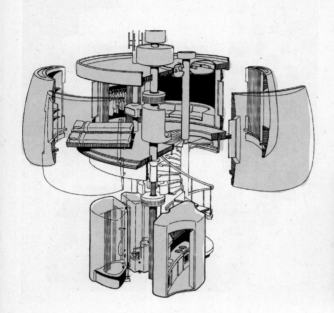

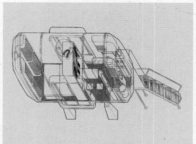

Interior of one half of a Hermit Crab.

1964

1969

## Pumpkin House
Ekuan

Designed, initially, for a couple, the Pumpkin House has capsules ("organs") that swivel around a core ("skeleton"). A room can be added when the couple has a child.

## Yadokari Hermit Crab Capsule Lodge
Ekuan

A mobile capsule perched, for the moment, on top of a hill. Like the Ski Lodge, it is designed to be moved around by truck.

Capsule road trip.

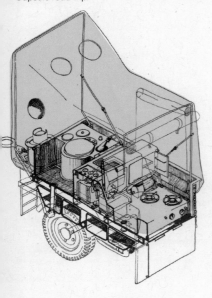

|1970|1972|

## Moving Capsule
**Kurokawa**

In *Casabella*, Kurokawa unveils a jeep and trailer equipped with kitchen and toilet precariously adjacent. An erectable canvas roof creates shelter for the homo moven / camper. "Enjoy your own handmade instant house, which brings you the stars, the sun, the river, and the trees," Kurokawa implores. The moving capsule, towed around by jeep, recalls a critical moment in Kurokawa's youth, when he witnessed a convoy of American jeeps and felt the overwhelming material substance and undeniable strength of the American culture."

## Capsule Summer House K
**Kurokawa**

Kurokawa's own summer vacation house (even though he claims he hasn't taken a vacation since 1964), on a hillside near the wealthy holiday resort of Karuizawa, Nagano Prefecture. Even in the countryside, without pressure on space, discipline is maintained: the four capsules have the standardized dimensions of the Nakagin Capsule Tower in Tokyo. One of them is a reconstruction of a tea room designed by early 17th-century artist Kobori Enshu. Kurokawa intends to change the configuration of the capsules over time.

Metabolism develops a deeply ambivalent attitude towards Japan's ground, which is usually too densely populated, expensive, mountainous, flood-prone, beautiful, or seismically unstable to build on. So the Metabolists conceive "artificial ground" structures that hover over the ground on platforms or pilotis, still in a close relation with the topography even in its attempts at defiance, and occasionally lunging upwards, desperate for liberation. Kawazoe writes: "The very difficulty of obtaining land is actually unfolding a new possibility for housing…"

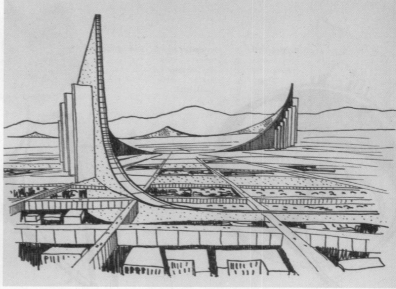

1958

1959

## Sky House
Kikutake

For his own family to inhabit, Kikutake builds artificial ground on a small scale. The dispossessed landowner claims his land again, this time perching on stilts 6.6 meters above the tainted surface of Japan.

## Wall City
Kurokawa

Repudiating the Corbusian doctrine of urban life in the Athens Charter (1943), which demanded separate areas to live, work, play, and travel, Kurokawa proposes integrating all city functions into a continuous ground-hugging wall, sometimes lurching up into a skyscraper before curving back down into an elevated city grid. Mobility is paramount: the wall features conveyor belts and monorail; plug-in housing units can also be moved.

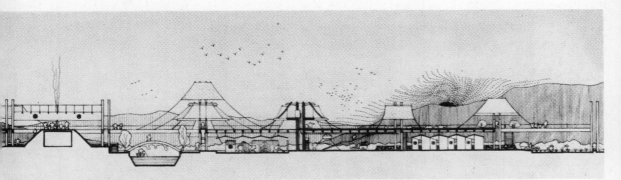

Agricultural City, with protruding Mushroom Houses.

1960

1960

## Agricultural City
Kurokawa

"The Ise Bay typhoon (1959) destroyed many villages in the Amagun region in Aichi Prefecture, and I happened to be in one of them," Kurokawa writes. "I witnessed an almost evenly distributed grid of thatched roofs above the vast sea of mud water covering paddy fields. It was an odd scene." The result of his experience is Agricultural City: a grid system on stilts raised four meters over flood-prone fields, allowing agriculture and communal life to exist, safely and unimpeded on two separate datum.

## Mushroom House
Kurokawa

"Mushroom Houses" (aka the K Residence) sprout from the ground and poke through the frame of Agricultural City. "Architecture, which hitherto was inseparable from the earth," Kurokawa writes, "is separating itself from it by expanding towards the universe." Kawazoe explains the origin of the mushroom form: "Standing on the rice paddy field, anyone is drawn to a deep sense of solitude. Kurokawa wrapped a house with something neither roof nor wall, so that the landscape is shuttered off and the sight line is guided to the ground. The tea room attached to the core underneath the living space, on the contrary, expands the view."

**1960**

**1964**

**1967**

## World Health Organization
Tange

For his (unsuccessful) competition entry for the WHO headquarters in Geneva, Tange employs the A-frame as a means of creating levels of artificial ground overlooking an interior plaza where people "can communicate visually and mentally."

## Tortoise House
Ekuan

Composed of repeatable orthogonal units—a filled-out space frame—facilitating future growth, Ekuan's tortoise both crawls along the ground and reaches up...

## Central Lodge
Kurokawa

Kurokawa gets to build a Mushroom House, as a "Central Lodge" in Kodomo-no-kuni (Children's land), Yokahama, masterplanned by Takashi Asada.

Section: urban platform on pilotis.

1967          1968

## Kodomo-no-kuni
### Kikutake

Asada, heading Artificial Land Subcommittee at the Architectural Institute of Japan, also commissions Kikutake for Children's Land. He builds a colony of diamond-shaped buildings—for summer school classes—demonstrating a way to inhabit Japan's hilly topography…

## Sakaide Artificial Ground
### Otaka

With Sakaide's tradition of salt production in decline and former farmers now living in slum conditions, Otaka attempts liberation from the chaotic, degraded urban plan by creating a housing complex on an urban platform raised six–nine meters. The platform stages social housing; below the platform, parking and shops. Otaka says: "Artificial ground is a means to create an artificial nature, using reinforced concrete. If carefully applied, reinforced concrete can last for more than 200 years, which allows us to use it just like natural ground. Artificial ground should be supplied to people for a very reasonable price as it should be built by infrastructural companies (gas, water, etc.). Artificial ground is ... an alternative means of creating new land without reclaiming the sea." The project grows in three more phases; the last is completed in 1986.

1969

1970

### Device Plaza
Ekuan

Artificial ground meets prefab: a readymade elevated transportation node, made in collaboration with Sumitomo Metal Industries, to be placed over any pinch point in any of Japan's growing cities. Ekuan's prototype is probably intended to play a role in the Second Comprehensive National Redevelopment Plan, launched by Atsushi Shimokobe in the same year.

### Main Gate, Expo '70
Otaka

A realized version of Ekuan's elevated plaza, Otaka's artificial ground straddles the new highway, connects Expoland in the south with the main Expo site, and links the train from Osaka with the entrance to Festival Plaza. At peak times, 48,000 people pass through the gate every hour.

**1972**

## tratiform Structure Module
ikutake

ikutake begins 20 years of research into the Stratiform
tructure Module, an A-frame megastructure accom-
nodating individual, varied houses. He envisions
tratiforms perching everywhere over the precarious
round of the Japanese Archipelago. Kikutake writes:
The A-frame structure, made of steel tubes, supports
ayers of artificial ground made of pre-stressed
oncrete slabs. The module would make it possible
o build on 'impossible' areas such as weak ground
r create ground over congested urban areas or
xisting roads or railways."

Since the precarious ground and its rules cannot be conquered, Metabolism spawns a series of buildings, megastructures, and even cities that instead find ways of adapting/submitting to their hostile host in a kind of desperate symbiosis: adding modules to answer unpredictable economic needs, creeping across impossible terrain in exponentially growing frameworks, even disappearing and reappearing on demand…

Linear City growing over Japan.

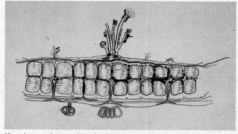

Kurokawa draws the city in a moment of organic growth.

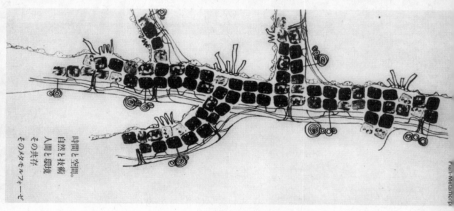

時間と空間。
自然と技術。
人間と環境。
その共存。
そのメタモルフォーゼ

1963

1965

### Nitto Food Cannery
Kurokawa

The factory, a purely functional space driven by economics, proves an apt typology for Metabolist principles of growth. Built in eight square modules, corner trusses are equipped with extruding steel flaps, standing ready to plug into new modules as required.

### Linear City: Metamorphosis
Kurokawa

Now projecting on a national scale, Kurokawa proposes the Linear City, growing like strings of bacteria, free from dependence on a choked urban center. Thin urban corridors consisting of repeated modules would efficiently transfer information, people, and products around a new network of cities stretching across the Japanese Archipelago. Kurokawa writes: "The concentric expansion of large cities has reached the limit of structural growth … In the linear city, nature and urban life exist in parallel; there is no city center and there is considerable growth potential." Kurokawa develops the idea while working on Plan for Tokyo at Tange Lab, drawing on his early research into road and street systems, which form, here, the boundary of each replicating cell / city block.

Single cell, realized.

Odakyu Drive-in Restaurant,
completed as single unit.

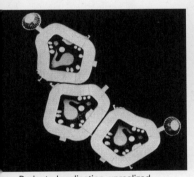

Projected replication, unrealized.

**1967**

Desired growth.

**1969**

## Yamagata Hawaii Dreamland
### Kurokawa

A holiday resort for the modern Japanese pilgrim, traveling for leisure rather than religion. The cell-shaped building encloses a swimming pool and recreation space—a process of "emwomb-ment" that, for Kurokawa, means bringing nature, and the public, within architecture. Kurokawa completes one cell, but it fails to multiply as planned.

## Odakyu Drive-in Restaurant
### Kurokawa

A year before his realizations at Expo '70, Kurokawa combines capsule and space frame on a small scale for a US-style roadside diner in the resort of Hakone, between Shizuoka and Kanagawa Prefectures. It is intended as a prototype for a larger, ground-hugging, capsule-holding space frame. Kurokawa writes: "Unlike those supported with columns, like Wachsmann's aircraft hanger, a space frame sitting on the ground can be extremely versatile as an urban structure, using prefabricated extension joints that allow for metabolism."

1970

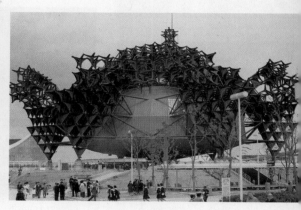

1970

## Takara Beautillion, Expo '70
Kurokawa

A cubic space frame made from over 200 prefabricated, six-pointed curved crosses. The capsules that plug into the system are designed to fit in standard trucks for easy transportation. Construction—a process merely of assembly and plugging-in—takes six days. The capsules function as interior showrooms, designed by Ekuan. As with the Odakyu structure, further growth is projected (and implied by the extrusions that are left ostentatiously "incomplete," as if caught in the process of replication), but not achieved.

## Toshiba IHI pavilion, Expo '70
Kurokawa

A sculptural space frame consisting of 1,444 tetrahedral units arranged with extravagant complexity, like a rampant cellular organism. Extrusions point towards expansion; erasure is also foreseen: Kurokawa embraces the idea of the immediate dismantling and recycling of the structure...

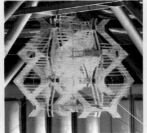
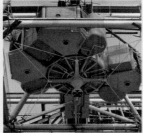

1970

**Big Roof, Tange et al, Expo '70**
One of the largest space frames ever built—292 meters long, 30 meters high, and 108 meters across—and with only six supporting beams, Tange's structure creates a huge plaza underneath and a structure in which capsules can be plugged above...

**Mid-Air Exhibition Expo '70**
Awazu
The graphic designer turns architect, creating an egg-like glass capsule.

**Golgi Structures Mid-Air Exhibition Expo '70**
Maki
Maki models his Golgi Structures concept from 1968, itself a framework in which capsules can be plugged, emphasizing connectivity as the structuring agent for the future city.

**Capsule for Living Mid-Air Exhibition Expo '70**
Kurokawa
Kurokawa's first proto-type for mass produced residential capsules. One of them is fur-lined.

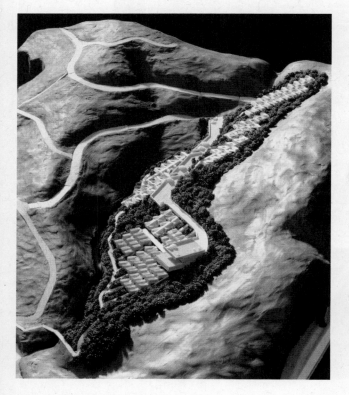

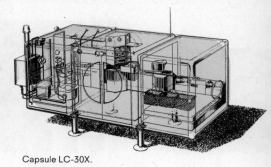

Capsule LC-30X.

1972

## Capsule Village
Kurokawa

A vacation colony of "leisure" capsules embedded in scaffolding—in order to protect plant life on the ground—creeping over a hillside in Usami, a weekend retreat southwest of Tokyo.

Instant city during the Hajj.

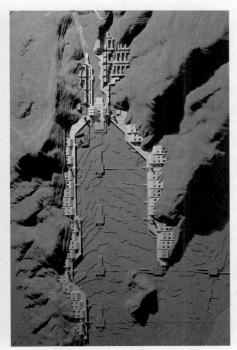

Post-Hajj, the city is stored away.

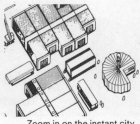

Zoom in on the instant city.

**1974**

## Mina (Muna) Pilgrim City, Mecca

ange with Ekuan

n a valley in Mina (Muna), the midpoint on the
nnual Hajj, a temporary city would be erected each
ear to accommodate pilgrims. When the Hajj is over,
n order to preserve the emptiness of the sacred
round, all equipment would be removed and stored
t the foot of the surrounding hills. Ekuan: "It was
n instant city indeed, made of Metabolic tools."

As an internal critique of the all-over aesthetic of some Metabolist projects, specifically megastructures, Maki and Otaka propose a flexible form of urban planning that can deal with the "amazingly heterogeneous" and rapidly transforming contemporary city: Group Form. Drawing on the ancient and the unplanned, Group Form anticipates a lessening of overall control in urbanism—and prefigures, weirdly, the actual unfinished aesthetic of many 21st-century masterplans initiated by developers. In Group Form, each element has an organic interdependence; incompleteness, the bugbear of modern masterplans, does not preclude a coherent overall image. Maki writes: "Cities, towns, and villages throughout the world do not lack in rich collections of collective form. Most of them have, however, simply evolved: they have not been designed."

1960

1964

### Shinjuku Project
Maki and Otaka

The first iteration of Group Form, containing a shopping city, offices, and entertainment centers on a platform of artificial ground over Shinkuku station. The entertainment centers are in the shape of a flower. If one "petal" is missing, they write, it does not effect the overall form of the flower—the essence of Group Form.

### K-Project
Maki

For a disused railyard in central Tokyo, Maki proposes "a complex of buildings, which consists of medium- and small-size stores, a terminal for local and express buses, a wholesale department store (one like the Merchandise Mart in Chicago), and education and social facilities." The main level would be lifted—introducing artificial ground as a protection against flooding. Maki calls the concept Master Form, "providing certain flexibility" while adhering to an overall vision.

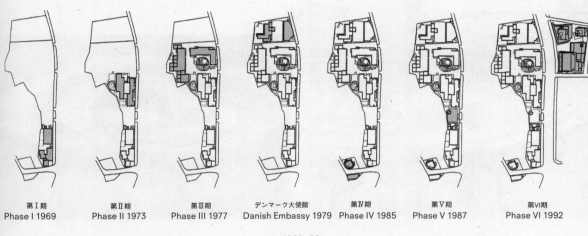

| 第Ⅰ期 | 第Ⅱ期 | 第Ⅲ期 | デンマーク大使館 | 第Ⅳ期 | 第Ⅴ期 | 第Ⅵ期 |
|---|---|---|---|---|---|---|
| Phase I 1969 | Phase II 1973 | Phase III 1977 | Danish Embassy 1979 | Phase IV 1985 | Phase V 1987 | Phase VI 1992 |

**1969–92**

## Hillside Terrace
### Maki

A forested, sloping tract of land owned by one family, the Asakuras, and containing only a few small wooden houses, stands in the path of the growth of Daikanyama, a fashionable district of Tokyo. In 1962 the Asakuras commission Maki to make a very long-term plan for developing the neighborhood so they can retain control of it. Maki begins building Hillside Terrace, an agglomeration of buildings arranged carefully over 23 years—the opposite of an instant city. As its own urban condition embracing and not rejecting the surrounding conditions, Hillside Terrace, which remains steadfastly low-rise, is also the opposite to the audacity of Metabolism's megastructures, looming over and implicitly condemning the city. Ironically, Group Form, a theoretically organic system of growth, is achieved in Hillside Terrace not through spontaneity, improvisation, and heterogeneity but through sensitive long-term planning, made possible by the singular ownership of the land.

"It is worth noting that Group Form evolves from the people of a society, rather than from their powerful leadership. It is the village, the dwelling group, and the bazaar which are Group Forms ... not the palace complex, which is compositional in character."

Maki, *Investigations in Collective Form*, 1964.

Through an alchemy of ambition and technology, Metabolism transforms what was previously felt as a limitation—Japan's islandness—into an opportunity. The Metabolists—especially Kikutake, who could be called monomaniacally devoted to marine architecture if it wasn't for a string of parallel obsessions on the land—plan to overlay artificial ground on water through a combination of reclamation, piers, platforms, floating megastructures, and floating islands. The drive is part utopian, part dystopian. Kikutake writes in *Metabolism 1960*: "… The civilization of continents has accumulated bloody struggles in human relations established within the limited land … a history of endless internecine war … The sea is waiting for a new discovery which will promise true happiness for human beings …"

1958

1959

### Marine City
Kikutake

After seeing the massive reclamation work underway on Yokkaichi's coastline in order to accommodate the sprawl of heavy industry, Kikutake feels the need to present an alternative proposal to protect the precious coastline. In *Metabolism 1960*, he explains Marine City as a response to human civilization's recurring crises, "ordained when man occupied, then clung to and expected too much from the land." Marine City, rendered here as a techno-romantic megastructure, floats free from the pressures of overpopulation on the land...

### Ocean City: Unabara
Kikutake

A new floating city for 500,000, published in *Metabolism 1960*, Unabara (meaning "ocean field") is mobile, and will cruise Japan's Pacific coast. When the city needs to grow, it will divide itself in the manner of self-replicating cells. In the center of two rings—the inner ring for housing, the outer ring for industry—a central control tower, 500 meters tall and plunging 1,000 meters beneath the sea, acts as Unabara's nucleus.

Koto Ward is replaced by a grid of piers that reaches out into Tokyo Bay.

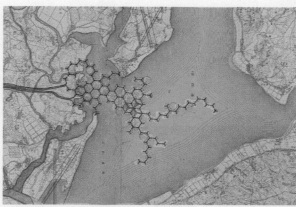

Helix Structures on Lake Kasumigaura.

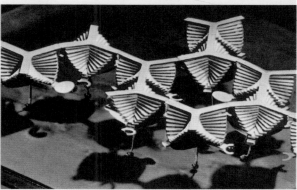

1961

1961

## isaster Prevention City
### ikutake

ocusing on a specific and land-based crisis, ikutake the frustrated landlord seeks to protect he Koto Ward of Tokyo (known as the "zero-meter rea") from persistent flooding through the onstruction of an elevated urban grid on six-meter- igh stilts. Each block measures 200 x 200 meters nd is capable of holding 20-story buildings.

## Floating City Kasumigaura
### Kurokawa

Kurokawa decides that his Helix Structures, original-ly designed as megastructures for Tokyo, can also float. As a counterproposal to the development going on around Kasumigaura, a lake northeast of the capital, he proposes his floating Helixes as an ideal settlement integrating modern living with nature. In 1964, Kurokawa presents his Helix in a short documentary, and the idea "is studied by the Government," according to the *Japan Times*.

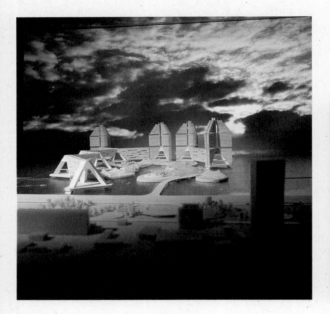

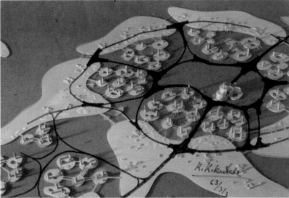

1963

1963

### Shallow Sea-Type Community
Kikutake

High-rise apartments that would balance on the periphery of Tokyo Bay using a "soft-landing system": the megastructure relies on partial flotation to mitigate its weight on the seabed. Again, defense against natural disaster and sound ecological stewardship are uppermost in Kikutake's mind: he sees the project as a way to protect against earthquakes and to minimize the impact of developments on the shoreline (avoiding destructive reclamation schemes).

### Marine City
Kikutake

A floating archipelago conceived for the middle of the ocean, made up of "mother cities" and "small cities" connected by bridges. The internal island clusters are residential, with large outer islands serving as wave buffers and accommodating industry. Towers are in various stages of growth. When one island becomes too old and unsuitable for living, it is dragged away and sunk. Kikutake draws communication and transportation networks over the model photo.

**1968**

**1969**

## Ocean City
### Kikutake

...owers are connected above and below
the water, eliminating the need for a
floating platform; now, rather than artificial ground, there is no ground at all.
Inspired by American naval technology,
the tower becomes a vertical submarine,
its nose poking above the water but its
main operations taking place beneath
the surface.

## Floating Factory: Metabonat
### Kurokawa

Commissioned by the newspaper *Asahi Shimbun* for a New Year's
Day supplement in 1970, Kurokawa makes a model of the floating
factories that will, he believes, have to accompany the floating
cities of the future. "Mankind was born in the oceans," he writes,
"and will have to return there." Metabonat is made up of square
floating modules to accommodate the expansion and replacement of factories. The name comes from the Soviet term *Kombinat*,
meaning a "state-planned industrial zone." Kombinat is already
commonly used in Japan to mean industrial complex—which are
usually located on the coast. Kurokawa metabolizes the Soviet/
Japanese concept, putting industry out to sea...

1971

1975

## Marine City, Hawaii
Kikutake

A collaboration with Professor Craven at the Department of Marine Programs at Hawaii University, where Kikutake is a visiting professor. The Hawaii Marine City would be located five kilometers from Waikiki beach, and would contain an exhibition plaza, hotel, and university.

## Aquapolis, Okinawa Ocean Expo '75
Kikutake

After nearly 20 years of research into marine cities, Kikutake finally gets to build a real one: the Aquapolis, a 100 x 100-meter floating city block resembling an oil rig or an aircraft carrier. In plans, Kikutake draws elaborate programs for the roof; in the end, it is left empty except for lawns and a helipad. The Aquapolis is the centerpiece of the Okinawa Ocean Expo '75, celebrating the handover of the the Okinaw islands from the United States to Japan in 1972. On a conveyor belt, visitors move around an exhibition exploring what a life at sea will look like. Eika Takayam. (veteran masterplanner of Datong) and co-master-planner Takashi Asada support the realization of Aquapolis.

1975

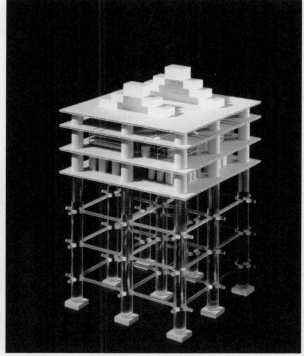

1983

## IC
### ikutake

collaboration of Kikutake, Ishikawajima-Harima
eavy Industry (IHI, who, with Toshiba, commissions
urokawa to design their pavilion at Expo '70), and
he Japan Long-Term Credit Bank, the KIC is part
hip, part architecture, plugging into Japan's harbors.
gain, it is a preparation for catastrophe: the KICs
an stock supplies and house the homeless after
oods or earthquakes.

## IT Aquapolis
### Kikutake

A floating city designed to house no less than one
million people on a rig of 25 square kilometers; architecture on a tectonic scale. Kikutake's lifelong obsession with living at sea suddenly coincides with a new
international maritime law expanding every nation's
territory 200 miles into its surrounding sea; gifting
Japan new territory to exploit in new ways...

As well as land and sea, Metabolism attempts the colonization of the air.
The means to do it is through a reinvention of the core: as a stand-alone tower into which living units can be plugged, and, in the "joint core" model, as one of several trunks supporting the branches of a new urban system, straddling the mess of the existing city beneath it. While in Tange Lab, Isozaki develops the joint core concept for Plan for Tokyo 1960 as a "three-dimensional-space network": the cores are "vertical streets" and "the horizontal spaces connecting them are like the buildings along streets in a city." The urban plan rotates 90 degrees. At the same time, he develops his own private version for Shinjuku, and Kikutake writes in *Metabolism 1960*: "It is incorrect, to say that the most sure means to live is to cling on to the land."

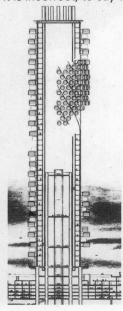

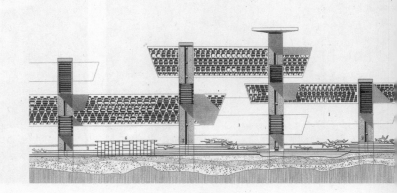

1958 | 1960

### Tower-Shaped Community
Kikutake

"A huge concrete cylinder will make a pleasant atmosphere in the neighbour-hood," Kikutake writes in *Metabolism 1960*. Up to 1,250 living units will be plugged into the central core like "leaves" on a tree (in pink here), providing living space for 5,000. Kikutake describes the moment when a new living unit is plugged into the core: "All ... inhabitants of the Tower and the people in the vicinity of the Tower will send their sincere and warmful congratulations for the starting of a new life of a fresh couple when they observe the lifting of new unit."

### Office buildings, Plan for Tokyo 1960
Tange and Isozaki

Along the central axis of a new city reaching over Tokyo Bay, 2.5 million people would work in megastructures made up of joint cores (yellow) and giant hovering slabs with massive spans, creating what Tange calls "columnless piloti" areas under the buildings. The joint cores have no urban mess below them to avoid; they are only for megastructural efficiency: artificial ground in the air, perched on a platform of artificial ground on the sea.

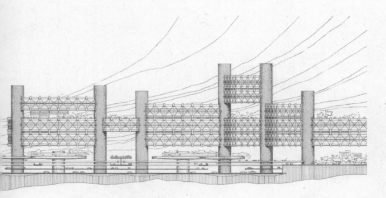

<table>
<tr><td>1960</td><td>1962</td></tr>
</table>

## City in the Air, Shinjuku
### Isozaki

Reaching over the chaotic Shinjuku station district of Tokyo, joint cores facilitate defiance of the existing urban (non) plan, potential for future growth, and practical architectural gain: floor plans uninterrupted by structural support. Isozaki writes: "[The] City in the Air grows with bridges spanning from column to column, which is the only element fixed to the ground." The scheme is a counterproposal to the redevelopment plan already underway in Shinjuku in the space liberated by the relocation of the Yodobashi Water Purification Plant.

## Ikebukuro Plan
### Kikutake

For the Ikebukuro district of Tokyo, which hosts a prison for war criminals (to be relocated in 1970) and has a regeneration plan already underway, Kikutake directly transplants one of the islands he is developing for his next Marine City. Here, the towers rest on massive podiums of artificial ground, and, in response to Tokyo's burgeoning population (which Kikutake researches himself), the towers preemptively break Tokyo's 31-meter height rule, which will be abolished in 1963.

1964

## Tsukiji Plan
Tange

For the Dentsu advertising firm, Tange proposes the urbanization of a building: a network of expandable structures, interconnected on multiple levels, with spans of 32 meters between joint cores and roads running underneath their liberated footprints. Design work begins in 1960, immediately after Plan for Tokyo, and is meant as a realization of its office megastructures, but this time over dry land. The petal form of one group of buildings echoes the "amusement square" in Maki and Otaka's plan for Shinjuku in *Metabolism 1960*.

Original state.

Growth, 1974.

1964

## amanashi Press and Broadcasting Center
ange

or a merger of newspaper, broadcasting, and printing
ompanies, Tange plans a three-dimensional building
etwork with "communications shafts" (joint cores)
ontaining human circulation and all mechanical systems.
he cores provide potential for future growth, which
ccurs in 1974 precisely as Tange envisions in the
60s, sprouting from the stubs of joint cores delib-
rately left unfinished in phase one.

1967

Expo '70

### Shizuoka Press and Broadcasting Center
Tange

A singular core next to the new elevated expressway in the dense downtown of Ginza—site of Japan's most expensive real estate—the tower stands alone, deprived of connections to a larger building system. Office space is attached to the core in stubs rather than fully-grown branches.

### Expo Tower
Kikutake

A denuded realization of the 1958 Tower-Shaped Community and the towers of the 1968 edition of Ocean City: a reduced budget (a result of inflation caused by Expo hype) means the core is only a space frame, and only a few capsules can be attached, 75 meters up, to serve as viewing areas over the Expo '70 site.

1972

1976

## Nakagin Capsule Tower
### Kurokawa

Two cores with 144 capsules plugged in, located near the nightlife district of Ginza, conceived as bolt holes for homo movens bachelors/commuters. All capsules are sold within a month of the building's completion: 30 percent to out-of-town companies looking for a cheap alternative to hotels for their salarymen; 30 percent to families seeking auxiliary studies or playrooms; 20 percent to bachelors; and the remaining 20 percent for miscellaneous uses. With their anonymity and convenience, the capsules seem to offer secret license within a rational, disciplined space. Kurokawa relishes the ambiguity. Capsules contain desk, color TV, telephone, tape deck, radio, and, in the bathroom, tub and toilet, all built into the architecture: a veritable control center in which appliances and architecture merge into one.

## Sony Tower
### Kurokawa

Showroom and offices for Sony, on the busiest intersection of Osaka. Like the Pompidou Center, then under construction (Kurokawa also entered the competition, but lost), pipes, elevators, and stairs are visible on the exterior. Capsules now play the role of appendages to more conventional office and showroom space. The site is sold and the building demolished in 2006.

**MEGAFOREST**

While the average building height in Tokyo is a paltry one and a quarter floors, the Metabolists envision forest-like megastructures that form a benevolent canopy over the squat city below. Composed of helixes, stacked tetrahedrons, branches, or cones, the megaforests create new categories of space: diagonal as well as vertical and horizontal, with the ability to reach across space onto neighboring "trees." Kikutake complains in *Metabolism 1960* that the Japanese still live in an age when "the buildings stand lower than the trees … It is time to separate from the horizontal city."

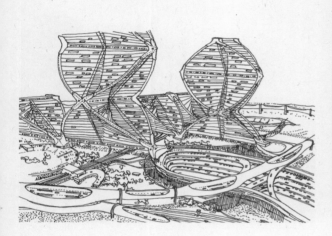

1961

1962

### Helix City
Kurokawa

Eight years after the double helix model of DNA is first published in *Nature* magazine, Kurokawa develops his Helix Structures, a modular system that can grow or shrink as required. Each spiral has the capacity for 10,000 people, and integrates various means of transportation into the structure. Kurokawa applies the concept to Tokyo, envisioning a new highway network linking numerous Helix Structures.

### Tetra Project
Kikutake

Inspired by the Pyramids, gothic churches, and Manhattan's skyscrapers, Kikutake proposes a structure capable of exploiting both vertical and horizontal space. Each "tetra" unit—which he wants to construct over the railyards of Shinagawa, Tokyo—is an expand- able artificial ground, 80 meters on each side, with 180–360 housing units clinging to the exterior. Kikutake writes: "Artificial ground so far has been a superimposition of additional horizontal layers over the ground and very much confined by the ground. This project takes off for a truly three-dimensional growth of the city."

1962

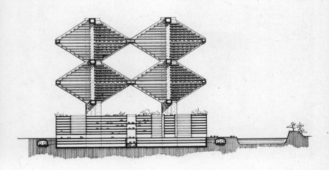

1963

## Clusters in the Air
### Isozaki

Isozaki proposes treelike linked structures that hover over the chaotic urban fabric of Shibuya. The shared cores are the "trunks," cantilevers "branches," and housing units "leaves." Inhabitation only begins at 31 meters: Isozaki takes the limit of the Tokyo's height law merely as a starting point for his plan.

## Marunouchi Project
### Isozaki

As a counterproposal to the redevelopment already underway, Isozaki designs structures that hover over the existing buildings in Tokyo's oldest and most authentic district, rather than destroying them: a forest of stacked tetrahedrons, 45 meters high, with multiple circulation routes.

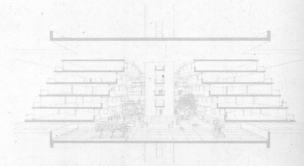

Child friendly: every fifth floor, an indoor park.

1964

1968

## Dwelling City
Ekuan

Ekuan escalates the scale of his ambitions from industrial design to megastructure. Each structure consists of two pyramids stacked bottom to bottom. Living units—capsules—are attached to the surface; the hollow area inside is designated as public space. The Dwelling City multiplies into clusters, forming cities within the city. Ekuan proposes the cluster for the flood-prone Koto district of Tokyo.

## Tree-shaped Community
Kikutake

Kikutake's version of the megaforest is motivated by children's welfare. Communities are organized into units of five terraced floors, which overlook an atrium with an internal park. The system is inspired by a report by Keiko Watanabe of the Building Research Institute in the Ministry of Construction. Her study finds that children living above the fifth floor in high-rises do not join other children playing in the park below; they just watch. So Kikutake creates a high-rise where, ostensibly, there are no floors above the fifth. Also: "This treelike housing is beautiful by itself, however ... several tens of towers together will appear like woods and forests and their appearance will be in harmony with nature."

1968

### olgi Structure
Maki

n exceptional project for Maki, who delves for once
to the techno/organic territory more familiar to his
etabolist colleagues. The Golgi Struture though
till carries Maki's characteristic concern with inter-
ependent entities and public space: it is a cluster
f stacked cones that accommodate capsules and,
ore importantly for Maki, shared space in between
em. The project is named after the Golgi Body, the
rganelle in plant and animal cells that processes
nd transports protein. The in-between, inside-outside
paces of the Golgi Structures let light in, facilitate
information transmission," and "allows real
xperience … participated in by many."

## References
### ON THE LAND / Capsule
GK Design Group et al., *GK Design 50 years 1952-2002* (Tokyo: Rikuyosha, 2002).

Kenji Ekuan, *Devoting Life to Design* (Tokyo: Shunjusha, 2009).

Kenji Ekuan, "My Metabolism: Past, Present and Future," *Approach Quarterly*, Takenaka Corporation, No.116, Winter 1991.

Kisho Kurokawa, *Metabolism in Architecture* (London: Studio Vista, 1977).

Kisho Kurokawa, "Oh! The law of cyborg," *SD*, March 1969.

Kisho N. Kurokawa, "Metamorphosis," *Casabella*, No.334, 1969.

Kisho Kurokawa, *Kurokawa Kisho no sekai* [The world of Kisho Kurokawa] (Toyko: Mainichi Shimbunsha, 1975).

Kisho Kurokawa, *Kisho Kurokawa Notes* (Tokyo: Dobun Shoin, 1994).

Kiyonori Kikutake and Satoru Kuji, "Move-net: till now and from here," *Kindai Kenchiku*, April 1960.

Masato Otaka and Noboru Kawazoe, eds., *Metabolism and the Metabolists* (Tokyo: Bijutsu Shuppansha, 2005).

"Japan: The Right Eye of Daruma," *Time*, February 10, 1967.

### Ground / Artificial Ground
*GK Design 50 years 1952-2002.*

Kenzo Tange Associates: 1946–1979 / *SD*, January 1980.

Kisho Kurokawa, "K Residence Plan," *Kindai Kenchiku*, April 1960.

Masato Otaka, "Group life: Artificial Land" (This will be your city), *Kindai Kenchiku*, November 1962.

Noboru Kawazoe, "Proposal: Let's liberate the ground," *Kindai Kenchiku*, April 1960.

Noboru Kawazoe et al., *Metabolism 1960* (Tokyo: Bijutsu Shuppansha, 1960).

Noboru Kawazoe, "Kisho Kurokawa," *Bijutsu Techo*, March 1961.

### Proliferation / Colonization
Kenzo Tange, *The Japan Architect*, 1985.

Kisho Kurokawa, "The architecture of the age of life principle," *The Japan Architect*, Summer 1995.

Kisho Kurokawa, "The method and realization of Metabolism," *Kenchiku Bunka*, November 1967.

Kisho Kurokawa, "Frame and Capsule," *Kenchiku Bunka*, January 1969.

Kurokawa, *Kisho Kurokawa Notes*.

Otaka and Kawazoe, eds., *Metabolism and the Metabolists*.

Kawazoe et al., *Metabolism 1960*.

*Official Report of the Japan World Exposition, Osaka, 1970* (Osaka: Commemorative Association for the Japan World Exposition 1970, 1972).

### Group Form
Fumihiko Maki, *Investigations in Collective Form* (St. Louis, Ill: Washington University, 1964).

Kawazoe et al., *Metabolism 1960*.

### ON THE SEA / Floating Cities
Kawazoe et al., *Metabolism 1960*.

Kiyonori Kikutake, *Megastructure* (Tokyo: Waseda Daigaku Shuppanbu, 1995).

Kiyonori Kikutake, *Kiyonori Kikutake: Concepts and Plans* (Tokyo: Bijutsu Shuppansha, 1978).

Takashi Asada, Eika Takayama, Kiyonori Kikutake, et al., "Having worked on the Okinawa Marine Expo," *SD*, August 1975.

Research Group for the Ocean Communications City, *Ocean Communications City 1985* (Tokyo: Sangyo Hochi Center, 1984).

Kurokawa, "The method and realization of Metabolism."
"City Planner Kurokawa Advocates Unusual Theory for Artificial Land," *The Japan Times*, January 28, 1965.

### IN THE AIR / Unicore / Joint Core
Arata Isozaki, "Structure: Shinjuku Plan" (This will be your city), *Kindai Kenchiku*, November 1962.

Kenzo Tange, *The Japan Architect*, October 1985.

Kenzo Tange Lab, "Plan for Tokyo," *The Japan Architect*, April 1961.

Kenzo Tange and Terunobu Fujimori, *Tange Kenzo* (Tokyo: Shinkenchikusha, 2002).

Kisho Kurokawa, *Metabolism in Architecture*.

### Megaforest
Fumihiko Maki, "The capsule is the king," *SD*, March 1969.

GA Architect 6: *Arata Isozaki: 1959–1978* (Tokyo: A.D.A. Edita, 1991).

Teiji Ito, "Moratorium and Invisibility," in David Stewart, ed., *Arata Isozaki: Architecture 1960–1990* (Los Angeles: Museum of Contemporary Art).

"Claiming to Mitsubishi Jisho," *Shukan Asahi*, February 1, 1963.

*GK Design 50 years 1952–2002.*

Kiyonori Kikutake & Architects, "Tetra Space—A scheme for vertical extension of a city," *Kindai Kenchiku*, October 1962.

Kiyonori Kikutake, *The Work of Kiyonori Kikutake 3: The Japanese House* (Tokyo: Kyuryudo, 1992).

Kurokawa, "Method and realization of Metabolism."

# Kisho Kurokawa 黒川紀章

**1934** born in Nagoya **1945** witnesses overnight destruction of Nagoya in US air raid **1957** graduates from Kyoto University and enters Tange Lab at Tokyo University graduate school **1958** visits Leningrad for International Conference of Architectural Students, then Moscow **1959** publishes New Tokyo Project: Human Type Plan in in *Kenchiku Bunka*; assigned by Tange to assist Asada and Kawazoe in organizing World Design Conference; joins Metabolism **1960** participates in World Design Conference and in "Visionary Architecture" exhibition at MoMA, New York; publishes first book, *Prefabricated House* **1961** proposes Helix City Plan for Tokyo **1962** sets up office in Tokyo; attends Team 10 meeting at Abbaye Royaumont, near Paris **1963** completes first commission: Nitto Food Cannery **1964** doctoral study at Tange Lab **1965** publishes *Homo Movens*; attends Team 10 meeting in Urbino **1967** publishes *Action Architecture*; joins Atsushi Shimokobe's study group for New Comprehensive National Development Plan; completes Yamagata Hawaii Dreamland **1969** establishes Institute for Social Engineering **1970** designs three pavilions at Expo '70; advisor to the Japanese National Railways **1972** Nakagin Capsule Tower; Capsule Summer House K; Capsule Village proposal; wins first international competition: Tanzania's new parliament and new capital **1973** interviews Prime Minister Kakuei Tanaka on NHK national television; masterplans for Vasto and San Salvo, Italy **1974–91** regular NHK commentator **1976** Capsule Tower, Osaka **1977** National Museum of Ethnology, Osaka; joins Central Council at Ministry of Education and the political-business-academic Liberal Society Study Group **1979** becomes advisor to Prime Minister Ohira; chairman, International Design Conference, Aspen; begins As-Sarir New Town, Libya **1985** designs five pavilions for Tsukuba Expo **1986** appointed lifetime visiting professor, Tsinghua University, Beijing **1987** New Tokyo Plan 2025; Richard Neutra Award **1988** Hiroshima City Museum of Contemporary Art **1991** publishes *Philosophy of Symbiosis* **1998** Kuala Lumpur International Airport; Astana masterplan, Kazakhstan; new wing, Van Gogh Museum, Amsterdam **2006** wins competition for new soccer stadium in St. Petersburg; publishes 100th book, *Revolution of City* **2007** residents vote to demolish Nakagin Capsule Tower; retrospective at Tokyo National Art Center, which he designed; runs for governor of Tokyo and for the Diet's Upper House as leader of his own Symbiosis Party; dies at age 73

**"Architects were living in such a small world and I thought this was foolish..."**

Twenty-six years old when Metabolism began, Kisho Kurokawa was the youngest, most precocious, and most photogenic member of the group, and would soon become the most prolific. Three revelations in the space of two years— post-graduate study at Tange Lab, disillusion after a visit to the USSR in 1958, and the collapse of CIAM and its static modern vision—turned Kurokawa into perhaps the exemplary Metabolist.

Witnessing the firebombing of Japan's cities in World War II was also fundamental: it made devastatingly clear to Kurokawa the impermanence of architecture. In our interview, Kurokawa insists that this apparently modern revelation—and a trigger for Metabolism—is actually a seamless continuation of Buddhist thought and Shinto Japanese tradition, evident in the reconstruction of Ise Shrine every 20 years since the seventh century.

Kurokawa started his own office in 1962, and through a series of unsolicited proposals and radical realizations in the '60s and '70s, he pioneered key Metabolist concepts: prefab, the capsule, cellular growth, biological metaphors for urban planning on a national scale...

In the run up to Expo '70, Kurokawa's metamorphosis from architect (only) into media icon and political player accelerated. With the establishment of his Institute for Social Engineering in 1969, he transcended architecture altogether to research politics, economics, science, and demographics, producing hundreds of reports for various government ministries and agencies over the years. Simultaneously, he pushed his ideas as a commentator on NHK TV from 1974–91.

In 2007, his last year of life, Kurokawa ran first for the governorship of Tokyo and then for a seat in the Diet; neither campaign was successful. The relentless rhetoric and flamboyance and the excessive production for which he was later criticized was all of a piece with his serious intentions as a public intellectual, a de facto government advisor, an author of, he claimed, 100 books, and a prolific builder inside and outside Japan. Everything was part of Project Kurokawa.

K-Systems and Kisho Kurokawa's home,
Akasaka, Tokyo, September 10, 2005

Kurokawa, often misunderstood...

**1958** Kurokawa, a 24-year-old student in Tange Lab, represents Japan at the Fifth International Conference of Architectural Students in Leningrad. On his first foreign mission, he instantly has the aura of a star—a status that, in Japan, he has to work harder to cultivate…

Behind the façade, Kurokawa suffers a crisis of faith in communism, searching the city for new examples of Constructivism, but finding only Stalin's legacy.

Mobbed at the Hermitage. Afterwards, he visits the city's first prefab-housing factory making *Khruschevkas*, inspiration or his next venture…

**International Conference of Architectural Students**
...aturing 130 students from ...countries; Oscar Niemeyer ...nds a greeting from the ...ost-complete Brasilia. ...e students' program in ...ningrad includes a visit ...a prefabricated-housing ...ctory, inspiring post-dinner ...cussions. (Kurokawa, ...eport on the 5th Interna-...nal Conference of ...chitectural Students," ...Tange Lab, 1958).

**...t-wing movement**
...rokawa's group was left ...ng and agitated for social ...tice, but did not belong ...the far left Zengakuren ...dent movement.

**...oscow**
...er Leningrad, the UIA ...ngress in Moscow ...thered attendants from ...re than 50 countries. In ...oscow, Kurokawa visits ...re prefab factories, which ...pires his first book ...efabricated House in 1960. ...oshi Dezain [Urban design], ...kyo: Kinokuniya Shoten, ...65.)

**...AM collapsed**
...e Congrès Internationaux ...Architecture Moderne ...arted in 1928 and collapsed ...1959 with the creation of ...am 10. See p. 126.

**...anifesto**
...agine—he was just a ...aduate student who sud-...nly found himself among ...ures like Otaka, already ...espected partner of Kunio ...aekawa, and Kikutake, ...ising star thanks to his ...y House. This "manifesto" ...uld have been his attempt ...push himself forward. ...e best he could do at that ...he was to write and draw ...anifestos.
...ajime Yatsuka

**REM KOOLHAAS** What we're trying to do is not so much reconstruct the history of Metabolism, but to understand how a Metabolist like you now thinks of Metabolism in retrospect. So far the interviews have really surprised us.

**HANS ULRICH OBRIST** One thing that came out on numerous occasions was that you were by far the youngest member of the group. Everyone seems to mention that you'd been to Moscow in 1958, two years before the World Design Conference. How did that Moscow trip happen? Were you invited? Was it a research trip?

**KISHO KUROKAWA** I was invited to Leningrad to attend the International Conference of Architectural Students as chairman of the Japanese group. This was during the left-wing movement among Japan's students. One of the groups I admired most was the Constructivist avant-garde, so while there I tried to find out what had happened since the early 20th century, and whether anyone was continuing in that line. Unfortunately I found nothing. But I met Nikita Khrushchev along with several students and the chairman of the Youth Committee, and we had a heated discussion.

**RK** About what? Do you remember?

**KK** When interviewed by Moscow television, I criticized Stalinist design ideas and Socialist Realism, which we saw in Moscow University and also in the subway stations, where they copied imperial-period decoration from before the revolution. What I saw was very strange to me, so different from the Russian avant-garde of Leonidov, Tatlin, and Mayakovsky. I was really disappointed, and that's why I came back to Japan. You know, Khrushchev tried to reassess the avant-garde movement, including modernism, as part of his Thaw policy.

**RK** He tried to reinstate it?

**KK** Yes, Khrushchev himself tried. After Stalin, he invited foreign architects and students to Moscow, even European architects. But he soon changed his mind and opposed modernism. Picasso was a member of the Communist Party, but when a Picasso exhibition was held in Moscow, Khrushchev was very critical.

**RK** He turned against it?

**KK** Yes, he said Picasso's art could have been painted by a donkey with his tail. Khrushchev went back to Socialist Realism in art and architecture.

### Two Collapses

**HUO** What was your relationship to Marxism? There are traces of Marxism throughout the Metabolist literature.

**KK** Well, I myself was an activist student at Kyoto University, but after 1958 I was completely disappointed with Communism. I changed my mind.

**RK** Does that mean that there was no Marxist component in Metabolism at all?

**KK** None at all. And the next year, CIAM collapsed. It was a great shock for me.

**RK** So two collapses in a very short space of time.

**KK** CIAM and the Bauhaus were great "texts" for us, so I couldn't understand what was happening, what went wrong with modernist theory. In 1959 I wrote a short polemic about how we were now facing a paradigm shift from the CIAM move-ment to another stage, but what was it to be?

**RK** How did you phrase it? Because the term "paradigm shift" wasn't yet...

**KK** The title was From the Machine Age to the Life Age. Or more precisely, a shift away from mechanical principles towards living principles.

**HUO** Did you consider it a manifesto?

**KK** Yes, it was a manifesto.

**HUO** We're very curious about the notion of a manifesto. Manifestos have become rare in the world of art and architecture in the last 10 to 20 years. Obviously, Metabolism being a movement, one can see Metabolism 1960 as a kind of collective manifesto.

**1962** Kurokawa, 28, on the road again: at the Team 10 meeting at l'Abbaye Royaumont, near Paris, he presents Box Type Apartments, a Japanese take on prefab and a way to bring architecture "closer to a changing form." His audience includes Christopher Alexander and James Stirling. Team 10 meetings are "so thorough and tough, it was like being attacked by a lynch mob… But it was good discipline for me."[1]

Adaptation: with a plug-in system and changeable configuration, Kurokawa sees Box Type Apartments as a modern echo of Katsura Detached Palace (ca. 1620), always changing and always "perfect." The Box Type project is initiated by the Nippon Prefabrication housing company, to which Kurokawa, Otaka, and Kikutake are technical consultants.

Prefab mentor: on the same trip, Kurokawa meets Jean Prouvé at one of the houses he designed.

## This is Metabolism!

**KK** In 1958 we didn't know each other. I knew the name of Kiyonori Kikutake, and Fumihiko Maki was in the United States. I was writing books, trying to understand the paradigm shift at that moment. Then I was invited by Takashi Asada, a friend of Tange's.

**RK** And a collaborator.

**KK** Yes, a collaborator. They were trying to put together a World Design Conference in Tokyo in 1960. Kawazoe formed a preparatory committee for the Conference, which became a starting point for the Metabolism group. In 1959, the first year of Metabolism, I met Kawazoe and Asada. We were all trying to understand what was going on in the world and what we could do, what we found interesting, what could be the theme for the conference. Then Kawazoe and I invited the industrial designer Kenji Ekuan, the photographer Shomei Tomatsu, the architect Kikutake, and the graphic designer Kiyoshi Awazu. We also contacted Maki and Masato Otaka, but Maki was not so willing to participate.

**HUO** He was reluctant?

**KK** His thinking was slightly different to the other Metabolists. In maybe his second month in the United States suddenly he and Otaka formed a team.

**RK** A small cell.

**KK** Yes, a small cell within the Metabolist group. They proposed their "group form" ideas. We thought these were similar to our Metabolist ideas. Do you know why we invited Shomei Tomatsu? His photo collection *Asphalt* from 1960 appealed to me: it was focused on details of Tokyo streets. Looking at his photographs of street surfaces, one sees many things in the asphalt: nails, rubbish, Coca-Cola caps, stones. The images showed a very disorganized reality. I thought, this is Metabolism! I proposed he should be a member. The photographs represented our image. As the group was more or less formed, we started meeting at six every evening.

**RK** Meeting where? In what kind of environment?

**KK** Sometimes at Ryugetsu in Ginza, a very small inn where Asada was staying. His house was quite far away in Kamakura, so he usually stayed in this very typical Japanese inn. At five or six o'clock, Kawazoe would get a phone call from Asada: "Come over. Let's start a discussion." Or Kawazoe would phone us with another venue: "We have a meeting at International House." There, Asada, who became the secretary-general of the conference, and his assistant Tsune Sesoko had their offices. Sometimes we just went out anywhere for discussions.

## Change Perfectly

**HUO** We heard that sometimes the meetings went on very late into the night.

**KK** Sometimes until the morning, yes. But then the next day, I'd be doing sketches and continuing to write books. At the meetings, we spent long hours discussing what should be the text for the Metabolist group, always trying to pick examples from Japanese traditional architecture. Katsura Detached Palace, for instance, was a very interesting text for the Metabolists because it was extended twice over 150 years into an asymmetrical plan, with modules for the old part, the middle part and the last part. Very interesting. In our tradition, we have metabolic and cyclical ideas of growth. People always admired the Katsura Detached Palace: they worshipped it during the first phase, then when the second phase was completed they said that was perfect beauty, and then again after the second extension. At each stage, people said it was perfect beauty. We thought it made an excellent text.

**RK** Text? You mean, a kind of prototype?

**KK** Well, "prototype" or "model" is antithetical to what I mean by 'text,' as in Roland Barthes's *Le plaisir du texte* (1973). A new interpretation, if you will,

Still at Tange Lab, Kurokawa works privately on his first megastructure. "Just as in the case of chromosomes ... the helix structure acts as a space frame for data transmission,"[2] he writes. The self-assigned project is an attempt to fulfill his own prophesy of a paradigm shift "from the machine age to the life age"—a necessity Tange does not feel as urgently as his student. Initially designed, in 1961, as a solution to Tokyo's congestion—with a looping integrated highway system and space for 10,000 people in each helix—Kurokawa also transplants the structure to the waters of Tokyo Bay and Lake Kasumigaura, northeast of the city.

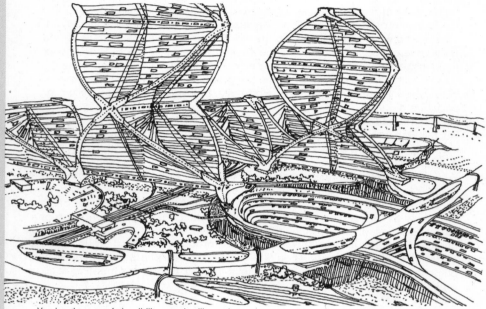

Varying degrees of plausibility: utopian illustration...

...model made from dried noodles...

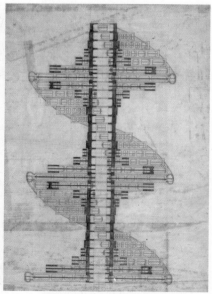

...traditional architectural section, showing embedded capsules.

**2** Rejecting Tange's pleas to stay at the Lab for two more years to ̶ish his education, Kurokawa, 27, sets up his own office. Howard Roark-̶ existential struggles ensue: "Those days, I ate only twice a day. ̶onlighting didn't occur to me as I believed an architect had to wait ̶iently for a client's visit. Eventually, I ate only once a day. I played a game ̶h a faux commission, spending a month seriously preparing drawings."³

**1963** Finally, a real commission arrives, a direct result of Kurokawa's as-yet unfounded bravado: he appears in *Asahi Shimbun* under the headline "World Famous Without Any Work" (January 18, 1963). Suitably provoked, Nitto Food asks him to build their new cannery in Sagae, Yamagata Prefecture.

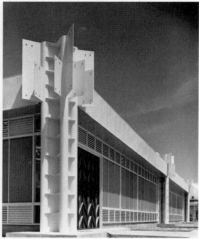

Kurokawa designs Nitto Food cannery around his theory of nodes, or "connectors": each corner truss has protruding flaps, ready to plug into future modules as required.

Eight modules so far...

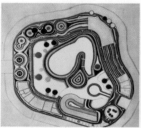

Cell wall, organelles, nucleus.

Future multiplication of leisure cells.

**1967** Yamagata Hawaii Dreamland, a weekend tourism spot for the farmer families of northern Japan who cannot afford to go to Hawaii itself. To avoid encroaching on the natural landscape, Kurokawa designs a sealed cell as an urban environment for fun. Dreamland is demolished in 1975.

"Leisure"—the English word, pronounced *rejaa*—becomes a buzzword in the early 1960s.

m scratch
as still a university student
en my house was destroyed
an air raid. But the store-
use survived the fire, so
uilt a toilet and a cooking
ea to try to make it livable.
those conditions, I eval-
ted via my own body the
ppositions of modern
chitecture for solutions
problems of ventilation
d hygiene, which gave me
e impetus to ponder the
estion: what is a dwelling
people in a city?
chio Otani

a kind of problématique. People think of Metabolist architecture growing and changing, but it has to grow and change perfectly. It has to be beautiful.

**RK** **Again, perfect.**

**KK** Yes, perfect as a constantly changing process. Impermanent beauty, immaterial beauty. So we found a new theory. European beauty was supposed to be eternal, but perhaps we could discover a new aesthetic based on movement. We thought we could make moving architecture. This is where Metabolism related to Futurism. The Futurists had this same idea and so did the Russian avant-garde.

### City from Scratch

**RK** **I want to look at a window of only two years: 1958 to 1960. This period feels something like a very busy airport with many planes departing and landing at the same time. You lose faith in Communism, and at the same time CIAM collapses—or the belief in modernity. It's only 13 years after the war, so build-ings are just beginning to rise from the ashes, yet you're studying Ise and Katsura.**

**KK** Especially Katsura, which was always a topic. At every Metabolist meeting we discussed Katsura; Ise only came up occasionally.

**RK** **It's so hard for us to imagine. You were part of a legendary movement with an incredible visual production that is still very eloquent today, yet you tell us you were looking at palaces and temples. How could you combine those things into one?**

**KK** It's like how things are linked to so many other things today. I think we were synthesizing many things, including contradictions. So many things were happening then.

**RK** **Were you exposed to the Futurists and the Soviet avant-garde in school?**

**KK** Yes, in high school. My father was an architect and his studio was full of books.

**RK** **So you're saying that part of your cultural information came from your father rather than from school?**

**KK** Yes, and also from first-hand experience. I started thinking about architecture around the very end of primary school. I grew up in the center of Nagoya, but during the war we fled to the suburbs. One night, two or three hundred bombers flew over the city and nothing remained. Nagoya's population of 1.5 million and its 230-year history disappeared overnight. I was shocked. Standing amidst the rubble, my father said, "Now we must build the city from scratch." I thought, we can build a city? Unbelievable! At the time, I didn't believe in architecture— I thought architecture and cities would just disappear.

### Consciousness Only

**RK** **How old were you then?**

**KK** Ten. Then in middle school I became interested in philosophy. Every week I listened to lectures at the Tokai Gakuen Buddhist School by the principal, Benkyo Shiio, who was a famous philosopher. After entering Kyoto University, I started studying philosophy and the Consciousness-Only School of Buddhism, which became a starting point for my philosophy of symbiosis.

The Consciousness-Only teachings arose in India in the fourth century, then were transmitted through China, and arrived in Japan together with Mahayana Buddhism to become a foundation of Japanese culture. I'm interested in this philosophy for its anti-purist approach. In contrast, European modern-ization was based on rational purism or dualism, from Aristotle up through Kant. Catholicism, for instance, typically dichotomizes good and evil. The purist approach helped to foster science, technology, and economics, but something else is needed.

**RK** **When were you exposed to Marxism in this sequence?**

**1969** Kurokawa, 34, is handed the perfect project for the newly motorized Japanese Archipelago: the Odakyu roadside restaurant, where customers transfer from one capsule—their car—to another, lodged in a space frame.

Producing reality—Kurokawa's turn.

"We must make cities of drive-ins. It's the philosophy of the drive-in that will unfold our future."[4]

**KK** As I mentioned before, I had been an activist at university, but I became disappointed in Communism in 1958. I concentrated on philosophy during my postgraduate studies at Tokyo University and began to write a text that ended up in my *Philosophy of Symbiosis*.[5] The book took 50 years to complete.

### Philosophy of Impermanence

**RK** Was your father a modern architect?

**KK** Yes.

**RK** Hardcore?

**KK** Yes, a classic modernist.

**RK** With any experience outside Japan?

**KK** No, strictly in Japan, and only in the Aichi area.

**HUO** You once told me that your father switched from traditional to Modernist architecture.[6]

**KK** I believe I said that during the war people were forced to be traditionalist—even Tange made an Ise Shrine–type project. Under the military regime, many architects were forced to design Shinto-style architecture, my father included. During the war he designed several buildings in a Shinto style, but I don't think he ever actually believed in it. After the war, he became a modernist.

**RK** This is one of the hardest things for me to understand. During the war, architects were forced to design Shinto-style, Ise-style, then after the war the avant-garde continued to study Ise?

**KK** No, it's not like that.

**RK** Kawazoe talks about this.

**KK** Yes, but it was the philosophy behind style that he was talking about. It was the aestheticism manifest in Ise and Katsura, the philosophy of impermanence.

**RK** Rather than method or ideology? It's still totally incomprehensible. It would be like the Nazis forcing classicism on a generation of architects, then the sons of those Nazi-against-their-will architects studying classicism.

**KK** The point is this: Consciousness-Only versus Western material-only views.

**RK** Was it part of the recovery, then, or in any way related to the war?

**KK** The shrine is 1,200 years old, it's true, but it's reconstructed every 20 years. Do you understand? Everything we see is impermanent. Whole cities can vanish in a day of warfare. It's this idea that the Japanese believe in, not the outward form. It's the philosophy. Kawazoe talked about the concept of Ise because of the simplicity it shares with the modern style. Hitler was obsessed by neo-classical style and tried to copy Karl Friedrich Schinkel. That is the difference. It's scandalous that Tange proposed a Shinto shrine–style project for the Greater East Asia Co-Prosperity Sphere Monument competition during the war.

**RK** Yes, we wanted to talk about that, too.

### Invisible Continuity

**HUO** If one looks at Tange and Kawazoe's interests in the '50s, drawing on Ise as a prototype for Japanese architecture, it actually explains retrospectively that they found modernist themes in the traditional Ise prototype—the use of natural materials for functional design, the whole notion of prefabrication. Were they seeking modernity within tradition?

**KK** No. Finding modernity in philosophy, not in style. There are, of course, traditions that are visible. But what's important here is that we conceive of our tradition and philosophy as invisible, which is very different from Europeans. The European way of thinking is rooted in materialistic civilization, so they're always talking about visible traditions.

**RK** Things.

**KK** A materialistic sense of order. We were talking about Ise as an invisible continuity: every 20 years the visible—the architecture—is rebuilt. We say

**1970** In the run up to Expo '70, Kurokawa's star rises, both in terms of architecture and celebrity. Working on three major commissions for the expo (Takara Beautillion, the Toshiba IHI pavilion, and the Capsule for Living, embedded in Tange's Big Roof—see Expo '70, p. 518 onwards) is not enough; Kurokawa also seizes the opportunity to mediate his work and himself, collaborating with artists, graphic designers, and a musician to forge the image of an effortless polyglot genius...

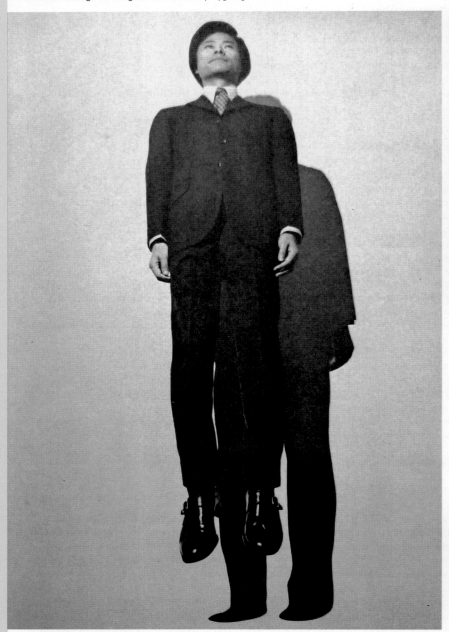

Achieving levitation.

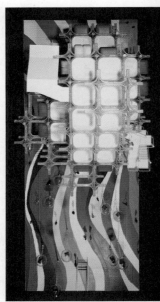

For the Takara Beautillion, a showroom for a furniture conglomerate at Expo '70 composed of capsules in a space frame, Kurokawa assembles a team of friends including Tadanori Yokoo (graphic design) and Motoko Ishii (lighting design), and creates a new Japanese Pop aesthetic, presaged by a model-as-artwork.

> The book-in-a-box also contains a poster and a record, "Music for Living Space," a surreal clash of old and new, composed by Toshi Ichiyanagi: choral chanting overlayed incomprehensible robotic voice.

Timed to coincide with Expo '70, fellow Metabolist Kiyoshi Awazu is given apparent free reign to design *The Work of Kisho Kurokawa*, a merger of theory (capsule, space frame, metamorphosis) and graphic audacity—a McLuhanesque medium as massage.

**1972** Kurokawa completes the icon of Metabolism: 144 capsules, prefabricated in a factory normally producing shipping containers, are plugged into two cores at the rate of five to eight per day; according to *The Japan Architect*, "all work is finished in 30 days." Kurokawa's motivation is ideological as well as technological, spelled out in his 1969 "Capsule Declaration" in *SD* magazine…

"Just as an astronaut is protected by a perfect shelter from solar winds and cosmic rays, individuals should be protected by capsules in which they can reject information they do not need and in which they are sheltered from information they do not want, thereby allowing an individual to recover his subjectivity and independence." (Article 6.) A capsule is a terminal for the networked cosmopolitan nomad, *and* a fort defending against information overload…

"The capsule stands for the emancipation of a building in relation to the ground, and heralds the era of moving architecture" (Article 2). Nakagin capsule, plugged into the core with only four bolts, theoretically removable…

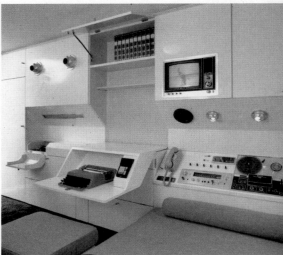

"Architecture from now on will increasingly take on the character of equipment" (Article 1). Toilet, bathtub, bed, desk, appliances, all embedded into the architecture…

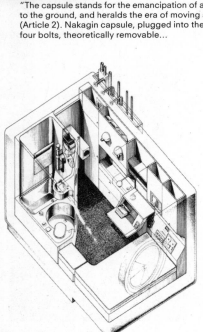

"The capsule is intended to institute an entirely new family system centered on individuals … The housing unit based on a married couple will disintegrate" (Article 4). Adjacent to the nightlife district of Ginza, Capsule Tower is a Japanese pied-à-terre for the salaryman who prefers not to return home to his suburban bedroom community…

"...the landscape of future cities will be determined not by express-ways or skyscrapers, but by a colossal aggregation of individual unit spaces" (Article 4). Nakagin, next to the new elevated expressway, a solitary time traveler from a thwarted future...

**1972** The same year as Nakagin, Kurokawa builds Capsule Summer House K—his own vacation home (though he also claims never to vacation)—with countryside capsules built to the same specs and size as the tower in Tokyo.

Surrounding forest not yet grown (see p. 426).

Rural vista beyond rooftop car park.

Capsules accommodate the future (bedroom capsule with electronic devices)...

...and the past (tea ceremony capsule).

Meiji Restoration

67: after three centuries
feudal rule under the
kugawa shogunate, impe-
l rule was restored, leading
modernization and open-
g to the outside world.
eiji means "enlightened
e."

ainst this attitude

experienced the end of
e war when I was a very
pressionable juvenile. The
merican occupation army
ould arrive boisterously,
ewing gum, and spread
ound candy for the chil-
en. This gave me, even
a child, a strong sense
humiliation. Japan indeed
st the war, but maybe it
ll held something that
uld not be defeated—that
came a central theme in
y mind since childhood.
e reason I entered Kyoto
iversity was to study the
d capital of Japan." From
isho Kurokawa bets his
!" *Playboy* (Japan),
arch 23, 1976.

am Tokyo
e p. 96

the tradition has been maintained for 1,200 years, though the material is always new. We say it's a very old, traditional building, but we mean something essentially different from the material preservation of the Acropolis.

In Japan, during the Meiji Restoration, we started to copy Western culture in dress, constitution, education, and architecture—everything mimicked European models. I am strongly against this attitude. Modernization should not mean copying European culture. But from the 19th century on, all developing countries tried to copy the West. It was a proven way to develop technology and the economy, and Japan succeeded in copying the European way. But now China, Singapore, Malaysia, and other Asian countries no longer believe that copying Europe is the best way to modernize. What we need is a philosophy of symbiosis between globalism and localism. Instead of leaving our future to a hegemonic competition for modernization, we must let diverse cultures flourish symbiotically. Neither Islamic fundamentalism nor ethnocentrism; it should be a whole new world.

**Way outside Architecture**

HUO  **The Metabolists, as we are finding out through these interviews, were not a homogenous group. It was more of a heterogeneous collective of very strong individuals. Compared to other avant-garde movements, Metabolism seems more organic, with rather softer edges and boundaries.**

KK  Otaka and Maki were thinking of architecture in terms of form or configuration, but I was thinking in a more philosophical way. Kawazoe was trying to find what the Japanese culture is, studying Ise Shrine, Izumo Shrine, and Jomon culture— an ancient people on the islands. He was at the hardcore of tradition.

Tange had no real relationship to Metabolism. Tange and Isozaki were very interested in the Metabolist group, but Isozaki's sense of order was always skewed, so we started without him. He used to say, "I'm an anti-Metabolist." I think he was more intent to form a group with avant-garde artists. He himself was a true avant-garde artist and very different from our group. He still has this artist attitude.

I started to make contacts with people way outside art and architecture. I had contact with people in sociology, economics, mathematics, and biology, as well as philosophers, business people, and industrialists.

RK  **So Tange was nowhere. It's refreshing to hear that.**

KK  After the Metabolist group began, Tange invited us to International House and declared, "We're forming Team Tokyo, including the Metabolist group, and inviting Sachio Otani, Arata Isozaki, and some others." So I asked, "What's the idea behind Team Tokyo? What does Tange-sensei envision about the future of architecture? How would it differ from Metabolist ideas? Do you even agree with Metabolism?" But we received no answer, so it was over.

RK  **Was *Metamorphosis* another name for Team Tokyo?**

KK  No, that was a title I prepared for the second Metabolist book.

HUO  **Which never came out?**

KK  Well, we tried. I made a huge amount of content and Ekuan did his own content based on our discussions, but Kikutake, Otaka, and Maki couldn't produce content.

RK  **Why not?**

KK  I don't know. The idea of metamorphosis made sense to me after Metabolism. I thought it would be interesting to take Metabolism to the next level. I'd already published my Helix Plan (1961) and Metamorphosis Plan (1965). But Maki, Otaka and Kikutake didn't really agree, even though there'd been a consensus about the title and the idea of the publication.

RK  **So there was no consensus after 1962?**

KK  We collaborated on a housing project competition for Peru in 1969 and did the masterplan for the 1985 Tsukuba Expo together. When Otaka had his

**1972** Further expansion of the capsule's domain: the Capsule Village leisure resort in Usami, southwest of Tokyo. Kurokawa predicts the abandonment of fixed residence and a new society of hypermobile "homo movens," moving freely between their urban and rural capsules—by means of another capsule, their cars.

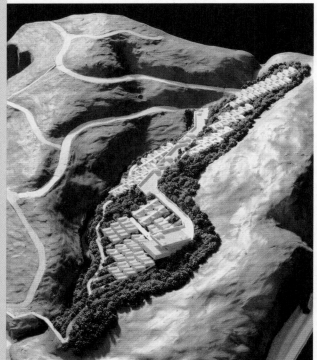

Hillside colony.

Leisure Capsule LC-30X: machine for living in.

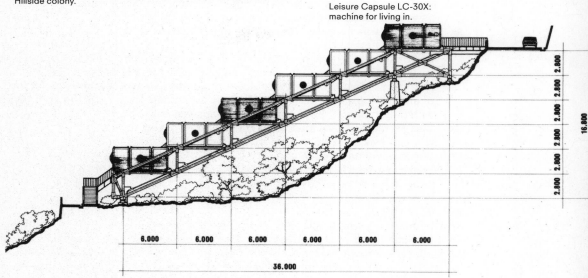

Terrace of leisure capsules plugs into hillside scaffolding to preserve vegetation below.

titute

panese futurology could
ly envision a bright future,
it was extremely enjoyable
d rewarding working for
e Institute for Social
gineering. Our research
ojects included a study of
elfare engineering" using
oots, undertaken with the
ience and Technology
ency and based on the
ea of "ecotechnology."
e also made a proposal
h the Tokyo Electric Power
mpany for a "system for
ng multiple sources of
ergy," which anticipated
day's environmental prob-
ns. The institute began as
enuine think tank. We had
direct ties to the Japanese
vernment, but we were
le to exert a major influence
the government as indi-
ual members of various
encies. However, few of
r reports were utilized.
e reason was the govern-
nt did not adopt a global
rspective in its relationship
foreign countries. The
onomic world was pre-
cupied with domestic
osperity. It was trapped
a bubble.
uhei Aida

siness sphere

he Institute for Social
gineering calls itself an
telligent group that takes
tion.' The founding capital
¥200 million is equally
ided among 26 investing
mpanies, which include
ose in major infrastructure,
general contractors,
velopers, and electrical
nufacturers. The ISE
dertook the first urban
nning commission from
road, the plan to merge
e cities of Vasto and San
vo in Italy in 1974. Within
ISE, an elite group called
Year 2000 Committee
ludes Takeshi Umehara
ilosopher), Tadao
nesao, Atsushi Shimokobe
ational Planning Agency),
asaru Ibuka and Akio
orita (co-founders of
ny), Shoichiro Toyoda
ce president of Toyota),
ma Dan (composer),
d the most prominent
onomists at the time,
asataka Kosaka and
oshi Kato." A dream team.
hink tanks of Japan", Jiyu
nshu (Liberal democratic),
bruary 1978.

80th birthday in 2003, all the members got together. And in 2005 we published our new book.[7]

### Principle of Life

**HUO** **One thing Kikutake and Kawazoe pointed out was their scientific inspiration, which became an important toolbox for Kikutake. I was wondering if Mitsuo Taketani's book, *Problems of Dialectics* (1946)[8] was also a toolbox for you, or if you had other scientific inspirations.**

**KK** My thinking was different. As I said, I was trying to understand the coming era, the shift from a mechanical to a biodynamic age.

**RK** **So basically the answer is less science and more towards philosophy.**

**KK** I'd always been exploring the life sciences and philosophy. Metabolism is a principle of life; symbiosis is one of the concepts most important to life. Cycles are a principle of life, ecology is a principle of life, information is a principle of life, ambivalent intermediate zones are a principle of life. Since Metabolism I continued to explore recycling, ecology, information, and symbiosis—all keywords based on living principles. My orientation was clear.

**RK** **If we look at your career now and the way you expanded the architectural field in the 1960s with television appearances, exhibitions and events, and becoming a public figure, was that all part of including life within architecture? Would you see it as part of the Metabolist mentality and philosophy in action?**

**KK** I tried to change the age.

### Institute for Social Engineering

**RK** **Can you explain how you did that and what you were thinking as your world expanded?**

**KK** Well, architects were living in such a small world and I thought this was foolish. Architecture and urbanism should engage with philosophy, economics, sociology, politics, science, art, culture, and other fields.

**HUO** **Who exactly did you work with?**

**KK** I sought out well-known academics, including the philosopher-anthropologist Tadao Umesao, who later became the first director of the National Ethnological Museum, which I designed in 1977. I tried to meet people and create interdisciplinary relationships. In 1969 I established the Institute for Social Engineering and invited people from different fields for discussions on futurology. It was a whole new scheme of "activity." The institute existed as a basic research organization for the Japanese government: the Ministry of Finance, the Ministry of Defense, the Ministry of Welfare.

**RK** **Was it entirely your idea to establish the institute? Or were you encouraged by the government?**

**KK** No, I established it in the business sphere, with the companies Mitsui, Mitsubishi, Sumitomo, and so on as backers.

**RK** **How did a young person like you get in contact with all those corporations? How did you have so much credibility?**

**KK** Because two of my books were bestsellers, I guess. I was addressing society via every medium available. Kikutake was a pure architect, Maki was an educator and architect, Kawazoe was a pure historian, so I thought I had to broaden the scope.

I worked through this Institute for Social Engineering for marketing, research, discussions, and public debate every time I had a project. Meanwhile, I worked on architecture in a very different way. It actually worked, and eventually the government asked us to play an important role in basic research comparing new airplane systems to train systems, simulations of Japanese demographic growth, as well as economic projections for the Ministry of Finance. These were very important experiences for me.

**1969** Trying to broaden his scope beyond architecture, Kurokawa starts a think tank with corporate backing—Mitsui, Mitsubishi, Sumitomo—that quickly becomes a resource for the government's optimistic and incessant national planning… (also see p. 683)

"Research on the role of V/STOL aircraft in city-to-city transportation," 1972. Proposal for drastically reducing travel time through a vertical and short take-off and landing aviation system.

"Long-term diachronic analysis of demographic distribution over the Japanese Archipelago," 1974, commissioned by Atsushi Shimokobe, then at the Economic Planning Agency, as part of his ongoing Comprehensive National Development Plan. The research team includes archaeologists and historians.

"Research on the public use of land in Tokyo," 1975, commissioned by the Ministry of Finance.

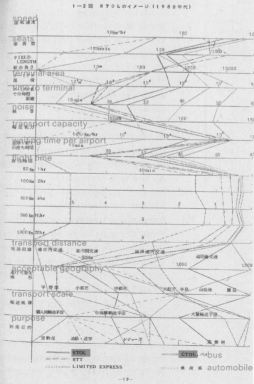

"How STOL will be in the 1980s": Kurokawa's report sets out the advantages of Short Take-Off and Landing versus Conventional TOL at a glance.

**V/OL and STOL**

The study of V/STOLs at the Institute for Social Engineering aimed at the development of convenient air routes over the Japanese Archipelago. We believed that planes of this type, which required only short runways, were indispensable for a mountainous country such as Japan. But the project never materialized because research and development of the aircraft itself was too narrowly focused. The present state of aviation in Japan is regrettable.
**Shuhei Aida**

**Lots to explain**

Shimokobe, a lifelong bureaucrat in various ministries, frequently commissions Kurokawa and his ISE to produce studies that contribute to his comprehensive National Development reports (see Project Japan, p. 684).

**Declined**

A number of technocrats showed great insight in the 1960s, and they contributed a lot alongside the Metabolists' projects in architecture magazines. It's a pity that this no longer happens today. The public sector has lost its daring spirit; so have architects and planners.
**Hajime Yatsuka**

RK  **Can you explain what the research on planes and trains was about?**

KK  It was research on hybrid transportation networks to combine systems for VTOL (vertical take-off and landing) and STOL (short take-off and landing) suitable for Japan's mountainous geography, linked with the Shinkansen bullet train and highways on the one hand, and with airplane development on the other hand. There were many other subjects. The research that led to the development of pollution reduction technologies for the automobile industry was sponsored by Toyota.

RK  **How many studies have you done?**

KK  We've actually done 480 studies over 36 years.

HUO  Fascinating. Have these been published?

KK  They were for the government, so no, they weren't published. The documents were distributed only among the investors and the government.

RK  **How many subscribers were there to these reports? How many investors were your 480 reports disseminated to?**

KK  They were produced as basic study materials from which to create plans for bureaucrats in various ministries. The Institute had a capitalization of $2 million and the investors shared the results of our research.

RK  **$2 million at that time?**

KK  Yes, it was big. Our reports were the most cutting-edge dossiers available to the government.

HUO  **Do you have any examples here?**

KK  Not here, but you can see the titles. They're all archived at the Institute.

RK  **You said you reacted against European dualism and were more interested in symbiosis and philosophy. But doesn't an "Institute for Social Engineering" sound frighteningly European and dualistic?**

KK  I'm not denying dualism. I just think dualism alone cannot answer everything. I happen to think the name is very Oriental, because sociology and engineering are opposing ideas. "Social engineering" was what I coined to describe research that symbiotically bridges sociology and engineering.

RK  **Well, the term also exists in America, and there it simply means the very calculated manipulation of social patterns. So you have an entirely different interpretation of social engineering.**

KK  Please understand that America didn't have this phrase half a century ago. It was completely new back then.

RK  **Can you tell me how the Institute grew? How did you achieve it, here within Japan?**

KK  Eighty percent of the Institute's clients were governmental, so it was very clear to us what exactly the government was trying to change. Through such connections I was invited to sit on government steering committees, to be an advisor to the National Railways, Japan Airlines, Mitsubishi Real Estate, and Mori Building, and to be a commentator on a news program on NHK TV.

RK  **Atsushi Shimokobe was a source of support for many of the Metabolists in the government. Did you encounter him? Did he support you or did you have other channels?**

KK  I have lots to explain. [laughs]

RK  **In the 1960s, you focused your intelligence on various government efforts or directives, even helping them to define their policies. You were able to expand while the public sector was very strong, when it had a lot of money and was deciding almost everything. In the last 10 or 15 years, however, the public sector has declined in power and there has been a corresponding shift to the private sector, to private developers who never have that kind of broad perspective.**

KK  Now I look at you and see you doing things similar to what I did when I was young, expanding into many countries, trying to bridge many fields.

RK  **Yes, but entirely without the support that you had. It strikes me that your career was so entwined with government.**

From *Prefabricated House* in 1960 to *Revolution of City* in 2006, Kurokawa writes, translates, and publishes 100 books—a relentless stream of ideas and ideology...

**1965** *Toshi dezain* (Urban design).

**1972** *The Death and Life of Great American Cities*, Jane Jacobs. Translated by Kurokawa.

**1967** *Kodo kenchiku ron: Metabolizumu no bigaku* (Action architecture: Aesthetics of Metabolism).

**1972** *Metabolism no hassou* (Concept of Metabolism).

**1972** *Joho rettou Nihon no mirai* (Information archipelago: The future of Japan).

**1969** *Homo Movens: The future of the city and man.*

**1973** *Toshigaku nyumon* (Introduction to urbanism: How to recover Tokyo and the archipelago).

**1975** *Kurokawa Kisho no sekai* (The world of Kisho Kurokawa).

**1976** *Introduction to Modern Architecture* by Charles Jencks. Translated by Kurokawa.

**1977** *Metabolism in Architecture*.

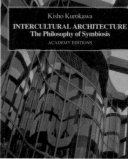

**1991** *Intercultural Architecture: The Philosophy of Symbiosis.*

**1996:** *Kyousei no shisou* (Philosophy of Symbiosis).

**2006** *Toshi kakumei* (Revolution of city), book #100.

ew projects

is true that the role of
agnostician and imple-
enter do not mix well.
e public does not like the
oncept of ideas emerging
duously, from analysis;
prefers the idea of virgin
rth, i.e., genius. Compare
e Corbusier and Mies:
erbose diagnostician vs.
rong, silent maker/*macher*.
em Koolhaas

## Improvised Live Broadcast

**HUO** **One of the things you used, which obviously made a big difference, was television. What you did would be almost impossible today. Could you tell us how you found opportunities to enter the space of television?**

**KK** NHK, the Japan Broadcasting Corporation, had a system back in the 1970s where they invited seven people from different fields to sit on a commentators' committee. I was architecture. The duties of a committee member were to discuss the orientation of news comments on NHK channels and to present a short program. My *Window on the News* ran for 15 minutes, where I talked on any subject. In any case, my ideas as a social commentator were well known through the books I'd written, which have now reached 100.

**RK** **Was your commentary program a monologue?**

**KK** Yes. No interviews.

**RK** **Improvised?**

**KK** Yes, improvised live broadcast.

**RK** **And you didn't write it out?**

**KK** Of course I used notes. It was all very heavy-duty, because this was Channel One, broadcast nationwide.

**RK** **When did it begin and when did it end?**

**KK** I did it from 1974 to 1991.

**RK** **For the same channel and in the same format?**

**KK** Yes. And not only on television—it was broadcast on radio at the same time. I also appeared on TV abroad, both national and private and on radio.

**RK** **So that must have contributed enormously to the expansion of your reputation?**

**KK** I think so. I was probably nominated to the committee because I'd also written books and made interesting proposals about future society. I think people were intrigued by my ideas, so they invited me to various forums for debate. However, doing TV news commentaries or speaking on TV never got me any new projects. It wasn't helpful for me in that sense, though of course I gained recognition and influence.

## Write, Write, Write

**HUO** **There was an interesting parallel in Europe, even if Japan is obviously very different in terms of media space. In the early '60s, the nouveau roman author Alain Robbe-Grillet had a huge weekly space in *l'Express*. Here was a very experimental writer given a huge platform and these mass media spaces for experiments. It was a unique moment.**

**RK** But that's also because there's no public television system anymore. It's the disappearance of the public sector everywhere.

**HUO** **Your books *Urban Design* (1965) and *Action Architecture* (1967) became bestsellers and made you a pop star in Japan overnight. This is really rare in the field of architecture. How did it happen?**

**KK** The secret was that my books [*reaches for* Information Archipelago: The Future of Japan (1972) *and* Homo Movens (1969)] addressed a general readership beyond the architectural profession. Now this book, Information Archipelago: The Future of Japan (*Joho rettou Nihon no mirai*), is very famous, but nobody ever read it. [*laughs*]

**RK** **One that wasn't a bestseller. [*laughs*]**

**KK** It discusses the future of Japanese society. It failed because it was the first book to talk about the information society. The critics said, "Why is an architect talking about spying?" Back then, the word *joho* meant intelligence. Nobody bought it.

**HUO** **This reminds me of my first visit to your office in 1997. You pointed out the window and said, all of these buildings will disappear, but writing is forever.**

As his fame and activities outside architecture increase in the late '70s, Kurokawa's core Metabolist ideas reappear in simplified form...

**1976** Capsule goes corporate: a tower of showrooms for Sony in downtown Osaka, with capsules as decorative apendages embellishing a corporate identity, rather than guiding ideology and structuring principle.

**1977** Built on the totally cleared site of Expo '70 in Osaka, the National Museum of Ethnology expands twice in six years, following the grid/cellular pattern.

Curving information capsules protrude into the Escher-like central courtyard, designed by Awazu.

i
shijin Labor Center, Kyoto,
62 (below), possibly
rokawa's first built work,
architecture conceived
part of a street.

naka
akuei Tanaka, charismatic
ime minister from 1972–74,
ublished the bestselling book
an for Remodeling the
panese Archipelago in
72 as a manifesto for his
ection. For Kurokawa's
interview, see Media
chitect, p. 460.

**KK** In my view, an architect must essentially be a thinker, whose mission is not only to realize works, but also to put forth images of the city's future and society's future. Whenever I have no immediate design work, I write, write, write.

The book *Urban Design* has been reissued and has been selling for nearly half a century. This is striking. I argued that roji—urban corridors—are superior to plazas and that the city of the future must be a city of narrow passageways, not open squares. This entered into popular discussion, not just among city planners and architects. I began a study of narrow *roji* in Kyoto and Tokyo, and made news documentaries. Pedestrian street preservation became an important urban issue at that time, when streets everywhere were being widened for cars. So my comments went against the grain and people were interested. In 1973 I was invited to debate with Prime Minister Tanaka on television and kept strongly…

**RK** **Pushing.**

**KK** Pushing the authorities to change their thinking about cities. People became interested and gradually began to understand my ideas. That's why my books became bestsellers.

**HUO** **How many copies are you talking about for your bestsellers?**

**KK** Probably 100,000 to 300,000 copies. Another bestseller, *Homo Movens*, does not talk about architecture, but about mobility. I talked about the future of the information society and time-sharing communities. If people are always moving, how can we maintain community-wide communications?

**HUO** **In 1960, the Metabolist group made itself public through a book. The publication was small but had worldwide impact—a butterfly effect—which we know very well from the art world too. Books that penetrate society as textbooks, mostly small textbooks, show how ideas travel differently outside the closed world of architectural bookshops. Don't you think so?**

**KK** Well, maybe. As you say, my books are not for architects, but for ordinary people. My ideas penetrated public consciousness directly, not through the architectural field. The book *Metabolism 1960*, our first one, didn't go anywhere in Japan; it only reached international architectural society.

**HUO** **It created a rumor.**

**KK** This book, *Revolution of City*, is number 100.

**HUO** **Is writing a daily practice for you?**

**KK** Thinking is the essential part of the architect's profession. I read and write in parallel with planning and designing every day.

### Import Godard

**HUO** **One thing fascinates me tremendously: the expansion of your practice has a strong resonance today, not only in the field of architecture, but also in my field. In contemporary art there are artists who do what Raymond Loewy calls the MAYA thing—Most Advanced and Yet Acceptable. It's the idea of being experimental yet mainstream.[9] Think about Matthew Barney's film *Drawing Restraint 9* with Björk (2006), or Philippe Parreno and Douglas Gordon doing a feature film about Zinedine Zidane (*Zidane: Un Portrait du XXIe Siecle*, 2006).**

**I was traveling this summer with Alain Robbe-Grillet and he was telling me that in France in the early 1960s there was a climate where one could be MAYA. The early works of Godard had this magical quality: mainstream movies that were yet cutting edge. In the field of architecture there are no comparisons—only you ever achieved that. We had Godard in cinema, Robbe-Grillet in literature. What if it wasn't pure coincidence that those very same years—**

**KK** Hiroshi Teshigahara, who directed *Woman of the Dunes* (1964), the art critic Yusuke Nakahara and 13 others including myself established a company called Film Art in 1968. It was a company to import films only by Godard, and we published a magazine on them, *Film Quarterly*. A beautiful magazine. We imported nearly 20 films and then the company went bankrupt.

Establishing credentials as man-about-town and entrepreneur, before turning his attention to the political scene…

Awazu, also on the board of Film Art alongside Hiroshi Teshigahara, poses with the poster for Teshigahara's *Face of Another* (1965), for which Isozaki works on the mise-en-scene and Awazu on graphic design.

New wave: Kurokawa helps establish Film Art Inc (1968), which imports *only* Godard movies to Japan, and publishes *FILM Quarterly*, designed by Awazu. In this issue: Anna Karina in *La Chinoise*, and, unsurprisingly, a feature on Godard.

"A capsule is for those who want to release what is pent up inside them."[10] Tange and Isozaki are regulars at Kurokawa's Space Capsule Disco in Akasaka, Tokyo. Stainless steel surfaces, computer-controlled lighting, chandelier made of televisions, each tuned to a different channel. Novelist Shintaro Ishihara, poet Shuntaro Tanikawa, lighting designer Motoko Ishii, and composer Toshi Ichiyanagi collaborate with Kurokawa to produce a seamless, hermetic, hedonistic experience. Composite image made by Awazu for *The Work of Kisho Kurokawa* (1970).

**RK** Did you meet Godard?

**KK** No.

**RK** Do you speak French?

**KK** No, I'm hopeless. I was trying to push the Metabolism movement towards different fields. The graphic designer Awazu, another member of the Metabolist group, was also on the board of directors.

In the '60s I also designed Space Capsule, Japan's first discotheque, in the Akasaka district of central Tokyo. It was the salon of the age: Tange, Isozaki, and everyone came to this discotheque almost every night. Everyone was there: the famous playwright Shuji Terayama, the poet Shuntaro Tanigawa, the composer Toshi Ichiyanagi, the novelist Shintaro Ishihara, who is now governor of Tokyo, Kazuko Shiraishi, another poet.

**RK** Was there much political coloring at that point?

**KK** We usually criticized the government, the political system.

**RK** Was there a leftist dimension to it?

**KK** Not ideologically, but the scene was very avant-garde and anti-academic. Space Capsule had a stainless steel floor and a chandelier made of TV sets. I tried to push in many ways.

**RK** In every direction, as usual.

### Geographic Expansion

**HUO** I would like to understand a bit more how this expansion really worked. You even went into the translation of seminal texts. You translated Jane Jacobs's *The Death and Life of Great American Cities* (1972) and that became a bestseller in Japan, which is incredible because it was never a real bestseller in the original.

**KK** After I wrote *Urban Design*, I found the Jacobs book. She was presenting similar ideas to mine about small streets. I felt I had found my comrade. So I asked her if I could translate it.

**RK** Have you ever felt the same about other writers?

**KK** Another book I translated was Charles Jencks's *Modern Movements in Architecture* (1977). I thought it would be a good text for students. Right now I'm translating John Howkins's book *The Creative Economy* (2002), the most advanced economics book out now.

**HUO** We've talked a lot about media expansion, about venturing into other fields. But your work includes another form of outreach: geographic expansion. Looking at the 1960 conference, it was really what in art we'd call Westkunst: basically just the Western countries and Japan. But you've ventured a lot into other Asian countries.

**KK** In 1986 I was suddenly invited to design Hainan Island, in the South China Sea, as the Hawaii of the Orient. This idea came from Deng Xiaoping, and through this invitation I met high profile people in the Chinese government. Then again I started criticizing urban planning policy in Beijing. They started constructing the Third Ring Road, which I strongly opposed. And I was very vocal about keeping the city wall, the hutongs, and the narrow streets —they're treasures. They were shocked, because nobody said such things back in the 1970s. Architects and professors from Russia and other countries were coming to China and always said: you must develop. While I said, keep the old town, reconstruct the walls! Then at the same time, in 1982, I was named a lifetime visiting professor to Tsinghua University.

Leveraging political connections to expand operations outside Japan...

**1983** In Beijing, Kurokawa meets Zhou Peiyuan (right; physicist and vice chairman of the eighth Chinese People's Political Consultative Conference [CPPCC] National Committee) and Sun Pinghua (key player in the "normalization" of Sino-Japanese relations in 1972). A year later, Kurokawa is invited to design one of the largest hospitals in Beijing; in 1990, he builds the Chinese-Japanese Youth Center, also in Beijing.

**1993** With Malaysian prime minister Mahathir, inspecting the model for the new Kuala Lumpur airport. Kurokawa merges several offices to make space for the (Albert Speer-esque?) model.

**RK** And how often did you go there?

**KK** Sometimes three or four times a year, sometimes once a year. Intensive lectures. I once did eight hours of lecturing, with lunch. So that was the start of very intimate contacts with the Chinese government.

**HUO** **In China, right away the politicians. In Singapore, right away the politicians. The last time I visited you, in 1997, Mahatir, the prime minister of Malaysia, was about to arrive.**

**KK** Some of my books have been translated in various countries. Before China entered the WTO, they could copy and translate anything. Only afterwards did I see the books being read, and I was very surprised; I never had any contracts with publishers in China. But among those who read my books as a student was the mayor of Shenzhen, who showed up at my office one day and said, "We held two international competitions, but couldn't find the right idea, so we gave up on competitions. I'd like to invite you to design this." Although I'm no stranger to winning big projects through international competitions, this was a very direct invitation. I guess he came to me because any country's government needs an urban planning policy.

**RK** **So much impressive work, so much impressive thinking, so much impressive ambition. Let's just say that your current status in architecture is based on a misunderstanding: it relates only to your buildings, not to the rest. It is depressing that, in architecture, the rest does not seem to count. So many of your activities are completely unknown, or to some extent even discredited.**

## Concentrate

**KK** Oh, I don't know, I don't care…[*laughs*]

**RK** **When did the rift between the profession and you actually start? Or don't you feel it? For instance, do you have friends who are architects at this point?**

**KK** I do meet important people quite often, though I find what they say boring. But I do make efforts to introduce younger architects to others outside Japan.

**RK** **Are you saying you hardly have a social life?**

**KK** I'm so busy. All I do is write and work on projects. I concentrate intensively. I suppose I am appreciated despite personal criticism, having received all the important awards in Japanese architecture. I've won first prizes in various international competitions over 45 years. For me that's one form of evaluation, not only from the competition organizers, but also the architect jurors, even if some projects are never realized. Then also my books have been translated and read. I receive constant requests for interviews, lectures and exhibitions.

**HUO** **Do you ever sleep?**

**KK** Very short hours.

**HUO** **How many?**

**KK** Sometimes five hours, sometimes three hours. I have no Saturday or Sunday, no New Year's, no summer holidays.

**HUO** **How many people work in your office? What are the maximum and minimum numbers?**

**KK** Including advisors, I once had 230 people. But now only 80 people.

**HUO** **Another statistical question. How many projects of yours have been realized versus unrealized?**

**KK** I win maybe one in eight or ten competitions for large-scale projects.

**HUO** **And how many projects have you realized so far?**

**KK** I don't know exactly. I've never counted, but somewhere between 100 and 200.

**RK** **Fifty percent of the Metabolist architects count and fifty percent don't. [*laughs*]**

**HUO** **Another question, my recurring question. Do you have a favorite unrealized project that you regret has not been realized so far?**

**ca. 1963** As the Tokyo Olympics approaches, Kurokawa (29 years old, 35 kilos, no major buildings to his name) is invited to explain his Helix City on Channel 3—the future shared with mass audience.

**KK**    I regret all those that won first prize yet went unrealized: UAE University City (1987), Osaka City Hall (1989), the parliamentary headquarters in Tanzania (1972), Abu Dhabi conference city (1975), the new capital of South Korea (1978). With the Pompidou Center in 1971, I received a telegram saying we won the first prize, and the next day…

**RK**    **The same thing happened to me with Parc de la Villette!**

**KK**    The next day I was told our project won second prize.

**RK**    **Was your project better?**

**KK**    I still think my project was more interesting than Pompidou Centre as actually built. And the odd thing is, they gave me prize money twice! Very strange. [*laughs*]

**HUO**    **The poet Rilke offered advice to young poets. I'd be curious to know what your advice might be to young architects.**

**KK**    My only advice is to go for the challenge, as I did as a young man with no experience. Getting projects means competition. It's a pity that the young generation is so cunning. [*laughs*] They're not doing any competitions. Competitions are time- and money-consuming and very tiring, so they avoid them. They design houses, they do interior designs or façade design. Things they can do easily, without writing books or challenging the government.

### Physical Beauty

**RK**    [*Looking at a photo of Kurokawa posing beside a car*] How much of a role do you think your physical beauty played in your career?

**KK**    Physical beauty? [*surprised*] You know, in my 20s, every weekly magazine was coming to me.

**RK**    **For your physical beauty?**

**KK**    Not beauty, but my lifestyle, my assertive way of talking. Everyone wanted my face. Cars were always prepared by magazines. I was so lean then because I was poor. I had no money to eat. I weighed only 35 kilos.

**RK**    **So that's the secret. A beautiful, sensual moment. Thirty-five kilos—and now?**

**KK**    Fifty-five! [*laughs*] Quite different, but still avant-garde.

**RK**    **Not a pop star, a serious intellectual. Was this the time you started the Institute for Social Manipulation? [*laughs*]**

**KK**    That was the end of the 1960s. You know, the public loves a poor man, a challenging poor man. But when the poor man becomes successful, that changes to jealousy. All too typical. If I keep losing competitions, I'll be poor again. It's easy to become poor, but I'm not afraid of that.

**References**

1   Kisho Kurokawa, *Kisho Kurokawa Notes* (Tokyo: Dobun Shoin, 1994).

2   Kisho Kurokawa, *Metabolism in Architecture* (London: Studio Vista, 1977).

3   *Kisho Kurokawa Notes*.

4   Kisho Kurokawa, *Car Graphic*, October 1967.

5   Kisho Kurokawa, *Each One A Hero: The Philosophy of Symbiosis* (Tokyo: Kodansha International, 1997, English edition).

6   Hans Ulrich Obrist's interview with Kisho Kurokawa for "Cities on the Move," 1997.

7   Kawazoe and Otaka ed, *Metabolism and Metabolists* (Tokyo: Bijutsu Shuppansha, 2005).

8   Mitsuo Taketani, *The Problems of Dialectics* (Tokyo: Rigakusha, 1946).

9   Raymond Loewy, *Never Leave Well Enough Alone* (Baltimore: The Johns Hopkins University Press, 2002).

10   Kisho Kurokawa, *Homo Movens* (Tokyo: Chuo Koronsha, 1969).

**1972** Nakagin Capsule Tower, in the natural habitat of the homo moven. By 2007, with capsules never added, removed, or refreshed as planned, the tower falls into disrepair. Just before his death, Kurokawa fights for rejuvenation according to his original intention for the building; residents vote for demolition anyway, which in 2011 is still pending. While it still exists, Nakagin Capsule Tower "stands as a powerful reminder of paths not taken, of the possibility of worlds shaped by different sets of values." ("Future Vision Banished to the Past," Nicolai Ouroussoff, *New York Times*, July 6, 2009.)

## Team X

I met Kurokawa in September 1966, when we were both going to Urbino to the Team X meeting overseen by Giancarlo De Carlo. Kurokawa was there because he had invited Peter Smithson to Japan, and knew other Team 10 members. Kurokawa was always the rainmaker, an organizer of things. The three of us—Hans Hollein, Kurokawa, and I—were the Young Turks (as far as the mainstream members were concerned), and because Team 10 at that moment was looking inward and trying to "faire école," they looked on us with a bit of resentment and perhaps jealousy. Particularly Kurokawa, because he was more beautiful than the others and more facile and constructing a lot of buildings. So there was productive and creative jealousy as well as the fact that Kurokawa didn't have the hang-ups of the Europeans. He seemed to be from outer space, a superman, an alien doing things no one else was achieving and carrying through these unlikely projects with a suave Italian nonchalance, a sprezzatura.

At the Urbino meeting he presented the Metabolic system, with various biological drawings and diagrams: this framework, by 1966, had already shifted for him to the idea of metamorphosis. Kurokawa could feed to Team 10 theory and imagery and show completed buildings. No one else did the three at such a high level of competence (even if one questioned some of the results).

These buildings were extremely important given the nature of the European avant-garde. In the European ideal, the avant-garde was there to be ahead of the army, ahead of the masses. It was not to do paper projects or pontificate, but test ideas. Here were the Metabolists, who had actually built buildings, while European groups like Archigram hadn't. Reyner Banham has said that Metabolism was "Archigram Lite." Well, it was the other way around. Hollein and I and Kurokawa discussed this: we said we have to test ideas in practice. You have an obligation to speak to more than the converted, the students. There was a kind of decadence to the Western avant-garde because they were posturing more than trying to build.

## Brother

Kurokawa was like a brother. We would be alone together for 10 hours at a time, sometimes traveling in bullet trains across to Hiroshima, and we would never speak, because there was a deeper understanding at the tacit level. This part was telepathic, although often I couldn't understand his Japanese values or some of his assumptions. He would say to me: "I can be Buddha, but you can't be Christ"— a big philosophical joke about the snobbism of the West versus the general connectedness of the East. Laughter was our middle name, the kind of explosive humor you find in a Kurosawa film when the tension is relieved. He famously worked 19 hours a day, so I said laughingly, "Then you sleep one hour less than Napoleon." He said, "Yes, that's right. I woke him up." He moved on five separate levels during the day, like a multi-speed demon, from big business to philosophy to pop star to politics to writing to architecture and city planning.

In these interviews we had we would just laugh at his outrageous statements. For instance, on a bullet train once, I asked him if he had children. He said "Yes, I have two children: one is called 'the past' and the other is named 'the future.'" I asked the obvious question, "Where is the present?" and he answered the expected, "Me." He said it with a straight face and then burst into a grin, like a samurai. And he loved a fight, as long as it wasn't humiliating for either side; he liked the battle of wits. So in our disagreements there was a kind of slapstick idiocy, the tall, straight American versus the short, more agile Japanese. We had nothing against each other, everything to play for; I am not a threat to him and he is not one to me.

## Facile

He translated Jane Jacobs, then three of my books: *Architecture 2000* (1971), *Modern Movements in Architecture* (1973), and *Le Corbusier and the Tragic View of Architecture* (1974). He boasted that he wrote 100 books, the kind of puffed up advertisement that drove people crazy. When Vasari boasted to Michelangelo that in one summer he painted a hundred frescoes, the master answered "it looks it." Kurokawa was occasionally swallowed by this persona of success. In our 1974–76 interviews he said, "I am the third most famous person in Japan." I said, after who? "The emperor is the first, the prime minister is the second, and I am the third." "Oh come on, Kisho-san, give me a break." He said, "It's true. I have this television show and that is why I am the third most famous person in this country." This provocation was delivered with a characteristic giggle.

He had a debate with the prime minister in 1973. Tanaka wanted to decentralize and industrialize. Kurokawa said you can't decentralize or industrialize, that will destroy Japan; what you have to do is have cities of all scales. Instead, fractal cities. I think he looked to science in a positive way and to the intellect to grapple with the problems of Japan. Other architects say that Kurokawa could out-talk and out-think them—he was quicker on his feet. That is why he could run circles around the prime minister. In his prime he was really well rehearsed.

## Outbreeder

He had a thousand slogans and architectural concepts, each given a moniker. But his time as a TV presenter took away some of his poetic qualities and turned him towards propaganda. For understandable reasons this upset the architectural community. The problem was that he became so successful at other things that he didn't concentrate enough on architecture. He was so productive and had such facility that he often didn't know what his best buildings were, or why. I came to him once after a lecture at the RIBA in 2001 or so and said, "You mustn't push that mega-building which is so stereotyped, but this other one." He would say, "Why? Why do you think so?" He was so over-productive, it was as if his critical facility wasn't operating. But he was exemplary as an outbreeder. For me, his and Le Corbusier's lesson and those of hybrid architects is that architecture is a wonderfully wide profession, but you have to breed with the outside world. We are so internalized a profession that it's hard to get sustenance, but we must in order not to lose touch with our art form.

## Upstaging

In 2006, he finished his National Art Center in Tokyo, the undulating building, and when I was there in January 2007 it opened with an exhibition of his own work. The prime minister and his entourage came in, and every single person, including the politicians and architects, was in Western black suits. Kurokawa and his wife were dressed in traditional colorful costume. The prime minister looked very unhappy as he got on the stage surrounded by his cabinet all in black, and we listened to an orchestra play various Western pieces by Mozart and Beethoven. Then we were ushered into another large abstract room of the museum and waited for half an hour for the emperor and the empress to come. Two hundred journalists with cameras were herded into a corner like animals. Toyo Ito, Kengo Kuma, and some other architects were introduced to the emperor by Kurokawa. He was running the show; and dressed in his resplendent costume it was as if he had taken over the evening, and the country, giving it a sense of dash and individuality.

## Death

When I last saw him, it was very upsetting. He had these amazing fantasies about his samurai past which he recounted as he showed me his (perhaps) family swords. In the mid-70s, we talked about Mishima. He said, "In Japan suicide is honorable, and I don't want my office going on after me because it won't be what I believe in and fought for." But in the end he allowed his family to carry it on. I think he was authentically himself, till the end. You could see him as a little emperor, maybe, internalizing Japanese history like Mishima. He internalized the many contradictory problems of Japan—that was what his philosophy of symbiosis allowed him to do, as it did Robert Venturi in America. And his ego—I don't want to overstress this because I did love him—but I think his ego often got the better of him. Nonetheless, Kurokawa has to be judged as the impresario architect who made things happen, a director or producer who helped a lot of young Japanese architects like Kengo Kuma. He was always cutting across cultures and working on different levels that other mortal architects never reach, and one could love him for his laugh alone.

Kurokawa with Jencks's children, Cosmo
and Justin, and his wife Maggie Kenswick.

**2007** Empress Michiko greets Kurokawa at the inauguration of his National Art Center in Tokyo. Next to him, his wife, legendary actress Ayako Wakao; in back, Bunmei Ibuki, minister of education and science; and Charles Jencks, his friend since 1966.

The end: Isozaki, lifelong colleague and rival, says goodbye to Kisho Kurokawa, April 8, 1934–October 12, 2007.
In his eulogy, Isozaki calls Kurokawa the first and the only "media architect" of Japan.
Left: condolences from Emperor Akihito. Right: a plaque confers the status of National Cultural Contributor.

1963 Kisho Kurokawa: Nitto Food cannery (now Nitto Best), Sagae
2009 Photos by Charlie Koolhaas

**1972** Kisho Kurokawa: Nakagin Capsule Tower, Tokyo
**2009** Photos by Charlie Koolhaas

**1972** Kisho Kurokawa: Capsule Summer House K, Karuizawa
**2009** Photos by Charlie Koolhaas

**1977** Kisho Kurokawa: National Museum of Ethnology, Osaka
**2009** Photos by Charlie Koolhaas

# Media Architects
## Tange and Kurokawa create and exploit the spotlight

"Through the swivel door, past the cloakroom, a guy in a three-piece black suit dashes into an elevator ... His black suits are made of British wool. The striking tie in archaic indigo blue and white is plant-dyed. The shirt is a subtle hue of ivory ... Perfect everywhere."

"Life in Three Colours: The Prince of Architecture," *Playboy*, Japanese edition, February 12, 1974.

A professional in Japan with a solid reputation earns the right to add the suffix "ka" to their title: a famous architect therefore becomes a *kenchiku-ka*. This might be an early, non-pejorative version of the dreaded Western neologism, starchitect. Long before the negative correlation between celebrity and credibility is established, from the late 1950s to the '70s Japan's media lionizes its architects with full sincerity. The growth of TV (95 percent of households own one by 1970), popular weekly magazines, and the architecture press itself transforms architects from fusty technicians or mere assistants to builders into gurus capable of reorganizing the nation. Serious attention is paid in extravagantly illustrated articles and on lengthy TV specials to the Metabolists' schemes, and, soon, to their clothes, cars, accessories, and leisure time.

In tandem with the architectural reimagining of Japan, a project is underway to create a new postwar, postimperial model of Japanese masculinity, part Samurai, part dandy. Yukio Mishima, the novelist and nationalist, is both; Kurokawa calls him "my only rival" in fashion and perhaps fame...

Tange, in the late 1950s, is the first to set the stage and benefit from the media spotlight, but Kurokawa quickly emerges as the perfect figure to exploit the increasing (and increasingly personal) attention. How did Kurokawa dislodge his former teacher? The two giants represent opposite poles, and different generations: Tange, the middle-aged bow-tied dandy, the public servant and pedagogue with the clout of Tokyo University behind him, wheeled out whenever the nation needs to assert its economic and cultural power (Hiroshima Peace Memorial in 1955, Yoyogi National Gymnasia in 1964, Expo '70); Kurokawa the handsome youth who makes up for what he lacks in authority with audacity, knows how to speak on TV (compared with Tange's fragile voice), and presents seemingly outlandish scenarios for the future with both deadpan seriousness and knowing playfulness. Kurokawa, unlike Tange, also transcends his discipline of architecture altogether in interviews with politicians (including the prime minister, Kakuei Tanaka) and in a TV spot on the national channel NHK, in which he monologues on his latest activities and theories; he systematically exploits this 15 minutes of fame for the next 20 years, before taking the next step, from media to politics...

**1961** First media architect: Tange presents Plan for Tokyo in a special New Year's Day broadcast on NHK

**Master of Tange School: An International Architectural Art Award Bestowed on Tange**

"The Sogetsu Kaikan is one of the architectural works that brought Tange the Pan-Pacific Art Award [from the American Institute of Architects]. Sofu Teshigahara asked Tange to design the building completely as he liked, and so he did. 'When you make a building full of creative ideas, you'll get 80 percent of people around you complaining at the beginning. But in half a year, the proportion will be reversed. After all, the appreciation of living space is a lot about getting accustomed to it… It makes me happier to be complimented on a building after 10 years of usage rather than immediately after completion,' says Tange."

The lauded Sogetsu Kaikan Art Center.

First pose: Tange smokes thoughtfully in front of his recently completed Sogetsu Kaikan Art Center on Aoyama-dori Avenue, Tokyo; in one of his first major magazine features, the image of architecture and architect already begin to merge…

**Avant-garde Is Japan's Favorite: Four Kings in Architecture, Drama, Photography and Painting** by Soichi Oya

On the avant-garde: "A new religious sect and the avant-garde members share several things in common. Both contain gurus, meaning that they have passionate supporters but no ears for criticism; they are left-wing, at least in speech; they are often surprising, which is a tactic to get recognition; they are good at mystifying people by using buzzwords drawn from other disciplines, typically literature, philosophy, and sociology; they exercise showmanship, constantly displaying new or bizarre gestures; they are essentially journalists and entertainers; they have a good sense of business. In short, they succeeded in reversing the common sense that avant-garde doesn't sell."

On Tange: "The leap from ancient plan to glazed modernism is brilliant, exercising if you will the 'dialectic synthesis of tradition and destruction.' Based on his theory that 'the ground surface belongs to people and therefore must be liberated,' his buildings [raised on pilotis] give free passage underneath, like a treehouse in a jungle. In Japan, this space sometimes serves as a home to hobos."

Last stand: a nascent media elite, initially confronted with sarcasm as an avant-garde that sells, will soon be celebrated in popular magazines and then galvanized by the emergence of TV, which Soichi Oya, the skeptical commentator writing here, dismisses as a sum total of "one billion in total idiocy."

**Best-Dressed Man in the Architecture Circle: Kenzo Tange**
"Kenzo Tange is acclaimed as the best-dressed man in the architecture circle. And the architecture he conceives is as urbane and articulate as his dressing style. Most of his works, including his own house in Seijo, Tokyo, sit on pilotis (lifted above the ground with columns) ... Tange is very popular internationally. The World Health Organization of the United Nations will be building its new gigantic headquarters in Geneva, Switzerland. Tange has been chosen from Japan among 15 competitors from around the world. Will he be able to step up to the world stage?"

東大丹下研究室　自作の設計図前で。

戦後のはなばなしい活躍で　日本建築学会賞　汎太平洋建築賞　国際建築美術賞を受賞。国際的にも大変な人気がある。今度　新しく（スイスのジュネーブに　国連の下部機構であるWHO（ワールド・ヘルス・オルガニゼーション世界保健機構）の巨大なビルが建てられる。この建物の設計にあたる世界の建築家15人に　日本の丹下氏が選ばれた。各国一流の建築家から集まるデザインのうち一つが採用されるわけである。日本の丹下氏が　世界の檜舞台に進出できるかどうか……。

Photographed in Tange Lab,
in front of his own drawing.

By 1960, Tange's architecture is described in terms
of his dressing style: "urbane" and "articulate..."

**Future City Floating on the Sea: The Dream of Kenzo Tange**
"At his studio, Kenzo Tange studies the model of a housing cluster on a man-made island … Cars approach the cluster via high-speed motorways surrounding it. Yachts are also seen in the model … The cluster is supported with a gigantic truss structure, which contains a large open space for communal activities and facilities, including schools. On the outer surfaces are attached 'cells' for living."

海に浮かぶ未来都市

丹下健三氏の夢

Tange's strategic absence from Tokyo in 1959, at the moment of Metabolism's gestation, is time well spent. He returns from MIT with the notion of the A-frame, a slab pulled apart to create public space and a passage for high-speed transit running through the structure—and applies it as a new typology in Plan for Tokyo...

## The Guru Pioneer: A Whirlwind in Architectural Society

週刊朝日

1月31日号

定価40円

Olympian: the upcoming Tokyo Olympics provide the media with an occasion for transforming Tange into a national hero: he poses for the cover of *Shukan Asahi*—confident, sharp, yet avuncular—as his iconic Yoyogi National Gymnasia (left) are about to be completed...

**Future Figure Of Japan's Architecture Circle Revives Japan's Ancient Beauty in Contemporary Design** "At the age of 36, Kiyonori Kikutake is already a recipient of two prestigious art awards. The renowned governor of Shimane Prefecture recalls that when he brought Kikutake to the Grand Shrine for the first time, the architect did not sleep for the entire night, astonished by the ancient architecture."

One of which is the Pan-Pacific award of the AIA, following in Tange's footsteps.

設計中の建築物の模型をみる菊竹さん（菊竹清訓建築設計事務所で）

Visionary: for the article, Kikutake inspects his Tokoen Hotel, under construction.

Reverant: eight weeks later, *Shukan Asahi* again gives its cover to an architect, this time to a Metabolist. Kikutake though still plays the role of serious, classic architect. On the left of the cover: his administrative building for the Izumo Shrine, Shimane, completed in 1963.

**1962, January 30** Using a diagram (right), Asada explains "the problem of urbanization that could be expected in a society where high economic growth has become the norm, and the potential effects of these urban problems on people's personal income."

**1963** Otaka presents Sakaide Artificial Ground, a social housing project on Shikoku island. Next to him, Kurokawa presents Helix City (a small model sits next to the ashtray on the table).

From ink to screen: after the attention of the popular press, the Metabolists' plans become a form of worthy TV entertainment for an exponentially bigger national audience: their presentations are alternately theoretical (Asada's lecture on economic and urban growth), fantastical (Kurokawa's Helix City), and actually under construction (Sakaide Artificial Ground)...

**Building the Dream Future City**
"'We need a city over a city.' Multiple, diverse ... these are the philosophies of this man. He has the ability to imagine the infinite, and the ability to integrate the imagination or vision of the future firmly into reality. He is also gifted with the ability to construct thoughts logically, the ability to make compelling arguments, and also political power..."

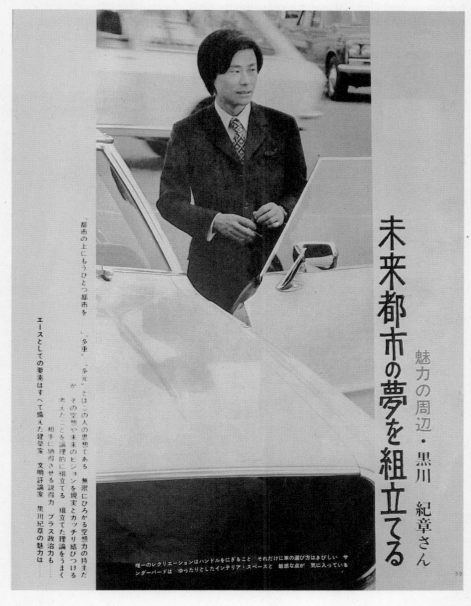

魅力の周辺・黒川 紀章さん

未来都市の夢を組立てる

"都市の上にもうひとつ都市を、"多重"、"多元"とはこの人の思想である 無限にひろがる空想力の持主だ が その空想や未来のビジョンを現実とカッチリ結びつける 考えたことを論理的に組立てる 組立てた理論をうまく 相手に納得させる説得力 プラス政治力も…… エースとしての要素はすべて備えた建築家 文明評論家 黒川紀章の魅力は

唯一のレクリエーションはハンドルをにぎること それだけに車の選び方はきびしい サンダーバードは ゆったりとしたインテリア・スペースと 敏感な点が 気に入っている

Enter Kurokawa: as the hype builds for Expo '70, the media finds a new, younger architect suitable for a new mode of character study and lifestyle coverage: the stylish, visionary 35-year-old Kisho Kurokawa. His "political" power is already sensed by *Mainichi Graph*...

## Building the Dream Future City ... cont'd

"Novelist Itaru Kikumura describes Kurokawa as 'guru-ish' and 'a new type of youth borne by our time.' Unconventionally, he thinks of architecture 'not in terms of everyday life but more metaphysically.' Social engineering professor Yujiro Hayashi points to Kurokawa's 'articulate and pleasant speech, avant-garde look, with the affableness of a 3-year-old and the modesty of an 80-year-old ... Besides his own occupation, TV stations compete for his voice on marine development, space after Apollo, etc. ... Is it TV's magic that makes Kurokawa's hard theory accessible to anyone?"

In sunglasses:
"A philosophical mask.
He is extremely popular
among young females."

Within one article, the emphasis begins to shift from the
architect-at-work (left page) to the architect-at-play (right);
the author also acknowledges the alchemy of TV. Soon,
the focus will shift away from architecture altogether...

"For a break, he goes out to Shinjuku at midnight once or twice a month. Not that he loves drinking, but he enjoys the atmosphere..."

**1969 July** Another man, another mirror: Yukio Mishima.

Kurokawa with the "enigmatic" Mariko Furuta at her legendary Shinjuku bar, Nadja. According to Furuta, Kurokawa always takes the corner seat, quietly sipping a glass ... Kurokawa later writes that "many of those who were introduced to me [at the bar] became leaders in various creative fields." (*Kisho Kurokawa Notes*, 1994.)

Meanwhile, Yukio Mishima—man of letters, actor, nationalist, and the first person the Japanese media calls a "superstar"—is never far from Kurokawa's mind. Mishima "was the first to dance in a psychedelic club; had ranks in body building, boxing, and kendo; honorably became Japan's first male nude model; experienced a supersonic flight on a jet fighter; sent out his party invites on Tiffany paper; spent a fortune to make his own army—while avidly writing novels to become the first Japanese candidate for the Nobel prize for literature." Occupying different fields, Mishima and Kurokawa's profiles nevertheless align through a shared dandyism, polemical flare, ability to manipulate the media, and a sensibility for engineering the identity of Japan ... to the extent that, in 1969, Kurokawa calls Mishima "my only rival." **

* Yamato Shiine, *Yukio Mishima in Heibon Punch*, (Tokyo: Shinchosha, 2007).
** "A Revolutionary Who Calls upon Mobile Home," *Shukan Yomiuri*, July 25, 1969.

**Western decadence, Eastern purism:** Mishima poses in a sharp modern suit in a colonial parlour, and in a tailored military uniform during a parade of his small private army in 1969. (One year later, he makes a farcical coup attempt, which ends with his suicide by *seppuku*.) In his military mode, Mishima, angry at the loss of traditional Japanese values during its rapid postwar modernization (and at the emasculation of the Joint Security Treaty with the US, which prohibits the development of Japan's army), campaigns for the restoration of the Emperor's powers and a resurrection of the samurai mentality. Inside the uniform is a product of incessant toil...

"Nothing strikes me as more fundamentally fashionable than Yukio Mishima in his military outfit. For him, the body is inseparable from the spirit: the body exists to discipline the spirit. As such, Mishima in his military look is disciplining his spirit. That is truly the philosophy of fashion." (Kurokawa, *Fujin Koron*, January 1969).

### Sex Appeal of a Man Who Intoxicates Me
### Kisho Kurokawa: Like a Fountain that Never Stops Gushing

by Junko Koshino, fashion designer

"Step into a bar in Shinjuku, and he is always there, sitting in a corner, quiet. If I don't find him, the corner feels strange, missing something. Among the regulars of the bar, he is a type who talks at length on one subject, and it could be about a love affair, an eye for fashion, an episode from a journey ... But whatever subject he picks, his story is so fresh it's as if it washes one's eyes. Is it just me who sees in the depths of the eyes of this pioneer of architecture a certain toughness, which comes from seeing to the farthest distance, and also the pain of a top runner?"

建築・黒川紀章　尽きない泉を見る思い　コシノジュンコ（デザイナー）

新宿の酒場へ繰り込むと、すみっこのほうに必ず、ひっそりとすわっている。彼がいない日の、そのコーナーは妙に格好がつかなくてさびしい。

飲み仲間の中でも、じっくり型の彼が話す恋の行くえ。モードの目。旅で拾ったエピソード。どれもが目を洗われるようにフレッシュで、心に残る。この建築界の旗手のひとみの奥には、はるかかなたを見つめるタフさと、トップ走者の哀歓があると思うのは、私だけだろうか。

★黒川氏は、こどもの国のセントラルロッジや万博の「東芝IHI館」など、数々のユニークな作品で知られる若手建築家のトップ。

協力　千代田生命

66

Architecture to celebrity: Kurokawa is one of several men (including a photographer, a novelist, a tennis player) picked out as a muse by a board of celebrated women in the magazine *Shufu-no-tomo* (Housewife's companion). The new Japanese creative man still harbors something of the samurai...

**The Man: Kisho Kurokawa, Creator of the Expo**
**What kind of a person are you?** Hmm, I'm a novice architect with a salary of one million yen [$10,000] a month. My biggest dream is to design time. I want to be someone who challenges time, like a movie director. I'm also a man of the future.
**Nixon?** Fail. I feel nothing.
**Napoleon?** Pass. He slept no more than three hours a night. No one knows where he is, but he can do anything. I respect him—I wish I could be like him. But I am I. If I was to be reborn, I definitely want to be me again.
**What is the Homo Moven you are advocating?** I can't but feel that the turbulence of our life—the city, architecture, art, technology—is actually swirling around the firm spine of a "movement." And I wonder what would the new value in such a condition would be. Those who carry such new value are what I call "homo movens."

**Cars he owns** Porsche 911S, Lincoln Continental
**Clothes he owns** About 30 sets
**Favourite fashion designers** Cardin, Saint-Laurent, Lapidus, Courèges
**Favourite colour** Black
**Height** 162 cm
**Weight** 45 kg

Kurokawa "THE MAN" appears perfectly alongside an ad for the fragrance, Dandy.

Like a rapper, Kurokawa celebrates the end of his youthful poverty with cars, clothes, and bravado. He already leads the exemplary lifestyle of the homo moven—the man who values mobility for its own sake.

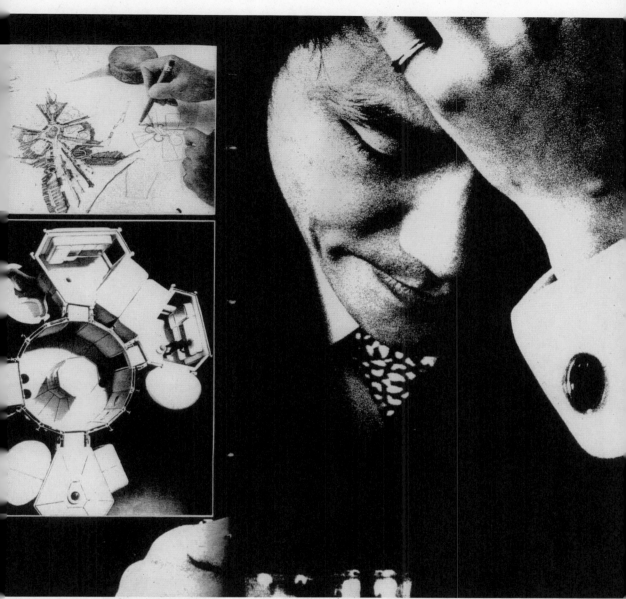

Laboring over the Capsule for Living, which he has one month to finish before Expo '70 starts. Article 8 of his "Capsule Declaration," made in 1969, offers philosophical clues to Kurokawa's ability to exploit the media: "The capsule mentality is opposed to uniformity and systematic thinking. The age of systematic thinking has ended. Thought disintegrates, is dissolved into separate, powerful words, and is capsulized. A single word, or single name, can spread, transform, permeate, stimulate an entire society and help to mould the thinking of the age…"

Science fiction novelist Sakyo Komatsu discusses Kurokawa's Takara Beautillion.

Pondering Taro Okamoto's *Tower of the Sun*.

1971 DECEMBER 4 **NHK CHANNEL 1**

**Kurokawa interviews New York Mayor John Lindsay**

Serious: in the build up to Expo '70, Kurokawa builds his TV profile as a spokesman for the nation-building event. A year later, in a national broadcast, he plays guest host to Mayor Lindsay. Two cities in crisis, Tokyo and New York, exchange wisdom, condolences...

## 11PM Show

Frivolous: after the Expo '70 fever, the 11 p.m. Show, a nightly talk
show targeted at men, is the unlikely venue for Kurokawa to present his
Metamorphosis project (1965–), which is used as a table. The host,
Ayuro Miki, a jazz critic, points to one of the show's models, who holds
a plan of Kurokawa's Hishino New Town, now under construction.
Japan itself serves as the TV backdrop...

## Dialogue with Prime Minister Tanaka

Transcending architecture: at age 38, Kurokawa is chosen by NHK
to interview Prime Minister Kakuei Tanaka, also a qualified architect
and a polemicist, fresh from the publication of his book *Plan for
Remodeling the Japanese Archipelago* (1972).

"It was just before I became a commentator for NHK, and the topic of conversation was a book the prime minister had written. In that book, Kakuei Tanaka had written enthusiastically about creating 150 to 300 cities with populations of about 150,000 to 300,000 over the Japanese Archipelago. Land with picturesque natural scenery where not many people lived, such as the vicinity of Lake Akan or the foot of Mount Fuji, would be purchased and entirely new cities constructed. I boldly told him that his thinking was basically wrong. I was all for invigorating local areas as an alternative to centralization around metropolises such as Tokyo, but was it right to make 150,000 or 300,000 the uniform target for all new cities and to create a lot of small, similar cities competing against each other? I remember arguing rather forcefully that, as we were entering an era of diversification, a better alternative might be network cities: cities linked by a communication network that promoted synergy, in which each city, whether an existing city of a million or 500,000 or a newly created city of 500,000, was allowed to make the most of its own distinctive size, history and character and to serve a unique function.

I was later admonished by various individuals for having spoken so plainly on an NHK television program to a prime minister known for his fiery disposition. I had no previous acquaintance with Prime Minister Tanaka but we became close after that meeting. After the program, he told me, "I found your ideas quite interesting and enlightening." When newspaper reporters huddled around us to ask him for his reaction, he deliberately called over his private secretary and ordered him to bring some paper. The prime minister then began drawing an architectural plan on the paper and told me, "Mr. Kurokawa, did you know that I was the one who created the first-class architects law [as a congressman in 1950] and that I am registered as the first first-class architect of Japan?"

I was summoned by the prime minister a number of times after that. And when I for my part felt a policy of the Liberal Democratic Party was questionable, I would telephone or visit him at his home in Mejiro and argue my case. The day after the [TV] conversation, the private secretary visited me to say, "Thank you for yesterday. The prime minister said it was highly enlightening." The secretary left behind a package. Wondering what it could be, I opened it to discover inside a bolt of splendid English cloth complete with a tailor's voucher. I was astonished. This was before there was talk of Tanaka's so-called "money politics." I was already acquainted with many politicians by then but that was the first time a conversation with one was followed by the delivery of the makings for a bespoke suit."

From *Kisho Kurokawa Notes* (1994).

## Life in Three Colours: The Prince of Architecture

"Through the swivel door, past the cloakroom, a guy in a three-piece black suit dashes into an elevator. Stepping out on the eighth floor, he begins walking more slowly... His black suits are made of British wool. The striking tie in archaic indigo blue and white is plant-dyed. The shirt in a subtle hue of ivory...
Perfect everywhere.

Why do you live in a hotel? I am out of town for almost half a year. For one third I'm outside Japan, and for the rest moving back and forth between Tokyo and outside. I need to stay in a hotel to meet writing deadlines.
Why do you wear black, navy blue and white only? Because I like them.
Do you wear suits also on construction sites? No, I do wear jeans.
Shall I put them on?

He changes for us, but it turns out to be a soft-cotton jeans blazer jacket, bell-bottoms, and light blue shirts. He then changes again for us, into a white turtleneck sweater and an Italian double-sided long leather jacket. Brown is a rare color for him ... His large Gucci travel bag is ready to go. He is departing Japan the next day. So I ask, 'where to this time?' 'Tanzania for development. Then, a lecture at Cambridge, followed by an international conference...'"

As much as he is adored by young women, Kurokawa is also a role model and icon for men. Appearing in Japanese *Playboy*, the sexuality simmering beneath the surface in all his media appearances threatens to fully emerge...

"'When Yukio Mishima was alive, an Italian came to document his eyes and mine in a film...' he [Kurokawa] said, suddenly defreezing his look into a smile. His eyes became smaller and gentler."

# 人生3色主義＝黒川紀章

建築界のプリンス

「三島由紀夫が生きていた頃イタリア人が、ぼくと三島の目を映画に撮っていって…」と彼はいった。

そのとき彼の冷たいまなざしが突然くずれて笑った。小さくやさしい目になった。だから、ブラックの堅いスーツ姿さえ、一瞬ピンク色に思えたほどだった。

ホテルの回転ドアを軽くまわして、少し小走りにクロークへ向う男がいた。三ツ揃いの黒いスーツに身を包んだその男は、やがて背を向けてエレベーターの中へ消えていっ

た。8階で男は降りた。が、また背を向けて、今度はゆっくりと歩いてゆく。

建築家、黒川紀章との出あいはここから始まった。

Q何故ホテル住いを……?

FASHION LIFE《9》黒川紀章

三色は外に置いてくれた系色。イタリア製のダブル S M C　

撮影／川仁 忍

Accessories of the homo moven, including eight (8) bunches of keys for various cars and properties.

床屋嫌いで、自分でカットする。もちろんヒゲも毎朝。

ホワイトゴールドのカフスボタンは、エルメスのもの。パリで求む。

15年使ったモンブランの万年筆とボールペン。ドイツ製のサングラス。タバコは普段葉巻を2箱。常備する東照宮の御守。

パセロンコンスタンチンの腕時計は彼の行動を正確に…。

今年、40才を迎える彼は、まだまだとても若く、そして建築界のちょっぴりキザなプリンスでありました。

そうこなくちゃウソだ！とばかり小躍りしたら、何んとまたもやソフトコットンのブルージーンズのブレザーに、ややベルボトムズのパンタロン姿。そして、Yシャツもやっぱり水色でありました。もちろん、値段なんてヤボなこと聞きません。伝票にただサインするだけでオーケーなんですから……。

A ぼくは、1年のうち約半年は東京にいません。1/3は海外ですし、あとの残りは地方と東京の往復です。……原稿に追われるとホテル泊りになるんですよ。

黒いスーツは英国製のウール。古代色の藍に白い模様の、鮮やかなネクタイは、草木染め。消え入る程に薄い象牙色をおびた白いYシャツ姿。そして、Yシャツもやっぱり水色でありました。もちろん、値段なんてヤボなこと聞きません。伝票にただサインするだけでオーケーなんですから……。

Q 英雄、色を好むって言いますよ。三色だけではありませんでしょ？

A アッハッハッ……。素晴らしく大きな声で笑ったかと思うと、彼はサッと着がえてくれた。白いセーター、茶色の皮のブレザー。こげ茶のパンタロン。洋服ダンスもチラリとのぞかせてくれた。薄茶色の毛皮のコート。皮のジャケット。数枚のYシャツとセーターがきちんとかけてあった。大きなグッチの旅行カバンには、旅の用意ができていた。明日、彼はまた日本を発つ。今度はどちらへ？とサヨナラした背中に問いかけたら、ヒョイと振りむいてこう言った。「タンザニアの開発にアフリカへ。その後ケンブリッジ大学でレクチャー。あとは国際会議に出席して……」

Q それでは、食事や酒もここで？

A ぼくはアルコールに弱くて……。でも好きですよ。ビール1杯で真赤になるけど……。ブランディーならナポレオンより、レニマルタンのほうがいいとか、ワインならシャトーもいいけど、モーゼが口に合うとかはありますが……。彼は、白いレースの窓ごしに、ホテルの庭を眺めながら

Q どんな色がお好きですか？

A スーツは三ツ揃いの紺と、また黒。ネクタイは紺と白のコンビネーション。Yシャツはホワイトですね。

スーツは銀座のヤジマという店です。あくまでもYシャツは布地で変化を出します。デザインは、ほとんど同一。値段？……さあ……知りません。だって伝票にサインするだけですから。15～16年前から作ってます。ええ、一度に5～6着まとめて……。

Q 何故、黒、紺、白だけなんでしょう？

A 好きだからです。

なるほど、単純にして且つ明快な答えが返ってきた。しかし、こうなると、こちらは意地でも他の色のファッションを見たくなる。

Q 建築現場でもスーツ姿で？

A いいえ、ジーンズですよ。ちょっと着てみましょうか。

手帳、名刺入れ、サイフ。これらがビシッと着こなしたスーツのポケットから出てきた。まるで手品のように。

大きな二つ折りのグッチの旅行ケースと、黒い皮のアタッシェケース。幾度も彼の旅の思い出をつめて運んだ。

**Friendship through Tanzania: Yoshiko Yamaguchi
Member, House of Councillors**
"When I first met Kurokawa, at a reception given by an ambassador from the Middle East, he was designing Tanzania's new parliament. Friendship began: he invited me to lecture at his forum and I consulted him on political issues. Sharing the same way of thinking, I felt relaxed talking to him from the beginning... At his office, I find him taking actions in various parts of the world —Middle East, Africa, Italy... Which reminds me of Chaplin's film, *Dictator*."

As the young homo moven enters middle age (he is now 43), he begins to develop his political network, meeting: Yoshiko Yamaguchi (now Otaka, no relation), a member of the Diet who made a similar transition from the world of culture to media to politics. Before marrying Isamu Noguchi in 1958, Yamaguchi was an actress and singer in Manchukuo, in Japan, and in the US, and was famous during the war as Li Xianglan; she later hosted a TV talk show; in 1982, Yamaguchi and Kurokawa visit Libya together on a diplomatic and architectural mission...

山口淑子氏（参議院議員）

黒川紀章氏（建築家）

山口淑子

中東の大使に招かれたレセプションで、当時、タンザニアの国会議事堂を設計なさってた黒川さんと出会ったのが始まり。以来、「紀章会」で講演させていただいたり、政治、政策でいろいろ知恵を拝借する縁となりました。

初めてお会いしたとき、ただ、一言も話さなくても以前から考え方の似ているところにいらっしゃって、異和感なくリラックスできる方という印象でした。

"建築は空間での凍れる音楽"と誰かが言ってましたが、一つの設計をなさるとき、いろいろな制約の上にたち、あらゆる矛盾するファクターを調整し、その中に自分の哲学、夢、オリジナリティを加えて、美しく燃焼させていく、なんともドラマチックな職業である建築家は、オーケストラのコンダクターのようです。

事務所を訪れると、日本はもとより、中東、アフリカ、イタリア……と世界の空間に行動している姿があり、さながら、チャップリンの映画「独裁者」を思い出しました。

（写真は黒川氏の事務所にて）

## Prime Minister Nakasone's main network

In his column "Eyes of a Reporter," Taro Maki diagrams the "brains" behind Prime Minister Yasuhiro Nakasone (in power from 1982–87). Kurokawa's Institute for Social Engineering, formed in 1969 and now producing regular reports for various ministries, is identified as Nakasone's academic and cultural brain. The ISE is also closely connected to former Premier Masayoshi Ohira's policy research group. Kurokawa himself plays up his growing relationship to political power since the late '60s: "A political policy research group was formed at the time of Prime Minister Sato (1964–72), comprising of experts in various disciplines. It discussed various topics from international politics and domestic politics to foreign policy, and presents advice to the Chief Cabinet Secretary, who has even attended the group's meetings. The group has continued for nearly 20 years to date. What's unique about this group is that no matter who comes into the position of prime minister, or into his regime, it has remained neutral and continued its activity." The members besides Kurokawa included political scientists, economists, sociologist, a playwright, and a natural scientist. (*Kisho Kurokawa Notes,* 1994)

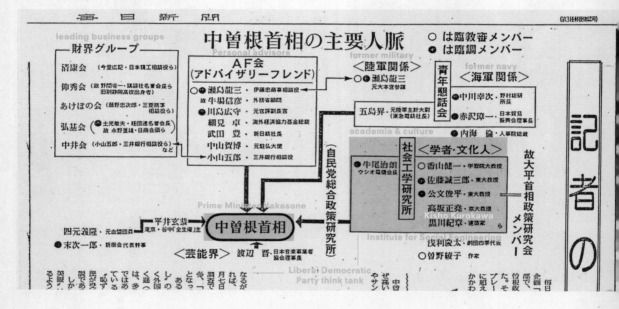

Media to politics: Kurokawa gradually leverages his media profile to acquire presence and a voice in the political scene. Unlike Tange, Kurokawa maintains his image as a private architect, and a businessman, well aware that it is this very independence which allows him to exercise a more politicized role...

**At the Prime Minister's official residence, Tokyo**
Nakasone's "brain": Representing hundreds of guests chosen from the cultural
and entertainment world, Kurokawa addresses Prime Minister Yasuhiro Nakasone
and the highest ranking politicians in the incumbent Liberal Democratic Party:
(from left) Chikage Ogi (member of the House of Councillors and former actress),
Sosuke Uno (later prime minister, June–August 1989), Noboru Takeshita (later
prime minister, 1987–89), Shintaro Ishihara (member of the House of Representatives;
later governor of Tokyo), Kurokawa, Yasuo Fukuda (prime minister, 2007–08),
Ayako Wakao (Kurokawa's wife and actress), Prime Minister Nakasone, and
Masajuro Shiokawa (minister of education).

**Kurokawa and Takeshi Kitano**
Kurokawa, now an official commentator on NHK, moonlights on Nihon TV to launch another private initiative designed to help the nation ... The overheated *minkatsu* (free market) economy resurrects the idea of building on Tokyo Bay; Kurokawa discusses his new scheme for the bay with the comedian Takeshi Kitano, two years before he appears in and directs *Violent Cop* (1989)...

Transformations: on popular TV show, Kurokawa presents his New Tokyo Bay 2025 plan for artificial ground on the bay to Takeshi Kitano, before he turns movie director.

**Kurokawa, TV Column**
The property bubble also resurrects the decentralization debate that started in the mid '60s. Kurokawa seizes the moment to present his concept of two national axes (*kokudojiku*). His hope is that Japan's regional cities, if they are better connected, can absorb some of the demand for, and reduce the prices of, real estate as the bubble threatens to burst...

"NHK commentator Kisho Kurokawa (architect)..."

"First national axis / second national axis," Kurokawa's 1990 scheme for connecting Japan's cities.

One and a half years after we interview him, Kurokawa announces that he will run for governor of Tokyo, under the banner of his own Symbiosis New Party. Dropping his longstanding refusal to enter politics, he says he is enraged by the performance of his "long-term friend" Shintaro Ishihara, Tokyo's governor. His manifesto includes plans to decentralize government functions to other cities, construct more parks and affordable housing, and—the culmination of a lifelong quiet rivalry—sell Tange's Tokyo Metropolitan Government buildings as commercial real estate. Kurokawa loses to Ishihara, coming in fourth with 2.9 percent of the vote. Soon after the defeat, he runs for the House of Councillors and loses again. Three months later, he passes away at the age of 73.

**1999, September** Confidante: Kurokawa and Tokyo Governor Shintaro Ishihara, an old friend, are invited to the Diet to debate the relocation of Congress and other capital functions.

**2007** Announcing his candidacy and manifesto for the governorship of Tokyo, running against Ishihara.

Until the bitter end: three months before his death, Kurokawa canvasses outside Tange's Tokyo Metropolitan Government buildings. It is a double rebellion: against his friend-turned political-rival Shintaro Ishihara, and against his mentor, now professional competitor.

# Kenji Ekuan 栄久庵憲司

**1929** born in Tokyo, father a Buddhist priest **1945** visits Hiroshima soon after atomic bombing, feels "the call of all things manmade"; continues practicing as monk at his father's former temple **1950** leaves the temple to study industrial design at Tokyo University of Fine Arts **1952** forms GK design collective with fellow students **1953** GK designs S1B Yamaha upright piano, and telephone booth for NTT, which becomes ubiquitous in Japan **1954** decides to continue with industrial design rather returning to the temple **1955** graduates from university; designs Yamaha's first motorcycle, the YA1; participates in Wachsmann Seminar at Tokyo University as the only industrial designer among architects; studies at Art Center College of Design, Pasadena, Los Angeles **1957** GK Industrial Design formally incorporated **1960** speaks at World Design Conference on role of automobiles in the city; elected board member of Japan Industrial Designers' Association **1961** designs Kikkoman soy sauce bottle **1963** three bicycles by GK exhibited at the Louvre, Paris **1964** creates Dwelling City and Metabolist Furniture concepts for unrealized second book of Metabolism, receives the Kaufmann International Design Award for them **1967** joins architects committee for Expo '70 with Tange **1969** Hermit Crab Capsule Lodge; publishes *Dougu-ko* (Thoughts on tools); begins exchange program with Philips (Netherlands) **1970** directs design of street furniture, signage, monorail, electric cars for Expo '70 **1972** designs indoor and outdoor equipment and furniture for Kyoto Shinyo Kinko bank branches **1973** Yokohama Municipal Subway; executive director, World Industrial Design Conference **1974** works with Tange on masterplan for Pilgrims' Accommodation, Muna, near Mecca, Saudi Arabia **1975** GK Tokyo Shibuya Shop opens **1976** elected president of International Council of Societies of Industrial Design **1980** publishes *Dougu-no-shiso* (The philosophy of tools) **1985** directs design of street furniture and facilities for Tsukuba Expo; establishes GK Graphics **1986** establishes GK Design Europe in Amsterdam **1987** coproducer of World Design Exposition, Nagoya **1989** divides GK into 12 companies upon becoming 60; *Neural Object II: Symphonic Object* mechanical interactive sculpture; signage for JR Line's Shinjuku Station **1991** designs Narita Express train connecting Tokyo airport with downtown **1995** chairman of Japan Institute of Design **1997** Akita Shinkansen Komachi bullet train **1998** founding chairman, Design for the World; publishes in English *The Aesthetics of the Japanese Lunchbox* **1999** GK school opens; designs Intelligent Bus Stop for Berlin **2002** passenger seating in Japan Air Lines aeroplanes; JR Yamanote Line train E231 **2007** designs logo for Tokyo Olympics promotion **2009** publishes *Dezain ni Jinsei o Kakeru* (Devoting life to design)

"By giving them rides in my car I was showing them exactly what industrial design was about. They'd often comment on how constrained architecture was. Kikutake would complain that architecture has no movement, it's not dynamic..."

Kenji Ekuan brought compelling professional experience and personal conviction when he joined the Metabolists not as an architect but as an industrial designer at the 1960 World Design Conference. Ekuan had decided to devote his life to design after convincing the Buddhist monks at the temple whose leadership he had inherited from his father that he could convey the teachings of Buddha "through the world of things." Visiting Hiroshima after the bomb—at the age of 16—was the formative experience for this belief: what was left of the man-made world assumed a massive, desperate significance; design, Ekuan thought, could help relaunch the shattered nation. While agitating for the elevation of industrial design as an academic discipline and a democratic tool while studying, Ekuan started the designers' collective GK in 1953. It was this pedigree, together with his participation in Konrad Wachsmann's Tokyo seminar in 1955—an incubator of technological awareness prefiguring Metabolism—and his leadership of Japan's nascent design community that made Kawazoe invite Ekuan into Metabolism. Seemingly unburdened by the pressure of the historical record at stake in this interview, Ekuan discusses, with un-Japanese frankness, the hierarchies among the Metabolists, and identifies Takashi Asada as the (invisible) core of the group.

Tsugihagi restaurant, Hibiya,
Tokyo, September 10, 2005

**1955** Ekuan, 26, just graduated in industrial design, commutes to Konrad Wachsmann's seminar at Tokyo University on one of his first works: the Yamaha YA1. He gives a demonstration of the bike to the gathering of architects, surprised at the speed and artistry of industrial design compared with their own profession…

Takashi Asada

Kenzo Tange

Rehearsal for Metabolism: Asada, Tange, Isozaki are also at the Wachsmann Seminar with Ekuan.

Space frame connector demonstrated by Wachsmann, featured by Kawazoe in *Shinkenchiku*, February 1956.

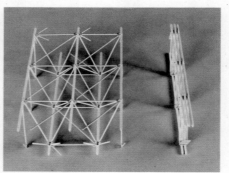

Space frame model.

**REM KOOLHAAS** **Can you tell us how you as an industrial designer were involved in Metabolism, basically a movement of architecture?**

**KENJI EKUAN** In the 1950s Japan was in pretty dire straits, and I felt like I wanted to do something to help save the country from those conditions. I thought we all needed to pitch in, to somehow recover the honor Japan had lost in defeat so we could be recognized again as a proper member of the world community.

**RK** **Save? This is the first time we've heard this word in these interviews.**

**KE** Yes, I wanted to help save our country both materially and spiritually. I think a lot of others felt that way, too. Then, during the run-up to the World Design Conference in 1960, the professional society in my field opposed participation on the grounds that Japanese industrial designers weren't yet established enough to involve ourselves in an international event of that kind. When I raised my voice to object that we shouldn't shrink from involvement, I soon heard from Kawazoe, who was the leader of the Metabolists.

Kawazoe was the editor of *Shinkenchiku* when the Wachsmann Seminar was held in Tokyo in 1955, and he had gotten to know me then as one of the participants. Of the seminar's 21 members, I was the only industrial designer. It was 20 architects—Isozaki was one of them—plus me. I was more accustomed to working with machinery and equipment, but it was a time when people were being drawn into all sorts of new things, and I decided to try my hand at industrial design in the world of architecture, which had become a very active field.

**HANS ULRICH OBRIST** **Can you tell us about Wachsmann?**

**KE** Konrad Wachsmann belonged to the Bauhaus school. He moved to America before the war like Walter Gropius and Mies van der Rohe, and he actually even taught alongside Mies at the Illinois Institute of Technology for a time. He'd gotten his start as a carpenter, so his background was that of a technician. He was a true master at building space frames. He went around the world talking tirelessly about how space frames were ideal educational tools for building a fundamental understanding of space. The connectors and other parts used in space frames are pure industrial design, of course.

**RK** **He made the space frames with his own hands, like a carpenter?**

**KE** Yes. So even though you might normally rely on machines, I built space frame parts by hand, too. And since I couldn't do them all by myself, I drafted a crew of students from Japan Women's University in Tokyo, lining them up assembly-line style.

**HUO** **This is interesting, and something we never thought about—the space frame connecting industrial design and architecture.**

## What Is Design?

**RK** **Were you politically active or interested in politics at that moment? I think an architect who is political is typical, but a designer who is political is much rarer.**

**EK** I suppose one way I was politically involved was in getting a definition of design into the Ministry of International Trade and Industry regulations. When the technocrats were drafting some new law, they started by asking "What is design?" And from there the discussions moved on to what kinds of protections and subsidies were needed.

**RK** **You were in contact with the technocrats of MITI in the late '50s?**

**EK** Yes. As I said before, the professional society for industrial design was pretty weak, and I was really determined to change that situation, so I developed a relationship with MITI officials in an effort to get support from the government.

**RK** **There seems to be a two-way access between the state and designers and architects. That perhaps explains the success of the Metabolists.**

**EK** The first thing we had to do was build up the occupational identity and standing of industrial designers. Actually, when I stood in the ruins of Hiroshima shortly

**1945** Ekuan visits Hiroshima 20 days after the bomb and has an epiphany: "In a world where there was nothing left at all, I felt the call of all things man-made." Destruction paradoxically forces him to commit to that which was destroyed, the designed world... this gives life to that...

After witnessing this scene, Ekuan continues studying Buddhism for the next five years, always harboring the desire to design...

**1950** Merging the spiritual and the material, Ekuan signs up for industrial design at Tokyo University of Fine Arts.

Twenty days

"Drop everything and go
to Hiroshima," is what Tange
said to me. I went there and
found that, rather than just
being burned by the atomic
bomb, everything had been
melted flat and made featureless.
Sachio Otani

after the atomic bombing, I was suddenly overcome by this sense of personal mission. This is a true story. I lost some of my own family to the bomb. I was away in the navy so I wasn't there when the bomb hit, but when I stood in the ruins of the city after losing my father and sister to the bomb, there, in a world where there was nothing left at all, I felt the call of all things man-made. The burned-out shell of a streetcar, an overturned truck, a half-melted bicycle… I felt like they were all calling out to me, saying, "Hear us, O traveler!"

**HUO**   **How long after the bomb?**

**EK**   Twenty days. When evening came, the setting sun was just so amazingly beautiful, setting the horrific ruins aglow in its crimson light—it was as if the light of the western sun upon the atomic hellscape transformed it into a dazzling vision of paradise. The setting sun saved the relationship between the realm of things and the realm of people. That scene has continued to have a primal significance in all that I've done since. Experiences like that redirected my perception of the mutability of life from a sense of vanity and desolation to the sense that change drives new growth. I vowed to pursue the kind of change that fit the needs of postwar Japan through industrial design.

**RK**   **Change for the better?**

**EK**   Yes. So in 1950 I enrolled in the Tokyo National University of Fine Arts. It was a narrow-minded old school, and I rebelled against the status quo much like young people today. They didn't have any courses in industrial design, so a bunch of us got together on our own and designed bicycles and things. We were basically saying that bicycle design was artistic expression, too. The traditional craft items everybody made at school were absolutely first rate—things like tea caddies and containers for tea ceremony utensils and such—but we thought it might appeal to people if we turned the duraluminum left over from making airplanes during the war into beautiful new pots and pans. And this is the part I really love: back when the war started, Japan had the world's best fighter plane, the Zero Fighter. The Americans were so surprised. It was just so amazingly beautiful.

**RK**   **Beautiful?**

**EK**   Beautiful and strong. Strong and beautiful. Anyway, we used the duralumin that had gone into these planes to make pots and pans.

**RK**   **That kind of beauty, shared by everyone, every day.**

### Relationships with Bureaucrats

**KE**   That was the sort of thing we wanted to do, so we produced this tract about how important design is, and how the university should be teaching it, and we sold it at the main gate for 20 yen a copy. Like you'd often see poets selling their poems on the street in those days. We said just as this country embraced all manner of new things after the Meiji Restoration many years ago, so this old university should embrace the new today! Pretty soon people started to know who we were and what we were about. I guess a sense of leadership was beginning to emerge from the younger set. You have to remember: most of the people older than us had died in the war.

**HUO**   **How old were you?**

**KE**   About 23. So I was rabble-rousing with a bunch of others my age who wanted industrial design to be recognized, and pretty soon the bureaucrats noticed and decided they wanted to find out who these mavericks were.

**RK**   **More and more we are beginning to understand that the Japanese bureau-cracy in the 1950s and maybe the '60s was very intelligent and I think helped Japanese culture move forward.**

**KE**   So getting back to that sense of mission I was talking about before, I realized that in order to carry it out, I would need the help of business. I would need the help of industry. But I also realized immediately that the bureaucracy was the first hurdle I had to jump. So I figured the quickest way to win recognition

**1952** Encouraged by his professor, Iwataro Koike (who imparts a Buddha-like aphorism: "Design is the figure of a leaf on the ground in the autumn sun"), Ekuan and fellow students launch the GK (Group Koike) design collective.

東京・上野　芸術大学　旧美校図案科教室で
撮影　岡松出版写真部員

Laughing Buddha: Ekuan reunites with his mentor for an article in *Shukan Asahi*, 1965.

**1953** Democratization of music: GK designs Yamaha's first mass-produced, affordable upright piano, the S1B, finished in unvarnished wood.

Group Koike: Ekuan (third from right) and Koike himself (right) plan the redevelopment of Tokyo Station Plaza.

bureaucrats
In those years Japan was
strongly criticized for copying products designed
elsewhere. In his September
1957 visit to the UK, the
minister of foreign affairs,
Aiichiro Fujiyama, encoun-
tered a tense moment in a
TV interview: he was shown
two ball bearings and asked
which he thought was made
in the UK and which one
Japan. In the following year
the department of inspection
and design was set up in the
Ministry of International
Trade and Industry. This was
the first time 'design' was
integrated in the official
system of the country."
Kuan, Devoting Life to
Design, Shunjusha, 2009.

Iwataro Koike
Iwataro Koike (1913–92)
taught design at Tokyo
National University of Fine
Arts and Music 1942–1969.
Koike was also director
of the Japanese Industrial
Designers' Association
1957–58 and again 1965–66.

President of Yamaha
Genichi Kawakami
(1912–2002) was president
of Yamaha from 1950–1983,
during which time he expanded
the company beyond the
manufacture of musical
instruments to the design
of motorcycles, boats and
even holiday resorts.

for the field of industrial design was to cultivate relationships with the bureaucrats. I think after the war the same could be said for architecture and for pretty much any other field as well.

### The World of Things

**RK** **I'm very surprised by the very early connection between an individual designer and the state as a sponsor. What happened from the moment in Hiroshima up until entering the art university?**

**KE** Before I went to the art school, I was at a Buddhist school.

**RK** **Was that your choice?**

**KE** No, I came from a line of priests, and I had to succeed my father at his temple. In fact, I'd already officially succeeded him as chief priest of the temple when I was a student. Then after Buddhist school I went to art school, and when I graduated from there I had to decide once and for all whether to pursue design or Buddhism. I told the temple board: "I want to give up my position as chief priest in charge of this temple. Please let me pursue a career in design. I will strive to convey the teachings of the Buddha through the world of things." This became my foundation, and it still is today. This was in 1954.

**RK** **At some point you started a commercial company. What is the chronology?**

**KE** The GK group was already formed as an independent design collective in 1952, while I was still at the Buddhist school. It was formally incorporated in 1957. I was 27 that year.

**RK** **What does GK mean?**

**KE** *G* is for "group," and *K* is not for "Kenji" [*laughs*], but for a professor who was so supportive of us students: Iwataro Koike. So it essentially stands for "Group Koike." Professor Koike used to say, "You know, design is the figure of a leaf on the ground in the autumn sun." It seemed like such a peaceful and serene image.

**RK** **We were just at Kurokawa's and serenity was definitely not on the agenda.**

**KE** But tranquility was definitely one of Professor Koike's virtues.

### Yamaha

**RK** **Was starting a company a shift so that you would be able to retain the initiative?**

**KE** We agonized a lot about that. We wanted to be able to freely pursue our own interests but also to be of service to others, doing things that would make them happy but would also be satisfying to ourselves. The president of Yamaha, who was a very interesting man, came to our school saying that with the war over we had entered a new age and he wanted us to give musical instruments a makeover. Professor Koike happened to be there, and—

**RK** **The piano company? They wanted to reinvent or design instruments?**

**KE** Redesign.

**RK** **I think Yamaha achieved a kind of ultimate democracy by making a pastime that previously belonged only to the bourgeoisie available to everyone. You could almost say they gave a political dimension to creativity.**

**KE** Yes, their Yamaha Schools were part of that. Japan was a poor country, and playing musical instruments traditionally had a kind of aristocratic flavor. So Yamaha was offering people a chance to have a taste of the high life. At the time, Yamaha was building motorcycles. During the war they made airplane propellers, so once the war ended, they had to find something else, and decided on motorcycles. Then our GK group teamed up with them. The currents of the times and Yamaha's own corporate currents brought us together.

GK develops its design ethic: rather than pursuing beauty for its own sake, Functionalism, or the high tech, they aim to make things—Ekuan prefers to call them "tools"—more accessible and more appealing...

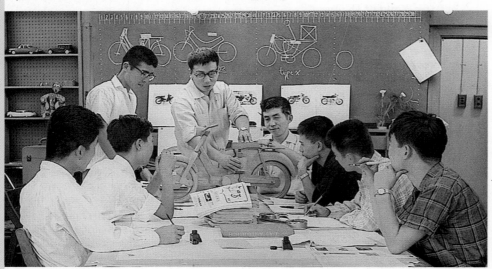

Designing bicycles for the manufacturer Maruishi, as tools of postwar development and individual liberation...

**1957** Yamaha YD-1. "Designing a motorcycle is a lot of fun. A motorcycle is like an insect: it haslegs, chest and a backside. All organs are exposed, so it has a natural logic."[1]

**1962** The "Sunday" bicycle. "We designed bicycles in red, white, pink or light gray. Our catchphrase was: 'The days of air-raid sirens are behind us. Darkness is gone. Light is back!'"[2]

Design for life: the GK collective enjoy motorcycles of their own making.

## Plodding Architecture

**RK**    **Are you saying that since you started in 1953 and became successful in 1957, you'd already had a much more adventurous career than the Metabolists had when they formed three years later?**

**KE**    You could say that. When Kawazoe called me and I joined the planning sessions that ultimately led to the birth of Metabolism, my first impression was: What kind of ancient history are these guys talking about? That's the absolute truth. [*laughs*] I mean, the field of industrial design is always on the move, and it's unfettered, and it's involved in making large quantities of products to provide for entire populations. By comparison, I couldn't believe how plodding the field of architecture seemed to be.

**RK**    **So you played your role as a supporter of it very seriously?**

**KE**    Yes. Since I was surrounded by architects, I decided, alright, I'm going to see what I can do with industrial design to make architecture movable. That was when I thought up "walking architecture." It's also when I came up with capsules that could be attached and removed or shifted around within a structure. I think it's generally believed that the capsule concept was something Kurokawa first came up with, but actually I was already doing capsules before that. I created modules that contained all the plumbing facilities in a single unit, and I designed telephone booths—things like that.

**RK**    **Did the capsule for you have anything to do with Japanese tradition? Because that is one of the things we hear again and again but which I find totally tiring and unbelievable: that the capsule goes back to the original Japanese house.**

**KE**    Well, I'm sorry, but there really is a connection. For me, the original capsule was the traditional Japanese tea hut. In this little tea hut in the garden you have all these different tea utensils, and you go inside it to mix bowls of tea. That's the image I had in my head. But Kurokawa had a way with words, and he wrote a lot, and there was just no way I could keep up with him. [*laughs*] I'm the type who works with his gut, following my instincts, and I wasn't very good at analyzing what I was doing or talking about it. Kurokawa was definitely a cut above me on that.

**RK**    **We have had the incredible privilege to experience within three hours these two extremes and to be impressed by both. [*laughs*]**

### An Object with Spirit

**RK**    **When you were active as a Metabolist, were you aware that Japan was actually more advanced than Europe or America? Were you confident that you were a real avant-garde or did you not compare yourselves to anything in America or in Europe?**

**KE**    I didn't think we were more advanced, but I definitely didn't think we lagged behind either. After all, to be plain about it, we had put up a pretty good fight against America and England and China. Even if we did lose.

**RK**    **So that's a positive thing. So there was still some adrenaline left.**

**KE**    Yes, I'd say so. Or an inner soul—some kind of heart or spirit, like bushido. We still had something like that. And on the material side, there were things like the Zero Fighter that I talked about before.

**RK**    **That is the gold standard, the beginning. Is the Zero Fighter the first capsule?**

**KE**    I don't know about that, but at least there's no question that it was a very powerful object. An object with spirit.

**JG**    **When industry started again after the war, Japanese products were considered to be copies of European products.**

**KE**    Civilian manufacturing in Japan had fallen way behind, all across the board. But when you look back historically to the Edo period, standards used to be at a very high level, so even if quality dropped off for a while, American products in particular provided a good stimulus, and it didn't take long to recover to

Ekuan—not Kurokawa—is the first to intuit the significance of the capsule as a hybrid piece of industrial design and architecture. Before, and simultaneously with his Metabolist peers, he designs several lesser-known prototypes…

**1953** First modern capsule? Ekuan's ubiquitous phone booth for the Nippon Telegraph and Telephone Corporation.

**1963** Designed to be carried on the back of a truck, the Plastic Ski Lodge encapsulates four beds and washing facilities.

**1964** Village Housing, adaptable agglomeration of prefab units/capsules.

**1969** Yadokari Hermit Crab Capsule Lodge: three years before Kurokawa's rural version, Ekuan creates the countryside capsule.

Tange, masterplanner of Expo '70, commissions GK to oversee the design of outdoor facilities; Ekuan goes further and launches the concept of "street furniture"—urban identity defined not by buildings but by smaller elements. GK's designs give visual and practical coherence to the jamboree of Expo '70; cities throughout Japan soon take up the idea of street furniture…

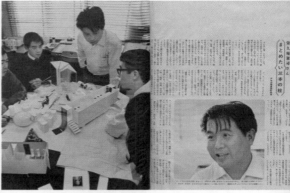

"Kenji Ekuan is excited to design some 150 different kinds of street furniture in a consistent style for Expo '70." *Mainichi Graph*, January 5, 1969.

Monorail—"I had a particular attachment to railways and pitched to Expo '70 to design the monorail. I saw a future in it."[3]

Street lighting and PA systems.

Multi-face clock.

Mise-en-scène of street furniture—parasols, seating, trash cans, planters—for pedestrians outside the Japanese pavilion.

Electric car for Kunio Maekawa's Automobile Pavilion.

Mailbox, which becomes ubiquitous in Japan.

Phone booths.

Wayfinding.

zaki was not, and
urokawa was left out, too.
evertheless, Kurokawa and
ozaki still played crucial
les in Expo '70: Kurokawa
esigned three pavilions;
ozaki collaborated with
ange on Festival Plaza,
nderneath the Big Roof.
ee Expo '70, p. 506.

hat's what Expo '70 was
me
hile large-scale projects
led the impression of the
xpo, smaller objects that
ere distributed over the
te—all designed or direct-
d by GK—played a decisive
le in controlling the massive
ow of visitors.
ajime Yatsuka

ross-disciplinary
sada was senior to me. His
ist knowledge was useful
nd I liked to ask him about
ings. I don't know when he
und time to study the New
eal policies of the US presi-
ent, but he lectured us on
ose policies and develop-
ent plans that seemed to
ing about economic leaps.
achio Otani

former levels. That's what led to the kind of explosive economic growth that wowed the whole world, and to Expo '70 in Osaka.

### Expo '70: 12 + 1

**HUO** **I want to ask you about Expo '70, which has become a big myth in Europe. None of us actually saw it. One of the things I was very surprised about in our interviews is the rather negative assessment about Osaka. I had thought the Expo was somehow the fulfillment of the Metabolist generation's utopia, but that does not seem to be the case. Did you do anything for the Expo?**

**KE** To put it in a word, I think Expo '70 restored our confidence as a people. And I think that became the foundation for today's Japan. For that to happen, we needed something visible. And the person responsible for giving shape to something on that scale was Tange.

Now, what impressed me about Tange was his relentless pursuit of possibility, of what the future might hold. He turned to his most trusted disciple Isozaki and asked, "What are the things that join us with the future?" And he did much the same with the Metabolist group, asking me in particular to take on the design of items for the urban environment. Street furniture, public toilets, information centers, signage, lighting, trash receptacles, fountains—all those sorts of things that are part of life in the city, he declared me in charge of. Isozaki had suggested my name to him because he knew me from the Wachsmann Seminar.

Tange selected 12 architects plus one to be on his masterplanning commit-tee—the "plus one" being me. Kikutake was one of the 12. Isozaki was not, and Kurokawa was left out, too.

It was very interesting to see. A very delicate balancing act. Befitting his position as professor at a national university, his selections were very even-handed so nobody could complain about the makeup of the committee.

**RK** **It was probably your triumph because it was the triumph of the street furniture of industrial design.**

**KE** Together with Isozaki and Tange, my GK Industrial Design group tried out all kinds of things, and we worked hard to bring out some of the ideas that came from Metabolism in the way of urban design issues. That's what Expo '70 was to me.

### Asada Mystical Sage

**HUO** **You've said that Takashi Asada was the leader of Metabolism. I'm interested in knowing more about the role of Asada and in all the questions in relation to it—how Metabolism evolved with Tange and Kawazoe.**

**KE** Tange recommended Asada—the person closest to him—to serve as secretary-general of the World Design Conference while he was at MIT in 1959, and Asada became the one who stood at the intersection of all the different person-alities and groups that were involved. But he wasn't the sort of person to really take charge like a normal secretary-general; he was more like a mystical sage who just went around spinning profound statements about the quality of the future and such. Fortunately he had plenty of admirers to support him, and two of them in particular, Kawazoe and Kurokawa, served as the main brains for making the World Design Conference a success.

In order to bring something fresh and unique to the conference, Asada wanted to create a cross-disciplinary structure. For example, to put an architect and a graphic designer and an educational specialist side by side. But as I said before, the Japan Industrial Designers' Association opposed the conference, so Asada asked Kawazoe to persuade me to get involved.

**RK** **It was Asada's initiative?**

**KE** When Asada asked him about designers, Kawazoe told him he knew this guy

After leaving Tange Lab, Takashi Asada continues to creates a scene, and generates work for himself and his Environmental Development Center, through relentless networking, constant curiosity, and gnomic proclamations; he does not summon crowds, but draws them wherever he goes...

**1952** with Yukio Futagawa, photographer and founder of *GA* magazine, cruising on the Sumida river, near Tokyo Bay, conducting "urban research."

**1962** with acolytes working on the masterplan for *Kodomono-kuni* (Children's land), Yokohama. Asada commissions Kikutake, Kurokawa, and Otani, among others to design buildings for the site.

**1966** with Eika Takayama (holding octopus), professor of urban planning at Tokyo University; and Akira Tamura (left), who later directs urban planning in Yokohama, implementing plans by Asada's Environmental Development Center.

**1963** with Prince Akihito and Princess Michiko at the completed *Kodomono-kuni*.

**1965** with Kanagawa prefecture governor Masanori Kaneko, culture-lover, who commissions Tange, Isamu Noguchi, and Genichiro Inokuma for major buildings and artworks in his prefecture.

**1966** with Isamu Noguchi, who donates a "sculptural toy" to a playground designed by Asada in Kagawa Prefecture.

**1967** with Charles and Ray Eames, Santa Monica.

**1974** with Ekuan (right); Aiko Hasegawa, editor of *SD* magazine (left); and Finnish architects Heikki and Kaija Siren in Helsinki.

**1964** With a grant from the American Kaufmann Foundation, GK produces a body of work in which they operate at every possible scale, insisting on fluidity between object, architecture, and urbanism...

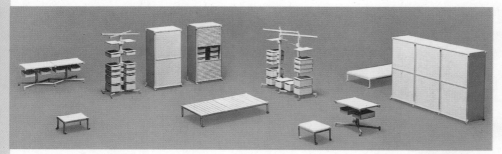

Metabolic Furniture, designed for adaptation with its structure of "skeleton," "organs," and "skin."

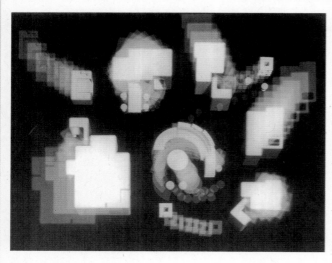

Movable Furniture Room.

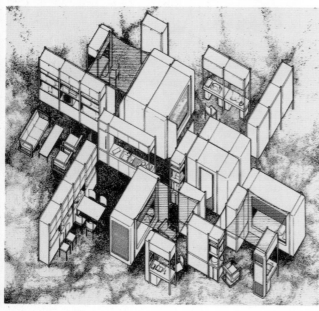

Furniture House—in which the house, without walls, is defined instead by the composition of the furniture.

theoretician who didn't
rite, and an architect who
dn't build

Kawazoe described Asada
s "an architect who doesn't
uild, a writer who doesn't
rite, a professor who
oesn't teach." (Takashi
sada, *Kankyo Kaihatsuron*
Discourse on environmental
evelopment), Kajima
huppankai, 1969.)

nvironmental issues
vas cautious of my uncle's
eculiar forays into environ-
ental concerns. This concern
aybe started during the war,
th exposure to different
imates. He established the
nvironmental Development
enter, and he was very
uch into bureaucratic and
olitical affairs. He was
robably influenced by the
yoto school of philosophy,
hich was around in the '30s
nd '40s. It was the Japanese
ounterpart to Heidegger.
ne member, Nishita Kitaro,
ctured the emperor, saying
at the Greater East Asia
o-Prosperity Sphere had to
e based on an ecological
otion: "Your Highness, you
now that the forest is not
whole, nor merely an
nsemble of mere parts.
's a complex ecological
etwork, a system. We need
concentrate on net-
orking and ecological
rinciples." Of course, this
nd of thinking was just a
retext of Japanese imperi-
ist aggression, which was
upposed to contrast with
Western vulgar imperialism.
hey talked about "over-
oming the modern"—the
odern meaning Western
odernity, which was sup-
osed to be this fatal conflict
etween holism and atomism
r German totalitar- ianism,
oviet totalitarianism, and
nglo-Saxon individualism.
My uncle was probably aware
f this kind of rhetoric. Even
ith Tange, there was this
roto-ecological concern.
Akira Asada

called Ekuan, and took me to see him. Asada was one of the elites from Tokyo University and a disciple of Tange. He was an interesting character—he really reminded me of a mystical Chinese sage. He wasn't the sort to summon an audience, but rather to go out into the street and declaim to anyone who would listen. Kawazoe heard him and took note. Asada didn't really care who was listening. He wasn't selective about who he talked to.

**RK** **He just needed a crowd, and then he came to life.**

### People Bleed

**HUO** **What was his background?**

**KE** He grew up on the island of Shikoku and was the son of a doctor, so he'd been exposed to the essence of life and death from an early age. Then he became an officer in the navy during the war, and although he never saw the battlefront, he did things like fix bomb-damaged airports overnight, and he knew a lot of people who died in bombing raids. One of his pet phrases used to be: "People bleed." The way I see it, that's Metabolism right there.

**RK** **People bleed...**

**KE** He was talking about circulation.

**HUO** **That is a new definition.**

**KE** We have bleed-ocracy. The sage said, "People bleed. Because they have circulation, if you cut them, blood spurts out."

**RK** **It's impossible to imagine that a mystical sage talking about human circulation would trigger such massive events. What was so unique about saying that humans circulate? What else did he say?**

**KE** He'd start by talking about how circulation was the nature of human beings, and pretty soon he'd be talking about the nature of space or the mutability of the world. That's how he was; his mind would go off in every imaginable direction. It wasn't his style to pursue just one thing deeper and deeper like a scholar. He'd go off this way, then off that way, talking about all sorts of different things.

**RK** **So he was preaching?**

**HUO** **But he did not really publish it, because he wasn't present in the 1960 book. He was in a way an invisible man.**

**RK** **An oral man, by the mouth.**

**KE** A theoretician who didn't write, and an architect who didn't build.

**RK** **Do you think that all Metabolists saw him as a sage?**

**KE** I don't really know, but that's how I saw him. Not so much as a Buddhist sage per se; more like a cross between Buddhism and Taoism. Definitely not like Mencius or Confucius.

**RK** **That is, much more magnetic?**

**KE** Yes. Everyone would crowd around him in a theater wanting to hear more because they found what he had to say so interesting.

**RK** **Also handsome?**

**KE** Yes, he was a tall fellow, what you might call a stalwart. Fair-skinned, though not in the sense of pale, and very well-featured. With his ramrod-straight posture, he'd probably look great in a samurai topknot.

**HUO** **Very nice. We have been circling around this center of the movement, which we haven't been able to find until now.**

**RK** **But it's also about charisma.**

**HUO** **Charisma and utopia—something that is missing, as Ernst Bloch defined.[4]**

### Environmental Development Center

**RK** **What was Asada doing between 1960 and 1990?**

**KE** He was one of the earliest to raise his voice on environmental issues. As I recall, he started out by declaring that Japan was on course to becoming one giant trash heap and we needed to do something about it. So he created the

**1964** Increasing the scale of his ambition, Ekuan does not consider architecture as off-limits to the industrial designer...

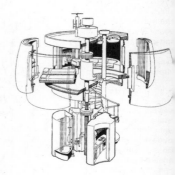

Pumpkin House: designed for a couple, expandable to include a mini-capsule for a child, and featuring outdoor space, Ekua's conception of the capsule is fundamentally different from the communications node that Kurokawa conceived and built for the itinerant, hedonistic single occupant.

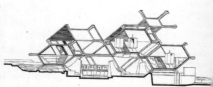

Tortoise House: inhabitable space frame also designed for a family, with rooms as discrete yet connected orthogonal units.

Environmental Development Center. It had a membership of one! I'd say he was what you call a dreamer. He asked me to introduce him to the president of Yamaha, so I did. Well, I'd always thought the president of Yamaha was a bit of an oddball, too, but in any case, he sat there quietly listening to what Asada had to say. Asada was going on and on about the environment and the world and outer space and so on. So finally the president asks, "How many members does your Center have?" and Asada answers, "Just one." [*laughs*]

Afterwards, when Asada and I were having a cup of tea, I asked him why he didn't count Otaka and Maki and Kikutake and Kurokawa and GK and me when the president asked him how many members he had. He said, "Oh, I suppose I could have, couldn't I?" [*laughs*] That's the sort of man he was. You couldn't help worrying about him sometimes. Otaka was the one who tried more than anyone to help him out. I really respected Otaka for that.

**RK** **Kawazoe seems the absolute opposite of Asada. We met him yesterday and he seems to have no charisma.**

**KE** Yes, he's a complete contrast.

**RK** **How did that contrast work?**

**KE** Asada always seemed to be looking far off in some unexpected direction when he spoke. He wasn't concerned about the smaller details. But Kawazoe looked at people up close. He had a fine eye for human sensitivities. I think it was that fine eye that I succumbed to. [*laughs*]

**RK** **Seduced by Asada and attracted to Kawazoe.**

**KE** Kawazoe was good at praising, encouraging my work. Asada didn't do that.

**HUO** **And what about Tange?**

**KE** By the time we all got to know Tange, the Hiroshima Peace Memorial Park was already done. He was like the ultimate authority, so no matter what anybody said, all he'd do was quietly state his opinion, and that would be that. Kind of like when the dead scream all sorts of things at the Buddha, and the Buddha just says, "Is that so?" But I imagine that inside, he probably was the type to go out of his mind in the fires of hell. When I asked some people who'd studied with him, they told me his nickname was "Shark." Not because he looked like a shark, but because once he sank his teeth into some goal he had, he'd never let go.

**HUO** **Did you know Atsushi Shimokobe?**

**KE** Yes, I think of him as a nationalist.

**RK** **Do you mean in the sense of promoting Japan, rather than right-wing nationalism?**

**KE** Well, I think of Asada as being a little like Shoin Yoshida 150 years ago, who tried to break through Japan's closed doors and go to America. From a certain perspective, Yoshida looked like an ultranationalist, but at the same time he had this powerful desire to sneak behind the government's back and get to know the world.

Shimokobe, on the other hand, was very knowledgeable, and he was extremely focused on domestic policies. He had a strong voice in housing policy issues. He'd been a standout as a student in the architectural program and became a top candidate for the bureaucracy. So it was no surprise that he ultimately rose to be vice minister. Asada was a little older than Shimokobe, and he had no interest in stepping up the ladder. But at any rate, it was very reassuring to have people like them working above us.

**RK** **Did Asada the sage smoke?**

**KE** Yes, he did. And on that score, you might say he treated Kurokawa and me like his personal servants. We were at the bottom of the totem pole, so when someone had to buy cigarettes or run some other errand, it was always Kurokawa or me. [*laughs*] I was an outsider, since I wasn't an architect, while Kurokawa was the most junior of the architects, so you could say he and I felt a certain affinity for each other.

**1964** In the final escalation of "House to the City," Ekuan conjures a megastructure: Dwelling City is formed of two stacked tetrahedrons (a shape also used by Kikutake and Kurokawa), with capsules attached to the surface and designated public space inside.

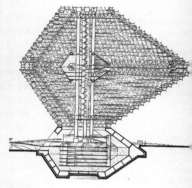

Section.

The colony expands across Tokyo.

## Hierarchy

**KAYOKO OTA** **What exactly was the hierarchy among the Metabolists?**

KE Well, Asada and Otaka were at the top, of course.

RK **Why Otaka? In chemistry or age or talent?**

KE Age plus Tokyo University. [*laughs*] Kawazoe was the one who mediated between the two, and based on age, he was number three and Kikutake number four. Maki was next—a little lower even though he was the same age as Kikutake.

RK **Why? Because he was not there, because he lived abroad? Or because he was Americanized?**

KE Because he was frequently away in America. After Maki was me. And then finally, Kurokawa.

RK **Can you do the same rating in terms of talent?**

KE Well, let me tell you, Kikutake was the outright genius. Kurokawa was extremely capable all around. The one who knew the most about what was going on in the world was Maki. Otaka was kind of a strong grandfather figure. He was older, and he had a very solid track record.

RK **Was he creative or not?**

KE It gets a little complicated, but he was the most involved with social issues, and he was kind of like a standard-bearer in the farmers' liberation movement. He was more of a country boy than a city boy, and he had a strong attachment to the earth. He was the wise old man who commanded everybody's respect.

RK **Now, the most intelligent?**

KE I suppose I'd have to say Kawazoe. It takes more than knowledge to bring together a bunch of eccentric architects and somehow keep them working together. So there must be something special there. Some kind of special wisdom.

RK **The most entertaining?**

KE I suppose the one who was generally most entertaining for people in the city was Kurokawa.

RK **Because of a sense of humor or a passion for performance?**

KE He was spectacularly flamboyant. [*laughs*] So flamboyant that his older colleagues found him pretty hard to take sometimes.

RK **He told us that he weighed 35 kilos. Could you blow him away? [*laughs*]**

KE But he looked really sharp.

RK **Smart or beautiful?**

KE Smart. For example, we'd all be going on about this or that, and he'd be sitting there writing something in his lap. Then when we finished talking, he'd snap a page from his writing pad and present us with a clearly organized summary of what we'd just talked about.

RK **So he always had a narrative.**

KE Kurokawa had technical skills that were very important in sustaining the Metabolists as a group. I, on the other hand, came from a field the architects didn't know much about, so I could be more happy-go-lucky—cheerfully playing the clown, you might say.

### First Metabolist to Own a Car

W

RK **A symbiotic comedian? [*laughs*]**

KE I think on the whole everybody liked me and treated me well. I may have been the comedian, but I also had my own company. So I was the first of the Metabolists to own my own car. I bought a car in 1959, the year before the World Design Conference. Kurokawa and Kawazoe and Kikutake would all pile in, and vroom—off we'd go.

RK **What kind of car?**

KE It was a Subaru 360. A tiny little Japanese car. Built with technologies developed for the Zero Fighter.

**1961** GK's Kikkoman soy sauce bottle relieves housewives of the burden of handling the traditional two-liter barrel.

"My staff used to call me *shocho,* which means 'director', but now they call me *shi,* which is like 'reverend.'"

Ekuan employs industrial design as a solution
to the growing pains of Japan's cities...

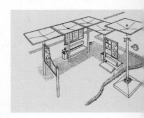

**1963** Shelter Unit for Bus Stop,
prefabricated, shipped to a city
in need, and easily assembled.

**1969** Device Plaza is not a
pedestrian bridge but a "harbor
in the constant stream of automobiles," Ekuan says, providing
gas, drinking water, phone booth
and public lounges. "It will be
a highly functional node of
urban culture."[5]

Commodore Perry
Matthew Calbraith Perry
(1794–1858), US Navy
commodore who compelled
the opening of Japan to the
West with the Convention
of Kanagawa, 1854.

MacArthur
Douglas MacArthur (1880–
1964), head of US occupa-
tion of Japan from 1945–
1948 as Supreme Command-
er of the Allied Powers.

Walking trade shows
After the war, a national
policy of modernization
permeated the whole of
Japanese society. Architecture was modernized more
or less, but there was greater
modernization going on in
industry, especially in electronics. There were no doubt
many extremely able people
who made modernization
possible, even though their
names don't get mentioned.
You hear about individuals in
architecture because architecture was manifestly a field
of activity for individuals,
as opposed to corporations
such as Toyota, Sony, and
Canon.
Hiroshi Hara

**RK**  It was the closest you came to the Zero Fighter? [*laughs*]

**KE**  That's right. Anyway, after our meetings, I'd drive the others home, dropping them off one by one.

**RK**  So they were the bombs that were dropped…

**KE**  There was the sense that by giving them rides in my car I was showing them exactly what industrial design was about. It seems funny today, but the guys were always so impressed when I drove them places in my Subaru. "What a great car!" "This is really cool!" They were totally impressed by all the qualities that make up a car. They'd often comment on how constrained architecture was. Kikutake would complain that architecture has no movement, it's not dynamic.

**RK**  So they were inspired by the flexibility of industrial design?

**KE**  Yes. As I recall, after me, Kurokawa was the next one to get a car. And after him was Kikutake.

**RK**  Kurokawa had an American car. We saw the picture today.

**KE**  No, Kurokawa had a Renault. That was one noisy car—clatter clatter, clatter clatter! [*laughs*] Then Kikutake bought a Chevy. So my Japanese car was followed by a French car and an American car.

**JOSEPH GRIMA**  Did Maki have a car?

**KE**  Maybe he didn't care so much about cars because he'd spent so much time in America. Oh, I remember now, he used to drive around in a dirty old black Mercedes.

**RK**  A German car! That makes sense. [*laughs*]

**KE**  He seemed to be really proud of that car.

**RK**  I can understand entirely, very sober German…

**KE**  It's not often I talk about things like this. [*laughs*]

### Democracy

**RK**  It's very interesting that you are the first Metabolist we've spoken to who talks about Japanese people and not about Japanese tradition. And it's particularly interesting that supposedly the ambition of industrial designers is smaller yet you're both more mystical than anyone we've heard so far and more generous, or less abstract, than anything we've heard so far. More mystical and more concrete—maybe that's the interesting combination.

**KE**  In those days a lot of people were talking about bringing democracy to our material world, bringing democracy to material goods. That is, about making things accessible to everyone through mass production. And the same for beauty: items of beauty were not just for the rich, but for everyone. I thought: "That's exactly what industrial design can facilitate."

**RK**  This is only the second time we've heard the word "democracy." Some of the Metabolists are very anti-American and therefore democracy seems to be a suspect area. Others seem to be simply authoritarian and want to impose their will on the world. It seems that industrial design was an easier bridge to an American program of modernization, democracy and so on. In a way, it was much more modern than architecture.

**KE**  Well, not to go into too much detail, but as you know, Japan's modernization got its start a century and a half ago, when Commodore Perry showed up and set off a big bang. Even though that was a huge shock to us, I think the people of Japan developed a powerful respect for America. And then we got MacArthur after the war—that was another big bang.

**RK**  Super bang.

**KE**  The occupying GIs were like walking trade shows for the United States. They were the ambassadors of American civilization. The jeeps they drove had all kinds of fancy accessories, and the things they carried, from pistols to canteens, represented the latest in American engineering. The people of Japan saw all these things, and naturally, just like nearly a century earlier, they felt—

**RK**  Was it like a Noh play? Costumes?

**1974** Ekuan collaborates with Tange on a collapsible colony for two million pilgrims on the Hajj in Muna, near Mecca, Saudi Arabia. After its four-day use, the city would be dismantled and stored on the periphery of the valley. "All of these pieces of a city would move around," Ekuan recalls, "which would make Tange suddenly a Metabolist!"[6] The project ends abruptly when the client, King Faisal, is assassinated in 1975. According to Ekuan, Tange laments the cancellation of this project more than any other.

Assembling the temporary city.

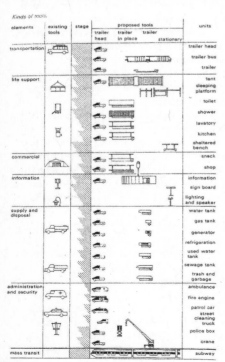

*Kinds of tools.*

| elements | existing tools | stage | proposed tools | | | units |
|---|---|---|---|---|---|---|
| | | | trailer head | trailer in place | trailer stationary | |
| transportation | | | | | | trailer head |
| | | | | | | trailer bus |
| | | | | | | trailer |
| life support | | | | | | tent |
| | | | | | | sleeping platform |
| | | | | | | toilet |
| | | | | | | shower |
| | | | | | | lavatory |
| | | | | | | kitchen |
| | | | | | | sheltered bench |
| commercial | | | | | | snack |
| | | | | | | shop |
| information | | | | | | information |
| | | | | | | sign board |
| | | | | | | lighting and speaker |
| supply and disposal | | | | | | water tank |
| | | | | | | gas tank |
| | | | | | | generator |
| | | | | | | refrigeration |
| | | | | | | used water tank |
| | | | | | | sewage tank |
| | | | | | | trash and garbage |
| administration and security | | | | | | ambulance |
| | | | | | | fire engine |
| | | | | | | patrol car |
| | | | | | | street cleaning truck |
| | | | | | | police box |
| | | | | | | crane |
| mass transit | | | | | | subway |

The city unpacked.

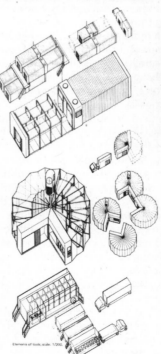

Elements of tools; scale: 1/200.

Storage in the side of the mountain.

| | |
|---|---|
| **KE** | No, what I'm trying to say is just how dire things were for Japan at that point. So everything we saw provoked feelings of envy, which then turned into feelings of respect. And I think that ultimately provided the basis for communication. |
| **RK** | **Visual communication through the shine of material goods?** |
| **KE** | Yes, I think it did have that power. Looking at the canteens, for example, you suddenly realize that they're curved, to match the shape of your hip. |
| **RK** | **Behind their pistol and hand grenade were industrial designers at work on the human scale.** |
| **KE** | Yes. In the Japanese Navy we carried our canteens over our shoulders, so when we got the order to double time, we'd have to run holding our rifles in our right hand and our left hand on our canteens. [laughs] But the GIs' canteens were strapped snugly to their hips, so they could run without having to hold them down. It may seem trivial, but it's the sort of thing that opens all kinds of new vistas. |

### State vs. Marketing Department

| | |
|---|---|
| **HUO** | **It reminds me of Roger Tallon, whom I recently interviewed in Paris. I was wondering if it's not by coincidence that you designed the bullet train in Japan and that Tallon designed the TGV in France. There was an obsession with the idea of democratization. It's the opposite of what we have now, where everything is becoming design. Could you tell me if my feeling that you and Roger Tallon had some invisible connections is somehow right, or if it's a wrong intuition?** |
| **KE** | Tallon is like my double. When I talk to him, I feel like I'm talking to myself. [laughs] |
| **RK** | **That's so beautiful!** |
| **KE** | He and I are exactly the same age, too. |
| **HUO** | **What about the train? How do you feel about the bullet train and the TGV?** |
| **KE** | To be honest, Tallon's whole design for the interior seems a lot like the bucket seat, sculpted to wrap tightly around your body. I rode the TGV right after it was introduced, and my immediate impression was of how cramped it looked. Like there was a futon pressing in around me. [laughs] Our design for the train was more like sitting on a bench seat. Square and roomy. |
| **RK** | **I have the feeling that when you were active in this period, the state was a very important client, and there was an intimate relationship with the public sector. I think the problem for Philippe Starck, for example, is that he operates in the moment that the market economy dominates every single issue. So would you say that the same is true in industrial design as in architecture, which has lost a lot of seriousness in the last 10 years simply because the market dominates?** |
| **KE** | Yes, I think the same is true. Just when people seem to be looking more than ever for unconstrained experimentation, it's such a shame we can't respond to that sentiment. Something's wrong when we can't respond to what people are looking for. There's also the problem of excesses driven by commercialism, such as adding all sorts of unnecessary stuff. |
| **RK** | **My interpretation is different: you're given unlimited freedom to express yourself except the freedom to address any serious issue.** |
| **KE** | I think that's a problem we face within the industry rather than in society at large. It's so disappointing to see the most interesting ideas discarded in favour of the expeditious. When you start trying to satisfy all the criteria and specifications demanded by the marketing department, the results always end up looking pretty much the same. That's why they lack the dynamic beauty of a lovely flower popping open in the middle of a deep forest. |
| **RK** | **This is totally incredible. Can you tell us what kind of work environment you are in right now?** |
| **KE** | Right now, we have a holding company called GK Design Group at the centre, with about 12 other companies in its orbit. |
| **RK** | **What is your position?** |

**1991** Narita Express N'EX, one of GK's several train designs.

"Square and roomy": N'EX cars from Narita airport to Tokyo.

Back to Buddhism: Ekuan during an eight-day ascetic retreat in which "man acquires pride by discovering the spirit of creating things." Robe by Issey Miyake.

**KE** Chairman. It's mostly a symbolic position. I spend most of my time talking about philosophy.

**RK** **To keep it pure.**

**KE** Yes, a bit like a priest.

**RK** **Back to the temple. So you never resigned?**

**KE** Not until I die. Strangely enough, that's what my people seem to want. They used to call me *shocho*, which basically means "director," but now they call me *shi*, which is like "reverend."

**RK** **A sage? [*laughs*]**

**KE** That seems be the consensus. What can I do? [*laughs*]

**RK** **Did you ever live in a capsule? In what kind of situation do you live?**

**KE** I live in an old, traditional Japanese house.

**RK** **You have been incredibly honest in a very un-Japanese way. [*laughs*] Thank you.**

**KE** I may have been digging up all these things from my past, but it felt more like I was talking about the future. I have truly enjoyed myself today.

**References**

1 Kenji Ekuan, *Dezain ni jinsei wo kakeru* (Devoting life to design) (Tokyo: Shunjusha, 2009).

2 Ibid.

3 Ibid.

4 Ernst Bloch (1885–1977), German Marxist philosopher, author of *Principle of Hope* (three volumes, 1938–47).

5 Kenji Ekuan, *Industrial Design: Dougu sekai no genkei to mirai* (The Archetype and Future of the World of Tools), Tokyo: Nihon Hoso Shuppan Kyokai, 1971.

6 Interview with the editors, Tokyo, August 2009.

# Expo '70
## Apotheosis
## of Metabolism

**"No country has a stronger franchise
on the future than Japan."**

*TIME,* March 2, 1970.

Japan originally wanted to host an international expo in 1940, at the peak of its imperial ambitions. The one million people who bought tickets for Expo '40, canceled with the escalation of the war, are allowed to use the same tickets to enter Expo '70. Now, the Expo represents a different kind of power: in combination with the 1964 Tokyo Olympics, Expo '70 marks the completion of Japan's postwar moral and economic rehabilitation—the "miracle" which had made it richer than any nation apart from the US—and the beginning of the shift in the world's center of gravity from West to East. Japan has the confidence to predict the future form of the city under the benevolent theme "Progress and Harmony for Humankind." Expo '70 is also the apotheosis of Metabolism: Tange, the Expo's masterplanner, commissions Kikutake to design the Expo Tower; he ask Ekuan to oversee the design of Expo's street furniture and transportation, and Otaka to build a transport node on artificial ground. Independently, Kurokawa wins commissions for two corporate pavilions, one composed of capsules, the other modules. Tange also works with Isozaki, plus his colleagues Koji Kamiya and the independent structural engineers Yoshikatsu Tsuboi and Mamoru Kawaguchi to create the Expo's center-piece, the colossal Big Roof and the open-air Festival Plaza beneath it.

Taro Okamoto, an Expo producer, commissions Kawazoe to curate the Mid-Air Exhibition, embedded in the space frame of the Big Roof (for which the Metabolists and the international avant-garde collaborate for the first time).

With government and private sector largesse that would shortly evaporate (the Expo costs, in 1970 terms, $2.9 billion), the Metabolists are able to realize some of their earliest dreams and inventions in an arena that embodies many of their fundamental ideas: a high-tech city, pumping with vitality (64 million people visit over six months, an average of about 345,000 per day), unburdened by any pretense of permanence.

As an apotheosis, Expo '70 is also the beginning of a decline: it is the most intensive realization of Metabolist ideas and a thrilling flourish of globalization, before the darker side of global interdependence reveals itself in the oil crisis three years later and the Japanese economy contracts for the first time since 1945, suspending utopia indefinitely…

**1968** Groundwork begins on Expo '70. The 330-hectare site—one of the few slivers of tabula rasa in Japan—is an undeveloped tract adjacent to the new town of Senri Hills, created from scratch over a former bamboo forest 15 kilometers outside of Osaka. Senri's masterplanner a decade earlier was, appropriately, Eika Takayama,[1] protégé of Manchukuo masterplanner Yoshikazu Uchida.

## MASTERPLANNERS

In 1966, the Expo masterplan is assigned, in a characteristically Japanese compromise, to two masterplanners: Professor Uzo Nishiyama of Kyoto University and Professor Tange of Tokyo University. But the physical and ideological distance between the two camps—Nishiyama has a Marxist background, Tange is seen as representing the establishment—soon renders collaboration impossible, so the work is divided: Nishiyama makes the initial concept, and Tange will flesh out the masterplan. Nishiyama wants a city of the people, based around a "Festival Plaza," a public space for 150,000, and the center of a new city that will grow on the site. When Tange assumes full control of the project, he assembles a team of 13 architects—including Kikutake, Isozaki, Kamiya, and Otaka—to help complete the masterplan, which is structured as a "tree" with a trunk (the symbol zone), branches (moving walkways and streets), and "petals" (pavilions). Tange, shrewd as ever, keeps Nishiyama's concept of a Festival Plaza, which becomes the icon of Expo '70…

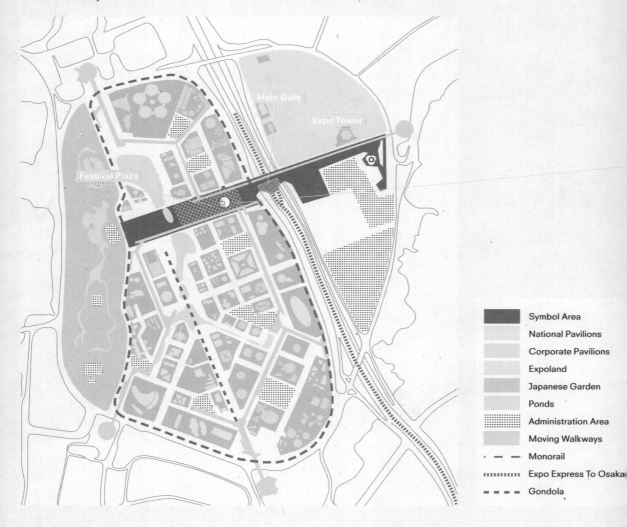

Symbol Area
National Pavilions
Corporate Pavilions
Expoland
Japanese Garden
Ponds
Administration Area
Moving Walkways
Monorail
Expo Express To Osaka
Gondola

## ICON: THE BIG ROOF

To give Festival Plaza shelter (Isozaki points out that it rains a lot in Osaka, especially in June—Expo '70 runs March–September), and to give Expo '70 an icon, Tange conceives the Big Roof: a futuristic and benevolent canopy—the largest space frame in the world*—over the 29,170 square meter Festival Plaza. To build such a thing, Tange turns to Koji Kamiya, chief of his company URTEC, and independent structural engineer Mamoru Kawaguchi. Kawaguchi invents a welding-free, cast iron ball joint which distributes 500 tons safely; he also creates a system for building the space frame flat on the ground and raising it up on mobile jacks that climb up the structure "like monkeys." The covering itself consists of 274 air-inflated transparent panels (the design of which is used 38 years later in the Water Cube for the 2008 Beijing Olympics and for Japan's pavilion at Expo 2010 in Shanghai). Like the Crystal Palace, made for the first expo in 1851, the Big Roof is an all-over structure fostering unity; at the heart of Expo '70 it stands in opposition to the closedness, fragmentation, and rivalry of the 116 individual pavilions...

It is 30 meters tall, 108 x 292 meters, weighing 4,800 tons, bearing loads 10 times bigger than a conventional space frame, and supported on only six pillars...

Tange and his group listen to Kunisuke Ito, producer of events, explain how events will unfold under the Big Roof.[2]

**1969** "Koji Kamiya challenging the limits of the giant scale," *Mainichi Graph*, January 12.

Support the Big Roof are 640 ball joints. Peter Rice picks ups the idea for the Pompidou Center...

**Space frame precedents** Tange and the Metabolists are intimately familiar with the prototypes for the Big Roof, all of them Western, most of them unrealized...

**1953** Konrad Wachsmann's aircraft hangar, a collapsible and bombproof structure for the US Air Force.

**1958** Yona Friedman, Ville Spatiale, space frame canopies over countryside and cities, a framework in which everything is permitted to take place."

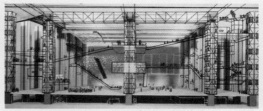

**1961** Cedric Price, Fun Palace, open framework for events and leisure, which Price repeatedly tries to get built in London until 1970.

## TANGE VS. OKAMOTO: PIERCING THE BIG ROOF

Artist Taro Okamoto is offered the position of Expo producer, in charge of the exhibitions underneath, in, and over Festival Plaza. He accepts on the condition that Tange's hi-tech, futuristic Big Roof is pierced with a brutal and populist monument: the *Tower of the Sun*. Tange resists at first but is convinced of Okamoto's contrarian logic after repeated visits to his studio. The unlikely collaboration creates a monumental juxtaposition in Festival Plaza that goes to the heart of Japan-ness: the refined Yayoi (Tange) vs. the primal Jomon (Okamoto)…

Expansive/defensive: opposite even in their gesticulations, Okamoto explains to Tange how the *Tower of the Sun* should penetrate his Big Roof. (They must also now deal with a major reduction in budget.) Helping negotiate is Shigeomi Hirano, right, Okamoto's business partner and sub-producer of the Expo.

Having secured Tange's agreement, Okamoto discusses with Isozaki the best orientation for *Tower of the Sun* in Festival Plaza.

**1967** Trickster: Okamoto puts himself where his *Tower of the Sun* will be. "When I first saw the model of the Big Roof, I was struck with an impulse that this grand horizon is there to be raptured" Okamato says. "Bang! The elegant plane of the Big Roof had to be juxtaposed with something outrageous. When the architects first saw the drawing [of the *Tower of the Sun*], they didn't look very happy. The tower was totally incongruent with modernism. But true collaboration, after all, comes through total confrontation." Tange and his staff gradually become convinced by Okamoto's tower, "so much so that I was almost taken aback."[3]

雨降って地固まる Ground firms after hard rain (adversity creates character): Tange points out the Big Roof, punctured by the *Tower of the Sun*. The president of the Expo '70 organization, Taizo Ishizaka (wearing waistcoat), is immediately charmed. From left: Taro Okamoto (president of the Expo '70 organization), Shozo Hotta (vice president, silver hair), Tange, and Kunisuke Ito (producer for events).

## HYPE

Ten years after the World Design Conference, Tange again mobilizes promising new architects, and the now well-established Metabolists, for a massive collective effort—this time in building the image of their nation. In the years leading up Expo '70, multiple expertises, authorities, and professions combine for the grand production, and every step of the preparations is carefully mediated...

**1967, March** Wise men's council: Tange mobilizes his protegés to assist Okamoto: (from left) Kurokawa (architectural consultant), Kikutake (masterplanning consultant, appointed by Tange), Okamoto himself (producer), Inui Hidejima (urban planning advisor and veteran of Manchukuo) and Isozaki (masterplanning consultant).

**1968** The curatorial team for Festival Plaza meet in Kyoto. Sakyo Komatsu (third from left) works with Okamoto on the exhibition inside the *Tower of the Sun* and underneath Festival Plaza; sociologist Hidetoshi Kato (center) works on the Expo's overall concept; Kawazoe (bag on knee) curates the Mid-Air Exhibition in the Big Roof; Kurokawa (hand on knee) assists Kawazoe and designs capsules to plug into the Big Roof; Isozaki (looking awry) works on the masterplan and designs the lighting system and the two giant robots who will occupy Festival Plaza.

**1969** Sumiko Sakamoto, a singer, takes stock of the Expo site on MBS Osaka Channel 4. Isozaki (left) watches with writer Rokusuke Ei, and—apt for the temporary city that will be built in Osaka and the illustrations behind them—the science fiction novelist Sakyo Komatsu.

Komatsu scrutinizes the masterplan with Kurokawa on TV, the space frame of the Big Roof pictured behind them.

"There is no land (or not enough land) in Tokyo. The Big Roof as therefore conceived as a city in the air, where buildings could be suspended," Kurokawa writes. The "buildings," including Kurokawa's Capsule for Living, hang on the left side of the roof, in the Mid-Air Exhibition.⁴

## MEETING OF THE AVANT-GARDES

In the run up to the Expo, Kawazoe, Maki, and Kurokawa travel to Europe to invite their Western contemporaries to participate in the Mid-Air Exhibition embedded in Tange's Big Roof. (On the plane, seniority customs dictate that Kurokawa, 36, sits in the middle seat—the worst position.) Their mission is successful: Archigram, Yona Friedman, Moshe Safdie, and others making similar explorations with capsules and space frames contribute to Kawazoe's quadrant of the exhibition, officially titled "Encounter with Life," in which he asks for their visions of the city of the future.

Big Roof from above.

Thirty meters up inside the Big Roof, the 11 installations by the Eastern and Western avant-garde (many of them associated with Team 10) grapple with the simultaneous and apparently contradictory forces that they think cities will be subject to in the future: increasing isolation (in capsules) and increasing connectivity through technology. The westerners have a generally more anxious response to these issues than the Metabolists, asserting citizen participation as an antidote to the top-down control implicit in the networked megastructural city of the future. In the other three areas of the Mid-Air Exhibition, capsules still dominate: a model of the Intelsat 4 satellite (a capsule) and two "body" capsules: one a model of a foetus as a "capsule of life," the other a coffin capsule being launched into space. Everything is a capsule.

East and West avant-gardes meet for the opening of the Mid-Air Exhibition: (from left) Dennis Crompton (Archigram), Moshe Safdie, unknown, Yona Friedman (in beret and sunglasses), Taro Okamoto, Giancarlo De Carlo, Kurokawa, Hans Hollein, Toshiko Okamoto, and Yuji Ono and Shigeomi Hirano (sub-producers of Festival Plaza).

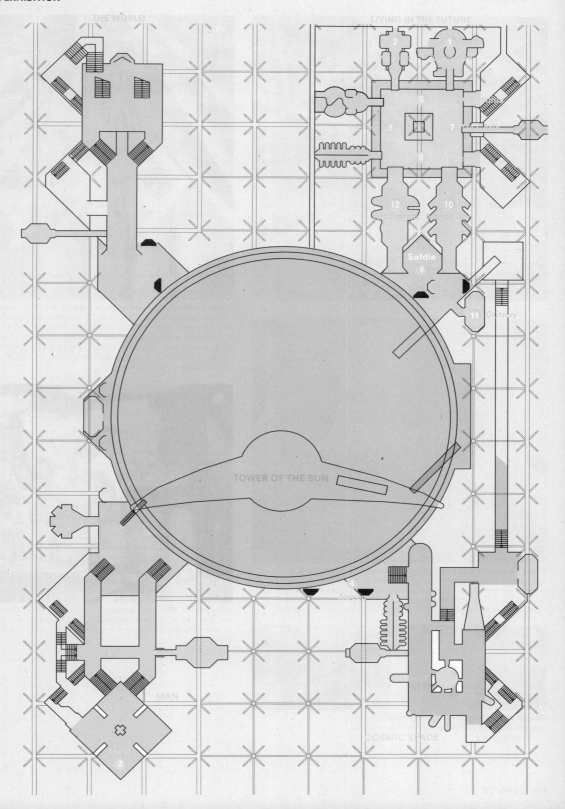

THE WORLD

LIVING IN THE FUTURE

TOWER OF THE SUN

Safdie

Gutnov

MAN

COSMIC SPACE

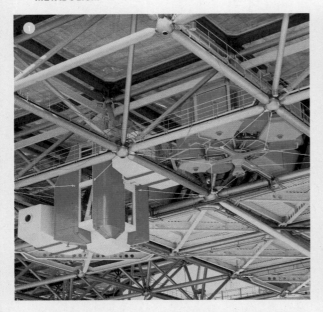

**Fumihiko Maki, Capsule of Network City** An elaboration of his 1968 Golgi Structures, Maki makes a miniature model of the future city, its form determined by information networks. The structure is a framework in which capsules can be embedded; for Maki, the areas in between capsules—functioning as public spaces—are just as important as the capsules themselves, which his contemporaries tend to fixate on.

**Kisho Kurokawa and Koji Kamiya, Capsules for Living, A & B** Kurokawa builds prototype bedroom, kitchen, and bathroom capsules fanning out from a central core (1). One of Kurokawa's capsule is lined with fur à la *Barbarella* (1968), extremely popular in Japan (above). Kamiya, chief of Tange's URTEC, builds a neighboring capsule (2).

**Metabolists, Wall of Capsules** A rare collaborative work by the Metabolists: an attempt to illustrate the archetypal and biological importance of the capsule in a gallery of its natural and artificial iterations...

**Kiyoshi Awazu** Metabolism's illustrator makes his own orb-like capsule and a parade of interactive "cosmo capsules."

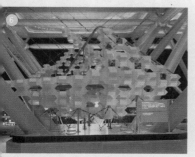

**Montreal: Moshe Safdie, Residential City** An elaboration of his Habitat '67 for the Montreal Expo three years earlier (which excited the Metabolists), the arrangement of capsules is now geometric rather than (seemingly) haphazard.

**Milan: Giancarlo De Carlo, Participation City** De Carlo thinks control of the future city should be bottom-up rather than top-down: his interactive installation allows visitors to pull levers to rotate images on the wall, creating new compositions of colors and shapes.

**Paris: Yona Friedman, Ring City** Inside the space frame, Friedman creates one of his own, made from rings hanging from the ceiling. Stretched over the rings are Friedman's primitive symbolic drawings.

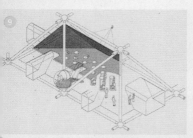

**Vienna: Hans Hollein, Vision of Tomorrow's City** Visitors stand in tubular capsules, where their heads poke through into a second level and they watch a film projected onto the roof.

**San Francisco: Christopher Alexander, Exit Capsule: Path of Pattern Language** Alexander, a British architect teaching at Berkeley, gathers proposals, strategies, diagrams, and slogans for the future city: "Stop isolating old people!" "Resist the mindless sprawl of cities!" "Don't break a teenager's spirit!" It is the systematic thinking that produces, in 1977, *Pattern Language*, Alexander's typology of "harmonious" (i.e. traditional, anti-modernist) buildings and their various components, and a guide for how to build them.

**Moscow: Alexei Gutnov, Spiral City** The author of *The Ideal Communist City* (1968) contributes a model of a megastructural city assuming a natural spiral form.

**London: Archigram, Dissolving City** A "capsule" passage, made of pink fake rock. Visitors are confronted with five questions about the city of the future. Though the Big Roof echoes Archigram ideas—a techno-utopian instant city devoted to social gatherings and entertainment; a realization, in the East, of what they were never able to build in the West—their skepticism and playful embrace of dystopia is very unMetabolist. "We expect," they say, "the implication of each [question] will be to suggest that the hallowed role of the 'city' will not remain quite so hallowed. It may soften, or dissolve." Question one immediately illuminates something that never troubles the Metabolists (except perhaps Maki): "Do you like a highly organized city? It may be obviously structured or dependent upon social constraints unseen." Archigram wanted to include screens showing scenes of city life, and polling stations for people to record their answers to the questions—but none of the electronics are installed; the questions hang in the air, and are printed in a special edition of Archigram, "Osakagram"...

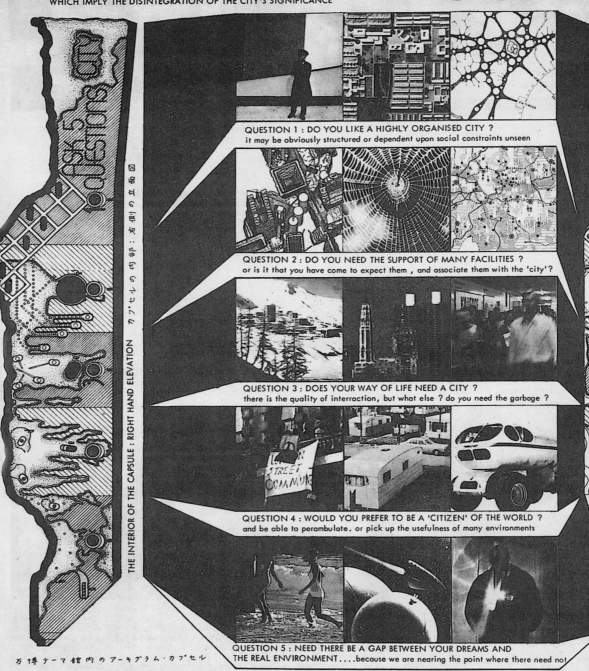

THE ARCHIGRAM CAPSULE IN THE THEME PAVILION   EXPO 70   OSAKA

# FIVE QUESTIONS ABOUT THE CITY   OSAK

WHICH IMPLY THE DISINTEGRATION OF THE CITY'S SIGNIFICANCE

QUESTION 1 : DO YOU LIKE A HIGHLY ORGANISED CITY ?
it may be obviously structured or dependent upon social constraints unseen

QUESTION 2 : DO YOU NEED THE SUPPORT OF MANY FACILITIES ?
or is it that you have come to expect them , and associate them with the 'city'?

QUESTION 3 : DOES YOUR WAY OF LIFE NEED A CITY ?
there is the quality of interraction, but what else ? do you need the garbage ?

QUESTION 4 : WOULD YOU PREFER TO BE A 'CITIZEN' OF THE WORLD ?
and be able to perambulate , or pick up the usefulness of many environments

QUESTION 5 : NEED THERE BE A GAP BETWEEN YOUR DREAMS AND
THE REAL ENVIRONMENT....because we are nearing the point where there need not

万博テーマ館内のアーキグラム・カプセル

都市の重要性の崩壊を意味する

都市に関する五つの質問

アーキグラム

Osakagram: special edition of Archigram for Expo '70.

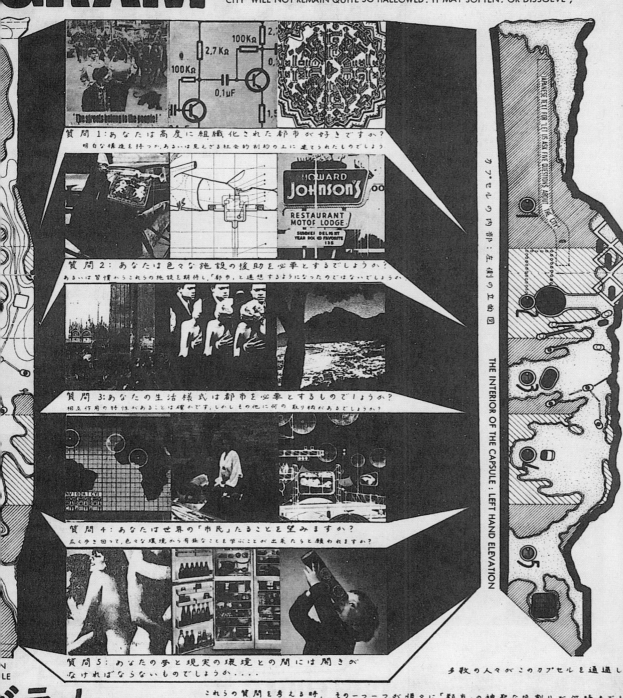

# GRAM

WE EXPECT THAT AS THE MAJORITY OF PEOPLE PASS THROUGH THE CAPSULE AND ASK THEMSELVES THESE QUESTIONS, THE IMPLICATION OF EACH ONE AFTER THE OTHER WILL BE TO SUGGEST THAT THE HALLOWED ROLE OF THE 'CITY' WILL NOT REMAIN QUITE SO HALLOWED . IT MAY SOFTEN . OR DISSOLVE ,

質問 1：あなたは高度に組織化された都市が好きですか？
明白な構造を持つか、あるいは見えざる社会的制約の上に建てられたものでしょう

質問 2：あなたは色々な施設の援助を必要とするでしょうか？
あるいは習慣からこれらの施設を期待し、「都市」と連想するようになったのではないでしょうか？

質問 3：あなたの生活様式は都市を必要とするものでしょうか？
相互作用の特性があることは確かです。しかしその他に何の取り換えがあるでしょうか？

質問 4：あなたは世界の「市民」たることを望みますか？
広くさき回って、色々な環境から見識なことも学ぶことが出来たらと願われますか？

質問 5：あなたの夢と現実の環境との間には開きがなければならないものでしょうか....

JAPANESE TEXT FOR "TELL US ASK THE QUESTIONS ABOUT THE CITY"

カプセルの内部：左側の立面図

THE INTERIOR OF THE CAPSULE : LEFT HAND ELEVATION

多数の人々がこのカプセルを通過し

これらの質問を考える時、その一つ一つが段々に「都市」の神聖な役割りが何時までも

そう神聖ではあり得ないことを意味することに気付くでしょう。軟化するか溶解するので

ラム

## UNDER THE ROOF: FESTIVAL PLAZA

When Uzo Nishiyama first suggested a Festival Plaza for the Expo, Isozaki, with characteristic skepticism, thought it a "cheesy term one would even hesitate to pronounce."[5] But he twists the idea, and, working with Tange, makes the Plaza a techno-utopia with stadium seating for various spectacles, computer-controlled lighting, and two giant robots that choreograph both. Isozaki imagines Festival Plaza as an "invisible monument": a fluid, high-tech space for transient events (the Plaza hosts performances by Sammy Davis Jr., Sergio Mendes, Andy Williams, and the Gutai artist group) and random encounters. But the political engagement Isozaki envisaged never manifests itself. In 1969, there is a large demonstration in Osaka held by the "Joint Struggle Committee to Crush the 1970 World Exposition," (which also protests the Vietnam War and the renewal of Japan's security treaty with the US). But by the time the Expo opens, the Joint Struggle Committee's power has diminished, and there is only a minor demonstration outside as Emperor Hirohito opens Expo '70 in a massive ceremony in Festival Plaza on March 15. Too much reality does not infiltrate the utopian city...

Isozaki photographs his two major innovations for Festival Plaza: the lighting system...

...and one of his robots, participating in Gutai's light performance.

RK and RM: two 20-meter tall robots designed by Isozaki (their Japanese names are Démé and Déku). The pair emit smoke, control lighting, and set up and disassemble the stage for daily events such as fashion shows and concerts.

## PLAZA VS. PAVILION

Even fierce critics like Ichiro Hariu ("Expo: this grandiose fake festival") applaud Isozaki's concept of an "invisible monument" as a correction to the expo syndrome of monumentality. Hariu writes: "Amid all the opportunistic technological fantasies of the 'future' prevalent in this Expo, [Isozaki's idea] is something to be valued ... it looks at the unpredictable 'present'; it tries to bring day-to-day life to our consciousness." But Hariu is not sure if the concept of Festival Plaza really works in reality: "In such an open space with nowhere to hang about and no shade, do people really meet, respond to each other, or intensify their experiences?"[6]

While Expo '70 marks the peak of the pavilion, Tange thinks that Festival Plaza points the way beyond it, to a new mode of exhibition. At a symposium two weeks after the Expo opens, he says:

"Hundreds of thousands of visitors are rushing to two or three pavilions just to look at a lunar stone and other displays ... in the Festival Plaza, people can have an environmental experience. To spend time in these exterior spaces and to experience the feeling of participation in some events or some happenings might be an unforgettable and psychologically satisfying moment."[7]

The type of spontaneous encounter—"an unforgettable and psychologically satisfying moment"—for which Festival Plaza was made.

Festival Plaza parade, photographed by Ekuan.

Public space: picnics, street vendors, groups on tour (all members wearing hats), and crowds milling, sitting on steps, and ascending from Festival Plaza to enter the Roof.

### Expo Tower, Kikutake

Kikutake seizes the possibility of finally realizing
something like his Tower-Shaped Community from
1958 (drawing below): a tower made of a central
core and capsules (or move-nets, as he calls them)
that can plug in like leaves on a tree. But a budget
crisis—ironically caused in part by the inflation that
accompanies the Expo hype—forces a drastic reduction of his ambition, and the Expo Tower becomes
a hollow vertical space frame, holding only a few capsules, used as viewing platforms, 120 meters high.

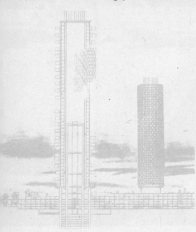

### Main Gate, Otaka

Otaka pursues his fixation with artificial ground,
first expressed in his plan for Shinjuku station with
Maki in *Metabolism 1960* (below). For the Expo's
main gate—through which 48,000 people pass every
hour on peak days—he designs a raised urban node
straddling the new highway, just as his Shinjuku plan
straddled the train tracks. The platform links the main
Expo site in the north with Expo Land (an amusement
park) in the south, and connects to the new metro
to downtown Osaka.

## Takara Beautillion, Kurokawa with Ekuan/GK ③

With the Takara conglomerate of furniture and beauty companies providing a budget, Kurokawa builds the Beautillion. It is an elaboration of his single capsule-in-space-frame project, the Odakyu roadside restaurant, and his 1962 plan for prefab Box-Type Apartments. The capsule, which started life as a democratic—and even mobile/pioneering—tool for individual living and individual freedom, becomes here the ideal unit for showcasing Takara's beauty products in luxury mini-showrooms (with interiors designed by Ekuan and sound design by Toshi Ichiyanagi). Capsules plug into a framework of six-pointed crosses, with multiple "unfinished" extrusions, indicating the (inevitably unrealized) possibility of adding more capsules and more framework in the future. Thanks to the ease of the construction system, the Beautillion is assembled on site in only six days, and is disassembled just as quickly after the Expo. Kurokawa later describes the Beautillion, a structure planned for impermanence, as "a classic example of Metabolism, and one in which Japan's Buddhist aesthetics can be seen."[8]

Prototypes: Box-Type Apartments, 1962; and Odakyu Drive-inn Restaurant, 1969.

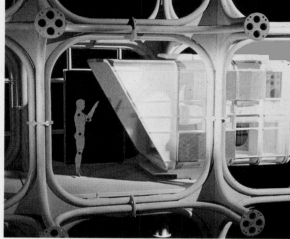

Plug-in system.

The most effeminate megastructure?
The Takara Beautillion, originally conceived in pink.

Showroom interiors, designed by Ekuan.

Unfinished aesthetic.

Kurokawa gives a tour to Takara executives.

## Toshiba IHI pavilion, Kurokawa ④

For Toshiba and the IHI heavy industry and shipbuilding company, Kurokawa develops a space frame comprised of tetrahedron units, supporting a giant Global Vision Theater raised and lowered by hydraulics. A small-scale application of the modular principle of his Helix City, the framework can grow in 14 different directions, and Kurokawa flaunts the formal possibilities with extrusions that resemble natural growth. As with the Takara Beautillion, ease of dismantling is key; after the Expo, Kurokawa sends the steel tetrahedrons back to the furnaces for recycling.

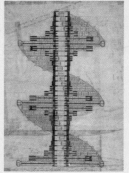

Helix City, 1961.

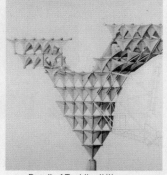

Detail of Toshiba IHI's tetrahedron units.

Toshiba IHI pavilion, composed of 1,444 tetrahedron units.

The Global Vision Theater is suspended from the tetrahedral framework and contains nine screens showing films produced by Shinya Izumi; the audience sits underneath in the 500-seat auditorium, which rises and lowers.

## Transportation and Street Furniture, Ekuan/GK ⑤

Rather than miscellaneous elements, Ekuan treats street furniture and transportation as intrinsic, unified tools which bring to the Expo all the functions of a city. He designs postboxes, which become ubiquitous throughout Japan, multi-face clocks (110 of them), electric cars both for Kunio Maekawa's automobile pavilion and for the Expo taxis, telephone booths, lighting, public address systems, and signage. The concept of street furniture as a crucial urban element is born as a result of Ekuan's endeavor at Expo '70.

Monorail.

Cars outside Kunio Maekawa's automobile pavilion.

Public address systems, which play classical music.

Multi-face clock.

Phone booths.

Wayfinding.

"SEND MORE SAND STOP PAVILION PROVING POPULAR" writes Saudi
Arabia's pavilion commissioner to his seniors in Riyadh.[9] In the first month of
the Expo, one million people visit the Saudi pavilion, pocketing some of the red
Dahna sand on display along the way. Saudi Arabia is the biggest exporter of oil
to Japan, and is making its international expo debut in Osaka. Other Arab nations,
fresh from or about to establish independence (Kuwait, 1961; Algeria, 1962;
Abu Dhabi, 1971) announce themselves on the world expo stage with debut
pavilions, all of them traditional forms compared with the innovation and
gaudiness of most national pavilions.

Saudi Arabia (center, white domes) designed by local architects
Kawashima with exhibition design by Dainippon. Inside are films
showcasing Saudi Arabia, a fragment of the covering of the
Kaabah, and a model of an oil well complete with gushing oil.

United Arab Republic
(Egypt): a miniature pyramid.

Kuwait: mosque domes. Inside, the exhibition
includes a pool and model of a pearling dhow.

Abu Dhabi: a desert fort designed by
Abdul Rahman Makhlouf, urban planner
of Abu Dhabi itself.

Algeria, the biggest of the Arabian pavilions.
Designed in Paris; includes a French restaurant.

## NATIONAL PAVILIONS

The national pavilions form a parade of icons, an architectural Olympics post-Tokyo '64. The spirit is benevolent, populist, and competitive: the USSR shows Tchaikovsky's piano (the theme of the pavilion is "Harmonious Development of the Individual under Socialism"); the United States shows a moon rock fresh from the 1969 Apollo 11 mission; Turkey an enlarged version of the 1274 BCE Kadesh peace treaty; Tanzania a replica of the skull of the oldest man on earth. Germany is an exception, with a sound installation by Stockhausen and live performances of his music. The Swiss pavilion is a sculpture not a building, but proves to be one of the most popular not only for its beauty but for the shade it gives in day and the light is gives at night...

Switzerland: Willi Waltar, Charlotte Schmid & Paul Leber.

USSR: M. Poshokin (chief), V. Svirsky (engineer), A.Kondratyev (painter), and K. Rozhdestvensky.

Netherlands: Jaap Bakema and Carel Weeber.

USA: Davis-Brody with de Harak, Chermayeff, Geismar.

## CORPORATE PAVILIONS

...But queues for corporate pavilions are even longer than those for the nation-states. The Expo '70 planning committee lifts all restrictions on corporate pavilions, encouraging sponsors to make their showcases as "individualistic, expressionistic and colourful as possible." The pavilions are inflatable (Fuji), shrouded in mist (Pepsi), levitating (Ricoh), flying saucer–like (Hitachi), modular (Kurokawa's modular Toshiba IHI pavilion), and capsular (Takara Beautillion). Inside, the focus is on experience rather than objects: Hitachi has a flight simulator, Fuji the world's first IMAX movie, Toshiba the first videophone. The proliferation of corporate pavilions reflects the deeper structural movement in Japan from the public to the private sector, a movement that will soon extinguish the very utopia that corporations ride on at Expo '70. The lofty ideas of the Expo are in fact under attack on both sides: the competing flamboyance of the national pavilions suggests a spirit of nationalism as much as international brotherhood; the consumerist spirit of the corporate pavilions overwhelms any more noble intentions. The aim of both types

Ricoh: Nikken Sekkei Komu.

Steel: Kunio Maekawa.

Fuji: Yukata Murata with Mamoru Kawaguchi, structural engineer.

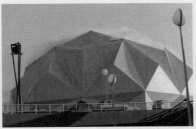

Pepsi: shrouded in mist, Takenaka Corporation and EAT (Experiments in Art and Technology).

Hitachi: Tonichi Construction Consultants.

Sumitomo Fairytale Pavilion: Sachio Otani.

Suntory whiskey pavilion: with the theme "Water of Life," Yasui Architects & Engineers.

Sanyo: demonstrating how well the capsule functions as a vessel of corporate futurology as well as the "Buddhist aesthetics" cited by Kurokawa, Sanyo's pavilion contains a "living capsule" with ultrasonic bathing and drying.

Final day: "Goodbye Expo '70!"
*Yomiuri Shimbun,* September 13, 1970.

**Number of visitors** 60,000,000
(64,220,000, according to official Expo figures)
**Number of participating countries** 77
**Number of pavilions** 110
**Profit** ¥10,000,000,000 ($100 million)

## AFTERMATH

Expo '70 is an unadulterated success in terms of media coverage, popularity, and profitability. But it turns out to be a point of no return in a series of modern transitions: from the nation-state to globalism, from the West to the East, from the public sector to the private, and, most critically for the Metabolists, from master-planning on a grand scale to much more limited ambitions. Isozaki laments how the burgeoning neoliberalism under the Tanaka government, together with the oil crisis, drains the state money available for grand-scale planning and optimism…

"How to represent the will of the nation was the fundamental framework of Tange's architectural conception up to Expo '70. His national-scaled 'megastructure' planning concept in the '60s also stemmed from this framework of thought. Entering the 1970s, Prime Minister Kakuei Tanaka (1972–74) besieged the regime and began restructuring the nation's physical organization, calling it *Retto kaizo*—remodeling of the Japanese Archipelago. Tange was among many of those who were involved in the operations of the government, and proposed ideas. The power of the nation itself began waning right after its peak at Expo '70. Then came the global oil shock of 1973, followed by the Lockheed bribery scandal of 1976. This was the time when the US had begun recovering from defeat in the Vietnam War and was introducing the concept of neoliberalism into global capital. This had such a significant impact on Japan as a modern nation-state that it also had to change its fundamental flow of capital. In my view, Tanaka was the first victim of this turbu-lence, 'shot down' by the Lockheed affair. And so were the Metabolists, at least so it seemed to an outsider. In fact, the power of the Japanese nation-state waned gradually. In the case of the US, Reagan and Thatcher collaborated in the so-called Reaganomics of the '80s. In the case of Japan, capital gradually and inconspicuously integrated with the nation-state. It was Prime Minister Yasuhiro Nakasone (1982–87) who articulated this trend in his new *Minkatsu* policy or mobilization of private resources. This policy was nothing but a means to allow a nation-state to be taken over by capital. Japan then plunged into the Bubble Economy, which came to an end almost at the same time as the bipolar confrontation. The Soviet Union dissolved, but the nation-state of Japan? I wonder if it had already ceased to exist by then."

**Arata Isozaki in conversation, April 2010**

**1970** Expo in full swing. Tange says: "I imagine that the trunk elements can remain and that a new city can grow up in the areas where the pavilions now stand. When this happens, what is now the Expo site will become either the heart of a city with a population of 500,000 or will become that city in its entirety."[10]

**1995** Back to nature. All that remains of Expo '70 is Okamoto's *Tower of the Sun* and Maekawa's Steel Pavilion. Kurokawa's National Museum of Ethnology springs up in 1977 (center left).

**References**

1 Tetsukazu Akiyama, "Senri New Town: The first experimental city," *Kenchiku Bunka,* September 1993.

2 "New art beyond imagination," *Asahi Shimbun,* December 9, 1967.

3 Taro Okamoto, "My wager on the Expo" in Akiomi Hirano, *Okamoto Taro to Taiyo no toh* (Taro Okamoto and the Tower of the Sun) (Tokyo: Shogakukan, 2008).

4 Kisho Kurokawa, "Young people should see the Expo this way!" *Heibon Punch,* March 9, 1970.

5 Arata Isozaki, *Japan-ness in Architecture* (Cambridge, MA: MIT Press, 2006).

6 Ichiro Hariu, "Expo: this grandiose fake festival," *Sekai,* June 1970.

7 "International symposium: The city of tomorrow," *approach '70,* Takenaka Corporation, Summer 1970.

8 Kisho Kurokawa, *Metabolism in Architecture* (London: Studio Vista, 1977).

9 "The Arabs at Osaka," Paul F. Hoye, *Aramco World magazine,* July/August 1970.

10 "Osaka Expo: Half a year of 'progress' hype," *Asahi Shimbun,* April 11, 2009.

11 Kenzo Tange, "Some thoughts about Expo '70," *The Japan Architect,* May/June 1970.

**Bibliography**
**Masterplanners**
Kenzo Tange and Terunobu Fujimori, *Tange Kenzo* (Tokyo: Shinkenchiku-sha, 2002).

Kenzo Tange, "The planning of the Expo and the future city," *Kenchiku Bunka,* April 1970.

**Icon: The Big Roof**
*Official Report of the Japan World Exposition, Osaka, 1970* (Osaka: Commemorative Association for the Japan World Exposition 1970).

Kisho Kurokawa, "The potential of a future city: the experimental architecture of the Expo," *Yomiuri Shimbun,* January 26, 1970.

Interview with Mamoru Kawaguchi by Rem Koolhaas, November 15, 2008.

Mamoru Kawaguchi, *Kozo to kansei* (Structure and sensibility) (Tokyo: Hosei University, Alumni of Architecture Department, 2007).

Construction supervisors' consortium for Festival Plaza, *Omatsurihiroba kenchiku koji no gaiyo* (Outline of the construction work of Festival Plaza) (Osaka: Obayashi Corporation, Takenaka Corporation, Fujita Corporation).

**Tange vs. Okamoto:**
**Piercing the Big Roof**
Akiomi Hirano, *Okamoto Taro to Taiyo no toh.*

**Hype**
Taro Okamoto et al, "Making the entire site a place to celebrate the human kind," *Nippon Bankokuhaku* (Japan World Expo), March 1967.

**Meeting of the Avant-Gardes**
Noboru Kawazoe, *Omoide no ki* (Notes of Memories) (Tokyo: Domesu Shuppan, 1996).

Noboru Kawazoe, "Capsule as an antithesis to value," *SD,* March 1969.

"International symposium: The city of tomorrow,"

Official Report of the Japan World Exposition, Osaka, 1970.

**Living in the Future**
*Official Report of the Japan World Exposition, Osaka, 1970.*

"The man who lives in 'the future,'" *Sankei Shimbun,* March 26, 1970.

Archigram (produced by Arata Isozaki), "ARCHIGRAM 9," *Toshi Jutaku,* December 1970.

Under the Roof: Festival Plaza
"Dancing Android or tomorrow's slave?" *AD,* June 1970, 293.

Metabolism, Built
Masato Otaka, "Main Gate," *Kenchiku Zasshi,* March 1970.

Kisho Kurokawa, *Kisho Kurokawa Notes* (Tokyo: Dobun Shoin, 1994).

"Kenji Ekuan: Three poles I want to consolidate," *Mainichi Graph,* January 12, 1969.

**National Pavilions/**
**corporate Pavilions**
Kisho Kurokawa, Taro Okamoto, Kenzo Tange, eds., *Nihon Bankokuhaku – kenchiku zokei* (Expo '70: Architecture & Form) (Tokyo: Kobunsha, 1971).

**1970** *Tower of the Sun* (Taro Okamoto) and Big Roof
remnant (Kenzo Tange), Expo '70 Park, Osaka
**2009** Photos by Charlie Koolhaas

# Takako Tange 丹下孝子
# Noritaka Tange 丹下憲孝

**Discussed in this interview:**
**Kenzo Tange, part II, (part I on p.84)**

**1965** international practice begins: wins UN competition for reconstruction of Skopje, Macedonia, after earthquake; invited to Saudi Arabia with structural engineer Yoshikatsu Tsuboi **1966** appointed masterplanner for Expo '70; publishes Tokaido Megalopolis scheme in a pocket book, *Future Image of the Japanese Archipelago* **1967** Shizuoka Press and Broadcasting Center in Tokyo; Yamanashi Press and Broadcasting Center; design for Kuwait International Airport begins; masterplans for Bologna's New Northern Development, San Francisco's Yerba Buena Center, and New York's Flushing Meadows Sports Park; commissioned to design stadium in Riyadh **1969** wins competition for Kuwait Sports City; commissioned by UN Secretary-General U Thant to masterplan Lumbini Sacred Garden, Nepal **1970** masterplans Expo '70 and designs Big Roof and Festival Plaza (with Isozaki et al); Kuwait Embassy, Tokyo; presents Tokaido Megalopolis scheme to Prime Minister Eisaku Sato **1971** marries Takako Iwata; design for University of Oran campus; masterplans for Bologna's Fiera District and Catania's Librino New Town begin **1974** masterplan for Pilgrims' Accommodation, Muna, Saudi Arabia, with Ekuan (GK); designs Farah Park Hotel and three apartment towers in Tehran; collaborates with Louis Kahn on masterplan for Abbas Abad new town, Tehran; Minneapolis Arts Complex **1976** opens office in Paris; design for Yarmouk University, Jordan **1977** designs palace for Emir of Qatar; proposal for New City Hall of Tehran; masterplan for Government Center, Doha; new Sogetsu Hall, Tokyo **1978** masterplan for government complex, Morocco; Hanae Mori Building, Tokyo **1979** masterplan for Abuja, new capital of Nigeria; completes Kuwait International Air Terminal, first realization in the Middle East; campaigns for Shunichi Suzuki's election to governorship of Tokyo **1980** masterplan for Napoli Administration Center; Order of Cultural Merit **1981** People's Palace, Damascus **1982** Royal Palace of Saudi Arabia, Jeddah; King Faisal Foundation, Riyadh (Phase I); Akasaka Prince Hotel, Tokyo **1983** Kenzo Tange Visiting Professorship starts at Harvard Graduate School of Design; masterplan for Federal Twin Capital, Malaysia **1984** commissioned by Paris mayor Jacques Chirac to redevelop Place d'Italie **1985** commissioned by King of Brunei to design capital and government buildings **1986** wins competition for new Tokyo City Hall; Tokyo Plan 1986; OUB Center and Nanyang Technological Institute, Singapore **1987** Pritzker Prize **1988** Arabian Gulf University, Bahrain **1989** Hiroshima International Conference Center, completing his plans for the Peace Center after nearly 40 years; Singapore Indoor Stadium **1990** commissioned by mayor of Rome to masterplan the city **1991** New Tokyo City Hall **1994** renovates Hiroshima Peace Memorial Museum main and east buildings **1995** UOB Plaza, Singapore **1996** Fuji Television Headquarters, on Tokyo Bay **1997** succeeded by Paul Noritaka Tange as president of his company **1998** University of Bahrain **2002** Tange Associates is set up **2005** dies at age 91

**"All of a sudden, everybody around wanted Tange to build a palace or something. So from Saudi Arabia they went on to Syria, Qatar, Iran, Algeria... commissions started coming in..."** Noritaka Tange

At a moment when Kenzo Tange's attentions were beginning to turn abroad, it is apt that he met Takako Iwata, his second wife, on a plane from leaving Japan. He was probably on his way to Skopje to work on the 1965 masterplan; he and Iwata would marry in 1973. In the same year, Tange retired from Tokyo University to focus on his private office, URTEC (URbanists and archiTECts), which was the catalyst for the expansion of his operations beyond Japan into the Middle East, Africa, Europe, and southeast Asia. (Also in 1973, the oil crisis struck, providing the impetus for stronger relations between Japan and the Middle East). At the age of 60, Tange had a second wind.

Over 34 years of marriage, Iwata traveled loyally with Tange, mingling with Saudi royalty and heads of state, supporting her husband socially and spiritually (he became Catholic) as he entered his international phase. Her son, Noritaka, born in 1958, was groomed by Tange to become an architect himself (the first lesson Tange taught him: know what the client wants). Noritaka Tange succeeded his stepfather as president of Kenzo Tange Associates in 1997.

After the ingenious audacity, the generous grooming, the professional organization, and even the playfulness of his earlier years as the instigator of Metabolism, the Tange of the 1970s and '80s became a serious diplomat, duty-bound, and maybe more Japanese as he started nation building for other countries.

Hotel Okura, Toranomon,
Tokyo, November 16, 2008

Already established as Japan's iconic architect by the mid-60s, Tange begins to seek opportunities further afield: reconstructing Skopje, and learning from Doxiadis...

**1966** The UN charges a Japanese architect with remodeling a medieval Balkan city—Skopje, post-earthquake. He is flanked by local architects Radovan Mishevic and Fedor Wenzler.

**1966** Traveling south from Skopje to Athens, Tange and his colleague Koji Kamiya visit the first global urban planner, Constantinos Doxiadis. He has offices in 11 countries, and according to *Time* magazine, has "helped resettle 10 million humans in 15 countries." Using a hanging contraption, the Japanese are treated to an overhead view of a city Doxiadis is about to operate on. Tange, later crosses paths with Doxiadis in Riyadh and Abuja, Nigeria...

Organizing system for a new city? Tange, developing the Tokaido Megalopolis scheme back home (see p.678), takes note.

**REM KOOLHAAS I would like to discuss one essential part of Tange's life. Until the late 1960s, he was involved in a practical way in form and shape in his design. It seems to me that in the '70s he became more interested and** involved in globalization **and in projecting something that was initially Japanese onto the world.**

**NORITAKA TANGE** It was the reconstruction of Skopje after the earthquake in 1963 that triggered his movement outward from Japan.

**RK** **For a disaster in Europe, a Japanese person was asked to solve it. In that sense the word "globalization" is right. What I find interesting is how he suddenly went from working strictly in Japan—in a very Japanese way, and in a very Japanese political climate—to being active in Europe, then very soon the Arab world, then Nepal, then the African world, then Singapore. I need to understand what happened, or what it was in his character that enabled him to make that step. Was he always oriented towards the outside world, or was this a sudden shift in his mentality? What prepared him, and did the marriage help?**

**TT** He had quite an international mind. He was always thinking not only of Japan but of the whole world. And he was always thinking not only about architecture but also about education and other such issues. He read a lot, especially philosophy.

**RK** **I see that you wear a cross. I heard that Tange was also a Catholic. Would that have helped orient him to the outside?**

**NT** He became a Catholic very late in his life, so that was not a factor. My mother is Catholic, but his family was Shintoist. He didn't necessarily believe in Catholicism.

## Leaving Japan

**HANS ULRICH OBRIST** [*to Takako Tange*] **When did you meet Tange for the first time?**

**TT** I met him in an airplane.

**RK** **Leaving Japan or returning to Japan?**

**TT** Leaving. The person who was waiting for me was also waiting for him. By coincidence, we stayed in the same hotel in Paris.

**RK** **You already had a relationship with countries outside Japan?**

**TT** No.

**RK** **Did you have a profession?**

**TT** I had studied psychology. I just wanted to see the whole world.

**RK** **I said that I wanted to discuss the switch in Tange's life from a preoccupation with Japan to a preoccupation with the outside world. Then it turns out that you had studied psychology and that you are interested in the outside world. There must be a connection.**

**TT** I didn't know about him at all. I wasn't so interested in architecture. He looked at me—my face is exactly the same as his mother's. It was like he saw a ghost or something.

**NT** There is a photograph of his mother in which she looks exactly like my mother. He was very much loved by his mother. And all of a sudden, there is this person who looks so similar to his late mother. They met just around the time of Skopje in the mid '60s, exactly the time that he started going abroad.

**RK** **So that coincidence is there. It sounds as if you were already confident in traveling and addressing the outside world. Did your confidence help him?**

**TT** He was a scholarly person and he was an architect. He didn't want to speak a lot. He was not so sociable.

**NT** Ever since getting married, my mother always traveled with him. He never traveled alone.

**RK** **They were a team.**

**NT** Yes.

**RK** **Would you also discuss with him the background of different countries? Would you explore things together, like the mentalities you found in Skopje, the mentalities in Saudi Arabia?**

## GLOBALIZING

Starting with a realization for Kuwait on his home soil, in the '70s, with the economy at home flailing, Tange starts work in a total of 30 countries…

**1970** Kuwaiti: Tange builds the newly independent nation's embassy in Tokyo—harbinger of the direction of his activities…

**1972** Singapore: Tange visits just as the Metabolist-inspired megastructures of the Golden Mile Complex (a colossal half A-frame) and the People's Park Complex (including a Maki-esque "city room" atrium) are being completed. After a decade of rampant development, founding prime minister Lee Kuan Yew (in power since 1959) still treats the island like tabula rasa, showing Tange a map titled "CONCEPT PLAN." Tange participates in the next wave of development, completing the first of his five skyscrapers in the CBD a decade later.

**1978** Nepal: asked by UN secretary general U Thant to masterplan Lumbini, birthplace of the Buddha, Tange designs a mandala and a classically Tangean central axis connecting international temples, public facilities, and gardens.

NT He never asked my mother her opinion on architecture or professional things, but they were very close.

RK **But certainly on diplomatic things—**

NT Yes.

RK **—because he must have been diplomatic if he worked for the king of Saudi Arabia, if he was invited by U Thant to masterplan Lumbini, if he did a city for the leaders of Nigeria. Whenever I see pictures of him in the outside world, he is always surrounded by power, by presidents, kings. It must have been a particular part of his character that enabled him to do that. Which part of his character was that?**

NT He was not an outgoing person. He was very professional; he was a scholar. I think these leaders were fascinated by his knowledge, his professional abilities and his unique aura.

RK **What was your role when you were visiting these leaders?**

TT My husband could speak and explain professional things, but in social events he didn't want to speak. Thus I used to make my whole body an antenna.

NT He was rather shy.

TT So I had to make everybody happy on his behalf. That was my job. But the top-of-country people were almost the same type as my husband. The King of Saudi and U Thant—they had peace, gentleness, and severity.

RK **The king was Faisal?**

TT Yes. It seems he had the same nature as my husband!

RK **So it was the similarity? The king was similar to your husband in the sense that he was also a scholar and also introverted?**

TT Yes, very similar. The queen was a very open person. We became such good friends.

HUO **So a personal relationship of trust had been established?**

TT Yes, the relationship of trust continued to the end.


**Thirty Countries**

NT The King of Saudi Arabia was the father figure in the Arab world. All of a sudden, everybody around wanted Tange to build a palace or something. So from Saudi Arabia they went on to Syria, Qatar, Iran, Algeria… commissions started coming in.

RK **Snowballed.**

TT That may be overstating it, but he was also called to African countries.

NT He was a good listener. As much as people think that he was determined and did whatever he wanted to—yes, he had that character as well—he was a very good listener. The first thing that I learned as an architect was whether the design was really what the client wanted.

RK **From him?**

NT Yes, from him. He would send me to a meeting and would then want to know exactly what happened. His first question was: what does the client want? Or when we did an architectural work in a group, he would patiently listen to both young staff and senior staff on an equal level. It didn't matter who it was as long as good ideas were proposed that he could explore. That was his way of designing.

HUO **Did he read a lot?**

NT He was a well-read person so he always knew about the history and traditional background. He was very interested in and learned a lot about the world. Regarding Metabolism in the Middle East, he was much more concerned about the history and about the tradition of these countries.

That is what my father taught all of us. Even today after he is gone, that is what we strongly try to do in our company. If you are comfortable in an environment, you can be productive and creative. But there is no universal comfort: your background and my background are different. If you want to ensure comfort in an individual-oriented society, you need to touch upon the

"The same nature as my husband": after the 1964 Olympics, Tange strikes up a relationship of trust with Saudi Arabia's modernizer, King Faisal. After proposing a stadium in Riyadh and a temporary city for pilgrims near Mecca, Tange is able to complete three buildings—each one nationally symbolic—only after Faisal's assassination in 1975...

**1976–1982** Tange is selected to build Faisal's philanthropic memorial, the King Faisal Foundation Headquarters Complex in Riyadh.

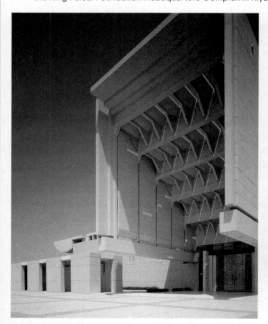

**1982** Left: beginning in 1972 as a palace for King Faisal in Jeddah, ten years later the project becomes a palace for his successor, King Khalid. Above: at the same time, Tange designs a palace across the bay for Crown Prince Fahd.

Aside from designing isolated marvels, Tange is also engaged in urban planning for the new capital of Nigeria, Abuja, symbol of the nation's independence and (still unstable) democracy...

**1981** Nigerian president Shehu Shagari (wearing glasses) approves Tange's masterplan for Abuja's central district.

Abuja's mall: Tange's signature linear urban planning culminates in the Three Arms Zone—presidential complex, parliament, supreme court.

**1960** "A good era": Kurashiki City Hall, concrete in a still-wooden city—
one in a series of public commissions that slows to a halt in the '70s,
forcing Tange to look further afield…

Pierre El Khoury
One of the first Lebanese
modernist architects, El
Khoury (1930–2005) later
became minister of public
works.

governor
Masayoshi Kaneko (1907–96),
formerly a judge, became
governor of Kagawa prefecture in 1950 and commis-
sioned Tange to design the
new prefectural government
building (1958) and the
gymnasia (1964). Kaneko
also employed the creative
talents of artists Isamu
Noguchi and Genichiro
Inokuma, and architects
around Tange, including
Takashi Asada and Hiroshi
Oe in various public works
in the prefecture.

Yoyogi National Gymnasia
At first the roof surface
of the Yoyogi National
Gymnasia was composed
of a network of cables, and
only when we'd entered
the construction stage did
we learn that the design
was not feasible. Mamoru
Kawaguchi saved the day:
he had the idea of using
a steel frame instead of
suspension cables. There
were a number of other occasions when things were
uncertain, but I wasn't scared
at the time because so many
outstanding people were
involved in both design
and construction. Now, it
scares me to remember.
Koji Kamiya

background, upbringing, or cultural tradition of the people who you design for.
I think these are the reasons why he was able to work in over 30 countries.

### Collaborators

**TT**    What we shouldn't forget is that he also had the good fortune to meet excellent collaborators in every country he worked in.

**NT**    Yes, he had good collaborators all over the world who gave us their input and helped us. If you are working all over the world, you don't learn the history overnight. You have active discussion. I think that was also his methodology.

**RK**    **Could you name some of the collaborators? For instance, who worked with you in the Middle East?**

**TT**    In the Middle East, Pierre El Khoury, for instance, from the Khoury family of the president of Lebanon. And also, the Syrian—

**NT**    When he worked on the Syrian presidential palace, there was a collaborator. But my father had very good collaborators in each country. He was also lucky in Japan to have very good collaborators.

### Meanwhile in Japan

**HUO**    **What was his working method inside Japan?**

**NT**    My father was quite fortunate with commissions. In the '60s, he was doing a lot of public buildings in Japan, municipality-type buildings. I think these public buildings set a model for office buildings in Japan. The story goes that a governor of a prefecture met him in some gathering and said: "Oh, Tange-san, I was looking for you. Can you do our prefecture government headquarters?" That was a good era, when these kinds of things really happened.

**RK**    **It was organized in that way.**

**NT**    Yes. They would just think, he is so talented, so why can't we ask him to do the work?

**RK**    **Sort of a no-competition thing.**

**NT**    Right, there was no competition. Now, if you did that, they'd say, oh, there's a conflict of interest. So, I see a lot of luck, timing-wise. He always said that luck was something that you create. You see a lucky thing coming and you just grab it.

**TT**    He always said that luck comes from the back, never from the front. If you keep on studying and making an effort, you can sense the luck coming. Luck comes up beside him, he feels it and takes it. [*gestures grabbing something from the side*]

**HUO**    **Ekuan, the industrial designer, said that he was a man of determination: when he wanted something, he would never let it go. So it was not only luck but also determination. Can you talk a little bit about that feature, which seems to be a strong part of his character?**

**NT**    I think Ekuan is right—he was a very determined man. He tried to think of ways to realize what he had envisioned, not only for getting a job but also for what he wanted to achieve in architecture. To build the Yoyogi National Gymnasia obviously required a good quarrel with a structural engineer.

**TT**    Talking of luck, for example, Saudi Arabia was one of the most important and majestic countries at that time. Once my husband was invited by King Faisal, he was eventually invited by the other kings of the neighboring countries, including Jordan.

**HUO**    **Maybe for Tange the world was his platform after the '60s, but I'm curious about your experience in the local context here. With which Metabolist architects did he have the most intense dialogue in the second half of the '60s and in the '70s? Or was the dialogue more with architects around in the world, and less with those in Japan?**

**NT**    I don't think my mother knows much about the movement. But in the '60s my father was researching how the industrial-oriented society was going to be an information-oriented society, and he was also working on projects like

**1964** Kagawa Prefecture Gymnasium—the same year as the Yoyogi National Gymnasia—commissioned by Governor Masayoshi Kaneko, patron of progressive architects and artists.

**1978** Tange, 65, returns to Bologna, where he masterplanned a new development in 1967, to write another chapter in the city's modernization; le grand maître japonaise is also invited by mayor Jacques Chirac to Paris…

**1987** Nine years later, the Fiera District as backdrop to the 12th century Asinelli Tower.

A static Tange, pleased with the presentation of the Fiera District Center model (featuring his already signature tubular cores). The increasing agency of his URTEC colleagues becomes clear.

**1986–88** Tange, 73, presents the Grand Écran, part of the Place d'Italie masterplan, to his private commissioner, Jacques Chirac (there is no public competition for the project). Artist Thierry Vide, responsible for the preembedded sculpture, stands right.

Plan for Tokyo 1960. He was much more involved in urban situations, and how those issues should be developed, than in architecture. Of course, Kurokawa, Isozaki, Kikutake—everybody was around as my father's student, in a way. I think that this kind of thinking expanded in their mind into the form of Metabolism. My father treasured conversation with young people and he would collaborate with them on actual projects.

TT   When he met young architects at various conferences, they would exchange ideas and opinions enthusiastically. In those times, people in the "Tange School" used to spend a lot of time together.

RK   **Did the dialogue continue over time? And was it, at some point, abandoned? Our question is: was the moment of orientation to the rest of the world also the moment when the school in Japan diminished or contact with the Japanese diminished?**

NT   At the time of Plan for Tokyo 1960 the body of his company was actually Tange Lab, which was within Tokyo University. Then it became more independent and eventually, around 1964, became a company called URTEC, which was run by Koji Kamiya, while my father kept his position as a university professor, leading the Tange Lab. As a professor of a national university, you cannot found a private company. The studio became more actively involved in the architectural world when it became a private limited company. From there, they produced architectural and urban works.

RK   **Until when was he a university professor?**

NT   Till after Expo '70. In 1973 he turned 60 and retired from the university. After that, he moved on to the office of URTEC.

### Businessman

RK   **In our research, we found that Yoshio Taniguchi said that he learned architectural principles from his father and business sense from Tange the opposite of what you would expect.[1]**

NT   I think my father was always an academic person. I don't think that he was thinking of business per se.

RK   **Never?**

NT   I don't think so.

RK   **What was the maximum scale of the office?**

NT   A hundred-plus?

RK   **Is it possible to not think about business if you have a hundred-plus office?**

NT   Of course, one has to think about it.

RK   **Or did other people think for him?**

NT   Actually, yes, Kamiya was running the office for some time, but it was much more out of a sense of necessity. A university professor could propose ideas but they would not be realized because they were not allowed to do business. Having said that, my father was a brilliant businessman in some ways. [laughs]

RK   **Can you say a little more about that? What makes a brilliant businessman?**

TT   He was very good at numbers. I believe he had a natural gift for business.

RK   **Can you say something about Atsushi Shimokobe as a kind of supporter? We hear that it's not only good collaborators but also civil servants, bureaucrats, people like Shimokobe, who genuinely constructed a place for Tange.**

TT   Did you meet Shimokobe?

RK   **Yes.**

TT   Did you think that he was a bureaucratic person?

RK   **Officially yes, but I think that he also created a lot of opportunities for other people. So his bureaucracy took a form of creativity. I think he must have done a lot for your husband.**

NT   Indeed, he gave my father opportunities.

TT   Sure, but in Japanese society men would not reveal such scenes to their families.

**2000** Changing of the guards: Noritaka Tange, now president of Tange Associates.

sukiji
We have based the Tsukiji
proposal on the concept
of having business district
buildings raised above the
urban axis—an idea first
used in Plan for Tokyo 1960."
Tange, "From Architecture
to Urban Design," *Japan
Architect*, May 1967.

**NT** In Japanese society men are much more together, so unfortunately she would not know. But I know that Shimokobe helped many people.

## Father Figure

**KAYOKO OTA Did Tange see the work of the Metabolists as an extension of his own work or did he believe that they were trying to break away from his school?**

**NT** Unfortunately, as we never exchanged opinions on the topic, it is just conjecture, but he might see his influence in their works. For example, looking at Kikutake's Marine City or Tower-Shaped Community in *Metabolism 1960*, they may have been developed or reinterpreted later based on my father's thoughts on urban structure in Plan for Tokyo 1960 or his Plan for Tsukiji in 1964.

**KO It seems that many of the most important postwar Japanese architects can trace their lineage back to Tange. Do you think he sensed that he was becoming a father figure for a much broader circle of Japanese architects? And do you think he felt a certain responsibility to support the work of these younger designers?**

**NT** I think my father felt a responsibility to support the work of young architects, including current world-leading architects, from a variety of standpoints: as an architect, an educator, and a man of culture.

**RK We have discussed some of Tange's qualities, but for me, it is mysterious how somebody with such an obviously strong character and strong convictions can find so many supporters. Usually, strong characters put people off. What was it in his character that drew so much support?**

**TT** I would assume it was because my husband was a good person. As they say, a good person attracts good people.

**RK But was he kind?**

**NT** Yes!

**RK Was he funny?**

**NT** Oh, he was not funny; he was very serious. But he was very charming in his own way.

**RK Was he very formal?**

**NT** Very sincere and very formal. He only had a suit and pajamas in his life and nothing in between. If he had one spot on his suit, he would excuse himself and change the entire outfit. But that was cute in a way. Isn't that sweet in his own way?

**Reference**
1  Yoshio Taniguchi, "Tange's
DNA Discovered," *Casa Brutus*,
September 2005.

**1967** Kenzo Tange: Yamanashi Press and Broadcasting Center
**2009** Photos by Charlie Koolhaas

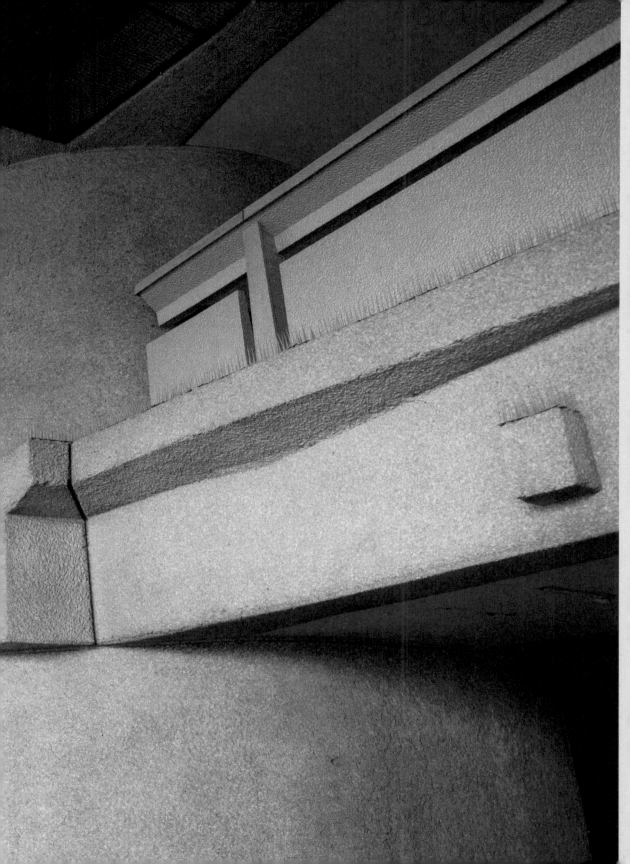

**1967** Kenzo Tange: Shizuoka Press and Broadcasting Center, Tokyo
**2009** Photos by Charlie Koolhaas

# Expansion/Exile
## Tange and Kurokawa's globalization

**"I think it is the duty of Japan, which already has industrialized know-how ... to export design and techniques to the third world, and help them in sustaining man-made environments."**

Tange, *Asahi Shimbun*,
April 23, 1974.

Post-Expo '70, Tange and the Metabolists—mostly Kurokawa—embark on a full-scale globalization of their practice, triggered by apparently contradictory forces: accumulated triumphs on their home turf, and the simultaneous deterioration of conditions within Japan itself. The 1973 oil crisis pushes Japan's economy, and large parts of the West, into recession for the first time since 1945, but also coincides with the acceleration of globalization and a wave of decolonization across the Middle East and Africa.

Middle Eastern and newly independent African nations in search of modernity and flush with oil money after the crisis begin consulting foreign architects to plan buildings and cities from scratch. For Tange and the Metabolists, the project of nation building elsewhere becomes a welcome alternative to stagnation at home. A combination of factors drives Japan into a deeper relationship with the Middle East, consummated in architecture: Japan's need for a secure oil supply, guaranteed through non-oil-based economic relations; the Middle East's need for architectural and urban-planning expertise, and the fact that Japan is a developed nation with this knowledge, but it is not the West; and a subtle cultural attraction: Japanese politeness and instinctive understanding of the Middle East's honor culture, plus Middle Eastern fascination with Japan, a culture so alien that adherence to Islam is not an issue?

The stately Kenzo Tange is able to export his proficiency in creating national symbols. Political tumult—an assassination (Saudi Arabia), a coup (Nigeria), and a revolution (Iran)—scupper many of his projects; dictatorial stability ensures the completion of some (Syria), Tange's patience and tenacity others still (Abuja).

Kurokawa, once again representing the new way of doing things, operates in the Middle East more as businessman than statesman, benefitting from the growth of international architectural competitions as well as increasing economic interdependence between Japan and the region. Both of them use foreign territories —often, the tabula rasa of the desert—to try to realize ideas that could no longer-be entertained in Japan...

**Riyadh, 1965** On their first visit to Saudi Arabia, Tange and structural engineer Yoshikatsu Tsuboi (left) diligently wear the ghutra at a "dinner reception" in the desert, after submitting a report to the government...

Immediately as the oil crisis hits and Japan's GDP growth plummets in 1973, Tange and the Metabolists take advantage of opportunities arising in the Middle East for the exact same reasons; a concurrent wave of modernization and independence in Africa also brings new projects... After the Iranian Revolution and the second oil crisis, Asia, particularly Singapore, begins to emerge as the next most hospitable environment...

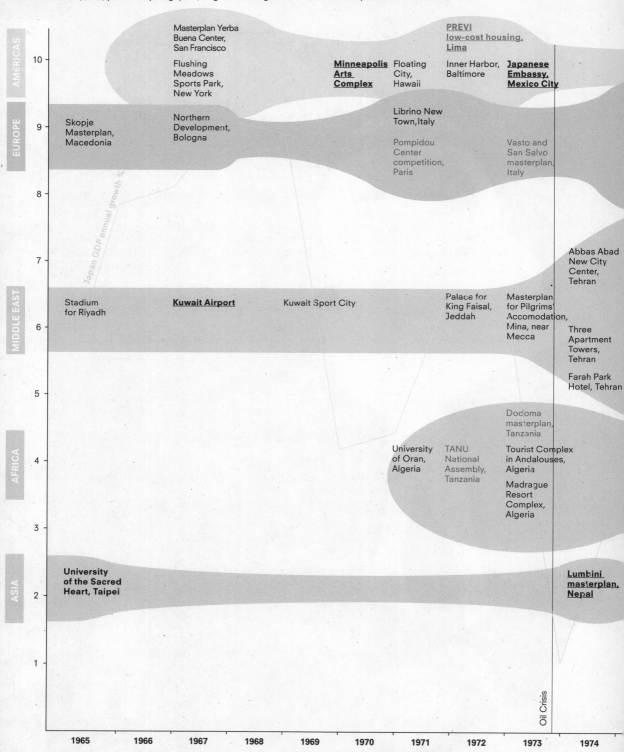

AMERICAS

Masterplan Yerba Buena Center, San Francisco

Flushing Meadows Sports Park, New York

**Minneapolis Arts Complex**

Floating City, Hawaii

Inner Harbor, Baltimore

PREVI low-cost housing, Lima

**Japanese Embassy, Mexico City**

EUROPE

Skopje Masterplan, Macedonia

Northern Development, Bologna

Librino New Town, Italy

Pompidou Center competition, Paris

Vasto and San Salvo masterplan, Italy

Japan GDP annual growth %

MIDDLE EAST

Stadium for Riyadh

**Kuwait Airport**

Kuwait Sport City

Palace for King Faisal, Jeddah

Masterplan for Pilgrims' Accomodation, Mina, near Mecca

Abbas Abad New City Center, Tehran

Three Apartment Towers, Tehran

Farah Park Hotel, Tehran

AFRICA

University of Oran, Algeria

TANU National Assembly, Tanzania

Dodoma masterplan, Tanzania

Tourist Complex in Andalouses, Algeria

Madrague Resort Complex, Algeria

ASIA

**University of the Sacred Heart, Taipei**

**Lumbini masterplan, Nepal**

Oil Crisis

1965  1966  1967  1968  1969  1970  1971  1972  1973  1974

**Japanese
Embassy,
Brasilia**

South
Friedrichstadt,
Berlin

Serdica
Complex,
Sofia,
Bulgaria

Librino
New Town,
Catania, Italy

Place
d'Italie,
Paris

Le Colisée,
Paris

Sports Center,
Vasto, Italy

Festival Hall
and Congress
Center, Cannes

Business and
Administrative
Center, Napoli

Fiera Center
Headquarters,
Bologna

Hotel in
Sofia, Bulgaria

Government
Center, Doha

**Palace for
King Khalid,
Jeddah**

**Public Garden,
Damascus**

**Palace for
Crown Prince
Fahd, Jeddah**

**People's
Palace,
Damascus**

Yarmouk
University,
Amman

Emir's
Palace,
Doha

Conference
City, Abu
Dhabi

**King Faisal
Foundation,
Riyadh**

City Hall at
Abbas Abad,
Tehran

Arabian Gulf
University,
Bahrain

Jordan Royal
Palace,
Amman

King Saud
University,
Al-Gassim,
Saudi Arabia

National
University,
Abu Dhabi

Floating
Hotel, Abu
Dhabi

Floating
Luxury Hotel,
Saudi Arabia

**Japanese
Embassy and
Chancellery,
Riyadh**

Um-Al
Kanhazeer
Hotel,
Baghdad

Floating
Infra-Cassette,
Iraq

Ministry of
National
Planning,
Abuja

National
Theater, Abu
Dhabi

**Central
Area of
Abuja,
Nigeria**

El-Fateh
University,
Rabat,
Morocco

Supreme
Court, Abuja

University of
Constantine,
Algeria

Institute of
Architecture,
Oran, Algeria

Algeria
International
Airport

Capital
Complex
Hall, Rabat

As Sarir
New Town,
Libya

East Coast
Corniche,
Benghazi,
Libya

**Presidential
Complex,
Abuja,
Nigeria**

Federal Twin
Capital, Pahang

Bandar Beri
Segawan,
Brunei

7,000
Housing
Units,
Benghazi,
Libya

King's
Center,
Singapore

Jalan Tuank
Abdul
Rahman,
Kuala Lumpur

Parkland
Condo-
minium,
Jakarta

**Singapore
Indoor
Stadium**

Floating
Infra-
Cassette,
Libya

New Capital
Planning,
Seoul

**City Tele-
comunication
Center,
Singapore**

Shah Alam
Hotel,
Malaysia

OCBC
Condo-
minium,
Singapore

New World
Complex,
Singapore

International
Conference
Center,
Brunei

Peace Memorial,
Malaysia

Kota
Kinabaru
Sports
Complex,
Malaysia

**GB
Building,
Singapore**

Shah Alam
Town Center,
Malaysia

**United
Overseas
Bank Plaza,
Singapore**

Asoke
Project,
Bangkok,
Thailand

**Overseas
Union Bank,
Singapore**

International
Petroleum
Center,
Singapore

Marina South,
Singapore

**Nanyang
Technology
Institute,
Singapore**

Peace
Memorial,
Malaysia &
Marshall Is.

MRT Raffles
Place Station,
Singapore

Iranian Revolution

1979 Energy Crisis

Iran–Iraq War

| 1975 | 1976 | 1977 | 1978 | 1979 | 1980 | 1981 | 1982 | 1983 | 1984 | 1985 |
|------|------|------|------|------|------|------|------|------|------|------|

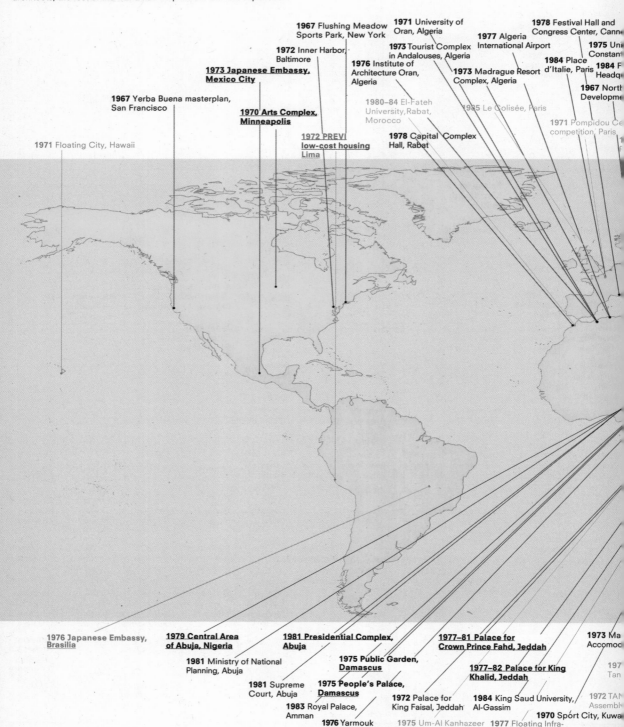

After the relatively modest involvement in the construction of the
Greater East Asia Co-Propserity Sphere, the global involvement of
Japan from the late '60s is massive. While in the West it was difficult,
at least until the '90s, to confide important projects to German
architects, the rest of the world had no problem with the Japanese...

**1967** Flushing Meadow
Sports Park, New York

**1971** University of
Oran, Algeria

**1978** Festival Hall and
Congress Center, Canne

**1972** Inner Harbor,
Baltimore

**1973** Tourist Complex
in Andalouses, Algeria

**1977** Algeria
International Airport

**1975** Uni
Constan

**1973 Japanese Embassy,
Mexico City**

**1976** Institute of
Architecture Oran,
Algeria

**1973** Madrague Resort
Complex, Algeria

**1984** Place
d'Italie, Paris

**1984** F
Headq

**1967** Yerba Buena masterplan,
San Francisco

**1970 Arts Complex,
Minneapolis**

**1967** North
Developme

1980–84 El-Fateh
University, Rabat,
Morocco

1985 Le Colisée, Paris

1971 Pompidou Ce
competition, Paris

**1972 PREVI
low-cost housing**
Lima

**1978** Capital Complex
Hall, Rabat

1971 Floating City, Hawaii

**1976 Japanese Embassy,
Brasilia**

**1979 Central Area
of Abuja, Nigeria**

**1981 Presidential Complex,
Abuja**

**1977–81 Palace for
Crown Prince Fahd, Jeddah**

1973 Ma
Accomod

**1981** Ministry of National
Planning, Abuja

**1975 Public Garden,
Damascus**

**1977–82 Palace for King
Khalid, Jeddah**

197
Tan

**1981** Supreme
Court, Abuja

**1975 People's Palace,
Damascus**

**1972** Palace for
King Faisal, Jeddah

**1984** King Saud University,
Al-Gassim

1972 TAN
Assembl

**1983** Royal Palace,
Amman

1975 Um-Al Kanhazeer
Hotel, Baghdad

**1977** Floating Infra-
Cassette, Iraq

**1970** Sport City, Kuwa

**1976** Yarmouk
University, Amman

**1977–82 K**

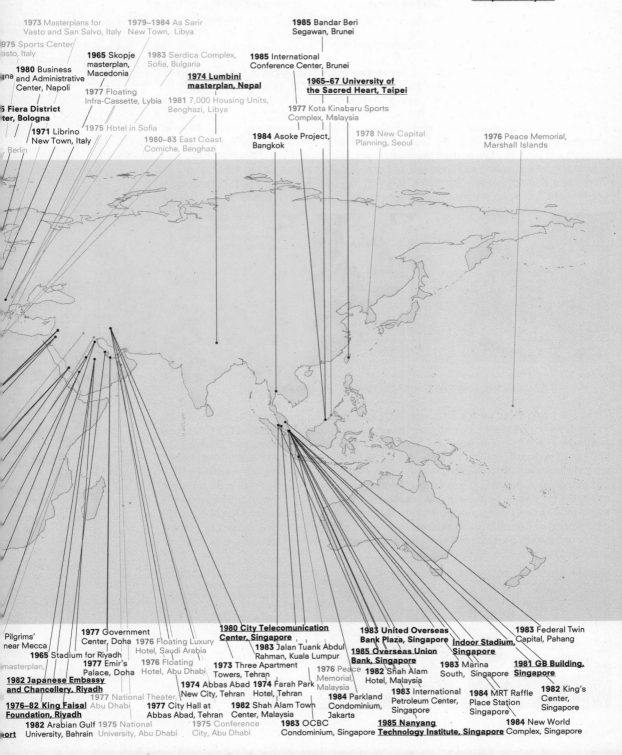

**1973** Masterplans for
Vasto and San Salvo, Italy

**1979–1984** As Sarir
New Town, Libya

**1985** Bandar Beri
Segawan, Brunei

**975** Sports Center
asto, Italy

**1965** Skopje
masterplan,
Macedonia

**1983** Serdica Complex,
Sofia, Bulgaria

**1985** International
Conference Center, Brunei

**1980** Business
and Administrative
Center, Napoli

**1977** Floating
Infra-Cassette, Lybia

**1974 Lumbini
masterplan, Nepal**

**1965–67 University of
the Sacred Heart, Taipei**

**5 Fiera District
ter, Bologna**

**1981** 7,000 Housing Units,
Benghazi, Libya

**1977** Kota Kinabaru Sports
Complex, Malaysia

**1971** Librino
New Town, Italy

**1975** Hotel in Sofia

**1984** Asoke Project,
Bangkok

**1978** New Capital
Planning, Seoul

**1976** Peace Memorial,
Marshall Islands

Berlin

**1980–83** East Coast
Corniche, Benghazi

Pilgrims'
near Mecca

**1977** Government
Center, Doha

**1976** Floating Luxury
Hotel, Saudi Arabia

**1980 City Telecomunication
Center, Singapore**

**1983 United Overseas
Bank Plaza, Singapore**

**1983** Federal Twin
Capital, Pahang

**1965** Stadium for Riyadh

**1983** Jalan Tuank Abdul
Rahman, Kuala Lumpur

**1985 Overseas Union
Bank, Singapore**

**Indoor Stadium,
Singapore**

**1977** Emir's
Palace, Doha

**1976** Floating
Hotel, Abu Dhabi

**1973** Three Apartment
Towers, Tehran

**1983** International
Petroleum Center,
Singapore

**1983** Marina
South,
Singapore

**1981 GB Building,
Singapore**

**1982 Japanese Embassy
and Chancellery, Riyadh**

**1974** Abbas Abad
New City, Tehran

**1974** Farah Park
Hotel, Tehran

**1976** Peace
Memorial,
Malaysia

**1982** Shah Alam
Hotel, Malaysia

**1984** MRT Raffle
Place Station
Singapore

**1982** King's
Center,
Singapore

**1977** National Theater,
Abu Dhabi

**1984** Parkland
Condominium,
Jakarta

**1976–82 King Faisal
Foundation, Riyadh**

**1977** City Hall at
Abbas Abad, Tehran

**1982** Shah Alam Town
Center, Malaysia

**1984** New World
Complex, Singapore

**1982** Arabian Gulf
ort University, Bahrain

**1975** National
University, Abu Dhabi

**1975** Conference
City, Abu Dhabi

**1983** OCBC
Condominium, Singapore

**1985 Nanyang
Technology Institute, Singapore**

## JAPAN AND THE MIDDLE EAST
## OIL, ECONOMICS, ARCHITECTURE

The expansion of Tange and the Metabolists into the Middle East is the result not only of their private initiative and talents, but the byproduct—and the crucial symbolic manifestation—of three key stages in Japan's diplomatic efforts, at the highest level, to deepen economic relations, in order to keep the oil flowing...

### 1958 FIRST FORAY: THE ARABIAN OIL COMPANY

The 1956 Suez crisis, and Japan's accelerating economic growth prompts Japan to launch its first major foray into the Middle East. In 1957, Taro Yamashita, founder of the Japan Petroleum Trading Company, meets King Saud in Riyadh, carrying a letter of introduction from Japanese Prime Minister Tanzan Ishibashi.[1] In the face of competition from Western oil companies, Yamashita wins a 44-year concession to extract Saudi Arabian oil by shrewdly promising the Saudis 56 percent of revenue (rather than the customary 50 percent). The Arabian Oil Company, which is in fact Japanese, is born. Production begins in 1960, and Yamashita develops, near the wells, housing, offices, and facilities for shipping—the first link between architecture and oil.[2]

**1957** Taro Yamashita, of the the Japan Petroleum Trading Company, secures a deal with King Saud in Riyadh.

### 1960–73 FUELING THE ECONOMIC MIRACLE: ENTER THE SHOSHAS

As Japan's economy grows between 1961 and 1973, its demand for oil quadruples. Japan buys 70 percent of its oil from the majors, mostly the Arabian Oil Company, putting it in a vulnerable position. Japanese *shoshas*—like Mitsui and Mitsubishi—step in, working directly with Middle Eastern governments as they nationalize their oil industries to help them develop refineries. Shoshas are massive conglomerates operating in a range of industries, expert in setting up distribution channels overseas, supplying raw materials, and creating consortiums to make large-scale contracting more efficient. By the early '70s, all major Shoshas have a presence in Saudi Arabia and Iran, working on refinery expansion projects that are paid for with oil itself and providing the framework in which industrial and architectural projects can be organized...

Leading shosha Mitsui Bussan helps build the Das Island oil facility 250 kilometers offshore from Abu Dhabi.

After the Fourth Arab-Israeli War in October 1973, OPEC defines Japan, with its ties to Israel and the US, as an "unfriendly" nation. The classification is disastrous: Japan gets 90 percent of its oil from OPEC states; in the embargo that follows, oil prices in Japan increase 217 percent, and its economy contracts for the first time since 1945. The crisis forces Japan to reenter the international political arena in a serious way for the first time since the war: the government realizes that it can no longer afford to have a passive economic and diplomatic relationship with the oil producing countries, and launches an intense campaign of oil diplomacy.

In November 1973, the secretary-general of the Japanese cabinet, trying to appease OPEC, declares that "Israel must withdraw from the occupied territories," and says it supports the "legitimate rights of the Palestinian people." But OPEC demands more: Japan must sever all ties with Israel. Henry Kissinger immediately visits Tokyo and tells Japan not to accept. In exchange, Japan asks Kissinger to guarantee oil from America's emergency stocks if the flow from the Middle East dries up completely. When Kissinger refuses, Japan continues on its track of appeasing OPEC. Deputy Prime Minister Takeo Miki is dispatched to eight Middle Eastern countries to explain Japan's neutral position vis-à-vis Israel and the Arab states. In January 1974, Minister of International Trade and Industry Nakasone arranges a loan of $1 billion to Iran in exchange for 160 million tons of oil over 10 years; he pledges $1.5 billion to Iraq for a similar exchange. In return, Arab countries start sending missions to Japan seeking technical assistance in industrial and refinery projects. Nearly a year later, in December 1974, OPEC reclassifies Japan as a "friendly nation" and lifts the embargo; in March 1975 Japan reaches an Economic Cooperation Agreement with Saudi Arabia.[3]

**1973** Deputy Prime Minister Takeo Miki (right) embarks on a mission to the Middle East carrying a letter from Prime Minister Tanaka explaining Japan's neutrality in the Israel-Arab conflict.

**1975** In Tokyo, Hisham Nazer, Saudi Arabia's minister of state, signs the Economic Cooperation Agreement with Kiichi Miyazawa, minister of foreign affairs.

## JAPAN AND THE MIDDLE EAST: THE FOUNDATIONS OF ARCHITECTURAL EXPORT...

Japan's diplomatic and economic activism succeeds in creating deeper links with the Middle East throughout the 1970s. The Middle East continues to provide the oil Japan needs to fuel its industry—the top country is Saudi Arabia. In return, the region—particularly Saudi Arabia—starts buying Japanese cars, motorcycles, household appliances (there is a shift from American to Japanese products), iron, steel, and architectural expertise. In 1970, Japanese goods account for 10 percent of the Middle East's total imports; in 1980, the figure is 18 percent,[4] making Japan the single biggest exporter of goods to the region. Tange and the Metabolists are a small part of the growing wave of Japanese exports...

**Exports: Japan to Middle East**

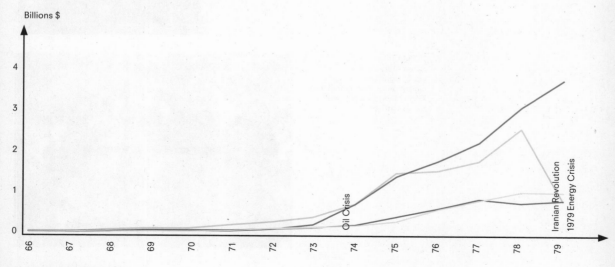

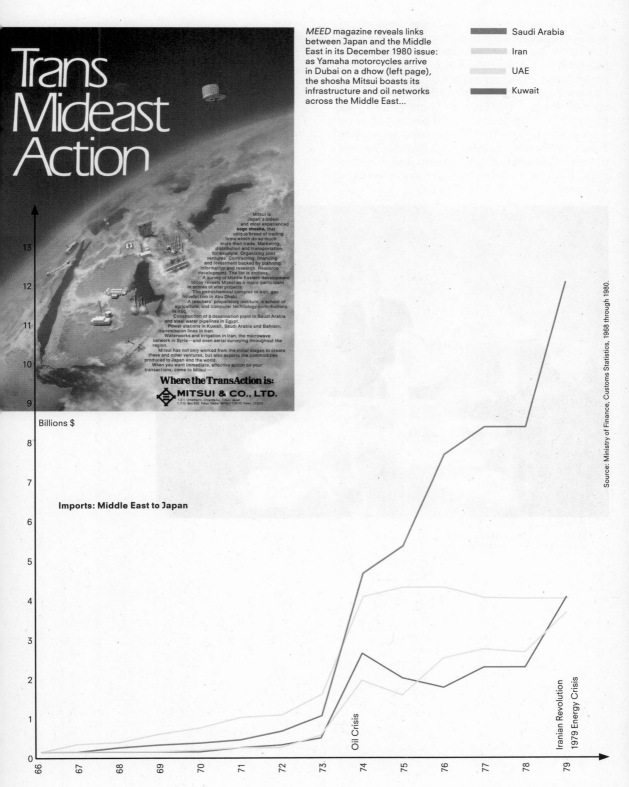

*MEED* magazine reveals links between Japan and the Middle East in its December 1980 issue: as Yamaha motorcycles arrive in Dubai on a dhow (left page), the shosha Mitsui boasts its infrastructure and oil networks across the Middle East...

▬▬▬ Saudi Arabia

▬▬▬ Iran

▬▬▬ UAE

▬▬▬ Kuwait

Trans
Mideast
Action

Mitsui is Japan's oldest and most experienced **sogo shosha,** that unique breed of trading firms which do so much more than trade. Marketing, distribution and transportation, for example. Organizing joint ventures. Contracting, financing and investment backed by planning, information and research. Resource development. The list is endless.

A survey of Middle Eastern development today reveals Mitsui as a major participant in scores of vital projects:

The petrochemical complex in Iran, gas liquefaction in Abu Dhabi.

A teachers' preparatory institute, a school of agriculture, and computer technology contributions in Iraq.

Construction of a desalination plant in Saudi Arabia and steel water pipelines in Egypt.

Power stations in Kuwait, Saudi Arabia and Bahrain; transmission lines in Iran.

Waterworks and irrigation in Iran, the microwave network in Syria—and even aerial surveying throughout the region.

Mitsui has not only worked from the initial stages to create these and other ventures, but also exports the commodities produced to Japan and the world.

When you want immediate, effective action on your transactions, come to Mitsui—

**Where the TransAction is:**

**MITSUI & CO., LTD.**
1-2-1 Ohtemachi, Chiyoda-ku, Tokyo, Japan
C.P.O. Box 822, Tokyo Cable: MITSUI TOKYO Telex: J22253

Billions $

**Imports: Middle East to Japan**

Oil Crisis

Iranian Revolution

1979 Energy Crisis

Source: Ministry of Finance, Customs Statistics, 1968 through 1980.

13

12

11

10

9

8

7

6

5

4

3

2

1

0

66  67  68  69  70  71  72  73  74  75  76  77  78  79

## TANGE'S MISSION

After the triumph of Expo '70, Tange the de facto architect laureate suffers his first major reversal of fortune: in Japan, with its economy slowing down, he becomes a marginalized figure, struggling for new projects and even for recognition. But "silence" at home is only the flip side to a massive expansion abroad. Through URTEC—his English-named and English-speaking company—80 percent of Tange's work at one point in the '70s comes from outside Japan.[5] It is a mission that Tange approaches with the same ambition, insight, paternalistic responsibility, and dignity that he brought to the rebuilding of Japan...

**1969** Tange negotiates to build Kuwait's new international airport, with Kuwait City as backdrop.

**Silence since Expo**
*Asahi Shimbun*, April 23, 1974

Since four years ago when he sent out a rosy fantasy of the future city as a producer of the Expo, Tange has realized almost no work in Japan. After a long silence, he and his office URTEC are beginning to work on an increasing number of gigantic-scaled projects in the Middle East...

The domestic situation is severe. Since Expo 70, major general contractors became so powerful that they are now almost entirely monopolizing the market, including architectural design. Individual talents like Tange, who is known to "exceed budgets by using new experimental methods," tend to be avoided ... Under such circumstances, however, Tange is receiving a number of invitations from abroad, mainly Middle Eastern countries that are trying to speed up modernization thanks to oil revenue...

He is popular perhaps because among the "master" architects today he has the most compelling experience of urban design. In 1961 he publicized Plan for Tokyo 1960 ... This vision lay full trust in technological progress; the worship of industrial civilization was also adopted in the Skopje reconstruction plan, and likewise in the urban planning of Bologna, Italy, before Tange began directing the construction of a futuristic city at Expo 70. In the projects currently under way in Oran, Algeria, and in Tehran, Iran ... the Plan for Tokyo is applied here and there ... but now in the 1970s we are beginning to question our optimistic aspiration for the progress of industry and technology. Would it really benefit the happiness of developing countries to sympathize and provide them with design based on industrialization?

Tange replies: "We are beginning to criticize progress and growth, development and construction as they result in the destruction of our environment. But that is a luxurious problem of developed countries ... Developing countries do need growth and technology in order to undo technical, economic and cultural imbalance, and to redistribute wealth. Thanks to the progress of technology, I think we can manage to create a development model free of pollution. ...I think it is the duty of Japan, who already has industrialized know-how in energy conservation, to export design and technique."

1964    Tanganyika merges with Zanzibar to form Tanzania after independence from UK in 1961; Japan
joins OECD (Organization of Economic co-Operation and Development); Tokyo Olympics Faisal
becomes king of Saudi Arabia, launches modernization agenda.

1967    Japan's GDP becomes world's second largest; Six-Day War between Israel and Egypt,
Jordan and Syria.

1968   **Kuwait International Airport.**

1968   **Riyadh stadium.**

1969   **Kuwait Sports City.**

    Qaddafi takes power in coup in Libya, nationalizes oil industry.

    Concorde flies; man lands on the moon.

1970    Expo '70: Saudi Arabia, Kuwait, Abu Dhabi debut with pavilions. Algeria, Tanzania,
Egypt make their world expo debut.

    Hafez al-Assad resumes power in Syria.

1971    UAE forms; Qatar independence from UK.

1972    Saudi government acquires 20% stake in Aramco oil from United States.

    Khalifa bin Hamad Al Thani takes power in Qatar in palace coup.

    **Tanzania's Parliament and TANU Headquarters, Dar es Salaam.**

1973   Qaddafi announces "cultural revolution."

    **Masterplan for Dodoma, Tanzania's new capital.**

    **Abbas Abad New City Center, Tehran.**

    Oil crisis: OPEC embargo after 4th Arab–Israeli War. Japan's oil supply decrease 10–30%,
price of crude oil increase 217%.

    Attempting to mitigate the embargo, Japan calls for Israel to withdraw from territories gained
in 1967.

1974   **Farah Park Hotel, Three Apartment Towers, Tehran.**

    **Masterplan for Pilgrims' Accommodation, Muna, Mecca.**

    Nakasone, minister of international trade and industry, visits Saudi Arabia; Ahmed Yamani,
Saudi Arabia's minister of oil, visits Japan; Honda (motorcycles) and Nissan (trucks) begin manufacturing in Saudi Arabia; Japan recognizes PLO.

    Iran–Japan Tourism Company forms; NEC, Bridgestone, and Kubota begin manufacturing in Iran.

    **Palaces for the King and Crown Prince, Jeddah.**

1975   Japan's GDP declines for first time since 1945.

    **People's Palace and Public Garden, Damascus.**

    Toshiba, Matsushita (Panasonic), Honda, Suzuki, and Yamaha begin manufacturing in Iran;
Sony launches in Saudi Arabia.

    King Faisal of Saudi Arabia assassinated by his half-brother's son, Faisal bin Musa'id.

    Mayor of Tehran passes "Shahestan Pahlavi" (Abbas Abad) project to Llewelyn Davies.

    Nigeria announces it will move its capital from Lagos to Abuja.

    **Conference City, Abu Dhabi.**

    **Al Khanazeer Island Tourist Development, Baghdad.**

1976   **King Faisal Foundation, Riyadh.**

    Obayashi Corporation sets up in Saudi Arabia; Mitsubishi sets up in UAE.

    Nigeria's military ruler Murtala Mohammed assassinated; Olusegun Obasanjo takes over,
introducing presidential constitution.

    **Floating Hotel, Abu Dhabi.**

1977   **Floating Luxury Hotel, Saudi Arabia.**

    **Floating Infra-Cassette, Libya and Iraq.**

    **Tehran City Hall.**

    **Palace for the Emir, Doha.**

    **Qatar Government Center, Doha.**

1979    Japanese contractors Kajima, Hazama, Takenaka, and Sato Kogyo set up local consortiums in Iran.

    Iranian Revolution: Khomeini deposes the shah; collapse of Japan's investment in petrochemical
complex at Bandar Shahpur.

    Nigeria returns to democracy: Obasanjo transfers power to Shehu Shagari after elections.

    **As-Sarir New Town, Libya.**

    **Abuja masterplan.**

1980   Gulf Cooperation Council (GCC) launches with Saudi Arabia, Kuwait, Bahrain, Qatar, Oman,
and UAE.

    Second oil crisis, triggered by Iranian Revolution.

    **El Fateh University, Tripoli; Benghzai East Coast Development; 7,000 Housing Units in Benghazi**

1980   Iran–Iraq War starts.

1984   **King Saud University, Al-Gassim.**

Kenzo Tange
Kisho Kurokawa
Kiyonori Kikutake

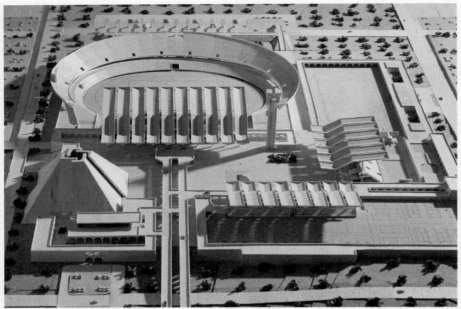

Ziggurat and bowl: Tange's monumental first design for Saudi Arabia.

## Nation Building Abroad

Faisal, having deposed his brother Saud in 1964, commissions Tange to design stadia in Riyadh, Jeddah, and the oil base Dhahran. The connection is made through the Tokyo Olympics: according to Tange's account, a Saudi royal attends, and is impressed by the Yoyogi gymnasia. The minister of labor and social welfare invites Tange and Tsuboi (pictured in the desert, p. 592) to Saudi Arabia in 1965 to review and advise on already existing stadia proposals.[6] But Faisal is apparently so impressed by Tange, and his emphasis on the symbolic power of stadia for a nation, that he commissions him to design all three of them. With characteristic generosity, Tange agrees to take one stadium and gives the other two away: to Jørn Utzon (struggling to get his Sydney Opera House constructed), and to Paul Rudolph. Tange's design for Riyadh includes a 57,000-seat stadium, gymnasium, swimming pool, and second athletics track. The four components are linked by a shaded arcade—Isamic-style—and a plaza. Doxiadis, already working in Riyadh, helps Tange with urban planning and traffic management. The project is halted, according to Tange "by the out-break of the Middle East War"—presumably, the Fourth Arab-Israeli War of 1973 between Israel and Egypt with Syria, Iraq, and Jordan.

Plane-shaped.

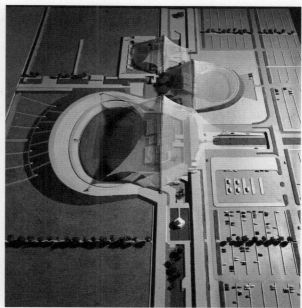

Big Roofs: Sports City.

## Symbols of Modernization

Kuwait's independence from the UK in 1961 triggers three nation-building projects that Tange is selected for: the Kuwaiti Embassy in Tokyo completed in 1970, Kuwait's new international airport, and Kuwait Sports City for the Pan-Arab Games. The airport is Tange's first commission outside Saudi Arabia, probably aided by his relationship with King Faisal. He designs an emblematic form—a terminal building shaped like a plane (Concorde?)—for the newly independent nation state. "I think of an airport terminal building as a long corridor," Tange writes. "That is why it is so interesting to me. In schools as well, the halls are more important than the classrooms; halls and corridors are excellent means of communications."[7] (Here Tange echoes Louis Kahn's remarks in a conversation at Kikutake's Sky House during the World Design Conference in 1960.) Twelve years after beginning the design, the airport is complete…

## Collaboration

For Kuwait's Sports City, planned for the 1974 Pan Arab Games, Tange invites Frei Otto—master of tensile canopies, architect of the Germany pavilion at Expo '67 and the Munich Olympic stadium in 1972—to collaborate. Working with Tange in Tokyo, Otto designs three massive structures to shield the main athletics stadium, soccer stadium, and swimming pool from the desert sun. The three fields are connected by an artificial oasis, a valley sunken by 3.6 meters beneath the ground. Tange and Otto's design wins the competition, but, as with the Riyadh stadium, the project is canceled along with the Games when the Fourth Arab–Israeli War breaks out in 1973.

Local sensitivity: Islamic facade detailing.

## Architecture of independence

Tanganyika (like Qatar) wins independence from
the UK in 1961; two years later it absorbs the island
of Zanzibar to form the new nation of Tanzania.
Kurokawa, 38, wins his first international competition
—for the new headquarters of the Tanzania African
National Union (TANU) party, and the national
parliament it controls, in Dar es Salaam. He presents
the design to president Julius K. Nyerere: it is based
on his long-held concept of *kairo*, "architecture of
the street," in the form of an A-Frame that creates
an interstitial zone between the urban and the architectural, the inside and the outside. The structure
considers sustainability avant la lettre: the huge
"urban roof," with ventilation slots, provides shade
and generates a breeze…

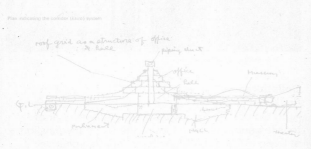

Section showing "roof grid."

Simulation.

"Architecture of the
street": a slab pulled
apart to create an atrium
and a passage through
the building…

## Building ⟶ city

One year after the competition, the Tanzanian government decides to move the parliament project—and the entire capital—from Dar es Salaam, the tainted center of operations under British colonial rule, inland to Dodoma, a small city at the foot of Mount Kilimanjaro. Kurokawa's plan becomes more ambitious, growing from a single structure into a masterplan for the new capital: the TANU Headquarters and Parliament is positioned along the central avenue cutting across the core of the city. A combination of the oil crisis and political wrangling (Nyerere is busy consolidating his power) kills the project.[8] It takes another 23 years before Dodoma is finally inaugurated as Tanzania's capital.

Kurokawa arrives in Tanzania and "800 Refugees Enter Kigoma after unrest in neighboring Burundi."

Celebrating the completion of the model before dispatch to Tanzania.

Skeleton of Tanzania's new capital.

## Dream team

In November 1973, Queen Farah Pahlavi receives Tange and Louis Kahn in Tehran, sharing her vision for Abbas Abad, a new 500-hectare development for the north of Tehran with government, financial, and residential buildings. Tange and Kahn are treated to a helicopter tour of the site and invited to collaborate on a masterplan. They go straight from Tehran to Tokyo to start working on a "Common Agreement on the Parts and Their Relation."[9] Continuing his obsession with the central axis, Tange plans a north–south double avenue. Kahn, back in the United States, produces a drastically different proposal: where Tange rides roughshod over the natural topography, presumably flattening it, Kahn preserves it and develops instead the southern part of the site. In February 1974, Kahn sends the plan to Tange, and Isozaki is tasked with integrating the two masters' plans. But the following month, Kahn dies. In 1975, the British firm Llewelyn Davies takes over the project after winning a competition, but preserves Tange's central axis. Jacquelin Robertson directs the project, which takes the new, more Shah-centric name Shahestan Pahlavi. After the revolution in 1979, the project is shelved.

Isozaki's integration of the masters' plans.

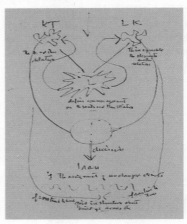

Kahn sketches the collaborative structure, leading to a "Common Agreement on the Parts and Their Relation."

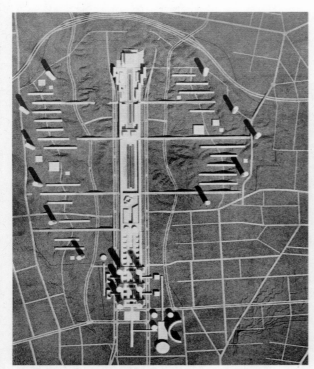

Tange's spine-inspired masterplan.

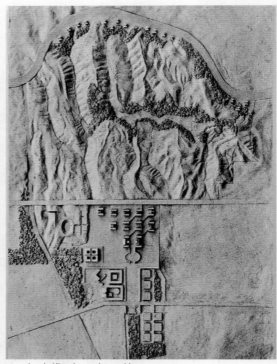

Louis Khan's version, taking account of the mountains....

## The Shah's Modernization Drive

In 1974, Tange is back in Iran, this time for its second International Congress of Architecture, an event triggered by the shah's modernization drive (funded by increasing oil revenues) and queen Farah Pahlavi's interest in architecture (she studied at the École Spéciale d'Architecture in Paris). Tange joins a stellar array of architects and urban planners in Persepolis, including B.V. Doshi, Josep Lluís Sert and his former student Fumihiko Maki, Moshe Safdie, Buckminster Fuller, I.M. Pei, James Stirling, and Hans Hollein. After the conference, Tange is commissioned by a consortium, of Iranian, French, and Japanese companies to design three high-rise apartments (of which nothing comes). At the same time, the unlikely sounding Iran–Japan Tourism Company (composed of Iran's Ministry of Tourism and National Mining Industry Bank together with Japan's Industrial Bank and Fujita Kanko tourism company) commissions Tange to design a 700-room Sheraton hotel tower in a park named after the Queen, in downtown Tehran. Construction begins...

**1977** Japanese at Persepolis, result of the bilateral tourism strategy.

1974 Farah Park Hotel, Tehran.

Void in Farah Park (now Laleh park).

**2011** Thirty-two years after the '79 revolution halts construction (with 80 percent of the excavation and 20 percent of the foundations complete), the hotel remains on hold...

## Masterplan for Islam

Emboldened by the oil embargo, Faisal turns to Tange with a second crucial commission. In a valley five kilometers southeast of Mecca, Tange works with Ekuan to plan a temporary city for the two million pilgrims on the Hajj each year. The 635-hectare valley is sacred ground and must be kept free of permanent structures, so Tange and Ekuan design equipment—tents with sleeping bunks, showers, toilets, water tanks, gas tanks, generators, refrigeration cars, sewage tanks, garbage cans—that can be stored under platforms at the edge of the valley and rolled out every year for four days before going into hibernation again. Combining industrial design, architecture, and masterplanning, Tange and Ekuan suddenly receive offers from Japanese auto manufacturers, including Isuzu, excited by the prospect of making special vehicles for the site.[10] King Faisal wants to implement the scheme immediately but is assassinated in 1975 before construction can begin, and the project is shelved. The Metabolist idea of a temporary city, so close to realization, remains a dream…

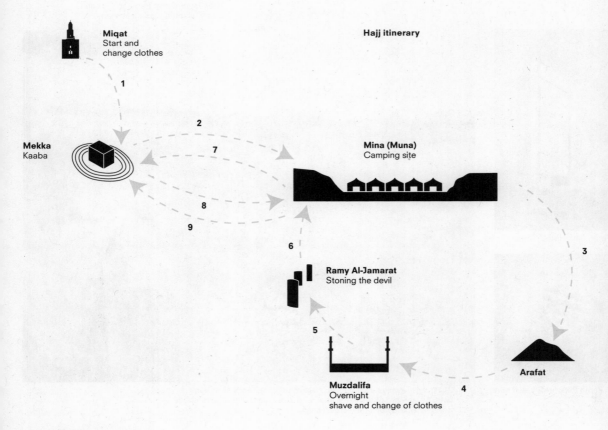

Hajj itinerary

**Miqat**
Start and change clothes

**Mekka**
Kaaba

**Mina (Muna)**
Camping site

**Ramy Al-Jamarat**
Stoning the devil

**Muzdalifa**
Overnight shave and change of clothes

**Arafat**

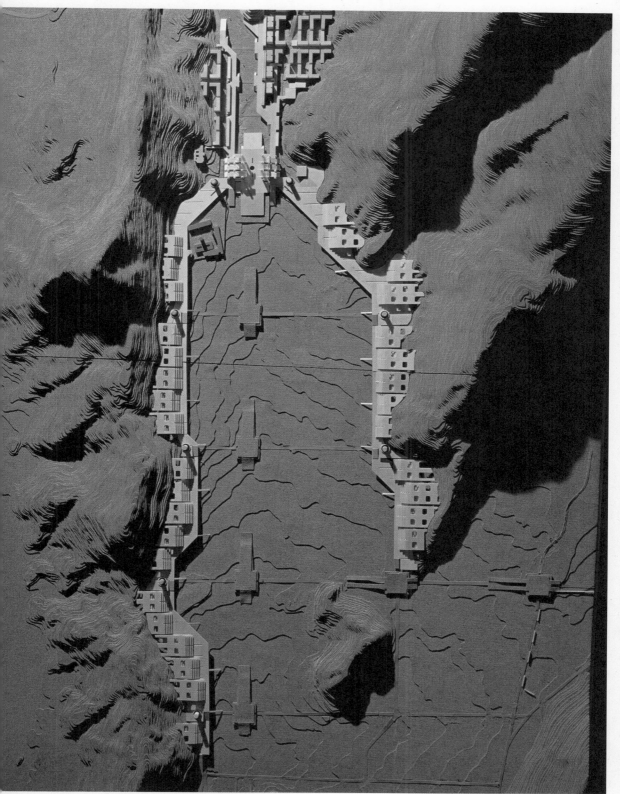

Pre-Hajj: the invisible city.

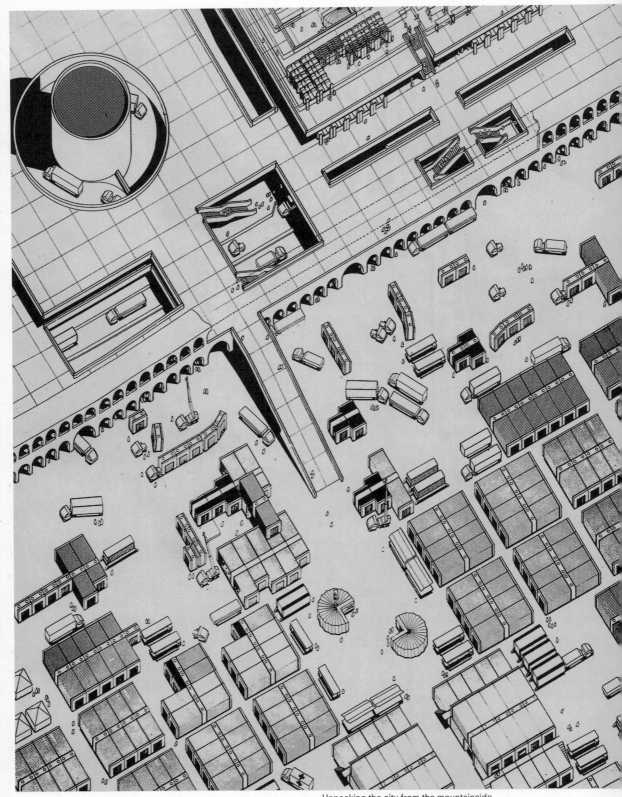

Unpacking the city from the mountainside.

During the Hajj: temporary city.

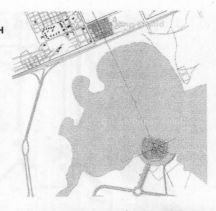

## Royal architect

Faisal's assassination also halts Tange's project to build a private house for the queen. Nevertheless, with the nation flush after the oil crisis, the Saudi royal family continues its relationship with the Tange, commissioning him to build palaces for King Khalid (Faisal's successor), and for Crown Prince Fahd. Fahd's palace is on an artificial island, overlooked with a "watchful, guarding eye,"[11] by Khalid's larger palace across the Jeddah inlet.

Like father...

...like son.

Islamodernism.

## Shelved

As part of a masterplan for Doha's corniche (see p. 629), Tange is asked to design a palace for Qatar's Emir Khalifa bin Hamad Al Thani. Tange's modern design, lacking in traditional Islamic qualities, is rejected.

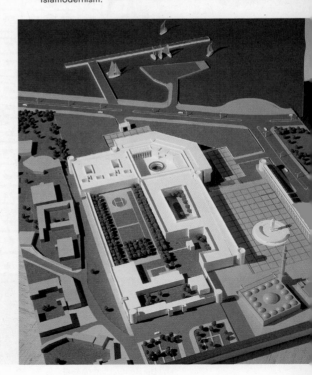

## Monumental philanthropy

The King Faisal Foundation, the largest philanthropic body in the Middle East, becomes Tange's first realization in Saudi Arabia. "The heir who set up the Foundation entrusted me to design the entire complex," Tange writes.[12] At the end of a long courtyard, two monumental triangular towers are connected by bridges; The complex includes a mosque, religious library and school, plaza, apartment building, hotel, and shops. Tange tries to create a city within a city, using his characteristic central axis.

Model of the complex, front ....

... and back.

Twin towers.

Blue mosque.

Lobby.

**2001** Photos by Rem Koolhaas.

## Public space

Tange's royal commission from Assad includes a
public element: in the valley at the foot of the new
palace, its benevolence spilling over, Tange designs
a four-hectare park on the site of a former orchard
irrigated by Roman canals. The park features a central
boulevard—echoing the shape of the presidential
gardens—with amphitheater, nightclub, restaurant,
café, children's playground, and Japanese Garden.

People's palace

Public garden

Mise-en-scène: Damascus
propped up on a Tokyo rooftop.
A default Middle East earth color
emerges in Tange's models, the
same as the valley in Muna...

## Friend of a friend

King Faisal gives Syria's Hafez al-Assad—leader of the Baath Party, whose dictatorial power is consolidated by the 1970 "Corrective Revolution"— a new palace, along with his court architect to build it, Kenzo Tange. On a western hill overlooking Damascus—visible from everywhere in the city— the "People's Palace" is a complex of low, flat slabs lined with large windows.

**2010 November** Photos by Rem Koolhaas.

## Kurokawa: businessman abroad in the UAE

Whereas Tange acts as a court architect in the
Middle East, Kurokawa—again, representing the next
generation—acts as an entrepreneur. In 1977, he sets
up a local office in Abu Dhabi, Kurokawa & Partners,
as a launchpad for Middle East operations. Kurokawa
tries to create a structure where he can operate
autonomously, without the mediation of governments
or Japanese shoshas. The plan pays off, to a degree:
in 1977, Kurokawa wins the competition for Abu
Dhabi's National Theatre (unbuilt), designs a guest
house for a Sheikh, and a new town for emirate of
Ajman. In 1987, he wins the competition for the UAE
National University in Al Ain. The campus, similar
in plan to Conference City, is a city in itself, for a
population of 33,000. But Kurokawa is undercut by
an American contractor and the plan is abandoned.[14]

**1977** NHK documents his
presentation of a new town
in Ajman, an emirate of UAE.

**1987** Fourth time lucky: after the
Abu Dhabi National Theatre,
sheikh's guest house, and new
town in Ajman fall through,
Kurokawa tries again with the
UAE National University in Al Ain.

## Supranational hub

Kurokawa wins the competition for Conference City, built on reclaimed (artificial) land in Abu Dhabi. The complex, a "city in architecture," would include a presidential residence and the national assembly, and host OPEC and Gulf Cooperation Council meetings. Like Tange's urban masterplans, Conference City is planned around a central axis, but Kurokawa's uses his own theory of *kairo*, or "architecture of the street," with separate levels for cars and covered corridors/streets for pedestrians.

A polemicist even abroad, Kurokawa claims the lofty intention of melding Japanese and Islamic tradition, claiming to draw on Japanese temples and Islamic palace compounds for the semi-enclosed spaces and integration of disparate elements into a whole. According to Kurokawa, when Dubai becomes nervous about Abu Dhabi assuming all the functions of a capital city for the UAE, the project is put on permanent hold.[13] Nevertheless, Kurokawa establishes enduring relations with the ruling family....

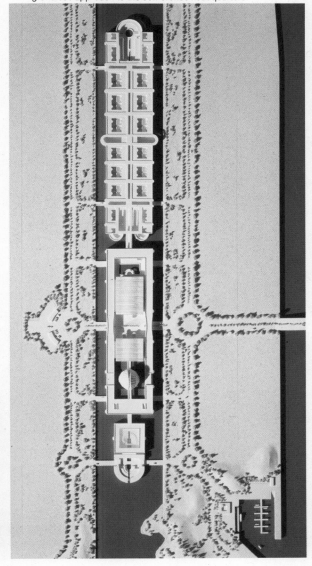

Second iteration? Buildings move onto the island; less grandiose approach to the conference headquarters.

"City in Architecture": sequence of compounds surrounded by water.

## Exporting the Capsule

On a grassy island in the Tigris occupied until recently only by hogs (*khanazeer*)—the same island for which Frank Lloyd Wright proposed an opera house in 1957—the Baathist government of Ahmed Hassan al-Bakr wants to establish a special economic zone for international tourism and licensed gambling. Kurokawa wins the competition with a plan for a tower made up of large, luxury capsules. A shosha, called Tomen, forms a consortium around Kurokawa and plans to undertake construction and supply materials and equipment.

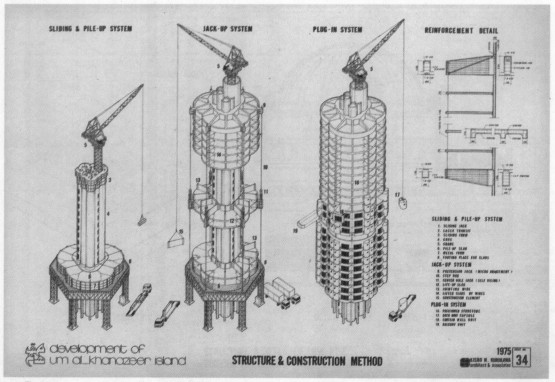

Three steps to constructing the capsule hotel: sliding and pile-up, jack-up, plug-in...

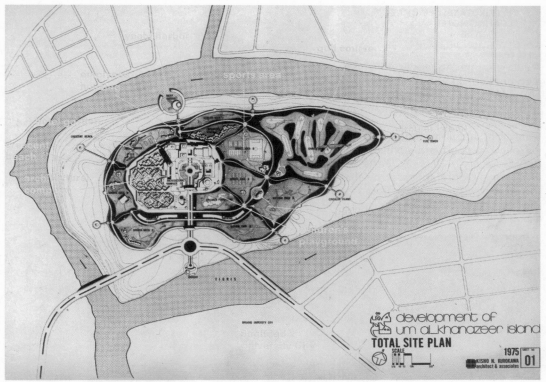

Site of repeated architectural experiments.

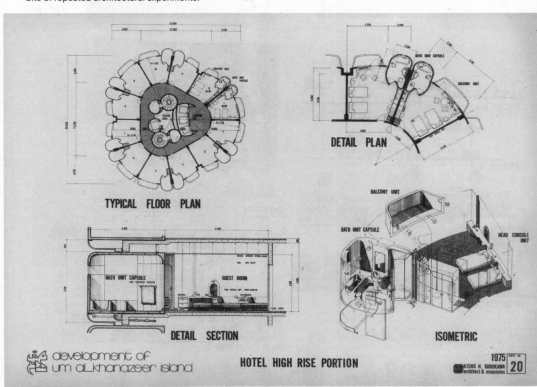

Capsules the size of regular hotel rooms.

## Last resort

A year after the Aquapolis, Kikutake is invited to a competition in Abu Dhabi, which has a growing appetite for luxury and leisure. Collaborating with Mitsui Ocean Development & Engineering, he designs a crescent-shaped hotel for Abu Dhabi's waterfront that floats independently of its surrounding courtyard, so that it can rotate 360 degrees every 8–10 hours. Parts above the water level would be prefabricated by shipbuilders and towed to the site by boats. Rooms are plugged in the semicylindrical structure—a vertical ground, like Kikutake's earliest tower proposals.[15]

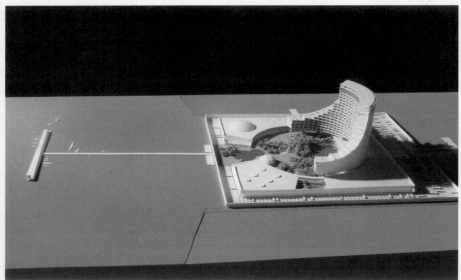

Courtyard includes a waterfall, woods, and swimming pool.

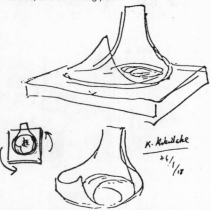

Rotation, which seems implausible, takes place "with a simple system," according to Kikutake: the circular inner courtyard and hotel move together while the surrounding square platform remains static.

## Free zone

A year later, Kikutake develops the Floating Luxury
Hotel: part barge, part hulking cruise ship; easy-build
luxury, constructed in shipbuilding factories and
towed to shore. The 500-room hotel, designed for
an American client, is a "free zone" moored just
offshore, where gambling is legal. It is a city in
microcosm, with its own energy, water, and waste
disposal systems.

"Fantastic and attractive space is produced by quiet
music and artificially controlled environments."[16]

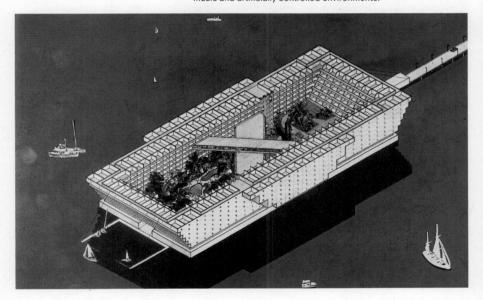

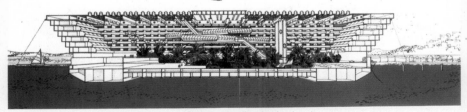

Floating city disguised as hotel.

## Japanese fleet

Sixteen years after his "Disaster Prevention City" flood protection scheme for the Koto Ward of Tokyo, Kikutake performs the role of benevolent landlord outside of Japan. Through a Japanese bank, he meets Qaddafi, looking for foreign talent to help implement the social housing and industrial measures in his "Five-Year Transformation Plan" of 1976–1980. Kikutake proposes an "urban belt" of floating factories and residences, made of precast concrete, along the coast from Tripoli to Benghazi. The structures would be made in shipbuilding factories in the Mediterranean and towed to Libya...

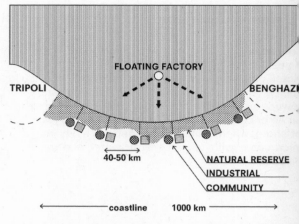

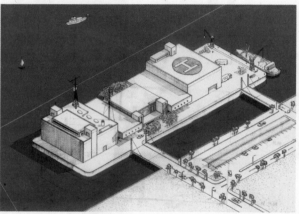

Offshore industry.

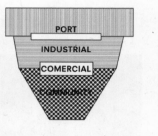

**TYPICAL CITY ZONING**

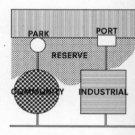

**NEW COMMUNITY**

An environmental effort: Kikutake illustrates how floating cassettes free up access to the waterfront; nature reserve and industry co-exist peacefully.

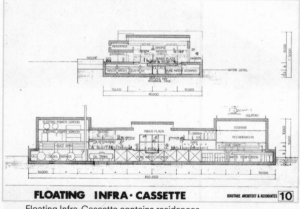

**FLOATING INFRA·CASSETTE**

Floating Infra-Cassette contains residences, library, shops, restaurant, plaza, power station, oil tanks, water purification system.

Plan for Libya.

## 1978 KIKUTAKE: IRAQ
## FLOATING INFRA-CASSETTE

**Iraqi edition**
The shipbuilding innovator Hisashi Shinto of IHI
(for whom Kurokawa built a pavilion at Expo '70)
supports the infra-cassette project; so does the
leading shosha Sumitomo, which enables the proposal to be exported to Iraq for flood protection
along the Tigris and Euphrates. There, floating infra-
cassettes (miniature versions of the Marine Cities
that Kikutake has been planning since 1958) would
be pontooned to the shore—the surest way to
avoid flooding is to float in the first place...

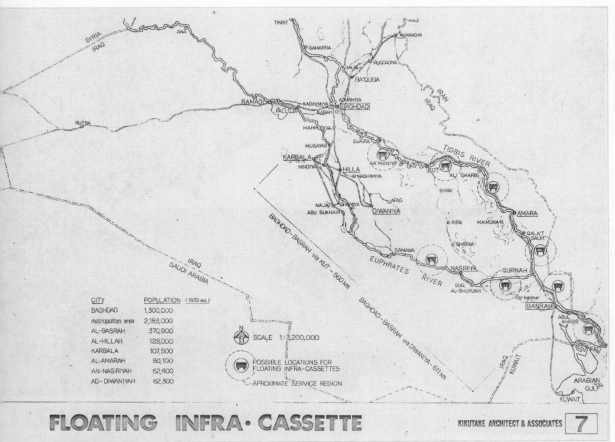

FLOATING INFRA·CASSETTE    KIKUTAKE ARCHITECT & ASSOCIATES  7

Floating Cassettes at key points on the
Tigris from Fao upriver to Na'Maniya, and
on the Euphrates up to Nasiriya.

## Continuation

As the Abbas Abad plan he developed with Louis
Kahn is taken over by Llewelyn Davies, Tange is
invited to design a key element in the masterplan:
the new Tehran city hall. He asks Isamu Noguchi, his
friend since their collaboration for Hiroshima 26 years
earlier, to design a monument for the plaza. Tange
bends the rules of the commission in order to project
his building beyond the obligatory row of colonnades,
forming "urban shelter in this land of brilliant sunlight"
and a means of "strong symbolization in the plaza."[17]
Using the model / sublime photo collage effect mas-
tered by Kikutake, Tange envisions the city hall in the
context of Tehran's surrounding mountains...

Persian sublime.

## Government center

Five years after Qatar's independence, Tange beats James Stirling, Gunther Behnisch, and Walter Gropius's The Architects Collaborative (TAC) in the competition for the new Government Center in Doha. Tange's masterplan—including the palace, courthouse, national assembly, People's Square, 15 ministry buildings, and cultural facilities—consists of orthogonal buildings with his trademark tubular cores, arranged in a grid system on land to be reclaimed along the corniche. Buildings are connected by a public moving walkway (from Expo '70) five meters above ground, called the Corniche Corridor. Difficulties coordinating ministries kill the scheme, but URTEC is able to complete an extension to the Ministry of Finance in 2003.

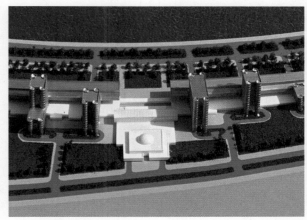

Tubular cores.

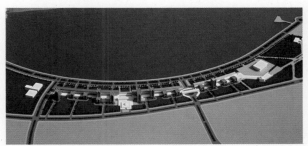

Doha's new corniche.

In a later wave of development on Doha's corniche, Tange achieves a completion on a smaller scale: the Ministry of Economy and Finance, with a similar overhang to his design for Tehran's city hall.

## City in the Desert

When an aquifer is discovered in Sarir, in the Sahara south of Libya's third largest city, Benghazi, Kurokawa wins a competition to masterplan a 330-hectare new town, and design homes for 60,000 people. Kurokawa draws on his bad experience of American-designed housing in Abu Dhabi, insensitive to desert conditions and the transition of the Bedouin to permanent housing (they kept their livestock in their unbearably hot new homes, Kurokawa claims, and slept in tents outside). The houses would be organized in dense streets—unlike Tange, Kurokawa always favors streets over boulevards and plazas—which also protect against the desert heat.

**1982** Diplomatic mission: Kurokawa in Libya with Yoshiko Otaka (formerly Yamaguchi) (left), Isamu Noguchi's ex-wife, now a representative in the Japanese Diet.

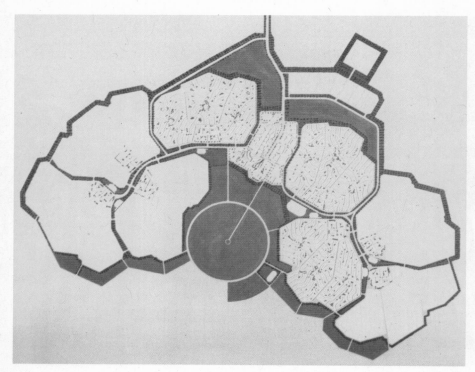

Green city, with zones still to be filled in.

## DIY housing

As an antidote to the impositions usually enforced by foreign architects, Kurokawa develops a design template (including wind towers for cooling) for the houses of As Sarir that would-be residents can construct themselves. He spends three years with English scientists developing adobe "sand bricks," an inexhaustible building material in the desert. After concrete walls containing infrastructure are set up (and kitchen and bathroom capsules installed), Kurokawa imagines that anyone—even housewives or children—can build their houses by themselves, and in any way they wish, using these sand bricks.[18] Only one prototype house is completed by the time oil prices drop and constructions stops for good. But the project is the first of several for Kurokawa in Libya: the East Coast Corniche Development in Benghzai (1980–1983), El Fateh University in Tripoli (1980–1984), and the 7,000 Units Housing Development in Benghazi, completed in 1988.

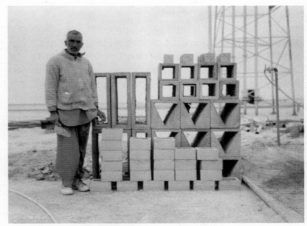

Fulfillment of Kurokawa's vision: a local, with sand bricks, ready to construct his own house.

The single completed house of As Sarir.

## New Capital

Nigeria, seeking a tabula rasa free from the colonial legacy and overcrowding of Lagos, plans a new capital, Abuja, in the neutral center of the country. Conceived as a city for three million, with construction phases spanning 20 years, Abuja is part of the global wave of new capitals and new cities asserting modernity and national self-confidence: Brasilia (Lucio Costa and Oscar Niemeyer, 1956), Chandigarh (Le Corbusier, 1952–59), Dakar (Michel Ecochard, 1963–67), Islamabad (Doxiadis, 1959–60), Dodoma, Tanzania (Kurokawa, 1972).

Under the rubric of the International Planning Associates, three American firms (Planning Research Corporation; Wallace McHarg Roberts & Todd; and Archisystems) begin work on Abuja, and in 1979 Tange wins the competition to design the central district. He envisions a Plan for Tokyo–style central axis, the 250-meter-long National Mall, with democratic, open public spaces. The mall would connect the Central Business District and ministries with the Three Arms Zone, which includes the presidential complex, national assembly, and supreme court circumnavigated by a massive crescent road.

Either side of the mall, Tange plans housing; cutting the mall at 90 degrees, a cultural axis would include a national museum and conference center at either end, with cathedral, theatre, library, and mosque in between.

Construction begins in 1980, and the URTEC team lives and works within a barbed-wired compound protected by the military.[19] A military coup in 1983, followed by a purging of the civil service and the federal budget, forces the URTEC team out of Abuja in 1984 and slows construction almost to a halt. When Olusegun Obasanjo returns to the presidency in 1999, the project is brought back to life and Abuja's central district is completed according to the outline of Tange's masterplan, with the Three Arms Zone completed at the top and the stadium at the bottom (though the buildings are not designed by him); the National Mall though remains largely unfilled and the cultural axis totally unrealized.

Ziggurats either side of Abuja's municipal headquarters: a daring form of stacked, cantilevering boxes.

Ministry buildings with trademark Tangean tubular cores.

Abuja's mall: Tange's signature linear urban planning culminates in the Three Arms Zone, consisting of the presidential complex, parliament, and supreme court.

## Masterplanning education

Tange is invited to design a university campus, a city
in itself, on tabula rasa in Al-Gassim, 100 kilometers
north of Riyadh. Approaching the site for the first time
by airplane, Tange is struck by sporadic green circles
in the desert—efforts to create agriculture—and takes
this pattern as the motif for the masterplan.[20] Tange
accommodates 25,000 residents in a city grid with
several circular hubs (faculty buildings). He is also
asked to step beyond the boundaries of architecture
and draft the university's academic plan itself.

Oasis/mosaic.

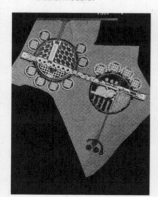
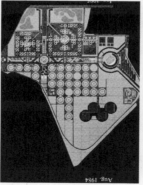
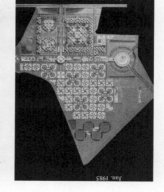

Phasing: the masterplan, growing like
circular fields of green in the desert...

## Bibliography

1 Arabian Oil Company, Ltd., "Taking hold in the desert," Arabian Oil Co. News (May 2002), www.aoc.co.jp/his/ayumi_fr01.html

2 Ministry of Culture and Information of Saudi Arabia, *The Kingdom of Saudi Arabia: A young modern nation with traditions* (Tokyo: Embassy of Saudi Arabia, 2004).

3 Kaoru Sugihara and J.A. Allan, eds., *Japan in the Contemporary Middle East* (London: Routledge, 1993).
Kaoru Sugihara, *East Asia, Middle East and the World Economy: Further Notes on the Oil Triangle* (Kyoto: Afrasian Centre for Peace and Development Studies, 2006).

4 Ibid.

5 Kenzo Tange, *Ippon no empitsu kara* [From one pencil] (Tokyo: Nihon Tosho Center, 1997).

6 Yoshikatsu Tuboi, "Saudi Arabia," *Seisan-Kenkyu*, February 1966.

7 *Kenzo Tange Associates, SD 2*, (September 1983).

8 Kisho Kurokawa, *Kisho Kurokawa Notes* (Tokyo: Dobun Shoin, 1994).

9 Presentation panel by URTEC, 1974.

10 Interview with Kenji Ekuan, August 2009.

11 "Kenzo Tange and URTEC: Works of the Late 1970s," *The Japan Architect*, July/August 1979.

12 Tange, *From one pencil*.

13 *Kisho Kurokawa Notes*.

14 Ibid.

15 Kiyonori Kikutake, *Kiyonori Kikutake: Concepts and Planning* (Tokyo: Bijutsu Shuppansha, 1978).

16 Ibid.

17 Kenzo Tange and URTEC, *Shinkenchiku*, October 1970.

18 Kisho Kurokawa, *Intercultural Architecture: The Philosophy of Symbiosis* (London: Academy Editions, 1991).

19 Kenzo Tange and Terunobu Fujimori, *Tange Kenzo* (Tokyo: Shinkenchiku-sha, 2002).

20 Ibid.

21 Kenzo Tange Associates, Vol.3 / SD, April 1987.

22 Rem Koolhaas, *S,M,L,XL* (New York: Monacelli Press, 1995).

**Sources** (for pp. 594–597)
*Kenzo Tange Associates*, Vol.1 to 4, *SD*, 1980–1991.

Kisho Kurokawa, *Metabolism in Architecture* (Studio Vista, 1972).

**Sources** (for p. 598–601)
*Japanese Multinationals Facts & Figures* (Tokyo: Toyo Keizai, 1973 through 1980 editions).

Ministry of International Trade and Industry, *Research on the Overseas Activities of Japanese Firms*, 1975 edition, 1976.

*Facts about the Overseas Expansion of Sogo Shoshas* (Kobe University: Research Institute for Economics and Business Administration, 1979).

Independent since 1959, Singapore, in a Japan-like spasm of growth, and with Japan-like population and spatial pressures and lack of natural resources, sets out on a massive program of nation building. Here though, the moment is post-colonial rather than postwar. After creating several new towns from scratch, creating and exploiting tabula rasa through slum clearance and land reclamation, by the early '80s, the focus shifts to the market economy and the Central Business District; enter Tange. He is handed the opportunity to define downtown's skyline with four towers designed and built over the course of 15 years. Three are cor-porate headquarters for banks, and mark his evolution into a builder of towers in aluminum, glass, and steel; the other tower, the City Telecommunications Center, is a building not for people but for machines: it contains 32 stories of communi-cations equipment.[21] As in Japan, Tange plays a major role in constructing the image and infrastructure of a nation (he also completes the sprawling Nanyang Technology Institute, the Yoyogi-like canopy of the Singapore Indoor Stadium, and the GB office building). But now, the vision is not his, and the tools are not Japanese; rather, a generic corporate postmodernism begins to take hold. The joint core, Tange's signature concept, only appears in an unbuilt project: the massive campus planned for the International Petroleum Center (1982).

Tange's Skyline

Overseas Union Bank Centre,
1980–86

United Overseas Bank Plaza 2,
1992–95

UOB Plaza 1,
1986–92

City Telecommunications Centre,
1980–86

## Flashback: Singapore Songlines

Metabolism occurs in Singapore ten years earlier, by the hands of local architects. In the atmosphere of intensive, almost metabolic growth, William Lim and Tay Kheng Soon—exposed to Maki at Harvard--are able to realize the first Asian megastructures: buildings as vast accumulations, containers of multiplicity, rather than discrete entities; nodes within a continuous urban system teeming with "street" life brought indoors. Lim and Tay's People's Park Complex (1972) has 264 apartments resting on a podium that contains 300 shops and huge interior spaces with indeterminate structure and program—Maki's City Room, realized. With bridges extending in all directions, the complex also forms a Makian City Corridor with the adjacent People's Park Center (Ng Chee Sen, 1970), another enormous agglomeration of apartments and stores—shopping as the Asian agora.

On Beach Road, a "Metabolist Mile" emerges: the Plaza (built by a firm naming themselves after their heroes: Design Metabolist Architects); the 22-story Golden Mile Tower (by Goh Hock Suan, containing cinema, shops, 16-story office tower, parking); and at the end of the road, Lim and Tay's Golden Mile complex: one half of a Metabolist A-Frame—half-city, half architecture. Maki inspects Singapore's new model of Asian urbanism and declares: "We theorized and you people are getting it built..."[22]

People's Park Complex, Lim and Tay, 1972; the City Room inside.

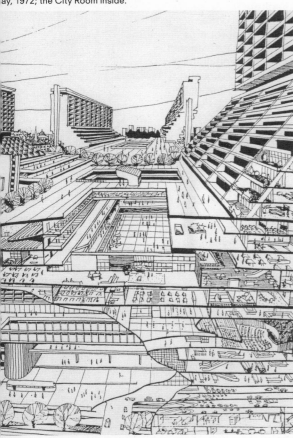

**1973** Metabolism in Singapore: the half A-Frame of the Golden Mile complex, by local architects Design Partnership (Gan Eng Oon, William Lim and Tay Kheng Soon). It is a realization of their own "Future Urban City" (left), sketched four years earlier.

# Atsushi Shimokobe 下河辺淳

**1923** born in Tokyo in year of Great Kanto Earthquake **1944** enters Tokyo University to study urban planning, spends time in Tange Lab; surveys Tokyo's war damage for police student program **1945** visits Hiroshima after atomic bombing; researches industrial development and urbanization, focusing on the waterfront as a site typology **1947** graduates from Tange Lab; enters Institute for War Recovery **1952** enters Economic Planning Agency **1957** enters Department of Planning in the Ministry of Construction, specializes in waterfront planning, including Tokyo Bay **1961** critiques Tange's Plan for Tokyo 1960 in *Shinkenchiku* symposium **1962** enters Economic Planning Agency as the first Comprehensive National Development Plan begins **1967** appoints Kurokawa to large-scale projects and information network research group **1968** supports Otaka's efforts for artificial ground in *Nikkan Kensetsu Kogyo Shimbun* (Daily construction industry journal) **1969** issues New Comprehensive National Development Plan, organizes related study groups, appoints Kurokawa to two of them **1970** publishes *Dialogues with Information Society*, compilation of research he assigned to specialists including Kurokawa **1971** sends young architect Toyo Ito to research computer networks in US and Europe **1972** director, Department of Comprehensive National Development Plan, Economic Planning Agency; leads study group for Prime Minister Kakuei Tanaka's *Plan for Remodeling the Japanese Archipelago*; contrary to legend, Shimokobe is not the ghost writer; through the Economic Planning Agency, commissions Kurokawa's Institute for Social Engineering to study vertical and short take-off and landing aviation network **1974** enters National Land Agency; commissions ISE study on demographics **1977** vice minister, National Land Agency; issues Third Comprehensive National Development Plan; commissions Kawazoe's CDI think tank to research cultural development of regional cities **1979** president of National Institute for Research Advancement (NIRA); advisor, National Land Agency; issues Third Comprehensive National Development Plan; commissions Kikutake to research floating artificial ground for Japan's coasts **1981** appointed director of basic planning for Tsukuba Expo '85, commissions Metabolists to formulate masterplan **1982** organizes reunion of the Metabolists (plus Isozaki and Shinya Izumi) for a roundtable discussion **1983** joins JAPIC (Japan Project–Industry Council), a public-private-academic consortium for national regeneration, in charge of artificial ground project in Tokyo **1985** producer, Tsukuba Expo '85 **1987** Fourth Comprehensive National Development Plan **1988–2000** chairman of Hakushu art festival **1992** president, Tokyo Marine Research Institute **1994** publishes *Sengo kokudo keikaku no shogen* (Testimony on postwar national land planning) **1995** chairman of Kobe Earthquake recovery committee **1998** Fifth Comprehensive National Development Plan **2003** chairman of his own corporation, Aoi-umi (Blue Sea), and Shimokobe Lab

**"I thought they were like children, so I thought it was my task to raise them... As a parent."**

Atsushi Shimokobe was a reluctant, but ultimately pioneering lifelong bureaucrat, lured from Tange Lab and a career in architecture into nation building on a political level—nearly always working backstage, and frequently with the Metabolists themselves. Starting at the Institute for War Recovery in 1947, Shimokobe rose through the ranks of the Ministry of Construction, the National Economic Planning Agency, the National Land Agency, and the National Institute for Research Advancement. Successive Japanese governments and prime ministers valued his vision of a decentralized Japan, relieving pressure on the overburdened capital, and spreading evenly the benefits of the nation's rapid modernization. Turning bureaucracy into a form of creativity, over forty years Shimokobe produced and commissioned a slew of reports, radical proposals, events, and projects, often turning to Kurokawa, Kikutake, Otaka, Kawazoe, and Tange for their visionary ideas for redesigning the nation. Shimokobe was a committed, charismatic player (allegedly he drove a red Ferrari at the peak of his power in the '70s) who relished his role as a connector of politicians, industrialists, planners, architects. He facilitated—behind the scenes, subtly—a historically rare confluence of avant-garde and government. His nickname was *Kaihatsu tenno*—emperor of development.

Hotel Okura, Toranomon,
Tokyo, September 9, 2005

Center of intrigue: Shimokobe reveals
his role in the nation-building of Japan...

Working for the Tokyo police student mobilization program, Shimokobe, 22, surveys the damage in Hiroshima. Entering the Institute for War Recovery two years later, the young bureaucrat is one of a new generation drafted to solve Japan's postwar housing crisis: 2.1 million houses lost in atomic firebombing; a further 2.1 million homes needed by those returning from war and former colonies...

**1945** Recovery at Ground Zero, working on Japan's thin crust.

**1941** Under the aegis of Kunio Maekawa's office and the mentorship of Hideto Kishida, Tange completes his first building, the all-wood Kishi Memorial Hall, Tokyo.

**HANS ULRICH OBRIST While you were an engineering student, you were a member of Tange Lab—is that right?**

ATSUSHI SHIMOKOBE That's right. This was during World War II, when Tange was an assistant professor. At that time I never saw him delving into architectural subjects—he was reading philosophy all the time. So he wasn't very well liked by people who were really focused on architecture. [*laughs*]

**HUO I think it is rare that a studio develops into something almost like a school. The inverse often happens, but in the case of Tange, the studio was somehow a place of ideas, and Tange was a trigger. With the World Design Conference in 1960, Tange put all these young people on the job and that created or led to Metabolism. It seems that Tange Lab was a knowledge production facility, as Isozaki and Kikutake described it to us.**

### Backing Tange

**REM KOOLHAAS Do you think Tange invented the role of architect in Japan after the war, or reconstructed the role?**

AS In the period immediately after the war, building designers talked like they were nothing but sales reps for the builders. [*laughs*] Times were hard, and they had difficulty putting food on the table. So even if Tange wanted to be an architect, he had to depend on a university salary to make ends meet. As a matter of fact, Ministry of Education regulations prohibited professors from moonlighting for extra money, but Tange labored as much as he could to support himself and Tange Lab.

At one time we decided on the government side to throw our weight behind Tange—to work behind the scenes in ways that would help him be recognized internationally as an architect. From my perspective as a government official, we needed to work through politicians, we needed money and it was all very complicated.

**HUO The idea was basically to construct a global trajectory? How was this plot developed?**

AS Well, I can tell you, and all the people it casts in a bad light are no longer with us. [*laughs*] Jurors of international competitions—unless we gave them money, we couldn't achieve our goal. We had a plan to make Tange an internationally recognized architect, but the trouble was that there really weren't any world-class buildings he'd designed that we could show off. In those days there was only a small all-wood gymnasium in Tokyo's Ochanomizu district called the Kishi Memorial Hall, and for a long time we were presenting that to the world as Tange's most important work. That was the best we could do.

**RK There was just one piece of evidence.**

AS Yes.

**RK So, you are saying that in a way Tange is an invention, and that the construction of Tange was a plot. Were people like Kikutake or Isozaki also supported in a similar way?**

AS No, Otaka's group [the Metabolists] were not yet architects: we are talking about during the war and postwar periods, so one generation, one decade before.

Another way to look at the whole issue is that it simply took a very long time to lift the social standing of architects in Japan and establish an appropriate level of remuneration for them. To begin with, our goal as government officials was to raise the social standing of all architects, and we saw backing Tange as a step towards accomplishing that. As part of that same effort, we also worked to get the 1950 Kenchikushi (architects) law on the books. It all took a lot of time.

## HOUSE FOR A MILLION PEOPLE

The Institute for War Recovery stimulates Kunio Maekawa—employer of Tange and later Otaka—to develop a pioneering prefab housing system: PREMOS, for Prefab-Maekawa-Ono-Sanin; the final two names being the structural engineer and wood manufacturer. Maekawa calls PREMOS a "house for a million people," but the system is used in the end only for housing coal miners at Japan's increasingly exploited mines—economic recovery trumps social housing.[1]

**1949** Inside the PREMOS house.

Prefabrication in progress.

**1950** PREMOS compound for coal miners of Shakubetsu, Hokkaido.

**1946** Prototype of the all-wood PREMOS.

**plot two**
Tange received the full support of the state. The state equaled Kenzo Tange. At the 1964 Olympics, it was the state that told him to design the Yoyogi National Gymnasia; at Expo '70, the state told him to do the masterplan. But the state never gave Metabolism its full support. I believe there were people—Shimokobe, Asada, newspaper people, and a number of sympathizers—who helped by supporting, for example, the 1960 World Design Conference, where the Metabolists made themselves known. But that doesn't mean the state helped. If that were the case, I think the movement would have lasted a little longer, and a lot more would have been realized. For example, what might have happened had the state helped a little more when Kikutake tried to create a marine city in Okinawa in 1975? And Kurokawa was an extremely politically active person throughout his life, but in the end the state did not provide him with support.
**Hiroshi Hara**

**involved**
Kawazoe later wrote: Metabolism is deeply indebted to Shimokobe, especially at the time of Tsukuba Expo among other occasions." (*Metabolism and the Metabolists*, Bijutsu Shuppansha, 2006.)

**psyche**
The destruction of a city by aerial bombardment is awful, but in particular, I think that the dropping of an atomic bomb represents unspeakable violence. With regard to the sense of despair of the victims—whose skin was scorched by the heat and was peeling off in swathes, which they dragged as they wandered the streets searching for help—how could we survivors, with nothing to offer, make up for this? I could do nothing but maintain my own self-respect. At the same time, I remained aware that I should not allow myself to become debilitated by my wartime experiences.
**Sachio Otani**

## Three Plots

**HUO**   If we could say plot one was to make Tange a global architect, Metabolism was plot two: as we discussed with Kikutake, this was a plot to get this time not an individual like Tange but the whole group of Japanese architects into the world. And the plot functioned brilliantly.

I would then see plot three, which led to Kurokawa becoming a national celebrity in Japan by the '70s. This is something I've always found extremely fascinating. Even if you look at what happened to architecture in recent years, it's incredible, this celebrity dimension. Could you comment upon that? And were you involved in plot three as well?

**AS**   Hmm, that's kind of a tough one…

**RK**   No comment is also… [*laughs*]

**AS**   Well, I suspect thinking of it as any kind of national thing is blowing it out of proportion. I think it's more a Kurokawa personality thing. He was always very fond of young pretty women, you know.

## Civil Servant

**RK**   Can you tell me how you ended up in the civil service even with an architectural degree? Why did you not become an architect?

**AS**   As you suggest, no one with an architecture degree had any desire to join the civil service. But the government was faced with an emergency: they needed to do something as quickly as possible about all the housing that was destroyed in the war. So in 1947, two years after the war ended, they recruited students graduating from architectural programs in large numbers. I didn't want to apply, but a prior graduate of my program twisted my arm, saying "Look, you don't have to accept the job if you decide it's not for you, but at least apply so that I don't lose face." So I took the employment exam and was offered a job in the Institute for War Recovery, which soon became the Ministry of Construction. It's funny how these things turn out, since I wound up staying in the civil service the longest of anyone, all the way to full retirement age. It wasn't at all out of youthful idealism.

**RK**   You were in Tange Lab when the war ended. Is it true that you were involved in the aftermath of Hiroshima and that you were looking there as part of a damage control research scheme?

**AS**   Yes.

**RK**   If that is the case, what effect did it have on your psyche? And particularly on your idealism, if by 1947 you already didn't have any idealism?

**AS**   I was working for the Tokyo Metropolitan Police under the student mobilization program, and I was involved in surveying bomb damage. Then word came that America had dropped some kind of special bomb on Hiroshima, so I went there almost right away. Official confirmation that it had been an atomic bomb actually didn't come until sometime later, but I had done a certain amount of research related to atomic bombs, so I figured that's what it had to be. And then I actually went and saw the damage and knew that's what it was. In fact, because of what I saw there, I still can't forgive President Truman and America for dropping those bombs.

## Bitterness

**RK**   A private question: Did you think about Hiroshima when you heard about 9/11?

**AS**   If we'd been able to have a discussion about it at the time, I think a lot of people would have viewed the bomb as a terrorist act perpetrated by the American government. What else could dropping an atomic bomb on Hiroshima be if not terrorism? It's hard for me to believe that any nation could sanction such an act. Yet President Truman and his war advisors saw fit to launch a terrorist attack

**1963** Now at the Economic Planning Agency, trying to keep up with annual GDP growth of ca. 10 percent, Shimokobe writes a "prospectus" for the decade 1965–75, containing both a promise and a crisis: "the second period of capital accumulation will unfold in our country, allowing for a new system of national land use to be born. And I assume that the system will provide Japan's economy with new conditions as well as stimulation beyond our imagination... In the current rush of urban construction, a battle with land shortage emerges. I find that there are many problems in the proposals regarding land ownership, usage, and price. There are those who abandon old cities or those who have no alternatives. Then there are those who try to promote artificial ground, which is a form of architecture that accommodates all kinds of urban facilities. While these battles go on, people still live in the same conditions."[2]

Bureaucratic sympathy with the avant-garde: Shimokobe joins a panel with Kikutake (center) as Tange presents his Plan for Tokyo in 1961, the most radical land-use plan yet... "Rather than criticizing the plan," Shimokobe says, "we should find a way to back up the proposal."[3]

Sprawl: Meikou Industrial Belt. One of Shimokobe's principal battlegrounds in land-use planning is Japan's coastline, site of rampant reclamation and unchecked industrial development.

Ise Bay Industrial Waterfront Belt, Japan's largest oil processing *kombinat* (term borrowed from the USSR, meaning industrial belt). Shimokobe's New Comprehensive National Development Plan, issued in 1969, attempts to solve a new industrial problem: pollution.

huge numbers of small landholders
After the war there was an urban design competition for the fire-devastated areas in central Tokyo, for which I assisted on Professor Kiyoshi Ikebe's entry. He became excited by the new forms of human habitation that suddenly emerged in these areas. As I surveyed the form of land ownership in Tokyo's destroyed areas, I found that it had been determined by small site divisions. There was no way all these holdings would be nationalized in order to be consolidated, as if under a dictatorship. So I wrote a graduation thesis suggesting that, for such clusters of sites, independent buildings would be placed on each one and these would aggregate into a single form. However, this thesis went astray in the postwar turmoil. **Masato Otaka**

Kiichi Miyazawa
Minister of the Economic Planning Agency when Shimokobe joined in 1962.

first Security Treaty renewal
Continuing the 1951 treaty, which was signed upon the end of the US occupation, disarming Japan and establishing US military bases in Okinawa. The new Treaty of Mutual Cooperation and Security was forced by the Diet in May 1960 after rioting by students and trade unions and a boycott of the Diet by the Japan Socialist Party.

Kunio Maekawa
I learned everything I needed to know to create real architecture under Maekawa, especially a great knowledge about the "technical approach," as he liked to call it. He said that unless shapes are created based upon solid techniques, they would not endure time. Maekawa continued to realize that principle right until the end. Yet I don't think I studied much urban planning in his office. That is why I set out on a journey, together with some friends, leaving Le Corbusier behind and following the ideas of the 1960 World Design Conference. **Masato Otaka**

and drop the bomb. That's why my bitterness towards America will never go away. That's why I hate America so.

**HUO** **That's interesting because Kikutake told us in a similar way that at the beginning of his whole work was anger and protest.**

**RK** **Anger and protest against the Americans, but in his case not about the atom bomb but about the elimination of land ownership and the aristocracy.**

**AS** Under Japan's private property system we used to have tenant agriculture with large landlords, but the revolutionary land reforms after the war turned the land owned by the landlords over to the tenants. The great landholders disappeared, and huge numbers of small landholders were born.

This was basically true even for residential land in the cities. You were no longer allowed to own more than a certain amount of land. The concept of "my own independent estate" died. It was a revolutionary redistribution of land, and I was pretty heavily involved in promoting the changes.

### Kept for Japan

**RK** **At what point did you begin to discover that as a civil servant you would have certain powers that were actually interesting—and potentially more interesting than those that somebody outside the government would have?**

**AS** I was bound to be involved in promoting those changes because the bureaucracy now had to intervene in every relationship between the owners and their use of land.

In all the years since the Meiji Restoration, I'm the only architect by training who has risen to be a vice minister in the government. Building designers have traditionally worked in the private sector, and it's civil engineers who were the ones to work for the government.

Since I stayed on in the ministry longer than any of the others, it may seem ironic for me to say this now, but I never dreamed I'd stick it out so long. In private, I was always wanting to quit, wanting to go overseas, but somehow the time just slipped by. Actually, my heart was set on Italy. I applied to study architecture at the Giovanni Agnelli Foundation in Turin, and I even got accepted, but Kiichi Miyazawa refused to let me go.

**RK** **Kept you for Japan. And that was in the '50s?**

**AS** It was 1962, shortly after the first Security Treaty renewal, when the *Zengakuren* and other student radicals were very active. Waseda University was one of the most active campuses leading the student revolt, and a class in the architectural program there once called me in as a representative of the government, in effect to interrogate me and rake me over the coals. But the funny thing was, as I spoke, students regarded as radicals found themselves agreeing with me, and it turned into a rather odd meeting. [*laughs*]

### Maekawa

**RK** **We are very interested in the particular moment when the Metabolists were formed. When was the group of individuals that were previously autonomous consolidated into a movement? And did you play any role in that?**

**AS** I'd have to say one of the most important actors at the outset was Kunio Maekawa. His office played a decisive role.

**HUO** **Kunio Maekawa belongs to the generation before the Metabolists. Can you describe how his office played an important role?**

**AS** I think it's fair to say that Maekawa was the one who originally laid the foundations of a new architectural movement in Japan. A group led by Otaka in Maekawa's office then used those ideas to promote themselves. Metabolism at first was just the name of this group. It wasn't until a little later that Kurokawa joined them.

**1968 October 29** Shimokobe and Otaka share their frustrations with planning in the *Nikkan Kensetsu Kogyo Shimbun* (Daily construction industry journal; the fact that such a niche publication is daily in itself hints at the ferocity of Japan's growth). Meanwhile Otaka is on the brink of completing the first phase of a radical solution to the fragmented ownership of urban land: Sakaide Artificial Ground…

Shimokobe: "A scientific approach and empirical background for urban planning is still immature in Japan, which is what I'm personally suffering from…"

Otaka: "Land ownership is often too complicated to allow for modern industry. Even if we tried to move forward, there are too many knots in our urban fabric…"

**1969** Otaka's Sakaide Artificial Ground, a "three-dimensionalization of land ownership … as a method for solving the problem of tiny subdivisions of land ownership." One of Ekuan's NTT phone boxes perches on the new urban platform, above the mess on the ground.[4]

### "Metabolism"

**RK** **Are you suggesting that there are different families in Metabolism?**

**AS** The thing is, Metabolism wasn't something that had clear philosophical underpinnings. It was basically just a bunch of colleagues who decided to work together, so I really don't think they were all that concerned about how they should interpret the word. It was just a convenient word they latched onto.

**RK** **Convenient for whom? For their discussions or their presentations to the outside?**

**AS** For presenting themselves to the outside. Kawazoe was the one who used the name "Metabolism" in his writing and spread the word about it.

**RK** **Was there at that point an explicit relationship between you and this movement or the individuals?**

**AS** Yes, I was meeting with some of them on an individual basis.

**RK** **And who were your most intimate contacts?**

**AS** Otaka. We'd been in the same class at Tokyo University.

### Remodeling the Japanese Archipelago

**RK** **Can you talk about Tanaka's *Plan for Remodeling the Japanese Archipelago*?[5] Were you the ghostwriter?**

**AS** The plan was, in effect, a national land development plan that reflected the concerns of the times in which it appeared. But I should say that I did not contribute a single word to the volume.

**RK** **Not a single word. That's the ultimate ghostwriter! [*laughs*]**

**AS** The book was essentially a compilation of speeches written by a Ministry of International Trade and Industry official and a journalist for Kakuei Tanaka when he was running for prime minister in 1972. It wound up being such a big hit that he had a really hard time disavowing it. There were actually a lot of things in the book that Tanaka himself didn't agree with.

One of the things Tanaka was gnashing his teeth about most in connection with remodeling the Archipelago was the council the government set up to discuss the concept. It wound up with 120 members! When Tanaka heard the council had 120 members, he really hit the roof. He called me in and said, "This is ridiculous. I want the group closed down. You can have three meetings, and that's it." I told him a group with 120 members can't possibly finish its business in three meetings, but he wouldn't budge, so I really did put an end to it in three meetings.

At the first meeting I addressed some opening remarks to Tanaka, and that was pretty much it. For the second meeting, I had asked the 120 members to submit their views in writing. They'd all done this beforehand, so I had all the papers compiled and printed up together, and I offered my commentary on them at the meeting, and that was that. Then the third meeting was basically "Thank you for your cooperation. Please keep in touch. Goodbye." [*laughs*]

**RK** **Very efficient. [*laughs*]**

**AS** There are a number of journalistic misconceptions about Tanaka's government that have never been corrected. The conventional view is that Tanaka became prime minister precisely in order to promote the remodeling of the Archipelago. The truth is, Tanaka didn't think it was the right time to push for it. It's not widely known that he said he wouldn't move ahead on remodeling the archipelago until things like land issues and environmental pollution and our relationship with China were resolved.

### Speak His Mind

**HUO** **I'm very interested in whether you feel an infiltration of power within your work, an infiltration of administration in terms of effecting change.**

**AS** I always thought a good bureaucrat should speak his mind plainly. I also

**1969** While Japan's economy continues to accelerate (GDP growth this year: nine percent), distribution of development is still uneven across the Archipelago and unrest intensifies in the Diet and in Japan's universities over the imminent renewal of the US-Japan security treaty. Shimokobe's New Comprehensive National Development Plan tries to create a better-planned, fairer future...

**1969** The *Zenkyoto* (All Campus joint struggle, heirs to the *Zenga-kuren*) shuts down universities across Japan and sets fire to Tokyo University's Yasuda auditorium (designed by Manchuria master-planner Yoshikazu Uchida in 1925).

**1972** Manifesto: Shimokobe, with a growing reputation as mastermind of the nation's planning, is rumored—incorrectly—to be ghostwriter of Kakuei Tanaka's *Nihonrettou kaizoron* (Plan for remodeling the Japanese Archipelago). The book sells 910,000 copies in its first four years and propels Tanaka from minister of International Trade and Industry to prime minister.

**1972** Prime Minister Tanaka addresses the unwieldly group of politicians discussing his Plan for Remodeling the Japanese Archipelago. Behind the scenes, believing that the moment is not yet ripe for total transformation, he instructs the meetings' chairman, Shimokobe, to bring them to a premature close.

thought bureaucrats needed to be more than just an instrument of the state; they needed to foster a revolution as well as keep an eye out for the interests of private industry. So I often made statements that disagreed with the incumbent administration. I wasn't inclined to defer to politicians who are only thinking about the next election.

**HUO** I have a question which I ask in all my interviews: do you have any unrealized projects, projects that were utopian or impossible to realize within the ministry?

**AS** Well, I don't really have a simple answer. It seems like there were a lot of things we failed spectacularly at, and yet somehow the failure wound up working to the good. I fought long and hard against pollution from heavy industry up and down the Archipelago, but before I gave up the ghost in that fight, the heavy industries themselves began to die off. As you know, Japan's manufacturing industries were always heavily concentrated in the industrial belt running along the Pacific seaboard, from Tokyo Bay to Ise Bay to the Inland Sea. As we were trying to disperse these industries, the industries themselves underwent changes that made it less urgent for them to be dispersed.

### Incendiary

**RK** It's a real privilege to meet someone like you, and I'm particularly struck by your straightforwardness and your honesty. Is that something you always had? Or is it a recent development now that you don't owe anyone any allegiance?

**AS** Oh, I've been getting scolded for statements that people think are incendiary ever since I was young. So I think I can say I've always been talking like this.

**RK** What sign are you?

**AS** I was born September 30, 1923.

**RK** Libra.

**AS** Of course, I'm over 80 and retired now, and I don't have to be accountable to anyone anymore, so maybe that helps loosen my tongue a bit, too.

### Second Interview: February 28, 2008

**RK** The last time we met, I was not fully aware of your importance, and I thought that you would be able to give us background information on the Metabolists. But during that conversation, I realized that you were actually one of the main brains of this entire operation, if not the puppet master. So now we want to talk to you about you.

**AS** I was very much looking forward to seeing you again.

**RK** Thank you. In the meantime, we have read some of your reports, and it's only now that I'm aware of the phenomenal amount of research that you were able to orchestrate, and the depth of that research. When I look at the research you helped produce, or when I look at the efforts of reconstructing the demographics of Japan, I am stunned by your ambitions. Looking back, do you think the research was a viable effort? Did it have an importance at that time, and does it still have an importance?

**AS** Clearly, the Japanese Archipelago was concentrated in one location, Tokyo. Some people call Japan a two-poled society, with the presence of Osaka, or tri-poled with Nagoya. Anyway, we have concentration over the belt stretching from Tokyo to Fukuoka, with Nagoya and Osaka in between, while all the other territories are allowed to lose population. The first motivation for changing the Archipelago was to correct this structure.

**RK** I think I understand it. What I'm trying to understand is how somebody in your position would suddenly feel a responsibility for the fate of Japan as a whole,

**1974** Such is the faith in planning and research that Shimokobe commissions Kurokawa's Institute for Social Engineering to create a diagrammatic prediction of every known factor affecting procreation and population, including "libidinal-action freedom," suicide, vegetation, and mineral resources…

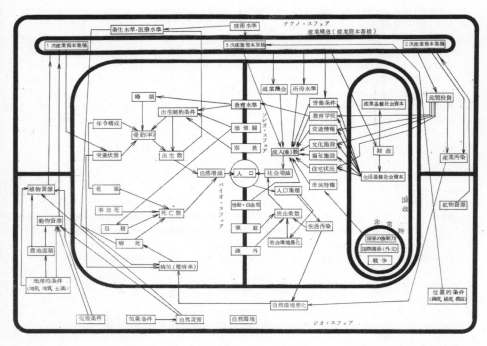

"Long-term diachronic analysis of demographic distribution over the Japanese Archipelago," made for Shimokobe's Economic Planning Agency.

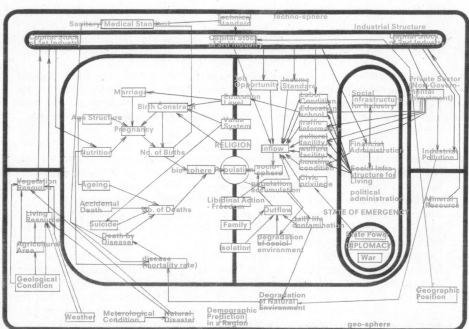

**1974** Shimokobe commissions Kurokawa's Institute for Social Engineering to produce a report for the Economic Planning Agency. Kurokawa attempts to diagram the relationships between social, demographic, geographic, technological and political forces that can produce change in Japan.

income. I think that his greatest talent was an ability to charm bureaucrats and politicians. For example, the aforementioned two tasks became the immediate goals for the many civil engineers involved in public projects. Their work became easier thanks to Shimokobe's advocacy and bureaucrats felt they were given opportunities by Shimokobe to practice their ability.
**Takashi Onishi**

Kazue Kobata
Dean of Intermedia Art Department at Tokyo National University of Fine Arts and Music. Worked with Shimokobe since 1982 on Tsukuba Expo '85 and at the National Institute for Research Advancement. Translator of this interview.

artificial ground
Sakaide was packed with buildings, as in many of Japan's cities, and was in desperate need of public space. It was clear that if left untouched it would end up becoming not far from a slum. As a solution, we proposed creating new space on an artificial ground with a three-dimensional division of ownership of urban space.
**Masato Otaka**

and develop almost a sense of injustice when you see one area of Japan growing and one shrinking. I see in all your work an interest more in network than in concentration. There's a feeling that there should be a different kind of distribution, with less hierarchy.

### Outside Tokyo

**AS** I never lived outside of Tokyo, and never worked outside of Kasumigaseki, the government district, and so I was never qualified to speak as one of the Japanese population. In other words, I never had the same environment as the general public: I only knew of Kasumigaseki, and that was a limitation. But my job was really to do something in the field, so on weekends I traveled a lot outside of Tokyo. For me, the central government was someone nice who would cover my travel money on weekends.

**RK** **So, are you saying that a part of this colossal effort is an attempt to undo your own ignorance?**

**AS** Yes, you could say so. But of course, that's what I can say now. At the time, I had no idea. I couldn't see. Yet I really loved walking around outside of Tokyo.

**RK** **I can imagine. But for instance, can we relate this to a project like vertical and short take-off and landing?**

**AS** Yes.

**RK** **Can we understand that as walking through Japan on a massive scale? Just what was it that created these grand schemes?**

**AS** I never had such a lofty idea. But I loved the Japanese Archipelago, and so I would be going all over the place all the time.

**KAZUE KOBATA** **Were you usually playing alone in the government?**

**AS** During the 1960s, only 10–15 years after the country was defeated, I did not have to feel restricted by my seniors. They were in jail. I did what I liked.

**RK** **So it was a sort of free-for-all.**

### Groundless

**KAYOKO OTA** **In the 1960s, the architects Kurokawa, Maki, Otaka, and Kikutake were in their 30s and asserted projects that were more visionary than realistic.**

**AS** Well, they intended to have their visionary projects realized but there was no knowing of the future. They were groundless.

**RK** **Groundless? So, even you thought there was no ground for them to realize the projects? I understood your role as trying to offer them a ground.**

**KO** **For example, there was the artificial ground project proposed by Otaka and others in the '60s. We understand that when you were at the Economic Planning Agency you tried to support such ideas.**

**AS** That's correct. Back then, artificial ground was a minor project. They were excited just to have one ground put on top of another! But now artificial ground has became realistic, finally. High-rise buildings are a kind of artificial ground, aren't they? Let's say, 50-story buildings—they increased the ground, and that is one kind of artificial ground.

**RK** **So you supported the Metabolists but you still thought they were deeply naïve. Were you critical to their face about their naivety?**

**AS** Well, I thought they were like children, so I thought it was my task to raise them. [*laughs*] As a parent.

**RK** **That's beautiful.**

### Tsukuba Expo

**KO** **After you became director of the National Institute for Research Advancement (NIRA) you were involved with the planning of the 1985 Tsukuba Expo as executive director. You commissioned the Metabolists, who set up an**

**1976** By now the backstage player is widely recognized as the mastermind of Japan's major planning efforts. Shimokobe moves to a newly created ministry that would ostensibly increase his power: the National Land Agency. But Japan's economic growth has passed its peak, and his plans start to have less purchase on reality...

**March 31** Wise men: Shimokobe (third from right) with property developers and academics at a symposium on "land revolution"—what to do now that real estate prices and demand are dropping—convened by the newspaper Yomiuri Shimbun. by the newspaper *Yomiuri Shimbun*. Even Shimokobe is at a loss: "One of the confusions caused by the decentralization policy was that the 'receptacles' of decentralization were not fully prepared for new population"; now, the receptacles cannot afford to develop...

**October 2** *Asahi Shimbun*: "Scenario writer of development: Shimokobe, 52, is the one the prime minister [Takeo Miki] favors to invite to breakfast. The high GDP growth-rate days are over, but the chief [Shimokobe] is confident he can navigate through this time of low growth."

independent firm called Keikaku Rengo (Planning Union) to draw a blueprint for a new model city in Tsukuba. It was in a way a project to convert an expo into a new city. Is that correct?

**AS**  Yes. The Tsukuba Expo had the theme of science and technology. It was meant to show how much corporations understood and supported the development of science and technology.

**KO**  You had a vision of Tsukuba City as a model of a new city that wouldn't have a fixed status but would keep being regenerated with temporary structures.[6] That was your concept. Wasn't it Metabolist?

**AS**  The basis of the Tsukuba Expo was the idea of things moving away from Tokyo. At that time, I was very interested in decentralization by means of developments in science and technology. I relished the idea that decentralization from Tokyo could go hand in hand with the development of science and technology.

### The Market and Globalization

**RK**  So as a parent of the children to be raised, I want to ask you again the question about then and now. Then, the state had enormous power and enormous initiative. Now, you have all collectively given that power away, and we expect that the market will replace the kind of intelligence we had then with its own intelligence. The result is that there is no vision, no initiative, no centre, no nothing. Can you comment on that situation, on that difference between your period and the current period?

**AS**  I don't agree. Globalization means that things go beyond national boundaries. We would think about everything based on the nation-state. I really can't imagine the world that is not based on nation-state. Yet, I have big expectations for people in their 30s that through exposure to this new condition they will gain something drastically new and significant.

**KK**  Do you think the current situation, after deregulation, has had a negative effect?

**AS**  No, I don't think it's bad. I think the 20th and 21st centuries are essentially different. I think the market economy took over the idealism in planning and the privilege of the government. I think it's OK.

### China

**AS**  I am interested in your observations of China, because it has undergone enormous transformation. It is important that people like you have good insight into China. Right now they are having a big debate over the internationalism of companies operating under the Communist regime. Supporters and opponents of internationalism are fighting now in Shanghai, which has become more of an international city than a Chinese city. It's also impressive to see how executives in any organization in China have become so much younger. You rarely see anyone older than 60. China has become a country of young leaders, but Japanese leaders are the eldest!

**RK**  Yes. When did you first go to China? Did you ever work with them or for them?

**AS**  The first time I made contact with China was in January 1980, when I stayed in Beijing for about a month. Actually, my visit to China on a serious engagement from Japan was exceptional: I was a technocrat from a state that was sort of their enemy, still. But because I went there, they were impressed and valued highly what I did. So they started a habit of always consulting me as a Japanese.

**KK**  Then you organized many symposia and exchange research programs with China.

**RK**  Were you involved in the establishment of the Special Economic Zones? Or in conceiving that model?

**AS**  I guess I could say so, in various ways. But if you ask whether we could influence them much—that depends. China and Japan used to have an antagonistic

When major growth begins again, in the '80s, it is under
a different regime, less intent on planning: the free market...

**1981** Internationalist: like Tange and the
Metabolists, Shimokobe turns his attentions
abroad late in his career. Removed from the front
lines of national planning at the National Institute
for Research Advancement, he visits New York for
the Japan-US Intellectual Interchange Program,
organized by Tokyo's International House (where
*Metabolism 1960* was written); he also assists in
Japanese efforts to "help China on the way to
modernization."[7]

**1985** Reprise: Shimokobe reconvenes the
Metabolists to masterplan Tsukuba Expo '85.
Shimokobe's vision of temporary architecture
metamorphosing into a science city post-Expo
remains unrealized due to bureaucratic wrangling; the Metabolists are only able to build four
blocks of pavilions and the main gate, with
greatly reduced ambitions since Expo '70.
Still, sociologist Munesuke Mita captures the
essence of Shimokobe's, and Metabolism's,
mission: "[He] has a revealing vision: the idea
of keeping architecture permanently is hypo-
critical, whereas considering architecture as
temporary is authentic. Perhaps our desire
of imprinting the ground with something imperish-
able is a manifestation of gross civilization."[8]

normalization
In 1972 Tanaka brokered
the resumption of diplomatic
relations between Japan and
China. China dropped de-
mands for war reparations in
return for Japan's recog-
nition of China's claim on
Taiwan.

relationship, but as soon as Tanaka became prime minister there was suddenly a growing pro-China policy, so I assume there was great expectation on the Chinese side for me to be a—

**RK**   **Go-between?**

**KK**   **Didn't you have a lot of contacts with the Chinese Department of Foreign Affairs?**

**AS**   At the beginning, I was still in contact with the Communist Party line, the Party people, because it was prior to the normalization. It was later that I began seeing the government officials.

**KK**   **After the normalization, the Tanaka cabinet took an open, pro-China policy and you started being in contact with more wide-ranging people: academics, researchers, planners, but not necessarily party-line people. NIRA also sponsored a number of big joint research projects or sometimes financially supported research by Chinese people and organized international conferences where five or six North Pacific countries got together. That was very special.**

**RK**   **Visionary.**

### Build

**RK**   **On another note, why did you not write your autobiography? And why isn't there a biography of you? Have you sabotaged that?**

**AS**   I'm saying no. But I was criticized for not leaving a document, so I said I would answer if questions were posed. Hence I made a book of my answers working with some editors.[9] I do draw over the ground, but I do not draw pictures on paper.

**RK**   **You mean you build, but do not describe?**

**AS**   Right.

**KK**   **Your tabula rasa is the ground.**

**RK**   **Maybe we can end on that note.**

**AS**   When you are back, please let me know of your observation of China.

**RK**   **I will, because I still don't have the feeling that we have the full penetration into your mystery.**

**References**

1  Hiroshi Matsukuma et al, eds., *The Work of Kunio Maekawa: A Pioneer of Japanese Modern Architecture* (Tokyo: Bijutsu Shuppansha, 2006).

2  Atsushi Shimokobe, "Understanding our time and the architectural today," *Kenchiku Bunka*, June 1983.

3  "Report: Symposium on Plan for Tokyo 1960," *Shinkenchiku*, July 1961.

4  Masato Otaka in text interview by Hans Ulrich Obrist and Kayoko Ota, May 2008.

5  Kakuei Tanaka, *Nihon retto kaizo-ron* (Plan for remodeling the Japanese Archipelago) (Tokyo: Nikkan Kogyo Shimbunsha, 1972).

6  Atsushi Shimokobe and Kisho Kurokawa in conversation, "Temporary City: The concept of the Expo '85 Masterplan," *Shinkenchiku*, May 1985.

7  The International House of Japan ed., *Cultural Bridge between East and West* (Tokyo: The International House of Japan, 2009).

8  Munesuke Mita, "Rondan jihyo" (Current arguments), *Asahi Shimbun*, February 25, 1985.

9  Atsushi Shimokobe, *Sengo kokudo-keikaku eno shogen* (Testimony on the post-war national land planning) (Tokyo: Nihon Keizai Hyoronsha, 1994).

大高さん80才（2003）
metabolismの仲間たち

Kawazoe 川添 ○

Shimokobe 下河辺

Maki ○ 槇
Ekuan ○ 栄久庵

Kikutake 菊竹
Otaka 大高

# Project Japan
## Rebuilding/reimagining the nation

**"We did nothing but long-term, deficit-making projects. This is today almost entirely denied. I see no one presenting such a vision. It's deplorable how human beings are only interested in profit-making projects ... I tell you that once a planner begins to think about profit, the plan can never be good. Think of the Great Wall of China, think of the 16th-century Japanese castles. These things would never come out of a profit calculation."**

Atsushi Shimokobe in conversation with Kiyohide Terai, *Ocean Communications City 1985,* (Tokyo: Sangyo Hochi Center, 1984).

When Prime Minister Hayato Ikeda announces the Income Doubling Plan in 1960, it sparks a decade of unprecedented economic growth—peaking at 10 percent in 1970—and engenders a solid faith in the efficacy of governmental planning... perfect conditions for a historically rare confluence of state, business, and architecture/planning. Americans, nervous, call this semi-planned economy, with its state sponsorship of private initiative, "Japan Incorporated." The Japanese call it smart.

The structural weaknesses of the nation—unstable ground, lack of space and resources, pixelated land ownership, a population overconcentrated in Tokyo—are addressed in a systematic redesign of the Archipelago: Project Japan. The Metabolists, with their ambitions escalating to a national scale, are key participants.

From 1962, Atsushi Shimokobe—already supportive of Tange's rise to prominence—is the creative bureaucrat who oversees a boom in large-scale planning "visions" in tandem with the economic boom. Shimokobe shapes a series of Comprehensive National Development Plans (1962, 1969, 1976, 1987, and 1998) that call on an array of experts, including the Metabolists, to think and act as nation builders. Architects and bureaucrats enable each other through a slew of think tanks, deeply researched reports, concrete building projects, and visionary proposals—even the most radical of which are seriously funded and seriously considered. Shimokobe and the Metabolists work together in a growing mutual dependence: with a mission to create a decentralized Japan, with Tokyo relieved of its burdens and development spread more evenly across the Archipelago, Shimokobe needs the young and talented to help produce the government's planning scenarios.

After Expo '70, the oil crisis, and the rise of neoliberal *minkatsu* deregulation in the '80s, the spirit of collaboration and the limitless ambition begins to decline, and ends altogether in 1985 with a disappointing reprise of Metabolism: the Tsukuba Science Expo, planned by Shimokobe but realized in a denuded, budget-slashed form. Project Japan—the postwar fervor for reimagining the entire nation—is over, replaced by a new regime: the free market...

The strategic collusion of government, bureaucracy,
business, and architecture, 1960–1985.

GOVERNMENTAL

| Ministry of Foreign Affairs | Ministry of International Trade and Industry | Prime Minister's Cabinet | Ministry of Construction | Economic Planning Agency | Land Planning Agency | Science & Technology Agency | Na Insti Res Advan |

World Design Conference

Income Doubling Plan

Plan for Tokyo (TV launch)

Artificial Land Sub-Committee

First Comprehensive National Development Plan

Tokaido Megalopolis

Tokyo Olympics

Saikade Artificial Ground

Export excess over import ranks the world's highest

Artificial ground research for areas below sea level

Japan's GNP ranks second in the world

New (Second) Comprehensive National Development Plan

Expo '70: Big Roof / Mid-Air exhibition, Main Gate, Expo Tower, Urban Furniture, Pavilions

Expo '70

Japan in the 21st Century

Stratiform Structure Module

*Plan for Remodeling the Japanese Archipelago, Tanaka*

Vertical/Short Take-Off and Landing network

| 1960 | 1961 | 1962 | 1964 | 1965 | 1966 | 1968 | 1969 | 1970 | 1971 | 1972 |

**KENZO TANGE**

**TAKASHI ASADA**

**MASATO OTAKA**

**FUMIHIKO MAK**

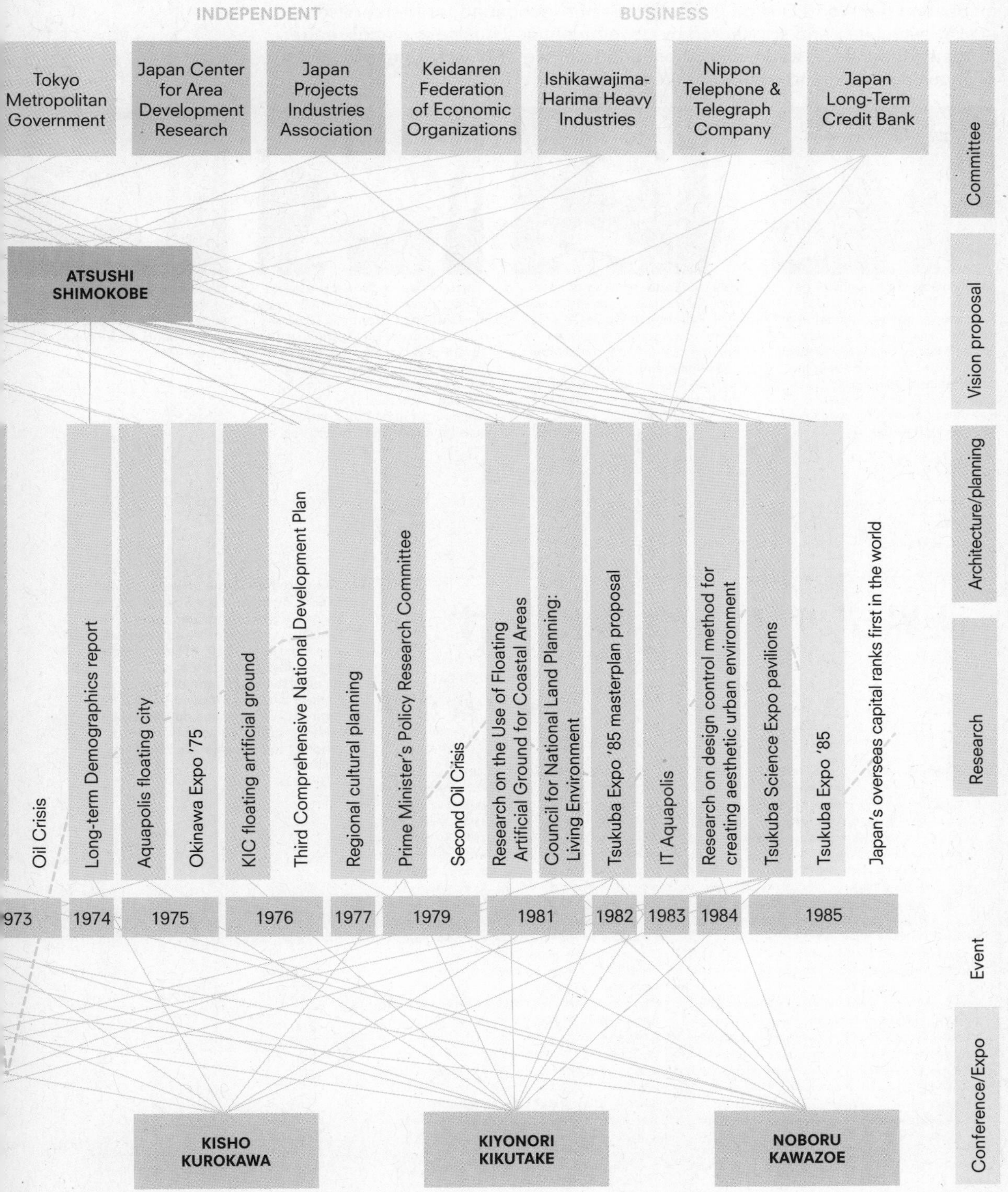

Tokyo Metropolitan Government

Japan Center for Area Development Research

Japan Projects Industries Association

Keidanren Federation of Economic Organizations

Ishikawajima-Harima Heavy Industries

Nippon Telephone & Telegraph Company

Japan Long-Term Credit Bank

Committee

**ATSUSHI SHIMOKOBE**

Vision proposal

Architecture/planning

Research

Oil Crisis

Long-term Demographics report

Aquapolis floating city

Okinawa Expo '75

KIC floating artificial ground

Third Comprehensive National Development Plan

Regional cultural planning

Prime Minister's Policy Research Committee

Second Oil Crisis

Research on the Use of Floating Artificial Ground for Coastal Areas

Council for National Land Planning: Living Environment

Tsukuba Expo '85 masterplan proposal

IT Aquapolis

Research on design control method for creating aesthetic urban environment

Tsukuba Science Expo pavilions

Tsukuba Expo '85

Japan's overseas capital ranks first in the world

| 1973 | 1974 | 1975 | 1976 | 1977 | 1979 | 1981 | 1982 | 1983 | 1984 | 1985 |

Event

Conference/Expo

**KISHO KUROKAWA**

**KIYONORI KIKUTAKE**

**NOBORU KAWAZOE**

## Constructing a World Stage

Ostensibly a showcase made for and by architects and designers, on close inspection the World Design Conference—the launchpad for Metabolism—is also stimulated and sponsored by government and business circles, eager to foster Japanese design innovation, and to prove the quality and originality of Japan's products to an initially skeptical world…

**Aiichiro Fujiyama**, minister of foreign affairs, takes time out from preparing the ratification of the US–Japan Security Treaty (steamrollered into law one week after WoDeCo), to endorse the conference. Design is his first love: in 1953, he translated Raymond Loewy's *Never Leave Well Enough Alone*…

**Hayato Ikeda**, minister of international trade and industry, speaks after Fujiyama at WoDeCo's opening ceremony. Becomes prime minister two months later and immediately issues the Income Doubling Plan, triggering for Japan's economic miracle.

**Taizo Ishizaka**, former president of Toshiba and head of the Keidanren Federation of Economic Organizations, serves on WoDeCo's board of directors, ensuring the collaboration and sponsorship of Japan's leading companies. Ishizaka later leads the Tokyo Olympics funding foundation and the Expo '70 Organization.

**Hisaakira Kano**, chairman of WoDeCo's preparatory committee and of the Japan Housing Corporation, addresses the conference.

世界デザイン会議に寄す

国務大臣 科学技術庁長官

中曽根康弘

このたび世界デザイン会議が5月11日より10日間にわたつて　世界一流の優れたデザイナーや評論家をあつめて　東京でひらかれることになりましたが　私は大いなる喜びをもつて皆様とともにこれを迎えるものであります。これも産業界の強力な後援のもとに　各関係者の方々の苦心の結果に他なりません。あと数日にせまつたこの会議が　大きな成果をあげることを祈つております。

さてこのたびの世界デザイン会議は　新時代のトータル・イメージは何かということがテーマとなつております。思うに　原子エネルギーの解放と電子工学の飛躍的な発達は　第三の産業革命といわれる人類の生産力の発達をもたらしました。またさらに月ロケットによる宇宙空間の探求は　人類の未来の生活への限りない可能性を菜啓するものでありましょう。このような自然科学的な方法によつて物質を支配することが　私たちに大きな希望を与えてくれる反面　私たちのますます複雑化してゆく人間生活はしだいに多くの矛盾を孕んできているのではないでしょうか。いかんながら私たち人類は　科学という新しい仏をつくつて魂をふきこんではいないのでしょうか。物質の洪水のなかで人間精神は溺れかかつているのではないでしょうか。この物と精神のギャップがますます大きくなつているのが二十世紀の特徴だといえましょう。このような物質と人間をむすぶものがデザインであり　今日はどデザインということが重大な意味と任務を負つたことはなかつたと私は思うのであります。このときにあたり　世界を代表するデザイナー諸氏が一堂に集まり　人と物をむすぶ　世界のトータル・イメージについて論じあうことは　人類の未来への一里塚をうちたてるうえに　大きな成果が期待されるものと思います。

またこの会議が日本の東京でひらかれる　ということも偶然ではありません。我国が　今日東洋での工業的先進国であるからばかりでなく　古い伝統と文化の国だからであります。衆知のごとく我国は　正倉院の御物にもみられるように　遠くはペルシヤやインドの文化が流入し　また中国・朝鮮とは不断の密接な関係を保ち　しかもそれが甚だしい戦乱で消滅することもなく　いわば国全体が東洋の美術館と呼ばれるほど　豊かな文化遺産をうけついできたのです。受けつぐことは　また常にそのなかに生きることです。このようにして我国の文化はかもされ熟し　そして洗練されて世界にも独特な一文化園をかたちづくつたのでした。このような土壌があつたからこそ　明治からの西欧的な近代文明にも迅速に反応し抵取することができたのです。これは精神文化一般についてもいえることですが　とくに生活環境に関係した面では　日本の抽象的デザインは19世紀のヨーロッパ美術に強い影響を与えたように　はなはだすぐれた作品が残されております。このような日本的な　ひろくは東洋的な伝統文明が　今日の世界の人類の文化のために　特に大きな寄与をすることは何人も疑い得ないところでありましょう。

このような意味でも　このたび東京で世界デザイン会議が行われることには　重大な意味と期待がよせられる次第であります。そして　この根元的な問題が　そのまま近代産業のなかで生かされることを併せて希望して止まないものであります。日本のデザインの独自性と創意をひろく海外のデザイナー諸氏に理解して戴くことはまた当面の急務でもあります。

**Yasuhiro Nakasone**, minister of state affairs, director of the Science and Technology Agency, and later prime minister, writes a congratulatory address in *Kindai Kenchiku*, May 1960. "The conference bears great significance, and guests will discuss the integration of oriental traditions with modern industries, and the creativity of Japanese design will be widely recognized and understood among the professionals visiting from abroad."

WoDeCo 1

A Project Japan: The first in a series of WoDeCo reports, with graphic design by emerging talent Ikko Tanaka and art direction by design critic Masaru Katsumi.

The relationship between government, business, and design is choreographed by two crucial figures in the birth of Metabolism: one a businessman/bureaucrat, and one an architect/theoretician. Hisaakira Kano, chief of the Japan Housing Corporation (a government agency), and the visionary behind the first massive reclamation proposal for Tokyo Bay, serves as chairman of WoDeCo's preparatory committee.[1] Takashi Asada, Tange's right-hand man, is WoDeCo's secretary-general, responsible for mobilizing not only the nascent Metabolists in the run-up to the conference but also key figures in business and government—for whom the problem of Japan's reputation for producing counterfeit goods is reaching crisis point.

For a country so dependent on exports, the government is desperate for Japan's products to remain competitive on the world market. After a string of humiliating incidents—protests in the US; Foreign Minister Aiichiro Fujiyama subject to a grilling by the press on a visit to London in 1957—the realization spreads that "design" is a precious commodity worthy of investment.

One month after Fujiyama's ordeal, the Japan Committee on International Design (a key organizer of WoDeCo) is cofounded by Kano.[2] In 1958, the Ministry of International Trade and Industry (MITI) launches a "Design Section" in order to promote innovation and quality. Ekuan is consulted for a legal definition of design. The Section organizes an exhibition showing pairs of authentic and counterfeit goods, which creates controversy in Japan's domestic industry but appreciation by foreign media like *Life* magazine.[3]

The government realizes that Japanese architecture—especially in the form of Tange, with a growing international reputation—has a key role to play in its design renaissance...

**Aiichiro Fujiyama, minister of foreign affairs**
"This conference is, as I understand it, very unique, for it is a meeting of the most active experts in the field of concrete and creative design, in order to incorporate artistic needs and industrial techniques in our environment. I am convinced that this conference, through the common word 'design,' will form a basis for strong mutual confidence and cooperation, and will also brilliantly serve as a guide for humanity in the coming age."

**Hayato Ikeda, minister of international trade and industry**
"The attendence of a large group of foreign designers will contribute to promoting mutual understanding between East and West ... I also hope that the foreign participants will adjust their knowledge of Japan by studying modern industrial Japan as well as traditional Japan with the keen eyes of a specialist."

Politicians endorsing WoDeCo.

Business brains behind WoDeCo.

## Urban Platform

Searching for new surfaces on which to build, the Ministry of Construction latches onto a new avant-garde concept: "The idea of artificial land," says bureaucrat Terumi Kitabatake, "which has been explored by well-known architects like Tange, Kikutake, Otaka and Maki, can indeed provide a solution that is neither utopian nor complacent but effective for urban problems…"[4]

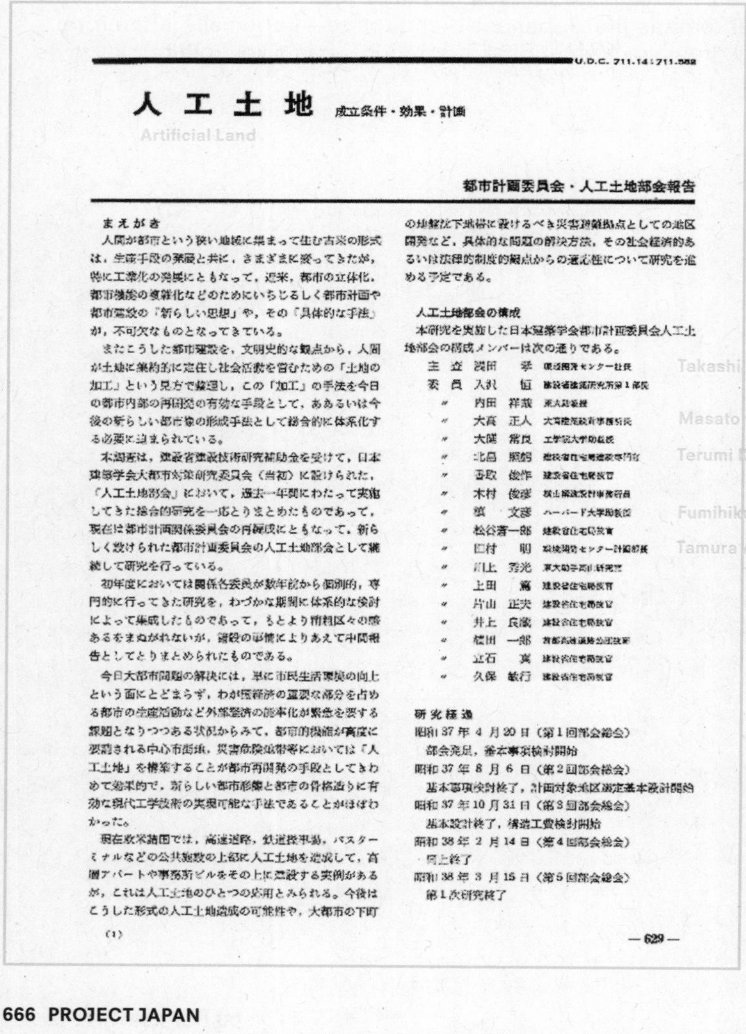

U.D.C. 711.14:711.582

# 人 工 土 地 成立条件・効果・計画

Artificial Land

都市計画委員会・人工土地部会報告

**まえがき**

人間が都市という狭い地域に集まって住む古来の形式は，生産手段の発展と共に，さまざまに変ってきたが，特に工業化の発展にともなって，近来，都市の立体化，都市機能の複雑化などのためにいちじるしく都市計画や都市建設の「新らしい思想」や，その「具体的な手法」が，不可欠なものとなってきている。

またこうした都市建設を，文明史的な観点から，人間が土地に集約的に定住し社会活動を営むための「土地の加工」という見方で整理し，この「加工」の手法を今日の都市内部の再開発の有効な手段として，あるいは今後の新らしい都市像の形成手法として綜合的に体系化する必要に迫まられている。

本調査は，建設省建設技術研究補助金を受けて，日本建築学会大都市対策研究委員会（当初）に設けられた，「人工土地部会」において，過去一年間にわたって実施してきた綜合的研究を一応とりまとめたものであって，現在は都市計画関係委員会の再編成にともなって，新らしく設けられた都市計画委員会の人工土地部会として継続して研究を行っている。

初年度においては関係各委員が数年前から個別的，専門的に行ってきた研究を，わずかな期間に体系的な検討によって集成したものであって，もとより前後区々の感あるをまぬがれないが，諸般の事情によりあえて中間報告としてとりまとめられたものである。

今日大都市問題の解決には，単に市民生活環境の向上という面にとどまらず，わが国経済の重要な部分を占める都市の生産活動など外部経済の能率化が緊急を要する課題となりつつある状況からみて，都市的機能が高度に要請される中心市街地，災害危険地帯等においては「人工土地」を構築することが都市再開発の手段としてきわめて効果的で，新らしい都市形態と都市の骨格造りに有効な現代工学技術の実現可能な手法であることがほぼわかった。

現在欧米諸国では，高速道路，鉄道操車場，バスターミナルなどの公共施設の上部に人工土地を造成して，高層アパートや事務所ビルをその上に建設する実例があるが，これは人工土地のひとつの応用とみられる。今後はこうした形式の人工土地造成の可能性や，大都市の下町の地盤沈下地帯に設けるべき災害避難拠点としての地区開発など，具体的な問題の解決方法，その社会経済的あるいは法律的制度的観点からの適応性について研究を進める予定である。

**人工土地部会の構成**

本研究を実施した日本建築学会都市計画委員会人工土地部会の構成メンバーは次の通りである。

| | | |
|---|---|---|
| 主査 | 浅田　孝 | 環境開発センター社長 |
| 委員 | 入沢　恒 | 建設省建築研究所第1部長 |
| 〃 | 内田　祥哉 | 東大助教授 |
| 〃 | 大高　正人 | 大高建築設計事務所長 |
| 〃 | 大隅　常良 | 工学院大学助教授 |
| 〃 | 北畠　照躬 | 建設省住宅局建築専門官 |
| 〃 | 香取　俊作 | 建設省住宅局技官 |
| 〃 | 木村　俊彦 | 横山建築構造設計事務所員 |
| 〃 | 槇　文彦 | ハーバード大学助教授 |
| 〃 | 松谷蒼一郎 | 建設省住宅局技官 |
| 〃 | 田村　明 | 環境開発センター計画部長 |
| 〃 | 川上　秀光 | 東大助手高山研究室 |
| 〃 | 上田　篤 | 建設省住宅局技官 |
| 〃 | 片山　正夫 | 建設省住宅局技官 |
| 〃 | 井上　良蔵 | 建設省住宅局技官 |
| 〃 | 植田　一郎 | 首都高速道路公団技師 |
| 〃 | 立石　真 | 建設省住宅局技官 |
| 〃 | 久保　敏行 | 建設省住宅局技官 |

Takashi Asada

Masato Otaka

Terumi Kitabatake

Fumihiko Maki

Tamura Akira

**研究経過**

昭和37年4月20日（第1回部会総会）
部会発足，基本事項検討開始

昭和37年8月6日（第2回部会総会）
基本事項検討終了，計画対象地区選定基本設計開始

昭和37年10月31日（第3回部会総会）
基本設計終了，構造工費検討開始

昭和38年2月14日（第4回部会総会）
同上終了

昭和38年3月15日（第5回部会総会）
第1次研究終了

（1）　— 629 —

**Artificial Land Subcommittee: "Artificial Land: Prerequisites, effects and planning"**
Commissioner: Ministry of Construction / Architectural Institute of Japan. "We are desperately in need of a new way of thinking and a specific means for urban planning and construction," November 1963.

Networking: Asada invites the next visionary to his Environmental Development Center... the Metabolists, Shimokobe, Shinya Izumi, academics, and journalists meet frequently at the EDC, in Ginza, around 1963.

In 1963, the ministry funds the Artificial Land Sub-Committee within the Architectural Institute of Japan. The group's mission is to establish an alternative datum—on the land, on the sea, in the air—to the overcrowded, fragmented, and geologically unstable ground plane of Japan. Takashi Asada (who has now left Tange Lab to set up the Environmental Development Center), heads the subcommittee, which includes Akira Tamura of the EDC, nine members from the Ministry of Construction, and Otaka and Maki as pioneers of artificial ground. In the group's first report, artificial land is defined in political terms, as "a means to process land by which men can live collectively and engage in social activities." Otaka's plans for Tokyo's Kanda and Otemachi districts and Maki's K-Project for Tokyo appear in the report as exemplars of artificial land.

The group's primary project is Otaka's plan to build, over a slum in Sakaide, Kagawa Prefecture, a social housing complex on a raised urban platform—solving the myriad problems connected with the land in one all-over gesture. In 1964, Asada plays the role of facilitator, convincing the Sakaide municipality of the virtues of Otaka's scheme (it helps that Asada already works as a consultant on tourist development for Kagawa Prefecture). The Ministry of Construction subsidizes the project, and the first phase of Sakaide Artificial Ground is completed in 1968. Research into artificial ground continues for the next two decades, with the assistance of the government, desperate for alternatives to Japan's saturated and uninhabitable land...[5]

Urban platform.

**1968** Otaka's Sakaide Artificial Ground rises over surrounding slum.

## Artificial Ground Colonization

Kikutake finds long-term government support for his life's pursuit of artificial ground, this time in the form of megastructural frameworks dotted over the Archipelago, safely straddling the most congested, the most pristine, and the most earthquake-prone ground...

Stratiform Structure Module

層構造モジュール

ⓑk 財団法人 機械振興協会
新機械システムセンター
〒105 東京都港区芝公園3−5−8

層構造モジュールの開発は、財団法人機械振興協会が、日本自転車振興会から機械工業振興資金の交付を受け、通商産業省の指導のもとに、
昭和47年から進めている開発プロジェクトです。この資料は、日本自転車振興会から機械工業振興資金の交付を受けて作成したものです。
ⓒkikutake architects

**1977 Stratiform Structural Module**
Commissioner: Ministry of International Trade and Industry / Mechanical Social Systems Foundation. "Our proposal is to generate inexpensive artificial land equipped with urban infrastructure in the middle of a congested city, which makes it essentially different from other urban improvement proposals—a land that allows you to build a house, plant a tree and grow flowers."

1:1 Test construction, earthquake, and fire testing.

The Mechanical Social Systems Foundation (MSSF), supervised by the Ministry of International Trade and Industry, sponsors the Stratiform project, directed by Kikutake, as one of many infrastructure technology development programs. With the support of a veritable wise men's committee for artificial ground—including Yoshichika Uchida (expert on construction technology; second son of Yoshikazu Uchida, masterplanner for Manchuria), Soichiro Honda (founder of the car company), Genko Uchida (formerly of the Ministry of International Trade and Industry), major contractors, engineering firms, and electric companies—the MSSF, from 1972 onwards pursues Kikutake's endeavour through nearly two decades of experimentation.[16]

Stratiform Structures are steel trusses supporting platforms of artificial ground made of prestressed concrete. Upon these platforms, Western-style houses perform like (individualized) capsules embedded in a space frame. Ever conscious of the environment, Kikutake selects structural materials that could be reused and recycled after a Stratiform is dismantled. The system is fast to build, flexible, and apparently viable in a country where the technology for producing sophisticated steel and concrete members is already in place (Japan becomes the world's biggest producer of steel in 1973). After years of making increasingly ambitious models, collages, and renderings of the Stratiform in various picturesque locations in Japan, Kikutake gets to the point of actually doing earthquake and fire tests on 1:1 prototypes...

Stratiform modules would be placed over existing roads and railways.

## Stages of an Obsession

Over 20 years, Kikutake plots the Stratiform's
colonization of the Japanese Archipelago...

...in the shadow of Mount Fuji...

...in the countryside in Shikoku, 1972...

...with Western-style suburban houses functioning like capsules in the midst of an elevated forest, 1971...

...for the Japanese government pavilion, containing all facilities at Tsukuba Science Expo '85 (the proposal is thwarted)...[17]

...and exported to the Amazon in 1992 in a project for the Rio Earth Summit: Habitat Infrastructure, a city for 15,000 raised 10–15 metres above the delicate ground—"It is a city coexisting with nature, not destroying it."[18]

## Floating Artificial Ground

With his own research program at Hawaii University, Kikutake develops a new type of marine city, inspired by new submarine technology. The project evolves into a government commission, and his first realization of a floating city: the Aquapolis. Meanwhile, there is a rumor of a US–Japanese floating project that may require Kikutake's expertise...

**1975 Kikutake: Aquapolis, Okinawa Ocean Expo**
Commissioner: Ministry of International Trade and Industry / Prime Minister's Cabinet.
The world's first floating pavilion. Kikutake writes: "The decision [to build the floating pavilion in a typhoon-prone area and season] reflected the government's firm determination to tackle marine development in earnest and, to be sure, confidence in shipbuilding technology. It was also remarkable that different ministries worked together to clear problems and direct the project."[9]

Okinawa, via Hawaii: Kikutake's team tests an Aquapolis model on Kaneohe Bay, 1973.

Floating cities become a subject for bilateral discussions: Tanaka and Nixon meet in 1971 and discuss an education city (to be designed by Kikutake?) in the Atlantic.

The same year: Obama returns to Hawaii.

**Hawaii explorations**
Vertical flotation research at Hawaii University, used for the Aquapolis and another version of the ever-evolving Marine City...

At Hawaii University, Kikutake leads a marine city research team that includes engineers, sociologists, and the military: former US Navy lieutenant John Craven brings his knowledge of the new Philips submarine, which turns 90 degrees to stand upright (a vision Kikutake had for floating towers in 1958). Kikutake uses this vertical flotation system in a new design for a floating city, to be stationed five kilometers off Waikiki Beach and contain an outpost of Hawaii University for ocean research, hotels, offices, and exhibition space.[19]

Kikutake also applies vertical flotation to his plans for the Aquapolis, which will be realized at the Okinawa Ocean Expo in 1975 (celebrating the handover of the islands from the US back to Japan). The Hawaii team successfully tests a model of the oil rig-like structure (but an oil rig that floats) on Kaneohe Bay.

The projects coincide with an invitation for a private audience with Prime Minister Kakuei Tanaka. With his architectural background, Tanaka pays serious attention to Kikutake's concepts for floating cities and offers his support. Later, Kikutake learns that Tanaka and US President Nixon had been planning to construct a floating school as a US Bicentennial project, for which Japan would collaborate as a final confirmation of the postwar reconciliation. But when Nixon insists on the Atlantic as the site rather than the more logical Pacific, the project collapses, along with Kikutake's potential involvement.

MARINE

SUBMARINE

Flotation test.

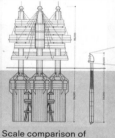

Scale comparison of Hawaii Marine City and the Philips submarine.

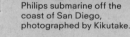

Philips submarine off the coast of San Diego, photographed by Kikutake.

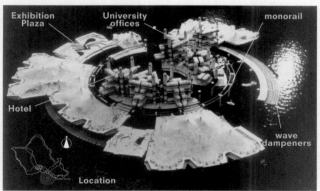

Exhibition Plaza · University offices · monorail · Hotel · wave dampeners · Location

**Floating city, Hawaii edition** Composed of 28 modules suspended from "milk bottle" concrete cylinders, which control stability and flotation by taking water in and out using compressed air—the same mechanism as the Philips submarines. Modules, suspended from the cylinders by tension cables, contain a 1,200-room hotel, Hawaii University outpost, offices, housing, shopping, and marine research center. An exhibition will take place on the fanlike platforms surrounding the modules; afterwards, the city will be used as a mobile recreation facility at sea.

**Plug-in Floating Urban Unit**

Just as the Aquapolis is being tugged into place in Okinawa, Kikutake, supported by a conglomerate of industrialists, is already planning an escalation of his ambition: KIC, a Stratiform Structure Module that has taken to sea, ready to plug into Japan's harbors. As the UN's convention of the sea takes shape—potentially increasing Japan's ocean territory—the National Institute for Research Advancement commissions Kikutake for further research into ways of exploiting the new tabula rasa...

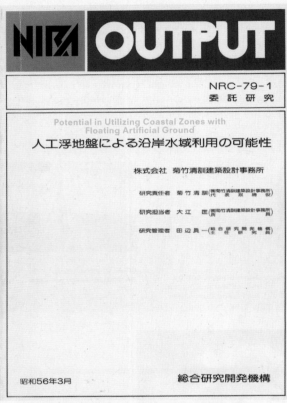

**NIRA OUTPUT**

NRC-79-1
委託研究

Potential in Utilizing Coastal Zones with
Floating Artificial Ground
人工浮地盤による沿岸水域利用の可能性

株式会社　菊竹清訓建築設計事務所

研究責任者　菊竹清訓（株菊竹清訓建築設計事務所 代表取締役）

研究担当者　大江　匡（株菊竹清訓建築設計事務所 所員）

研究管理者　田辺員一（総合研究開発機構 主任研究員）

昭和56年3月　　　総合研究開発機構

**1979 Potential in Utilizing Coastal Zones with Floating Artificial Ground**
Commissioner: National Institute of Research Advancement (NIRA).
"In the new maritime order, our nation now has territorial waters more than 10 times as wide as its land. The seafront of congested cities is the last remaining, precious, free space that will be indispensable in national land planning, together with sea area." Kikutake's introduction to the report "Potential in Utilizing Coastal Zones with Floating Artificial Ground."

KIC floating A-frames docking in their specially made ports.

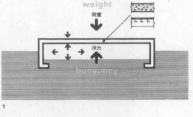

weight
荷重

浮力
buoyancy

1

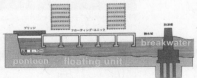

ブリッジ　　フローティング・ユニット　防波堤
bridge　　floating unit　　breakwater
pontoon　floating unit

2

KIC port: floating platforms, hollow underneath.

A KIC floating A-frame contains housing and offices, and can also be used to stock supplies and house the homeless after floods or earthquakes—as with his 1961 Koto Plan (Disaster Prevention City), catastrophe and benevolence are Kikutake's motivation more than a conception of utopia. The KIC is named after the collaborators behind the scheme: Kikutake himself, Ishikawajima-Harima Heavy Industry (IHI, Japan's major shipbuilding firm and a pioneer in tanker-building technology), and the Japan Long-Term Credit Bank. The system is designed for excellent stability, structural and material durability (100 years), and cost efficiency thanks to its prefabrication in shipbuilding yards. In 1977 and '78, Kikutake develops a similar plug-in system for floating structures Libya's coast and for the Tigris and Euphrates in Iraq: the "Infra-Cassette" (see p. 66). As Kikutake develops the KIC, the UN's Law of the Sea Convention is under the process of ratification. The Law would grant every nation an Exclusive Economic Zone (EEZ) within 200 miles of its coast. Japan, so obsessed with the limitations of its islandness for so long, would suddenly gain massive new territories, becoming the seventh largest country in terms of its EEZ. Kikutake's latest marine venture in a lifetime of exploits suddenly gains geopolitical relevance...

Kikutake maps Japan's new marine territory under the UN's Law of the Sea Convention, Japan suddenly changes shape...

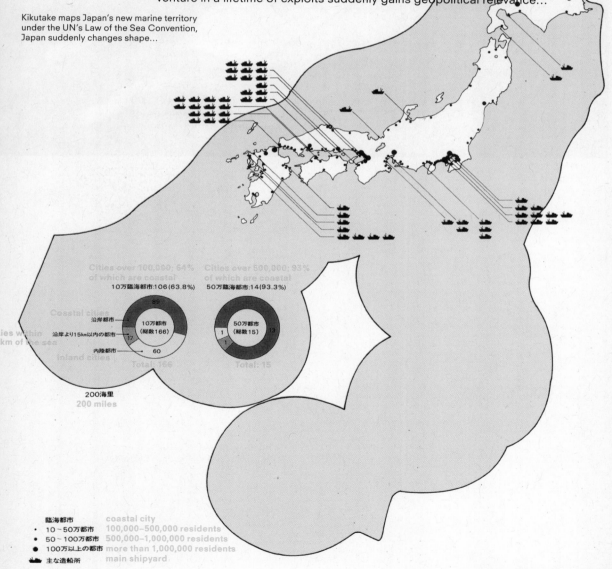

Cities over 100,000; 64% of which are coastal
10万臨海都市:106(63.8%)

Cities over 500,000; 93% of which are coastal
50万臨海都市:14(93.3%)

Coastal cities
沿岸都市

ties within km of the sea
沿岸より15km以内の都市

Inland cities
内陸都市

89
10万都市
(総数166)
17
60
Total: 166

1
50万都市
(総数15)
13
1
Total: 15

200海里
200 miles

臨海都市    coastal city
·   10～50万都市    100,000–500,000 residents
●   50～100万都市    500,000–1,000,000 residents
⬤   100万以上の都市    more than 1,000,000 residents
⛴   主な造船所    main shipyard

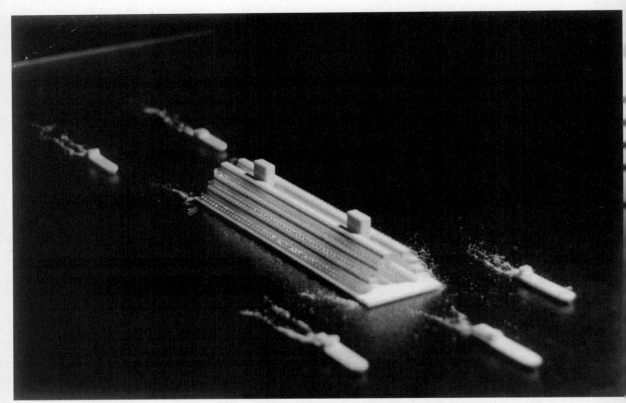

A freshly made KIC is
towed to its harbor...

KIC, plugged into the urban
fabric on the waterfront.

## Masterplanning the Nation

Tange's career as a visionary starts in earnest with Tokyo Bay but quickly—aided, abetted, and critiqued by figures in the government and the bureaucracy—extends from the capital to an evolving masterplan for the entire Japanese Archipelago...

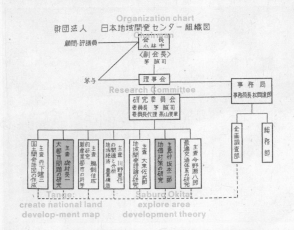

**1964 Japan Center for Area Development Research**
A merger of academia and industry, cofounded by Tange, the JCADR reports to the Ministry of Construction. Saburo Okita, author of the Income Doubling Plan, has just left the Economic Planning Agency, where Shimokobe now leads the Comprehensive National Development Plans.

**"Tokaido Megalopolis Starts to Move,"** *Asahi Graph*, **November 17, 1967**
Shimokobe, now director of national land planning at the Economic Planning Agency, interviews Tange:
**Shimokobe**: "The government has so far aimed at distribution, but we need a more tactful balancing of distribution and concentration."
**Tange**: "Tokyo's CBD can be distributed along the Tokaido belt. The capital itself could be moved to somewhere else, like at the foot of Mt. Fuji. It would be ideal if Japan had a spine with ribs stretching out."

**1971 Prime Minister's Cabinet**
Tokaido Megalopolis takes a leading role in a project reflecting Prime Minister Sato Eisaku's hunger for visions of the future: *Japan in the 21st Century: A Socioeconomic and Physical Proposal for the Future Japan* (left). Tange (front row, left) is photographed with Prime Minister Sato after receiving an award for the Megalopolis.

The reception of Tange's audacious Plan for Tokyo 1960, which he presents on national television on New Year's Day 1961, is one of the first tests of the new relationship between government and avant-garde. In a symposium organized by *Shinkenchiku*, in front of an audience of bureaucrats and architects, Tange leads a panel that includes Kikutake, Eika Takayama of Tokyo University (veteran of urban planning in Datong, Inner Mongolia in 1939), and Shimokobe, Tange's former student, now representing the Ministry of Construction. Shimokobe remarks: "Without a good historical analysis of how Tokyo has come to hold 10 million residents, Tange's argument would be a mere discussion of how to design a bucket." But the research is indeed in place. Shimokobe asks the audience to "bear with" Tange and his grand plans, for their own benefit in the future—Shimokobe clearly treats him as a national treasure worth nurturing. He continues: "Everyone agrees that Tokyo needs a solution. Rather than criticizing the plan, we should find a way to back up the proposal. We must come up with a fundamentally different idea for urban planning based on this proposal. The fiscal budget for such a mission is rather abundant..."[10] Encouraged by Shimokobe's remarks, Tange enlarges the frame. In 1964, he co-founds the Japan Center for Area Development Research, a collaboration of the academic and industrial spheres to guide national land planning. The group reports to the Ministry of Construction. In one of the first meetings, Tange presents Tokaido Megalopolis: a web of infrastructure connecting cities from Tokyo to Osaka in a single urban corridor 600 kilometers long. In a lecture to the group, Tange says: "We don't need to limit the 'Tokaido Megalopolis' concept literally to the Tokaido area. We could think of two lines: one from Mito to Tokushima, and the other from Utsunomiya to Okayama—crossing with Tokyo, Nagoya and Osaka. We could see the Tokaido area as the central nervous system or spinal cord of Japan, from which arms and legs stretch out to the Tohoku, Hokuriku, Chugoku, and Shikoku regions, forming altogether the Japanese Archipelago."[11]

In 1966, Tange appears again on national TV, again on New Year's Day—seemingly, the day for grand schemes. He presents Tokaido Megalopolis on the show "Designing the 21st Century," featuring various "visions"—a new buzzword— for the future Japan. Four months later, Tange publishes Tokaido Megalopolis in another "visionary" vehicle: a popular pocket book titled *Future Image of the Japanese Archipelago...*

**1960** Plan for Tokyo, with its "spine" ready to grow across the mainland...

**1961** Interrogation: Tange (standing, far right) presents Plan for Tokyo at the *Shinkenchiku* symposium, 1961.

TOHOKU

HOKURIKU

CHUGOKU

Okayama

SHIKOKU

Tokushima

Nagoya

Osaka

Utsunomiya

Mito

Tokyo

I

II

II

I

**1964** Tokaido Megalopolis: the urban axis from Plan for Tokyo extends into a new axis (I-I, above). The perpedicular II-II axis is devoted to green spaces. The axes grow into Tokaido Megalopolis, a linear amalgamation of Tokyo, Nagoya, and Osaka, and then into a nationwide urban web.

"The Tokaido Megalopolis will be the central nervous system of Japan,"[12] Tange writes. The Tokaido region already contains 50 percent of Japan's wealth and 70 percent of Japan's urban population; Tange's research shows that 80 percent will live there by the end of the century, making the development of infrastructure and communication networks imperative. He proposes strategic corridors of urban conurbation, which would increase mobility, spread development more evenly across Japan, and heighten the contrast between the (continuous) city and the countryside. Land for the spinal growth of cities would be acquired with government money; private money would fund construction itself. "Tokyo, Nagoya, and Osaka are already strengthening their links," Tange writes, "which I value as a sign that the Japanese land is beginning to have a highly organic structure in itself. And I hope the government will shift its policy to support this direction."[13]

In 1966, Tokaido Megalopolis is debated in parliament by the Ministry of Municipalities and related ministers. But the idea is perceived as an attempt to create a new megacity sprawling from Tokyo, rather than redistributing power and population density to the regions.[14] Nevertheless, during the regime of Prime Minister Eisaku Sato (1964–1972), Tange is among nine groups commissioned to make a proposal for a "vision for the 21st century"—a subject of increasing concern for politicians and bureaucrats. Tange receives financial support for his research directly from the prime minister's office: ¥9.8 million over three years to 1971.[15] In 1972, Sato is replaced by Tanaka, who in turn brings his own "vision"…

"Perhaps more energy than has been invested by all mankind in the past several thousand years will be needed for the next 35 years towards the end of the 20th century. At a crossroads of civilization, we are undergoing revolutionary changes in the structure of the metropolis." Tange's pocket book, *Future Image of the Japanese Archipelago: Construction for the 21st Century* (Tokyo: Kodansha, 1966).

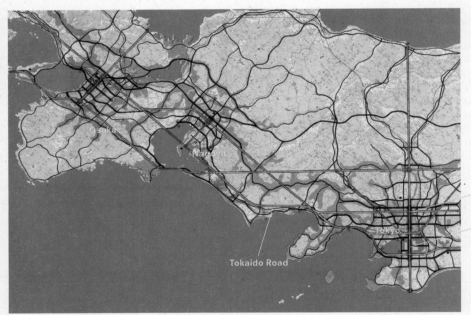

Spine growing from Plan for Tokyo 1960

Plan for Tokyo 1960, implemented

Tokaido Road

Zoom in on Tokyo-Nagoya-Osaka. "Tokaido Megalopolis will become one large continuous urban zone. Wherever one is along Tokaido, one should be able to access the same information and the same degree of urbanity as in Tokyo or in Osaka. The new capital could be moved to anywhere in the Tokaido Megalopolis, either on Tokyo Bay or at the foot of Mount Fuji."[12]

**Tokaido Megalopolis, 1971 edition** Presenting the final evolution of his scheme in his book *Future Image of the Japanese Archipelago*, Tange projects, for the year 2000, three types of infrastructure webs—creating a hyperconnected, efficient, responsive, fluid Japanese Archipelago...

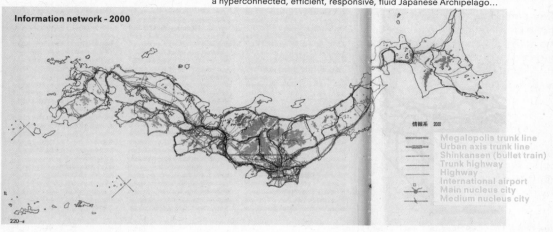

**Information network - 2000**

情報系 2000
Megalopolis trunk line
Urban axis trunk line
Shinkansen (bullet train)
Trunk highway
Highway
International airport
Main nucleus city
Medium nucleus city

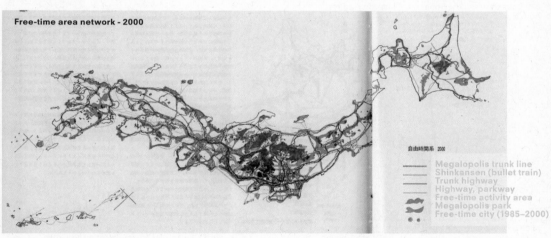

**Free-time area network - 2000**

自由時間系 2000
Megalopolis trunk line
Shinkansen (bullet train)
Trunk highway
Highway, parkway
Free-time activity area
Megalopolis park
Free-time city (1985–2000)

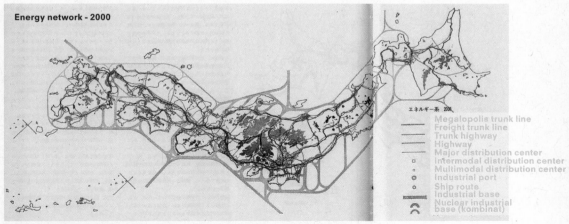

**Energy network - 2000**

エネルギー系 2000
Megalopolis trunk line
Freight trunk line
Trunk highway
Highway
Major distribution center
Intermodal distribution center
Multimodal distribution center
Industrial port
Ship route
Industrial base
Nuclear industrial base (kombinat)

"Tokaido Megalopolis is an organic entity, or a fluid city. The system of the fluidity is comprised of three networks. We propose that the Megalopolis trunk line would be a bundle of various transportation lines running together in tunnels through the mountains or under the sea. In order to avoid the difficulty of purchasing land or to avoid noise pollution, and in order to build freely and keep the inside under control, it is advised to construct the Megalopolis either under the ground or in the air."[13]

## Masterminding the Future Archipelago

In the New National Comprehensive Development Plan, Shimokobe scripts the nation's industrialization, urbanization, preservation, transportation, and communication, and enlists the help of Kurokawa and his new think tank, the Institute for Social Engineering. "Both Shimokobe and I were full of zeal at the time..."

**New Comprehensive National Development Plan**
**Atsushi Shimokobe at the Economic Planning Agency**

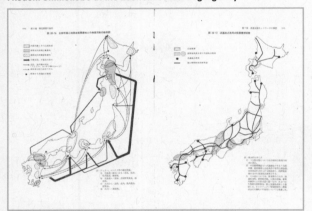

Left: conceptual diagram of freight transport to large cities and remote industrial bases. Right: distribution of ports.

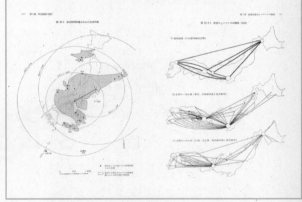

Left: Japan redrawn according to flight times. Right: plan for new aviation networks connecting major and regional cities.

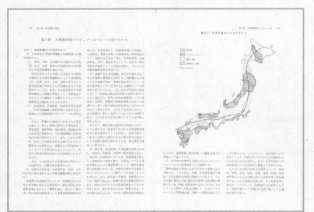

"In this Plan, special efforts are being made to integrate people's free time in the national land planning, which needs further research..."

The plan for greater Tokyo (left) does not include Tange's Tokaido Megalopolis proposal, but places the capital within a continuous coastal city zone. It also admits sprawl will occur towards the north.

The Income Doubling Plan of 1961 in fact leads to a quadrupling of income, causing severe urban congestion, sprawl, and pollution—problems that can only be addressed, Shimokobe believes, on the national scale. His 1969 National Comprehensive Development Plan attempts to give form, direction, and a degree of justice to Japan's rampant economic growth: Shimokobe's personal crusade is to spread Japan's development more evenly between its burgeoning cities and the relative poverty of its countryside (while Japan's gross GDP hovers around second in the world, its GDP per capita remains relatively low: the United States is nearly three times higher than Japan's).

He plans to do this through a vision similar to Tange's Tokaido Megalopolis: an urban belt running the length of Honshu; new networks for shipping and transportation; the Shinkansen bullet train... Japan itself becomes a canvas for new ideas. Preparing for the plan, Shimokobe appoints Kurokawa to the Research Committee for Large-Scale Development Projects and Information Networks. Kurokawa recalls the group's meetings, which are chaired by Saburo Okita (scriptwriter of the Income Doubling Plan):

"We would ask ourselves such questions as: What about building a bridge between the Chugoku region and Shikoku island? What about creating a major petrochemical center in Shibushi Bay between Shikoku and Kyushu? What about digging a large harbor in the Kashima Sea and creating a large industrial area? What about a large industrial estate somewhere in Mutsu in the Tohoku region?

At committee meetings, a white map of the Japanese Archipelago was placed in the middle and a picture was drawn on it with pens. Drawing a picture on a map of the Japanese Archipelago was something that had never been done before ... Both Atsushi Shimokobe and I were full of zeal at the time. Why be so cheap as to build just a single bridge over the Inland Sea? Build three, and in the future build a bridge between Shikoku and Kyushu as well. We thought all isolated regions in the Japanese Archipelago should be linked by a network of expressways and Shinkansen ... It was asserted in the discussions that the era of metropolises may gradually come to a close, making it possible for local areas including areas now subject to depopulation to preserve a balance..."

*Kisho Kurokawa Notes, 1994*

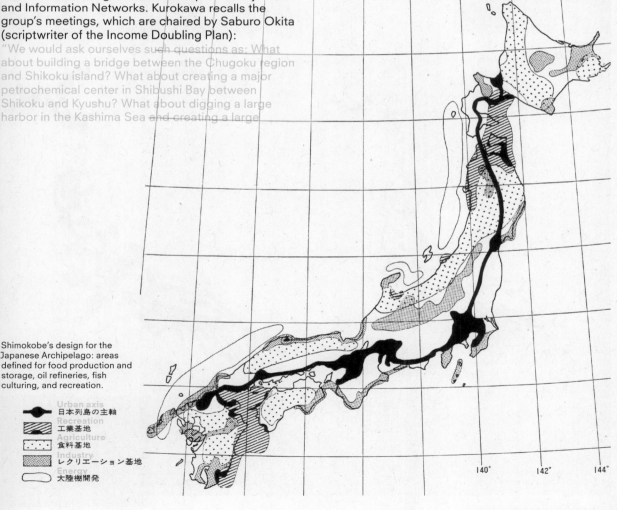

Shimokobe's design for the Japanese Archipelago: areas defined for food production and storage, oil refineries, fish culturing, and recreation.

Urban axis
日本列島の主軸
Recreation
工業基地
Agriculture
食料基地
Industry
レクリエーション基地
Energy
大陸棚開発

## Shrinking Japan

Kurokawa, a member of the Information Network Study Committee, set up to implement Shimokobe's 1969 Plan, is commissioned to research a radical new aviation system for leisure and for decentralization, redrawing the map of Japan entirely...

**Institute for Social Engineering: "Research on the Role of V/STOL Aircrafts in City-to-City Transportation."**
Commissioner: Ministry of International Trade and Industry / Mechanical Social Systems Foundation.
"The New Comprehensive National Development Plan underlines the necessity of improving the transportation and communications system—Shinkansen bullet train, highways, and aviation facilities— in order to fundamentally solve the congestion as well as thinning problems, and also to enhance the civil economy further."

**1990** Short Take-Off and Landing network (projected)

**1970** City Constellation

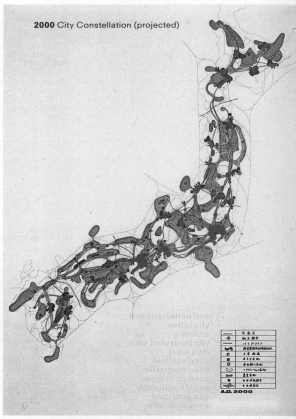

**2000** City Constellation (projected)

Archipelago within an archipelago:
Japan's disconnected cities.

Connecting the blobs: an organic network
of various infrastructures, 30 years later.

The British, French, and Germans are already developing V/STOL planes, predicted to come into service by the late '70s.

British V/TOL: Hawker Siddeley HS-141, 1969.

Kurokawa's report, made with his Institute for Social Engineering, envisions a network of airports for a new generation of Vertical and Short Take-Off and Landing passenger aircraft, capable of operating in mountainous and dense urban areas where it is impossible to build conventional airports with long runways. V/STOL is designed to meet the 4,900 percent projected increase in demand for air travel by 1985 (a daunting statistic gleaned by the ISE itself). As part of Japan's new transport system, including Shinkansen bullet trains and new highways, V/STOL would "fundamentally solve the congestion [in cities] as well as thinning problems [in the countryside], and also ... enhance the economy further." V/STOL would drastically shrink the distance between cities, supposedly contributing to Shimokobe's vision of a decentralized Archipelago, but also, unwittingly, working against it—allowing people to remain in major urban centers and simply commute to the regions.

Kurokawa's second, interlocking, motivation is to accelerate the coming "leisure" lifestyle. Citing Tange's Tokaido Megalopolis research, the ISE claims that: "The hypothetical view that people's time will be equally divided between work and leisure time from the latter half of the 1980s is becoming widely accepted." The ISE adopts Tange's idea of giving various small cities entirely over to leisure. But unlike the Megalopolis, V/STOL removes the burden of having to build physical conurbations/spines between cities; Kurokawa instead proposes a dematerialized continuous city, linked through the air...

**1980** Passenger flows: plane (blue) and train (red) (projected)

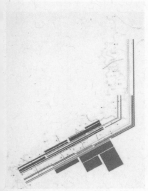

The coming supremacy of the air.

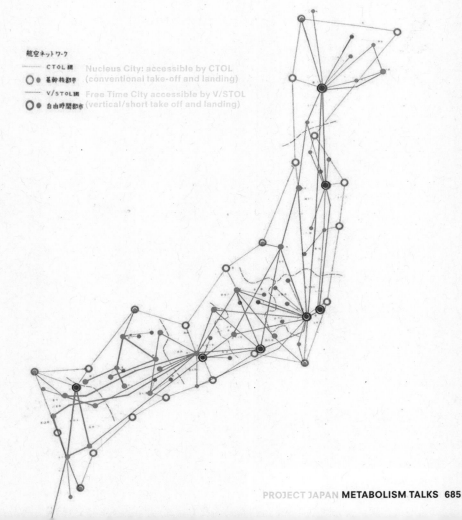

Cities surrendered to leisure, connected to working cities by next-generation aircraft.

## Demographics as Destiny

After picturing people and architecture as pixels, Kurokawa, commissioned again by Shimokobe, now pixelates Japan...

**Institute for Social Engineering: "Long-Term Diachronic Analysis of Demographic Distribution in the Japanese Archipelago."** Commissioner: Economic Planning Agency.

"According to the 1970 census, 43 percent of the national population lives in the three largest cities. If the pace continues, it will be 56 percent in 1985... This research intends to provide a basic understanding of the demographic past so that a comprehensive policy of demo - graphic distribution can be pursued. Historical analysis of demographic distribution over such a long term has rarely been done..."

９００K㎡（１辺３０Km）メッシュで
描いた日本列島

Default Japan: divided
into pixelated regions
of 900 km² each

**Japan's Population Homunculus**
Population density, 700–1970
1 pixel = 82,000 people.

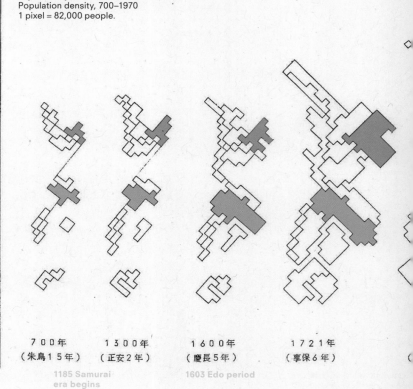

| ７００年 | １３００年 | １６００年 | １７２１年 |
|---|---|---|---|
| （朱鳥１５年） | （正安２年） | （慶長５年） | （享保６年） |

1185 Samurai
era begins

1603 Edo period

The ISE, usually acting as futurologists, now explore the history of Japan's demographics in the hope of finding causes of the overpopulation in Japan's major cities. Each region is represented as a pixelated unit, as if Kurokawa's capsule has proliferated across Japan. The pixelation generates a population homunculus: Japan rendered according to its increasingly lopsided population density, concentrating more and more over the years in Tokyo and Osaka. Shimokobe is determined to rectify the imbalance. Having just moved to the newly created National Land Agency in 1974, he is interviewed by the popular weekly *Shukan Asahi*:[18]

**Reporter**: After the oil crisis, didn't the archipelago remodeling idea return to square one?
**Shimokobe**: Unlike the short-cycled economic planning, national land planning takes a 50- or 100-year time span, so it's not immediately affected by a temporary economic crisis. So, for instance, the National Land Agency is analyzing and extrapolating where people have moved or will move to live, and how they have done or will do so between 700 AD and 2000. Historians and other academics are also mobilized for the research.
**Reporter**: But that's too long-term...
**Shimokobe**: Well, we want to understand the mechanism of congestion, as a natural phenomenon, learning from history. We say we want demographic distribution, but it wouldn't necessarily mean forced relocation. It seems to me that demographic convergence into a big city is hitting a limit. I feel that people will soon begin to find quality life in countryside...

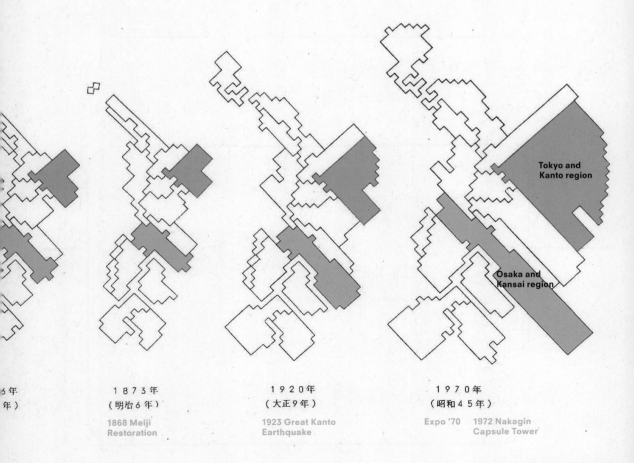

Tokyo and
Kanto region

Osaka and
Kansai region

１８７３年
（明治６年）

**1868 Meiji
Restoration**

１９２０年
（大正９年）

**1923 Great Kanto
Earthquake**

１９７０年
（昭和４５年）

**Expo '70    1972 Nakagin
Capsule Tower**

## 1. Ancient and Medieval period: factors shaping demography

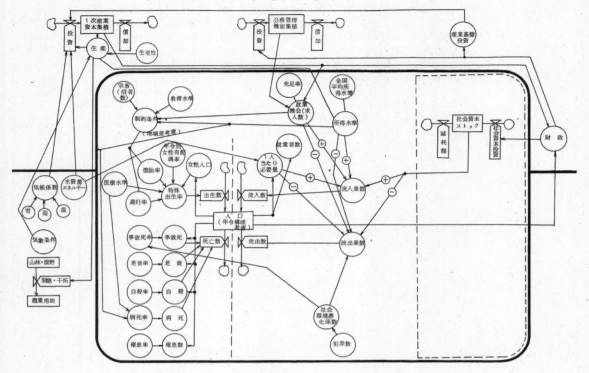

## 2. Early modern period: accumulation of new factors

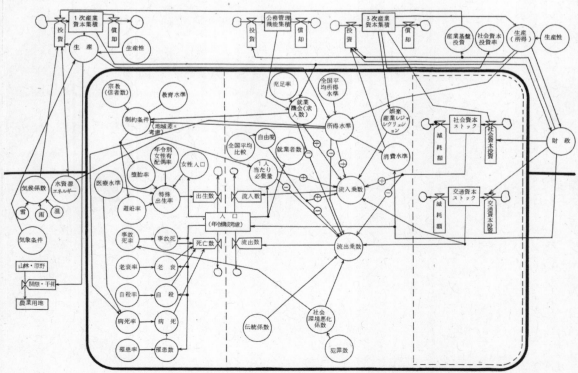

### The Meaning of Life and Death in Japan

In the same report, the ISE attempts to diagram the increasingly complex forces shaping Japan's demography through the ages. Modern confidence with the scientific management of knowledge and its powers of analysis remain, as yet, undaunted. The ISE's obsessively systematic diagram is probably a computer model meant to predict future demographic trends. The one scenario that remains hidden in the analysis is Japan's *actual* approaching demographic crisis, low birth rate and population decline, the unimaginable opposite of the overpopulation they are desperately planning for...

3. Modern day: maximum complexity

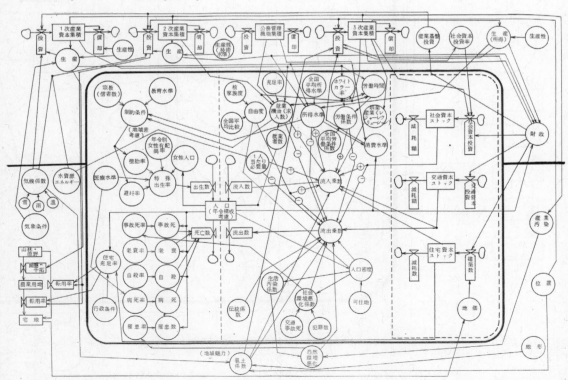

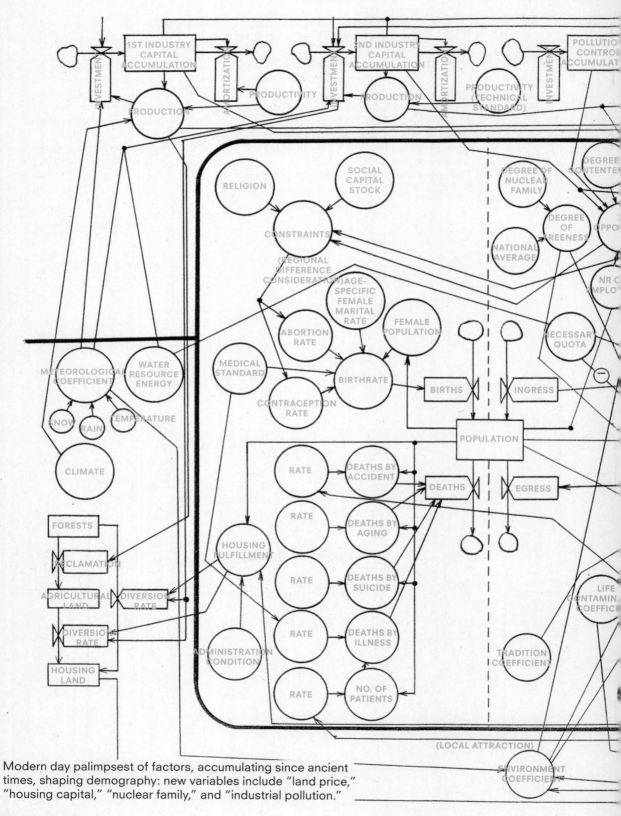

Modern day palimpsest of factors, accumulating since ancient times, shaping demography: new variables include "land price," "housing capital," "nuclear family," and "industrial pollution."

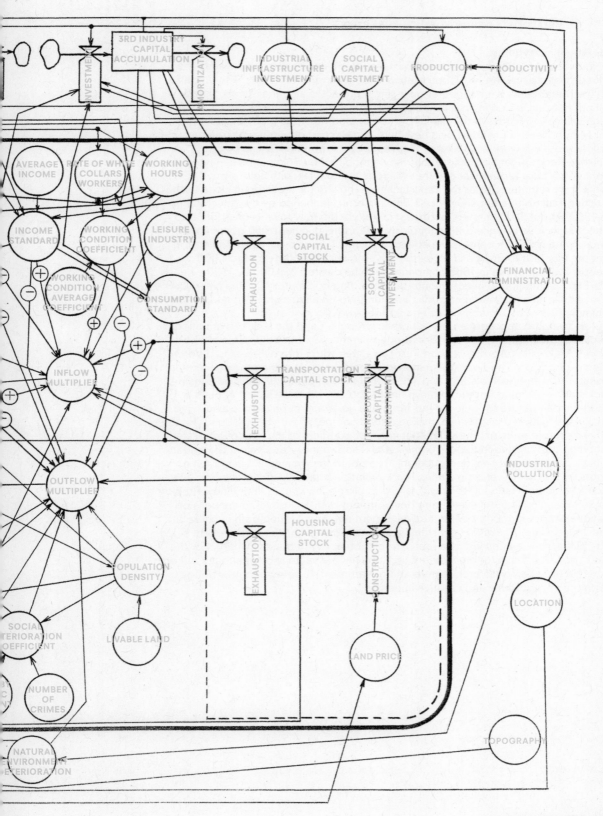

## Metabolism in Hiding

Shimokobe, now producer of the 1985 Tsukuba Science Expo, reconvenes the Metabolists to masterplan Japan's latest Expo as a renewable city. The first time all the Metabolists work together on a single project is also their final collaboration. (Isozaki is also invited to the project, but pulls out, maintaining his lifelong ambivalence towards Metabolism.) But the original Tsukuba plan, a last hurrah for Metabolism, is thwarted by a new bureaucratic and governmental regime. To carry out the work on Tuskuba, the Metabolists form their own company, Keikaku Rengo (Planning union), but they are guided by Shimokobe's masterplan concept: a pure Metabolist city that will regenerate itself with new, always temporary structures after the Expo finishes. The site for the Expo is close to the existing Tsukuba Science City, a $5.3 billion effort launched by the government in 1963. About 60 kilometers northeast of Tokyo, the new town is an attempt to boost Japanese science and technology research—it includes 50 government and private research centers, an affiliated university, and a particle accelerator. But the city fails to grow as fast as the government expected—only 34,000 people live in the area in 1985 compared with the desired 220,000 by 1990—hence the Expo's ambition to inject life into the sprawling commuter city (the New York Times calls it "a planned metropolis that tends to be all too gray"[19]), and, under Shimokobe's plan, a means of permanent renewal.[20]

But as the Expo approaches, bureaucratic wrangling and the reduced ambitions and budgets of the Ministry of Construction in the '80s frustrates Shimokobe's plan.[21] Maki, Kikutake, Otaka, and Kurokawa are reduced to overseeing different blocks of pavilions and designing individual pavilions rather than the masterplan; compared with the innovation and self-confidence of Expo '70, their designs are lackluster—basic geometric forms in neutral colors. Kikutake's plan to build a Stratiform Structure Module for the Japanese government pavilion is also killed. Tsukuba's failure to inspire—20 million attend compared with 64 million for Expo 70—is symptomatic of a new national mindset skeptical of the kind of organized ambition that produced Expo '70: *minkatsu*. The Japanese equivalent of Reaganomics, *minkatsu* involves deregulation, "reorganizing urban space in pursuit of economic growth," relaxing zoning laws, privatizing national industries (for example, Japan National Railways), and liberalizing the market. In the new Project Japan, planning is out; laissez-faire development is in. The government sells off national land, triggering rampant development and speculation both in cities and the countryside. *Minkatsu* intensifies a national obsession with land present since the 1930s, now expressed as a real estate bubble, which bursts in 1990. For the next two decades, economic stagnation sets in. The same shortage that sparked a heroic group effort in architecture and government 40 years ago now brings Japan to an economic and creative impasse...

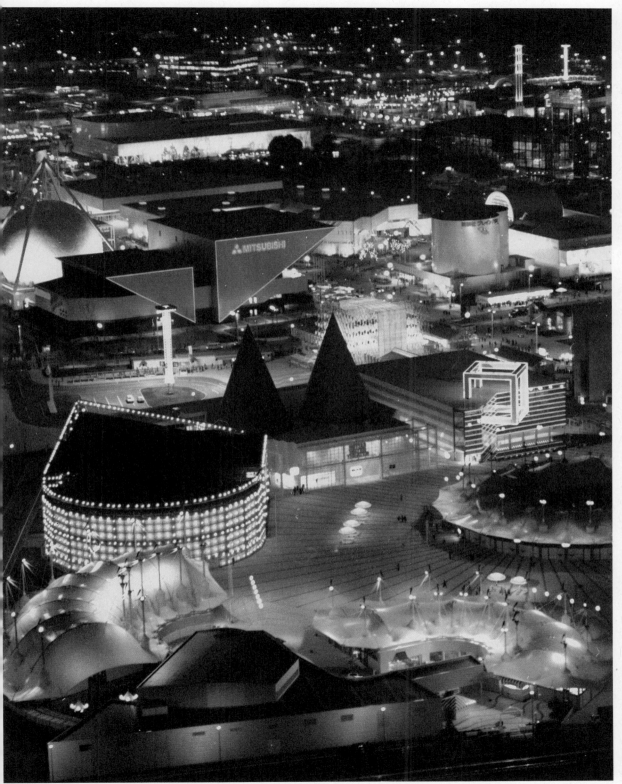

Night falls on Tsukuba '85. In the foreground, curving tents designed
by Maki; the cones of Kurokawa's Mitsui Water Theater behind.

## Hyper-Artificial Ground

Kikutake, 68, launches a next-generation artificial ground project for the age of the megacity. The Hyperbuilding Research Society, supported by the government, stimulates research into the possibility of super-tall structures in cities with a minimum population of 10 million.[footnote: 22] In 1996, OMA is invited to contribute, and designs a cluster of towers one kilometer high, some of them leaning, linked at multiple levels by platforms and diagonal struts reaching out into the surrounding area: a city in the air. 120,000 people could live there. The location would be Bangkok, not Tokyo; but Kikutake continues to use the city, with its intractable problems continuing into the '90s, as his canvas. Without knowing it, OMA is mobilized by Kikutake in a rearguard action to continue Project Japan, even in foreign climes...

Kikutake's Hyperbuilding, 1997. The Tower-Shaped Community, 600 m high, accommodates 4,500 housing units on 150 floors; 30,000 people by day and 15,000 by night. Kikutake writes: "One may think that a hyperbuilding would not be comfortable to live in. But it has hanging gardens every 10th or 20th floor flight, and a high degree of freedom inside. But it must be made as a megastructure with a renewal system."[23]

Fellow travelers: OMA's Hyperbuilding, artificial ground for Bangkok, 1996.

## References

1  Kazuto Tanabe, "The Process of Realizing the World Design Conference," *Kenchiku Zasshi*, October 1960.

2  Foundation for the World Design Conference Organization, "The process of organizing the World Design Conference in Japan," Notes dated December 1, 1959. Asada Archive at Tohoku University of Art and Design.

3  Japan Patent Office: Design Section, *Isho seido 120-nen no ayumi* [120 years of design institution], 2009.

4  Terumi Kitabatake, "Artificial land is no dream tale," *Shinkenchiku*, November 1963.

5  Terumi Kitabatake, "The Complexity of Architecture and Artificial Land," *Kenchiku Zasshi*, July 1967.

6  Shizuo Harada, *Toshi kyoju no frontier design—Sokozo module* [Frontier of urban habitation design: Stratiform structure module] (Tokyo: Riko Tosho, 1991).

7  Mechanical Social Systems Foundation, apple thinking— *Uchuteki-shiya kara chikyu wo kangaeru* [Apple Thinking: thinking of the Earth from the perspective of the universe], brochure, June 1989.

8  Kiyonori Kikutake Architects & Associates, Technological Developments for Realization of Habitat Infrastructure, brochure for the Rio Earth Summit, 1992.

9  Kiyonori Kikutake, *Koso to Keikaku* [Concepts and plans] (Tokyo: Bijutsu Shuppansha, 1978).

10  "Report on the symposium on Plan for Tokyo 1960," *Shinkenchiku*, July 1961.

11  Kenzo Tange, "The future image of the Japanese Archipelago," *Chiiki Kaihatsu* [area development], Japan Center for Area Development Research, November 1964.

12  Kenzo Tange, *Future Image of the Japanese Archipelago* (Tokyo: Kodansha, 1966).

13  Kenzo Tange, "The future image of the Japanese Archipelago," *Chuo Koron*, January 1965.

14  Record of proceedings of Budget Committee at House of Councillors, March 10, 1966.

15  Tange Group, "Japan in the 21st Century: A Socio-economical and Physical Proposal for Future Japan," proposal for Prime Minister's Cabinet, June 1971.

16  Tange, *Future Image of the Japanese Archipelago*.

17  Tange Group, "Japan in the 21st Century: A Socio-economical and Physical Proposal for Future Japan."

18  "Logic on the developing side: Atsushi Shimokobe, man behind the scenes at the National Land Agency," *Shukan Asahi*, July 12, 1974.

19  "A Flawed Science Showplace," *New York Times*, September 11, 1984

20  Atsushi Shimokobe and Kisho Kurokawa in conversation, "Temporary City: the masterplan concept of Expo '85," *Shinkenchiku*, May 1985.

21  Kimio Fukushima, "The long process of the Science Expo— Tsukuba '85," *Kensetsu Geppo*, February 1985.

22  Hiroshi Hayami, "Hyper Building Study Society," *Rapido*, The Building Center of Japan, no. 8, 2001.

23  Kiyonori Kikutake, *Megastructure* (Tokyo: Waseda University Press, 1995).

**Japan, Inc.** (pp. 485–486)
**Sources**
Noboru Kawazoe, *Omoide-no-ki* [Chronicle of memories] (Tokyo: Group of 70/70/Domesu Shuppan, 1996).

Masato Otaka and Noboru Kawazoe, eds., *Metabolism and Metabolists* (Tokyo: Bijutsu Shuppansha, 2005).

Masato Otaka, "Artificial Land and Group Form," Kikan Obayashi: Metabolism 2001 [*Obayashi quarterly*], no. 48, 2001.

"Artificial Land to Receive Subsidy," *Asahi Shimbun*, July 5, 1972.

Kisho Kurokawa, *Kisho Kurokawa Notes* (Tokyo: Dobun Shuppan, 1994).

Japan Architecture Center, "Research for the Development of the Building Systems of Artificial Land, Chapter 1," *Periodical Reports of Research*, No.58, Japan Housing Corporation, February 1978.

Atsushi Shimokobe, *Testimony on the Postwar National Land Planning* (Tokyo: Nihon Keizai Hyoronsha, 1994).

Atsushi Shimokobe, "Discourse on the globe environment," *Dezain-no-sozo* (Creation of design) (Tokyo: Fuhdosha, 1970).

Kiyonori Kikutake "Metabolism 2001," Kikan Obayashi: Metabolism 2001 [*Obayashi quarterly*], no. 48, 2001.

# Toyo Ito 伊東豊雄

**April 2011** "The fragile state of things." Ito observes the ruins of the Tohoku earthquake and tsunami.

## Postscript

The reported scene of a fishing village in Sanriku* devoured in seconds by the tsunami struck me and made me wonder what Japan's 60 years of modernization since the war was all about. Back in the Edo period, fishing villages disappeared in tsunamis; now it has happened again.

The Tohoku Shinkansen bullet train is still closed and the Fukushima nuclear plant continues to be in a tightrope crisis. I am amazed by the fragile state of things despite all the economic and technological "strength" Japan has been so proud of. If the disaster had happened in Tokyo, the situation would no doubt be even more devastating. Was our achievement of the past several decades a house of cards?

The media often uses the phrase "beyond assumption" for the disaster, meaning that its force was beyond architectural requirements. But I can't help sensing a more fundamental disruption between our norm and the reality. I think we design things in a mechanical manner as a "complete machine," complying with nature defined in quantities or abstract definitions; we do not engage with the natural environment as something constantly affected by the varying forces of ground, sea, or wind. Public architecture or private house, we design strictly within an abstract framework.

I think our task now is to rethink how we "assume" design conditions, rather than reviewing the conditions. We need to start by questioning the way we relate to nature. The people or community which we always argue for in our architecture—aren't they just an abstracted scheme?

Any proposal for tackling this issue, however visionary, should be an encouragement for the towns and villages reconstructing with the possibility of natural disaster always looming. And we architects should find it an invaluable opportunity to work on such a proposal, where we can question the norm of modernism that is so embedded in us.

Being an architect from outside, I had a hesitation in getting involved in reconstruction planning for towns and villages washed away on the coast. But after visiting the area and witnessing the devastating condition, my mind is changing. I feel I should be involved in various issues on various levels. Since around the time I set up my own office in 1971, urban proposals such as those made by the Metabolists are rarely seen. We are still in the mode of introversion and abstraction. I think now is a good moment for us architects to break away from this mode and regain a viable relationship with nature.

Tokyo, July 2011

---

\* Sanriku: Northern coast of the Tohoku
region facing the Pacific Ocean.

**PROJECT JAPAN**
**1940–1985**

Cultural, political, economic, and architectural* events in postwar Japan...

Sources for economic and demographic data:
Statistics Bureau of Japan, www.stat.go.jp (2010)
United Nations Statistic Division (2010)

* grey = completed buildings

**KENZO TANGE**
1913–2005

Kishi Memorial Hall, Tokyo

Greater East Asia Co-Prosperity Sphere monument

Japanese-Thai Culture Center, Bangkok

Tange Lab launched at Tokyo University

**EVENTS**

**ARATA ISOZAKI**
1931–

**ECONOMY**

Roosevelt imposes US trade embargo on Japan

40% of industrial plants and infrastructure destroyed by US bombing

Federation of Economic Organizations (*Keidanren*) established

**FUMIHIKO MAKI**
1923–

Japan's population    71.6 million                                                               73.1 million

**POLITICS**

Joins Axis powers, establishes puppet government in China.

Japanese attack US base at Pearl Harbor

Japanese Americans moved to internment camps

Japan conquers Philippines, Malaysia, Dutch East Indies, and Burma

US firebombing of Japan's cities

"Little Boy" and "Fat Man" dropped on Hiroshima and Nagasaki

39 women elected to upper house of Diet. Emperor Hirohito repudiates divinity of the Emperor

Prime Ministers ⟶

DOUGLAS MACARTHUR – supreme commander for allied pow

**MASATO OTAKA**
1923–2010

**INTERNATIONAL EVENTS**

Germany invades Norway, Denmark, Netherlands, Belgium, Luxembourg, and France

World Bank, GATT, and IMF created at Bretton Woods Conference, US

United Nations established

**KIYONORI KIKUTAKE**
1928–

**CULTURE**

*China Nights*, with Li Xianglan (Yoshiko Yamaguchi)

*The 47 Ronin*, Kenji Mizoguchi

*The War at Sea, from Hawaii to Malay* Kajiro Yamamoto

*Sugata Sanshiro*, Akira Kurosawa

Shochiku Kagekidan girls operetta dissolves

*Soyokaze (Breeze)*, first postwar movie

Coca-Cola introduced in Japan

**KISHO KUROKAWA**
1934–2007

**INVENTION**

Tokyo's population    ● 7.3 million

**NOBORU KAWAZOE**
1928–

**700  PROJECT JAPAN, 1940–1985**

Japan's GNP    0.5 billi

| | 1947 | 1948 | 1949 | 1950 | 1951 | 1952 | 1953 | 1954 | 1955 |
|---|---|---|---|---|---|---|---|---|---|
| Architecture | Reconstruction masterplan for Hiroshima; New Architect's Union of Japan established | World Peace Memorial Cathedral, Hiroshima | Wins competition for Hiroshima Peace Memorial Park | Kenchikushi (architect) law establishes professional standards | Tange attends CIAM meeting, Hoddesdon, UK | | Hiroshima Children's Library | Tsuda College Library, Tokyo; Walter Gropius visits Japan; Graduates from Tokyo University | Hiroshima Peace Memorial Museum; Wachsmann Seminar, Tokyo University |
| Economy | Antimonopoly Law breaks up keiretsu conglomerates | | Ministry of International Trade and Industry (MITI) established | Korean War sparks economic growth as MITI implements Foreign Capital Law | Japan Development Bank formed, launches Fiscal Investment and Loan Plan | Industrial output returns to prewar levels. MITI begins regulating imports. Japan joins IMF | Export and Import Trading Act allows price and import cartels | 40% of labor force in agriculture. Keiretsu reemerge | Economic Deliberation Agency announces five-year plan to promote exports |
| Education | | | | | | Bachelor of Architecture, University of Tokyo | Master of Architecture, Cranbrook Academy of Art | Master of Architecture, Harvard | |
| Politics | Democratic constitution. Standing army abolished. *Nochi Kaiho* law ends feudalism | Economic Recovery Plan spurred by US aid | | Comprehensive National Land Development Act for national reconstruction | US-Japan Security Treaty established US military bases "in and about" Japan | US grants Japan independence. Since 1945, US has given $1.9 billion in aid. | | New Land Reform Act gives government more power to expropriate | Government officially declares end of postwar period |

TSU KATAYAMA   HITOSHI ASHIDA   SHIGERU YOSHIDA →   → MATTHEW RIDGWAY (MILITARY GOVERNOR)   ICHIRO HATOYAMA →

| | 1947 | 1948 | 1949 | 1950 | 1951 | 1952 | 1953 | 1954 | 1955 |
|---|---|---|---|---|---|---|---|---|---|
| World events | US establishes Marshall Plan to aid Europe | Israel declared a state | Establishment of NATO. Mao Zedong proclaims the People's Republic of China | Korean War begins | King Abdullah of Jordan assassinated in Jerusalem | European Coal and Steel Community (ECSC) established | Korean War armistice | Southeast Asia Treaty Organization (SEATO) formed in Manila | Vietnam War |
| Career | | 3rd place in Hiroshima World Peace Memorial cathedral competition, after Tange in 2nd | | Bachelor in Architecture, Waseda University | | | Opens office in Tokyo | | |
| Culture | *Snow Country*, Yasunari Kawabata | *Confessions of a Mask*, Yukio Mishima | First Japanese Nobel Prize: Hideki Yukawa | *Rashomon*, Akira Kurosawa | Akari lamps, Isamu Noguchi | *Astro boy*, Osamu Tezuka | *Tokyo Story*, Yasujiro Ozu | Gutai group founded | Yayoi Kusama's first exhibition overseas, at Brooklyn Museum |
| Products | | First Nikon camera | | Sony Type G tape recorder | Sony TR-55 transistor radio | Sanyo SS52 plastic radio | Yahama S1B Piano, GK Design | Electric rice cooker | Suzuki Suzulight lightweight car |

5 million   5 million   ¥4.4 billion

Becomes editor of *Shinkenchiku*

| | 1956 | 1957 | 1958 | 1959 | 1960 | 1961 | 1962 |
|---|---|---|---|---|---|---|---|
| **KENZO TANGE** 1913–2005 | | Tokyo Metropolitan Government Building  | Kagawa Prefectural Government Office  | Sogetsu Art Center, Tokyo  | Plan for Tokyo 1960  | Totsuka Country Club  | Nichinan Cultural Center, Miyazaki  |
| **EVENTS** | | | Tokyo Tower, first structure higher than 31 meters  | CIAM, Otterlo | World Design Conference; *Metabolism 1960* | Tange presents Plan for Tokyo 1960 on TV  | "This will be your city," Metabolism exhibition, Tokyo  |
| **ARATA ISOZAKI** 1931– | | | | | Oita Medical Hall  | Peugeot Building competition, Buenos Aires | Clusters in the Air, Tokyo  |
| **ECONOMY** | | New Long-Term Economic Plan by Economic Deliberation Agency. Toyota Crown is first Japanese car sold in the US | MITI establishes Japan External Trade Organization | First use in US of phrase "Japan Inc." to describe mix of state planning and private enterprise | | Income Doubling Plan announced by Prime Minister Hayato Ikeda | "Consider Japan: Economic lessons of the world's most extraordinary growth economy" |

Japan's population — 89.9 million  ... 94 million

| | 1956 | 1957 | 1958 | 1959 | 1960 | 1961 | 1962 |
|---|---|---|---|---|---|---|---|
| **FUMIHIKO MAKI** 1923– | | Assistant Professor, Harvard | | | Nagoya University Toyoda Memorial Hall  | Wins Architectural Institute of Japan Prize | Chiba University Memorial Auditorium  |
| **POLITICS** | | Japan admitted to United Nations | First National Capital Region Development Plan | | New Treaty of Mutual Cooperation and Security with US leads to mass protests and political upheaval | | Atsushi Shimokobe works on First Comprehensive National Land Development Plan |

TANZAN ISHIBASHI → NOBUSUKE KISHI → ... HAYATO IKEDA →

| | 1956 | 1957 | 1958 | 1959 | 1960 | 1961 | 1962 |
|---|---|---|---|---|---|---|---|
| **MASATO OTAKA** 1923–2010 | | | Harumi High-rise Apartments, Tokyo (for Kunio Maekawa's office)  | | | | |
| **INTERNATIONAL EVENTS** | Nikita Khrushchev begins "de-Stalinization" | USSR launches Sputnik satellite | NASA founded  | Fidel Castro seizes power in Cuba. Yasser Arafat establishes Fatah | OPEC (Organization of Petroleum Exporting Countries) founded | Berlin Wall built. Yuri Gagarin, first man in space. Non-Aligned Movement founded | Cuban Missile Crisis. Nelson Mandela imprisoned |
| **KIYONORI KIKUTAKE** 1928– | Bridgestone Tongaya Apartments, Tokyo  | Mothers' and Children's Dormitory, Kyushu | Sky House, Tokyo  | Shimane Prefectural Museum  | Marine City: Unabara  | Disaster Prevention City, Tokyo Bay  | Ikebukuro, Tokyo  |
| **CULTURE** | *Temple of the Golden Pavilion,* Yukio Mishima  | *Throne of Blood,* Akira Kurosawa | *I want to be a shell,* live TV drama  | *Forbidden Colors.* Tatsumi Hijikata's first butoh dance  | *Magnificent Seven,* US remake of Kurosawa's *Seven Samurai*  | First Meijin (Go) tournament  | *Woman in the Dunes,* Kobo Abe  |
| **KISHO KUROKAWA** 1934–2007 | | Graduates from Kyoto University | Visits USSR for architecture students congress | New Tokyo Project: Human-Type Plan  | Agricultural City, Aichi | Helix City, Tokyo | Box-Type Apartments |
| **INVENTION** | Fujitsu sells first Japanese computer  | Casio 14 A, first electric compact calculator | Instant noodles invented by Momofuku Ando  | Nikon F  | Sony TV8 transistor TV  | Kikkoman Soy Sauce bottle, GK Design  | |

Tokyo's population — ¥9.7 billion — 8.6 million — ¥20.2 billion — 10.2 million

| | 1956 | 1957 | 1958 | 1959 | 1960 | 1961 | 1962 |
|---|---|---|---|---|---|---|---|
| **NOBORU KAWAZOE** 1928– | Japan's GNP | Starts English edition of *Shinkenchiku, The Japan Architect* | Quits *Shinkenchiku* | Chooses name Metabolism1 | 'Material and Man,' *Metabolism 1960, Extinction of Architecture, House for People and the Gods* | *What is Design?*  | |

**702  PROJECT JAPAN, 1940–1985**

| 1963 | 1964 | 1965 | 1966 | 1967 | 1968 | 1969 | 1970 | 1971 |
|---|---|---|---|---|---|---|---|---|

**1963**
St. Mary's Cathedral, Tokyo

Ville Spatiale, Yona Friedman

Maronouchi Project, Tokyo

**1964**
Yoyogi National Gymnasia, Tokyo

Tokyo Olympics

Iwata Girls High School, Oita

Joins OECD. Exports more to US than it imports from it.

**1965**
Skopje masterplan

Kasumigaseki Building, Tokyo's first skyscraper

Set for Face of Another

25% of labor force atill in agriculture.

**1966**
Yamanashi Cultural Center

Seaside Bubbles, Archigram

Oita Prefectural Library

**1967**
Taipei University of Sacred Heart, Taiwan

Habitat 67, Moshe Safdie

Fukuoka City Bank, Oita

**1968**
International School of the Sacred Heart, Tokyo

Student occupation of Milan Triennale/ May '68 in Paris

*Electric Labyrinth* Installation shut down, Milan Triennale

GNP second highest in the world, over-taking Germany. Japan produces 4.1 million cars. Economy grows 11%

**1969**
Yerba Buena masterplan, San Francisco

Kurokawa forms Institute for Social Engineering

Arai House (Responsive House), Fukuoka

Student demon-strations; New Comprehensive National Develop-ment Plan.

**1970**
Expo '70 Big Roof

Yukio Mishima attempts coup, commits suicide

Expo '70: Festival Plaza and Robots

Share of world trade increases to 7%. Wages increased annually by 11–12% in '60s. Tokyo real estate prices up 670% since 1960.

**1971**
University of Oran, Algeria

Bretton Woods canceled, unfixing $–¥ exchange rate. Service industry overtakes agriculture

---

Lecturer, University of Tokyo

Japan admitted to GATT; signs partial nuclear test ban treaty

Japanese citizens allowed to freely travel overseas for the first time

Japan and South Korea sign Normal-ization Treaty

EISAKU SATO →

Rissho University Kumagaya Campus, Saitama

GATT Kennedy Round is completed

Rinkai Center, Osaka

Anti-Land Reform movements form All-Japan Land Readjustment Op-position League

Hillside Terrace Phase I, Tokyo

New comprehen-sive National Development Plan, Atsushi Shimokobe

Senri Civic Center, Osaka

Kanazawa Ward Offices, Yokohama

Okinawa returned to Japan; US military bases remain

---

Otemachi Artificial Land plan, Tokyo

Kennedy assassinated. Organization of African Unity founded

Tanganyika merges with Zanzibar to form Tanzania, US increases troop levels in Vietnam

Hanaizumi Agricul-tural Cooperative, Ichinoseki

Singapore independence from Malaysia

Mao launches Cultural Revolution

Sakaide Artificial Ground, Tokyo

Che Guevara killed in Bolivia. Six-Day War between Israel and Arab states

Chiba Prefectural Conference Hall

*Whole Earth Catalog*

Tochigi Prefectural Assembly Hall

Neil Armstrong, first man on moon US and USSR sign Nuclear Non-Proliferation Treaty

Chiba Prefectural Central Library

Japanese Red Army hijack domestic flight using swords and a bomb as weapons

Shizuoka Agricultural Cooperative Center

Idi Amin coup in Uganda. United Arab Emirates formed. Qatar independence

---

Administrative Building, Izumo Shrine

California roll born in LA

Tokoen Inn, Yonago

*Godzilla against Mothra, Honda/ Tsuburaya*

Tree-Shaped Community

Yoko Ono *Cut Piece,* Carnegie Hall, New York

Miyakonojo Civic Center

*Tattoo,* Yasuzo Masumura with Ayako Wakao

Sado Grand Hotel

*Face of Another,* Hiroshi Teshigahara

Hagi Civic Centre

Yasunari Kawabata wins Nobel Prize for Literature

Kurume Civic Center

Comme des Garçons founded

Expo Tower

*Empire of Signs,* Roland Barthes

Kyoto Community Bank

*Shura (Demons),* Toshio Matsumoto

---

Nitto Food Cannery, Sagae

Jun'ichi Nishizawa, fiber-optic com-munication

Tokaido Shinkansen bullet train

Central Lodge, Children's Land, Yokohama

¥39.6 billion

11.1 million

Sony Trinitron

Hishino New Town

Yamagata Hawaii Dreamland

Seiko Astron, first Quartz wristwatch

Fujisawa New Town

Suzuki 4x4 Jimny

Odakyu Drive-In Restaurant, Otome

Honda CB750

Expo '70: Takara Beautilion and Toshiba IHI pavilion

Cup Noodles

Curates Mid-Air Exhibition, Expo '70

Pompidou Center competition, Paris

Karaoke

CDI (Creative Design Institute) designs Kyoto Shinyo Kinko Bank branches

---

*Ise: Prototype of Japanese Architec-ture,* with Tange

*Design Hihyo* magazine with Kiyoshi Awazu

|  | 1972 | 1973 | 1974 | 1975 | 1976 | 1977 | 1978 |
|---|---|---|---|---|---|---|---|
| **KENZO TANGE** 1913–2005 |  Baltimore Inner Harbor |  Masterplan for pilgrims, Mina (Muna), Saudi Arabia |  Abbas Abad masterplan, Tehran | People's Palace, Damascus, Syria |  Government Center, Doha |  Sogetsu Hall and Office, Tokyo |  Hanae Mori Building, Tokyo |
| **EVENTS** | Venturi, Scott Brown, and Izenour | Kazuo Shinohara, House in Higashi-tamagawa, Tokyo | IAUS periodical *Oppositions* | Okinawa Ocean Expo | Toyo Ito, White U | *The Language of Post-Modern Architecture*, C. Jencks | "MA: Space/Time in Japan" exhibition, organized by Isozaki, Paris |
| **ARATA ISOZAKI** 1931– |  Oita Medical Hall Annex | |  Museum of Modern Art, Gunma |  Dismantling of Architecture |  Installation for ManTransform in New York City | |  MA: Space/Time in Japan, Festival d'Automne, Paris |
| **ECONOMY** | Remodeling the Japanese Archipelago, Kakuei Tanaka | Oil crisis: price of gasoline up 220%. First economic downturn since 1945. Investment in small, fuel efficient cars | First convenience store (7- Eleven) opens in Koto Ward, Tokyo | | New 5-year plan targets annual growth of 6% | Increase in public debt leads to establishment of market for government bonds | 10.7% of labor force in agriculture; 17.3% in services |
| **FUMIHIKO MAKI** 1923– | Kato Gakuen Elementary School, Numazu | Hillside Terrace Phase II, Tokyo | Kuragike Memorial Hall, Toyota | Marine Life Park, Okinawa Expo '75 | Japanese Embassy, Brasilia | Kota Kinabaru Sport Complex, Malaysia | Iwasaki Art Museum, Kagoshima Prefecture |
| **POLITICS** | Normalization of Sino-Japanese relations | Kidnapping of Kim Dae-Jung (later president of South Korea) in Tokyo | Prime Minister Tanaka arrested in Lockheed bribery scandal | US, Japan, Germany, France, Britain, and Italy form G6 | | Fukuda Doctrine of military non-aggression | China-Japan Peace and Friendship Treaty |
|  | KAKUEI TANAKA → | | TAKEO MIKI → | | TAKEO FUKUDA → | | MASAYOSHI ŌHIRA |
| **MASATO OTAKA** 1923–2010 | | | | | Motomachi and Chojuen Housing, Hiroshima | Tama New Town planning, Tokyo | |
| **INTERNATIONAL EVENTS** | 11 Israeli athletes killed at Munich Olympics | US President Nixon declares the end of Vietnam War | | Pol Pot takes over Cambodia. King Faisal of Saudi Arabia assassinated | Concordes make first commercial flights from London and Paris | Japan ratifies International maritime law claiming territory in 12-mile and 200-mile radius | Deng Xiaoping becomes leader of China, begins market reforms, says "To get rich is glorious" |
| **KIYONORI KIKUTAKE** 1928– | Museum Bernard Buffet, Surugadaira | Yokohama District Project | Pasadena Heights | Aquapolis, Okinawa Expo | Floating Hotel, Abu Dhabi | Floating Infra-Casette, Libya and Iraq | |
| **CULTURE** | | Issey Miyake Paris debut | *Heidi, Girl of the Alps* | Akira Kurosawa wins Oscar for *Dersu Uzala* | *The sailor who fell from grace with the sea* based on Mishima's novel | Jun'ichiro Tanizaki's *In Praise of Shadows* in English | Yellow Magic Orchestra |
| **KISHO KUROKAWA** 1934–2007 | Nakagin Capsule Tower, Tokyo | Vasto and San Salvo masterplans, Italy | Koito Building, Tokyo | Fukuoka Bank | Sony Tower, Osaka | National Museum of Ethnology, Osaka | |
| **INVENTION** | Technics SL-1200 turntable | Canon color copier | Pikkari Konica with built-in flash | Sony Betamax | Sony compact disc | Nintendo color video game console | Credit card–sized calculator |
| **NOBORU KAWAZOE** 1928– | | | | | | National Land Planning Agency begins commissioning CDI for research | |

 Japan's population

 LEARNING FROM LAS VEGAS

 Japan's GNP

    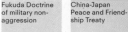 ¥171.2 billion

 Tokyo's population 11.6 million

112.8 million

| 1979 | 1980 | 1981 | 1982 | 1983 | 1984 | 1985 |
|------|------|------|------|------|------|------|

University of Tokyo headquarters

*The Postmodern Condition*, J-F Lyotard,

Napoli Administration Center

¥260.3 billion

Abuja Central Area District, Nigeria

Memphis Milano movement

Akasaka Prince Hotel, Tokyo

Metabolists reunite to form *Keikaku Rengo* (planning federation) for Tsukuba Science Expo '85

Hyogo Prefectural Museum of History

Buzzwords of the year in Japan: light, thin, short, and small

Tsukuba Center

King Faisal Foundation Complex, Saudi Arabia

Philip Johnson, AT&T Building, New York

Japanese Embassy, Riyadh, Saudi Arabia

Tsukuba Science Expo

Palladium Club, New York

Plaza Accord between France, West Germany, Japan, US, and UK depreciates $ in relation to ¥

G7 summit, Tokyo

GDP per capita: Japan $9 US $12

MITI import promotion department. Honda opens first plant in US. Nakasone enacts minkatsu (deregulation) laws.

Royal Danish Embassy, Tokyo

GATT Tokyo Round completed

Kawawa Lower Secondary School Kanagawa

Sudden death of Prime Minister Masayoshi Ohira. Foreign Exhange Law eases foreign exchange controls

Keio University Library, Mita Campus, Tokyo

Maezawa Garden House, Kurobe

International Whaling Commission suspends commercial whaling

Dentsu Kansai Branch, Osaka

Tanaka found guilty of accepting bribes from Lockheed

Fujisawa Municipal Gymnasium

*Minkatsu* deregulation policy sells public land for private development

Spiral Building, Tokyo

ZENKŌ SUZUKI ⟶   YASUHIRO NAKASONE ⟶

Gunma Prefectural Museum of History

Iranian revolution. Saddam Hussein president of Iraq. USSR invades Afghanistan

Iraq invades Iran; eight-year war ensues

UN Convention of the Law of the Sea

ARPANET begins developing the Internet

Kanagawa Museum of Art, Annex, Kamakura

UK and China sign agreement to transfer sovereignty of Hong Kong

Mikhail Gorbachev president of USSR, launches perestroika

Saison Modern Art Museum, Karuizawa

Kumamoto Arts and Crafts Center

*Nausicaa of the Valley of the Wind*

IT Aquapolis

Chris Marker, *Sans Soleil*

*Karate Kid*: karate becomes international

Tsukuba Expo '85

Studio Ghibli founded

*Hear the Wind Sing*, Haruki Murakami's first novel

*Pac-Man*

*Donkey Kong*

As-Sarir New Town, Libya

South Friedrichstadt, Berlin

Japan Art Bank

Saitama Museum of Modern Art

National Bunraku Theatre, Osaka

Wacoal Building

Mitsui Pavilion, Tsukuba Expo '85

Sony Walkman

Flash memory

Sony digital camera

Sony CD Player

Nintendo Famicom

Epson Handheld Color TV

Super Mario Bros

Keikaku Rengo with other Metabolists

# INDEX

Numbers in **bold** = sidenote
Numbers in *italics* = image

## CAST OF CHARACTERS

The predecessors, collaborators, mentors, family, and offspring of Metabolism; all participants in Project Japan...

| **PREDECESSORS** | **SHINPEI GOTO**<br>1857–1929<br>**Statesman**<br>Infrastructural planner in colonized Taiwan and Manchuria; home minister and then foreign minister; implements modernization masterplan for Tokyo after 1923 Great Kanto Earthquake; a beacon for Tange and other urban planners. | **JUNZO SAKAKURA**<br>1901–1969<br>**Architect**<br>Returns from Le Corbusier's studio in Paris in 1940 to become Japan's pioneering modern architect, inspiring the young Tange; chairman of 1960 World Design Conference. | **HIDETO KISHIDA**<br>1899–1966<br>**Architect**<br>Tange's teacher at Tokyo Imperial University; remains his mentor and collaborates on several of his buildings. |

**TANGE**
**+**
**COLLABORATORS**

**KENZO TANGE**
1913–2005
**Architect**

**TAKASHI ASADA**
1921–1990
**Architect**
Tange's right hand at Tange Lab, secretary-general of World Design Conference, initiator of Metabolism, pioneer of environmentalism.

**MAMORU KAWAGUCHI**
1932–
**Structural engineer**
Collaborator with Tange 1960–89, most notably on Yoyogi National Gymnasia and breakthrough engineering of Big Roof at Expo '70; works on projects by Maki and Kurokawa.

**FAMILY**

**TOSHIKO KATO**
Marries Tange in 1947, helps his diverse social activities outside architecture.
**Interview** p. 84

**MICHIKO UCHIDA**
Daughter of Toshiko Kato and Tange.

**TAKAKO TANGE**
Tange's second wife, married in 1973; helps his international activities as partner.
**Interview** p. 550

**TANGE LAB**
**+**
**Maki**
**Isozaki**
**Kurokawa**
**Hiroshi Hara**
**Takashi Asada**
**Hajime Yatsuka**

**ATSUSHI SHIMOKOBE**
1923–
**Bureaucrat**

**Interview** p. 638

**SACHIO OTANI**
1924–
**Architect**
Member of Tange Lab; worked with Tange on Hiroshima Peace Memorial Park and all major projects from 1947–1960 before starting own practice; pursues his anti-megastructrual approach.

**AKIRA TAMURA**
1926–2010
**Urban planner**
Tange Lab graduate; Asada sends him to implement their ideas in participatory town planning in Yokohama; the system they establish becomes a national model.
**+ Metabolism collaborator**

**METABOLISTS**

**MASATO OTAKA**
1923–2010
**Architect**

**NOBORU KAWAZOE**
1926–
**Critic**

**Interview** p. 222

**FUMIHIKO MAKI**
1928–
**Architect**

**Interview** p. 294

**COLLABORATORS**
**OF METABOLISM**

**SHOMEI TOMATSU**
1930–
**Photographer**
Invited by Kawazoe to join Metabolism, though he never did; Isozaki uses his photos of Hiroshima in the installation *Electric Labyrinth* (1968).

**SHINYA IZUMI**
1930–
**Industrial designer**
Attends Metabolism meetings and collaborates with Kurokawa et al on Expo '70; producer of all subsequent Expos in Japan.

**HIDETOSHI KATO**
1930–
**Sociologist and critic**
Works with Kawazoe, Awazu, and Izumi on Expo '70 as a thematic planner; sets up Communication Design Institute with Kawazoe in 1970, works with Kikutake and Ekuan.

**COMMENTATORS**

**HIROSHI HARA**
1936–
**Architect**
Tange Lab graduate, co-founds alternative journal *Design Criticism* with Kawazoe, Izumi and Awazu (and designs Awazu's house).

**CHARLES JENCKS**
1939–
**Architect and writer**
Lifelong friends with and scribe for Kurokawa; writer on modern and postmodern architecture.

**TOYO ITO**
1941–
**Architect**
Spends four years working for Kikutake before setting up own office in 1970; debuting with works antithetical to Metabolism.
**Postscript** p. 696

**KUNIO MAEKAWA**
1905–1986
**Architect**
Returns from Le Corbusier's studio in 1930; Tange and later Otaka work in his office; invents Japan's first prefab housing system.

**YOSHIKAZU UCHIDA**
1885–1972
**Architect**
Masterplans Datong, Inner Mongolia, represents conservative modernist mainstream of architecture and urban planing.

**EIKA TAKAYAMA**
1910–1999
**Urban planner**
Works with Uchida in Datong; runs Takayama Lab for urban planning at Tokyo University as Tange's senior; leads urban planning academy and large projects in postwar Japan.

**ISAMU NOGUCHI**
1904–1988
**Artist**
Born in Los Angeles with Japanese and American parentage; first visits Japan in 1951, works with Tange on Hiroshima Peace Park; remains close friend and collaborator.

**TARO OKAMOTO**
1911–1996
**Artist**
Designs artificial "Island of Leisure" in Tokyo Bay in 1957; advocates ancient Jomon culture in modern Japan; keeps dynamic friendship with Tange as opponent in debate over tradition; his *Tower of the Sun* sculpture pierces Tange's Big at Expo '70.

**HISAAKIRA KANO**
1886–1963
**Bureaucrat and planner**
Proposes infilling most of Tokyo Bay in 1958, sparking series of artificial ground proposals; supports Maekawa, Otaka and Tange as chairman of Japan Housing Corporation; instigates World Design Conference.

**NORITAKA TANGE**
1958–
**Architect**
Having learned architecture and urban planning under his step father, succeeds Tange in 1997.
**Interview** p. 550

**KOJI KAMIYA**
1928–
**Architect**
Core member of Tange Lab from 1951; prominent role designing Kagawa Prefectural Government Offices; leads Tange's office, URTEC, 1964–71, works on Yoyogi National Gymnasia and Expo '70.

**KIYONORI KIKUTAKE**
1928–
**Architect**

**Interview** p. 128

**KIYOSHI AWAZU**
1929–2009
**Graphic designer**

**KENJI EKUAN**
1929–
**Industrial designer**

**Interview** p. 474

**KISHO KUROKAWA**
1934–2007
**Architect**

**Interview** p. 372

**ARATA ISOZAKI**
1931–
**Architect**

**Interview** p. 24

**SHUHEI AIDA**
1932–
**Scientist**
Collaborates with Kurokawa at the Institute for Social Engineering; specialist in systems engineering; opinion leader on environmental science.

**TAKASHI ONISHI**
1946–
**Urban planner**
Successor to Eika Takayama at Tokyo University; specialises in national land planning and sustainable development.

**HAJIME YATSUKA**
1948–
**Architect and critic**
One of the last students at Tange Lab; also studies under Otani and works with Isozaki from 1978–83; author of two books on Metabolism (1997 and 2011).

**AKIRA ASADA**
1957–
**Critic and curator**
Nephew of Takashi Asada; writer on art, music, literature, and architecture.